From *Apocalypse*

To **Glory**

Written by Ellen G. White

Compiled by Michael D. Haus

Information about this Book

- The compiler assumes full responsibility for the accuracy and interpretation of the Ellen White quotations cited in this book.
- A list of acronyms for the sources can be found on page 550.
- *From Apocalypse to Glory* is the second book of a two-part series. While this volume is a stand-alone book, readers who want to read about the Shaking, the Sunday Law, and the Latter Rain, should purchase the first book in the series, titled: *The Global Worship Crisis.*

Copyright Notice

TABLE OF CONTENTS

Preface

When I was a youngster, I would go with my friends and build end-time survival shelters in the local rock piles left behind by farmers. We would dig holes between the stones and form a roof out of sticks and leaves. Then we would talk in whispered tones about the Time of Trouble and how dreadfully awful the Seven Last Plagues would be.

My interest in adventure and survival skills led me to spend a month in the Colorado wilderness, practicing knot-tying skills and learning how to navigate whitewater safely. Then one day, I turned to the Spirit of Prophecy, expecting to find a wealth of information about living off the grid and how to hide from armed soldiers.

Instead, I found that Mrs. White's writings paint a completely different picture. She wrote that houses and lands will be of no use during the time of trouble, and our only safety will be to hide in Jesus. While she emphasized the value of country living before probation closes, her writings clearly state that when the great tribulation occurs, only Christ will be able to protect us. This revelation negated some of the things I had previously believed.

Filled with a new-found interest in the end times, I began to put together what would become a two-volume compilation on final events. There were many places to pull quotes from, but the most helpful resource proved to be the online Ellen White database. Three and a half years later, a project that was only supposed to last several months was completed.

The finished book is one that both pastors and laypeople should appreciate. Whatever teachings you have heard about the end times—be prepared to have those ideas challenged as you read *From Apocalypse to Glory*.

— Michael Haus

4

The Lesser

Time of Trouble

— 1 —

Prepare Spiritually

"God is our refuge and strength, a very present help in trouble." — Psalm 46:1

| Psalm 9:9, 10 | Proverbs 3:5, 6 | Romans 10:13 | Eph. 3:17-19 | Colossians 3:16 | 1 Peter 5:8 |
| Psalm 56:4 | Mark 11:22-24 | Galatians 2:20 | Eph. 6:10-20 | Hebrews 11:1 | Rev. 3:10 |

Focus on Jesus

The time has come when every soul who trusts in false hopes will be shaken out. It will not answer to take the eye off Jesus for one moment. — *Lt 2, 1889*

Israel's God Guides Us

I am encouraged and blessed as I realize that the God of Israel is still guiding his people and that He will continue to be with them, even to the end.

— *9T, p. 8*

Remember Gethsemane

When the servants of God are tried and tempted; when they are disappointed in obtaining human sympathy, they may remember Jesus in his hour of greatest agony in Gethsemane. — *Lt 7, 1885*

Rely on Jesus for Safety

Our only safety is in doing our work for each day as it comes, working, watching, waiting, every moment relying on the strength of Him who was dead and who is alive again, who lives forevermore. — *Lt 66, 1894*

Know Christ Personally

If you would stand through the time of trouble, you must know Christ, and appropriate the gift of his righteousness, which He imputes to the repentant sinner. Human wisdom will not avail to devise a plan of salvation.

— *RH, Nov. 22, 1892*

Unite with Jesus in Love

Persecution is coming, and God calls upon all to stand firm in Christian love, their hearts knit together, of one mind and one judgment. His people are to cleave to Him, and they are to love one another as He has loved them. Christ's life is to be their example. In love, in meekness, in humility, they are to follow Him. *— ST, Oct. 31, 1900*

Be Rooted and Grounded in Christ

The only way in which men will be able to stand firm in the conflict, is to be rooted and grounded in Christ. They must receive the truth as it is in Jesus. And it is only as the truth is presented thus that it can meet the wants of the soul. The preaching of Christ crucified, Christ our righteousness, is what satisfies the soul's hunger. *— GCDB, Jan. 28, 1893*

Make Truth a Shield and Buckler

All heaven is looking upon the remnant people of God, to see if they will make truth alone their shield and buckler. Unless the truth is presented as it is in Jesus, and is planted in the heart by the power of the Spirit of God, even ministers will be found drifting away from Christ, away from piety, away from religious principle. They will become blind leaders of the blind. *— Ms 15, 1886*

Choose Death before Dishonor

Choose poverty, reproach, separation from friends, or any suffering, rather than to defile the soul with sin. Death before dishonor or the transgression of God's law, should be the motto of every Christian. As a people professing to be reformers, treasuring the most solemn, purifying truths of God's Word, we must elevate the standard far higher than it is at the present time.

— Ms 9, 1880

Pray Fervently for God's Protection

If the messengers who bear the last solemn warning to the world would pray for the blessing of God, not in a cold, listless, lazy manner, but fervently and in faith, as did Jacob, they would find many places where they could say: "I have seen God face to face, and my life is preserved." Genesis 32:30. They would be accounted of heaven as princes, having power to prevail with God and with men. *— GC, p. 622*

7

We are under God's Charge

We are to remember that we are in the hands of him who created us. Whatever Satan may inspire evil men to do, we are to rest in the assurance that we are under God's charge, and that by his Spirit He will strengthen us to endure. —*RH, Dec. 28, 1897*

Study Psalm 91

In the ninety-first Psalm is a most wonderful description of the coming of the Lord to bring the wickedness of the wicked to an end, and to give to those who have chosen Him as their Redeemer the assurance of his love and protecting care. —*Ms 151, 1901*

The Lord Works on Our Behalf

The man of sin, who thought to change times and laws, and who has always oppressed the people of God, will cause laws to be made enforcing the observance of the first day of the week. But God's people are to stand firm for Him. And the Lord will work in their behalf, showing plainly that He is the God of gods. —*9T, p. 229*

Special Tokens of the Holy Spirit

In the future we shall have special tokens of the influence of the Spirit of God—especially at times when our enemies are the strongest against us. The time will come when we shall see some strange things; but just in what way—whether similar to some of the experiences of the disciples after they received the Holy Spirit following the ascension of Christ—I cannot say. —*Ms 115, 1908*

God's Glory Penetrates Prison Walls

Where two or three are present who love and obey the commandments of God, Jesus there presides; let it be in the desolate place of the earth, in the wilderness, in the city enclosed in prison walls. The glory of God has penetrated the prison walls, flooding with glorious beams of heavenly light the darkest dungeon. His saints may suffer, but their sufferings will, like the apostles of old, spread their faith and win souls to Christ and glorify his holy name. The bitterest opposition expressed by those who hate God's great moral standard of righteousness should not and will not shake the steadfast soul who trusts fully in God. —*Lt 108, 1886*

A Personal Experience is Needed

Personal religious experience is needed in every church. Why? Because those who are not under the working of the Holy Spirit will not stand amid the perils of the last days. — *Lt 148, 1899*

Lives Hidden in Christ will Stand

When God's people seek Him with all the heart, He will be glorified in them. Self will not be regarded as a precious article, which must necessarily be handled with great care, lest it be broken. Would that every soul who has had the light would break by falling in Christ. Only those whose lives are hidden with Christ in God will stand firm, rooted, and grounded, and established in the truth for this time. Everything is to be shaken that can be shaken, that those things which cannot be shaken may remain. — *Lt 163, 1900*

Tribulation Cannot Take Jesus Away

No amount of tribulation can separate us from Christ. If He leads us to Rephidim, it is because He sees that it is for our good and for his name's glory. If we will look to Him in trusting faith, He will, in his own time, turn the bitterness of Marah into sweetness. He can open the flinty rock, and cause cooling streams to flow forth. Then shall we not lift our voices in praise and thanksgiving for past mercies, and go forward with full assurance that He is an ever-present help in time of trouble? He has been with us in our past experiences, and his word to us is, "Lo, I am with you alway, even unto the end of the world." — *ST, Sept. 17, 1896*

Remember Calvary's Awful Sacrifice

Remember that everyone who shall be found with the wedding garment on will have come out of great tribulation. The mighty surges of temptation will beat upon all. But the long night of watching, of toil, of hardship, is nearly past. Christ is soon to come. Get ready! The angels of God are seeking to attract you from yourself and from earthly things. Let them not labor in vain. Faith, living faith, is what you need; the faith that works by love and purifies the soul. Remember Calvary and the awful, the infinite sacrifice there made for man. Jesus now invites you to come to Him, just as you are, and make Him your strength and your everlasting Friend. — *RH, Apr. 17, 1894*

Believe Life will be Restored

Terrible trials are to come upon our world, and the world is preparing itself for this. We too must be prepared, that we may have the protection of our heavenly Father. And if we lose our life in the conflict, let us have faith to believe that it will be restored to us again. —*Ms 19, 1909*

Keep the Word of God's Patience

"Because thou hast kept the word of my patience." Revelation 3:10. Does this apply to the men who persecute those who conscientiously keep the commandments of God, who refuse to bow down to an idol sabbath and worship an institution of the papacy? Who is keeping the Word of God's patience? This is a question of intense interest—a question which none of us can afford to ignore; because God has said of those who do keep the word of his patience, "I also will keep thee from the hour of temptation."

—*RH, June 19, 1900*

Secure the Oil of Grace Now

Study the parable of the wise and foolish virgins. There were ten that went forth to meet the bridegroom, but five of them were wise, and five were foolish. The foolish virgins took no oil in their vessels with their lamps. Are there not many who are following this same foolish course? In probationary time we are to secure the oil of grace. It will be too late to secure it when the last great emergency comes upon us. If we neglect the day of salvation, we may come like the foolish virgins and seek an entrance to the marriage supper, and find that the door is shut. I can hardly express the trouble of my soul.

—*Lt 16, 1895*

Jesus Strengthens His People

The Captain of our salvation will strengthen his people for the conflict in which they must engage. How often when Satan has brought all his forces to bear against the followers of Christ, and death stares them in the face, have earnest prayers put up in faith brought the Captain of the Lord's host upon the field of action and turned the tide of battle and delivered the oppressed. Now is the time when we should closely connect with God, that we may be hid when the fierceness of his wrath is poured upon the sons of men. We have wandered away from the old landmarks. Let us return. If the Lord be God, serve Him; if Baal, serve him. Which side will you be on? —*5T, p. 137*

Consecrate Yourself Individually

The stake and scaffold are not appointed for this time to test the people of God, and for this very reason the love of many has waxed cold. When trials arise, grace is proportioned for the emergency. We must individually consecrate ourselves on the very spot where God has said He would meet us.

—RH, Apr. 4, 1882

The Assurances of Corinthians

I am so thankful that we have a faith that will stand the test of trial and opposition. As trouble in the world increases, the Lord's children will have to suffer; but the Word of God affords comfort and encouragement for such a time. Read the first and second chapters of First Corinthians; there are precious assurances here for the child of God. *—Lt 266, 1907*

Live the Life of Faith Daily

Live the life of faith day by day. Do not become anxious and distressed about the time of trouble, and thus have a time of trouble beforehand. Do not keep thinking, "I am afraid I shall not stand in the great testing day." You are to live for the present, for this day only. Tomorrow is not yours. Today you are to maintain the victory over self. Today you are to live a life of prayer. Today you are to fight the good fight of faith. Today you are to believe that God blesses you. And as you gain the victory over darkness and unbelief, you will meet the requirements of the Master, and will become a blessing to those around you. *—ST, Oct. 20, 1887*

Reformation Prepares Families

In the night season there was represented to me the great need of thorough changes among us as a people, and especially in our households. I was shown that reformations must be wrought in families that have long professed to serve the Lord, but whose lives have not been acceptable in his sight. There is need of repentance and conversion; and in every family there needs to be a diligent seeking unto God; for we are living amidst the perils of the last days. Soon the time of trouble will break upon us; and unless decided changes are made, there will be few prepared to meet the Lord. Many will lose the eternal rewards prepared for the people who walk in all the ways of the Lord.

—Ms 78, 1912

Trust Fully in God

The bitterest opposition expressed by those who hate God's great moral standard of righteousness should not and will not shake the steadfast soul who trusts fully in God. All things shall work together for good to those who love God. "This is the love of God, that ye keep his commandments." 1 John 5:3. They that will be doers of the Word are building securely, and the tempest and storm of persecution will not shake their foundation, because their souls are rooted to the eternal rock. —*Lt 108, 1886*

Grasp the Hand of Infinite Power

Now, brethren, we are coming to the crisis. Let us stand the test manfully, grasping the hand of Infinite Power. God will work for us. We have only to live one day at a time, and if we get acquainted with God, He will give us strength for what is coming tomorrow, grace sufficient for each day, and every day will find its own victories, just as it finds its trials.

We shall have the power of the Highest with us; for we shall be clad with the armor of Christ's righteousness. We have the same God that has worked for his people in ages past. Jesus stands by our side, and shall we falter? No, as the trials come, the power of God will come with them. God will help us to stand in faith on his word, and when we are united, He will work with special power in our behalf. —*RH, Apr. 29, 1890*

A Guide to Escaping God's Wrath

A book has been given us to guide our feet through the perils of this dark world to heaven. It tells us how we can escape the wrath of God, and also tells of the sufferings of Christ for us, the great sacrifice that has been made that we might be saved and enjoy the presence of God forever. And if any come short at last, having heard the truth as they have in this land of light, it will be their own fault; they will be without excuse.

The Word of God tells us how we may become perfect Christians and escape the seven last plagues. But they took no interest to find this out. Other things diverted the mind, idols were cherished by them, and God's Holy Word was neglected and slighted. God has been trifled with by professed Christians, and when his Holy Word shall judge them in the last day, they will be found wanting. —*1T, p. 125*

Fall upon the Rock of Christ

Many persons are by their own endeavors hewn, polished, and beautified; but they cannot become "living stones," because they are not connected with Christ. Without this connection, no man can be saved. Without the life of Christ in us, we cannot withstand the storms of temptation. Our eternal safety depends upon our building upon the sure foundation. Multitudes are today building upon foundations that have not been tested. When the rain falls, and the tempest rages, and the floods come, their house will fall, because it is not founded upon the eternal Rock, the chief cornerstone Christ Jesus.

—DA, p. 599

Understand the Will of God

Those who endeavor to obey all the commandments of God will be opposed and derided. They can stand only in God. In order to endure the trial before them, they must understand the will of God as revealed in his word; they can honor Him only as they have a right conception of his character, government, and purposes, and act in accordance with them. None but those who have fortified the mind with the truths of the Bible will stand through the last great conflict. To every soul will come the searching test: Shall I obey God rather than men? The decisive hour is even now at hand. Are our feet planted on the rock of God's immutable word? Are we prepared to stand firm in defense of the commandments of God and the faith of Jesus? *— GC, p. 593*

Jesus Traveled before Us

It is not the fear of punishment, or the hope of everlasting reward, that leads the disciples of Christ to follow Him. They behold the Saviour's matchless love, revealed throughout his pilgrimage on earth, from the manger of Bethlehem to Calvary's cross, and the sight of Him attracts, it softens and subdues the soul. Love awakens in the heart of the beholders. They hear his voice, and they follow Him. As the shepherd goes before his sheep, himself first encountering the perils of the way, so does Jesus with his people.

"When He putteth forth his own sheep, He goeth before them." The way to heaven is consecrated by the Saviour's footprints. The path may be steep and rugged, but Jesus has traveled that way; his feet have pressed down the cruel thorns, to make the pathway easier for us. Every burden that we are called to bear He Himself has borne. *— DA, p. 480*

Rivet the Soul to Christ

Nothing short of real, genuine faith will survive the strain that will come upon every soul of man in these last days to test and try him. God must be our refuge; we cannot trust in form, profession, ceremony, or position, or think that because we have a name to live, we shall be able to stand in the day of trial. Everything that can be shaken will be shaken, and those things that cannot be shaken by the deceptions and delusions of these last days, will remain. Rivet the soul to the eternal Rock; for in Christ alone there will be safety. — *YI, Aug. 3, 1893*

Listen for the Watchman's Trumpet

All should be prepared to hear the signal trumpet of the watchman, and be ready to pass the word along the walls of Zion, that the people may prepare themselves for the conflict. The people must not be left to stumble their way along in darkness, not knowing what is before them, and unprepared for the great issues that are coming. There is a work to be done for this time in fitting a people to stand in the day of trouble, and all must act their part in this work. They must be clothed with the righteousness of Christ, and be so fortified by the truth, that the delusions of Satan shall not be accepted by them as genuine manifestations of the power of God. — *RH, Dec. 24, 1889*

Children to Prepare for the Plagues

Children, if any of you are without a hope in Christ, and you fear or tremble when any storm shall now arise, ask yourselves this question: If I fear now, how shall I stand in the great and dreadful day of God's wrath? None of the wicked can escape then. There will not be an hour, a moment lent you then to get prepared for that dreadful day. You will then witness, not merely rain, lightning and thunder; but every island will flee away, and the mountains will not be found. "And there fell upon men great hail out of heaven, every stone about the weight of a talent." Revelation 16:21.

The storm of God's wrath is soon coming upon a guilty world, and can you endure the thought of coming up to such a scene without a hope in God, and feeling that his withering frown is upon you? If you want a shelter, you must seek it now, and then you will be hid when the fierce anger of the Lord shall come. — *YI, Dec. 1, 1852*

There are Wellsprings of Joy

All the way up the steep road leading to eternal life are well-springs of joy to refresh the weary. Those who walk in wisdom's ways are, even in tribulation, exceeding joyful; for He whom their soul loveth, walks, invisible, beside them. At each upward step they discern more distinctly the touch of his hand; at every step brighter gleamings of glory from the Unseen fall upon their path; and their songs of praise, reaching ever a higher note, ascend to join the songs of angels before the throne. "The path of the righteous is as the light of dawn, that shineth more and more unto the perfect day." — *MB, p. 140*

We are Safe in God's Hands

Brethren, it is no time now for mourning and despair, no time to yield to doubt and unbelief. Christ is not now a Saviour in Joseph's new tomb, closed with a great stone and sealed with the Roman seal; we have a risen Saviour. He is the King, the Lord of hosts; He sitteth between the cherubim; and amid the strife and tumult of nations He guards his people still. He who ruleth in the heavens is our Saviour. He measures every trial. He watches the furnace fire that must test every soul. When the strongholds of kings shall be overthrown, when the arrows of God's wrath shall strike through the hearts of his enemies, his people will be safe in his hands. — *5T, p. 754*

Receive Grace Daily for Emergencies

We will not be able to meet the trials of this time without God. We are not to have the courage and fortitude of martyrs of old until brought into the position they were in. The Lord proportions his grace to meet every emergency. We are to receive daily supplies of grace for each daily emergency. Thus we grow in grace and in the knowledge of our Lord Jesus Christ, and if persecution comes upon us, if we must be enclosed in prison walls for the faith of Jesus and the keeping of God's holy law, "As thy days, so shall thy strength be." Should there be a return of persecution, there would be grace given to arouse every energy of the soul to show a true heroism.

But there is a large amount of nominal Christianity which has not its origin in God, the Source of all power and might. God gives us not power to make us independent and self-sufficient. We must ever make God our only dependence. — *Ms 22, 1889*

"Get Ready! Get Ready! Get Ready!"

I saw that the remnant were not prepared for what is coming upon the earth. Stupidity, like lethargy, seemed to hang upon the minds of most of those who profess to believe that we are having the last message. My accompanying angel cried out with awful solemnity, "Get ready! Get ready! Get ready! For the fierce anger of the Lord is soon to come. His wrath is to be poured out, unmixed with mercy, and ye are not ready. Rend the heart, and not the garment. A great work must be done for the remnant. Many of them are dwelling upon little trials." — *EW, p. 119*

Cherish the Presence of Christ

Let us look the future decidedly in the face, and say, "I can do all things through Christ which strengtheneth me." We must cherish the presence of Christ, for we need Him in the less as well as the greater trials. By a willingness for his sake to endure shame and reproach, by learning the meekness and lowliness of Christ, we shall prove the sincerity of our Christianity. When we are called to imprisonment and shame, when degraded by our fellow-beings, who are inspired by the spirit of Satan, God will give his grace to sustain us. His promise is, "As thy days, so shall thy strength be." — *ST, Sept. 2, 1897*

Study Scriptures to Survive

Just before us is a time of trouble such as never was, and those who are weaving the principles of truth into their practical life will soon understand what the wrath of the dragon means. Every soul who loves God will be tested in regard to his sacred law. Christians must stand on the elevated and holy ground which advanced truth has given them.

The light shining forth from the Scriptures for these last days, will qualify those who walk in it, to stand before magistrates and rulers, and will enable them to lift up the true standard of religion by their intelligent knowledge of the Word of God. The Word of God has been neglected, but it is high time to wake to the necessity of diligent and prayerful study of the Scriptures. God would have us study the history of his dealing with men and nations in the past, that we may learn to respect and obey his messages, that we may take heed to his warnings and counsels. — *RH, Nov. 5, 1889*

Receive Strength from Jesus

The True Witness declares: "Behold, I have set before thee an open door." Let us thank God with heart and soul and voice; and let us learn to approach unto Him as through an open door, believing that we may come freely with our petitions, and that He will hear and answer. It is by a living faith in his power to help that we shall receive strength to fight the battles of the Lord with the confident assurance of victory. —*Ms 35, 1908*

Gather Strength and Courage

Said Jesus: "No man can serve two masters: for either he will hate the one, and love the other; or else he will hold to the one, and despise the other. Ye cannot serve God and mammon." Matthew 6:24. If we are true servants of God, there should be no question in our minds as to whether we will obey his commandments or consult our own temporal interests. If the believers in the truth are not sustained by their faith in these comparatively peaceful days, what will uphold them when the grand test comes and the decree goes forth against all those who will not worship the image of the beast and receive his mark in their foreheads or in their hands? This solemn period is not far off. Instead of becoming weak and irresolute, the people of God should be gathering strength and courage for the time of trouble. —*4T, p. 251*

Deny Self and Agonize before God

The season of distress and anguish before us will require a faith that can endure weariness, delay, and hunger—a faith that will not faint though severely tried. The period of probation is granted to all to prepare for that time. Jacob prevailed because he was persevering and determined. His victory is an evidence of the power of importunate prayer. All who will lay hold of God's promises, as he did, and be as earnest and persevering as he was, will succeed as he succeeded.

Those who are unwilling to deny self, to agonize before God, to pray long and earnestly for his blessing, will not obtain it. Wrestling with God—how few know what it is! How few have ever had their souls drawn out after God with intensity of desire until every power is on the stretch. When waves of despair which no language can express sweep over the suppliant, how few cling with unyielding faith to the promises of God. —*GC, p. 621*

"Lo, I am with You Always"

The assurance of success is ours, because of the provision made by Christ. We shall meet with obstacles and difficulties; bitter and relentless will be our enemies; but as we follow on to know the Lord, we shall know that his going forth is prepared as the morning. Christ's presence is promised to us in our labors. "Lo, I am with you alway," He says, "even unto the end of the world." In his presence there is fullness of joy; at his right hand there are pleasures forevermore. —*RH, Aug. 12, 1909*

Fight in God's Army

You are to fight as in the presence of the universe of heaven. You are to fight the battles of the Lord. Then He tells you that more than human beings compose that army; He tells you that the angels that excel in strength are the warriors there; He tells you, as Captain of the Lord's host, He is there. They are to do the warring. You are to stand in the army of God, and they will gain for you the victory; they will give power to everyone that is fighting the battles of the Lord to the very gate. The power of God shall be upon every soldier that is true and that will bear hardness as good soldiers. But we cannot meet the evil angels and overcome them. It is the divine power, it is partaking of the divine nature. —*Ms 49, 1894*

God Protects Commandment Keepers

All the symbolical representations serve a double purpose. From them God's people learn not only that the physical forces of the earth are under the control of the Creator, but also that under his control are the religious movements of the nations. Especially is this true with reference to the enforcement of Sunday observance. He who gave his people, through his servant Moses, instruction in regard to the sanctity of the Sabbath—as recorded in Exodus 31:11-18—will in the hour of trial preserve those who keep this day as a sign of loyalty to Him.

God's commandment-keeping people believe that He will fulfill his promise to protect them. By actual experience they know that the Lord sanctifies them and grants to them the seal of his approval as commandment keepers. Those who read the Scriptures with an intense desire to know what the Spirit saith unto the churches know that God lives and reigns. —*Ms 153, 1902*

Humble the Soul before God

When trials come, we are not to fret and complain, not to rebel, not to worry ourselves out of the arms of Christ, but humble the soul before God. Cry unto Him that He may give rest and peace. We should bear the yoke of Christ in time of trouble, and instead of allowing ourselves to be repulsed, we should hear the voice that invites us, saying, "Come unto Me, all ye that labor and are heavy laden, and I will give you rest." Matthew 11:28. *—Ms 38, 1895*

"I Know in Whom I Have Believed"

The question is asked, "Who shall separate us from the love of Christ? Shall tribulation, or distress, or persecution, or famine, or nakedness, or peril, or sword?" Hear the triumphant cry of victory from the apostle Paul, that hero of faith: "I am persuaded, that neither death, nor life, nor angels, nor principalities, nor powers, nor things present, nor things to come, nor height, nor depth, nor any other creature, shall be able to separate us from the love of God, which is in Christ Jesus our Lord." "I know in whom I have believed."

We are not to be ignorant as to whose precious blood was shed for us, in order that we may rejoice in a personal Saviour. Satan desires to sift us, everyone, as wheat; but thank God, our Advocate is praying for us. *—Lt 44, 1894*

Nobody Abiding in Christ will Fall

When the world makes void the law of God, what will be the effect upon the truly obedient and righteous? Will they be carried away by the strong current of evil? Because so many rank themselves under the banner of the prince of darkness, will God's commandment-keeping people swerve from their allegiance? Never! Not one who is abiding in Christ will fail or fall. His followers will bow in obedience to a higher authority than that of any earthly potentate.

While the contempt placed upon God's commandments leads many to suppress the truth and show less reverence for it, the faithful ones will with greater earnestness hold aloft its distinguishing truths. We are not left to our own direction. In all our ways we should acknowledge God, and He will direct our paths. We should consult his word with humble hearts, ask his counsel, and give up our will to His. We can do nothing without God.

—Ms 48, 1891

Come up into the Mount

The Lord wants us to come up into the mount—more directly into his presence. We are coming to a crisis, which, more than any previous time since the world began, will demand the entire consecration of every faculty of the mind and every power of the being on the part of all who have named the name of Christ. —*Ms 32, 1890*

Trust God as Daniel Did

From the story of Daniel's deliverance we may learn that in seasons of trial and gloom God's children should be just what they were when their prospects were bright with hope and their surroundings all that they could desire. Daniel in the lions' den was the same Daniel who stood before the king as chief among the ministers of state and as a prophet of the Most High. A man whose heart is stayed upon God will be the same in the hour of his greatest trial as he is in prosperity, when the light and favor of God and of man beam upon him. Faith reaches to the unseen, and grasps eternal realities. —*PK, p. 545*

Pray Faithfully like Elijah

Time is very short, deliverance is coming and Satan knows it and is working in great power. I can see the restraint is being taken off from the wicked, and very soon when Jesus steps out from between the Father and man it will be entirely gone. Now is the time we must watch on every hand, against the wiles of Satan and have steady, abiding faith in God, faith that will stand the trial, such faith as Elijah had when he prayed for rain. He prayed once and sent his servant to see if there was any sign of his prayer being answered, and although there was none, outward appearance was against him, yet he did not give up in discouragement but bid his servant to go again yet seven times. Elijah had faith that holds on and that would stand the trials seven times. At last the cloud appeared and the heavens gave rain.

Bless God the prayer of faith will bring the dew of heaven and our souls will be watered by it. Hold on to faith, let your feelings be what they will. Oh, how my soul feels for the flock of God. I long to be out among them. I often awake myself crying to God's people to get ready, get ready that the cloak of Almighty God may be thrown around them and they be hid in the time of trouble. —*Lt 8, 1849*

Trust Implicitly in God's Power

Courage, fortitude, faith, and implicit trust in God's power to save do not come in a moment. These heavenly graces are acquired by the experience of years. By a life of holy endeavor and firm adherence to the right the children of God were sealing their destiny. Beset with temptations without number, they knew they must resist firmly or be conquered. They felt that they had a great work to do, and at any hour they might be called to lay off their armor; and should they come to the close of life with their work undone, it would be an eternal loss. They eagerly accepted the light from heaven, as did the first disciples from the lips of Jesus.

When those early Christians were exiled to mountains and deserts, when left in dungeons to die with hunger, cold, and torture, when martyrdom seemed the only way out of their distress, they rejoiced that they were counted worthy to suffer for Christ, who was crucified for them. Their worthy example will be a comfort and encouragement to the people of God who will be brought into the time of trouble such as never was. *—5T, p. 213*

Gather Strength from Past Victories

Great things are before us, and we want to call the people from their indifference to get ready. Things that are eternal crowd upon my vision day and night; the things that are temporal fade from my sight. We are not now to cast away our confidence, but to have firm assurance, firmer than ever before. Hitherto hath the Lord helped us, and He will help us to the end.

We will look to the monumental pillars, reminders of what the Lord hath done, to comfort and to save us from the hand of the destroyer. We want to have fresh in our memory every tear the Lord has wiped from our eyes, every pain He has soothed, every anxiety removed, every fear dispelled, every want supplied, every mercy bestowed, and thus strengthen ourselves for all that is before us through the remainder of our pilgrimage.

We can but look onward to new perplexities in the coming conflict, but we may look on what is past as well as what is to come, and say, "Hitherto hath the Lord helped us. As thy days, so shall thy strength be." The trial will not exceed the strength which shall be given us to bear. Then let us take up our work just where we find it, without one word of repining, believing nothing can come but that strength will come proportionate to the trial.

—RH, Mar. 25, 1884

Prepare Families for the Great Crisis

The law of God is made void in the world, and iniquity prevails; but light is shining from the open door of the temple of God. Open your heart, and let the bright beams of the Sun of Righteousness shine into your soul, that you may be softened, subdued, and sanctified. The enemy of all righteousness is on our track. Satan is marshaling his host; and are we individually prepared for the fearful conflict that is just before us?

Are we preparing our children for the great crisis? Are we preparing ourselves and our households to understand the position of our adversaries, and their modes of warfare? Are our children forming habits of decision, that they may be firm and unyielding in every matter of principle and duty? I pray that we all may understand the signs of the times, and that we may so prepare ourselves and our children that in the time of conflict God may be our refuge and defense. — *RH, Apr. 23, 1889*

Only Disciplined Characters will Stand

God would have his people prepared for the soon-coming crisis. Prepared or unprepared, we must all meet it. Only those whose characters are thoroughly disciplined to meet the divine standard will be able to stand firm in that testing time. But when enemies shall be on every side, watching them for evil, the God of heaven will be watching his precious jewels for good.

When secular rulers unite with the ministers of religion to come between God and our conscience, then those who cherish the fear of God will be revealed. When the darkness is deepest, then the light of a noble, Godlike character will shine the brightest. When every other trust fails, then it will be seen who have an abiding trust in God.

The stronger and purer the faith of God's people, and the firmer their determination to obey Him, the more will Satan stir up the rage of those who claim to be righteous, while they trample upon the law of God. In that coming emergency, rulers and magistrates will not interpose in behalf of God's people. There will be a corrupt harmony with all who have not been obedient to the law of God. In that day, all time-servers, all who have not the genuine work of grace in the heart, will be found wanting. It will require the firmest trust, the most heroic purpose, to hold fast the faith once delivered to the saints. — *LP, pp. 251, 252*

Expect to be Persecuted like Jesus

The world's Redeemer was scorned as a deceiver, hunted down as a malefactor, and shall those who become the servants of Christ expect to be treated any better than was their Lord? If they work the works of Christ, relatives and friends will rise up against them. They will persecute, forsake, and betray them. Let the believer not become discouraged because of the things he must suffer. Let his only anxiety be that hatred is kindled against him for no other reason than that of faithfulness in the discharge of his duty for Christ's sake. The true child of God will say, "I know I have to do with God, who trieth the heart, and hath pleasure in uprightness. I will set the Lord ever before me, and follow in the footsteps of Jesus." — *BE, Mar. 19, 1894*

Educate Children to Honor God's Law

The present hour, involving our dearest interests, is an hour of momentous importance. Our rights as individuals and churches are brought into question in the agitation on the enforcement of Sunday observance. Conflicting opinions are disturbing the minds of the religious world, and the people are at variance in regard to what should be done in the matter. Events of a startling character are fast thickening, and the anxious inquiry is already arising, "What shall be the end?"

Those who keep the law of God look upon their children with indefinable feelings of hope and fear, wondering what part they will act in the great conflict that is just before them. The anxious mother questions, "What stand will they take? What can I do to prepare them to act well their part, so that they will be the recipients of eternal glory?" Great responsibilities rest upon you, mothers. Although you may not stand in national councils, or cast your vote, you may do a great work for God and your country. You may educate your children. You may aid them to develop characters that will not be swayed or influenced to do evil, but will sway and influence others to do right.

By your fervent prayers of faith you can move the arm that moves the world. You can teach your children to pray effectually as they kneel by your side. Let your prayers arise to the throne of God, "Spare thy people, O Lord, and give not thine heritage to reproach, that the heathen should rule over them: wherefore should they say among the people, Where is their God?" Joel 2:17. — *RH, Apr. 23, 1889*

Thank God that Jesus is Alive

You will always find Satan on the side of the oppressor. God does not oppress. God does not bring people in by persecution, for He has let them live all this time, but when Satan gets the lines in his hands, he takes the spurious sabbath and sets it up against the perfection of Christ and says you have got to keep it. That is the spirit of persecution, and oppression and bondage. It goes right with the spurious sabbath that has not one syllable for its sanctity in the Word of God. "If you do not keep Sunday, you shall not buy or sell." And not only that, but they work their oppression in every way possible, but thank God, He lives. — *Ms 11, 1894*

Prepare Now for the Tribulation

I saw that we must be willing to go alone, and that we must cut loose from everyone that will not walk godly in Christ Jesus. I saw that the unbelief of brother or sister, father or mother, husband, wife or children was no excuse for any, to hinder them from doing their duty. And that those will lose their souls, if they seek to please their unbelieving friends, more than God, and they will be counted unworthy to be partakers of Christ's glory.

I saw that Jesus was rejected by his own nation, and if Jesus suffered we must be partakers of his sufferings. Said the angel, "Cut clear, cut clear, cut clear from everything or anyone that hinders thy progress." I saw that the ties of nature between man and wife, parents and children need not be severed. Still those who believe God and his truth, must obey God even if it displeased their nearest and dearest friend.

I saw that there would be no chance to get ready after Jesus leaves the most holy place, therefore we must get right now, while there is a chance. Very soon it will be too late. I saw that God's people must press together and not be too willing to see faults in each other, for where there is union there is strength. I saw that the people of God were generally too dull, too dormant and unbelieving.

The angel said, "Watch, watch, watch." I saw a crown of glory laid up for those who make a covenant with God by sacrifice. I saw that a sacrifice would not increase but decrease and consume. I was then pointed to him who had defied the armies of Israel; that truth would overcome error; and that light would shine out of darkness. — *Ms 4, 1850*

Do Not Be Discouraged

Although we are now passing through the night of tribulation, yet we need not be discouraged by the surrounding darkness. The Lord desires us to exercise faith, and with spiritual eyesight pierce through the gloom to the scenes of the morning so soon to dawn. With faith and hope we may confidently say, "The morning cometh, when there will be no more night." Soon we shall see the dawn of the eternal day in all its splendor and glorious beauty. —*Lt 177, 1901*

Pray to God in the Day of Trouble

The Lord says, "Call upon Me in the day of trouble." Psalm 50:15. He invites us to present to Him our perplexities and necessities, and our need of divine help. He bids us be instant in prayer. As soon as difficulties arise, we are to offer to Him our sincere, earnest petitions. By our importunate prayers we give evidence of our strong confidence in God. The sense of our need leads us to pray earnestly, and our heavenly Father is moved by our supplications.

Often those who suffer reproach or persecution for their faith are tempted to think themselves forsaken by God. In the eyes of men they are in the minority. To all appearance their enemies triumph over them. But let them not violate their conscience. He who has suffered in their behalf, and has borne their sorrows and afflictions, has not forsaken them.

The children of God are not left alone and defenseless. Prayer moves the arm of Omnipotence. Prayer has "subdued kingdoms, wrought righteousness, obtained promises, stopped the mouths of lions, quenched the violence of fire"—we shall know what it means when we hear the reports of the martyrs who died for their faith—"turneth to flight the armies of the aliens." Hebrews 11:33, 34.

If we surrender our lives to his service, we can never be placed in a position for which God has not made provision. Whatever may be our situation, we have a Guide to direct our way; whatever our perplexities, we have a sure Counselor; whatever our sorrow, bereavement, or loneliness, we have a sympathizing Friend. If in our ignorance we make missteps, Christ does not leave us. His voice, clear and distinct, is heard saying, "I am the Way, the Truth, and the Life." John 14:6. "He shall deliver the needy when he crieth; the poor also, and him that hath no helper." Psalm 72:12. —*COL, pp. 172, 173*

25

A Short Time to Learn Truth

Heaven will be cheap enough, if we obtain it through suffering. We must deny self all along the way, die to self daily, let Jesus alone appear, and keep his glory continually in view. I saw that those who of late have embraced the truth would have to know what it is to suffer for Christ's sake, that they would have trials to pass through that would be keen and cutting, in order that they may be purified and fitted through suffering to receive the seal of the living God, pass through the time of trouble, see the King in his beauty, and dwell in the presence of God and of pure, holy angels.

As I saw what we must be in order to inherit glory, and then saw how much Jesus had suffered to obtain for us so rich an inheritance, I prayed that we might be baptized into Christ's sufferings, that we might not shrink at trials, but bear them with patience and joy, knowing what Jesus had suffered that we through his poverty and sufferings might be made rich.

Said the angel, "Deny self; ye must step fast." Some of us have had time to get the truth and to advance step by step, and every step we have taken has given us strength to take the next. But now time is almost finished, and what we have been years learning, they will have to learn in a few months. They will also have much to unlearn and much to learn again. Those who would not receive the mark of the beast and his image when the decree goes forth, must have decision now to say, "Nay, we will not regard the institution of the beast." — *EW, p. 67*

Discussion Questions

1. Why is it critical to remember Gethsemane when we are going through difficult trials?

2. What can we do to secure the oil of grace immediately?

3. How can we keep the Word of God's patience?

4. What does it mean to hide in Christ?

5. Why will some people have a very short time to learn truth?

— 2 —

Invest in God's Work

"Sell that ye have, and give alms; provide yourselves bags which wax not old, a treasure in the heavens that faileth not, where no thief approacheth, neither moth corrupteth. For where your treasure is, there will your heart be also." — Luke 12:33, 34

| Prov. 3:27, 28 | Matt. 6:19-21 | Matt. 19:21, 22 | 2 Cor. 5:1 | James 5:1-3 |
| Eccl. 5:13-15 | Matt. 6:31-33 | Luke 12:15-21 | 1 Tim. 6:6-10 | Rev. 13:16, 17 |

Sell Printing Presses
The time will come when the many presses in our publishing houses will not be needed. They will be disposed of, and the proceeds will go toward the advancement of the Lord's work. *— Ms 101, 1901*

Properties will be Useless
It is now too late to cling to worldly treasures. Soon houses and lands will be of no benefit to anyone, for the curse of God will rest more and more heavily upon the earth. The call comes, "Sell that ye have, and give alms." This message should be faithfully borne—urged home to the hearts of the people, that God's own property may be passed on in offerings to advance his work in the world. *— Lt 177, 1901*

Do Not Plan Selfishly
We are only selfishly wise when we plan for the future, and make resolutions and bring them in, and we ourselves arrange matters, as we think in all wisdom; for in so doing we are in danger of getting in the way of the Lord. Stand out of the way with your many resolutions, and when the time comes for God to bring his people into trying places to test and prove them, He will help them, and He will not fail or be discouraged, but will be a present help in trouble. *— RH, Apr. 15, 1890*

No Home is Impenetrable

In the neighborhood where we are, and in the country round about, all kinds of wickedness is practiced. That may be, for wicked people are found everywhere. No mountain home or secluded location in the bush or woods can enclose us from the enemy who found his entrance at the gates of Paradise. No seclusion from the companionship of the world can sanctify and cleanse from moral defilement of sin. —*Ms 181, 1897*

God May Destroy Property

Acquire what you may, preserve it with all the jealous care you are capable of exercising, and yet the mandate may go forth from the Lord, and in a few hours a fire which no skill can quench may destroy the accumulations of your entire life and lay them a mass of smoldering ruins. This was the case with Chicago. God's Word had gone forth to lay that city in ruins. This is not the only city that will realize the visible marks of God's displeasure. He has made a beginning, but not an end. — *4T, p. 52*

God Passes by Greedy Christians

I saw that at present God did not call for the houses his people need to live in, unless expensive houses are exchanged for cheaper ones. But if those who have of their abundance do not hear his voice, and cut loose from the world, and dispose of a portion of their property and lands, and sacrifice for God, He will pass them by, and call for those who are willing to do anything for Jesus, even to sell their homes to meet the wants of the cause. God will have a free-will offering. Those who give must esteem it a privilege to do so.

—*RH, Nov. 26, 1857*

Sabbathkeepers Face Starvation

We pray that the Lord will inspire with faith these souls who are convinced of the truth that the seventh day is the Sabbath of the Lord, that they shall not confer with their own feelings, and let the enemy lead them to decide that the sacrifice is too great. They will suffer loss in temporal matters, and a helping hand must not be wanting. Many ask, "How can we support our families? We shall lose our positions as soon as we decide to keep holy the seventh day, and do no work on the Sabbath. Our families, shall they starve?"

—*Ms 19, 1894*

Money Loses Its Value

Money seems to them to be a dead loss that does not bring immediate returns when invested in the work of saving souls. The very means that is now so sparingly invested in the cause of God, and that is selfishly retained will, in a little while, be cast with all idols to the moles and to the bats. Money will soon depreciate in value very suddenly when the reality of eternal scenes opens to the senses of man. God will have men who will venture anything and everything to save souls. — *TM, Jan. 1, 1874*

Invest in God's Work Now

If in the providence of God you have been given means, do not settle down with the thought that you need not engage in useful labor, that you have enough, and can eat, and drink, and be merry. Do not stand idle while others are struggling to obtain means for the cause. If you do less than your duty in giving help to the perishing, remember that your indolence is incurring guilt.

Before it is forever too late, begin to reform. Invest less in worldly enterprises, and use your means in creating increased facilities for giving the third angel's message to the world. The time will soon come when no man can buy or sell, save he who has the mark of the beast. — *Lt 72, 1902*

Sell Possessions before Sunday Laws

The work must not stop for want of means. More means must be invested in it. Brethren in America, in the name of my Master I bid you wake up. You that are placing your talents of means in a napkin, and hiding them in the earth, who are building houses and adding land to land, God calls upon you, "Sell that ye have, and give alms."

There is a time coming when commandment-keepers can neither buy nor sell. Make haste to dig out your buried talents. If God has entrusted you with money, show yourselves faithful to your trust; unwrap your napkin, and send your talents to the exchangers, that when Christ shall come, He may receive his own with interest.

In the last extremity, before this work shall close, thousands will be cheerfully laid upon the altar. Men and women will feel it a blessed privilege to share in the work of preparing souls to stand in the great day of God, and they will give hundreds as readily as dollars are given now. — *HS, p. 292*

Stored Food Turns Wormy

The Lord has shown me that some of his children would fear when they see the price of food rising, and they would buy food and lay it by for the time of trouble. Then in the time of need I saw them go to their food and look at it and it had bred worms, and was full of living creatures and not fit for use.

—Ms 3, 1849

Rights Taken from Christians

The adherents of truth are now called upon the choice whether to disregard a plain requirement of God's Word or to forfeit their liberty. If we yield the Word of God, and accept human customs and traditions, we may still be permitted to live among men, to buy and sell, and have our rights respected.

But if we maintain our loyalty to God, it must be at the sacrifice of our rights among men. For the enemies of God's law have leagued together to crush out independent judgment in matters of religious faith, and to control the consciences of men. They are determined to put an end to the long continued controversy concerning the Sabbath, to prohibit all further spread of the truth upon this point; and to secure the exaltation of Sunday, in the very face of the injunction of the fourth commandment. *—Ms 100, 1893*

Refrain from Increasing Belongings

We ought now to be heeding the injunction of our Saviour: "Sell that ye have, and give alms; provide yourselves bags which wax not old, a treasure in the heavens that faileth not." It is now that our brethren should be cutting down their possessions instead of increasing them. We are about to move to a better country, even a heavenly. Then let us not be dwellers upon the earth, but be getting things into as compact a compass as possible.

The time is coming when we cannot sell at any price. The decree will soon go forth prohibiting men to buy or sell of any man save him that hath the mark of the beast. We came near having this realized in California a short time since; but this was only the threatening of the blowing of the four winds. As yet they are held by the four angels. We are not just ready. There is a work yet to be done, and then the angels will be bidden to let go, that the four winds may blow upon the earth. That will be a decisive time for God's children, a time of trouble such as never was since there was a nation.

—5T, p. 152

Hoarded Wealth is Worthless

Now is the time to invest the means which God has entrusted to his stewards for this very work. Time is short; hoarded wealth will soon be worthless. When the decree shall go forth that none shall buy or sell except they have the mark of the beast, very much means will be of no avail. God calls for us now to do all in our power to send forth the warning to the world.

—RH, Mar. 21, 1878

Many Keep Possessions from God

I could hardly bear the sight of the sheep dying for the want of saving, present truth, while some who professed to believe the present truth, were holding on to their property, and were letting them die, by withholding the necessary means to carry forward the work of God. As it was held up before me the sight was too painful, and I begged of the angel to take it away, and remove the painful sight from me.

I saw that when the cause of God called for their property, they were sorrowful; as the young man was who had great possessions, and who inquired what he should do to inherit eternal life. I saw that very soon the overflowing scourge would pass over, and sweep their possessions all away; and then it will be too late to sacrifice earthly goods, and lay up a treasure in heaven.

I then saw the glorious Redeemer, beautiful and lovely. That He left the realms of glory, and came to this dark and lonely world, to give his precious life and die, the Just for the unjust. He bore the cruel mocking, and scourging, and wore the plaited crown of thorns, and sweat great drops of blood, while the burden of the sins of the whole world were upon Him. The angel asked, "What for?" I saw, I knew it was for us; for our sins He bore all this, that by his precious blood He might redeem us unto God.

Then again was held up before me those who were not willing to sell their possessions, to save one fainting, starving soul; while Jesus stands before the Father pleading his blood, his sufferings and his death, for those souls, and while God's servants were waiting, ready to carry them the saving truth that they might be sealed with the seal of the living God, and yet it was hard for some who profess to believe the present truth to even do so little as to hand the messengers God's own money, that He had lent them to be stewards over.

—Ms 4, 1850

Ask God When to Sell Property

The Lord has shown me repeatedly that it is contrary to the Bible to make any provision for our temporal wants in the time of trouble. I saw that if the saints had food laid up by them or in the field in the time of trouble, when sword, famine, and pestilence are in the land, it would be taken from them by violent hands and strangers would reap their fields.

Then will be the time for us to trust wholly in God, and He will sustain us. I saw that our bread and water will be sure at that time, and that we shall not lack or suffer hunger; for God is able to spread a table for us in the wilderness. If necessary He would send ravens to feed us, as He did to feed Elijah, or rain manna from heaven, as He did for the Israelites.

Houses and lands will be of no use to the saints in the time of trouble, for they will then have to flee before infuriated mobs, and at that time their possessions cannot be disposed of to advance the cause of present truth. I was shown that it is the will of God that the saints should cut loose from every encumbrance before the time of trouble comes, and make a covenant with God through sacrifice. If they have their property on the altar and earnestly inquire of God for duty, He will teach them when to dispose of these things.

Then they will be free in the time of trouble and have no clogs to weigh them down. I saw that if any held on to their property and did not inquire of the Lord as to their duty, He would not make duty known, and they would be permitted to keep their property, and in the time of trouble it would come up before them like a mountain to crush them, and they would try to dispose of it, but would not be able. I heard some mourn like this: "The cause was languishing, God's people were starving for the truth, and we made no effort to supply the lack; now our property is useless. Oh, that we had let it go, and laid up treasure in heaven!"

I saw that a sacrifice did not increase, but it decreased and was consumed. I also saw that God had not required all of his people to dispose of their property at the same time; but if they desired to be taught, He would teach them, in a time of need, when to sell and how much to sell. Some have been required to dispose of their property in times past to sustain the Advent cause, while others have been permitted to keep theirs until a time of need. Then, as the cause needs it, their duty is to sell. —*EW, pp. 56, 57*

32

Sacrifice Self and Property

I was pointed to the remnant on the earth. The angel said to them, "Will ye shun the seven last plagues? Will ye go to glory and enjoy all that God has prepared for those who love Him and are willing to suffer for his sake? If so, ye must die that ye may live. Get ready, get ready, get ready. Ye must have a greater preparation than ye now have, for the day of the Lord cometh, cruel both with wrath and fierce anger, to lay the land desolate and to destroy the sinners thereof out of it. Sacrifice all to God. Lay all upon his altar—self, property, and all, a living sacrifice. It will take all to enter glory." —*EW, p. 66*

God's Servants Refuse Rich Gifts

Oh, I saw it was an awful thing to be thus forsaken by the Lord—a fearful thing to hold onto a perishable substance here, when He has said that if we will sell and give alms, we can lay up treasure in heaven. I was shown that as the work is closing up, and the truth is going forth in mighty power, these rich men will bring their means and lay it at the feet of the servants of God, begging them to accept it. The answer from the servants of God will be: "Go to now, ye rich men. Your means is not needed. Ye withheld it when ye could do good with it in advancing the cause of God. The needy have suffered; they have not been blessed by your means. God will not accept your riches now. Go to now, ye rich men." —*1T, p. 175*

Discussion Questions

1. Is there a possibility of selling all your belongings too soon?

2. What are some of the ways that money will someday be worthless?

3. Will off-the-grid shelters save anyone during the time of trouble?

4. How will those who withhold money from God feel at the end of time?

5. God does not require everyone to dispose of their possessions at the same time. What eschatological signs might indicate that it is time to sell our homes and give the proceeds to the Lord?

— 3 —

Brought before Courts

"But when they deliver you up, take no thought how or what ye shall speak: for it shall be given you in that same hour what ye shall speak. For it is not ye that speak, but the Spirit of your Father which speaketh in you." — Matthew 10:19, 20

Exodus 4:15	Ps. 119:41-46, 89	Jer. 1:6-9	Matt. 5:34, 35	Acts 5:27-29
Joshua 1:8	Isaiah 54:17	Jer. 9:2-5	Matt. 10:17-22	Rom. 12:14-21
Psalm 43:1, 2	Isaiah 55:10, 11	Matt. 5:10-12	John 14:26	1 Peter 3:15-17

Do Not Detract from Scriptures
In this perilous period, when we see universal contempt placed upon the law of God, when the world is choosing between the holy Sabbath of the fourth commandment and the spurious sabbath, shall we say one word that will detract from the words of the Lord of the Sabbath? — *RH, June 8, 1897*

Irrefutable Charges are Made
There is need of watching unto prayer. The evils we shall meet have long been gathering and like a storm, will come upon many when they least expect it. While they cannot be charged with originating the evil, they precipitated it. Charges will be made which believers cannot refute, because they have not shown wisdom in the use of either the pen or the voice. — *Ms 90, 1893*

Speak Truth and Righteousness
When men lose sight of Christ's example and do not pattern after his manner of teaching, they become self-sufficient and go forth to meet Satan with his own manner of weapons. The enemy knows well how to turn his weapons upon those who use them. Jesus spoke only words of pure truth and righteousness. If ever a people needed to walk in humility before God, it is his church, His chosen ones in this generation. — *9T, p. 243*

God Flashes Knowledge

We want the truth as it is in Jesus. He says, "It is not ye that speak, but the Spirit of the Father that speaketh in you." You need not be surprised that God will flash the knowledge obtained by diligent searching of the Scriptures, into your memory at the very time when it is needed. — *RH, April 15, 1890*

Keep Lifting up Christ

We must appear before these men as trying to help others, working on the lines of the Christian help work... Do not abruptly present the Sabbath; present Christ. Should they begin to oppose you, saying, "Oh, he is a Seventh-day Adventist," lift up Christ, higher and still higher. — *Ms 22c, 1895*

Satan Treasures Unwise Words

Satan is standing ready, burning with zeal to inspire the whole confederacy of satanic agencies, that he may cause them to unite with evil men and bring upon the believers of truth speedy and severe suffering. Every unwise word that is uttered through our brethren will be treasured up by the prince of darkness. — *9T, p. 241*

Do Not Manifest Bitterness

If ever we needed to manifest kindness and true courtesy, it is now. We may have to plead most earnestly before legislative councils for the right to worship God according to the dictates of conscience. Thus in his providence God has designed that the claims of his law shall be brought before men in positions of highest authority. But as we stand before these men, we are to show no bitterness of feeling. — *RH, Feb. 11, 1904*

How to React When Arrested

We should have nothing to do with the actions of the government. Our duty is to obey God. When you are arrested, take no thought what you shall say or do. You are to follow Christ step by step. You need not commence weeks beforehand to examine the question, and laying plans as to what you will do when the powers shall do this or that, neither need you think what you are to say. Study the truth, and the Spirit of the Lord will bring to your remembrance what you shall say. Our minds should be a treasure house, filled with the Word of God. — *Ms 22c, 1895*

Lawyers and Jurors are Converted

From those who thus boldly witness for Christ, men will hear truth who never heard it before. In some hearts the seed will take root. The converting power of God will win souls from darkness to light. Some of the very men on the judgment-seat—lawyers and jurors—will embrace the truth, and in their turn will confess Christ, and show their loyalty to all the commandments of God, especially the Sabbath command, which will be made, as it has ever been, the test question. —*RH, Dec. 7, 1897*

Jesus is with Christians on Trial

We may know that if our life is hid with Christ in God, when we are brought into trial because of our faith, Jesus will be with us. When we are brought before rulers and dignitaries to answer for our faith, the Spirit of the Lord will illuminate our understanding, and we shall be able to bear a testimony to the glory of God. And if we are called to suffer for Christ's sake, we shall be able to go to prison trusting in Him as a little child trusts in its parents. Now is the time to cultivate faith in God. —*RH, May 3, 1892*

Christ's Teachings are Remembered

Jesus promised his disciples: "The Comforter, which is the Holy Ghost, whom the Father will send in my name, He shall teach you all things, and bring all things to your remembrance, whatsoever I have said unto you." John 14:26. But the teachings of Christ must previously have been stored in the mind in order for the Spirit of God to bring them to our remembrance in the time of peril. "Thy word have I hid in mine heart," said David, "that I might not sin against thee." Psalm 119:11. —*GC, p. 600*

Speak Nothing but the Truth

I saw that the Lord still has something to do with the laws of the land. While Jesus is in the sanctuary, God's restraining Spirit is felt by rulers and people. But Satan controls to a great extent the mass of the world, and were it not for the laws of the land, we should experience much suffering. I was shown that when it is actually necessary, and they are called upon to testify in a lawful manner, it is no violation of God's Word for his children to solemnly take God to witness that what they say is the truth, and nothing but the truth.

—*1T, p. 202*

Do Not Plead for Civil Rights

When brought before courts, we are to give up our rights, unless by so doing we are brought in collision with God. We are not pleading for our rights, but for God's right to our service. Instead of resisting the penalties unjustly imposed upon us, it would be better to take heed to the Saviour's words, "When they persecute you in this city, flee ye into another; for verily I say unto you, Ye shall not have gone over the cities of Israel, till the Son of man be come." —*Ms 22c, 1895*

Judicial Oaths are Not Forbidden

Our Saviour did not... forbid the use of the judicial oath, in which God is solemnly called to witness that what is said is truth and nothing but the truth. Jesus Himself, at his trial before the Sanhedrin, did not refuse to testify under oath. The high priest said unto Him, "I adjure thee by the living God, that thou tell us whether thou be the Christ, the Son of God." Jesus answered, "Thou hast said." Matthew 26:63, 64.

If there is anyone who can consistently testify under oath, it is the Christian. He lives constantly as in the presence of God, knowing that every thought is open to the eyes of Him with whom we have to do; and when required to do so in a lawful manner, it is right for him to appeal to God as a witness that what He says is the truth, and nothing but the truth. —*MB, p. 67*

Stand Boldly for the Sabbath

We believe the Sabbath of the fourth commandment because it is written plainly and is the foundation of our religious faith. Let none of us be ashamed of this. We see the importance of believing the truth, and obeying the command of God, and not heeding the pope's instituted authority who claims he has a right to change the seventh-day Sabbath God gave to man to the first day of the week. We heed not the words that are reiterated in the pulpits throughout the land, that Sunday is the Sabbath. We accept not the authority of men's councils; but we go further back, even to the councils of heaven.

"Forever, O Lord, thy word is settled in heaven." Psalm 119:89. We take a "Thus saith the Lord." Here we stand. A doctrine that has not a "Thus saith the Lord" may be accepted by the whole world, but that does not make it truth. —*Ms 39, 1893*

Church Members Testify Publicly

The members of the church will individually be tested and proved. They will be placed in circumstances where they will be forced to bear witness for the truth. Many will be called to speak before councils and in courts of justice, perhaps separately and alone. The experience which would have helped them in this emergency they have neglected to obtain, and their souls are burdened with remorse for wasted opportunities and neglected privileges. — *5T, p. 463*

Learn the Reason for Sabbath Beliefs

Well, what shall we do? Shall we study and become conversant with the Bible? Or shall we have our minds occupied with things of minor importance and with things of this world's business? Shall we not study to know whereof we believe? The time is just before us when you will have to stand before the kings, to be criticized by learned men, and to give a reason of the hope that is within you. When asked for the reason of your hope, it will not do to say as some do, "We keep the Sabbath because our father did."

Do you know why you keep the Sabbath of the Lord your God? And if so, can you tell why you keep it? If so, you can plant your feet on the foundation and be able to understand every principle of your faith so as to give an intelligent reason for the hope that is within you, with meekness and with fear. — *Ms 4, 1888*

The Roles of God and Caesar

If, however, the magistrate transcends his civil authority and attempts against the citizen's conscience, conscientious enlightenment by the clear Word of God, to require wrong things, then the citizen, rising to a higher law, is justified in refusing obedience, saying with Peter and the other Apostles before the council, "We ought to obey God rather man." The discrimination is emphatically brought out by our Lord in the injunction, "Render therefore unto Caesar the things which are Caesar's; and unto God the things that are God's." Matthew 22:21.

Within the sphere of civil relations, Caesar is supreme; within the sphere of moral and religious duties, God alone is supreme. And so also, it is the duty of children to obey their parents and wives their husbands and servants their masters, each according to his sphere and its just limitation. — *Ms 8, 1884*

Obey God Rather than Men

Paul writes to the Romans, "If it be possible, as much as lieth in you, live peaceably with all men." But there is a point beyond which it is impossible to maintain union and harmony without the sacrifice of principle. Separation then becomes an absolute duty. The laws of nations should be respected when they do not conflict with the laws of God. But when there is collision between them, every true disciple of Christ will say, as did the apostle Peter when commanded to speak no more in the name of Jesus, "We ought to obey God rather than men." —*Ms 51, 1899*

Injustice Prevails in Courts

Those who live during the last days of this earth's history will know what it means to be persecuted for the truth's sake. In the courts injustice will prevail. The judges will refuse to listen to the reasons of those who are loyal to the commandments of God because they know the arguments in favor of the fourth commandment are unanswerable. They will say, "We have a law, and by our law he ought to die." God's law is nothing to them. "Our law" with them is supreme. Those who respect this human law will be favored, but those who will not bow to the idol sabbath have no favors shown them.

—*ST, May 26, 1898*

Our Words are Used against Us

The time will come when unguarded expressions of a denunciatory character, that have been carelessly spoken or written by our brethren, will be used by our enemies to condemn us. These will not be used merely to condemn those who made the statements, but will be charged upon the whole body of Adventists. Our accusers will say that on such and such a day one of our responsible men said thus and so against the administration of the laws of this government.

Many will be astonished to see how many things have been cherished and remembered that will give point to the arguments of our adversaries. Many will be surprised to hear their own words strained into a meaning that they did not intend them to have. Then let our workers be careful to speak guardedly at all times and under all circumstances. Let all beware lest by reckless expressions they bring on a time of trouble before the great crisis which is to try men's souls. —*6T, p. 394*

Accusers Manufacture Falsehoods

For want of Bible arguments, those who are making void the law of God will manufacture falsehoods to stain and blacken the workers. They did this to the world's Redeemer; they will do it to his followers. Reports that have not the least foundation will be asserted as truth. —*5T, p. 601*

Careless Words are Reproduced

May the Lord help his messengers who bear the last note of warning to our world, to speak from the very depth of wisdom. Guard every word, control every emotion, giving no occasion for Satan to triumph over the believers. The time will come when we shall be called to stand before kings and rulers, magistrates and powers, in vindication of the truth.

Then it will be a surprise to those witnesses to learn that their positions, their words, the very expressions made in a careless manner or thoughtless way, when attacking error or advancing truth, expressions that they had not thought would be remembered, will be reproduced, and they will be confronted with them, and their enemies will have the advantage, putting their own construction on these words that were spoken unadvisedly.

—*Lt 66, 1894*

Do Not Become Exasperated

When our enemies try to place upon us the black robes of unrighteousness, let us not become exasperated at their injustice. When your efforts are falsified, when your motives and your works are painted in colors black as ink, remember those who were treated the same before you. How have the saints of God in ages past been maligned, traduced, and persecuted! For centuries their names were covered with infamy. All that the hosts of hell could do was done to heap reproach upon them as the vilest of men.

But John in holy vision beholds the faithful souls that come up out of great tribulation, surrounding the throne of God, clad in white robes, and crowned with immortal glory. What though they have been counted the offscouring of the earth? In the investigative Judgment their lives and characters are brought in review before God, and that solemn tribunal reverses the decision of their enemies. Their faithfulness to God and to his word stands revealed, and heaven's high honors are awarded them as conquerors in the strife with sin and Satan. —*RH, Aug. 28, 1883*

Every Position is Severely Criticized

We see that efforts are being made to restrict our religious liberties. The Sunday question is now assuming large proportions. An amendment to our Constitution is being urged in Congress, and when it is obtained, oppression must follow. I want to ask, "Are you awake to this matter? And do you realize that the night cometh, when no man can work? Have you had that intensity of zeal, and that piety and devotion, which will enable you to stand when oppression is brought upon you?"

It does not seem possible to us now that any should have to stand alone; but if God has ever spoken by me, the time will come when we shall be brought before councils and before thousands for his name's sake, and each one will have to give the reason of his faith. Then will come the severest criticism upon every position that has been taken for the truth. We need, then, to study the Word of God, that we may know why we believe the doctrines we advocate. We must critically search the living oracles of Jehovah.

— RH, Dec. 18, 1888

Prepare No Set Speeches

Paul, writing of his own trial at the court of the Caesars, says, "At my first defense no one took my part, but all forsook me... But the Lord stood by me, and strengthened me; that through me the message might be fully proclaimed, and that all the Gentiles might hear: and I was delivered out of the mouth of the lion." 2 Timothy 4:16, 17.

The servants of Christ were to prepare no set speech to present when brought to trial. Their preparation was to be made day by day in treasuring up the precious truths of God's Word, and through prayer strengthening their faith. When they were brought into trial, the Holy Spirit would bring to their remembrance the very truths that would be needed.

A daily, earnest striving to know God, and Jesus Christ whom He has sent, would bring power and efficiency to the soul. The knowledge obtained by diligent searching of the Scriptures would be flashed into the memory at the right time. But if any had neglected to acquaint themselves with the words of Christ, if they had never tested the power of his grace in trial, they could not expect that the Holy Spirit would bring his words to their remembrance.

— DA, pp. 354, 355

The Remnant Vindicate the Truth

As the movement for Sunday enforcement becomes more bold and decided, the law will be invoked against commandment keepers. They will be threatened with fines and imprisonment, and some will be offered positions of influence, and other rewards and advantages, as inducements to renounce their faith. But their steadfast answer is: "Show us from the Word of God our error"—the same plea that was made by Luther under similar circumstances. Those who are arraigned before the courts make a strong vindication of the truth, and some who hear them are led to take their stand to keep all the commandments of God. Thus light will be brought before thousands who otherwise would know nothing of these truths. — *GC, p. 607*

Christ's Condemnation is Reenacted

"Thus saith the Lord" is of more value and is to be regarded more sacredly than any human laws that can be framed. But men will refuse to others the liberty of keeping the commandments of God according to his revealed will. As Roman Catholics have thought, they will still think that human laws should prevail.

From the record of Christ's trial we may see to what pass those come who have perverted ideas of what constitutes godliness, and who allow their passions and prejudices to rule. When men are inspired by Satan with false religious zeal, they have no sense of what true piety means.

The times are marked by extraordinary depravity. The religion of the churches of today is of a kind that should make every true follower of God afraid of it. The religious character of professed Christians makes them act like demons. "We have a law," they say, "and by our law he ought to die."

More than common contempt will be shown to those who make the Word of God their criterion. The scenes of Christ's condemnation will be acted out in the courts by the people of this age who claim to be serving God. They will be moved with fury against God's people. Those who follow the Lamb whithersoever He goeth will know what it means to feel the wrath of the dragon. A power from beneath will cooperate with the apostate churches against those who obey the truth. Men will do the deeds of their fathers, repeating as far as possible the course of action pursued against Christ.

— *ST, Jan. 31, 1900*

The Greatest Peril is to Stop Studying

There can be no greater peril to the souls of those who profess to believe the truth, than to cease their research for light and knowledge from the Scriptures. God has put the truth into our hands; and with faithful, thoughtful, prayerful study, and with the counsel of God-fearing teachers, we may become able in the exposition of the word of truth. You are to pray, and search for the truth on every point of faith and doctrine. You will be brought before critical, opposing councils. You will be tried for your faith, and you will want to know that you have good ground for every point of doctrine. God enjoins upon all men to search the Scriptures; but how doubly important is this injunction to those who teach the word to others. —*RH, Sept. 4, 1888*

The Example of Daniel and His Friends

"Then Daniel went to his house, and made the thing known to Hananiah, Mishael, and Azariah, his companions, that they would desire mercies of the God of heaven concerning this secret, that Daniel and his fellows should not perish with the rest of the wise men of Babylon. Then was the secret revealed unto Daniel in a night vision. Then Daniel blessed the God of heaven." ...

The close application of those Hebrew students under the training of God was richly rewarded. While they made diligent effort to secure knowledge, the Lord gave them heavenly wisdom. The knowledge they gained was of great service to them when brought into straight places. The Lord God of heaven will not supply the deficiencies that result from mental and spiritual indolence.

When the human agents shall exercise their faculties to acquire knowledge, to become deep thinking men, when they, as the greatest witnesses for God and the truth, shall have won in the field of investigation of vital doctrines concerning the salvation of the soul, that glory may be given to the God of heaven as supreme, then even judges and kings will be brought to acknowledge in the courts of justice, in parliaments and councils, that the God who made the heavens and the earth is the only true and living God, the author of Christianity, the author of all truth, who instituted the Seventh-day Sabbath when the foundations of the world were laid, when the morning stars sang together, and all the sons of God shouted for joy. All nature will bear testimony as designed for the illustration of the Word of God. —*Lt 67, 1894*

Reproach Falls upon Christ

When for the truth's sake the believer stands at the bar of unrighteous tribunals, Christ stands by his side. All the reproaches that fall upon him, fall upon Christ. Christ is condemned over again in the person of his disciple. When one is incarcerated in prison walls, Christ ravishes the heart with his love. When one suffers death for his sake, Christ says, "I am He that liveth, and was dead; and, behold, I am alive forevermore, ... and have the keys of hell and of death." Revelation 1:18. The life that is sacrificed for Me is preserved unto eternal glory. —*DA, p. 669*

Present Biblically Sound Arguments

Believers are not to rest in suppositions and ill-defined ideas of what constitutes truth. Their faith must be firmly founded upon the Word of God so that when the testing time shall come and they are brought before councils to answer for their faith they may be able to give a reason for the hope that is in them, with meekness and fear.

Agitate, agitate, agitate. The subjects which we present to the world must be to us a living reality. It is important that in defending the doctrines which we consider fundamental articles of faith we should never allow ourselves to employ arguments that are not wholly sound. These may avail to silence an opposer, but they do not honor the truth.

We should present sound arguments, that will not only silence our opponents, but will bear the closest and most searching scrutiny. With those who have educated themselves as debaters there is great danger that they will not handle the Word of God with fairness. In meeting an opponent it should be our earnest effort to present subjects in such a manner as to awaken conviction in his mind, instead of seeking merely to give confidence to the believer.

Whatever may be man's intellectual advancement, let him not for a moment think that there is no need of thorough and continuous searching of the Scriptures for greater light. As a people we are called individually to be students of prophecy. We must watch with earnestness that we may discern any ray of light which God shall present to us. We are to catch the first gleamings of truth; and through prayerful study clearer light may be obtained, which can be brought before others. —*5T, pp. 707, 708*

Great Men Test Adventist Beliefs

Every position of truth taken by our people will bear the criticism of the greatest minds; the highest of the world's great men will be brought in contact with truth, and therefore every position we take should be critically examined and tested by the Scriptures. Now we seem to be unnoticed, but this will not always be. Movements are at work to bring us to the front; and if our theories of truth can be picked to pieces by historians or the world's greatest men, it will be done. —*Lt 6, 1886*

The Holy Spirit Helps Men in Court

Persecution will spread the light. The servants of Christ will be brought before the great men of the world, who, but for this, might never hear the gospel. The truth has been misrepresented to these men. They have listened to false charges concerning the faith of Christ's disciples. Often their only means of learning its real character is the testimony of those who are brought to trial for their faith. Under examination these are required to answer, and their judges to listen to the testimony borne. God's grace will be dispensed to his servants to meet the emergency. "It shall be given you," says Jesus, "in that same hour what ye shall speak. For it is not ye that speak, but the Spirit of your Father which speaketh in you."

As the Spirit of God illuminates the minds of his servants, the truth will be presented in its divine power and preciousness. Those who reject the truth will stand to accuse and oppress the disciples. But under loss and suffering, even unto death, the Lord's children are to reveal the meekness of their divine Example. Thus will be seen the contrast between Satan's agents and the representatives of Christ. The Saviour will be lifted up before the rulers and the people. The disciples were not endowed with the courage and fortitude of the martyrs until such grace was needed. Then the Saviour's promise was fulfilled.

When Peter and John testified before the Sanhedrin council, men "marveled; and they took knowledge of them, that they had been with Jesus." Acts 4:13. Of Stephen it is written that "all that sat in the council, looking steadfastly on him, saw his face as it had been the face of an angel." Men "were not able to resist the wisdom and the spirit by which he spake." Acts 6:15, 10. —*DA, p. 354*

God's People Testify before Rulers

Kings, governors, and great men will hear of you through the reports of those who are at enmity with you, and your faith and character will be misrepresented before them. But those who are falsely accused will have an opportunity to appear in the presence of their accusers to answer for themselves. They will have the privilege of bringing the light before those who are called the great men of the earth, and if you have studied the Bible, if you are ready to give an answer to every man that asketh you of the hope that is in you with meekness and fear, your enemies will not be able to gainsay your wisdom. You now have an opportunity to attain to the greatest intellectual power through the study of the Word of God. But if you are indolent, and fail to dig deep in the mines of truth, you will not be ready for the crisis that is soon to come upon us...

If you have an eye single to his glory, you need not take thought as to how you shall witness for his truth. "Take no thought how or what ye shall speak: ... for it is not ye that speak, but the Spirit of your Father which speaketh in you." How can the Spirit of God communicate with you? It is the Holy Spirit that is to bring to your remembrance whatsoever Jesus has said unto you. Are you now hearing the words of Christ? Does the word of Christ dwell in you richly in all wisdom? The reason that we do not know more of the inspiration of the Holy Spirit is that men would be lifted up in self, and take the glory to themselves, if God should crown their efforts with success.

Oh if you were hidden in Christ, if you were on the Rock of Ages, when you are brought before kings and great men, it would be evident that Jesus was at your side, and you would know just what answer to give, for the Spirit would give you what you should utter. Praise God for this promise!

The time is not far off when the people of God will be called upon to give their testimony before the rulers of the earth. Not one in twenty has a realization of what rapid strides we are making toward the great crisis in our history. The angels of God are holding the four winds, and this leads many to cry, "Peace and safety;" but there is no time for vanity, for trifling, for engaging the mind in unimportant matters. We must empty the soul temple of every defilement, and let the Spirit of God take full possession of the heart, that the character may be transformed. —*RH, Apr. 26, 1892*

46

Do Not Point Out Foolish Errors

When we begin to work with parliaments, and with men holding high positions in governments, the enemy is roused to exert all his strength against us, and he will make the work hard. Do not let your work be known any more than is necessary; the best course to follow is that which will avoid opposition. The least said about the foolish errors of others, the better. — *Ms 22c, 1895*

We Cannot Depend on Earthly Rulers

Christ presented the character of the unjust judge to show the kind of judgment that was then being executed, and would soon be shown at his trial. He would have his people in all time realize what little dependence can be placed on earthly rulers or judges in the day of adversity.

The elect people of God will stand before men in official position, who do not make the Word of God their guide and counselor, but who follow their unconsecrated, undisciplined impulses. Those who have taken a position to be loyal and true, to do the commandments of God, will understand by their own experience that they have adversaries who are moved by a power from beneath. Such adversaries beset Christ at every step, how constantly and determinedly no earthly being can ever know. Christ's disciples, like their Master, will be followed by continual temptation. But Christ is their refuge, as He was the refuge of the importunate widow. — *Ms 33, 1898*

Discussion Questions

1. Do the courts in your home country judge fairly? How will justice be compromised after church and state unite?

2. Which of Christ's teachings could be helpful in court someday?

3. What are some of the ways we could share Jesus in a courtroom?

4. Why are Christians specially qualified to take the judicial oath?

5. Satan treasures every unwise word spoken. Could this include time-wasting conversations on social media?

— 4 —

Persecution Begins

"Then they will deliver you up to tribulation and kill you, and you will be hated by all nations for my name's sake." — Matthew 24:9

Psalm 59:1-4	John 15:18-20	2 Cor. 4:8-11	2 Timothy 3:12	Rev. 2:8-11
Psalm 116:15	John 16:2, 33	Phil. 3:8	1 Peter 3:12-18	Rev. 13:7
Daniel 11:44	Acts 14:22	Heb. 11:30-40	1 Peter 4:12-19	Rev. 20:4

A) Enmity from the Brethren

Rebellion Makes Men Bitter

There is danger now of men losing sight of the important truths applicable for this period of time, and seeking for those things that are new, strange, and entrancing. Many, if reproved by the Spirit of God through his appointed agencies, refuse to receive correction, and a root of bitterness is planted in their own hearts against the Lord's servants who carry heavy, disagreeable burdens. —*Ms 92, 1897*

The Hardest Type of Persecution

The Saviour bade his disciples not to hope that the world's enmity to the gospel would be overcome, and that after a time its opposition would cease. He said, "I came not to send peace, but a sword." This creating of strife is not the effect of the gospel, but the result of opposition to it.

Of all persecution the hardest to bear is variance in the home, the estrangement of dearest earthly friends. But Jesus declares, "He that loveth father or mother more than Me is not worthy of Me: and he that loveth son or daughter more than Me is not worthy of Me. And he that taketh not his cross, and followeth after Me, is not worthy of Me." —*DA, p. 357*

Family Ties are Broken

All who have genuine faith will be tested and tried. They may have to forsake houses and lands, and even their own relatives, because of bitter opposition.

—Ms 9, 1900

False Brethren Bring Great Perils

There will be perils by land and by sea; but the greatest of all perils will be brought in by false brethren. Privations, trials, discord, and strife will meet us to confuse and discourage. *—Lt 133, 1897*

Some Businessmen are Treacherous

Every man whom God has chosen to do a special work becomes a target for Satan... The only safety for any of us is in clinging to Jesus and letting nothing separate the soul from the mighty Helper. Those who have merely a form of godliness, and yet are connected with the cause in business relations, are to be feared. They will surely betray their trust. They will be overcome by the devices of the tempter and will imperil the cause of God. *—5T, pp. 428, 429*

Children and Parents Battle

Decisions will be called for and made; backsliders will either return decidedly to their allegiance to God, or they will be enrolled in the ranks of the enemy: Satan will have control of all who finally refuse to be controlled by the law of God. He will inspire parents to war against their children, and children to war against their parents—to betray and deliver those of their own household to enemies. Coming events are casting their shadows upon our pathway.

—RH, Apr. 23, 1889

Nominal Adventists become Traitors

Much so-called Christianity passes for genuine, faithful soundness, but it is because those who profess it have no persecution to endure for the truth's sake. When the day comes when the law of God is made void, and the church is sifted by the fiery trials that are to try all that live upon the earth, a great proportion of those who are supposed to be genuine will give heed to seducing spirits, and will turn traitors and betray sacred trusts. They will prove our very worst persecutors. "Of your own selves shall men arise, speaking perverse things, to draw away disciples after them; and many will give heed to seducing spirits." *—RH, June 8, 1897*

Many Make False Accusations

Many who were once conscientious and loved God and his Word have become so hardened by rejecting the light of truth that they do not hesitate to wickedly misrepresent and falsely accuse those who love the holy Sabbath, if by so doing they can injure the influence of those who fearlessly declare the truth. — *EW, p. 69*

Sabbathkeepers are Slandered

Satan will then inspire men, and even professedly Christian men who refused to receive the love of the truth, to accuse and slander those who keep the commandments of God and have the faith of Jesus. He will lead those who appear to be good men to accuse the servants of God who refuse to bow down to the image of Baal in observing the spurious Sabbath and will cause men to cast contempt upon the Sabbath which the Lord sanctified and blessed.

— *Ms 104, 1893*

Nominal Adventists are Enraged

At the commencement of the time of trouble, we were filled with the Holy Ghost as we went forth and proclaimed the Sabbath more fully. This enraged the churches and nominal Adventists, as they could not refute the Sabbath truth. And at this time God's chosen all saw clearly that we had the truth, and they came out and endured the persecution with us. I saw the sword, famine, pestilence, and great confusion in the land. The wicked thought that we had brought the judgments upon them, and they rose up and took counsel to rid the earth of us, thinking that then the evil would be stayed. — *EW, p. 33*

Some Christians Act like Judas

Some who profess righteousness will, like Judas, betray their Lord into the hands of his bitterest enemies. These self-confident ones, determined to have their own way and to advocate their own ideas, will go on from bad to worse, until they will pursue any course rather than to give up their own will. They will go on blindly in the way of evil, but, like the deluded Pharisees, so self-deceived that they think they are doing God's service. Christ portrayed the course which a certain class will take when they have a chance to develop their true character: "And ye shall be betrayed both by parents, and brethren, and kinsfolks, and friends." — *5T, p. 690*

Friends and Relatives will Betray Us

To meet the trials, perplexities, and persecution that are sure to come in various ways in regard to the sabbath law, and to distinguish the path of duty clearly, will require intelligent knowledge of the Scriptures, much faith, and divine wisdom, for righteousness and truth will be darkened by error and false theories.

We shall find that we must let loose of all hands except the hand of Jesus Christ. Friends will prove treacherous, and will betray us. Relatives, deceived by the enemy, will think they do God service in opposing us and putting forth the utmost efforts to bring us into hard places, hoping we will deny our faith. But we may trust our hand in the hand of Christ amid darkness and peril.

— Ms 21, 1889

Apostates Manifest Bitter Enmity

The warnings that worldly conformity has silenced or withheld must be given under the fiercest opposition from enemies of the faith. And at that time the superficial, conservative class, whose influence has steadily retarded the progress of the work, will renounce the faith and take their stand with its avowed enemies, toward whom their sympathies have long been tending. These apostates will then manifest the bitterest enmity, doing all in their power to oppress and malign their former brethren and to excite indignation against them. This day is just before us. The members of the church will individually be tested and proved. *— 5T, p. 463*

Men Send Wolves after the Brethren

"Little children, it is the last time," writes John, "and as ye have heard that Antichrist shall come, even now there are many Antichrists: whereby we know that it is the last time. They went out from us, but they were not of us; for if they had been of us, they would no doubt have continued with us: but they went out, that it might be made manifest that they were not all of us." 1 John 2:18, 19.

Those who apostatize in time of trial, will, to secure their own safety, bear false witness, and betray their brethren. They will tell where they are concealed, putting the wolves on their track. Christ has warned us of this, that we may not be surprised at the unnatural and cruel course of friends and relatives. *— Ms 78, 1897*

Spiritless Men Turn on Christians

The followers of Jesus Christ will understand, in the great crisis which is before us, what dependence can be placed upon men who have turned from the warnings and entreaties of the Spirit of God, to follow their own imaginings. It becomes every soul now to stand on the sure rock, to build for time and for eternity, and to understand what voice they are following. "Show us a sign," said the unbelieving Jews, but the Lord did not gratify their curiosity. Jesus gave them a statement, "They have Moses and the prophets. If they believe not these, neither will they believe although one rose from the dead, and should come to them with a message." —*Lt 14, 1897*

Lukewarm Members Help Enemies

I was shown in the vision given me of the judgment that God would send warnings, counsels, and reproof. Some would take heed to their ways and seek the Lord, while some would follow their own judgment because it was more convenient and pleasing to their own natural hearts to do so.

Some others would kick against the pricks, rise up against the testimonies of reproof, despise the warnings, choose their own wisdom, be ensnared and overcome by the enemy, and be so blinded by his infatuations that they would be utterly unable to discern the things of God and would work directly against the light, enshrouding themselves in darkness and error. Then these very ones would sustain and strengthen the hands of our bitterest enemies. —*Lt 14, 1883*

Former Adventists are Great Adversaries

The truth is to be presented in its native force and clearness, whether men will hear or whether they will forbear. This cannot be done without exciting opposition. Those who refuse to receive the love of the truth will not rest without attempting to retard its progress. They have been turned unto fables, and will unite with the great adversary of souls to bring the message of heaven into contempt.

The apostle Paul warns us that "some shall depart from the faith, giving heed to seducing spirits, and doctrines of devils." This is what we may expect. Our greatest trials will come because of that class who have once advocated the truth, but who turn from it to the world, and trample it under their feet in hate and derision. —*RH, Jan. 10, 1888*

Parents Turn against Children

Parents will turn harshly against their children who accept unpopular truth. Those who conscientiously serve God will be accused of rebellion. Property that was willed to children or other relatives who believe the present truth will be given into other hands. Guardians will rob orphans and widows of their just dues. Those who depart from evil will make themselves a prey, through laws enacted to compel the conscience. Men will take to themselves property to which they have no right. The words of the apostle will be verified in the near future: "All that will live godly in Christ Jesus will suffer persecution." 2 Timothy 3:12. —*Lt 30a, 1892*

Gather Courage from Cowardice

When God's wrath is poured out upon the earth, who will then be able to stand? Now is the time for God's people to show themselves true to principle. When the religion of Christ is most held in contempt, when his law is most despised, then should our zeal be the warmest and our courage and firmness the most unflinching.

To stand in defense of truth and righteousness when the majority forsake us, to fight the battles of the Lord when champions are few—this will be our test. At this time we must gather warmth from the coldness of others, courage from their cowardice, and loyalty from their treason. The nation will be on the side of the great rebel leader. — *RH, Jan. 11, 1887*

Brother Rises against Brother

Fewer and fewer will become the sympathetic cords which bind man in brotherhood to his fellow man. The natural egotism of the human heart will be worked upon by Satan. He will use the uncontrolled wills and violent passions which were never brought under the control of God's will. This man wants his own way; the next man wants his own way. Every man's hand will be against his fellow man. Brother will rise against brother, sister against sister, parents against children, and children against parents.

All will be in confusion. Relatives will betray one another. There will be secret plotting to destroy life. Destruction, misery, and death will be seen on every hand. Men will follow the unrestrained bent of their hereditary and cultivated tendency to evil. — *Lt 20, 1901*

Some Adventists are Unconsecrated

I say again, be of good courage, and watch unto prayer... We know something of what is before us. We know that trials await us. We know that unconsecrated Seventh-day Adventists, who have a knowledge of the truth, but who have linked themselves with worldlings, will depart entirely from the faith, giving heed to deducing spirits. The enemy will gladly hold out inducements to them, to lead them to carry on a warfare against the people of God. — *Lt 127, 1903*

Some Become Defiant Scoffers

Many at first appeared to receive the warning; yet they did not turn to God with true repentance. They were unwilling to renounce their sins. During the time that elapsed before the coming of the Flood, their faith was tested, and they failed to endure the trial. Overcome by the prevailing unbelief, they finally joined their former associates in rejecting the solemn message.

Some were deeply convicted, and would have heeded the words of warning; but there were so many to jest and ridicule, that they partook of the same spirit, resisted the invitations of mercy, and were soon among the boldest and most defiant scoffers; for none are so reckless and go to such lengths in sin as do those who have once had light, but have resisted the convicting Spirit of God. — *PP, p. 95*

Former Members Become Satan's Agents

As the storm approaches, a large class who have professed faith in the third angel's message, but have not been sanctified through obedience to the truth, abandon their position and join the ranks of the opposition... By uniting with the world and partaking of its spirit, they have come to view matters in nearly the same light; and when the test is brought, they are prepared to choose the easy, popular side.

Men of talent and pleasing address, who once rejoiced in the truth, employ their powers to deceive and mislead souls. They become the bitterest enemies of their former brethren. When Sabbathkeepers are brought before the courts to answer for their faith, these apostates are the most efficient agents of Satan to misrepresent and accuse them, and by false reports and insinuations to stir up the rulers against them. — *GC, p. 608*

Many are Stumbling Blocks

There are troublous times before us, when Satan will make every effort to call in among us the unconverted, that they may prove stumbling blocks to souls and workers whom Satan can use to deceive. I am instructed to say to our people, Satan holds the minds of not a few of those who pass among us as believers of the truth. — *Ms 99, 1908*

Some People Seek Revenge

There are those who will, through hasty, unadvised moves, betray the cause of God into the enemy's power. There will be men who will seek revenge, who will become apostates and betray Christ in the person of his saints. All need to learn discretion; then there is danger on the other hand of being conservative, of giving away to the enemy in concession. Our brethren should be very cautious in this matter for the honor of God. They should make God their fear and their dread. — *Ms 6, 1889*

Families Must be Divided

The fact that Jesus, innocent and pure, should suffer, that God should lay all his wrath upon the head of his dear Son, that the guiltless should bear the punishment of the guilty, the just endure the penalty of sin for the unjust, breaks the heart; and as Jesus is lifted up, conviction strikes to the soul, and the love that prompted the bestowal of the infinite gift of Christ, constrains the sinner to surrender all to God.

But how different is the case of him who refuses to receive the salvation purchased for him at infinite cost. He refuses to look upon the humiliation and love of Jesus. He plainly says, "I will not have this man to reign over me." To all who take this attitude, Jesus says, "I came not to send peace, but a sword." Families must be divided in order that all who call upon the name of the Lord may be saved.

All who refuse his infinite love will find Christianity a sword, a disturber of their peace. The light of Christ will cut away the darkness that covers their evil doings, and their corruption, their fraud, and cruelty, will be exposed. Christianity unmasks the hypocrisies of Satan, and it is this unmasking of his designs that stirs his bitter hatred against Christ and his followers.

— RH, July 24, 1894

Christians Betray Their Friends

"Then shall they deliver you up to be afflicted," Christ said, "and shall kill you; and ye shall be hated of all nations for my name's sake. And then shall many be offended, and shall betray one another, and shall hate one another."

Those who have been our companions in Christian association do not always maintain their fidelity. Envy and evil surmising, if cherished, will separate very friends. The words of Christ will be strictly fulfilled, "Then shall many be offended, and shall betray one another, and shall hate one another."

— Ms 87, 1897

A Vision of Persecution by the Brethren

That night I dreamed that I was in Battle Creek looking out from the side glass at the door and saw a company marching up to the house, two and two. They looked stern and determined. I knew them well and turned to open the parlor door to receive them, but thought I would look again. The scene was changed. The company now presented the appearance of a Catholic procession. One bore in his hand a cross, another a reed. And as they approached, the one carrying a reed made a circle around the house, saying three times: "This house is proscribed. The goods must be confiscated. They have spoken against our holy order."

Terror seized me, and I ran through the house, out of the north door, and found myself in the midst of a company, some of whom I knew, but I dared not speak a word to them for fear of being betrayed. I tried to seek a retired spot where I might weep and pray without meeting eager, inquisitive eyes wherever I turned. I repeated frequently: "If I could only understand this! If they will tell me what I have said or what I have done!"

I wept and prayed much as I saw our goods confiscated. I tried to read sympathy or pity for me in the looks of those around me, and marked the countenances of several whom I thought would speak to me and comfort me if they did not fear that they would be observed by others. I made one attempt to escape from the crowd, but seeing that I was watched, I concealed my intentions. I commenced weeping aloud, and saying: "If they would only tell me what I have done or what I have said!" My husband, who was sleeping in a bed in the same room, heard me weeping aloud and awoke me. My pillow was wet with tears, and a sad depression of spirits was upon me. *— 1T, pp. 577, 578*

56

B) Terrible Persecution Occurs

We May Lose Our Lives

There is before us a mighty conflict. God calls upon his people to stand firm upon the platform of eternal truth. He calls upon them to stand in oneness, in unity; and He promises that He will be with us, to help us by his mighty power. We may lose our lives in the conflict, but at the last great day we shall receive a crown of life, that fadeth not away. —*Ms 71, 1903*

Sunday Laws bring Civil Penalties

When the leading churches of the United States, uniting upon such points of doctrine as are held by them in common, shall influence the state to enforce their decrees and to sustain their institutions, then Protestant America will have formed an image of the Roman hierarchy, and the infliction of civil penalties upon dissenters will inevitably result. — *GC, p. 445*

Satan Uses Every Possible Device

Opposition we shall have as we voice the message of the third angel. Satan will bring in every possible device to make of no effect the faith once delivered to the saints. "Many shall follow their pernicious ways; by reason of whom the way of truth shall be evil spoken of. And through covetousness shall they with feigned words make merchandise of you: whose judgment now of a long time lingereth not, and their damnation slumbereth not." 2 Peter 2:2, 3.

—*8T, p. 199*

Diabolical Strategies are Utilized

Satan will use his agencies to carry out diabolical devices, to overpower the saints of God, as in times past he used the Roman power to stay the course of Protestantism; yet the people of God can look calmly at the whole array of evil and come to the triumphant conclusion that because Christ lives we shall live also. The people of God are to advance in the same spirit in which Jesus met the assaults of the prince of darkness in the past. The evil confederacy can advance only in the course which Jesus has marked out before them; every step of their advance brings the saints of God nearer the great white throne, nearer the successful termination of their warfare. The confederacy of evil will finally be destroyed. —*Ms 92, 1894*

Enmity towards the Godly

Those who love and keep the commandments of God are most obnoxious to the synagogue of Satan, and the powers of evil will manifest their hatred toward them to the fullest extent possible. — *RH, Apr. 14, 1896*

Worship God or Baal

God's law is regarded as of no consequence, while the first day Sabbath is acknowledged as supreme. And if men will not exalt this spurious sabbath, and allow it to take the place of the true, the stocks, the prisons, the fires will be the price of their obedience to the law of God. The question is, "Shall we worship God or Baal?" Shall we bow to an idol, or shall we reverence and obey a "Thus saith the Lord?" — *Ms 67, 1898*

Face the Same Trials as Esther

The trying experiences that came to God's people in the days of Esther were not peculiar to that age alone. The revelator, looking down the ages to the close of time, has declared, "The dragon was wroth with the woman, and went to make war with the remnant of her seed, which keep the commandments of God, and have the testimony of Jesus Christ." Revelation 12:17. Some who today are living on the earth will see these words fulfilled. The same spirit that in ages past led men to persecute the true church, will in the future lead to the pursuance of a similar course toward those who maintain their loyalty to God. Even now preparations are being made for this last great conflict. — *PK, p. 605*

The Danger of Worldly Friends

One of the dangers to be met, if we should link up with unbelievers, is that we cannot depend upon the opinions and judgment, regarding the sacred interests of the Lord's work, of men who, with the Bible open before them, are living in open transgression of the law of God. We cannot depend upon them, because the enemy of Christ influences their minds. They may be ever so favorable to our work now, but in the future there will come times of crisis; and then our people will be brought into a position of extreme trial, if they are bound up in any way with the worldlings. Our people may think that they can guard against these difficulties that would naturally arise in their union with worldlings, but in this they will be disappointed. — *Lt 283, 1905*

Churches Despise God's Laws

The churches are naked, and without a covering. Like the archdeceiver they are without excuse, for they have the Word of God, plain and clear and pointed. While they would rein up the faithful and loyal subjects of the kingdom of God, depriving them of their liberty of conscience, bringing them before magistrates and judges, and pronouncing sentence upon them, delivering them into prison, putting them into the chain gang, and even condemning them to death, they themselves before the universe are showing determined and obstinate contempt of the laws of the eternal Jehovah.

—Ms 7a, 1896

Every Soul is Tested

Our people have been regarded as too insignificant to be worthy of notice, but a change will come. The Christian world is now making movements which will necessarily bring commandment-keeping people into prominence. There is a constant supplanting of God's truth by the theories and false doctrines of human origin. Movements are being set on foot to enslave the consciences of those who would be loyal to God. The lawmaking powers will be against God's people. Every soul will be tested. Oh, that we would, as a people, be wise for ourselves, and by precept and example impart that wisdom to our children! Every position of our faith will be searched into; and if we are not thorough Bible students, established, strengthened, and settled, the wisdom of the world's great men will lead us astray. *—5T, p. 546*

Sabbathkeepers Face Prison

Those who desire to be refreshed in mind, and instructed in the truth, should study the history of the early church during and immediately following the day of Pentecost. They need to study carefully the experience of Paul and the other apostles; for God's people in these days must pass through similar experiences.

As the world becomes more imbued with the spirit of the enemy, there will be more vehement opposition of the Word. Some will be imprisoned because they refuse to desecrate the Sabbath of the Lord. Those who would hold the beginning of their confidence firm unto the end must bear a living testimony to the world. Their words are to have a convincing power upon minds, and many through them will be turned to the Lord. *—Lt 190, 1907*

Churches and Governments Persecute

Satan will work miracles to deceive those who dwell upon the earth. Spiritualism will do its work by causing the dead to be personated. Those religious bodies who refuse to hear God's messages of warning will be under strong deception, and will unite with the civil power to persecute the saints. The Protestant churches will unite with the papal power in persecuting the commandment-keeping people of God. This union constitutes the great system of persecution which will exercise spiritual tyranny over the consciences of men. — *Lt 28, 1900*

The Loud Cry Enrages the Wicked

What shall we do in this time when iniquity is prevailing? Those who will take their stand to stem the current will have reproach and persecution. When will this persecution come? When the message goes with a loud cry. Those who do not love the truth do not want to hear. The truth of God is aggressive.

Those who carry it must meet with opposition. They cannot submit to laws and to the powers that be when these are in opposition to God. After the resurrection, the disciples went forth and proclaimed Jesus, even though He had been proscribed and crucified. It was contrary to the law for them to do so, yet they did not desist even when thrust into prison and forbidden to preach. So we have decided to obey God rather than man. — *Ms 6, 1884*

Sunday Laws Lead to Tribulation

When the State shall enforce the decrees and sustain the institutions of the church, then will Protestant America have formed an image of the Papacy. Then the true church will be assailed by persecution as were God's people in ancient times. Almost every century furnishes instances of what human hearts, controlled by rage and malice, can do under a plea of serving God by protecting the rights of the church and State.

The Protestant churches that have followed in the steps of Rome by forming alliances with worldly powers have manifested a similar desire to restrict liberty of conscience. How many non-conformist ministers have suffered under the power of the Church of England! Persecution always follows a restriction of religious liberty on the part of secular governments.

— *ST, Nov. 8, 1899*

God's Purpose is Fulfilled

The same scorn and hatred that was manifested against Christ may be seen now to exist against those whom He has evidently chosen to be his co-workers. Those whose spirits rise up against the doctrines of truth make hard work for the servants of Christ. But God will make their wrath to praise Him; they accomplish his purpose by stirring up minds to investigate the truth. God may allow men to follow their own wicked inclinations for a time, in opposing Him; but when He sees it is for his glory, and the good of his people, He will arrest the scorners, expose their presumptive course, and give triumph to his truth. —*3SP, p. 273*

The Loud Cry Brings Persecution

The Lord will make his word powerful in the earth. New cities and villages and territories will be entered; the church will arise and shine, because her light has come, for the glory of the Lord is risen upon her. New converts will be added to the churches, and those who now claim to be converted will feel in their own hearts the transforming power of the grace of Christ. Then Satan will be aroused, and will excite the bitterest persecution against God's people. But those not of our faith, who have not rejected light, will recognize the spirit of Christ in his true followers, and will take their stand with the people of God. —*RH, Dec. 23, 1890*

Many Martyred for Christ's Sake

The two armies will stand distinct and separate, and this distinction will be so marked that many who shall be convinced of truth will come on the side of God's commandment-keeping people. When this grand work is to take place in the battle, prior to the last closing conflict, many will be imprisoned, many will flee for their lives from cities and towns, and many will be martyrs for Christ's sake in standing in defense of the truth.

They will be brought before kings and rulers, and before councils to meet the false, absurd, and lying accusations brought against them, but they must stand firm as a rock to principle, and the promise is, "As thy days so shall thy strength be." Deuteronomy 33:25. You will not be tempted above what you are able to bear. Jesus bore all this and far more. The express command of God must be obeyed, for God has been working. Luke 21:8-19. —*Ms 6, 1889*

Persecution is Fierce and Terrible

The combat of wrong against right will be fierce and terrible. The forms of evil, nursed by rebellion against God, and strong with the growth of centuries, will show what lawless transgressors can do in connection with their leader. Let Seventh-day Adventist remember that they are now to stand as men and women prepared for the issue. —*Ms 72, 1902*

Waldensian Experiences Repeated

Let the history of the Waldenses testify what they suffered for their religion. Though persecuted and driven from their homes, they conscientiously studied the Word of God, and lived up to the light which shone upon them. When their possessions were taken from them, and their houses burned, they fled to the mountains, and there endured hunger, fatigue, cold, and nakedness.

And yet the scattered and homeless ones would assemble to unite their voices in singing and praising God, that they were accounted worthy to suffer for Christ's name. They encouraged and cheered one another, and were grateful for even their miserable retreat. Many of their children sickened and died through exposure to cold, and the sufferings of hunger; yet the parents did not for a moment think of yielding their faith. —*RH, Feb. 12, 1880*

Branded as Disturbers of the Peace

Persecution cannot do more than cause death, but the life is preserved to eternal life and glory. The persecuting power may take its stand, and command the disciples of Christ to deny the faith, to give heed to seducing spirits and doctrines of devils, by making void the law of God. But the disciples may ask, "Why should I do this? I love Jesus, and I will never deny his name."

When the power says, "I will call you a disturber of the peace," they may answer, "Thus they called Jesus, who was truth, and grace, and peace. They rejected, insulted, and mocked my Saviour." Why? They were stirred with a power from beneath. Satan inspired men to make the work of Christ as hard and trying as possible. Christ was, to the Jewish people, a rock of offense, while if they had received Him, He would have been the rock of their salvation. —*Lt 116, 1896*

Catholics Imitate the Pharisees

The Catholic hierarchy is not tested and proved by having the Son of God in its midst to reprove its hypocrisy and rebuke its corruptions as Jesus did those of the priests and Pharisees. Its emissaries show the same spirit against Christ's followers and treat them exactly as they would treat the Son of God were He in their place. "Inasmuch as ye have done it unto one of the least of these my brethren, ye have done it unto Me." Matthew 25:40. —*Ms 55, 1886*

A Dragonic Spirit is Revealed

A spirit of hatred and opposition to the Hebrews formed the bond of union and created a mutual sympathy among different bodies of men who might otherwise have warred with one another. This well illustrates what we frequently witness in our day in the existing union of men of different denominations to oppose present truth, men whose only bond seems to be that which is dragonic in its nature, manifesting bitterness and hatred against the remnant who keep the commandments of God.

This is especially seen in the first-day, no-day, and all-days-alike Adventists, who seem to be famous for hating and slandering one another, when they can spare time from their efforts to misrepresent, slander, and in every way abuse Seventh-day Adventists. —*3T, p. 572*

Faithful Christians Excite Persecution

The spirit of persecution will not be excited against those who have no connection with God, and so have no moral strength. It will be aroused against the faithful ones, who make no concessions to the world, and will not be swayed by its opinions, its favor, or its opposition. A religion that bears a living testimony in favor of holiness, and that rebukes pride, selfishness, avarice, and fashionable sins, will be hated by the world and by superficial Christians.

Marvel not, then, my youthful Christian friends, if the world hates you; for it hated your Master before you. When you suffer reproach and persecution, you are in excellent company; for Jesus endured it all, and much more. If you are faithful sentinels for God, these things are a compliment to you. It is the heroic souls, who will be true if they stand alone, who will win the imperishable crown. —*YI, May 28, 1884*

Timid Souls Become Strong

When laws are enacted that bind the consciences of those whom God has made free, and men are cast into prison for exercising their religious liberty, many poor, timid, ignorant souls will be hindered from doing the will of God; but many will learn aright from Jesus Christ, and will maintain their God given freedom at any cost. — *RH, Jan. 28, 1896*

The Oppression of Bible Heroes

Through trial God leads his children to perfect trust. "In the world ye shall have tribulation," Christ says; "but in Me ye shall have peace." It is through much tribulation that we are to enter the kingdom of God. The followers of Christ will often be sorely tried and afflicted. Joseph was maligned and persecuted because he was determined to preserve his virtue and integrity.

David, God's chosen messenger, was hunted like a beast of prey by wicked enemies. Daniel was cast into a den of lions because he would not yield his allegiance to God. Jeremiah spoke the word that God gave him, and his plain testimony so enraged the king and the princes that he was cast into a loathsome pit. Stephen was stoned for preaching Christ and Him crucified. Paul was imprisoned, and finally put to death, because he obeyed Christ's command to carry the Gospel to the Gentiles. — *ST, Feb. 5, 1902*

Christians Act like Christ's Persecutors

Men professing to be representatives of Christ will take a course similar to that taken by priests and rulers in their treatment of Paul. All who would fearlessly serve God according to the dictates of their own conscience, will need moral courage, firmness, and a knowledge of God and his word, to stand in that evil day. Persecution will again be kindled against those who are true to God; their motives will be impugned, their best efforts misinterpreted, their names cast out as evil.

Then will it come to pass, as foretold by Christ, that whoever shall seek to destroy the faithful, will think that he is doing God service. Then Satan will work with all his fascinating power, to influence the heart and becloud the understanding, to make evil appear good, and good evil. Then it is that he is through his agents to "show great signs and wonders, insomuch that, if it were possible, they shall deceive the very elect." — *LP, pp. 251, 252*

Men are Angry like Cain

The Protestant world has taken this child of papacy, and cherished it, and called it Christ's day—the Christian Sabbath. But it is a spurious sabbath, an idol, placed where the Lord's day should be. And, like Cain, the transgressor is exceedingly angry because the whole world does not regard it with the sacredness of the Sabbath of the Lord. —*Ms 163, 1897*

A Loss of Property, Freedom, and Life

When God has given us light showing the dangers before us, how can we stand clear in his sight if we neglect to put forth every effort in our power to bring it before the people? Can we be content to leave them to meet this momentous issue unwarned?

There is a prospect before us of a continued struggle, at the risk of imprisonment, loss of property, and even of life itself, to defend the law of God, which is made void by the laws of men. In this situation worldly policy will urge an outward compliance with the laws of the land, for the sake of peace and harmony. And there are some who will even urge such a course from the Scripture: "Let every soul be subject unto the higher powers... The powers that be are ordained of God." —*5T, p. 712*

Persecution Reveals Satan's Spirit

If men will not agree to trample underfoot the commandments of God, the spirit of the dragon is revealed. They are imprisoned, brought before councils, and fined. "He causeth all, both small and great, rich and poor, free and bond, to receive a mark in their right hand, or in their foreheads." Revelation 13:16. "He had power to give life unto the image of the beast, that the image of the beast should both speak, and cause that as many as would not worship the image of the beast should be killed." Revelation 13:15.

Thus Satan usurps the prerogatives of Jehovah. The man of sin sits in the seat of God, proclaiming himself to be God, and acting above God. There is a marked contrast between those who bear the seal of God and those who worship the beast and his image. The Lord's faithful servants will receive the bitterest persecution from false teachers, who will not hear the Word of God, and who prepare stumbling blocks to put in the way of those who would hear.

—*Lt 28, 1900*

Support Taken from Adventists

Nations will be stirred to their very center. Support will be withdrawn from those who proclaim God's law as the only standard of righteousness, the only sure test of character. And all who will not bow to the decree of the national councils, and obey the national laws to exalt the sabbath instituted by the man of sin, to the disregard of God's holy day, will feel not only the oppressive power of the Papacy, but the oppression of the Protestant world, who will seek to enforce the worship of the image of the beast. —*RH, Mar. 9, 1911*

Martyrs Convert Many Souls

Now we see what those before us have suffered for the truth's sake. The worthies who refused to bow to the golden image were cast into a burning fiery furnace, but Christ was with them there, and the fire did not consume them. There was not even the smell of fire upon their garments.

Now some of us may be brought to just as severe a test. Will we obey the commandments of men, or will we obey the commandments of God? This is a question that will be asked of many. The best thing for us is to come into close connection with God; and if He would have us be martyrs for the truth's sake, it may be the means of bringing many more into the truth. —*Ms 83, 1886*

Many Lose Homes and Heritage

The future glory and elevation of the adopted sons and daughters of God is not now discerned. By the world they are scorned and despised. But God's people have the sympathies of a better world than this, even a heavenly. "And every man that hath this hope in Him, purifieth himself, even as He is pure." They have that faith that works by love, and purifies the soul. The Spirit of God brings every faculty, every organ of the body, into conformity with Him. Even the thoughts are brought into obedience to Christ.

In every habit and practice the living principle to be like Jesus, is cherished. The desires are upward; the heart is filled with joy at the anticipation of the future, for they looked "for a city which hath foundations whose maker and builder is God." Many, because of their faith, will be cut off from house and heritage here; but they may still be filled with joy, if they will give their hearts to Christ, receiving the message of his grace, resting upon their substitute and surety, even the blood of the Son of God. —*Ms 90, 1897*

Persecution to Intensify

Persecution will come more definitely and decidedly upon the people of God, because the godly are seeking for uprightness and holiness, and the disobedient are in sin. The sin-loving do not choose the will and ways of God; and the obedient, in their character and course of action, are a constant rebuke to the sinful. When the truth finds access to the heart, it must fight every inch of the way. —*Lt 2c, 1892*

A Brief History of Sunday Laws

As the papacy became firmly established, the work of Sunday exaltation was continued. For a time the people engaged in agricultural labor when not attending church, and the seventh day was still regarded as the Sabbath. But steadily a change was effected. Those in holy office were forbidden to pass judgment in any civil controversy on Sunday. Soon after, all persons, of whatever rank, were commanded to refrain from common labor on pain of a fine for freemen and stripes in the case of servants. Later it was decreed that rich men should be punished with the loss of half of their estates; and finally, that if still obstinate they should be made slaves. —*GC, p. 574*

Zealots Coerce the Conscience

The scenes of persecution enacted during Christ's life will be enacted by false religionists till the close of time. Men think that they have a right to take into their charge the consciences of men, and work out their theories of apostasy and transgression. History will be repeated. Christ declared that prior to his Second Coming the world would be as it was in the days of Noah, when men reached such a pass in following their own sinful imagination that God destroyed them by a flood.

Every power that has been exercised since the betrayal of Christ to force the consciences of men, every court that has taken upon itself to decide man's destiny by its measurement of what constitutes religion, has revealed satanic attributes. Men have betrayed and persecuted God's chosen ones. They have taken the life that God alone can give. They have done that which they will wish they had never done when they are asked, "Who gave you this authority? Who required this at your hands? Who authorized you to put God's children to death?" —*Ms 111, 1897*

Perplexities beyond Imagination

We are on the very verge of the time of trouble, and perplexities that are scarcely dreamed of are before us. A power from beneath is leading men to war against heaven. Human beings have confederated with satanic agencies to make void the law of God. — *9T, p. 43*

All Who Love God are Persecuted

Test and trial will come to every soul that loves God. The Lord does not work a miracle to prevent this ordeal of trial, to shield his people from the temptations of the enemy. If they are tempted severely, it is because circumstances have been so shaped by the apostasy of Satan that temptations are permitted. Characters are to be developed that will decide the fitness of the human family for the heavenly home,—characters that will stand through the pressure of unfavorable circumstances in private and public life, and that will, under the severest temptations, through the grace of God grow brave and true, be firm as a rock to principle, and come forth from the fiery ordeal, of more value than the golden wedge of Ophir. God will endorse, with his own superscription, as his elect, those who possess such characters.

—RH, Sept. 14, 1897

The Spirit of Torture Still Exists

"Ye shall be betrayed both by parents, and brethren, and kinsfolks, and friends; and some of you shall they cause to be put to death." … Every indignity, reproach, and cruelty that Satan could instigate human hearts to devise, has been visited upon the followers of Jesus. And it will be again fulfilled in a marked manner; for the carnal heart is still at enmity with the law of God, and will not be subject to its commands.

The world is no more in harmony with the principles of Christ today than it was in the days of the apostles. The same hatred that prompted the cry, "Crucify Him! Crucify Him!" the same hatred that led to the persecution of the disciples, still works in the children of disobedience. The same spirit which in the Dark Ages consigned men and women to prison, to exile, and to death, which conceived the exquisite torture of the Inquisition, which planned and executed the Massacre of St. Bartholomew, and which kindled the fires of Smithfield, is still at work with malignant energy in unregenerate hearts. The history of truth has ever been the record of a struggle between right and wrong. — *AA, p. 84*

Men Suffer Humiliation and Abuse

Satan and his angels determined to make Christ's death as humiliating as possible. They filled the hearts of the Jewish leaders with feelings of bitter hatred against the Saviour. Controlled by the enemy, priests and rulers stirred the multitude to take part against the Son of God. Aside from Pilate's declaration of his innocence, no one spoke a word in his favor. And even Pilate, knowing his innocence, gave Him over to the abuse of men under the control of Satan.

Similar events will take place in the near future. Men will exalt and rigidly enforce laws that are in direct opposition to the law of God. Though zealous in enforcing their own commandments, they will turn away from a plain "Thus saith the Lord." Exalting a spurious rest day, they will seek to force men to dishonor the law of Jehovah, the transcript of his character. Though innocent of wrongdoing, the servants of God will be given over to suffer humiliation and abuse at the hands of those who, inspired by Satan, are filled with envy and religious bigotry. —9T, p. 229

America becomes a Battlefield

The persecutions of Protestants by Romanism by which the religion of Jesus Christ was almost annihilated, will be more than rivaled when Protestantism and popery are combined. The darkest pages of history will be opened in that great day when it will be too late for wrongs to be righted. Registered in the book are crimes that have been committed because of religious differences. We are not ignorant of the history. Europe was shaken as though with an earthquake when a church, lifted up in pride and vanity, haughty and tyrannical, devoted to condemnation and death all who dared to think for themselves, and who ventured to take the Bible as the foundation of their faith.

Our own land is to become a battlefield on which is to be carried on the struggle for religious liberty to worship God according to the dictates of our own conscience. Then can we not discern the work of the enemy in keeping men asleep who ought to be awake, whose influence shall not be neutral but wholly and entirely on the Lord's side? Shall men cry, "Peace and safety," now, when sudden destruction is coming upon the world; when God's wrath shall be poured out? —Ms 30, 1889

Sabbathkeepers Suffer Greatly

During the past night I seemed to be enumerating in my mind the evidences we have to substantiate the faith we hold. We see that seducers are waxing worse and worse. We see the world working to the point of establishing by law a false sabbath and making it a test for all. This question will soon be before us. God's Sabbath will be trampled underfoot and a false sabbath will be exalted. In this Sunday law there is possibility for great suffering to those who observe the seventh day. The working out of Satan's plans will bring persecution to the people of God.

But the faithful servants of God need not fear the outcome of the conflict. If they will follow the pattern set for them in the life of Christ, if they will be true to the requirements of God, their reward will be eternal life, a life that measures with the life of God. —*Ms 11, 1909*

Evil Men Cannot Destroy the Soul

"I say unto you, my friends," Christ said, "be not afraid of them that kill the body, and after that have no more than they can do." Luke 12:4.

The priests and rulers did all that lay in their power against the only begotten Son of God and against all who acknowledged Him, for they were imbued with the spirit of him who is a liar and a murderer. But though Satan vented his spite against the children of God and their great Head, he could not control the conscience or tarnish the soul. He may cause all the suffering possible to the body, but he cannot change the character of the man who conscientiously serves God.

Today men may persecute even unto death in an effort to make their fellow men worship an idol sabbath which has been brought into existence by the man of sin, who thinks to change times and laws. But to torture and put to death the body is all they can do. Satan makes a continual effort to ruin the souls God is seeking to save. By his masterly inventions and crooked deceptions he seeks to confuse men's minds in regard to the Way, the Truth, and the Life. Under his direction men have inflicted untold pain and misery on their fellow men. But they have never been able to harm the soul. There is a power which can destroy both soul and body. "I will forewarn ye whom ye shall fear. Fear Him which, after He hath killed, hath power to cast into hell, yea, I say unto you, fear Him." Luke 12:5. —*Ms 42, 1899*

Pressure to Accept False Doctrines

The world is full of false teaching; and if we do not resolutely search the Scriptures for ourselves, we shall accept the world's errors for truth, adopt its customs, and deceive our own hearts. Its doctrines and customs are at variance with the truth of God. Those who seek to turn from its service to the service of God, will need divine help. They will have to set their faces like a flint toward Zion. They will feel the opposition of the world, the flesh, and the devil, and will have to go contrary to the spirit and influences of the world.

Since the time when the Son of God breasted the haughty prejudices and unbelief of mankind, there has been no change in the attitude of the world toward the religion of Jesus. The servants of Christ must meet the same spirit of opposition and reproach, and must go "without the camp, bearing his reproach." — *RH, July 6, 1911*

Satan Has a Thousand Masked Batteries

When we are in this position of oneness with Christ, Satan's enmity will be aroused. He who stands in defense of the truth will draw upon himself the dislike, the criticism, the decided opposition of relatives and professed friends; he will become a subject of ridicule. All opposition and persecution, whether in its mildest or most terrible forms, is only the development of a principle that originated with the first great rebel in heaven. This work will continue as long as Satan exists.

As we near the close of time, the opposing element will work in the same lines in which it has worked in times past. Every soul will be tested. Under persecution it will be made manifest just what banner every individual has chosen to stand under.

While sin remains, the offense of the cross will never cease. Satan has a thousand masked batteries which will be opened upon the loyal, commandment-keeping people of God to compel them to violate conscience. The followers of Christ must expect to encounter sneers. They will be reviled; their words and their faith will be misrepresented. Coldness and contempt may be harder to endure than martyrdom. With some persons it would require more courage to encounter a laugh than to be thrust through with a sword. But we must stand steadfastly for the truth, not returning railing for railing, but contrariwise, blessing. — *Lt 30a, 1892*

The Time of Trouble Has Begun

The time of trouble has already begun. We hear continually of riots and accidents, or murders and robberies. Human life is no longer safe unless under the protection of God. God's servants must not be surprised that they meet with great difficulties and persecution at this time. In his day, the world's Redeemer, the Son of God, was shamefully treated by the people He came to bless. He had to go from city to city to ensure his safety, and this persecution followed Him until his work on earth was accomplished. —*Lt 266, 1907*

Remember God's Promise When Arrested

When one is arrested for working on the first day of the week according to the commandment, do you hear him say I will not keep the Sabbath anymore? No he is glad that he can bring the truth before the people, even in this way.

He bears in mind the promise, "If thou take away thy foot from the Sabbath, from doing thy pleasure on my holy day, and call the Sabbath a delight, the holy of the Lord, honorable, and shalt honor Him, not doing thine own ways, nor finding thine own pleasure, nor speaking thine own words, then shalt thou delight thyself in the Lord, and I will cause thee to ride upon the high places of the earth, and feed thee with the heritage of Jacob thy Father, for the mouth of the Lord hath spoken it."

When Paul and Silas were thrown into prison, and their feet put into the stocks, the universe of heaven knew all about it. In the night the jailers heard these men singing praises to God. Then the army of heaven approached, and at their tread the earth began to quake, and the prison doors were thrown open. The jailers knew that those who had kept the prison when Peter escaped had been put to death, and they came in fear and trembling to Paul and Silas. He acknowledged the power of God and asked forgiveness for his cruelty. "What shall I do to be saved?" he asked. Right there the jailer gave himself to God.

The God who wrought for Paul and Silas lives today. If the prison is to be our home, we can sing within prison walls. We will not be called to endure more than the King of glory bore in our behalf. May God help us to establish the fear of God in our homes. May He help us to make straight paths for our feet. May He help us to help one another, and the Lord of hosts will be with us. —*EA, pp. 173, 174*

Tenfold Greater Difficulties

In the future we shall have to contend with difficulties tenfold greater than any we have yet had. Do you ask why I say this? Do you not realize that Satan's time is very short? He is working and planning with intensity of effort to place obstacles in the way of God's people and to hinder their progress. We have the powers of darkness to meet. At this time, more than ever before, willing, unquestioning obedience is needed if we come off conquerors.

—Ms 118, 1904

The Remnant Meet Goliath's Spirit

Those who are loyal to God, keeping all of his commandments, will meet a spirit of opposition similar to that which David encountered. Learned men, proud and boastful in their supposed superiority, will feel, as did Goliath, to despise the little band who are loyal to God. Many of these never graduated from a college; but, with the Bible in their hands, they stand in defense of the truth of God, and vindicate his Sabbath, which has been trodden beneath lawless feet. But the Lord can make his strength perfect in man's weakness. If, like David, men will forget self, and seek to honor God and to vindicate his name and his truth, He will work mightily with them, and crown their efforts with success.

But there are many who take the glory to themselves if the work of God is prospered in their hands. They become proud and self-sufficient, and flatter themselves that their success is owing to their own superior abilities. Prosperity would often prove the ruin of the one thus honored of the Lord. Our compassionate Father in heaven pities the weakness of our nature, and bears long with our follies. If this were not the case, He would not have given his Son to come to a fallen world and bear the buffetings and temptations of Satan, that He might show men how to overcome.

The enemies of the truth will grow stronger and more bitter in their opposition to the law of God. They will resort to ridicule and insult; they will wrest and misinterpret the Scriptures, and will sustain their positions by human opinions and arguments. They will present things in a false light, and thus pervert even honest minds. They will glory in their strength, as did the Philistine giant, and for a time they may appear to prosper. But their triumph will not always last; they will themselves fall into the pit which they have digged for others. *— ST, Mar. 4, 1886*

Persecution is Inevitable

With every rejection of truth the minds of the people will become darker, their hearts more stubborn, until they are entrenched in an infidel hardihood. In defiance of the warnings which God has given, they will continue to trample upon one of the precepts of the Decalogue, until they are led to persecute those who hold it sacred. Christ is set at naught in the contempt placed upon his word and his people. — *GC, p. 603*

The Papacy Uses Attraction before Force

History will be repeated. False religion will be exalted. The first day of the week, a common working day, possessing no sanctity whatever, will be set up as was the image at Babylon. All nations and tongues and peoples will be commanded to worship this spurious sabbath. This is Satan's plan to make of no account the day instituted by God, and given to the world as a memorial of creation. The decree enforcing the worship of this day is to go forth to all the world. In a limited degree, it has already gone forth. In several places the civil power is speaking with the voice of a dragon, just as the heathen king spoke to the Hebrew captives.

Trial and persecution will come to all who, in obedience to the Word of God, refuse to worship this false sabbath. Force is the last resort of every false religion. At first it tries attraction, as the king of Babylon tried the power of music and outward show. If these attractions, invented by men inspired by Satan, failed to make men worship the image, the hungry flames of the furnace were ready to consume them. So it will be now. The Papacy has exercised her power to compel men to obey her, and she will continue to do so.

We need the same spirit that was manifested by God's servants in the conflict with paganism. Giving an account of the treatment of the Christians by the emperor of Rome, Tertullian says, "We are thrown to the wild beasts to make us recant; we are burned in the flames; we are condemned to prisons and to mines; we are banished to islands—such as Patmos—and all have failed." So it was in the case of the three Hebrew worthies; their eye was single to the glory of God; their souls were steadfast; the power of the truth held them firmly to their allegiance to God. It is in the power of God alone that we shall be enabled to be loyal to Him. — *ST, May 6, 1897*

The Power of Persecution

The time in which we live is a time when the church militant will realize the oppressive power of persecution, because they keep the Sabbath of creation which God has sanctified and blessed. — *Ms 139, 1903*

The Spirit of Cain is Revived

These words of Christ have been fulfilled in the experience of those who have been loyal to the God of heaven according to the light received. "If they have persecuted Me," He said, "they will also persecute you; if they have kept my saying, they will keep yours also." "All that will live not merely profess to live godly in Christ Jesus, shall suffer persecution." "And these things will they do unto you, because they have not known by an experimental knowledge the Father, nor Me."

As Christ was hated without cause, so will his people be hated because they are obedient to the commandments of God. If He who was pure, holy, and undefiled, who did good, and only good, in our world, was treated as a base criminal, and condemned to death, his disciples must expect but similar treatment, however faultless may be their life and blameless their character.

Human enactments, laws manufactured by satanic agencies under a plea of goodness and restriction of evil, will be exalted, while God's holy commandments are despised and trampled underfoot. And all who prove their loyalty by obedience to the law of Jehovah must be prepared to be arrested, to be brought before councils that have not for their standard the high and holy law of God.

The same spirit that moved the priests and rulers had moved Cain to slay his brother. It is the apostasy from truth that works in the children of disobedience to silence the voice of those who are calling them to obedience. And today this spirit is manifested in the churches that are trampling upon the Word of God, transgressing his holy law. They know not what spirit they are of, nor the end of the dark tunnel through which they are passing.

Deceived, deluded, blind, they are hastening forward to the first and the second death. The vast tide of human will and human passion is leading to things they did not dream of when they discarded the law of Jehovah for the inventions of men, to cause oppression and suffering to human beings.

— RH, Dec. 26, 1899

A Surprising Storm of Opposition

In this time of persecution the faith of the Lord's servants will be tried. They have faithfully given the warning, looking to God and to his word alone. God's Spirit, moving upon their hearts, has constrained them to speak. Stimulated with holy zeal, and with the divine impulse strong upon them, they entered upon the performance of their duties without coldly calculating the consequences of speaking to the people the word which the Lord had given them. They have not consulted their temporal interests, nor sought to preserve their reputation or their lives.

Yet when the storm of opposition and reproach bursts upon them, some, overwhelmed with consternation, will be ready to exclaim: "Had we foreseen the consequences of our words, we would have held our peace." They are hedged in with difficulties. Satan assails them with fierce temptations. The work which they have undertaken seems far beyond their ability to accomplish. They are threatened with destruction. The enthusiasm which animated them is gone; yet they cannot turn back.

Then, feeling their utter helplessness, they flee to the Mighty One for strength. They remember that the words which they have spoken were not theirs, but his who bade them give the warning. God put the truth into their hearts, and they could not forbear to proclaim it.

The same trials have been experienced by men of God in ages past. Wycliffe, Huss, Luther, Tyndale, Baxter, Wesley, urged that all doctrines be brought to the test of the Bible and declared that they would renounce everything which it condemned. Against these men persecution raged with relentless fury; yet they ceased not to declare the truth.

Different periods in the history of the church have each been marked by the development of some special truth, adapted to the necessities of God's people at that time. Every new truth has made its way against hatred and opposition; those who were blessed with its light were tempted and tried. The Lord gives a special truth for the people in an emergency.

Who dare refuse to publish it? He commands his servants to present the last invitation of mercy to the world. They cannot remain silent, except at the peril of their souls. Christ's ambassadors have nothing to do with consequences. They must perform their duty and leave results with God.

— GC, pp. 608, 609

The Offense of the Cross

The character of the persecution changes with the times, but the principle—the spirit that underlies it—is the same that has slain the chosen of the Lord ever since the days of Abel.

As men seek to come into harmony with God, they will find that the offense of the cross has not ceased. Principalities and powers and wicked spirits in high places are arrayed against all who yield obedience to the law of heaven. Therefore, so far from causing grief, persecution should bring joy to the disciples of Christ, for it is an evidence that they are following in the steps of their Master.

While the Lord has not promised his people exemption from trials, He has promised that which is far better. He has said, "As thy days, so shall thy strength be." "My grace is sufficient for thee: for my strength is made perfect in weakness." Deuteronomy 33:25; 2 Corinthians 12:9.

If you are called to go through the fiery furnace for his sake, Jesus will be by your side even as He was with the faithful three in Babylon. Those who love their Redeemer will rejoice at every opportunity of sharing with Him humiliation and reproach. The love they bear their Lord makes suffering for his sake sweet. —*MB, pp. 29, 30*

Discussion Questions

1. Why is persecution by family and friends extremely difficult?

2. How will some Christians act like Judas when the tribulation begins?

3. Why must some families be divided? How will those married to unbelievers be tested?

4. What was the meaning of the vision where Mrs. White saw her familiar brethren change into a Catholic procession?

5. Why does the Loud Cry bring about bitter persecution?

— 5 —

God's Church is Purified

"His winnowing fan is in his hand, and He will thoroughly clean out his threshing floor, and gather his wheat into the barn; but He will burn up the chaff with unquenchable fire."

— Psalm 25:19

Job 23:8-12	Proverbs 17:3	Isaiah 57:12, 13	Ezek. 22:17-22	Malachi 3:1-3
Psalm 25:14-21	Isaiah 8:13, 14	Isaiah 48:10	Daniel 3:16-27	Revelation 3:18

A) Weak Believers Stumble

Warlike Christians Apostatize

Christianity is not manifested in pugilistic accusations and condemnations. Some who are now so ready to take up weapons of warfare, in times of real peril will make manifest the fact that they have not built upon the solid Rock themselves, and they will yield to temptation. — *Lt 36, 1895*

Men Break Every Commandment

The most trying times are to come upon the whole earth to try them that dwell upon the face of the whole earth. Whosoever shall be willing to break one of the least of God's commandments will be found unable in spirit and in truth to keep any one of the commandments. — *Lt 21, 1893*

Some are Scared into Serving Satan

Persecution has frightened many poor souls from the bloodstained banner of Prince Emmanuel to the black banner of the great apostate. For the sake of this life, they transgress the law of God, and in that day when all transgressors will be destroyed, they will be bound up with Satan to suffer the second death. All who continue to transgress after light has been given them will perish with the enemy of God. — *Ms 87, 1897*

Pride Leads to Apostasy

Many are holding on to the truth with only the tips of their fingers. They have had great light and many privileges. Like Capernaum, they have in this respect been exalted to heaven. But unless they put away their pride and self-confidence, in the time of trial that is approaching they will become apostates. Unless they have an entire transformation of character, they will never enter heaven. — *RH, Feb. 11, 1904*

Unfruitful Christians are Lost

Time is rapidly passing, and wickedness is increasing. If we refuse to do the good we may do, we place ourselves in a perilous position. If we delay to enter the ranks of those who are workers together with God, we will find ourselves in the ranks of those who oppose truth and righteousness, who have turned away from the truth and are turned unto fables. The condition of this class is a sad one; for unless some power shall break the spell that is upon them, they will be lost, eternally lost.

God's people will be called to pass through trying experiences. Many will fall at their post, betrayed and condemned by their fellow men. In such times of trial they can remember that the Saviour suffered in like manner, passed over that very ground in their behalf. — *Lt 230, 1907*

Unanchored Christians Uprooted

When men are willing to become intelligent in regard to the cause of God because they have invested faith and means in it, God will help them to understand, and they will be steadfast in the faith; but when they have merely a theory, a shallow faith they cannot explain, a sudden temptation will cause them to drift away with the current bearing toward the world. It is not always an easy matter to be steadfast and immovable, "always abounding in the work of the Lord."

In order to be firmly anchored, there must be something firm to hold us; and nothing will avail until Christ takes possession of the soul, until the cause becomes our property, and is made a part of ourselves. Many who now appear strong, and talk in vindication of the truth, are not rooted and grounded. They have no tap-root; and when the storms of opposition and persecution come, they are like a tree uprooted by the blast. — *RH, Apr. 29, 1884*

Tests and Trials Lead to Apostasies

When the test and trial comes to every soul, there will be apostasies. Traitors, heady, high-minded, and self-sufficient men will turn away from the truth, making shipwreck of the faith. Why? Because they did not dig deep and make their foundation sure. They were not riveted to the eternal Rock. When the words of the Lord, through his chosen messengers, are brought to them, they murmur, and think that the way is made too strait. Like those who were thought to be the disciples of Christ, but who were displeased by his words, and walked no more with Him, they will turn away from Christ. — *Ms 68, 1897*

Many Church Members are Offended

On every occasion that persecution takes place, the witnesses make decisions, either for Christ or against Him. Those who show sympathy for the men wrongly condemned, who are not bitter against them, show their attachment for Christ. Many will be offended because the principles of the truth cut directly across their practice or their income. Many will stumble and fall, apostatizing from the faith they once advocated. Many who have professed to love the truth will then show that they had no vital union with the true vine. They will be cut away, as branches that bear no fruit, and will be bound up with unbelievers, scoffers, and mockers. — *Ms 78, 1897*

Skeptics Struggle Tremendously

Those who feel at liberty to question the Word of God, to doubt everything where there is any chance to be unbelieving, will find that it will require a tremendous struggle to have faith when trouble comes. It will be almost impossible to overcome the influence that binds the mind which has been educated in the line of unbelief, for by this course the soul is bound in Satan's snare and becomes powerless to break the dreadful net that has been woven closer and closer about the soul.

In taking a position of doubt, man calls to his aid the agencies of Satan. But the only hope of one who has been educated in the line of unbelief is to fall all helpless upon the Saviour and, like a child, submit his will and his way to Christ that he may be brought out of darkness into his marvelous light. Man does not have the power to recover himself from the snare of Satan. He who educates himself in the line of questioning, doubting, and criticizing strengthens himself in infidelity. — *Ms 3, 1895*

Perilous Trials Thicken

We can never know our weakness or our strength until we have been tested by the furnace of trial. As trials thicken around us, those who have had great light, but have not improved it, will go out from us. Giving heed to seducing spirits, they will depart from the faith. — *Ms 117a, 1901*

God Leaves Idol Worshipers

Some are willing to receive one point; but when God brings them to another testing point, they shrink from it and stand back, because they find that it strikes directly at some cherished idol. Here they have opportunity to see what is in their hearts that shuts out Jesus. They prize something higher than the truth, and their hearts are not prepared to receive Jesus. Individuals are tested and proved a length of time to see if they will sacrifice their idols and heed the counsel of the True Witness.

If any will not be purified through obeying the truth, and overcome their selfishness, their pride, and evil passions, the angels of God have the charge: "They are joined to their idols, let them alone," and they pass on to their work, leaving these with their sinful traits unsubdued, to the control of evil angels. — *1T, p. 187*

Weak Men will Not Uphold Truth

I have been shown that many who profess to have a knowledge of present truth know not what they believe. They do not understand the evidences of their faith. They have no just appreciation of the work for the present time. When the time of trial shall come, there are men now preaching to others who will find, upon examining the positions they hold, that there are many things for which they can give no satisfactory reason. Until thus tested they knew not their great ignorance.

And there are many in the church who take it for granted that they understand what they believe; but, until controversy arises, they do not know their own weakness. When separated from those of like faith and compelled to stand singly and alone to explain their belief, they will be surprised to see how confused are their ideas of what they had accepted as truth. Certain it is that there has been among us a departure from the living God and a turning to men, putting human in place of divine wisdom. — *5T, p. 707*

81

Adversity Purges the Lukewarm

Every trial made by the refining, purifying process upon professed Christians proves some to be dross. The fine gold does not always appear. In every religious crisis some fall under temptation. The shaking of God blows away multitudes like dry leaves. Prosperity multiplies a mass of professors. Adversity purges them out of the church. As a class, their spirits are not steadfast with God. They go out from us because they are not of us; for when tribulation or persecution arises because of the word, many are offended.

—4T, p. 89

Many Prove to be Base Metal

"Because iniquity shall abound, the love of many shall wax cold" Matthew 24:12. The very atmosphere is polluted with sin. Soon God's people will be tested by fiery trials, and the great proportion of those who now appear to be genuine and true will prove to be base metal. Instead of being strengthened and confirmed by opposition, threats, and abuse, they will cowardly take the side of the opposers. The promise is, "Them that honor Me I will honor." Shall we be less firmly attached to God's law because the world at large have attempted to make it void? *—RH, Jan. 11, 1887*

Some Adventists Forsake the Sabbath

With some there is an outward show, a form of godliness, but there is no real power; and against them is pronounced the sentence, "Thou art weighed in the balances, and found wanting." They are deficient, yet, in false confidence, they are deceiving themselves and misleading others. Yielding to Satan's sophistry, they stand on a false track, and by their representations endeavor to tear down truths that God has made fast, never to be moved. By their course, the inexperienced are led to wonder whether these special truths are not, after all, errors that ought to be shunned.

When brought into strait places, they will give up the Sabbath and its powerful endorsement, and the more they are opposed in their apostasy, the more self-sufficient and self-deceived they become. They have lifted up their souls unto vanity, and God says, "Remember therefore how thou hast received and heard, and hold fast, and repent. If therefore thou shalt not watch, I will come on thee as a thief, and thou shalt not know what hour I will come upon thee." Revelation 3:3. *—Lt 95, 1905*

Many Cannot Bear Reproach

The hot summer sun, that strengthens and ripens the hardy grain, destroys that which has no depth of root. So he who "hath not root in himself," "dureth for a while"; but "when tribulation or persecution ariseth because of the word, by and by he is offended." Many receive the gospel as a way of escape from suffering, rather than as a deliverance from sin. They rejoice for a season, for they think that religion will free them from difficulty and trial.

While life moves smoothly with them, they may appear to be consistent Christians. But they faint beneath the fiery test of temptation. They cannot bear reproach for Christ's sake. When the Word of God points out some cherished sin, or requires self-denial or sacrifice, they are offended. It would cost them too much effort to make a radical change in their life. They look at the present inconvenience and trial, and forget the eternal realities. Like the disciples who left Jesus, they are ready to say, "This is a hard saying; who can hear it?" John 6:60. — *COL, p. 47*

God Removes Corrupt Individuals

God is sifting his people. He will have a clean and holy people. We cannot read the heart of man. But He has provided means to keep the church pure. A corrupt people has arisen who could not live with the people of God. They despised reproof, and would not be corrected. They had an opportunity to know that their warfare was an unrighteous one. They had time to repent of their wrongs; but self was too dear to die. They nourished it, and it grew strong, and they separated from the peculiar people of God, whom He was purifying unto Himself.

We all have reason to thank God that a way has been opened to save the church, for the wrath of God must have come upon us, if these corrupt individuals had remained with us. Every honest one that may be deceived by these disaffected ones, will have the true light in regard to them if every angel from heaven has to visit them, and enlighten their minds. We have nothing to fear in this matter. As we near the judgment all will manifest their true character, and it will be made plain to what company they belong. The sieve is going; let us not say, "Stay thy hand, O God." We know not the heart of man. The church must be purged, and will be. God reigns, let the people praise Him. — *2SG, p. 201*

Self-Indulgent Men are Lost

In the last days, Satan will come down in great wrath, knowing that his time is short, and will work with all deceivableness of unrighteousness in them that perish. Those who profess the religion of Jesus, but have not followed Him in self-denial, will be wholly unprepared for this time. Their religion is a religion of ease and convenience. They lift no cross; they fight no stern battles with the natural desires of the human heart. When the claims of God cross their self-indulgent desires, they choose to please themselves. They have not known Christ; for they have not accepted Him in his humiliation. These will be found with the company that oppose the truth, rather than with those who are suffering for the truth's sake. — *YI, May 28, 1884*

Some Face a Crisis like Achan

When a crisis finally comes, as it surely will, and God speaks in behalf of his people, those who have sinned, those who have been a cloud of darkness and who have stood directly in the way of God's working for his people, may become alarmed at the length they have gone in murmuring and in bringing discouragement upon the cause; and, like Achan, becoming terrified, they may acknowledge that they have sinned. But their confessions are too late and are not of the right kind to benefit themselves, although they may relieve the cause of God. Such do not make their confessions because of a conviction of their true state and a sense of how displeasing their course has been to God.

God may give this class another test, another proving, and let them show that they are no better prepared to stand free from all rebellion and sin than before their confessions were made. They are inclined to be ever on the side of wrong. And when the call is made for those who will be on the Lord's side to make a decided move to vindicate the right, they will manifest their true position. Those who have been nearly all their lives controlled by a spirit as foreign to the Spirit of God as was Achan's will be very passive when the time comes for decided action on the part of all. They will not claim to be on either side. The power of Satan has so long held them that they seem blinded and have no inclination to stand in defense of right. If they do not take a determined course on the wrong side, it is not because they have a clear sense of the right, but because they dare not. — *3T, pp. 271, 272*

Many Change Sides to Survive

Many who claim to believe the truth will change their opinions in times of peril and will take the side of the transgressors of God's law in order to escape persecution, because they are not established in the present truth—knowing it is truth because they have dug it out for themselves. There will be great humbling of hearts before God on the part of everyone who remains faithful and true to the end. But Satan will so work upon the unconsecrated elements of the human mind that many will not accept the light in God's appointed way. —*Ms 15, 1888*

Minor Affairs Become Critical

Satan leads many to believe that God will overlook their unfaithfulness in the minor affairs of life; but the Lord shows in his dealings with Jacob that He will in no wise sanction or tolerate evil. All who endeavor to excuse or conceal their sins, and permit them to remain upon the books of heaven, unconfessed and unforgiven, will be overcome by Satan. The more exalted their profession and the more honorable the position which they hold, the more grievous is their course in the sight of God and the surer the triumph of their great adversary. Those who delay a preparation for the day of God cannot obtain it in the time of trouble or at any subsequent time. The case of all such is hopeless.

Those professed Christians who come up to that last fearful conflict unprepared will, in their despair, confess their sins in words of burning anguish, while the wicked exult over their distress. These confessions are of the same character as was that of Esau or of Judas. Those who make them, lament the result of transgression, but not its guilt. They feel no true contrition, no abhorrence of evil. They acknowledge their sin, through fear of punishment; but, like Pharaoh of old, they would return to their defiance of heaven should the judgments be removed...

Those who exercise but little faith now, are in the greatest danger of falling under the power of satanic delusions and the decree to compel the conscience. And even if they endure the test they will be plunged into deeper distress and anguish in the time of trouble, because they have never made it a habit to trust in God. The lessons of faith which they have neglected they will be forced to learn under a terrible pressure of discouragement. —*GC, pp. 620, 622*

Unfruitful Adventists Apostatize

As trials thicken around us, separation and unity will both take place in our ranks. Those who have had great light and precious privileges, and who have not improved them, will go out from us under one pretext or another, for all will be tested. Not receiving the love of the truth, they will be taken in the delusion of the enemy, they will give heed to seducing spirits, and doctrines of devils, and will depart from the faith. — *Lt 36, 1895*

Nominal Sabbathkeepers Buckle

The time of trouble is soon to break upon us, and the decree will go forth that everyone who will not keep the first day of the week shall be put to death. Those who have not regarded the Sabbath as they should, who have exalted their business above God's commandment, will trample upon the Sabbath and keep the first day of the week, because they have consulted their own convenience before the honor of God. They did not learn to bring themselves into harmony with the Sabbath, but sought to bring the Sabbath to meet their own convenience.

With the preparation they have made, they are no more fitted to stand in the day of judgment than the greatest sinner. Their ideas are confused; they have tried to serve God and mammon; they received not the love of the truth, that they might be saved. Those who love God with all the heart, and their neighbor as themselves, will be the only ones who will stand the test of the decree.

When Satan brings his power to bear upon half-hearted professors, he will sweep them over to his side, he will claim his right to do with them as he pleases. But of those who honor God, the Lord says, "They shall be mine, ... in that day when I make up my jewels; and I will spare them, as a man spareth his own son that serveth him."

Those who are in the favor of God will not be deceived. Many now pass as Sabbathkeepers who, when the test comes upon the question, will no longer have a place among those who observe God's commandments. The prophet says, "Then shall ye return, and discern between the righteous and the wicked, between him that serveth God and him that serveth Him not." Those who are determined to have their own way, who measure themselves by their own standard, will have their time of trouble. — *ST, June 2, 1890*

B) The Remnant are Purified

True Christians Suffer

The time is hastening on when those who stand in defense of the truth will know by experience what it means to be partakers in Christ's sufferings.

—RH, May 29, 1900

The Godly Stay with Jesus

While persecution from those who worship at false shrines will cause some to yield up the truth, it will never induce a true child of God to separate from Christ, in whom his hopes of eternal life are centered. *—Ms 87, 1897*

Every Church Needs Refining

The Lord is soon to come. There must be a refining, winnowing process in every church, for there are among us wicked men who do not love the truth or honor God. There is need of a transformation of character. Will the church arise and put on her beautiful garments, the righteousness of Christ?

—Lt 15, 1892

Many Wrestle like Jacob

When tribulation comes upon us, how many of us are like Jacob. We think it the hand of an enemy; and in the darkness we wrestle blindly until our strength is spent, and we find no comfort or deliverance. To Jacob the divine touch at break of day revealed the One with whom he had been contending… We also need to learn that trials mean benefit, and not to despise the chastening of the Lord, nor faint when we are rebuked of Him. *—ST, Feb. 5, 1902*

Men are Purified Seven Times

These trials of life are God's workmen to remove the impurities, infirmities, and roughness from our characters, and fit us for the society of pure, heavenly angels in glory. But as we pass through these trials, as the fires of affliction kindle upon us, we must not keep the eye on the fire which is seen, but let the eye of faith fasten upon the things unseen, the eternal inheritance, the immortal life, the eternal weight of glory; and while we do this the fire will not consume us, but only remove the dross, and we shall come forth seven times purified, bearing the impress of the Divine. *—1T, p. 706*

Be Sifted like Wheat

Every child of God will be sifted as wheat, yet not a grain will fall to the ground—severely tempted, but never failing; though in the furnace, yet not consumed but refined as gold seven times purified. Because Christ lives, we shall live also. —*Lt 2, 1889*

The Difficult Path to Heaven

If you go forward toward heaven, the world will rub hard against you. At every step you will have to urge your way against Satan and his evil angels, and against all who transgress God's law. Earthly authorities will interpose. You will meet tribulations, bruising of the spirit, hard speeches, ridicule, and persecutions. Men will require your conformity to laws and customs that would render you disloyal to God. Here is where God's people find the cross in the way to life. —*Ms 3, 1885*

Trials Refine and Purify Christians

The watchful Christian is a working Christian, seeking zealously to do all in his power for the advancement of the gospel. As love for his Redeemer increases, so also does love for his fellow men. He has severe trials, as had his Master; but he does not allow affliction to sour his temper or destroy his peace of mind. He knows that trial, if well borne, will refine and purify him, and bring him into closer fellowship with Christ. Those who are partakers of Christ's sufferings will also be partakers of his consolation and at last sharers of his glory. —*AA, p. 261*

The Beauty of Truth is Revealed

There is a beauty and force in the truth that nothing can make so apparent as opposition and persecution. When this is revealed, many will be converted to the truth. Many who profess the truth do not know its preciousness, nor realize the richness of the assurances God has given. And they will not understand this until they are pressed into places of difficulty.

But then they will understand what the Saviour means when He says, "I will manifest myself unto them." When surrounded by those who have not the love of God, the Christian will realize how precious it is to have communion with God, and to obtain views of eternal redemption. —*Ms 15, 1896*

Tribulation is Required

All who reach the standard must learn the lesson that it is through much tribulation that we enter the kingdom of heaven. If we sit with Christ on his throne, we must be partakers with Him of his suffering. — *EA, p. 330*

Cling to God for Cleansing

The chaff and wheat are mingled in an indistinguishable manner. But when some crisis comes, when test and trial pass over the people, those who are symbolized by chaff are driven away; those who are represented by wheat remain. When God takes us in hand He will accomplish his purpose for our good. Though our past course may not have been in harmony with the Lord, though our paths have been turned aside from the ways of God, yet if we will cling to Him, He will change our course so that we shall keep the way of the Lord. — *Ms 52, 1896*

Purification is a Necessity

The followers of Christ know little of the plots which Satan and his hosts are forming against them. But He who sitteth in the heavens will overrule all these devices for the accomplishment of his deep designs. The Lord permits his people to be subjected to the fiery ordeal of temptation, not because He takes pleasure in their distress and affliction, but because this process is essential to their final victory. He could not, consistently with his own glory, shield them from temptation; for the very object of the trial is to prepare them to resist all the allurements of evil. — *GC, p. 528*

God's Servants Grow in Faith

As the opposition rises to a fiercer height, the servants of God are again perplexed; for it seems to them that they have brought the crisis. But conscience and the Word of God assure them that their course is right; and although the trials continue, they are strengthened to bear them. The contest grows closer and sharper, but their faith and courage rise with the emergency. Their testimony is: "We dare not tamper with God's Word, dividing his holy law; calling one portion essential and another nonessential, to gain the favor of the world. The Lord whom we serve is able to deliver us. Christ has conquered the powers of earth; and shall we be afraid of a world already conquered?" — *GC, p. 610*

Tests Come to All

The testing time will come to all... the humble in heart, who have daily felt the importance of riveting their souls to the eternal Rock, will stand unmoved amid the tempests of trial, because they trusted not to themselves. "The foundation of God standeth sure, having this seal, The Lord knoweth them that are his." — *RH, Jan. 18, 1881*

Self Must be Crucified

Oh, there is a great work to be done for the people of God, ere they are prepared for translation to heaven! The heat of the furnace upon some must be severe to reveal the dross. Self will have to be crucified. When each believer is to the very extent of his knowledge obeying the Lord, and yet seeking to give no just occasion to his fellow men to oppress him, he should not fear the results, even though it be imprisonment and death. — *Ms 6, 1889*

God Leads Men Step by Step

God leads his people on, step by step. He brings them up to different points calculated to manifest what is in the heart. Some endure at one point, but fall off at the next. At every advanced point the heart is tested and tried a little closer. If the professed people of God find their hearts opposed to this straight work, it should convince them that they have a work to do to overcome, if they would not be spewed out of the mouth of the Lord. Said the angel: "God will bring his work closer and closer to test and prove every one of his people." — *1T, p. 187*

True Christians Shine Brilliantly

When the testing time shall come, those who have made God's Word their rule of life will be revealed. In summer there is no noticeable difference between evergreens and other trees; but when the blasts of winter come, the evergreens remain unchanged, while other trees are stripped of their foliage.

So the falsehearted professor may not now be distinguished from the real Christian, but the time is just upon us when the difference will be apparent. Let opposition arise, let bigotry and intolerance again bear sway, let persecution be kindled, and the half-hearted and hypocritical will waver and yield the faith; but the true Christian will stand firm as a rock, his faith stronger, his hope brighter, than in days of prosperity. — *GC, p. 602*

Affliction Purifies God's Church

Soon there is to be trouble all over the world. It becomes everyone to seek to know God. We have no time to delay... God's love for his church is infinite. His care over his heritage is unceasing. He suffers no affliction to come upon the church but such as is essential for her purification, her present and eternal good. He will purify his church even as He purified the temple at the beginning and close of his ministry on earth. All that He brings upon the church in test and trial comes that his people may gain deeper piety and more strength to carry the triumphs of the cross to all parts of the world. —*9T, p. 228*

The Church is Sifted like the Disciples

"He that is not with Me," said Christ, "is against Me." It is wholehearted, thoroughly decided men and women who will stand now. Christ sifted his followers again and again, until at one time there remained only eleven and a few faithful women to lay the foundation of the Christian church. There are those who will stand back when burdens are to be borne; but when the church is all aglow, they catch the enthusiasm, sing and shout, and become rapturous; but watch them. When the fervor is gone, only a few faithful Calebs will come to the front and display unwavering principle. These are salt that retains the savor. —*5T, p. 130*

Tribulation Reveals Pure Characters

Let God be acknowledged as standing at the helm to guide and control at all times and under every circumstance. He will work by means that will be suitable and will maintain, increase, and build up his own people. His agents should have a sanctified zeal that is wholly under his control. Stormy times will come rapidly enough upon us, without our taking any special course of our own that will hasten them.

Tribulation will come of such a character as will drive all those to God who wish to be his and his alone. We do not know ourselves until we are tested and proved in the furnace of trial, and it is not proper for us to seek to measure the characters of men and condemn those who have not yet had the light of truth. Many who have not the privileges that we have had will go into heaven before those who have had great light, and who have not walked in it.

—*Lt 36, 1895*

Some are Saved from Heresy

Persecution, which is about to open upon us in so wonderful a manner, may save some of these souls that have gone into heresy, but we cannot afford to spoil God's heritage. —*Ms 160, 1904*

Godly Characters Shine the Brightest

God desires his people to prepare for the soon-coming crisis. Prepared or unprepared, they must all meet it; and those only who have brought their lives into conformity to the divine standard, will stand firm at that time of test and trial. When secular rulers unite with ministers of religion to dictate in matters of conscience, then it will be seen who really fear and serve God. When the darkness is deepest, the light of a godlike character will shine the brightest. When every other trust fails, then it will be seen who have an abiding trust in Jehovah. And while the enemies of truth are on every side, watching the Lord's servants for evil, God will watch over them for good. He will be to them as the shadow of a great rock in a weary land. —*AA, p. 431*

The True Sheep are United

When the storm of persecution really breaks upon us, the true sheep will hear the true Shepherd's voice. Self-denying efforts will be put forth to save the lost, and many who have strayed from the fold will come back to follow the great Shepherd. The people of God will draw together and present to the enemy a united front. In view of the common peril, strife for supremacy will cease; there will be no disputing as to who shall be accounted greatest. No one of the true believers will say: "I am of Paul; and I of Apollos; and I of Cephas." The testimony of one and all will be: "I cleave unto Christ; I rejoice in Him as my personal Saviour."

Thus will the truth be brought into practical life, and thus will be answered the prayer of Christ, uttered just before his humiliation and death: "That they all may be one; as thou, Father, art in Me, and I in thee, that they also may be one in Us: that the world may believe that thou hast sent Me." John 17:21. The love of Christ, the love of our brethren, will testify to the world that we have been with Jesus and learned of Him. Then will the message of the third angel swell to a loud cry, and the whole earth will be lightened with the glory of the Lord. —*6T, pp. 400, 401*

The Church will be Purged

The days of purification of the church are hastening on apace. God will have a people pure and true. In the mighty sifting soon to take place, we shall be better able to measure the strength of Israel. The signs reveal that the time is near when the Lord will manifest that his fan is in his hand, and that He soon will thoroughly purge his floor. —*RH, Jan. 11, 1887*

Sacred Truths Become Tests

God will test and prove his people. One sacred truth after another will be brought to bear upon their hearts, close and cutting, until their faith will be purified and tried like gold, until all their dross will be purged away, and Jesus will present them unto his Father without spot, or wrinkle, or any such thing. We must overcome through trials and sufferings, as Jesus overcame. We must not shun the cross or the suffering part of religion. The language of the heart should be, "Let me know the fellowship of the sufferings of Christ. Let me suffer with Him that I may reign with Him." —*RH, Sept. 16, 1862*

Men Brought into Trying Positions

The dreadful state of our nation calls for deep humility on the part of God's people. The one all-important inquiry which should now engross the mind of everyone is: Am I prepared for the day of God? Can I stand the trying test before me?

I saw that God is purifying and proving his people. He will refine them as gold, until the dross is consumed and his image is reflected in them. All have not that spirit of self-denial and that willingness to endure hardness and to suffer for the truth's sake, which God requires. Their wills are not subdued; they have not consecrated themselves wholly to God, seeking no greater pleasure than to do his will. Ministers and people lack spirituality and true godliness.

Everything is to be shaken that can be shaken. God's people will be brought into most trying positions, and all must be settled, rooted, and grounded in the truth, or their steps will surely slide. If God comforts and nourishes the soul with his inspiring presence, they can endure, though the way may be dark and thorny. For the darkness will soon pass away, and the true light shine forever. —*1T, p. 355*

Persecution Unites Men to Christ

Trouble is coming on us as a people. In view of the common peril, let there be no more strife among us. True believers will not say, I am of Paul, or, I am of Apollos. All will have one testimony to bear, "I cleave to Christ as my personal Saviour." When the storm of persecution comes, the true sheep, knowing the shepherd's voice, will gather to Him. — *Ms 117a, 1901*

Purified Men No Longer Boast

God has not changed toward his faithful servants who are keeping their garments spotless. But many are crying, "Peace and safety," while sudden destruction is coming upon them. Unless there is thorough repentance, unless men humble their hearts by confession and receive the truth as it is in Jesus, they will never enter heaven. When purification shall take place in our ranks, we shall no longer rest at ease, boasting of being rich and increased with goods, in need of nothing. — *8T, p. 250*

A Painful Process for the Remnant

The work of pruning and purifying, to fit us for heaven, is a great work, and will cost us a great deal of suffering and trial, because our will is not subjected to the will of Christ. We must go through the furnace till the fires have consumed the dross, and we are purified, and reflect the divine image. Those who follow their inclinations and are governed by appearances, are not good judges of what God is doing. They are filled with discontent. They see failure where there is indeed triumph, a great loss where there is gain; and, like Jacob, they have been ready to exclaim, "All these things are against Me," when the very things whereof they complained were all working together for their good.

"No cross, no crown." How can one be strong in the Lord without trials. To have strength, we must have exercise. To have strong faith, we must be placed in circumstances where our faith will be called forth. The apostle Paul, just before his martyrdom, exhorted Timothy, "Be thou partaker of the afflictions of the gospel, according to the power of God." It is through much tribulation we enter the kingdom of God. Our Saviour was tried in every possible way, and yet He triumphed in God continually. It is our privilege to be strong in the strength of God under all circumstances, and to glory in the cross of Christ. — *RH, May 18, 1886*

The Church Looks about to Fall

Satan will work his miracles to deceive; he will set up his power as supreme. The church may appear as about to fall, but it does not fall. It remains, while the sinners in Zion will be sifted out—the chaff separated from the precious wheat. This is a terrible ordeal, but nevertheless it must take place. None but those who have been overcoming by the blood of the Lamb and the word of their testimony will be found with the loyal and true, without spot or stain of sin, without guile in their mouths. We must be divested of our self-righteousness and arrayed in the righteousness of Christ.

The remnant that purify their souls by obeying the truth gather strength from the trying process, exhibiting the beauty of holiness amid the surrounding apostasy. All these, He says, "I have graven... upon the palms my hands" Isaiah 49:16. They are held in everlasting, imperishable remembrance. We want faith now, living faith. We want to have a living testimony that shall cut to the heart of the sinner. There is too much sermonizing and too little ministering. We want the holy unction. We need the spirit and fervor of the truth. —*Lt 55, 1886*

The Time of Trouble is a Crucible

The path to freedom from sin is through crucifixion of self, and conflict with the powers of darkness. Let none be discouraged in view of the severe trials to be met in the time of Jacob's trouble, which is yet before them. They are to work earnestly, anxiously, not for that time, but for today. What we want is to have a knowledge of the truth as it is in Christ now, and a personal experience now. In these precious closing hours of probation, we have a deep and living experience to gain. We shall thus form characters that will ensure our deliverance in the time of trouble.

The time of trouble is the crucible that is to bring out Christlike characters. It is designed to lead the people of God to renounce Satan and his temptations. The last conflict will reveal Satan to them in his true character, that of a cruel tyrant, and it will do for them what nothing else could do, uproot him entirely from their affections. For to love and cherish sin, is to love and cherish its author, that deadly foe of Christ. When they excuse sin and cling to perversity of character, they give Satan a place in their affections, and pay him homage. —*RH, Aug. 12, 1884*

95

The Furnace of Affliction

Said the Saviour to his disciples, foreseeing the doubts that would press upon their souls in days of trial and darkness: "Remember the word that I said unto you, The servant is not greater than his lord. If they have persecuted Me, they will also persecute you." John 15:20. Jesus suffered for us more than any of his followers can be made to suffer through the cruelty of wicked men. Those who are called to endure torture and martyrdom are but following in the steps of God's dear Son.

"The Lord is not slack concerning his promise." 2 Peter 3:9. He does not forget or neglect his children; but He permits the wicked to reveal their true character, that none who desire to do his will may be deceived concerning them. Again, the righteous are placed in the furnace of affliction, that they themselves may be purified; that their example may convince others of the reality of faith and godliness; and also that their consistent course may condemn the ungodly and unbelieving. — *GC, pp. 47, 48*

Soar Upwards like an Eagle

The path of duty and righteousness is not a path of peace and safety. By faith we must follow as the Lord leads us onward. But could we always discern the everlasting arms around and beneath us, there would be no occasion for the exercise of faith. The way of God's choosing may seem dark, yet it is the surest way to the light. In the midst of apparent disaster and defeat, God's providence is working out his purposes.

The eagle of the Alps is sometimes beaten down by the tempest into the narrow defiles of the mountains. Angry storm clouds shut in this mighty bird of the forest, their dense, dark masses separating her from the sunny heights where she has built her nest. For a time her efforts to escape seem fruitless. She dashes to and fro, beating the air with her strong wings, and waking the echoes of the mountains with her cries. At length, with a scream of triumph, she darts upward, and, piercing the clouds, she is once more in the clear sunlight, with the darkness and tempest far beneath.

Ever thus, by mighty efforts, have God's chosen servants urged their way upward, breasting opposition, reproach, and persecution, in their conflicts with principalities and powers, and spiritual wickedness in high places.

— *ST, July 26, 1883*

God Refines Characters with Trials

"In the world ye shall have tribulation," says Christ; "but in Me ye shall have peace." The trials to which Christians are subjected in sorrow, adversity, and reproach are the means appointed of God to separate the chaff from the wheat. Our pride, selfishness, evil passions, and love of worldly pleasure must all be overcome; therefore God sends us afflictions to test and prove us, and show us that these evils exist in our characters. We must overcome through his strength and grace, that we may be partakers of the divine nature, having escaped the corruption that is in the world through lust.

"For our light affliction," says Paul, "which is but for a moment, worketh for us a far more exceeding and eternal weight of glory; while we look not at the things which are seen, but at the things which are not seen: for the things which are seen are temporal; but the things which are not seen are eternal." Afflictions, crosses, temptations, adversity, and our varied trials are God's workmen to refine us, sanctify us, and fit us for the heavenly garner. —*3T, p. 115*

The World Hates Righteousness

The world loves sin, and hates righteousness, and this was the cause of its hostility to Jesus. All who refuse his infinite love will find Christianity a disturbing element. The light of Christ sweeps away the darkness that covers their sins, and the need of reform is made manifest. While those who yield to the influence of the Holy Spirit begin war with themselves, those who cling to sin war against the truth and its representatives.

Thus strife is created, and Christ's followers are accused as troublers of the people. But it is fellowship with God that brings them the world's enmity. They are bearing the reproach of Christ. They are treading the path that has been trodden by the noblest of the earth. Not with sorrow, but with rejoicing, should they meet persecution.

Each fiery trial is God's agent for their refining. Each is fitting them for their work as co-laborers with Him. Each conflict has its place in the great battle for righteousness, and each will add to the joy of their final triumph. Having this in view, the test of their faith and patience will be cheerfully accepted rather than dreaded and avoided. Anxious to fulfill their obligation to the world, fixing their desire upon the approval of God, his servants are to fulfill every duty, irrespective of the fear or the favor of men. —*DA, p. 306*

Trials Purified King David

Said my guide, "The contrite heart is known and accepted of God. Keep the way of the Lord. He alone can bring you forth from your present trial as gold purified from all dross. Let the lessons you now learn be lasting."

I was instructed by the case of David who had through his own course of action forfeited the favor of God, and like a funeral procession the uncrowned and unsandaled king, with head covered and eyes dim with tears, with his little handful of adherents, was pursuing his way along the precipitous road by the Mount of Olives. Yet God had his eye upon him every moment. His own course of action had brought the sure result. He had lost his self-respect and self-control. The man was humbled and mournful, but in his humiliation David, before the whole universe of heaven, was never more tenderly regarded than in this hour of his adversity. Never does he stand greater with God than when wrestling with the storm. —*Lt 61, 1890*

A Test of Faith and Obedience

The Lord often brings a crisis in the affairs of men that they may feel their need of his interposition, and when at such a time his people have sought Him, He has wrought deliverance for them. At times, He suffers persecution to make great havoc with the church, so that to human sight Satan appears to be on the point of extinguishing the light of truth in the earth.

But in these seasons of peril and distress, the faithful ones are led to rely less upon self and more upon God, their importunate prayers are heard in heaven, and when apparently weakest, they are strongest in the strength of their almighty Helper. God reserves the greatest manifestations of his power for exigencies when the necessity cannot be denied and men must acknowledge the interposition of a divine hand.

The test of faith and obedience will come to all the people of God. Like the apostle Paul, we must obey the divine voice, whatever that obedience may cost us. Upon all who are partakers of his grace, the Lord enjoins duties that involve peril and sacrifice. Christ Himself has trodden the path before us, and we should not expect to share his glory if we refuse to partake of his sufferings. The most exalted of the redeemed host that stand before the throne of God and the Lamb have gained their white robes and starry crowns only through "great tribulation." Revelation 7:13, 14. —*Ms 12, 1884*

Adventists are Tried by Fire

There is need of perfect unity in the church of God. All kinds of calamity are trying the nations that have so long trampled the law of God; and this is only the beginning of the end. Those who claim to be Seventh-day Adventists will be tried as by fire. There are tares among the wheat, and the untrue will be separated from the true. They will go out from us because they are not of us.

We are now living in perilous times. There is suffering in our world that is not dreamed of, bloodshed and revolt and crimes. We are living in times that try men's souls. We are in the crucible, and the dross will either be separated from us, or we will be consumed with the dross. The way in which we bear ourselves when the pruning of God is upon us will show what manner of people we are of. Bear your test and trial my children, that you may come forth as gold seven times purified. — *Lt 146, 1897*

More Precious than Fine Gold

Christ dwells in him who receives Him by faith. Though trials may come upon the soul, yet the Lord's presence will be with us. The burning bush in which was the Lord's presence did not consume away. The fire did not extinguish a fiber of the branches. Thus will it be with the feeble human agent who puts his trust in Christ. The furnace fire of temptation may burn, persecution and trial may come, but only the dross will be consumed. The gold will shine brighter because of the process of purification.

Greater is He that is in the heart of the faithful, than he that controls the hearts of unbelievers. Complain not bitterly of the trial which comes upon you, but let your eyes be directed to Christ, who has clothed his divinity with humanity, in order that we may understand how great his interest in us since He has identified Himself with suffering humanity. He tasted the cup of human sorrow, He was afflicted in all our afflictions, He was made perfect through suffering, tempted in all points like as humanity is tempted, in order that He might succor those who are in temptation.

He says, "I will make a man more precious than fine gold, even a man than the golden wedge of Ophir." He will make a man precious by abiding with him, by giving unto him the Holy Spirit. He says, "If ye then, being evil, know how to give good gifts unto your children, how much more shall your heavenly Father give the Holy Spirit to them that ask Him?" — *ST, Mar. 5, 1896*

A Crisis Reveals Character

It is in a crisis that character is revealed. When the earnest voice proclaimed at midnight, "Behold, the bridegroom cometh; go ye out to meet Him," and the sleeping virgins were roused from their slumbers, it was seen who had made preparation for the event. Both parties were taken unawares; but one was prepared for the emergency, and the other was found without preparation. So now, a sudden and unlooked-for calamity, something that brings the soul face to face with death, will show whether there is any real faith in the promises of God. It will show whether the soul is sustained by grace. The great final test comes at the close of human probation, when it will be too late for the soul's need to be supplied. — *COL, p. 412*

Sunday Laws Shake God's Church

An apostate church will unite with the powers of earth and hell to place upon the forehead or in the hand, the mark of the beast, and prevail upon the children of God to worship the beast and his image. They will seek to compel them to renounce their allegiance to God's law, and yield homage to the papacy. Then will come the times which will try men's souls; for the confederacy of apostasy will demand that the loyal subjects of God shall renounce the law of Jehovah, and repudiate the truth of his word.

Then will the gold be separated from the dross, and it will be made apparent who are the godly, who are loyal and true, and who are the disloyal, the dross and the tinsel. What clouds of chaff will then be borne away by the fan of God! Where now our eyes can discover only rich floors of wheat, will be chaff blown away with the fan of God. Everyone who is not centered in Christ will fail to stand the test and ordeal of that day. While those who are clothed with Christ's righteousness will stand firm to truth and duty, those who have trusted in their own righteousness will be ranged under the black banner of the prince of darkness.

Then it will be seen whether the choice is for Christ or Belial. Those who have been self-distrustful, who have been so circumstanced that they have not dared to face stigma and reproach, will at last openly declare themselves for Christ and his law; while many who have appeared to be flourishing trees, but who have borne no fruit, will go with the multitude to do evil, and will receive the mark of apostasy in the forehead or in the hand. — *RH, Nov. 8, 1892*

God Delivers a Bitter Cup

God has shown me that He gives his people a bitter cup to drink to purify and cleanse them. They can make it still bitterer by murmuring, complaining, and repining. But those who receive it thus, must have another draught, for the first does not have its designed effect upon the heart. And if the second does not affect the work, then they must have another, and another, until it does have its designed effect, or they will be left impure in heart. I saw that this bitter cup can be sweetened by patience, endurance and prayer, and that it will have its designed effect upon the hearts of those who thus received it, and God will be honored and glorified. —*2SG, p. 290*

Gold is Separated from the Dross

The time is not far distant when the test will come to every soul. The mark of the beast will be urged upon us. Those who have step by step yielded to worldly demands and conformed to worldly customs will not find it a hard matter to yield to the powers that be, rather than subject themselves to derision, insult, threatened imprisonment, and death. The contest is between the commandments of God and the commandments of men. In this time the gold will be separated from the dross in the church. True godliness will be clearly distinguished from the appearance and tinsel of it.

Many a star that we have admired for its brilliancy will then go out in darkness. Chaff like a cloud will be borne away on the wind, even from places where we see only floors of rich wheat. All who assume the ornaments of the sanctuary, but are not clothed with Christ's righteousness, will appear in the shame of their own nakedness.

When trees without fruit are cut down as cumberers of the ground, when multitudes of false brethren are distinguished from the true, then the hidden ones will be revealed to view, and with hosannas range under the banner of Christ. Those who have been timid and self-distrustful will declare themselves openly for Christ and his truth. The most weak and hesitating in the church will be as David—willing to do and dare. The deeper the night for God's people, the more brilliant the stars. Satan will sorely harass the faithful; but, in the name of Jesus, they will come off more than conquerors. Then will the church of Christ appear "fair as the moon, clear as the sun, and terrible as an army with banners." —*5T, p. 81*

The Refining Humbles the Remnant

The purification of the people of God cannot be accomplished without their suffering. God permits the fires of affliction to consume the dross, to separate the worthless from the valuable, that the pure metal may shine forth. He passes us from one fire to another, testing our true worth. If we cannot bear these trials, what will we do in the time of trouble? If prosperity or adversity discover falseness, pride, or selfishness in our hearts, what shall we do when God tries every man's work as by fire, and lays bare the secrets of all hearts?

True grace is willing to be tried; if we are loath to be searched by the Lord, our condition is serious indeed. God is the refiner and purifier of souls; in the heat of the furnace the dross is separated forever from the true silver and gold of the Christian character. Jesus watches the test. He knows what is needed to purify the precious metal that it may reflect the radiance of his divine love.

God brings his people near Him by close, testing trials, by showing them their own weakness and inability, and by teaching them to lean upon Him as their only help and safeguard. Then his object is accomplished. They are prepared to be used in every emergency, to fill important positions of trust, and to accomplish the grand purposes for which their powers were given them. God takes men upon trial; He proves them on the right hand and on the left, and thus they are educated, trained, disciplined.

Jesus, our Redeemer, man's representative and head, endured this testing process. He suffered more than we can be called upon to suffer. He bore our infirmities and was in all points tempted as we are. He did not suffer thus on his own account, but because of our sins; and now, relying on the merits of our Overcomer, we may become victors in his name. God's work of refining and purifying must go on until his servants are so humbled, so dead to self, that, when called into active service, their eye will be single to his glory.

He will then accept their efforts; they will not move rashly, from impulse; they will not rush on and imperil the Lord's cause, being slaves to temptations and passions and followers of their own carnal minds set on fire by Satan. Oh, how fearfully is the cause of God marred by man's perverse will and unsubdued temper! How much suffering he brings upon himself by following his own headstrong passions! God brings men over the ground again and again, increasing the pressure until perfect humility and a transformation of character bring them into harmony with Christ. —*4T, pp. 85, 86*

102

The Disciple's Night on the Boat

Dark hours of trial are before the church because they have not obeyed the warnings and reproofs and counsel of God. What a bewitching power comes upon human minds to do contrary to the oft repeated will of God, and close the eyes and stop the ears, when Jesus is calling to them to hear his voice. He says, "My sheep hear my voice." John 10:27.

That night in that boat was to the disciples a school where they were to receive their education for the great work which was to be done afterwards. The dark hours of trial are to come to everyone as a part of his education for higher work, for more devoted, consecrated effort. The storm was not sent upon the disciples to shipwreck them, but to test and prove them individually.

Before the great trouble shall come upon the world such as has never been since there was a nation, those who have faltered and who would ignorantly lead in unsafe paths will reveal this before the real vital test, the last proving, comes, so that whatsoever they may say will not be regarded as voicing the True Shepherd. The time of our educating will soon be over. We have no time to lose in walking through clouds of doubt and uncertainty because of uncertain voices. — *Lt 13, 1892*

Discussion Questions

1. Why do people who break one commandment find themselves unable to keep the rest?

2. Christians who are not anchored will be uprooted. What are some of the habits and beliefs that could help keep Adventists grounded?

3. How will lukewarm Christians imitate Achan when a crisis arrives?

4. What are some of the different ways the Remnant will grow and improve by being purified seven times during the time of trouble?

5. How will persecution unite men with Jesus? What will it be like to go through trials that are similar to the ones suffered by Christ?

The Close of Probation

— 6 —

Two Classes of People

"The field is the world; the good seed are the children of the kingdom; but the tares are the children of the wicked one." — Matthew 13:38

| Matt. 7:21-23 | Luke 12:8, 9 | Romans 1:18-20 | Romans 2:5, 6 | 2 Cor. 5:10 |
| Matt. 12:30 | Luke 12:47, 48 | Romans 2:1 | Romans 2:12 | Gal. 2:17-19 |

Tares amid the Wheat

Has God no living church? He has a church, but it is the church militant, not the church triumphant. We are sorry that there are defective members, that there are tares amid the wheat. — *RH, Aug. 29, 1893*

The Judgment Hall Scene

The scene in the judgment hall in Jerusalem is a symbol of what will take place in the closing scenes of this earth's history. The whole world will accept Christ, the truth, or they will accept Satan, the first great Rebel, an apostate, robber, and murderer. If they accept Satan, they identify their interests with the chief of all liars, and with all who are disloyal, while they turn from no less a personage than the Son of the infinite God. — *Ms 40, 1897*

Every Character is Developed

The warfare against God's law, which was begun in heaven, will be continued until the end of time. Every man will be tested. Obedience or disobedience is the question to be decided by the whole world. All will be called to choose between the law of God and the laws of men. Here the dividing line will be drawn. There will be but two classes. Every character will be fully developed; and all will show whether they have chosen the side of loyalty or that of rebellion. Then the end will come. God will vindicate his law and deliver his people. — *DA, p. 763*

The Decisive Hour is Here

To every soul will come the searching test, "Shall I obey God rather than men?" The decisive hour is even now at hand. Satan is putting forth his utmost efforts in the rage of a last despairing struggle against Christ and his followers. —*Ms 51, 1899*

One Party Honors the Sabbath

The point at issue is the observance of the Sabbath. Now these two parties are standing in opposition to each other. One company has the Sabbath sign, testifying their loyalty to God. They are a small company, but loyal and true, distinct from the world. —*Lt 118, 1900*

The Church Militant is Imperfect

Some people seem to think that upon entering the church they will have their expectations fulfilled, and meet only with those who are pure and perfect... But we need not be thus disappointed, for the Lord has not warranted us in coming to the conclusion that the church is perfect; and all our zeal will not be successful in making the church militant as pure as the church triumphant.

—*RH, Sept. 5, 1893*

Two Classes Oppose Each Other

There will be but two classes on the world, those who worship God and keep his commandments, and those who worship the beast and his image. These two classes are in decided opposition to one another. The worshippers of the beast will persecute those who keep the commandments of God. The members of the Roman Catholic Church and of the Protestant churches will unite against the remnant people of God. —*Ms 18, 1904*

Two Great Parties are Developed

If in one jot or title the law of God has been changed, Satan has gained on earth that which he could not gain in heaven. He has prepared his delusive snare, hoping to take captive the church and the world. But not all will be taken in the snare. A line of distinction is being drawn between the children of obedience and the children of disobedience, the loyal and true and the disloyal and untrue. Two great parties are developed, the worshipers of the beast and his image, and the worshipers of the true and living God. —*Ms 32, 1896*

One Class Wields the Bible

We are living in a time when there are but two classes in our world: those who trample upon the commandments of God and those who honor God and love his Word, using the weapon that Christ used in his battle with the great deceiver—the sword of the Spirit, "It is written." —*Ms 182, 1905*

All Christendom is Divided

The worshipers of God will be especially distinguished by their regard for the fourth commandment, since this is the sign of God's creative power and the witness to his claim upon man's reverence and homage. The wicked will be distinguished by their efforts to tear down the Creator's memorial and to exalt the institution of Rome. In the issue of the conflict all Christendom will be divided into two great classes, those who keep the commandments of God and the faith of Jesus, and those who worship the beast and his image, and receive his mark. —*9T, p. 16*

God's People Unite with Christ

The people of God will be consolidated as one with Christ in God, just in proportion as false theories become more and more prevalent. As we near the close of time, the distinction between those who are Christ's and those who are on the side of the apostate will become more marked. Only two great centers will appear—Christ, the Prince of heaven, the Prince of life and immortality, and Antichrist, the center of the rebel forces of apostasy. The separating line is now being drawn, and in that great conflict the parties will be forever separated. —*Lt 96, 1898*

Wheat and Tares Grow Together

We as a people profess to have truth in advance of every other people upon the earth. Then our life and character should be in harmony with such a faith. The day is just upon us when the righteous shall be bound like precious grain in bundles for the heavenly garner, while the wicked are, like the tares, gathered for the fires of the last great day. But the wheat and tares "grow together until the harvest." In the discharge of life's duties the righteous will to the last be brought in contact with the ungodly. The children of light are scattered among the children of darkness, that the contrast may be seen by all. —*5T, p. 100*

The Dividing Line Widens

And as we near the close of time, the demarcation between the children of light and the children of darkness will be more and more decided. They will be more and more at variance. This difference is expressed in the words of Christ, "born again," "created anew in Christ," "dead to the world and alive unto God." These are the walls of separation that divide the heavenly from the earthly and describe the difference between those who belong to the world and those who are chosen out of it, who are elect, precious in the sight of God. —*Lt 21, 1882*

The Obedient and the Disobedient

All society is ranging into two great classes, the obedient and the disobedient. Among which class shall we be found? Those who keep God's commandments, those who live not by bread alone, but by every word that proceedeth out of the mouth of God, compose the church of the living God. Those who choose to follow Antichrist are subjects of the great apostate.

Ranged under the banner of Satan, they break God's law, and lead others to break it. They endeavor so to frame the laws of nations that men shall show their loyalty to earthly governments by trampling upon the laws of God's kingdom. Satan is diverting minds with unimportant questions, in order that they shall not with clear and distinct vision see matters of vast importance. The enemy is planning to ensnare the world. —*Ms 24, 1891*

God Permits Men to Choose a Ruler

The Lord of heaven permits the world to choose whom they will have as ruler. Let all read carefully the thirteenth chapter of Revelation, for it concerns every human agent, great and small. Every human being must take sides, either for the true and living God, who has given to the world the memorial of creation in the seventh-day Sabbath, or for a false sabbath, instituted by men who have exalted themselves above all that is called God or that is worshipped, who have taken upon themselves the attributes of Satan, in oppressing the loyal and true who keep the commandments of God. This persecuting power will compel the worship of the beast by insisting on the observance of the Sabbath he has instituted. Thus he blasphemes God, "sitting in the temple of God, and showing himself that he is God."

—*Ms 7a, 1896*

The Classes of Cain and Abel

Cain and Abel represent the two classes, the righteous and the wicked, the believers and unbelievers, which should exist from the fall of man to the Second Coming of Christ. Cain slaying his brother Abel, represents the wicked who will be envious of the righteous, and will hate them because they are better than themselves. — *ST, Feb. 6, 1879*

Two Choices: Christ or Barabbas

The world is asleep. The people know not the time of their visitation. To them the words apply; "If thou hadst known, even thou, at least in this thy day, the things which belong unto thy peace! But now they are hid from thine eyes." All need to be aroused. We cannot afford to be rocked to sleep in the cradle of carnal security or indifference; for we are deciding our eternal destiny. The record of the shameful trial in the judgment hall has passed up to heaven, and is the standard by which all are measured, whether they stand under the blood-stained banner of Christ, or under the black banner of the prince of darkness.

There can be only two classes. Each party is distinctly stamped, either with the seal of the living God, or with the mark of the beast or his image. Each son and daughter of Adam chooses either Christ or Barabbas as his general. And all who place themselves on the side of the disloyal are standing under Satan's black banner, and are charged with rejecting and despitefully using Christ. They are charged with deliberately crucifying the Lord of life and glory.

Each one has an important question to answer for himself: Are you on the side of Satan, a transgressor of God's law, or are you loyal to that God who declared himself to be, "The Lord, The Lord God, merciful and gracious, long-suffering, and abundant in goodness and truth, keeping mercy for thousands, forgiving iniquity and transgression and sin, and that will by no means clear the guilty; visiting the iniquity of the fathers upon the children, and upon the children's children, unto the third and to the fourth generation."

God's character is here displayed as his glory. God has delivered all judgment into the hands of his Son; and as a righteous judge, Christ must pass sentence on every work whether it be good or bad. Justice is as much an expression of love as mercy. — *RH, Jan. 30, 1900*

Two Parties in the World

Lucifer made war in heaven and would not take the position God assigned him, therefore he fell from his high estate and has been in the world, a warring element against God's plans, and has had great power to allure and deceive souls to ruin them. There have been two parties in the world, the true and the false. —*Lt 189, 1909*

Two Groups Stand in Collision

Men are taking sides, according to their choice. These that are feeding on the Word of God will show this by their practice; they are on the Lord's side, seeking by precept and example to reform the world. All that have refused to be taught of God hold the traditions of men. They at last pass over on the side of the enemy, against God, and are written, Antichrist.

The people of God, who understand our position in this world's history, are with ears open and hearts softened and subdued, pressing together in unity, one with Jesus Christ. Those who will not practice the lessons of Christ, but keep themselves in hand, to mold themselves, find in Antichrist the center of their union. While the two parties stand in collision, the Lord will appear, and shine before his ancients gloriously. He will set up a kingdom that shall stand forever. —*Lt 73, 1896*

Discussion Questions

1. When will the tares leave the wheat? Has this process already begun?

2. How are the two opposing parties different from each other?

3. America has two political parties, and there are many different social classes. Does your denomination have two conflicting groups as well?

4. Why are godly people naturally at enmity with the world?

5. How are nominal Christians replacing Jesus with Barabbas?

The Seal of God

"Nevertheless the foundation of God standeth sure, having this seal, the Lord knoweth them that are his. And, let everyone that nameth the name of Christ depart from iniquity."

— 2 Timothy 2:19

Ex. 12:12-14	Isaiah 8:16, 17	Ezek. 20:12, 20	Eph. 1:13, 14	Rev. 7:2-4; 9:4
Ex. 16:4, 5	Isaiah 58:13	Daniel 6:17	Eph. 4:29, 30	Rev. 14:1, 12
Ex. 31:13-17	Ezek. 9:4	2 Cor. 1:21, 22	Heb. 4:4-11	Rev. 22:4, 14

A) The Sabbath Test

The Separating Wall

I saw that the holy Sabbath is, and will be, the separating wall between the true Israel of God and unbelievers; and that the Sabbath is the great question to unite the hearts of God's dear, waiting saints. *—EW, p. 33*

The Point of Truth Controverted

The Sabbath will be the great test of loyalty, for it is the point of truth especially controverted. When the final test shall be brought to bear upon men, then the line of distinction will be drawn between those who serve God and those who serve Him not.

While the observance of the false sabbath in compliance with the law of the state, contrary to the fourth commandment, will be an avowal of allegiance to a power that is in opposition to God, the keeping of the true Sabbath, in obedience to God's law, is an evidence of loyalty to the Creator. While one class, by accepting the sign of submission to earthly powers, receive the mark of the beast, the other, choosing the token of allegiance to divine authority, receive the seal of God. *— GC, p. 605*

The Great Point at Issue

In the warfare to be waged in the last days there will be united, in opposition to God's people, all the corrupt powers that have apostatized from allegiance to the law of Jehovah. In this warfare the Sabbath of the fourth commandment will be the great point at issue, for in the Sabbath commandment the great Lawgiver identifies Himself as the Creator of the heavens and the earth. —*Ms 24, 1891*

The Fourth Commandment Test

Man must wait patiently until the time when the work shall be accomplished, and every human being has had an opportunity to decide upon the light given. Decisions will be made for and against God. The Sabbath of the fourth commandment will be the test. Every man will decide his own case by his decision in regard to the law of Jehovah. Then the world will be ripened for the harvest. Both classes will be developed, the sentiment of every heart will be revealed. —*Ms 77, 1899*

A Test to This Generation

The Sabbath is a test to this generation. In obeying the fourth commandment in spirit and truth, men will obey all the precepts of the Decalogue. To fulfill this commandment one must love God supremely, and exercise love toward all the creatures that He has made. The Lord exhorts us to "remember the Sabbath day, to keep it holy;" and since this is his exhortation, will any one charge us with wearying them in bringing this commandment to their remembrance? —*ST, Feb. 13, 1896*

The Line of Demarcation

We have a message of solemn import to bear to the world. It bears a test, a close test, on its front. The Sabbath is the great test question. It is the line of demarcation between the loyal and true, and the disloyal and transgressor. This Sabbath, God has enjoined; and those who claim to be commandment keepers, who believe that they are now under the proclamation of the third angel's message, will see the important part the Sabbath of the fourth commandment holds in that message. It is the seal of the living God. They will not lessen the claims of the Sabbath to suit their business or convenience.

—*Ms 34, 1897*

Everyone Receives Sufficient Light

Not one is made to suffer the wrath of God until the truth has been brought home to his mind and conscience, and has been rejected. There are many who have never had an opportunity to hear the special truths for this time. The obligation of the fourth commandment has never been set before them in its true light. He who reads every heart and tries every motive will leave none who desire a knowledge of the truth, to be deceived as to the issues of the controversy. The decree is not to be urged upon the people blindly. Everyone is to have sufficient light to make his decision intelligently. — *GC, p. 605*

A Witness to Convert or Condemn

This time when there is such an effort made to enforce the observance of Sunday is the very opportunity to present to the world the true Sabbath in contrast to the false. The Lord in his providence is far ahead of us. He has permitted this Sunday question to be pressed to the front that the Sabbath of the fourth commandment may be presented before the legislative assemblies; thus the leading men of the nation may have their attention called to the testimony of God's Word in favor of the true Sabbath. If it does not convert them, it is a witness to condemn. The Sabbath question is the great testing question for this time. — *Ms 16, 1890*

An Issue of Vital Consequence

The Sabbath question is to be the issue in the great final conflict in which all the world will act a part. Men have honored Satan's principles above the principles that rule in the heavens. They have accepted the spurious sabbath, which Satan has exalted as the sign of his authority. But God has set his seal upon his royal requirement.

Each sabbath institution bears the name of its author, an ineffaceable mark that shows the authority of each. It is our work to lead the people to understand this. We are to show them that it is of vital consequence whether they bear the mark of God's kingdom or the mark of the kingdom of rebellion, for they acknowledge themselves subjects of the kingdom whose mark they bear. God has called us to uplift the standard of his downtrodden Sabbath. How important, then, that our example in Sabbathkeeping should be right. — *6T, p. 352*

B) The Godly are Sealed

Christ's Image on the Soul

As wax takes the impression of the seal, so the soul is to take the impression of the Spirit of God and retain the image of Christ. — *ST, July 18, 1911*

Happens before Probation Ends

The living righteous will receive the seal of God prior to the close of probation... these will enjoy special honors in the kingdom of God. — *Ms 4, 1883*

Men are Made Complete in Christ

The Lord would teach men the lesson that, though united in church capacity, he is not saved until the seal of God is placed upon him, and he is made complete in Christ. — *Lt 80, 1898*

Unexpected Tests will Occur

All are required to show a deep interest in the cause of God in its various branches, and close and unexpected tests will be brought to bear upon them to see who are worthy to receive the seal of the living God. — *5T, p. 382*

Discouraging Influences are Delayed

I tell you in the name of the Lord God of Israel that all injurious, discouraging influences are held in control by unseen angel hands, until everyone that works in the fear and love of God is sealed in his forehead. — *Lt 138, 1897*

Those Who Obey God are Sealed

The law of God, which is perfect holiness, is the only true standard of character. Love is expressed in obedience, and perfect love casteth out all fear. Those who love God, have the seal of God in their foreheads, and work the works of God. — *YI, July 26, 1894*

The Mark of Deliverance

The Lord is doing his work. All heaven is astir. The Judge of all the earth is soon to arise and vindicate his insulted authority. The mark of deliverance will be set upon the men who keep God's commandments, who revere his law, and who refuse the mark of the beast or of his image. — *5T, p. 451*

Men Must Honor the Sabbath

This is the distinction drawn between the loyal and the disloyal. Those who would have the seal of God in their foreheads must keep the Sabbath of the fourth commandment. This is what distinguishes them from the disloyal, who have accepted a man-made institution in the place of the true Sabbath. The observance of God's rest day is the mark of distinction between him that serveth God and him that serveth Him not. —*Ms 27, 1899*

The Signet of the Faithful

God will never, never allow any man to pass through the pearly gates of the city of God who does not bear the signet of the faithful, his government mark. Every soul who is saved will cherish pure principles, which proceed from the very essence of truth. He must fasten himself by golden links to the everlasting power and love of the God of truth. He must be loyal to the principles of God's Word, loyal to the everlasting covenant which is a sign between man and his Maker. —*Ms 63, 1899*

A Settling into the Truth

There is a spirit of desperation, of war and bloodshed, and that spirit will increase until the very close of time. Just as soon as the people of God are sealed in their foreheads—it is not any seal or mark that can be seen, but a settling into the truth, both intellectually and spiritually, so they cannot be moved—just as soon as God's people are sealed and prepared for the shaking, it will come. Indeed, it has begun already; the judgments of God are now upon the land to give us warning, that we may know what is coming.

—*Ms 173, 1902*

The Faithful Wear God's Signature

The Israelites placed over their doors a signature of blood, to show that they were God's property. So the children of God in this age will bear the signature God has appointed. They will place themselves in harmony with God's holy law. A mark is placed upon every one of God's people just as verily as a mark was placed over the doors of the Hebrew dwellings, to preserve the people from the general ruin. God declares, "I gave them my Sabbaths, to be a sign between Me and them, that they might know that I am the Lord that sanctify them." Ezekiel 20:12. —*RH, Feb. 6, 1900*

A Passport for the Holy City

Only those who receive the seal of the living God will have the passport through the gates of the Holy City. But there are many who take upon themselves responsibilities in connection with the work of God who are not wholehearted believers, and while they remain thus cannot receive the seal of the living God. They trust in their own righteousness, which the Lord accounts as foolishness and presumption. —*Lt 164, 1909*

The Sign of a Converted Mind

What is the seal of the living God, which is placed in the foreheads of his people? It is a mark which angels, but not human eyes, can read; for the destroying angel must see this mark of redemption. The intelligent mind has seen the sign of the cross of Calvary in the Lord's adopted sons and daughters. The sin of the transgression of the law of God is taken away. They have on the wedding garment, and are obedient and faithful to all God's commands.

—Lt 126, 1898

Sealed Christians are Protected

Every soul in our world is the Lord's property, by creation and by redemption. Each individual soul is on trial for his life. Has he given to God that which belongs to Him? Has he surrendered to God all that is his as his purchased possession? All who cherish the Lord as their portion in this life will be under his control, and will receive the sign, the mark of God, which shows them to be God's special possession. Christ's righteousness will go before them, and the glory of the Lord will be their reward. The Lord protects every human being who bears his sign. —*Lt 77, 1899*

Those Agonizing over Sin are Sealed

The day of God's vengeance is just upon us. The seal of God will be placed upon the foreheads of those only who sigh and cry for the abominations done in the land. Those who link in sympathy with the world are eating and drinking with the drunken and will surely be destroyed with the workers of iniquity. "The eyes of the Lord are over the righteous, and his ears are open unto their prayers: but the face of the Lord is against them that do evil." Our own course of action will determine whether we shall receive the seal of the living God or be cut down by the destroying weapons. —*5T, p. 212*

Angels Restrain Satan until Sealing

Angels are belting the world, refusing Satan his claim to supremacy, made because of the vast multitude of his adherents. We hear not the voices, we see not with the natural sight the work of these angels, but their hands are linked about the world, and with sleepless vigilance they are keeping the armies of Satan at bay till the sealing of God's people shall be accomplished. — *Lt 79, 1900*

Let God be Center of Your Thoughts

Unless the name of God is written in your forehead—written there because God is the center of your thoughts—you will not be meet for the inheritance in light. It is your Creator who has poured out to you all heaven in one wondrous gift—his only begotten Son. Will you withhold from God his own? Will you divert from the treasury the portion of means which the Lord claims as his? If so, you are robbing God, and every dollar is charged against you in the books of heaven. — *RH, Dec. 23, 1890*

Learn about the King's Mark

Christ, who came to our world to reveal the Father's heart of tender compassion, has shown us the methods which Sabbathkeepers are to follow in their work. These are plainly specified in the fifty-eighth chapter of Isaiah. The soul who keeps the Sabbath is stamped with the sign of God's government, and he must not dishonor this sign. By closely examining the Word of God, we may know whether we have the King's mark—whether we have been chosen and set apart to honor God. — *Ms 63, 1899*

One Commandment Has the Seal

To us as to Israel the Sabbath is given "for a perpetual covenant." To those who reverence his holy day the Sabbath is a sign that God recognizes them as his chosen people. It is a pledge that He will fulfill to them his covenant. Every soul who accepts the sign of God's government places himself under the divine, everlasting covenant. He fastens himself to the golden chain of obedience, every link of which is a promise.

The fourth commandment alone of all the ten contains the seal of the great Lawgiver, the Creator of the heavens and the earth. Those who obey this commandment take upon themselves his name, and all the blessings it involves are theirs. — *6T, p. 350*

Reflect the Image of Jesus

I also saw that many do not realize what they must be in order to live in the sight of the Lord without a high priest in the sanctuary through the time of trouble. Those who receive the seal of the living God and are protected in the time of trouble must reflect the image of Jesus fully. —*EW, p. 71*

Only Clear Minds are Sealed

That seal must be implanted in a clear mind. It is so engrossed there is no place for the seal. Who hath the image of the lovely Jesus? Holy God have mercy, have mercy upon thy Zion. Heal them, heal them. Watch them carefully, have everything done this side of the standing up of Michael. Those that now get established get fully established not to falter. —*Ms 5, 1849*

God Marks Peculiar People

Those who will be heirs of God, and joint heirs with Christ to the immortal inheritance, will be peculiar. Yes, so peculiar that God places a mark upon them as his, wholly his. Think ye that God will receive, honor, and acknowledge a people so mixed up with the world that they differ from them only in name? Read again Titus 2:13-15. It is soon to be known who is on the Lord's side, who will not be ashamed of Jesus. Those who have not moral courage to conscientiously take their position in the face of unbelievers, leave the fashions of the world, and imitate the self-denying life of Christ, are ashamed of Him, and do not love his example. —*1T, p. 287*

Godly Nonagenarians are Sealed

There are living upon our earth, men who have passed the age of four score and ten. The natural results of old age are seen in their feebleness. But they believe God, and God loves them. The seal of God is upon them, and they will be among the number of whom the Lord has said, "Blessed are the dead which die in the Lord."

With Paul they can say, "I have fought a good fight, I have finished my course, I have kept the faith; henceforth there is laid up for me a crown of righteousness, which the Lord, the righteous judge, shall give me at that day, and not to me only, but unto all them also that love his appearing." There are many whose gray hairs God honors because they have fought a good fight and kept the faith. —*Lt 207, 1899*

Perfect Characters are Sealed

We may talk of the blessings of the Holy Spirit, but unless we prepare ourselves for its reception, of what avail are our works? Are we striving with all our power to attain to the stature of men and women in Christ? Are we seeking for his fullness, ever pressing toward the mark set before us—the perfection of his character? When the Lord's people reach this mark, they will be sealed in their foreheads. Filled with the Spirit, they will be complete in Christ, and the recording angel will declare, "It is finished." —*RH, June 10, 1902*

Distracted Minds are Not Sealed

The Lord has shown me the danger of letting our minds be filled with worldly thoughts and cares. I saw that some minds are led away from present truth and a love of the Holy Bible by reading other exciting books; others are filled with perplexity and care for what they shall eat, drink, and wear. Some are looking too far off for the coming of the Lord. Time has continued a few years longer than they expected; therefore they think it may continue a few years more, and in this way their minds are being led from present truth, out after the world. In these things I saw great danger; for if the mind is filled with other things, present truth is shut out, and there is no place in our foreheads for the seal of the living God. —*EW, p. 58*

Commandment Keepers are Marked

Every soul who fastens himself to the divine, everlasting covenant, made and presented to us as a sign and mark of God's government, fastens himself to the golden chain of obedience, every link of which is a promise. He shows that he regards God's Word as above the word of man, God's love as preferable to the love of man. And those who repent of transgression, and return to their loyalty by accepting God's mark, show themselves to be true subjects, ready to do his will, to obey his commandments. True observance of the Sabbath is the sign of loyalty to God.

There are great lessons to be learned by all who minister for Christ. The Sabbath mark must be placed upon God's commandment-keeping people. The Sabbath, if kept in the spirit of true obedience, will show that all God's commandments are to be practiced, "that ye may know that I am the Lord that doth sanctify you." —*Ms 63, 1899*

Profound Humility is Required

Nothing is more essential to communion with God than the most profound humility. "I dwell," says the High and Holy One, "with him also that is of a contrite and humble spirit." While you are so eagerly striving to be first, remember that you will be last in the favor of God if you fail to cherish a meek and lowly spirit. Pride of heart will cause many to fail where they might have made a success.

"Before honor is humility," and "the patient in spirit is better than the proud in spirit." "When Ephraim spake trembling, he exalted himself in Israel; but when he offended in Baal, he died." "Many are called, but few are chosen." Many hear the invitation of mercy, are tested and proved; but few are sealed with the seal of the living God. Few will humble themselves as a little child, that they may enter the kingdom of heaven. —*5T, p. 50*

Growing Christians are Sealed

The Lord requires those who serve Him to show by word and action that they are sons of God. To show by the daily life that we are members of the royal family, children of the heavenly King, is of more value in God's sight than all learning, all wisdom, all high attainments. Any other course of action is dishonesty to the family of God, and will certainly be divorced from it.

When a man is filled with the Holy Spirit, the more severely he is tested and tried, the more clearly he proves that he is a true representative of Christ in word, in spirit, in action. Christ declares, "He that believeth on Me, the words that I do shall he do also; and greater works than these shall he do; because I go unto my Father." What is the promise to every true believer?— "Ye shall receive power, after that the Holy Ghost is come upon you."

Might we not better, my brethren and sisters, take ourselves to task for our unlikeness to Christ? He says, "Ye are my witnesses." What kind of witnesses are we for truth and righteousness? Are we striving with all our God-given powers to reach the measure of the stature of men and women in Christ? Are we seeking for his fullness, ever reaching higher and higher, trying to attain to the perfection of his character? When God's servants reach this point, they will be sealed in their foreheads. The recording angel will declare, "It is done." They will be complete in Him whose they are by creation and by redemption. —*Ms 148, 1899*

Sinful Christians are Not Sealed

I can tell you instance after instance that I know of, of men that have been warned and reproved, that have sat here in this house and listened to discourse after discourse; but in the place of being doers of the word, in the place of receiving the Word of God into good and honest hearts, in the place of working with all their might in harmony with heaven, they have hugged their sins to themselves.

And then what? The seal of God could not be upon them, and when calamities came, when placed in perilous positions, those very ones have gone down into the grave; and they will not come up in the first resurrection. They will not see the King in his beauty. They were lost simply because they took their own way. They broke away from the Spirit of God and kept venturing and venturing, and tasting and testing the wiles of the devil. — *Ms 1, 1890*

The Destroying Angel Sees the Seal

When the destroying angel was about to pass through the land of Egypt and smite the first-born of both man and beast, the Israelites were directed to bring their children into the house with them, and to strike the doorpost with blood; and none were to go out of the house, for all that were found among the Egyptians would be destroyed with them. We should take this lesson to ourselves.

Again the destroying angel is to pass through the land. There is to be a mark placed upon God's people, and that mark is the keeping of his holy Sabbath. We are not to follow our own will and judgment, and flatter ourselves that God will come to our terms. Suppose an Israelite had neglected to place the sign of blood upon his door, saying that the angels of God would be able to distinguish between the Hebrews and the Egyptians: would the heavenly sentinels have stood to guard that dwelling? That which looks unimportant to you may be of the highest consequence in God's special plans for the preservation of your life or the salvation of your soul.

God tests our faith by giving us some part to act in connection with his interposition in our behalf. To those who comply with the conditions, his promise will be fulfilled. But all that venture to depart from his instructions, to follow a way of their own choosing, will perish with the wicked when his judgments are visited upon the earth. — *Ms 3, 1885*

121

Reflect Christ's Image to be Sealed

We should study more earnestly the character of our Saviour. We should imitate the lovely Pattern that God has given us. We should dwell upon the matchless charms of Jesus until there will be nothing satisfying in this perishing world. We should desire to reflect his image in kindness, in courtesy, in gentleness, and love, then "when He shall appear, we shall be like Him; for we shall see Him as He is. And every man that hath this hope in Him purifieth himself, even as He is pure."

In a little while everyone who is a child of God will have his seal placed upon him. Oh that it may be placed upon our foreheads! Who can endure the thought of being passed by when the angel goes forth to seal the servants of God in their foreheads? — *RH, May 28, 1889*

Jesus Pleads for Men until the Sealing

I saw four angels who had a work to do on the earth, and were on their way to accomplish it. Jesus was clothed with priestly garments. He gazed in pity on the remnant, then raised his hands, and with a voice of deep pity cried, "My blood, Father, my blood, my blood, my blood!" Then I saw an exceeding bright light come from God, who sat upon the great white throne, and was shed all about Jesus.

Then I saw an angel with a commission from Jesus, swiftly flying to the four angels who had a work to do on the earth, and waving something up and down in his hand, and crying with a loud voice, "Hold! Hold! Hold! Hold! Until the servants of God are sealed in their foreheads."

I asked my accompanying angel the meaning of what I heard, and what the four angels were about to do. He said to me that it was God that restrained the powers, and that He gave his angels charge over things on the earth; that the four angels had power from God to hold the four winds, and that they were about to let them go; but while their hands were loosening, and the four winds were about to blow, the merciful eye of Jesus gazed on the remnant that were not sealed, and He raised his hands to the Father and pleaded with Him that He had spilled his blood for them. Then another angel was commissioned to fly swiftly to the four angels and bid them hold, until the servants of God were sealed with the seal of the living God in their foreheads. — *EW, p. 38*

A Test of Loyalty to God

The observance of the Lord's memorial, the Sabbath instituted in Eden, the seventh day Sabbath, is the test of our loyalty to God. Those who bring in, as there will be brought in, lords many and gods many, so that there is no distinct recognition of acknowledged loyalty to the Lord God, cannot have his mark, his seal of obedience. — *Lt 94, 1900*

The Blood on the Doorposts

The condition given to the Hebrews in Egypt on that night when the firstborn were slain was that every family should manifest that faith in the message given them of God that would lead them to act in perfect obedience to the directions given them of God. Every member of the family was to be gathered into the dwelling place of the Hebrews. They were to eat the Passover with their preparations all made for their departure, even with their staffs in their hands.

God was about to do his work in Judgment, and this was to bring Pharaoh to understand that the Lord, He was God, and beside Him there was none else. The angel of God was to pass over the houses of the Hebrews with the blood sprinkled on the lintels and doorposts. This sign was to be respected.

But suppose that the inmates of the house were careless and did not gather their children with them in the house? Or suppose the children who had been born and brought up in Egypt thought this only a whim, and altogether unnecessary, and should refuse the entreaties of their parents, making some excuse as did those called to the marriage supper? Then the judgment of God would not spare, but the stroke would as surely come upon the firstborn of the Hebrews as the firstborn of the Egyptians.

What is the condition of those who keep the commandments of God and have the faith of Jesus? If in families there are those who are refusing obedience to the Lord in keeping his Sabbath, then the seal cannot be placed upon them. The sealing is a pledge from God of perfect security to his chosen ones (Exodus 31:13-17). Sealing indicates you are God's chosen. He has appropriated you to Himself. As the sealed of God we are Christ's purchased possession, and no one shall pluck us out of his hands. The seal given in the forehead is God, New Jerusalem. "I will write upon him the name of my God, and the name of the city of my God" Revelation 3:12. — *Ms 59, 1895*

Ticketed for New Jerusalem

What need will there be of the solemn warning not to receive the mark of the beast, when all the saints of God are sealed and ticketed for the New Jerusalem? —*Lt 111, 1890*

A Story of a Firstborn Hebrew Girl

We are where the very last test is coming, as it was for the children of Egypt. It was the firstborn that was to be slain. From the king on his throne to the humble worker, they would not hear the Word of God. All the firstborn were to be slain. Now God says to the children of Israel, "Gather yourselves into your houses."

Suppose they had been disobedient. Suppose they had said, "God knows that I am not an Egyptian, and so I will not be particular to carry out this work." They would have been slain with the Egyptians. But God said, "Gather your families into your house and mark the lintel with blood, and thus mark your faith in Jesus Christ as the great antitype of all their offerings." See Exodus 12:22, 23.

How anxious those parents were! How they got their children into the house and counted them to see how many there were, and when one went to the door before the hour of midnight, how quickly they would snatch him away, to take him away lest he might be struck by the destroying angel. Were they any too careful? We want to consider, there they stood with their staves in their hands and their preparations made for the journey, so that when the word should come, they would not hesitate a moment, but start right on their way.

Imagine them. One child says, and she was the oldest daughter and an invalid, "Father, have you marked the door?" "I have given my servant direction that he shall do it, so do not worry any more." But the word comes again, "Father, Father, are you sure the door is marked?" He tells her that it is. But it comes again, "Father, take me in your arms and carry me to the door." He took her there, and lo, the door was not marked. With paling face the father gets the blood, and with his own hands puts the mark upon the door. It is important for every individual student to mark the door of their heart with the virtue of the blood of the slain Lamb. John said, "Behold the Lamb of God which taketh away the sin of the world." John 1:29. —*Ms 15, 1894*

Interweave Holiness into Character

Those that overcome the world, the flesh, and the devil, will be the favored ones who shall receive the seal of the living God. Those whose hands are not clean, whose hearts are not pure, will not have the seal of the living God. Those who are planning sin and acting it will be passed by. Only those who, in their attitude before God, are filling the position of those who are repenting and confessing their sins in the great antitypical day of atonement, will be recognized and marked as worthy of God's protection.

The names of those who are steadfastly looking and waiting and watching for the appearing of their Saviour—more earnestly and wishfully than they who wait for the morning—will be numbered with those who are sealed.

Those who, while having all the light of truth flashing upon their souls, should have works corresponding to their avowed faith, but are allured by sin, setting up idols in their hearts, corrupting their souls before God, and polluting those who unite with them in sin, will have their names blotted out of the book of life, and be left in midnight darkness, having no oil in their vessels with their lamps. "Unto you that fear my name shall the Sun of Righteousness arise with healing in his wings."

The same angel who visited Sodom is sounding the note of warning, "Escape for thy life." The bottles of God's wrath cannot be poured out to destroy the wicked and their works until all the people of God have been judged, and the cases of the living as well as the dead are decided. And even after the saints are sealed with the seal of the living God, his elect will have trials individually.

Personal afflictions will come; but the furnace is closely watched by an eye that will not suffer the gold to be consumed. The indelible mark of God is upon them. God can plead that his own name is written there. The Lord has shut them in. Their destination is inscribed—"God, New Jerusalem." They are God's property, his possession.

Will this seal be put upon the impure in mind, the fornicator, the adulterer, the man who covets his neighbor's wife? Let your souls answer the question, "Does my character correspond to the qualifications essential that I may receive a passport to the mansions Christ has prepared for those who are fitted for them?" Holiness must be inwrought in our character. —*TM, pp. 445, 446*

Those Who Cry over Abominations

The spirit of hatred which has existed with some because the wrongs among God's people have been reproved has brought blindness and a fearful deception upon their own souls, making it impossible for them to discriminate between right and wrong. They have put out their own spiritual eyesight. They may witness wrongs, but they do not feel as did Joshua and humble themselves because the danger of souls is felt by them.

The true people of God, who have the spirit of the work of the Lord and the salvation of souls at heart, will ever view sin in its real, sinful character. They will always be on the side of faithful and plain dealing with sins which easily beset the people of God. Especially in the closing work for the church, in the sealing time of the one hundred and forty-four thousand who are to stand without fault before the throne of God, will they feel most deeply the wrongs of God's professed people. This is forcibly set forth by the prophet's illustration of the last work under the figure of the men each having a slaughter weapon in his hand. One man among them was clothed with linen, with a writer's inkhorn by his side.

"And the Lord said unto him, Go through the midst of the city, through the midst of Jerusalem, and set a mark upon the foreheads of the men that sigh and that cry for all the abominations that be done in the midst thereof." Who are standing in the counsel of God at this time? Is it those who virtually excuse wrongs among the professed people of God and who murmur in their hearts, if not openly, against those who would reprove sin? Is it those who take their stand against them and sympathize with those who commit wrong?

No, indeed! Unless they repent, and leave the work of Satan in oppressing those who have the burden of the work and in holding up the hands of sinners in Zion, they will never receive the mark of God's sealing approval. They will fall in the general destruction of the wicked, represented by the work of the five men bearing slaughter weapons. Mark this point with care: Those who receive the pure mark of truth, wrought in them by the power of the Holy Ghost, represented by a mark by the man in linen, are those "that sigh and that cry for all the abominations that be done" in the church.

Their love for purity and the honor and glory of God is such, and they have so clear a view of the exceeding sinfulness of sin, that they are represented as being in agony, even sighing and crying. —*3T, pp. 266, 267*

126

Not All Sabbathkeepers are Sealed

Not all who profess to keep the Sabbath will be sealed. There are many even among those who teach the truth to others who will not receive the seal of God in their foreheads. They had the light of truth, they knew their Master's will, they understood every point of our faith, but they had not corresponding works. These who were so familiar with prophecy and the treasures of divine wisdom should have acted their faith. They should have commanded their households after them, that by a well-ordered family they might present to the world the influence of the truth upon the human heart.

By their lack of devotion and piety, and their failure to reach a high religious standard, they make other souls contented with their position. Men of finite judgment cannot see that in patterning after these men who have so often opened to them the treasures of God's Word, they will surely endanger their souls. Jesus is the only true pattern. Everyone must now search the Bible for himself upon his knees before God, with the humble, teachable heart of a child, if he would know what the Lord requires of him. —5T, pp. 213, 214

The Character Must be Spotless

Not one of us will ever receive the seal of God while our characters have one spot or stain upon them. It is left with us to remedy the defects in our characters, to cleanse the soul temple of every defilement. Then the latter rain will fall upon us as the early rain fell upon the disciples on the Day of Pentecost.

In this life we must meet fiery trials and make costly sacrifices, but the peace of Christ is the reward. There has been so little self-denial, so little suffering for Christ's sake, that the cross is almost entirely forgotten. We must be partakers with Christ of his sufferings if we would sit down in triumph with Him on his throne. So long as we choose the easy path of self-indulgence and are frightened at self-denial, our faith will never become firm, and we cannot know the peace of Jesus nor the joy that comes through conscious victory.

The most exalted of the redeemed host that stand before the throne of God and the Lamb, clad in white, know the conflict of overcoming, for they have come up through great tribulation. Those who have yielded to circumstances rather than engage in this conflict will not know how to stand in that day when anguish will be upon every soul, when, though Noah, Job, and Daniel were in the land, they could save neither son nor daughter, for everyone must deliver his soul by his own righteousness.

No one need say that his case is hopeless, that he cannot live the life of a Christian. Ample provision is made by the death of Christ for every soul. Jesus is our ever-present help in time of need. Only call upon Him in faith, and He has promised to hear and answer your petitions. Oh, for a living, active faith! We need it; we must have it, or we shall faint and fail in the day of trial. The darkness that will then rest upon our path must not discourage us or drive us to despair. It is the veil with which God covers his glory when He comes to impart rich blessings. We should know this by our past experience. In that day when God has a controversy with his people this experience will be a source of comfort and hope.

It is now that we must keep ourselves and our children unspotted from the world. It is now that we must wash our robes of character and make them white in the blood of the Lamb. It is now that we must overcome pride, passion, and spiritual slothfulness. It is now that we must awake and make determined effort for symmetry of character. "Today if ye will hear his voice, harden not your hearts." We are in a most trying position, waiting, watching for our Lord's appearing. The world is in darkness. "But ye, brethren," says Paul, "are not in darkness, that that day should overtake you as a thief." It is ever God's purpose to bring light out of darkness, joy out of sorrow, and rest out of weariness for the waiting, longing soul.

What are you doing, brethren, in the great work of preparation? Those who are uniting with the world are receiving the worldly mold and preparing for the mark of the beast. Those who are distrustful of self, who are humbling themselves before God and purifying their souls by obeying the truth, these are receiving the heavenly mold and preparing for the seal of God in their foreheads. When the decree goes forth and the stamp is impressed, their character will remain pure and spotless for eternity. Now is the time to prepare. The seal of God will never be placed upon the forehead of an impure man or woman. It will never be placed upon the forehead of the ambitious, world-loving man or woman. It will never be placed upon the forehead of men or women of false tongues or deceitful hearts. All who receive the seal must be without spot before God—candidates for heaven. —*5T, pp. 214-216*

Many Christians are Not Sealed

Many will not receive the seal of God because they do not keep his commandments or bear the fruits of righteousness. — *Lt 76, 1900*

Live in Constant Submission to God

All who earnestly desire to know whether they have the King's mark will examine his Word critically. A spurious sabbath is now exalted before the people. This is the mark, the sign, of a ruler who stands in opposition to the King of kings, the Lord of hosts. This ruler has sought to show his power and authority by taking a common working day, a child of the Papacy, and giving it to the world as the Sabbath of the Lord. He has sought to destroy the sign which God has said should be preserved to a thousand generations.

The observance of the Sabbath, the seventh day by God's people, is the sign to the world that they are linked to the God of heaven as his loyal subjects, who trust in his everlasting veracity and his power as the Creator of the heavens and the earth; and it is the sign that God recognizes them as his chosen people. Those who understand that the Sabbath is a sign between them and God will represent the principles of his government by bringing into their daily practice the laws of his kingdom. They will live in constant submission to his will, having the words of his law written in their hearts. His injunctions will be regarded as the spring of their existence. Faithful and true, they will heed every command given, and reveal in their daily lives the religion that emanates from God. — *ST, Nov. 22, 1899*

Discussion Questions

1. Why is the Sabbath the point of truth especially controverted?

2. How does the Sabbath separate the Remnant from worldly Christians?

3. What actions can we take to become like Christ?

4. How will the seal of God protect Christians at the end of time?

5. What does it mean to settle into the truth?

— 8 —

The Mark of the Beast

"And the smoke of their torment ascendeth up for ever and ever: and they have no rest day nor night, who worship the beast and his image, and whosoever receiveth the mark of his name." — Rev. 14:11

Job 10:14	Isa. 30:27, 28	Romans 16:17	Rev. 14:9-11	Rev. 19:19, 20
Psalm 130:3	Jer. 3:1-3	Rev. 13:16-18	Rev. 15:2; 16:2	Rev. 20:4

Sunday is Not a Test Yet

Sunday-keeping is not yet the mark of the beast, and will not be until the decree goes forth causing men to worship this idol sabbath. The time will come when this day will be the test, but that time has not come yet... The people will soon learn all you believe. — *Ms 118, 1899*

The Truth is Heard First

The sanctification of the Spirit signalizes the difference between those who have the seal of God and those who keep a spurious rest day. When the test comes, it will be clearly shown what the mark of the beast is. It is the keeping of Sunday. Those, who after having heard the truth continue to regard this day as holy, bear the signature of the man of sin, who thought to change times and laws. — *Lt 12, 1900*

Sunday Laws Bring the Mark

Satan and evil angels counsel to do away with God's sign. They said, "We will take Sunday, and make the world believe it is the Sabbath of the fourth commandment." When they will compel all to keep it, that is the mark of the beast and his image. All the lying signs and wonders, and mass of corruptions and slime, are the imprint of the satanic. They show blindness that is inconceivable. — *Ms 12, 1893*

Observing Sunday is the Mark

John was called to behold a people distinct from those who worship the beast or his image by keeping the first day of the week. The observance of this day is the mark of the beast. —*Lt 31, 1898*

Divisive Christians are Marked

God will open the eyes of honest souls to understand the cruel work of those who scatter and divide. He will mark those who cause divisions, that every honest one may escape from Satan's snare. — *1T, p. 333*

The Opposite of God's Seal

The sign, or seal, of God is revealed in the observance of the seventh-day Sabbath, the Lord's memorial of creation... The mark of the beast is the opposite of this—the observance of the first day of the week. This mark distinguishes those who acknowledge the supremacy of the papal authority from those who acknowledge the authority of God. —*8T, p. 117*

The Mark is Invisible

In the issue of the great contest two parties are developed, those who "worship the beast and his image," and receive his mark, and those who receive "the seal of the living God," who have the Father's name written in their foreheads. This is not a visible mark. The time has come when all who have an interest in their soul's salvation should earnestly and solemnly inquire, "What is the seal of God? and what is the mark of the beast? How can we avoid receiving it?" — *ST, Nov. 1, 1899*

Rebellious Minds are Marked

A refusal to obey the commandments of God, and a determination to cherish hatred against those who proclaim these commandments, leads to the most determined war on the part of the dragon, whose whole energies are brought to bear against the commandment-keeping people of God. "He causeth all, both small and great, ... to receive a mark in their right hand, or in their foreheads." Not only are men not to work with their hands on Sunday, but with their minds are they to acknowledge Sunday as the Sabbath. "And that no man might buy or sell, save he that had the mark, or the name of the beast, or the number of his name." —*RH, Apr. 27, 1911*

Many Fail the Loyalty Test

God has given men the Sabbath as a sign between Him and them, as a test of their loyalty. Those who, after the light regarding God's law comes to them, continue to disobey and exalt human laws above the law of God in the great crisis before us, will receive the mark of the beast. —*Lt 98, 1900*

The Wine of God's Wrath

With the issue thus clearly brought before him, whoever shall trample upon God's law to obey a human enactment receives the mark of the beast; he accepts the sign of allegiance to the power which he chooses to obey instead of God. The warning from heaven is: "If any man worship the beast and his image, and receive his mark in his forehead, or in his hand, the same shall drink of the wine of the wrath of God, which is poured out without mixture into the cup of his indignation." Revelation 14:9, 10. —*GC, p. 604*

Some Reject the Loud Cry

No one has yet received the mark of the beast. The testing time has not yet come. There are true Christians in every church, not excepting the Roman Catholic communion. None are condemned until they have had the light and have seen the obligation of the fourth commandment. But when the decree shall go forth enforcing the counterfeit sabbath, and the loud cry of the third angel shall warn men against the worship of the beast and his image, the line will be clearly drawn between the false and the true. Then those who still continue in transgression will receive the mark of the beast. —*Ms 51, 1899*

Prophecy Predicts a Papal Apostasy

The Sabbath of the fourth commandment is the seal of the living God. It points to God as the Creator, and is the sign of his rightful authority over the beings He has made. What, then, is the mark of the beast, if it is not the spurious sabbath which the world has accepted in the place of the true? The prophetic declaration that the Papacy was to exalt itself above all that is called God, or that is worshiped, has been strikingly fulfilled in the changing of the Sabbath from the seventh to the first day of the week. Wherever the papal Sabbath is honored in preference to the Sabbath of God, there the man of sin is exalted above the Creator of heaven and earth. —*ST, Nov. 1, 1899*

How to Receive the Beast's Mark

I saw all that "would not receive the mark of the beast, and of his image, in their foreheads or in their hands," could not buy or sell. I saw that the number of the image beast (666) was made up; and that it was the beast that changed the Sabbath, and the image beast had followed on after, and kept the Pope's, and not God's Sabbath. And all we were required to do, was to give up God's Sabbath, and keep the Pope's, and then we should have the mark of the beast, and of his image. — *WLF, p. 19*

Enemies of the Sabbath are Marked

John's prophetic eye sees a company who have not the mark of the beast. As he beholds them, he exclaims, "Here is the patience of the saints: here are they that keep the commandments of God, and the faith of Jesus."

Two parties are brought into view: one keeping the commandments of God, in distinction from the one breaking his commandments, enforcing the Sunday sabbath, and compelling the people to conform to the Sunday law. Through union with opposers of the Sabbath of the fourth commandment— the seventh day Sabbath—men will receive the mark of the beast. And all who have that mark will perish with the man of sin, who makes void the law of God. — *Lt 118, 1900*

Nominal Christians Receive the Mark

If the light of truth has been presented to you, revealing the Sabbath of the fourth commandment, and showing that there is no foundation in the Word of God for Sunday observance, and yet you still cling to the false sabbath, refusing to keep holy the Sabbath which God calls "My holy day," you receive the mark of the beast. When does this take place? When you obey the decree that commands you to cease from labor on Sunday and worship God, while you know that there is not a word in the Bible showing Sunday to be other than a common working day, you consent to receive the mark of the beast, and refuse the seal of God.

If we receive this mark in our foreheads or in our hands, the judgments pronounced against the disobedient must fall upon us. But the seal of the living God is placed upon those who conscientiously keep the Sabbath of the Lord. — *RH, July 13, 1897*

Beware of the Papal Sabbath

The change of the Sabbath is the sign or mark of the authority of the Romish church. Those who, understanding the claims of the fourth commandment, choose to observe the false sabbath in the place of the true, are thereby paying homage to that power by which alone it is commanded. The mark of the beast is the papal sabbath, which has been accepted by the world in the place of the day of God's appointment. —*Ms 51, 1899*

The World Worships the Beast

When Sunday observance shall be enforced by law, and the world shall be enlightened concerning the obligation of the true Sabbath, then whoever shall transgress the command of God, to obey a precept which has no higher authority than that of Rome, will thereby honor popery above God. He is paying homage to Rome and to the power which enforces the institution ordained by Rome. He is worshiping the beast and his image.

As men then reject the institution which God has declared to be the sign of his authority, and honor in its stead that which Rome has chosen as the token of her supremacy, they will thereby accept the sign of allegiance to Rome—"the mark of the beast." And it is not until the issue is thus plainly set before the people, and they are brought to choose between the commandments of God and the commandments of men, that those who continue in transgression will receive "the mark of the beast." —*GC, p. 449*

Discussion Questions

1. Why is Sunday not yet the Mark of the Beast?

2. What is the image of the beast?

3. Why does the Bible say that men will be marked in the hand or on the forehead?

4. Which major event will signal that men are in danger of being marked?

5. Why are Christians who reject the Loud Cry marked?

— 9 —

Time Runs Out

"When once the master of the house is risen up, and hath shut to the door, and ye begin to stand without, and to knock at the door, saying, 'Lord, Lord, open unto us;' and he shall answer and say unto you, 'I know you not whence ye are.'" — Luke 13:25

| Gen. 6:3; 7:16 | Daniel 5:25-31 | Matt. 23:36-39 | Luke 12:10 | Hebrews 4:7 |
| Isaiah 43:25 | Daniel 12:10 | Matt. 25:1-13 | 1 Thes. 5:1-7 | Rev. 22:11, 12 |

Probation Ends Suddenly

When probation ends, it will come suddenly, unexpectedly—at a time when we are least expecting it. —*Ms 95, 1906*

Even Satan Does Not Know

Satan sees that holy angels are guarding them, and he infers that their sins have been pardoned; but he does not know that their cases have been decided in the sanctuary above. —*GC, p. 618*

The Third Angel Binds the Wheat

I then saw the third angel. Said my accompanying angel, "Fearful is his work. Awful is his mission. He is the angel that is to select the wheat from the tares and seal, or bind, the wheat for the heavenly garner." These things should engross the whole mind, the whole attention. —*EW, p. 118*

Those Who Reject Truth are Lost

Those who have clearly seen and fully accepted the truth upon the fourth commandment and have received the blessing attending obedience, but have since renounced their faith and dared to violate the law of God, will find, if they persist in this path of disobedience, the gates of the city of God closed against them. —*Ms 4, 1883*

Character is Permanently Set

If you have become estranged, and have failed to be Bible Christians, be converted, for the character you bear in probationary time will be the character you will have at the coming of Christ. —*Lt 18b, 1891*

Men Answer for Their Talents

Everyone is accountable to God according to the ability and talent which he has received. Those who are on probation to see whether or not they are to be subjects of the kingdom of God, must be tried and proved now. Those who love God in spirit and in truth, will be pronounced fit subjects of the heavenly kingdom. — *YI, July 26, 1894*

God Knows When Probation Ends

God has not revealed to us the time when this message will close, or when probation will have an end. Those things that are revealed we shall accept for ourselves and for our children; but let us not seek to know that which has been kept secret in the councils of the Almighty. It is our duty to watch and work and wait, to labor every moment for the souls of men that are ready to perish. —*RH, Oct. 9, 1894*

More Solemn to Live than to Die

It is a solemn thing to die, but a far more solemn thing to live. Every thought and word and deed of our lives will meet us again. What we make of ourselves in probationary time, that we must remain to all eternity. Death brings dissolution to the body, but makes no change in the character. The coming of Christ does not change our characters; it only fixes them forever beyond all change. —*5T, p. 466*

Probation Ends as the Mediator Leaves

Many entertain the view that probation is granted after Jesus leaves his work as mediator in the most holy apartment. This is the sophistry of Satan. God tests and proves the world by the light which He is pleased to give them previous to the coming of Christ. Characters are then formed for life or death. But the probation of those who choose to live a life of sin, and neglect the great salvation offered, closes when Christ's ministration ceases just previous to his appearing in the clouds of heaven. —*2T, p. 691*

No Probation after Jesus Comes

There will be no probation after the coming of our Lord. Those who say that there will are deceived and misled. Before Christ comes, just such a state of things will exist as existed before the flood. And after the Saviour appears in the clouds of heaven, no one will be given another chance to gain salvation. All will have made their decisions. —*Lt 45, 1891*

The Door of Mercy Closes

When the work of investigation shall be ended, when the cases of those who in all ages have professed to be followers of Christ have been examined and decided, then, and not till then, probation will close, and the door of mercy will be shut. Thus in the one short sentence, "They that were ready went in with Him to the marriage: and the door was shut," we are carried down through the Saviour's final ministration, to the time when the great work for man's salvation shall be completed. —*GC, p. 428*

Prolonged Probation is a Fable

No literal devil, and probation after the coming of Christ, are fast becoming popular fables. The Scriptures plainly declare that every person's destiny is forever fixed at the coming of the Lord. "He that is unjust, let him be unjust still: and he which is filthy, let him be filthy still: and he that is righteous, let him be righteous still: and he that is holy, let him be holy still. And, behold, I come quickly; and my reward is with Me, to give every man according as his work shall be." Revelation 22:11, 12. —*5T, pp. 342, 343*

Transfer of Character is Impossible

The Lord is coming in power and great glory. It will then be his work to make a complete separation between the righteous and the wicked. But the oil cannot then be transferred to the vessels of those who have it not. Then shall be fulfilled the words of Christ, "Two women shall be grinding together; the one shall be taken, and the other left. Two men shall be in the field; the one shall be taken, and the other left." The righteous and the wicked are to be associated together in the work of life. But the Lord reads the character. He discerns who are obedient children, who respect and love his commandments.

—Lt 64a, 1895

Time Ends as the Party Continues

As the time of their probation was closing, the antediluvians gave themselves up to exciting amusements and festivities. Those who possessed influence and power were bent on keeping the minds of the people engrossed with mirth and pleasure, lest any should be impressed by the last solemn warning. Do we not see the same repeated in our day? While God's servants are giving the message that the end of all things is at hand, the world is absorbed in amusements and pleasure seeking. There is a constant round of excitement that causes indifference to God and prevents the people from being impressed by the truths which alone can save them from the coming destruction.

—PP, p. 103

Some Believe in a Second Probation

Those who love the world, and whose minds are carnal and at enmity with God, will flatter themselves that a period of probation will be granted after Christ appears in the clouds of heaven. The carnal heart, which is so averse to submission and obedience, will be deceived with this pleasing view. Many will remain in carnal security and continue in rebellion against God, flattering themselves that there is then to be a period for repentance of sin and an opportunity for them to accept the truth which now is unpopular and crossing to their natural inclination and desires. When they have nothing to venture, nothing to lose, by yielding obedience to Christ and the truth, they think they will take their chance for salvation. *—2T, p. 691*

Soon the Mandate will Go Forth

The Lord is proving and testing his people. Angels of God are watching the development of character and weighing moral worth. Probation is almost ended, and you are unready. Oh, that the word of warning might burn into your souls! Get ready! get ready! Work while the day lasts, for the night cometh when no man can work. The mandate will go forth: "He that is holy, let him be holy still; and he that is filthy, let him be filthy still."

The destiny of all will be decided. A few, yes, only a few, of the vast number who people the earth will be saved unto life eternal, while the masses who have not perfected their souls in obeying the truth will be appointed to the second death. "Oh Saviour, save the purchase of thy blood!" is the cry of my anguished heart. *—2T, p. 401*

Light from God Ceases

I was shown a bright light, given by God to guide all who would walk in the way of salvation, and also to serve as a warning to the sinner to flee from the wrath of God, and yield a willing obedience to his claims. While this light continued there was hope. But there was a period when this light would cease. When he that is holy will remain holy forever, and when he that is filthy will remain filthy forever. When Jesus stands up; when his work is finished in the Most Holy, when there will be not another ray of light to be imparted to the sinner. —*2SG, p. 275*

Choose Whom You will Serve

The Lord says to the people of the earth, "Choose you this day whom ye will serve." All are now deciding their eternal destiny. Men need to be aroused to realize the solemnity of the time, the nearness of the day when human probation shall be ended. God gives no man a message that it will be five years or ten years or twenty years before this earth's history shall close. He would not give any living being an excuse for delaying the preparation for his appearing. He would have no one say, as did the unfaithful servant, "My Lord delayeth his coming;" for this leads to reckless neglect of the opportunities and privileges given to prepare us for that great day. Everyone who claims to be a servant of God is called to do his service as if each day might be the last.

—RH, Nov. 27, 1900

Men Deceived by Fables are Lost

There is no work in our world so great and so glorious, no work which God honors as much, as the gospel work. The message presented is the last message of mercy for a fallen world. Those who have the privilege of hearing this message, and yet refuse to be enlightened, throw away their last chance. All will be tested and tried, according to the light they have had. Those who turn from the truth to fables can look for no second probation.

There will be no temporal millennium. If, after the Holy Spirit has brought conviction to their hearts, they resist the truth, and use their influence to block the way so that others will not receive it, they will never be convinced. They did not seek for transformation of character in the probation given them, and Christ will not give them opportunity to pass over the ground again. The decision is a final one. —*Lt 25, 1900*

More Probation Would be Pointless

We are living in the last days. God will be our Strength, our Support, our ever-present Helper, if we will only trust in Him. We are to make the best of our present opportunities. There will be no other probation given to us in which to prepare for heaven. This is our only and last opportunity to form characters which will fit us for the future home which the Lord has prepared for all who are obedient to his commandments. We can be saved only by forming characters like the character of Christ. — *Lt 20, 1899*

No Probation after the Judgment

There is to be no probation after the judgment. When the work of the gospel is completed, there immediately follows the separation between the good and the evil, and the destiny of each class is forever fixed.

God does not desire the destruction of any. "As I live, saith the Lord God, I have no pleasure in the death of the wicked; but that the wicked turn from his way and live. Turn ye, turn ye from your evil ways; for why will ye die?" Ezekiel 33:11. Throughout the period of probationary time his Spirit is entreating men to accept the gift of life. It is only those who reject his pleading that will be left to perish. God has declared that sin must be destroyed as an evil ruinous to the universe. Those who cling to sin will perish in its destruction. — *COL, p. 123*

The Angel of Mercy Folds Her Wings

There is not a second probation for any one. Now is probationary time, before the angel shall fold her golden wings, the angel of mercy, and shall step down from the throne, and mercy, mercy, is gone forever. But now everyone, he that hath the scarlet sin, he that hath the crimson sin, are not left out, for God says, "Though your sins be as scarlet, I will make them white as snow; though they be as crimson, I will make them like wool."

What precious promises are given to every one of us, if we will take hold of them. But we must lay hold of them, not by a casual faith, but lay hold of them as a personal blessing given to us, as a personal Saviour. We give ourselves to Him, surrender to Him, to have the mold and the fashion of our God upon us, that we may imitate his character. He does not want any there in heaven that do not represent his character. — *Ms 49, 1894*

No More Invitations to the Wedding

New life must enter into the churches. The last work of warning and mercy for a fallen world is being done. None are to be deceived, thinking to lay their individual work on somebody else. When this probationary time shall close, there is no opportunity for those who have received the warning message, the proclamation of pardon and salvation, and have refused—have turned from light and truth and accepted fables—to be justified. There is no second bidding to the marriage feast, no intermediate state when another call will be made to come to the heavenly feast. —*Ms 59, 1895*

Cries to God are Not in Vain

The faith and patience of those who have waited long, have been sorely tried. "Hope deferred has made the heartsick;" and the cry has come up before God, "Lord, how long?" But now the signs are fulfilling,—nation rising against nation, startling calamities by land and by sea, famine, pestilence, fearful storms, sweeping floods, and great conflagrations. All these testify that we are approaching the grand consummation. The cry going up to God from the waiting ones, will not be in vain. The response will come, "It is done." "He which is filthy, let him be filthy still; ... he that is holy, let him be holy still." Can the church contemplate this hour with calm indifference? —*RH, Jan. 1, 1889*

The End of Probation is Unnoticed

When God's presence was finally withdrawn from the Jewish nation, priests and people knew it not. Though under the control of Satan, and swayed by the most horrible and malignant passions, they still regarded themselves as the chosen of God. The ministration in the temple continued; sacrifices were offered upon its polluted altars, and daily the divine blessing was invoked upon a people guilty of the blood of God's dear Son and seeking to slay his ministers and apostles.

So when the irrevocable decision of the sanctuary has been pronounced and the destiny of the world has been forever fixed, the inhabitants of the earth will know it not. The forms of religion will be continued by a people from whom the Spirit of God has been finally withdrawn; and the satanic zeal with which the prince of evil will inspire them for the accomplishment of his malignant designs, will bear the semblance of zeal for God. —*GC, p. 615*

Jesus Leaves the Sanctuary

We must work while the day lasts, for when the dark night of trouble and anguish comes, it will be too late to work for God. Jesus is in his holy temple and will now accept our sacrifices, our prayers, and our confessions of faults and sins and will pardon all the transgressions of Israel, that they may be blotted out before He leaves the sanctuary.

When Jesus leaves the sanctuary, then they who are holy and righteous will be holy and righteous still; for all their sins will then be blotted out, and they will be sealed with the seal of the living God. But those that are unjust and filthy will be unjust and filthy still; for then there will be no Priest in the sanctuary to offer their sacrifices, their confessions, and their prayers before the Father's throne. —*EW, p. 48*

The Sanctuary Work Closes Soon

When Jesus ceases to plead for man, the cases of all are forever decided. This is the time of reckoning with his servants. To those who have neglected the preparation of purity and holiness, which fits them to be waiting ones to welcome their Lord, the sun sets in gloom and darkness, and rises not again. Probation closes; Christ's intercessions cease in heaven.

This time finally comes suddenly upon all, and those who have neglected to purify their souls by obeying the truth are found sleeping. They became weary of waiting and watching; they became indifferent in regard to the coming of their Master. They longed not for his appearing, and thought there was no need of such continued, persevering watching. They had been disappointed in their expectations and might be again. They concluded that there was time enough yet to arouse. They would be sure not to lose the opportunity of securing an earthly treasure. It would be safe to get all of this world they could.

And in securing this object, they lost all anxiety and interest in the appearing of the Master. They became indifferent and careless, as though his coming were yet in the distance. But while their interest was buried up in their worldly gains, the work closed in the heavenly sanctuary, and they were unprepared. If such had only known that the work of Christ in the heavenly sanctuary would close so soon, how differently would they have conducted themselves, how earnestly would they have watched! —*2T, p. 191*

God Passes by Lovers of Sin

The destroying angels have the commission from the Lord, "Begin at my sanctuary." And "they began at the ancient men which were before the house." If the warnings which God has given are neglected or regarded with indifference, if you suffer sin to be cherished, you are sealing your soul's destiny; you will be weighed in the balances and found wanting. Grace, peace, and pardon will be withdrawn forever; Jesus will have passed by, never again to come within the reach of your prayers and entreaties. While mercy still lingers, while Jesus is making intercession for us, let us make thorough work for eternity. — *RH, Jan. 11, 1887*

The Tares and Wheat are Separate

The looker-on may discern no difference, but there is One who said that the tares were not to be plucked up by human hands, lest the wheat be rooted up also. Let both grow together until the harvest. Then the Lord sends forth his reapers to gather out the tares, and bind them in bundles to burn, while the wheat is gathered into the heavenly garner. The time of the judgment is a most solemn period, when the Lord gathers his own from among the tares.

Those who have been members of the same family are separated. A mark is placed upon the righteous. "They shall be mine, saith the Lord of hosts, in that day when I make up my jewels; and I will spare them, as a man spareth his own son that serveth him." Malachi 3:17. Those who have been obedient to God's commandments will unite with the company of the saints in light; they shall enter in through the gates into the city, and have right to the tree of life. The one shall be taken. His name shall stand in the book of life, while those with whom he associated shall have the mark of eternal separation from God.

The tares and wheat are now commingled, but then the one hand that alone can separate them will give to everyone his true position. Those who have had the light of truth and heard the warning message, heard the invitation to the marriage supper—farmer, merchant, lawyer, false shepherds who have quieted the convictions of the people, unfaithful watchmen who have not sounded the warning or know the time of night—all who have refused obedience to the laws of the kingdom of God, will have no right therein. — *Lt 64a, 1895*

143

Probation Ends before Jesus Comes

Solemn are the scenes connected with the closing work of the atonement. Momentous are the interests involved therein. The judgment is now passing in the sanctuary above. For many years this work has been in progress. Soon—none know how soon—it will pass to the cases of the living. In the awful presence of God our lives are to come up in review. At this time above all others it behooves every soul to heed the Saviour's admonition: "Watch and pray: for ye know not when the time is." Mark 13:33. "If therefore thou shalt not watch, I will come on thee as a thief, and thou shalt not know what hour I will come upon thee." Revelation 3:3.

When the work of the investigative judgment closes, the destiny of all will have been decided for life or death. Probation is ended a short time before the appearing of the Lord in the clouds of heaven. Christ in the Revelation, looking forward to that time, declares: "He that is unjust, let him be unjust still: and he which is filthy, let him be filthy still: and he that is righteous let him be righteous still: and he that is holy, let him be holy still. And, behold, I come quickly; and my reward is with Me, to give every man according as his work shall be." Revelation 22:11, 12.

The righteous and the wicked will still be living upon the earth in their mortal state—men will be planting and building, eating and drinking, all unconscious that the final, irrevocable decision has been pronounced in the sanctuary above. Before the Flood, after Noah entered the ark, God shut him in and shut the ungodly out; but for seven days the people, knowing not that their doom was fixed, continued their careless, pleasure-loving life and mocked the warnings of impending judgment. "So," says the Saviour, "shall also the coming of the Son of man be." Matthew 24:39. Silently, unnoticed as the midnight thief, will come the decisive hour which marks the fixing of every man's destiny, the final withdrawal of mercy's offer to guilty men.

"Watch ye therefore: ... lest coming suddenly He find you sleeping." Mark 13:35, 36. Perilous is the condition of those who, growing weary of their watch, turn to the attractions of the world. While the man of business is absorbed in the pursuit of gain, while the pleasure lover is seeking indulgence, while the daughter of fashion is arranging her adornments—it may be in that hour the Judge of all the earth will pronounce the sentence: "Thou art weighed in the balances, and art found wanting." Daniel 5:27. *— GC, pp. 490, 491*

The Third Angel's Message Closes

When the third angel's message closes, mercy no longer pleads for the guilty inhabitants of the earth. The people of God have accomplished their work. They have received "the latter rain," "the refreshing from the presence of the Lord," and they are prepared for the trying hour before them. Angels are hastening to and fro in heaven. An angel returning from the earth announces that his work is done; the final test has been brought upon the world, and all who have proved themselves loyal to the divine precepts have received "the seal of the living God."

Then Jesus ceases his intercession in the sanctuary above. He lifts his hands and with a loud voice says, "It is done;" and all the angelic host lay off their crowns as He makes the solemn announcement: "He that is unjust, let him be unjust still: and he which is filthy, let him be filthy still: and he that is righteous, let him be righteous still: and he that is holy, let him be holy still." Revelation 22:11.

Every case has been decided for life or death. Christ has made the atonement for his people and blotted out their sins. The number of his subjects is made up; "the kingdom and dominion, and the greatness of the kingdom under the whole heaven," is about to be given to the heirs of salvation, and Jesus is to reign as King of kings and Lord of lords. — *GC, p. 613*

Discussion Questions

1. Why are lukewarm Christians described as tares?

2. Are there any final events coming that might allow Christians to infer that probation has already closed?

3. Do you think that probation will close early for Seventh-day Adventists?

4. Why would it be pointless for God to give men a second probation?

5. Are there any Bible characters who were spared from dying, and then failed to make the most of the extra time they received from God?

The Seven
Last Plagues

— 10 —

A Nation in Apostasy

"It is time for thee, Lord, to work: for they have made void thy law." — Psalm 119:126

| Joshua 24:20 | Ps. 94:20-23 | Isa. 10:1; 24:5 | Jer. 9:13-15 | Jer. 44:23 | Matt. 24:15, 16 |
| 2 Kings 22:16, 17 | Ps. 119:150 | Jer. 6:19 | Jer. 17:27 | Hosea 8:1 | Romans 4:15 |

The Protective Shield of God

The United States is a land that has been under the special shield of the Omnipotent One. God has done great things for this country; but in the transgression of his law, men have been doing a work originated by the man of sin. Satan is working out his designs to involve the human family in disloyalty. — *Ms 17, 1906*

God Works in a Special Manner

In the time of testing and trial the shield of Omnipotence will be spread over those whom God has made the depositaries of his law. When legislators shall abjure the principles of Protestantism, so as to give countenance and the right hand of fellowship to Romanism, then God will interpose in a special manner in behalf of his own honor and the salvation of his people. — *5T, p. 525*

Judgment Falls in the Streets

The time has come when judgment is fallen in the streets, and equity cannot enter, and he that departeth from evil maketh himself a prey. But the Lord's arm is not shortened that it cannot save, and his ear is not heavy that it cannot hear. The people of the United States have been a favored people; but when they restrict religious liberty, surrender Protestantism, and give countenance to popery, the measure of their guilt will be full, and "national apostasy" will be registered in the books of heaven. The result of this apostasy will be national ruin. — *RH, May 2, 1893*

Darkness Covers America

America, and especially Battle Creek, where the greatest light from heaven has been shining upon the people, can become the place of greatest peril and darkness because the people do not continue to practice the truth and walk in the light. —*Lt 23c, 1894*

National Apostasy Brings Ruin

When Protestant churches shall seek the support of the secular power, thus following the example of that apostate church, for opposing which their ancestors endured the fiercest persecution, then will there be a national apostasy which will end only in national ruin. —*ST, July 4, 1899*

Awful Sins Reach to Heaven

The sins of the world will have reached unto heaven when the law of God is made void; when the Sabbath of the Lord is trampled in the dust, and men are compelled to accept in its stead an institution of the papacy through the strong hand of the law of the land. In exalting an institution of man above the institution ordained of God, they show contempt for the great Lawgiver, and refuse his sign or seal. —*RH, Nov. 5, 1889*

America Receives Pure Wrath

Everything is preparing for the great day of God. Time will last a little longer until the inhabitants of the earth have filled up the cup of their iniquity, and then the wrath of God, which has so long slumbered, will awake, and this land of light (the United States) will drink the cup of his unmingled wrath. The desolating power of God is upon the earth to rend and destroy. The inhabitants of the earth are appointed to the sword, to famine, and to pestilence. —*1T, p. 363*

God Punishes Lawbreakers

The mingling of churchcraft and statecraft is represented by the iron and the clay. This union is weakening all the power of the churches. This investing the church with the power of the State will bring evil results. Men have almost passed the point of God's forbearance. They have invested their strength in politics, and have united with the papacy. But the time will come when God will punish those who have made void his law, and their evil work will recoil upon themselves. —*Ms 63, 1899*

Rulers are Guilty like Barabbas

Kings, and rulers, and governors have placed upon themselves the brand of Antichrist, and are represented as the dragon who goes to make war with the saints, with those who keep the commandments of God, and who have the faith of Jesus. In their enmity against the people of God, they show themselves guilty also of the choice of Barabbas instead of Christ.

—RH, Aug. 29, 1893

The World Has Legalized Sin

The Lord has rich stores, and He desires men to enjoy his blessing. Had men in the beginning rightly appreciated and appropriated the talents God gave them, the earth would not have been cursed by a flood. And we see the work of destruction still going on, and why? Because there has been a national apostasy. The world has thrown off the law of God, and has legalized transgression and sin. *—Lt 119, 1899*

America Fills up Its Cup of Iniquity

The land that has been abundantly blessed of God is fast filling up the cup of its iniquity. The figures on the side of iniquity are rapidly reaching the sum of corruption which was reached by the Amorites, and by the Jewish nation, once the elect people of God. In the days of Christ they made void the law of God, teaching for doctrines the commandments of men, and this led them to reject the Son of God. When the people accept and exalt a spurious sabbath, and turn souls away from obedience and loyalty to God, they will reach the point that was reached by the people in the days of Christ. *—Ms 15, 1896*

Church and State Void God's Law

Everything betokens the end is near. The churches are making void the law of God, rejecting the truth and choosing their delusions. They are not taking sides with the Prince of Peace. They are not ranging under the banner of the Lord God of hosts; and when church and state shall be united in restricting religious liberty, when the institution of the man of sin shall be taken up universally in preference to God's holy, sanctified day; when all men standing in church and state show strong respect for the man of sin in exalting the heathen day of worship and call it Christian, then it will be time for God to work, for they have made void his law. *—Ms 87, 1886*

Wrath Falls on Lawmakers

The Sabbath is the Lord's test, and no man, be he king, priest, or ruler, is authorized to come between God and man. Those who seek to be conscience for their fellow men, place themselves above God. Those who are under the influence of a false religion, who observe a spurious rest day, will set aside the most positive evidence in regard to the true Sabbath. They will try to compel men to obey the laws of their own creation, laws that are directly opposed to the law of God. Upon those who continue in this course, the wrath of God will fall. Unless they change, they cannot escape the penalty. — *9T, p. 234*

Laws Lead to a National Apostasy

Any fallacy is likely to be received by a people who make void the law of God. There is a crisis just ahead of those who are acting on a short-sighted policy. The rulers of the land will take their position above the great Creator of the world. The claims of a false sabbath will be brought to the front, and the rulers and the people will act upon the principle of a short-sighted policy. The false sabbath, the first day of the week, will be accepted, and the rulers will unite with the man of sin to restore his lost ascendancy.

Laws enforcing the observance of Sunday as the sabbath, will bring about a national apostasy from the principles of republicanism upon which the government has been founded. The religion of the Papacy will be accepted by the rulers, and the law of God will be made void. — *Ms 39, 1906*

God Keeps a Record against Nations

The Christian world has sanctioned his efforts by adopting this child of the papacy—the Sunday institution. They have nourished it, and will continue to nourish it, until Protestantism shall give the hand of fellowship to the Roman power. Then there will be a law against the Sabbath of God's creation, and then it is that God "will do a strange work in the earth."

He has borne long with the perversity of the race; He has tried to win them to Himself. But the time will come when they shall have filled their measure of iniquity; and then it is that God will work. This time is almost reached. God keeps a record with the nations: the figures are swelling against them in the books of heaven; and when it shall have become a law that the transgression of the first day of the week shall be met with punishment, then their cup will be full. — *RH, Mar. 9, 1886*

A Global Law Triggers Judgments

The wickedness of the inhabitants of the world has almost filled up the measure of their iniquity. This earth has almost reached the place where God will permit the destroyer to work his will upon it. The substitution of the laws of men for the law of God, the exaltation, by merely human authority, of Sunday in place of the Bible Sabbath, is the last act in the drama. When this substitution becomes universal, God will reveal Himself. He will arise in his majesty to shake terribly the earth. — *7T, p. 141*

Catholic Principles Lead to Ruin

The world has converted the church. Both are in harmony, and are acting on a short-sighted policy. Protestants will work upon the rulers of the land to make laws to restore the lost ascendancy of the man of sin, who sits in the temple of God, showing himself that he is God. Roman Catholic principles will be taken under the care and protection of the state. This national apostasy will speedily be followed by national ruin.

The protest of Bible truth will be no longer tolerated by those who have not made the law of God their rule of life. Then will the voice be heard from the graves of martyrs, represented by the souls that John saw slain for the Word of God and the testimony of Jesus Christ which they held; then the prayer will ascend from every true child of God, "It is time for thee, Lord, to work: for they have made void thy law." — *RH, June 15, 1897*

The Fate of Nadab and Abihu

This day so universally exalted is a spurious sabbath, a common working day. It is accepted in the place of the day that the Lord has blessed and sanctified; but the sure result of this course may be seen in the punishment which fell upon Nadab and Abihu, the sons of Aaron. As priests of God, these men had been commanded to offer always the fire of God's own kindling, which was kept burning before God day and night. This was ever to be strictly observed.

But Nadab and Abihu drank wine too freely; and because of this their minds were not keen, but confused, and they were unable to distinguish between the sacred and the common. They took their censers, "and put fire therein, and put incense thereon, and offered strange fire before the Lord, which He commanded them not. And there went out fire from the Lord, and devoured them, and they died before the Lord." — *RH, Dec. 20, 1898*

The Sunday Law Boundary

In this age men have gone to great lengths in arrogance and in blasphemous denunciation of God's law. They have accepted a false sabbath in the place of the day that God sanctified and gave to man as a memorial of creation. Their disobedience is great, and well may the prayer go forth from unfeigned lips, "It is time for thee, Lord, to work: for they have made void thy law." The boundary line will soon be reached. The crisis will soon come, and then God will interfere. When mercy's limits are passed, God will work, and show that He is God. The Judge of all the earth will vindicate his honor, and punish the rebellious inhabitants of the earth. —*RH, Aug. 14, 1900*

Our Extremity is God's Opportunity

Blindness and disloyalty to God so prevail that his law is made void, but the Psalmist says of such a condition, "It is time for thee, Lord, to work; for they have made void thy law." Psalm 119:126...

The man of sin thinks to change times and laws. He is exalting himself above God in trying to compel the conscience. But God's people should work with persevering energy to let their light shine upon the people in regard to the law and thus to withstand the enemies of God and his truth. When the law of God has been made void and apostasy becomes a national sin, the Lord will work in behalf of his people. Their extremity will be his opportunity. He will manifest his power in behalf of his church. —*Ms 18, 1888*

Nations Wear Out God's Patience

A more than common contempt is put upon the commandments of God, while the representative men of the Colonies have exalted the first day of the week to be observed by all men. They would have men bow down and worship it, as did Nebuchadnezzar when he exalted the golden image in the plains of Dura. When wickedness comes to this pass, it is fast reaching its height. Well may the prayer go forth from the people of God, calling for his interference...

It is a terrible thing for a nation to wear out the patience of God. Each century of profligacy has treasured up wrath for its iniquity against the day of wrath. Christ is now bidding the abandoned of our day to fill up the measure of their fathers in their iniquity. When that time shall come, and their cup of iniquity is filled up, it will be demonstrated that to wear out the patience of God brings tremendous consequences to the disobedient. —*Ms 127, 1897*

The Final Act of Apostasy

The world and the church are married. The ruling powers of earth have taken it upon themselves to compel the conscience of God's people who keep the commandments of God and have the faith of Jesus. They will seek by force to make them yield obedience to and worship the image of the beast, in keeping the spurious Sabbath, the child of papacy. But this final act of apostasy will bring upon the world and the church the doom of which the prophet writes, "In one hour she is made desolate. Rejoice over her, thou heaven, and ye holy apostles and prophets; for God hath avenged you on her."

—Ms 104, 1893

God will Punish Sunday Lawmakers

God declares, "If any man worship the beast and his image, and receive his mark in his forehead, or in his hand, the same shall drink of the wine of the wrath of God." God will punish those who attempt to compel their fellow men to keep the first day of the week. They tempt them to deny their allegiance to God. They accept the fruit of the forbidden tree, and try to force others to eat it. They will try to compel their fellow men to work on the seventh day of the week and rest on the first. God says of them, "They shall drink of the wine of the wrath of God, which is poured out without mixture into the cup of his indignation." *—Lt 98, 1900*

Idolatry Prevails as God's Law is Voided

The Lord has done more for the United States than for any other country upon which the sun shines. Here He provided an asylum for his people, where they could worship Him according to the dictates of conscience. Here Christianity has progressed in its purity. The life-giving doctrine of the one Mediator between God and man has been freely taught.

God designed that this country should ever remain free for all people to worship Him in accordance with the dictates of conscience. He designed that its civil institutions, in their expansive productions, should represent the freedom of gospel privileges. But the enemy of all righteousness has designs upon God's purpose for this country. He will bring in enterprises that will lead men to forget that there is a God. Worldliness and covetousness, which is idolatry, will prevail through the working of the archdeceiver, till the law of God, in all its bearings, shall be made void. *—Ms 17, 1906*

It is Time for God to Work

When the Christian world shall make void the law of God when church and state are united, when Protestantism shall reach its hands across the gulf to unite with Romanism, allegiance to the law of God will be fully thrown off and the decree will go forth against the people of God. But when men trample on the plainest requirements of God's Word, the prayer will go up to heaven, "It is time for thee, Lord to work; for they have made void thy law." Psalm 119:126. And God will work. —*Ms 104, 1893*

The United States is Greatly Favored

The greatest and most favored nation upon the earth is the United States. A gracious providence has shielded this country, and poured upon her the choicest of heaven's blessings. Here the persecuted and oppressed have found refuge. Here the Christian faith in its purity has been taught. This people have been the recipients of great light and unrivaled mercies.

But these gifts have been repaid by ingratitude and forgetfulness of God. The Infinite One keeps a reckoning with the nations, and their guilt is proportioned to the light rejected. A fearful record now stands in the register of heaven against our land; but the crime which shall fill up the measure of her iniquity is that of making void the law of God. —*4SP, p. 398*

Religious Liberty is Trampled

God has given a commandment to rest upon the seventh day. He has given this commandment to men to observe. It is God's memorial. What is Satan doing in our world? Why, he has been working for a long time to get control of the minds and emotions of the people that he might cause them to commit idolatry. He has them worked up where they want to put a working day right in the place of the Sabbath.

When that law shall be carried out, the very principles of liberty for which our fathers fought will be trampled upon. The reformers, the martyrs have died at the stake for these principles of religious liberty. When this law does go into effect, it is then that the nation's ruin will take place. It is then that it becomes universal that the law of God is made void by this nation of boasted liberty! What then? Why, Satan has done just what he wanted to. The man of sin has exalted himself above all that is called God or that is worshiped.

—*Ms 20, 1888*

A Sign of Impending Destruction

To secure popularity and patronage, legislators will yield to the demand for a Sunday law... By the decree enforcing the institution of the papacy in violation of the law of God our nation will disconnect herself fully from righteousness... As the approach of the Roman armies was a sign to the disciples of the impending destruction of Jerusalem, so may this apostasy be a sign to us that the limit of God's forbearance is reached, that the measure of our nation's iniquity is full, and that the angel of mercy is about to take her flight, never to return. —*5T, pp. 450, 451*

God's Law is Extinct in America

A time is coming when the law of God is, in a special sense, to be made void in our land. The rulers of our nation will, by legislative enactments, enforce the Sunday law, and thus God's people be brought into great peril. When our nation, in its legislative councils, shall enact laws to bind the consciences of men in regard to their religious privileges, enforcing Sunday observance, and bringing oppressive power to bear against those who keep the seventh-day Sabbath, the law of God will, to all intents and purposes, be made void in our land; and national apostasy will be followed by national ruin. —*RH, Dec. 18, 1888*

Rulers Unite with the Man of Sin

Men are prone to abuse the long-suffering of God, and to presume on his forbearance. But there is a point in human iniquity when it is time for God to interfere; and terrible are the issues. "The Lord is slow to anger, and great in power, and will not at all acquit the wicked." The long-suffering of God is wonderful, because He puts constraint on his own attributes; but punishment is none the less certain.

Every century of profligacy has treasured up wrath against the day of wrath; and when the time comes, and the iniquity is full, then God will do his strange work. It will be found a terrible thing to have worn out the divine patience; for the wrath of God will fall so signally and strongly that it is represented as being unmixed with mercy; the very earth will be desolated. It is at the time of the national apostasy, when, acting on the policy of Satan, the rulers of the land will rank themselves on the side of the man of sin—it is then the measure of guilt is full; the national apostasy is the signal for national ruin. —*Ms 48, 1891*

Nations Fill Their Cups of Iniquity

God's judgments will be visited upon those who are seeking to oppress and destroy his people. His long forbearance with the wicked emboldens men in transgression, but their punishment is nonetheless certain and terrible because it is long delayed. "The Lord shall rise up as in Mount Perazim, He shall be wroth as in the valley of Gibeon, that He may do his work, his strange work; and bring to pass his act, his strange act." Isaiah 28:21.

To our merciful God the act of punishment is a strange act. "As I live, saith the Lord God, I have no pleasure in the death of the wicked." Ezekiel 33:11. The Lord is "merciful and gracious, long-suffering, and abundant in goodness and truth, ... forgiving iniquity and transgression and sin." Yet He will "by no means clear the guilty." The Lord is slow to anger, and great in power, and will not at all acquit the wicked.

By terrible things in righteousness He will vindicate the authority of his downtrodden law. The severity of the retribution awaiting the transgressor may be judged by the Lord's reluctance to execute justice. The nation with which He bears long, and which He will not smite until it has filled up the measure of its iniquity in God's account, will finally drink the cup of wrath unmixed with mercy. When Christ ceases his intercession in the sanctuary, the unmingled wrath threatened against those who worship the beast and his image and receive his mark, will be poured out. — *GC, p. 627*

Discussion Questions

1. Over the last decade, how has God protected America?

2. How might God interpose for his people when a Sunday Law is passed?

3. Which cities in America, having been blessed with great truth, might someday receive a greater portion of God's judgments?

4. How is the United States filling its cup of iniquity? What will it be like to live in America when God pours out his unmingled wrath?

5. Why will national apostasy lead to national ruin in America?

— 11 —

God's Spirit Withdraws

"Behold, the days come, saith the Lord God, that I will send a famine in the land, not a famine of bread, nor a thirst for water, but of hearing the words of the Lord." —Amos 8:11

Exodus 7:4, 5	Eccles. 8:11	Isaiah 57:20, 21	Joel 1:15-20	2 Thes. 2:9-12
Deut. 28:65-67	Isaiah 26:9	Isaiah 59:12-15	Amos 8:1-12	2 Tim. 3:13
Deut. 31:17	Isaiah 33:14	Isaiah 66:4	Nahum 1:3	James 4:4
Prov. 1:24-33	Isaiah 55:6-9	Hosea 4:1-3	Malachi 1:4	1 John 5:19

God's Spirit is Withdrawn
The Spirit of God is gradually but surely being withdrawn from the earth. Plagues and judgments are already falling upon the despisers of the grace of God. *—9T, p. 11*

Armies Prepare for Armageddon
The four winds are held until the servants of God shall be sealed in their foreheads. Then the powers of earth will marshal their forces for the last great battle. *—6T, p. 14*

A Limit to God's Forbearance
The time is coming when in their fraud and insolence men will reach a point that the Lord will not permit them to pass, and they will learn that there is a limit to the forbearance of Jehovah. *—9T, p. 12*

Satan Fully Controls Sinful Men
When He (Jesus) leaves the sanctuary, darkness covers the inhabitants of the earth. In that fearful time the righteous must live in the sight of a holy God without an intercessor. The restraint which has been upon the wicked is removed, and Satan has entire control of the finally impenitent. *—GC, p. 614*

The Wicked Mirror Satan

Through yielding to satanic influences, men will be transformed into fiends; and those who were created in the image of God, who were formed to honor and glorify their Creator, will become the habitation of dragons, and Satan will see in an apostate race his masterpiece of evil—men who reflect his own image. —*RH, Apr. 14, 1896*

Men Reap as They Have Sown

The Spirit of God is being withdrawn from the earth, and unrepentant sinners are being left to the control of the enemy, to the destiny that they themselves have chosen. Those who persist in violating the holy Sabbath of the Lord, set apart by Him as a day of rest, will soon see that God will punish the transgressors of his law. Men are to reap as they have sown. —*Lt 99, 1904*

Soon All Evangelism will End

Soon it will be too late to do anything. Soon our opportunities to work will have passed by forever. The plagues of God are already beginning to be poured out upon the earth. The evidences before us indicate that God's Spirit is being withdrawn from the earth. Only a little while longer shall we be permitted to labor, and then in heaven it will be said, "It is done."

—*RH, May 27, 1902*

The Cloud of Judicial Wrath

Men cherish the attributes of the first great deceiver. They have accepted him as God, and have become imbued with his spirit. But the cloud of judicial wrath hangs over them, containing the elements that destroyed Sodom...

When the storm of God's wrath breaks upon the world, it will be a terrible revelation for souls to find that their house is being swept away because it is built upon the sand. —*6T, pp. 14-16*

Men Turn into Human Demons

A demoniacal spirit takes possession of men in our world. They combine the perverted animal life with the perverted human animal, intelligence making them human demons, detestable in the sight of God in proportion as they manifest the attributes of the satanic. Demon intelligence, by culture, will rend and destroy man formed in the divine similitude because man cannot control the conscience of his brother. —*Ms 104, 1897*

No Mediator for Mankind

As Jesus moved out of the Most Holy place, I heard the tinkling of the bells upon his garment, and as He left, a cloud of darkness covered the inhabitants of the earth. There was then no mediator between guilty man, and an offended God. — *1SG, p. 198*

The Witness of Sodom's Desolation

The fair vale of Siddim became a desolation, a place never to be built up or inhabited—a witness to all generations of the certainty of God's judgments upon transgression. The flames that consumed the cities of the plain shed their warning light down even to our time. We are taught the fearful and solemn lesson that while God's mercy bears long with the transgressor, there is a limit beyond which men may not go on in sin. When that limit is reached, then the offers of mercy are withdrawn, and the ministration of judgment begins. — *PP, p. 162*

We Cannot Reject God with Impunity

Men cannot with impunity reject the warning which God in mercy sends them. A message was sent from heaven to the world in Noah's day, and their salvation depended upon the manner in which they treated that message. Because they rejected the warning, the Spirit of God was withdrawn from the sinful race, and they perished in the waters of the Flood. In the time of Abraham, mercy ceased to plead with the guilty inhabitants of Sodom, and all but Lot with his wife and two daughters were consumed by the fire sent down from heaven. — *GC, p. 431*

The Four Winds are Unleashed

Four mighty angels hold back the powers of this earth till the servants of God are sealed in their foreheads. The nations of the world are eager for conflict; but they are held in check by the angels. When this restraining power is removed, there will come a time of trouble and anguish. Deadly instruments of warfare will be invented. Vessels, with their living cargo, will be entombed in the great deep. All who have not the spirit of truth will unite under the leadership of satanic agencies. But they are to be kept under control till the time shall come for the great battle of Armageddon. — *Lt 79, 1900*

The Restraining Spirit Leaves

When Jesus leaves the most holy, his restraining Spirit is withdrawn from rulers and people. They are left to the control of evil angels. Then such laws will be made by the counsel and direction of Satan, that unless time should be very short, no flesh could be saved. —*1T, p. 203*

People Desire God's Mercy

In that day, multitudes will desire the shelter of God's mercy which they have so long despised. "Behold, the days come," saith the Lord God, "that I will send a famine in the land, not a famine of bread, nor a thirst for water, but of hearing the words of the Lord: and they shall wander from sea to sea, and from the north even to the east, they shall run to and fro to seek the word of the Lord, and shall not find it." Amos 8:11, 12. —*GC, p. 629*

The Door of Mercy is Shut

Mercy had ceased its pleadings for the guilty race. The beasts of the field and the birds of the air had entered the place of refuge. Noah and his household were within the ark, "and the Lord shut him in." A flash of dazzling light was seen, and a cloud of glory more vivid than the lightning descended from heaven and hovered before the entrance of the ark. The massive door, which it was impossible for those within to close, was slowly swung to its place by unseen hands. Noah was shut in, and the rejecters of God's mercy were shut out. The seal of heaven was on that door; God had shut it, and God alone could open it. —*PP, p. 98*

God Laughs at Man's Calamity

The unbelieving world will soon have something to think of besides their dress and appearance; and as their minds are torn from these things by distress and perplexity, they will have nothing to turn to. They are not prisoners of hope, and therefore do not turn to the Stronghold. Their hearts will fail them for repining and fear. They have not made God their refuge, and He will not be their consolation then, but will laugh at their calamity, and mock when their fear cometh. They have despised and trampled upon the truths of God's Word. They have indulged in extravagant dress, and have spent their lives in hilarity and glee. They have sown to the wind; they must reap the whirlwind.

—*1T, p. 268*

God's Keeping Power is Removed

I have been shown that the Spirit of the Lord is being withdrawn from the earth. God's keeping power will soon be refused to all who continue to disregard his commandments. The reports of fraudulent transactions, murders, and crimes of every kind are coming to us daily. Iniquity is becoming so common a thing that it no longer shocks the senses as it once did. I have been shown that the whole world is fast becoming as it was in the days of Noah. —*Lt 258, 1907*

Deifying Satan Ends God's Mercy

Fallen angels upon the earth form confederacies with evil men. In this age Antichrists will appear as the true Christ, and then the law of God will be fully made void in the nations of our world. Rebellion against God's holy law will be fully ripe. But the true leader of all this rebellion is Satan clothed as an angel of light. Men will be deceived and will exalt him to the place of God, and deify him.

But Omnipotence will interpose, and to the apostate churches that unite in the exaltation of Satan, the sentence will go forth, "Therefore shall her plagues come in one day, death, and mourning, and famine; and she shall be utterly burned with fire: for strong is the Lord who judgeth her." Revelation 18:8. —*Lt 57, 1893*

A Limit to Divine Forbearance

Ere long there will be a sudden change in God's dealings. The Lord is preparing to visit the earth, for the iniquity of men is swelling to terrible proportions. "Because sentence against an evil work is not executed speedily, therefore the hearts of the sons of men are fully set in them to do evil." Ecclesiastes 8:11...

The Lord is teaching men that there are limits to his forbearance. In fires, in floods, in earthquakes, in the fury of the great deep, in calamities by sea and by land, the warning is given that God's Spirit will not always strive with men. The times in which we live are times of great depravity and crime of every degree. Why?—because men whom God has blessed and favored have reduced his holy law to a dead letter, making void the law of God by the traditions and inventions of the man of sin. —*Ms 127, 1897*

God Moves to Vindicate His Name

In connection with wicked men, Satan has attempted to make of none effect God's holy law. Because sentence against their evil work has not been "executed speedily, therefore the heart of the sons of men is fully set in them to do evil." Men are fast becoming imbued with an intense hatred of even hearing the law mentioned. They are fast approaching the bounds set by a longsuffering God. Soon the limits of his grace will be reached. Then He will interfere, vindicating his own name, and before all the world magnifying his law as holy, just, and good, as unchangeable as his own character. —*Ms 125, 1901*

Earth Has Almost No True Faith

The plainest precepts of Jehovah are turned from, to receive infidel fables. Man will be left without excuse. God has given sufficient evidence upon which to base faith if he wish to believe. In the last days the earth will be almost destitute of true faith. Upon the merest pretense, the Word of God will be considered unreliable, while human reasoning will be received, though it be in opposition to plain Scripture facts. Men will endeavor to explain from natural causes the work of creation, which God has never revealed. But human science can not search out the secrets of the God of heaven, and explain the stupendous works of creation, which were a miracle of Almighty power, any sooner than it can show how God came into existence. —*3SG, p. 94*

God's Patience for the Wicked Ends

The forbearance of God has been very great—so great that when we consider the continuous insult to his holy commandments, we marvel. The Omnipotent One has been exerting a restraining power over his own attributes. But He will certainly arise to punish the wicked, who so boldly defy the just claims of the Decalogue.

God allows men a period of probation; but there is a point beyond which divine patience is exhausted, and the judgments of God are sure to follow. The Lord bears long with men, and with cities, mercifully giving warnings to save them from divine wrath; but a time will come when pleadings for mercy will no longer be heard, and the rebellious element that continues to reject the light of truth will be blotted out, in mercy to themselves and to those who would otherwise be influenced by their example. —*PK, p. 276*

Satan Claims a Soul Harvest

The curse of sin has grown to such proportions that already the Spirit of God, insulted, refused, abused, is being withdrawn from the earth. Just as fast as God's Spirit is taken away, Satan's cruel work will be done upon land and sea. The air is filled with the poison of malaria. Judgments by fire and flood will increase in fearfulness, for Satan claims his harvest of souls in the destruction.

—Ms 134, 1898

Calamities Occur as the Spirit Leaves

He (Satan) acted out his principles, and showed what they would lead to, and we see the same acted out in our world today—what these lawless principles will lead to. The enemy has worked, and he is working still. He is come down in great power and the Spirit of God is being withdrawn from the earth. God has withdrawn his hand. We have only to look at Johnstown. He did not prevent the devil from wiping that whole city out of existence.

And these very things will increase until the very close of this earth's history, because he has come down in great power, and he works with all deceivableness of unrighteousness in them that perish. What is he doing? Going about like a roaring lion, seeking whom he may devour. And when he sees those who are resisting the light, and that God does not shelter them, he will exercise his cruel power upon them. This is what we may expect.

— Ms 5, 1889

Hearts Harden as God's Love is Removed

Conscientious obedience to the Word of God will be treated as rebellion. Blinded by Satan, the parent will exercise harshness and severity toward the believing child; the master or mistress will oppress the commandment-keeping servant. Affection will be alienated; children will be disinherited and driven from home. The words of Paul will be literally fulfilled: "All that will live godly in Christ Jesus shall suffer persecution." 2 Timothy 3:12.

As the defenders of truth refuse to honor the Sunday sabbath, some of them will be thrust into prison, some will be exiled, some will be treated as slaves. To human wisdom all this now seems impossible; but as the restraining Spirit of God shall be withdrawn from men, and they shall be under the control of Satan, who hates the divine precepts, there will be strange developments. The heart can be very cruel when God's fear and love are removed. *— GC, p. 608*

Nearly Every Mind is Perverted

The great controversy between the Prince of light and the prince of darkness has not abated one jot or tittle of its fierceness as time has gone on. The stern conflict between light and darkness, between error and truth, is deepening in its intensity. The synagogue of Satan is intensely active, and the deceiving power of the enemy is working in the subtlest way in this age. Every human mind that is not surrendered to God and is not under the control of the Spirit of God will be perverted through satanic agencies. — *Ms 39, 1894*

Men Give Themselves to Satan

You hear of calamities by land and by sea, and they are constantly increasing. What is the matter? The Spirit of God is taken away from those who have the lives of men in their hands, and Satan is coming in to control them, because they give themselves to his control. Those who profess to be the children of God do not place themselves under the guardianship of the heavenly angels, and as Satan is a destroyer, he works through those men and they make mistakes; and they will get drunk and because of intemperance, many times, bring these terrible calamities upon us. — *Ms 1, 1890*

Earth Sees the Results of Satan's Rule

The Saviour's prophecy concerning the visitation of judgments upon Jerusalem is to have another fulfillment, of which that terrible desolation was but a faint shadow. In the fate of the chosen city we may behold the doom of a world that has rejected God's mercy and trampled upon his law. Dark are the records of human misery that earth has witnessed during its long centuries of crime. The heart sickens, and the mind grows faint in contemplation. Terrible have been the results of rejecting the authority of heaven.

But a scene yet darker is presented in the revelations of the future. The records of the past—the long procession of tumults, conflicts, and revolutions, the "battle of the warrior... with confused noise, and garments rolled in blood" (Isaiah 9:5)—what are these, in contrast with the terrors of that day when the restraining Spirit of God shall be wholly withdrawn from the wicked, no longer to hold in check the outburst of human passion and satanic wrath! The world will then behold, as never before, the results of Satan's rule. — *GC, p. 36*

The Ministry of Wrath Begins

Jesus is about to leave the mercy seat of the heavenly sanctuary to put on garments of vengeance and pour out his wrath in judgments upon those who have not responded to the light God has given them. "Because sentence against an evil work is not executed speedily, therefore the heart of the sons of men is fully set in them to do evil." Ecclesiastes 8:11.

Instead of being softened by the patience and long forbearance that the Lord has exercised toward them, those who fear not God and love not the truth strengthen their hearts in their evil course. But there are limits even to the forbearance of God, and many are exceeding these boundaries. They have overrun the limits of grace, and therefore God must interfere and vindicate his own honor. With unerring accuracy the Infinite One still keeps an account with all nations. While his mercy is tendered with calls to repentance, this account will remain open; but when the figures reach a certain amount which God has fixed, the ministry of his wrath commences. The account is closed. Divine patience ceases. There is no more pleading of mercy in their behalf.

—5T, pp. 207, 208

A Parallel to Sodom's Final Night

The deadly lethargy of the world is paralyzing your senses. Sin no longer appears repulsive because you are blinded by Satan. The judgments of God are soon to be poured out upon the earth.

"Escape for thy life" is the warning from the angels of God. Other voices are heard saying: "Do not become excited; there is no cause for special alarm." Those who are at ease in Zion cry "Peace and safety," while heaven declares that swift destruction is about to come upon the transgressor. The young, the frivolous, the pleasure-loving, consider these warnings as idle tales and turn from them with a jest. Parents are inclined to think their children about right in the matter, and all sleep on at ease.

Thus it was at the destruction of the old world and when Sodom and Gomorrah were consumed by fire. On the night prior to their destruction the cities of the plain rioted in pleasure. Lot was derided for his fears and warnings. But it was these scoffers that perished in the flames. That very night the door of mercy was forever closed to the wicked, careless inhabitants of Sodom. *—5T, p. 233*

Sinners Make a Tremendous Mistake

There is a period of time just before us when the condition of the world will become desperate, when that true religion which yields obedience to a "Thus saith the Lord" will become almost extinct. Our youth should be taught that wicked deeds are not forgotten or overlooked because God does not immediately punish the perpetrators with extreme indignation.

God keeps a reckoning with the nations. Through every century of this world's history evil workers have been treasuring up wrath against the day of wrath; and when the time fully comes that iniquity shall have reached the stated boundary of God's mercy, his forbearance will cease. When the accumulated figures in heaven's record books shall mark the sum of transgression complete, wrath will come, unmixed with mercy, and then it will be seen what a tremendous thing it is to have worn out the divine patience. This crisis will be reached when the nations shall unite in making void God's law. — *5T, p. 523*

The Two Sides of God's Character

In all the dealings of God with his people there is, mingled with his love and mercy, a striking exactness and firmness of decision. This is clearly exemplified in the history of the Hebrew people. God had bestowed great blessings upon Israel. His loving-kindness toward them is thus touchingly portrayed by his own hand: "As an eagle stirreth up her nest, fluttereth over her young, spreadeth abroad her wings, taketh them, beareth them on her wings, so the Lord alone did lead them."

And yet what swift and severe retribution was visited upon them for their transgressions. How, then, can sinners in any age hope to escape the wrath of God? Again, more wonderful than his mercy toward Israel is the love which Christ has manifested in his infinite sacrifice to redeem a lost race. His earthly life was filled with deeds of divine tenderness and compassion.

And yet Christ Himself plainly declares, "Till heaven and earth pass, one jot or one tittle shall in no wise pass from the law till all be fulfilled." While He tells us of the love of God, He also pictures the awful scenes of the Judgment and the retribution that shall be visited upon the wicked. In all the Bible, God is presented not only as a being of mercy and benevolence, but as a God of strict and impartial justice. — *ST, Mar. 24, 1881*

Wonders of Spiritualism Intensify

Satan has a religion, he has a synagogue and devout worshipers. To swell the ranks of his devotees, he uses all manner of deception. The signs and wonders of spiritualism will become more and more pronounced as the professed Christian world rejects the plainly revealed truth of the Word of God, and refuse to be guided by a plain "Thus saith the Lord," accepting instead the doctrines and the commandments of men. Through rejecting light and truth, many are deciding their destiny for eternal death; and as men reject truth, the Spirit of God will gradually withdraw itself from the earth, and the prince of this earth will have more and more control over his subjects. He will show great signs and wonders as credentials of his divine claims, and through spiritualism will work against Christ and his agencies. — *Ms 92, 1894*

Satan's Power Grows as God Leaves

As the Spirit of God shall be withdrawn from the earth, Satan's power will be more and more manifest. The knowledge that he had through being in connection with God, as a covering cherub, he will now use to subordinate his subjects who fell from their high estate. He will use every power of his exalted intellect to misrepresent God and to instigate rebellion against Jesus Christ, the Commander of heaven.

In the synagogue of Satan he brings under his scepter, and into his counsels, those agents whom he can use to promote his worship. It is not a strange matter to find a species of refinement, and a manifestation of intellectual greatness, in the lives and characters of those who are inspired by fallen angels. Satan can impart scientific knowledge, and give men chapters upon philosophy. He is conversant with history, and versed in worldly wisdom.

Almost every phase of talent is now being brought into captivity to the prince of the power of darkness. Worldly-minded men, because they wish to exalt themselves, and have separated from God, do not love to retain God in their knowledge, for they claim to possess a higher, grander intellect than that of Jesus Christ. Satan envies Christ, and makes the claim that he is entitled to a higher position than the Commander of heaven. His self-exaltation led him to despise the law of God, and resulted in his expulsion from heaven.

— *ST, May 28, 1894*

Sinners Owe Life to the Godly

Hearts that respond to the influence of the Holy Spirit are the channels through which God's blessing flows. Were those who serve God removed from the earth, and his Spirit withdrawn from among men, this world would be left to desolation and destruction, the fruit of Satan's dominion. Though the wicked know it not, they owe even the blessings of this life to the presence, in the world, of God's people whom they despise and oppress. But if Christians are such in name only, they are like the salt that has lost its savor.

—DA, p. 306

The Wicked Long for Mercy

At any moment God can withdraw from the impenitent the tokens of his wonderful mercy and love. Oh, that human agencies might consider what will be the sure result of their ingratitude to Him and of their disregard of the infinite gift of Christ to our world! If they continue to love transgression more than obedience, the present blessings and the great mercy of God that they now enjoy, but do not appreciate, will finally become the occasion of their eternal ruin.

They may for a time choose to engage in worldly amusements and sinful pleasures, rather than to check themselves in their course of sin, and live for God and for the honor of the Majesty of heaven; but when it is too late for them to see and to understand that which they have slighted as a thing of naught, they will know what it means to be without God, without hope. Then they will sense what they have lost by choosing to be disloyal to God and to stand in rebellion against his commandments. In the past they defied his power and rejected his overtures of mercy; finally his judgments will fall upon them. Then they will realize that they have lost happiness—life, eternal life, in the heavenly courts. Surely they will say, "Our life was full of madness against God, and now we are lost!"

In the time when God's judgments are falling without mercy, oh, how enviable to the wicked will be the position of those who abide "in the secret place of the Most High"—the pavilion in which the Lord hides all who have loved Him and have obeyed his commandments! The lot of the righteous is indeed an enviable one at such a time to those who are suffering because of their sins. But the door of mercy is closed to the wicked, no more prayers are offered in their behalf after probation ends. *—Ms 151, 1901*

168

Disasters Show God's Spirit is Leaving

Already the restraining Spirit of God is being withdrawn from the earth. Hurricanes, storms, tempests, fire and flood, disasters by sea and land, follow each other in quick succession. Science seeks to explain all these. The signs thickening around us, telling of the near approach of the Son of God, are attributed to any other than the true cause. Men cannot discern the sentinel angels restraining the four winds that they may not blow until the servants of God are sealed. — *RH, Jan. 11, 1887*

The Angel of Mercy Folds Her Wings

I was shown that a terrible condition of things exists in our world. The angel of mercy is folding her wings, ready to depart. Already the Lord's restraining power is being withdrawn from the earth, and Satan is seeking to stir up the various elements in the religious world, leading men to place themselves under the training of the great deceiver, who work with all deceivableness of unrighteousness in the children of disobedience. Already the inhabitants of the earth are marshaling under the leading of the prince of darkness, and this is but the beginning of the end.

The law of God is made void. We see and hear of confusion and perplexity, want and famine, earthquakes and floods; terrible outrages will be committed by men; passion, not reason, bears sway. The wrath of God is upon the inhabitants of the world, who are fast becoming as corrupt as were the inhabitants of Sodom and Gomorrah. Already fire and flood are destroying thousands of lives and the property that has been selfishly accumulated by the oppression of the poor. The Lord is soon to cut short his work and put an end to sin. Oh, that the scenes which have come before me of the iniquities practiced in these last days, might make a deep impression on the minds of God's professing people.

As it was in the days of Noah, so shall it be when the Son of man shall be revealed. The Lord is removing his restrictions from the earth, and soon there will be death and destruction, increasing crime, and cruel, evil working against the rich who have exalted themselves against the poor. Those who are without God's protection will find no safety in any place or position. Human agents are being trained and are using their inventive power to put in operation the most powerful machinery to wound and to kill. — *8T, p. 49*

A Famine in the Land for Truth

I saw we are in the investigative judgment. Soon judgment will be pronounced on our works and our actions which are passing in review before God. A solemn, awful period! Who realize this great work? I saw that those who do not now appreciate, study, and dearly prize the Word of God, spoken by his servants, will have cause to mourn bitterly hereafter. I saw that the Lord in judgment will, at the close of time, walk through the earth; the fearful plagues will begin to fall.

Then those who have despised God's Word, those who have lightly esteemed it, shall wander from sea to sea, and from the north even to the east; they shall run to and fro to seek the Word of the Lord and shall not find it. A famine is in the land for hearing the Word. The ministers of God will have done their last work, offered their last prayers, shed their last bitter tear for a rebellious church and an ungodly people. Their last solemn warning has been given.

Oh then how quickly would houses and lands, dollars that have been miserly hoarded and cherished and tightly grasped, be given for some consolation by those who have professed the truth and have not lived it out, for the way of salvation to be explained or to hear a hopeful word, or a prayer, or an exhortation from their ministers.

But no, they must hunger and thirst on in vain; their thirst will never be quenched, no consolation can they get; their cases are decided and eternally fixed. It is a fearful, awful time. There can much be done now to bring in those jewels who are hid beneath the rubbish, who will highly prize the truth as it falls from the lips of God's servants.

I was shown that many of the church have at this time of peril more care for their farm and their cattle than they have for the servants of God, or the truth which they preach; their labors are so common among them that the laborers are not considered worthy of their hire. His strength must be exhausted, his life embittered by scarcely a well day, must spend and be spent, and yet the church asleep as to these things.

But I saw that God was not asleep. Said the angel, "Jesus says, I know thy works; yes, selfish, professed Sabbathkeepers. God knows thy works. Ye covetous, world-loving Sabbathkeepers," said the angel, "God knows thy works." —*Ms 1, 1857*

The Sweet Voice of Mercy Fades Away

While Jesus had been standing between God and guilty man, a restraint was upon the people; but when Jesus stepped out from between man and the Father, the restraint was removed, and Satan had the control of man. It was impossible for the plagues to be poured out while Jesus officiated in the Sanctuary; but as his work there is finished, as his intercession closes, there is nothing to stay the wrath of God, and it breaks with fury upon the shelterless head of the guilty sinner, who has slighted salvation, and hated reproof.

The saints in that fearful time, after the close of Jesus' mediation, were living in the sight of a holy God, without an intercessor. Every case was decided, every jewel numbered. Jesus tarried a moment in the outer apartment of the heavenly Sanctuary, and the sins which had been confessed while He was in the Most Holy place, He placed back upon the originator of sin, the Devil. He must suffer the punishment of these sins.

Then I saw Jesus lay off his priestly attire, and clothe Himself with his most kingly robes—upon his head were many crowns, a crown within a crown—and surrounded by the angelic host, He left heaven...

When the saints, and all heaven were interested for their salvation, they had no interest for themselves. Life and death had been set before them. Many desired life; but did not make any effort to obtain it. They did not choose life, and now there was no atoning blood to cleanse the sinner. No compassionate Saviour to plead for them, and cry, "Spare, spare the sinner a little longer." All heaven had united with Jesus, as they heard the fearful words, "It is done, It is finished." The plan of salvation had been accomplished. But few had chosen to accept the plan. And as mercy's sweet voice died away, a fearfulness and horror seized them.

With terrible distinctness they hear, "Too late! Too late!" Those who had not prized God's Word were hurrying to and fro. They wandered from sea to sea, and from the north to the east, to seek the word of the Lord. Said the angel, "They shall not find it. There is a famine in the land; not a famine of bread, nor a thirst for water, but of hearing the words of the Lord." What would they not give for one word of approval from God? But no, they must hunger and thirst on. Day after day have they slighted salvation, and prized earthly pleasure, and earthly riches, higher than any heavenly inducement and treasure. —*1SG, pp. 198-200*

Jerusalem's Fate is a Warning

A neglect to repent and to render willing obedience will bring upon men and women today as serious consequences as came upon ancient Israel. There is a limit beyond which the judgments of Jehovah can no longer be delayed. The desolation of Jerusalem in the days of Jeremiah is a solemn warning to modern Israel, that the counsels and admonitions given them through chosen instrumentalities cannot be disregarded with impunity. — *PK, p. 416*

God will Not Protect the Wicked

It is not wise to defer the preparation for eternity one day, no not an hour. This calamity speaks decidedly to every one of us to not neglect a vital connection with God. Satan is watching his chances to secure souls to himself, and unless we have God's protection, he will break forth in violence, and his angels will be set at work to do some marked mischief. The terrible tornadoes, the railroad disasters, the calamities at sea are because of Satan's wrath. The Lord does not work a miracle to protect those who are constantly working against Himself and strengthening the powers of darkness.

And this is only the beginning. Their hearts will not repent because they are fully set in them to do evil and that continually. These disasters, which should make men afraid, are now regarded only by those who fear for their own personal safety, themselves and those connected with them. — *Lt 3a, 1883*

Discussion Questions

1. Will it be immediately apparent that God's Spirit has been withdrawn?

2. In recent years, terrible disasters have desolated many wicked cities. Is God's Spirit currently vacating places where sinning is especially blatant?

3. Why will all evangelism end once God's Spirit leaves?

4. The prophet Amos wrote that there was going to be a famine in the land. What will be the experience of people searching for God at this time?

5. Why will the hearts of men someday become exceedingly cruel?

— 12 —

Plagues Ravage the Earth

"Judgment also will I lay to the line, and righteousness to the plummet: and the hail shall sweep away the refuge of lies, and the waters shall overflow the hiding place." — Isa. 28:17

Leviticus 26:21	Proverbs 11:4	Jer. 25:27-30	Haggai 2:6	Rev. 14:19, 20
Job 5:19-21	Isa. 34:5-8	Jer. 50:25-32	Matt. 24:7, 21	Rev. 15:1, 5-8
Job 38:22, 23	Isa. 54:10	Ezek. 33:28, 29	Luke 21:11	Rev. 16:1-12
Psalm 2:12	Isa. 61:2; 63:3, 4	Hab. 3:3-19	Rom. 1:18, 19	Rev. 18:4-8

A) God's Wrath is Poured Out

Plagues Fall as Jesus Leaves

I was shown that the seven last plagues will be poured out after Jesus leaves the sanctuary. Said the angel, "It is the wrath of God and the Lamb that causes the destruction or death of the wicked." — *EW, p. 52*

Property and Life is Destroyed

In the last scenes of this earth's history war will rage. There will be pestilence, plague and famine. The waters of the deep will overflow their boundaries. Property and life will be destroyed by fire and flood. We should be preparing for the mansions that Christ has gone to prepare for them that love Him.

— *RH, Oct. 19, 1897*

God's Wrath Grows over Time

The great day of God is nigh upon us, when it will be demonstrated that the righteous displeasure of God will be none the less terrible because of the long forbearance exercised for centuries. Instead of appreciating the goodness and mercy of God, men have made his forbearance an excuse for going into deeper and still more marked transgression, treasuring up wrath against the day of wrath. — *Lt 74, 1894*

The Straight Line of Justice

When the test is over, when men have taken sides for or against the law of Jehovah, the season of mercy and probation is ended. Then God will move in the straight line of justice to give to every man as his works have been. Some will receive the reward of well-doing, others the reward of their evil deeds. — *Ms 58, 1897*

God Consumes All Things

"I will utterly consume all things from off the land, saith the Lord. I will consume man and beast; I will consume the fowls of the heaven..." This is being literally fulfilled, and has been fulfilled for years in the course of some who have had great light and many opportunities to know and understand the ways and works of God. — *Ms 41, 1906*

God Reveals His Divine Majesty

In the days of Noah, violence filled the land; and thus Christ has told us that it will be in the last days. The history of the old world is to be repeated. The perversity and cruelty of men will reach such a height that God will reveal Himself in his majesty. Very soon the wickedness of the world will have reached its limit, and as in the days of Noah, God will pour out his judgments.

— *Lt 250, 1903*

Judgments Fall in Quick Succession

The time is nearing when the great crisis in the history of the world will have come, when every movement in the government of God will be watched with intense interest and inexpressible apprehension. In quick succession the judgments of God will follow one another—fire and flood and earthquake, with war and bloodshed. Oh, that the people might know the time of their visitation! — *9T, p. 97*

A Signal that Probation is Closed

Our own course of action will determine whether we shall receive the seal of the living God or be cut down by the destroying weapons. Already a few drops of God's wrath have fallen upon the earth; but when the seven last plagues shall be poured out without mixture into the cup of his indignation, then it will be forever too late to repent and find shelter. No atoning blood will then wash away the stains of sin. — *5T, p. 212*

The Plagues Intensify

The Egyptians were made to feel God's judgments. They were visited with plagues... Each visitation from God was more severe than the preceding one.

—1T, p 264

An Unimaginable Scene

Angels are now restraining the winds of strife, that they may not blow until the world shall be warned of its coming doom; but a storm is gathering, ready to burst upon the earth; and when God shall bid his angels loose the winds, there will be such a scene of strife as no pen can picture. *—Ed, p. 179*

A Minister of Vengeance

The love of a holy God is an amazing principle, which can stir the universe in our behalf during the hours of our probation and trial. But after the season of our probation, if we are found transgressors of God's law, the God of love will be found a minister of vengeance. God makes no compromise with sin. The disobedient will be punished. The wrath of God fell upon his beloved Son as Christ hung upon the cross of Calvary in the transgressor's place.

—RH, June 17, 1890

The Sword of God's Wrath

The sword of his wrath is stretched out over the people who by their pride and wickedness have provoked the displeasure of a just God. Storms, earthquakes, whirlwinds, fire, and the sword will spread desolation everywhere, until men's hearts shall fail them for fear and for looking after those things which shall come upon the earth. You know not how small a space is between you and eternity. You know not how soon your probation may close. *—4T, p. 52*

Nominal Churches are Punished

I was shown the pride of the nominal churches. God was not in their thoughts; but their carnal minds dwell upon themselves. They decorate their poor mortal bodies, and then look upon themselves with satisfaction and pleasure. Jesus and the angels looked upon them in anger. Said the angel, "Their sins and pride have reached unto heaven. Their portion is prepared. Justice and judgment have slumbered long, but will soon awake. 'Vengeance is mine, and I will repay,' saith the Lord." *—1SG, p. 190*

Plagues Destroy the Wicked

In the day of the Lord, just before the coming of Christ, God will send lightnings from heaven in his wrath, which will unite with fire in the earth. The mountains will burn like a furnace, and will pour forth terrible streams of lava, destroying gardens and fields, villages and cities; and as they pour their melted ore, rocks and heated mud into the rivers, will cause them to boil like a pot, and send forth massive rocks and scatter their broken fragments upon the land with indescribable violence. Whole rivers will be dried up. The earth will be convulsed, and there will be dreadful eruptions and earthquakes everywhere. God will plague the wicked inhabitants of the earth until they are destroyed from off it. —*3SG, pp. 82, 83*

Vials of God's Wrath are Emptied

Solemn events before us are yet to transpire. Trumpet after trumpet is to be sounded, vial after vial poured out one after another upon the inhabitants of the earth. Scenes of stupendous interest are right upon us, and these things will be sure indications of the presence of Him who has directed in every aggressive movement, who has accompanied the march of his cause through all the ages, and who has graciously pledged Himself to be with his people in all their conflicts to the end of the world. He will vindicate his truth. He will cause it to triumph. He is ready to supply his faithful ones with motives and power of purpose, inspiring them with hope and courage and valor in increased activity as the time is at hand. —*Lt 112, 1890*

Unrighteousness Brings the Plagues

The Psalmist marks the time in which he lived as that of great depravity, but what has it reached now? Centuries have been ripening up the harvest of the world for the sickle. "They have made void thy law." Psalm 119:126. They refuse to respect God's law, while they make human laws supreme. A more than common contempt is placed upon the holy law of Jehovah.

Men are fast exceeding the bounds prescribed by God. His interference must come, when He will vindicate his honor. Men are rushing on, to outrun the limits of his grace. God will not long delay. The swellings of unrighteousness have come to such a fearful pass that all the plagues that are prepared as revealed in Revelation will come upon a godless world. —*Lt 52, 1895*

God Punishes Rich Men

The cries of starving humanity are coming up before God, while these men bow down to their senseless idols as verily as do the heathen to their gods of wood and stone. Though the whole world were in league to prove it otherwise, every dollar gained in this unholy traffic wraps a curse up with it. The larger the bank stock the surer will be the judgment of God. Of these the words of Eliphaz will prove truth: "I saw him taking root, but I cursed his habitation." —Lt 89, 1898

Judgments Grow with Wickedness

The Saviour declared that before his Second Coming, there would be wars and rumors of wars, and earthquakes in diverse places. The reports that reached us of the terrible earthquakes in Italy and Sicily tell of another fulfillment of the signs of the end. These calamities are becoming more and more frequent, and each report of calamity by land or sea is a testimony to the fact that the end of all things is near. The world is filled with iniquity, and the Lord is punishing it for its wickedness. As crimes and iniquities increase, these judgments will become more frequent, until the time shall come when the "earth shall no more cover her slain." Isaiah 26:21. The judgments of God are hanging over our cities. —RH, Nov. 17, 1910

The Absence of Jesus Brings Plagues

Jesus clothes Himself with the garments of vengeance and takes his place upon the great white cloud before the plagues are poured out. The great white cloud, I saw, was not in the holy place but entirely separate from the holy and most holy, entirely separate from the sanctuary.

As Jesus passed through the holy place or first apartment, to the door to confess the sins of Israel on the scapegoat, an angel said, "This apartment is called the sanctuary." Then the angel repeated these words and said this is the time spoken of, and he saw that there was no man and wondered that there was no intercessor; we had no mediator between God and man and the plagues could be withheld no longer, for Jesus had ceased to plead for Israel, and they were covered with the covering of Almighty God and lived in his sight, and those who were not covered felt the plagues, for they had nothing to shelter them. —Ms 15, 1850

Seek Shelter Immediately

"And there fell upon men great hail out of heaven, every stone about the weight of a talent." Revelation 16:21. The storm of God's wrath is soon coming upon a guilty world, and can you endure the thought of coming up to such a scene without a hope in God, and feeling that his withering frown is upon you? If you want a shelter, you must seek it now, and then you will be hid when the fierce anger of the Lord shall come. — *YI, Dec. 1, 1852*

God's Sword is Unsheathed

It is time for the message of God's forbearance to be proclaimed to win men to repentance; and it is just as verily time for men to be warned that there are limits to God's forbearance. Men may advance, as did Belshazzar, in presumption and defiance, until they pass the boundary. Blasphemy may be so developed as to exhaust the patience of the longsuffering God.

In the midst of mirth, feasting, and forgetfulness of God, the command will go forth for the sword of the Lord to be unsheathed, that an end may be put to the insolence and disobedience of men. The prayers of God's people have ascended, "It is time, O Lord, for thee to work; for they have made void thy law." Psalm 119:126. These prayers will ere long be answered. When men pass the limit of grace, God must let the world see that He is God. — *Ms 50, 1893*

God Avenges Widows and Orphans

The time is right upon us when there will be sorrow in the world that no human balm can heal. Even before the last great destruction comes upon the world, the flattering monuments of man's greatness will be crumbled in the dust. God's retributive judgments will fall on those who in the face of great light have continued in sin. Costly buildings, supposed to be fireproof, are erected. But as Sodom perished in the flames of God's vengeance, so will these proud structures become ashes.

I have seen vessels which cost immense sums of money wrestling with the mighty ocean, seeking to breast the angry billows. But with all their treasures of gold and silver, and with all their human freight, they sank into a watery grave. Man's pride will be buried with the treasures he has accumulated by fraud. God will avenge the widows and orphans who in hunger and nakedness have cried to Him for relief from oppression. — *ST, Oct. 9, 1901*

178

A Scene of Universal Desolation

Everything has been moving on just as the Lord revealed in prophecy that it would. Something great and decisive is soon to take place, else no flesh would be saved. The character of God will not be compromised. Under the wrath of God, universal desolation will soon reach all parts of the known world.

— RH, Nov. 27, 1900

The Sun Scorches Men with Fire

In the plague that follows, power is given to the sun "to scorch men with fire. And men were scorched with great heat." The prophets thus describe the condition of the earth at this fearful time: "The land mourneth; ... because the harvest of the field is perished... All the trees of the field are withered: because joy is withered away from the sons of men." "The seed is rotten under their clods, the garners are laid desolate... How do the beasts groan! The herds of cattle are perplexed, because they have no pasture... The rivers of water are dried up, and the fire hath devoured the pastures of the wilderness."

"The songs of the temple shall be howlings in that day, saith the Lord God: there shall be many dead bodies in every place; they shall cast them forth with silence." Joel 1:10-12, 17-20; Amos 8:3. *— GC, p. 628*

God Violently Shakes the World

The Christian's hope is as an anchor to the soul, both sure and steadfast, and entereth into that which is within the veil, whither Christ the forerunner is for us entered. We have an individual work to do to prepare for the great events that are before us. The youth should seek God more earnestly. The tempest is coming and we must get ready for its fury by having repentance toward God and faith toward our Lord Jesus Christ.

The Lord will arise to shake terribly the earth. We shall see troubles on all sides. Thousands of ships will be hurled into the depths of the sea. Navies will go down, and human lives will be sacrificed by millions. Fires will break out unexpectedly and no human effort will be able to quench them. The palaces of earth will be swept away in the fury of the flames. Disasters by rail will become more and more frequent. Confusion, collision, and death without a moment's warning will occur on the great lines of travel. The end is near, probation is closing. Oh, let us seek God while He may be found, call upon Him while He is near! *— ST, Apr. 21, 1890*

John Saw the Last Plagues

John also was a witness of the terrible scenes that will take place as signs of Christ's coming. He saw armies mustering for battle, and men's hearts failing them for fear. He saw the earth moved out of its place, the mountains carried into the midst of the sea, the waves thereof roaring and troubled, and the mountains shaking with the swelling thereof. He saw the vials of God's wrath opened, and pestilence, famine, and death come upon the inhabitants of the earth. — *RH, Jan. 11, 1887*

The Shrieks of Dying Nations

"As it was in the days of Noah." Luke 17:26. In the future there will be broken thrones and great distress of nations with perplexity. Satan will work with intense activity. The earth will be filled with the shrieks of suffering, expiring nations. There will be war. The places of the earth will be in confusion, as from its bowels pour forth its burning contents, to destroy the inhabitants of the world, who in their wickedness resemble the inhabitants of the antediluvian world. — *Ms 72, 1902*

No Respite after Plagues Begin

The world is soon to be left by the angel of mercy, and the seven last plagues are to be poured out. Sin, shame, sorrow and darkness are on every side. God still holds out to men the precious privilege of exchanging darkness for light, error for truth, sin for righteousness; but his patience and mercy will not always wait. The storm is gathering; the bolts of God's wrath are soon to fall; and when He shall begin to punish the transgressors, there will be no period of respite until the end. He shall come forth to punish the inhabitants of the world for their iniquity, and "the earth shall disclose her blood, and shall no more cover her slain."

Only those will stand who are sanctified through the truth in the love of God. They will be hid with Christ in God until the desolation shall be overpast. Let no one think that he can escape God's wrath by hiding behind a lie; for God will strip from the soul the refuge of lies. That refuge for the covering up of sin must now be torn away, in order that poor deluded souls may not sleep on to their everlasting ruin. Let this work be done with faithfulness, and in love. — *Ms 122, 1899*

God Spoils the Entire Land

Once again the Lord God of Israel is to execute judgment upon the gods of this world as upon the gods of Egypt. With fire and flood, plagues and earthquakes, He will spoil the whole land. Then his redeemed people will exalt his name and make it glorious in the earth. Shall not those who are living in the last remnant of this earth's history become intelligent in regard to God's lessons? — *Ms 85, 1899*

The Plagues are Not Universal

These plagues are not universal, or the inhabitants of the earth would be wholly cut off. Yet they will be the most awful scourges that have ever been known to mortals. All the judgments upon men, prior to the close of probation, have been mingled with mercy. The pleading blood of Christ has shielded the sinner from receiving the full measure of his guilt; but in the final judgment, wrath is poured out unmixed with mercy. — *GC, p. 628*

A Terrifying Vision of the Plagues

Then I saw that the seven last plagues were soon to be poured out upon those who have no shelter; yet the world regarded them no more than they would so many drops of water that were about to fall. I was then made capable of enduring the awful sight of the seven last plagues, the wrath of God. I saw that his anger was dreadful and terrible, and if He should stretch forth his hand, or lift it in anger, the inhabitants of the world would be as though they had never been, or would suffer from incurable sores and withering plagues that would come upon them, and they would find no deliverance, but be destroyed by them.

Terror seized me, and I fell upon my face before the angel and begged of him to cause the sight to be removed, to hide it from me, for it was too dreadful. Then I realized, as never before, the importance of searching the Word of God carefully, to know how to escape the plagues which that Word declares shall come on all the ungodly who shall worship the beast and his image and receive his mark in their foreheads or in their hands. It was a great wonder for me that any could transgress the law of God and tread down his holy Sabbath, when such awful threatenings and denunciations were against them. — *EW, pp. 64, 65*

God Punishes with Hailstones

At his own will God summons the forces of nature to overthrow the might of his enemies—"fire, and hail; snow, and vapor; stormy wind fulfilling his word." Psalm 148:8. When the heathen Amorites had set themselves to resist his purposes, God interposed, casting down "great stones from heaven" upon the enemies of Israel. We are told of a greater battle to take place in the closing scenes of earth's history, when "Jehovah hath opened his armory, and hath brought forth the weapons of his indignation." Jeremiah 50:25.

"Hast thou," he inquires, "entered into the treasures of the snow? or hast thou seen the treasures of the hail, which I have reserved against the time of trouble, against the day of battle and war?" Job 38:22, 23. The revelator describes the destruction that is to take place when the "great voice out of the temple of heaven" announces, "It is done." He says, "There fell upon men a great hail out of heaven, every stone about the weight of a talent." Revelation 16:17, 21. —*PP, p. 509*

The Courts of Justice are Punished

All that the courts of justice have done in framing laws directly in opposition to God's law, in oppressing his people by compelling them to observe man-made statutes, will be visited upon them. While they enforce these statutes as supreme, they themselves are defying God, the Sovereign of the universe, to his face, by transgressing his law, obedience to which would have proved their highest good. The evil that results from ignoring the law of God and establishing human laws, executing them against those who are loyal and true to God, delights Satan, for it is working out his attributes.

God has borne long with the perversity of man, but a time is just before us which will make such a stir in our world as never has been made before. The proclamation goes forth, "Reward her even as she rewarded you, and double unto her double according to her works; in the cup which she hath filled, fill to her double. How much she hath glorified herself and lived deliciously, so much torment and sorrow give her; for she saith in her heart, I sit a queen, and am no widow, and shall see no sorrow. Therefore shall her plagues come in one day, death, and mourning, and famine; and she shall be utterly burned with fire; for strong is the Lord God who judgeth her." Revelation 18:6-8. —*Ms 71, 1896*

Blood Flows in Streams

I saw that professed friends had wounded the cause. Again I was compelled to cry for God to spare his people some of whom were fainting and dying. Then I saw the judgments of Almighty God were speedily coming. I begged of the angel to speak in his language to the people—said he, all the thunders and lightnings of Mount Sinai, cannot move those who will not be moved by the plain truths in the Word of God; neither would an angel's message move or awake them. I saw that the rebels must and will be purged out. The angel said, "Get ready, get ready, get ready." I saw that the judgments were just upon us, and that the trouble would soon be to this land, and that blood would flow in streams. The angel said it will soon be even to the horses' bridles. That was an awful time. — *Ms 4, 1850*

Unmingled Wrath is Poured Out

When Christ ceases his intercession in the sanctuary, the unmingled wrath threatened against those who worship the beast and his image and receive his mark (Revelation 14:9, 10), will be poured out. The plagues upon Egypt when God was about to deliver Israel were similar in character to those more terrible and extensive judgments which are to fall upon the world just before the final deliverance of God's people.

Says the revelator, in describing those terrific scourges: "There fell a noisome and grievous sore upon the men which had the mark of the beast, and upon them which worshipped his image." The sea "became as the blood of a dead man: and every living soul died in the sea." And "the rivers and fountains of waters... became blood." Terrible as these inflictions are, God's justice stands fully vindicated. The angel of God declares: "Thou art righteous, O Lord, ... because thou hast judged thus. For they have shed the blood of saints and prophets, and thou hast given them blood to drink; for they are worthy." Revelation 16:2-6.

By condemning the people of God to death, they have as truly incurred the guilt of their blood as if it had been shed by their hands. In like manner Christ declared the Jews of his time guilty of all the blood of holy men which had been shed since the days of Abel; for they possessed the same spirit and were seeking to do the same work with these murderers of the prophets.

— GC, p. 627

Now is the Time to Work

As we journeyed from Geneva to Basel, we passed through large and small cities; and my meditations were, "How are these people in these large cities to be warned?" In the vision of John, four mighty angels were shown him as holding the four winds, that they should not blow upon the earth until God's servants are sealed in their foreheads. Revelation 7:1-3. When this work is done, then the ministers of vengeance are called and commanded to pour upon the earth tempests, thunders, pestilences, calamities. Now then is the time to work when Jesus is interceding in the heavenly sanctuary. Now is our opportunity and privilege to be co-workers with God. — *Lt 38, 1886*

Mrs. White was Plagued by Hail

As we left the house we saw a storm coming. The blackness grew deeper—so pretentious that we drove as fast with our colts as we dared. When we were almost home the fury of the gale struck. Large hailstones began to fall—as large around as a hen's egg, but not as long.

This is the sharpest experience I have ever had in a carriage in a storm. When the blackness deepened, with the clouds in the south, I supposed it would be no ordinary storm that we should have, and I thought of the day when the judgment of God would be poured out upon the world, when blackness and horrible darkness would clothe the heavens as sackcloth of hair.

We have no question but our prayers were answered and the angel of God stood by the horses' heads. Nothing was broken. The Lord preserved us, and his name shall be glorified. But I was deeply impressed. My imagination anticipated what it must be in that period when the Lord's mighty voice shall give commission to his angels, "Go your ways, and pour out the vials of the wrath of God upon the earth." ...

When the plagues of God shall come upon the earth, hail will fall upon the wicked, about the weight of a talent. The hail had struck Brother Belden. One stone struck him on the back of the head, raising a large lump. Another stone struck him very near the temple. The bruise still shows upon the hands of Sister Belden. But what must it be when the hail shall be so much increased in size, falling upon those who would not care for and obey God but insulted Him and despised all his mercies? — *Ms 59, 1895*

B) The Wicked Suffer Dreadfully

Sinners are Punished

The seven last plagues are about to descend upon the disobedient.

—RH, July 23, 1895

Judgments Smite Lawbreakers

The seven last plagues will come upon all that unite with the one who has made void God's law. *—Lt 118, 1900*

Kings and Nobles are Humbled

I saw that soon the loftiness of man is to be brought down, and the pride of man humbled. Kings and nobles, rich and poor, alike shall bow, and the withering plagues of God shall fall upon them. *—1T, p. 140*

Doubters Now Understand

Those who seek to make it appear that there is no special meaning attached to the judgments that the Lord is now sending upon the earth will soon be forced to understand that which now they do not choose to understand.

—RH, Aug. 20, 1903

Hail and Fire Destroyed Egypt

The storm came as predicted—thunder and hail, and fire mingled with it, "very grievous, such as there was none like it in all the land of Egypt since it became a nation..." Ruin and desolation marked the path of the destroying angel. *—PP, p. 269*

Consequences of Sin Become Real

Soon the consequences of transgression will become to wrongdoers a living reality; for God's judgments will fall upon a disobedient world. Before the minds of sinners will be brought vividly the realization that sin is the transgression of the law of God. *—Ms 78, 1903*

Plagues Punish Independent Men

You who feel that you ought to have your own way, you will be among that company that will receive the seven last plagues of God. "Your way is not my way, neither are your thoughts my thoughts, saith the Lord." Isaiah 55:8. God makes no compromise with the enemy. *—Ms 14, 1894*

Satan Plagues Man and Beasts

Our only safety is in being wholly on the Lord's side. We cannot with any safety give place to the enemy, for if we are found on the enemy's side, we will perish with the wicked in the plagues the Lord shall allow Satan to create in the earth against men and against beasts. —*Lt 54, 1889*

Sunday Lawmakers are Punished

Then it is time for God to work in indignation and vengeance. To those who give their power to suppress religious liberty He says, "Therefore shall her plagues come in one day, death, and mourning, and famine; and she shall be utterly burned with fire; for strong is the Lord God who judgeth her."

—*Ms 71, 1896*

The Plagues Answer Awful Crimes

The end of all things is at hand. God will not much longer bear with the crimes and debasing iniquity of the children of men. Their crimes have indeed reached unto the heavens and will soon be answered by the fearful plagues of God upon the earth. They will drink the cup of God's wrath unmixed with mercy. —*3T, p. 473*

Those Unprepared are Shelterless

I saw that many were neglecting the preparation so needful and were looking to the time of "refreshing" and the "latter rain" to fit them to stand in the day of the Lord and to live in his sight. Oh, how many I saw in the time of trouble without a shelter! They had neglected the needful preparation; therefore they could not receive the refreshing that all must have to fit them to live in the sight of a holy God. —*EW, p. 71*

A Penalty Proportionate to the Sin

Merely being members of the church will avail nothing in the controversy before us. God is weighing men and their doings in the golden scales of the sanctuary. The time of trouble will surely search out and try every pretender. Those who claim to be Christians and yet act as sinners will be punished as sinners. Proportionate to the degree to which they have used their opportunities and talents to hinder the cause of God will be the severity of their punishment. —*Ms 18, 1903*

186

Vain Skeptics Have No Refuge

The spirit of opposition to reproof, that led to the persecution and imprisonment of Jeremiah, exists today. Many refuse to heed repeated warnings, preferring rather to listen to false teachers who flatter their vanity and overlook their evil-doing. In the day of trouble such will have no sure refuge, no help from heaven. — *PK, p. 437*

Angels Do Not Protect the Wicked

In the time of trouble, just previous to the coming of Christ, the lives of the righteous will be preserved through the ministration of holy angels. Those who come up to that trying time, neglecting to obey God's commands, will have no security of their lives. Angels cannot protect them from the wrath of their enemies while they are living in neglect of any known duty, or express command of Jehovah. — *3SG, p. 196*

Parents See Children Penalized

Look at these parents who heeded not the admonition of God for themselves and children. God wanted to save them and their children; they rejected the teachings of God, and while they were rejecting light from heaven their children became hardened and lost, without God and without hope in the world. What kind of an account will those parents have to render to God for children committed to their trust? How will they feel in the time of trouble as they see their children withering beneath the plagues of God unmixed with mercy? — *Lt 3, 1853*

Lukewarm Christians are Punished

Tribulation and wrath will surely come upon those who profess to be Christians, yet who accept the principles of Satan, departing from the commandments of God, in the daily life living a lie. Can we not see the uncertainty and shortness of time? There are many, many who are unready for the Lord's appearing. If they continue to act like the wicked, to cherish the principles of the wicked, they will be punished with the wicked. If they betray the truth of God, causing the messages given by Him to become an uncertain thing, can He shield them from disasters by sea and by land? No, no! — *Lt 195, 1903*

Multiple Plagues Fall on False Prophets

I saw that the priests who are leading on their flock to death are soon to be arrested in their dreadful career. The plagues of God are coming, but it will not be sufficient for the false shepherds to be tormented with one or two of these plagues. God's hand at that time will be stretched out still in wrath and justice and will not be brought to Himself again until his purposes are fully accomplished, and the hireling priests are led to worship at the feet of the saints, and to acknowledge that God has loved them because they held fast the truth and kept God's commandments, and until all the unrighteous ones are destroyed from the earth. — *EW, p. 124*

Men with Mocking Lips are Punished

As the words fell from mocking lips, "You have not gone up yet!" an angel wrote them. Said the angel, "They mock God." I was pointed back to a similar sin committed in ancient times. Elijah had been translated to heaven, and his mantle had fallen upon Elisha. Then wicked youth, who had learned from their parents to despise the man of God, followed Elisha, and mockingly cried, "Go up, thou bald head; go up, thou bald head." In thus insulting his servant, they insulted God and met their punishment then and there. In like manner, those who have scoffed and mocked at the idea of the saints' going up, will be visited with the wrath of God, and will be made to feel that it is not a light thing to trifle with their Maker. — *EW, p. 247*

Plagues Fall on Unconverted Adventists

When the Saviour saw in the Jewish people a nation divorced from God, He saw also a professed Christian Church united to the world and the papacy. And as He stood upon Olivet, weeping over Jerusalem till the sun sank behind the western hills, so He is weeping over and pleading with sinners in these last moments of time.

Soon He will say to the angels who are holding the four winds, "Let the plagues loose; let darkness, destruction, and death come upon the transgressors of my law." Will He be obliged to say to those who have had great light and knowledge, as He said to the Jews, "If thou hadst known, even thou at least in this thy day, the things which belong unto thy peace! But now they are hid from thine eyes?" — *RH, Oct. 8, 1901*

God Utilizes His Enemies

There is to be such a time of trouble as there never was since there was a nation. Already nations are angry, already Satan is working with signs and lying wonders, and this will increase until the end. God will use his enemies as instruments to punish those who have followed their own pernicious ways whereby the truth of God has been misrepresented, misjudged, and dishonored. These enemies of God are living evidences of the truth of his Word; they are fulfilling that which holy men of old spoke as they were moved by the Holy Ghost. — *Lt 44, 1894*

Nominal Christians Suffer Greatly

I pleaded before the angel for God to save his people who had gone astray, to save them for his mercy's sake. When the plagues begin to fall, those who continue to break the holy Sabbath will not open their mouths to plead those excuses that they now make to get rid of keeping it. Their mouths will be closed while the plagues are falling, and the great Lawgiver is requiring justice of those who have had his holy law in derision and have called it "a curse to man," "miserable," and "rickety."

When such feel the iron grasp of this law taking hold of them, these expressions will appear before them in living characters, and they will then realize the sin of having that law in derision which the Word of God calls "holy, just, and good." — *EW, pp. 64, 65*

The Wicked are Shelterless

Many have unsubdued, unhumbled hearts, and think more of their own little grievances and trials than of the souls of sinners. If they had the glory of God in view, they would feel for perishing souls around them; and as they realized their perilous situation, would take hold with energy, exercising faith in God, and hold up the hands of his servants, that they might boldly, yet in love, declare the truth and warn souls to lay hold upon it before the sweet voice of mercy should die away.

Said the angel, "Those who profess his name are not ready." I saw that the seven last plagues were coming upon the shelterless heads of the wicked; and then those who have stood in their way will hear the bitter reproaches of sinners, and their hearts will faint within them. — *EW, p. 120*

Sinful Men Beg for Mercy

I saw Jesus lay off his priestly attire and clothe Himself with his most kingly robes... Surrounded by the angelic host, He left heaven. The plagues were falling upon the inhabitants of the earth. Some were denouncing God, and cursing Him. Others rushed to the people of God, and begged to be taught how they should escape the judgments of God. But the saints had nothing for them. The last tear for sinners had been shed, the last agonizing prayer offered, the last burden had been borne. The sweet voice of mercy was no more to invite them. The last note of warning had been given. —*1SG, p. 199*

Many Neglected to Get Ready

I saw that many were neglecting the preparation so needful and were looking to the time of "refreshing" and the "latter rain" to fit them to stand in the day of the Lord and to live in his sight. Oh, how many I saw in the time of trouble without a shelter! They had neglected the needful preparation; therefore they could not receive the refreshing that all must have to fit them to live in the sight of a holy God. Those who refuse to be hewed by the prophets and fail to purify their souls in obeying the whole truth, and who are willing to believe that their condition is far better than it really is, will come up to the time of the falling of the plagues, and then see that they needed to be hewed and squared for the building. But there will be no time then to do it and no Mediator to plead their cause before the Father." —*EW, p. 71*

Former Ministers are Punished

No superiority of rank, dignity, or worldly wisdom, no position in sacred office, will preserve men from sacrificing principle when left to their own deceitful hearts. Those who have been regarded as worthy and righteous prove to be ring-leaders in apostasy and examples in indifference and in the abuse of God's mercies. Their wicked course He will tolerate no longer, and in his wrath He deals with them without mercy.

It is with reluctance that the Lord withdraws his presence from those who have been blessed with great light and who have felt the power of the word in ministering to others. They were once his faithful servants, favored with his presence and guidance; but they departed from Him and led others into error, and therefore are brought under the divine displeasure. —*5T, p. 212*

A Curse on Unfruitful Christians

As the priests and rulers, full of indignation and terror, sought refuge in flight at the cleansing of the temple, so will it be in the work for these last days. The woes that will be pronounced upon those that have had light from heaven, and did not heed it, they will feel, but will have no power to act. This is represented in the parable of the wise and foolish virgins. They cannot obtain a character from the wise virgins, and they have no oil of grace to discern the clear light, or to accept it, that they may join the procession going into the marriage supper of the Lamb. — *Lt 56, 1896*

Lukewarm Adventists are Plagued

Those who have had opportunities to hear and receive the truth and who have united with the Seventh-day Adventist Church, calling themselves the commandment-keeping people of God, and yet possess no more vitality and consecration to God than do the nominal churches, will receive of the plagues of God just as verily as the churches who oppose the law of God.

Only those that are sanctified through the truth will compose the royal family in the heavenly mansions Christ has gone to prepare for those that love Him and keep his commandments. All who claim to be Sabbathkeeping Adventists, and yet continue in sin, are liars in God's sight. Their sinful course is counterworking the work of God. They are leading others into sin.

— *Lt 35, 1898*

Evil Men Make False Confessions

When those who profess to love Him complain of his providence, despise his promises, and, yielding to temptation, unite with evil angels to defeat the purposes of God, the Lord often so overrules circumstances as to bring these persons where, though they may have no real repentance, they will be convinced of their sin and will be constrained to acknowledge the wickedness of their course and the justice and goodness of God in his dealings with them.

It is thus that God sets counter agencies at work to make manifest the works of darkness. And though the spirit which prompted to the evil course is not radically changed, confessions are made that vindicate the honor of God and justify his faithful reprovers, who have been opposed and misrepresented. Thus it will be when the wrath of God shall be finally poured out. — *PP, p. 393*

Evil Pastors are Punished Tenfold

Many of the wicked were greatly enraged as they suffered the effects of the plagues. It was a scene of fearful agony. Parents were bitterly reproaching their children, and children their parents, brothers their sisters, and sisters their brothers. Loud, wailing cries were heard in every direction… But I saw that the ministers did not escape the wrath of God. Their suffering was tenfold greater than that of their people. —*EW, p. 282*

False Shepherds Suffer the Greatest

In these last days the history of the Jewish nation is being repeated in the professed Christian world, and men are doing despite to the Spirit of God and, notwithstanding the example before them of the Jewish nation, they are doing as they did, and the time is now soon to come when it will be demonstrated that it is a fearful thing to have worn out the patience of God.

There shall be throughout the whole earth a time of trouble such as there never was since there was a nation, and the punishment will fall more surely upon those who have educated and deceived the people to accept of errors in the place of truth, to turn from the commandments of God to walk in paths God has not cast up for them to walk in. God keeps a reckoning with nations, and when the law of God is fully made void, then the destruction cometh.

—*Ms 69a, 1896*

The Christian World is Punished

"Behold, the Lord cometh out of his place to punish the inhabitants of the earth for their iniquity; the earth also shall disclose her blood and shall no longer cover her slain." Isaiah 26:21.

The professed Christian world is advancing as did the Jewish nation from one degree of sinfulness to a greater degree, refusing warning after warning, and rejecting a thus saith the Lord, while crediting the fables of men. The Lord God will soon arise in his wrath, and pour out his judgments upon those who are repeating the sins of the inhabitants of the Noatic world. Those whose hearts are fully set in them to do evil as were the hearts of the inhabitant of Sodom, will like them be destroyed. The fact that God has had long forbearance, patience, and mercy, the fact that his judgments have been long delayed will not make the punishments any less severe when it does come. —*Ms 105, 1894*

Retributive Judgments Fall

Among professed Christians there are idolaters, men and women who are not sealed by God. Many have subverted the Christian faith into idolatry, giving to a man-made institution the glory and honor that God requires for his Sabbath day, and compelling others to worship this idol. Such ones will surely be visited with God's retributive judgments, which are to be poured out without mixture of mercy upon the unrepentant despisers of God's law.

— Ms 24, 1891

Antichrist Feels God's Wrath

The greater man's influence for good, under the control of the Spirit of God, the more determined will be the enemy to indulge his envy and jealousy toward him by religious persecution. But all heaven is on the side of Christ, not of Antichrist. Those who love God and are willing to be partaker with Christ in his sufferings, God will honor.

Antichrist, meaning all who exalt themselves against the will and work of God, will at the appointed time feel the wrath of Him who gave Himself that they might not perish but have eternal life. All who persevere in obedience, all who will not sell their souls for money or for the favor of men, God will register in the book of life. *— Ms 9, 1900*

The Wicked Plead for Mercy

Mercy's sweet call is now sounding; but it will soon die away. Probation's hour will soon be ended. The seven last plagues will fall, and then those who have chosen the pleasures of the world and rebelled against God, will cry for mercy when there will be none to answer their prayers.

But a voice will be heard—"Thou art weighed in the balance and found wanting." And as they realize that they have no shelter from the dreadful storm of God's wrath, they will plead for one little hour of probation that they may again hear the sweet voice, inviting "every one that thirsteth, come ye to the waters."

It will then fall upon the ear, in that dreadful hour. "Too late! Too late! Because I have called, and ye refused; I have stretched out my hand, and no man regarded. But ye have set at naught all my counsel, and would none of my reproof. I also will laugh at your calamity, I will mock when your fear cometh." *— YI, Jan. 1, 1854*

Weak Christians Lose Divine Protection

I was shown that the time was in the near future that those whom God had warned and reproved and given great light but who would not correct their ways and follow the light, He would remove from them that heavenly protection which had preserved them from Satan's cruel power. The Lord would surely leave them to themselves to follow the judgment and counsels of their own wisdom.

They would be simply left to themselves, and the protection of God would be withdrawn from them, and they would not be shielded from the workings of Satan; that none of finite judgment and foresight can have any power to conceive of the care God has exercised through his angels over the children of men in their travels, in their own houses, in their eating and drinking. Wherever they are, his eye is upon them. They are preserved from a thousand dangers, all to them unseen. Satan has laid snares, but the Lord is constantly at work to save his people from them.

But from those who have no sense of the goodness and mercy of God, who refuse his merciful warnings, who reject his counsels to reach the highest standard of Bible requirements, who do despite to the Spirit of grace, the Lord would remove his protecting power. I was shown that Satan would entangle and then destroy if he could, the souls he had tempted. God will bear long, but there is a bound to his mercy, a line which marks his mercy and his justice.

I was shown that the judgments of God would not come directly out from the Lord upon them, but rather in this way: they place themselves beyond his protection. He warns, corrects, reproves, and points out the only path of safety; then, if those who have been the objects of his special care will follow their own course independent of the Spirit of God after repeated warnings, if they choose their own way, then He does not commission his angels to prevent Satan's decided attacks upon them.

It is Satan's power that is at work at sea and on land bringing calamity and distress, sweeping off multitudes to make sure of his prey. Storm and tempest both by sea and land will be, for Satan has come down in great wrath. He is at work. He knows his time is short, and if he is not restrained we shall see more terrible manifestations of his power than we have ever dreamed of.

—Lt 14, 1883

The Wicked Do Not Repent

When God's judgments shall fall upon the earth before its deluge by fire, the impenitent will know just where and what their sin is—the despising of his holy law. Yet they will have no more true repentance than did the old-world sinners. —*PP, p. 99*

The Agony of Skeptical Adventists

I saw the state of some who professed to stand on present truth, but disregarded the visions—the way God had chosen to teach, in some cases, those who erred from Bible truth. I saw that in striking against the visions, they did not strike against the worm—the feeble instrument that God spoke through, but against the Holy Ghost.

I saw it was a small thing to speak against the instrument, but it was dangerous to slight the words of God. I saw if they were in error and God chose to show them their errors through visions, and they disregarded the teachings of God through visions, they would be left to take their own way, and run in the way of error, and think they were right until they would find it out too late.

Then in the time of trouble I heard them cry to God in agony—"Why didst thou not show us our wrong, that we might have gotten right, and ready for this time?" Then an angel pointed to them, and said—"My Father taught but you would not be instructed. He spoke through visions but you disregarded his voice, and He gave you up to your own ways to be filled with your own doings." —*Ms 2, 1849*

Discussion Questions

1. Will the plagues punish men in proportion to the sins they committed?

2. Which plague could be God's response to the universal death decree?

3. How will the seven last plagues humble the rulers of church and state?

4. Why will the wrath of God fall on lukewarm Christians?

5. Who is protected from the plagues when the four winds are unleashed?

— 13 —

God Destroys Evil Cities

"The sword is without, and the pestilence and the famine within: he that is in the field shall die with the sword; and he that is in the city, famine and pestilence shall devour him."

— Ezekiel 7:15

Lev. 26:31	Jer. 4:26; 6:8	Ezek. 24:6-8	Micah 5:11	Jude 1:7
Proverbs 11:11	Jer. 9:11; 48:8	Ezek. 35:4	Zeph. 3:1-7	Rev. 16:19
Isa. 6:11; 32:19	Ezek. 12:20	Amos 3:6	2 Peter 2:6	Rev. 18:1-3

Plagues Fall on All Cities

The time is not far distant when every city will be visited by the plagues of God. — *Ms 41, 1902*

Thousands of Cities Destroyed

Oh that God's people had a sense of the impending destruction of thousands of cities, now almost given to idolatry. — *RH, Sept. 10, 1903*

Judged because of Apostates

Our cities are soon to feel the great displeasure of God because many have departed from the faith and, while professing to be children of God, have been doing a work contrary to the work that God has specified should be done. — *Ms 43, 1906*

Proud Structures Become Ashes

God has a storehouse of retributive judgments, which He permits to fall upon those who have continued in sin in the face of great light. I have seen the most costly structures in buildings erected and supposed to be fireproof. And just as Sodom perished in the flames of God's vengeance, so will these proud structures become ashes. — *Lt 20, 1901*

196

No Sign of Repentance

Even in the cities where the judgments of God have fallen in consequence of such transgression there is no sign of repentance. The saloons are still open, and many temptations are kept before the people. — *Lt 268, 1906*

Evil Cities are Justly Punished

The Lord calls for his people to locate away from the cities, for in such an hour as ye think not, fire and brimstone will be rained from heaven upon these cities. Proportionate to their sins will be their visitation. — *Lt 158, 1906*

San Francisco Suffers Greatly

The message of warning should be sounded in the large, wicked cities, such as San Francisco. San Francisco and Oakland are becoming as Sodom and Gomorrah, and the Lord will visit them. Not far hence they will suffer under his judgments. — *RH, July 5, 1906*

Fiery Arrows Fly Everywhere

Last Friday morning, just before I awoke, a very impressive scene was presented before me. I seemed to awake from sleep but was not in my home. From the windows I could behold a terrible conflagration. Great balls of fire were falling upon houses, and from these balls fiery arrows were flying in every direction. It was impossible to check the fires that were kindled, and many places were being destroyed. The terror of the people was indescribable. After a time I awoke and found myself at home. I see that the end is near, and I wish to do my work quickly. — *Lt 278, 1906*

Personal Property is Destroyed

In the future... I saw also that costly buildings in the cities, supposed to be fireproof, would be consumed by fire. The fire that lately swept through Patterson, N. Y., and the fires that have been in other places, are a fulfillment, in part, of the warning. God has not executed his wrath without mercy. His hand is stretched out still. His message must be given in Greater New York. The people must be shown how it is possible for God, by a touch of his hand, to destroy the property they have gathered together against the last great day. A little longer will the voice of mercy be heard; a little longer will the gracious invitation be given. — *Lt 42, 1903*

Chicago Loses Protection

Scenes that would soon take place in Chicago, and other large cities also, passed before me. As wickedness increased, and the protecting power of God was withdrawn, there were destructive winds and tempests; buildings were destroyed by fire and shaken down by earthquakes. I saw the expensive building, above referred to, fall, with many others. — *Ms 33, 1906*

Fireproof Buildings are Not Safe

On one occasion, when in New York City, I was in the night season called upon to behold buildings rising story after story toward heaven. These buildings were warranted to be fireproof, and they were erected to glorify their owners and builders... The scene that next passed before me was an alarm of fire. Men looked at the lofty and supposedly fireproof buildings and said: "They are perfectly safe." But these buildings were consumed as if made of pitch. The fire engines could do nothing to stay the destruction. The firemen were unable to operate the engines. — *9T, pp. 12, 13*

Wait before Issuing Scary Notices

Now do not issue notices so worded as to create an alarm. When the Lord is ready for the advanced denunciation of wicked cities, He will let his people know. But this will be after these wicked cities have had an opportunity to hear the Word and to receive the Word that is unto life eternal. Our work now is to enlighten and educate minds as to the sayings of the Scripture. Doors are now opened for the entrance of truth. Avail yourselves of the opportunity to reach those who have never heard the truth. Explain the truth, as did Christ, in many ways, by figures and parables. — *Lt 17, 1902*

Judged by the Light Rejected

The end is near, and every city is to be turned upside down every way. There will be confusion in every city. Everything that can be shaken is to be shaken, and we do not know what will come next. The judgments will be according to the wickedness of the people and the light of truth that they have had. If they have had the truth, according to that light will be the punishment. Christ pronounced his woes on the cities that had had most of his instruction. That is why I am so afraid of their putting up a great building in Battle Creek, or in any place where the truth has been known for years. — *Ms 173, 1902*

Fire Falls from Heaven

The cities will become worse and worse. In them will be strife and bloodshed, and at last they will be visited by earthquakes. Buildings will be thrown down and will be consumed by fire from heaven. — *Ms 76, 1905*

Wicked Cities Can Still Repent

The judgments of God will certainly fall upon all transgressors. The terrible earthquake that has visited San Francisco will be followed by other manifestations of the power of God. His law has been transgressed. Cities have become polluted with sin. Study the history of Nineveh. God sent a special message by Jonah to that wicked city... Many such messages as his would be given in our age, if the wicked cities would repent as did Nineveh.

— *Ms 61a, 1906*

Evil Forces Destroy Grand Buildings

The same Hand that kept the fiery serpents of the wilderness from entering the camp of the Israelites, until God's chosen people provoked Him with their constant murmurs and complaints, is today guarding the honest in heart. Were this restraining Hand withdrawn, the enemy of our souls would at once begin the work of destruction that he has so long desired to accomplish. And because God's long-continued forbearance is not now recognized, the forces of evil are already, to a limited degree, permitted to destroy. How soon human agencies will see blotted out of existence their magnificent buildings, which are their pride! — *Ms 153, 1902*

A Vision of Fireballs Hitting Nashville

When I was at Nashville, I had been speaking to the people, and in the night season, there was an immense ball of fire that came right from heaven and settled in Nashville. There were flames going out like arrows from that ball; houses were being consumed; houses were tottering and falling. Some of our people were standing there. "It is just as we expected," they said, "we expected this." Others were wringing their hands in agony and crying unto God for mercy. "You knew it," said they, "you knew that this was coming, and never said a word to warn us!" They seemed as though they would almost tear them to pieces, to think they had never told them or given them any warning at all.

— *Ms 188, 1905*

Cities Hit by Great Calamities

When God's restraining hand is removed, the destroyer begins his work. Then in our cities the greatest calamities will come. Is this because people do not keep Sunday? No; but because men have trampled upon the law of Jehovah. The Lord is slow to anger. This should inspire the heart with gratitude. "The Lord is slow to anger, and great in power, and will not at all acquit the wicked: the Lord hath his way in the whirlwind and in the storm, and the clouds are the dust of his feet." Nahum 1:3. — *Ms 127, 1897*

The Saving Hand is Strong to Destroy

The time is coming when in their fraud and insolence men will reach a point that the Lord will not permit them to pass, and they will learn that there is a limit to the forbearance of Jehovah...

I am instructed that when the Lord's time comes, should no change have taken place in the hearts of proud, ambitious human beings, men will find that the hand that had been strong to save will be strong to destroy. No earthly power can stay the hand of God. No material can be used in the erection of buildings that will preserve them from destruction when God's appointed time comes to send retribution on men for their disregard of his law and for their selfish ambition. — *9T, p. 13*

Modern Cities Suffer like Jerusalem

Said Christ, "As it was in the days of Noah, so shall it be also in the days of the Son of man." Let all read and understand the warnings given by the Saviour. And as He went out of the temple, one of the disciples saith unto Him, "Master, see what manner of stones and what buildings are here!" And Jesus answering said unto him, "Seest thou these great buildings? There shall not be left one stone upon another, that shall not be thrown down."

Men will continue to erect expensive buildings, costing millions of money; special attention will be called to their architectural beauty and the firmness and solidity with which they are constructed; but the Lord has instructed me that despite the unusual firmness and expensive display, these buildings will share the fate of the temple in Jerusalem. That magnificent structure fell. Angels of God were sent to do the work of destruction, so that one stone was not left one upon another that was not thrown down. — *Ms 35, 1906*

All Cities are Quickly Destroyed

The wrath of God will come upon all cities, upon dwellings, upon large buildings, so suddenly that they who have the slightest intimation have no safety in dallying at all. They are to flee at once.

We are living amid the perils of the last days. The wrath of God is preparing to come upon all the cities—not all at once but one after another. And if the terrible punishment in one city does not cause the inhabitants of other cities to be afraid and seek repentance, their time will come. When the Lord ariseth to shake terribly the earth, He will not cease until his work in punishment is done. The destruction will begin in certain places, and the destruction of life will be sudden and but few will escape.

There is not to be given an encouraging thought that the gospel of Jesus Christ will be accepted by the large majority of men prior to his coming again the second time with power and great glory. I am instructed by revelation to say that most solemn and overwhelming judgments are determined upon all people who have the light before them in the Word of God, but who do not follow it. —Ms 233, 1902

God Does Not Destroy Nations

The Lord will not suddenly cast off all transgressors or destroy entire nations, but He will punish cities and places where men have given themselves up to the possession of satanic agencies. Strictly will the cities of the nations be dealt with; and yet they will not be visited in the extreme of God's indignation, because some souls will yet break away from the delusions of the enemy and will repent and be converted, while the mass will be treasuring up wrath against the day of wrath.

The Lord bids the abandoned of this our day to fill up the cup of their iniquity to its full measure. God will arise speedily in his authoritative power and will pour out his wrath on those who have been working through Satan's science to deceive if possible the very elect.

Those who are deceiving souls will find that it is a most serious matter to have worn out divine patience. God's wrath will fall upon them signally, unexpectedly, fiercely. Though they may then humble themselves ever so much, there will be no further opportunity for repentance. They have persisted in leading souls to ruin. God's law has repeatedly been made void.

—Ms 35, 1906

Costly Mansions are Decimated

God is withdrawing his Spirit from the wicked cities, which have become as the cities of the antediluvian world, and as Sodom and Gomorrah. The inhabitants of these cities have been tested and tried. We have reached a time when God is about to punish the presumptuous wrong-doers, who refuse to keep his commandments and disregard his messages of warning. He who bears long with evil-doers gives every one an opportunity to seek Him and humble the heart before Him.

Everyone has opportunity to come to Christ and be converted, that He may heal them. But there will come a time when mercy will be no longer offered. Costly mansions, marvels of architectural skill, will be destroyed without a moment's notice when the Lord sees that the owners have passed the boundaries of forgiveness. The destruction by fire of the stately buildings supposed to be fireproof is an illustration of how in a short time the earth's architecture will lie in ruins. —*Lt 90, 1902*

Evil Cities Suffer like San Francisco

As we near the close of this earth's history, we shall have the scenes of the San Francisco calamity repeated in other places... The period of time in which we are living is a very solemn one... These things make me feel very solemn, because I know that the judgment day is right upon us. The judgments that have already come are a warning, but not the finishing, of the punishment that will come on wicked cities. Our cities are most terrible places, wherein are practiced all kinds of sin and iniquity of the most revolting character. The Lord's name is greatly dishonored...

San Francisco in ruins is the most complete, thorough, awful calamity I have ever looked upon. In the night season I have had many presentations of the judgments of God coming upon our cities; and now I can understand better the real meaning of these scenes that I have witnessed... Oh, how soon the scenes of destruction and desolation will come and be universal, we cannot tell. "Be ye also ready," saith the Lord; "for in such an hour as ye think not the Son of man cometh." ... These scenes will soon be witnessed, just as they are clearly described... The prophecies recorded in the Old Testament, are the word of the Lord for the last days and will be fulfilled as surely as we have seen the desolation of San Francisco. —*Lt 154, 1906*

Demolition in New York City

I have said, as I looked at the great buildings going up there, story after story. What terrible scenes will take place when the Lord shall arise to shake terribly the earth! Then the words of Revelation 18:1-3 will be fulfilled. The whole of the eighteenth chapter of Revelation is a warning of what is coming on the earth.

But I have no light in particular in regard to what is coming on New York, only that I know that one day the great buildings there will be thrown down by the turning and overturning of God's power. From the light given me, I know that destruction is in the world. One word from the Lord, one touch of his mighty power, and these massive structures will fall. Scenes will take place the fearfulness of which we cannot imagine. — *RH, July 5, 1906*

Balls of Fire Declare Christ's Coming

Little do we realize the strength of the forces that are now at work in this world. The whole heavenly host are seeking to save that which was lost; the fallen angels are working with a power from beneath to counteract the efforts of Christ and his co-laborers. Shall not we be faithful in doing our part? Shall we not strive to do everything in our power to carry the truth for this time to those who are in ignorance of God's commandments? Shall we not open the Scriptures to the understanding of those who have not yet learned the importance of obeying every precept and of preparing for the Lord's soon coming? Shall we not labor as do those that must give an account?

Last night a scene was presented before me. I may never feel free to reveal all of it, but I will reveal a little. It seemed that an immense ball of fire came down upon the world, and crushed large houses. From place to place rose the cry, "The Lord has come! The Lord has come!" Many were unprepared to meet Him, but a few were saying, "Praise the Lord!" "Why are you praising the Lord?" inquired those upon whom was coming sudden destruction.

"Because we now see what we have been looking for."

"If you believed that these things were coming, why did you not tell us?" was the terrible response. "We did not know about these things. Why did you leave us in ignorance? Again and again you have seen us; why did you not become acquainted with us, and tell us of the judgment to come, and that we must serve God, lest we perish? Now we are lost!" — *Ms 102, 1904*

Lordly Palaces Become Ruins

Terrible shocks will come upon the earth, and the lordly palaces erected at great expense will certainly become heaps of ruins. The earth's crust will be rent by the outbursts of the elements concealed in the bowels of the earth. These elements, once broken loose, will sweep away the treasures of those who for years have been adding to their wealth by securing large possessions at starvation prices from those in their employ. And the religious world, too, is to be terribly shaken, for the end of all things is at hand. —*Ms 24, 1891*

A Vision of Destroying Angels

While at Loma Linda, California, April 16, 1906, there passed before me a most wonderful representation. During a vision of the night, I stood on an eminence, from which I could see houses shaken like a reed in the wind. Buildings, great and small, were falling to the ground. Pleasure resorts, theaters, hotels, and the homes of the wealthy were shaken and shattered. Many lives were blotted out of existence, and the air was filled with the shrieks of the injured and the terrified.

The destroying angels of God were at work. One touch, and buildings, so thoroughly constructed that men regarded them as secure against every danger, quickly became heaps of rubbish. There was no assurance of safety in any place. I did not feel in any special peril, but the awfulness of the scenes that passed before me I cannot find words to describe. It seemed that the forbearance of God was exhausted and that the judgment day had come.

The angel that stood at my side then instructed me that but few have any conception of the wickedness existing in our world today, and especially the wickedness in the large cities. He declared that the Lord has appointed a time when He will visit transgressors in wrath for persistent disregard of his law.

Terrible as was the representation that passed before me, that which impressed itself most vividly upon my mind was the instruction given in connection with it. The angel that stood by my side declared that God's supreme rulership and the sacredness of his law must be revealed to those who persistently refused to render obedience to the King of kings. Those who choose to remain disloyal must be visited in mercy with judgments, in order that, if possible, they may be aroused to a realization of the sinfulness of their course. —*9T, pp. 92, 93*

God Uses Volcanic Eruptions

Coal and oil are generally to be found where there are no burning mountains or fiery issues. When fire and water under the surface of the earth meet, the fiery issues cannot give sufficient vent to the heated elements beneath. The earth is convulsed—the ground trembles, heaves, and rises into swells or waves, and there are heavy sounds like thunder underground. The air is heated and suffocating. The earth quickly opens, and I saw villages, cities and burning mountains carried down together into the earth.

God controls all these elements; they are his instruments to do his will; He calls them into action to serve his purpose. These fiery issues have been, and will be his agents to blot out from the earth very wicked cities. Like Korah, Dathan and Abiram they go down alive into the pit. These are evidences of God's power. Those who have beheld these burning mountains have been struck with terror at the grandeur of the scene—pouring forth fire, and flame, and a vast amount of melted ore, drying up rivers and causing them to disappear. They have been filled with awe as though they were beholding the infinite power of God. These manifestations bear the special marks of God's power, and are designed to cause the people of the earth to tremble before Him, and to silence those, who like Pharaoh would proudly say, "Who is the Lord that I should obey his voice?"

Isaiah refers to these exhibitions of God's power where he exclaims, "Oh that thou wouldest rend the heavens, that thou wouldest come down, that the mountains might flow down at thy presence as when the melting fire burneth. The fire causeth the waters to boil, to make thy name known to thine adversaries, that the nations may tremble at thy presence. When thou didst terrible things which we looked not for, thou camest down, the mountains flowed down at thy presence." Isaiah 64:1-3.

"The Lord is slow to anger, and great in power, and will not at all acquit the wicked. The Lord hath his way in the whirlwind and in the storm, and the clouds are the dust of his feet. He rebuketh the sea, and maketh it dry and drieth up all the rivers. Bashan languisheth, and Carmel, and the flower of Lebanon languisheth. The mountains quake at Him, and the hills melt, and the earth is burned at his presence, yea, the world, and all that dwell therein." Nahum 1:3-5. —3SG, pp. 80, 81

Worldly Cities Suffer Great Calamities

I am bidden to declare the message that cities full of transgression, and sinful in the extreme, will be destroyed by earthquakes, by fire, by flood. All the world will be warned that there is a God who will display his authority as God. His unseen agencies will cause destruction, devastation, and death. All the accumulated riches will be as nothingness. Notwithstanding the scientific care with which men safeguard buildings from destruction, one touch of the great and rightful Ruler will bring to nothingness the idolatrous possessions that have been laid up in a sightly and magnificent display. The devices of men will come to naught.

The injustice in our world, the masterly power man has taken unto himself, the oppressive, manmade unions that bring confusion and violence and strife, and the manipulation of a power to rule men and to acquire means through underhand deceptions—these conditions God cannot pass by with silence. Those who are under the influence and teaching of the great deceiver will find that although God has borne long with their deceptive acuteness, He has not been deceived, and He will reward every transgressor according to his works. He keeps a strict account of every lie framed; and when He takes matters in his hand, He will deal in accordance with every man's secret and hidden devising.

Bible history is to be repeated. Calamities will come, calamities most awful, most unexpected; and these destructions will follow one after another. If there will be a heeding of the warnings that God has given, and if churches will repent, returning to their allegiance, then other cities may be spared for a time. But if men who have been deceived continue in the same way in which they have been walking, disregarding the law of God and presenting falsehoods before the people, God allows them to suffer calamity, that their senses may be awakened.

It is in the exercise of his long-sufferance, that God gives man opportunity to come to his senses. A time of probation is granted; but if they go on making gold and silver their god, erecting their expensive buildings and accumulating iniquity by false dealings, they may expect nothing but an outbreak of the Lord's indignation to extinguish the sinner. And those who have been deceived by satanic agencies have often deceived others to their eternal ruin.

— *Ms 35, 1906*

Lawbreakers are Punished

There will be, not long hence, some demonstrations from the Lord God of heaven, greater than the burning of a sanitarium or a publishing establishment. Wicked cities will be visited. They will have an expression from the God of heaven as to how He regards the works and ways of those who have made void his law. They may be called to a realization of the offense they have been guilty of before God, the great Ruler of all worlds. —*Ms 43, 1906*

Ungodly Cities are Swept Away

The time is near when the large cities will be visited by the judgments of God. In a little while these cities will be terribly shaken. No matter how large or how strong their buildings, no matter how many safeguards against fire may have been provided, let God touch these buildings, and in a few minutes or a few hours they are in ruins.

The ungodly cities of our world are to be swept away by the besom of destruction. In the calamities that are now befalling immense buildings and large portions of cities God is showing us what will come upon the whole earth. He has told us: "Now learn a parable of the fig tree; When his branch is yet tender, and putteth forth leaves, ye know that summer is nigh: so likewise ye, when ye shall see all these things, know that it the coming of the Son of man is near, even at the doors." Matthew 24:32, 33. —*7T, p. 83*

Discussion Questions

1. Will cities with a sizeable Christian population be safe from God's plagues? How about Berrien Springs and Loma Linda?

2. What types of judgments might fall on wicked cities like San Francisco?

3. When the balls of fire arrive, people will wail that they never heard the gospel message. What can we do to warn our neighbors immediately?

4. Should we print pamphlets warning cities of God's judgments?

5. Why is the hand that was strong to save also strong to destroy?

— 14 —

Sabbathkeepers Blamed

"Blessed are ye, when men shall revile you, and persecute you, and shall say all manner of evil against you falsely, for my sake." — Matthew 5:11

Esther 3:5, 6	Psalm 35:20	Psalm 55:23	Prov. 25:18-22	1 Peter 3:16
Esther 5:14-6:4	Psalm 41:5-9	Psalm 119:69, 70	Daniel 6:4	1 Peter 4:12-16

Some Say the Affliction is from God
Satan has control of all whom God does not especially guard. He will favor and prosper some in order to further his own designs, and he will bring trouble upon others and lead men to believe that it is God who is afflicting them. — *GC, p. 589*

Men Warn against Defiling Sunday
Satan works under a guise of religion, and guided by him, the professed Christian world will be very zealous in working against the law of God. Satan is leading men and women to complete the ruin he began in heaven. He is willing for the world to declare that the calamity by land and sea and the destruction by flood and fire, are because Sunday is desecrated. Herein lies his deception. — *RH, June 4, 1901*

Ministers Blame Sabbathkeepers
In churches and in large gatherings in the open air, ministers will urge upon the people the necessity of keeping the first day of the week. There are calamities on sea and land: and these calamities will increase, one disaster following close upon another; and the little band of conscientious Sabbath-keepers will be pointed out as the ones who are bringing the wrath of God upon the world by their disregard of Sunday. — *RH, Mar. 18, 1884*

Men Already Cast Blame

The assertion that God's judgments are visited upon men for their violation of the Sunday sabbath, will be repeated; already it is beginning to be urged.

— GC, p. 579

The Object of Universal Hatred

As the Sabbath has become the special point of controversy throughout Christendom, and religious and secular authorities have combined to enforce the observance of the Sunday, the persistent refusal of a small minority to yield to the popular demand, will make them objects of universal execration.

— GC, p. 615

Hearts are Moved Away from Truth

The kingdom of darkness is extending over the world, and is embracing every sphere of action of men... The same spirit that was moving the priests and rulers had moved the heart and mind of Cain to slay his brother. It is the apostasy from truth that worketh in the children of disobedience to silence the voice of those who are calling them to obedience, and provoke the loyal to become disloyal as Cain tried to provoke Abel. *— Ms 104, 1897*

Godly Christians are Falsely Accused

Those who honor the law of God have been accused of bringing judgments upon the world, and they will be regarded as the cause of the fearful convulsions of nature and the strife and bloodshed among men that are filling the earth with woe. The power attending the last warning has enraged the wicked; their anger is kindled against all who have received the message, and Satan will excite to still greater intensity the spirit of hatred and persecution.

— GC, p. 614

Bogus Charges are Invented

In openly making void the law of God and exalting human laws, the church has been living in transgression of God's Word. She has turned away from the truth of God's Word. The words spoken from the cloudy pillar to Moses to give to the chosen people of God, and by them to be given to the world, have been discarded and disobeyed, while human laws and human traditions have been exalted. Those who keep God's memorial Sabbath are hated, and every charge which can be invented to make them trouble, is carried into effect. *— Ms 71, 1896*

Officials Lie about God's Workers

We are nearing the end. God has borne long with the perversity of mankind, but their punishment is no less certain. Let those who profess to be the light of the world depart from all iniquity. We see the very same spirit manifested against the truth that was seen in Christ's day. For want of Bible arguments, those who are making void the law of God will manufacture falsehoods to stain and blacken the workers. They did this to the world's Redeemer; they will do it to his followers. Reports that have not the least foundation will be asserted as truth. —*5T, p. 601*

The Remnant Blamed for the Plagues

When the angel of mercy folds her wings and departs, Satan will do the evil deeds he has long wished to do. Storm and tempest, war and bloodshed—in these things he delights, and thus he gathers in his harvest. And so completely will men be deceived by him that they will declare that these calamities are the result of the desecration of the first day of the week.

From the pulpits of the popular churches will be heard the statement that the world is being punished because Sunday is not honored as it should be. And it will require no great stretch of imagination for men to believe this. They are guided by the enemy, and therefore they reach conclusions which are entirely false. —*RH, Sept. 17, 1901*

Leaders Point to Natural Disasters

Men in responsible positions will not only ignore and despise the Sabbath themselves, but from the sacred desk, will urge upon the people the observance of the first day of the week, pleading tradition and custom in behalf of this man-made institution. They will point to calamities on land and sea—to the storms of wind, the floods, the earthquakes, the destruction by fire—as judgments indicating God's displeasure because Sunday is not sacredly observed.

These calamities will increase more and more, one disaster will follow close upon the heels of another; and those who make void the law of God will point to the few who are keeping the Sabbath of the fourth commandment as the ones who are bringing wrath upon the world. This falsehood is Satan's device that he may ensnare the unwary. —*ST, Jan. 17, 1884*

The Plagues Motivate Men to Kill

I saw that the four angels would hold the four winds until Jesus' work was done in the sanctuary, and then will come the seven last plagues. These plagues enraged the wicked against the righteous; they thought that we had brought the judgments of God upon them, and that if they could rid the earth of us, the plagues would then be stayed. —*EW, p. 36*

Satan's Agents Point to Adventists

In his work Satan pretends to be very religious. He finds this the most effective way of carrying on the work he began in heaven. Under his guidance the Christian world has made void the law of God by tearing down the seventh-day Sabbath, and exalting in its stead a common working day.

As men depart further and further from God, Satan is permitted to have power over the children of disobedience. He hurls destruction among men. There is calamity by land and sea. Property and life are destroyed by fire and flood. Satan resolves to charge this upon those who refuse to bow to the idol which he has set up. His agents point to Seventh-day Adventists as the cause of the trouble. "These people stand out in defiance of law," they say. "They desecrate Sunday. Were they compelled to obey the law for Sunday observance, there would be a cessation of these terrible judgments."

—*RH, July 16, 1901*

A False Interpretation of Events

Men may possess houses and lands of great money value; they may have obtained these honestly or dishonestly, but none of these things can make them happy and contended, sweet-tempered or self-controlled. They may at the same time be estranged from God by sin, their minds controlled by error and superstition. Under a false interpretation of events they think that the calamities that fill the land are the result of Sunday-breaking.

Thinking to appease the wrath of God, these influential men make laws enforcing Sunday observance. They think that by exalting this false rest day higher and still higher, compelling obedience to the spurious Sabbath, they are doing God's service. Those who honor God by observing the true Sabbath are looked upon as disloyal to God, when it is really those who thus regard them who are themselves disloyal, because they are trampling underfoot the Sabbath originated in Eden. —*Ms 83, 1902*

Men Despise Sabbathkeepers

There has been exercised against those who conscientiously observe the seventh-day Sabbath a spirit of enmity and hatred that reveals beyond a doubt that its possessors have no part in Christ, but are partakers of the spirit of the prince of the power of darkness. —*Ms 5, 1882*

Satan's Plan to Blame Sabbathkeepers

Says the great deceiver: "I will influence popular ministers to turn the attention of their hearers from the commandments of God. That which the Scriptures declare to be a perfect law of liberty shall be represented as a yoke of bondage. The people accept their ministers' explanations of Scripture, and do not investigate for themselves."

"Therefore by working through the ministers, I can control the people according to my will. But our principal concern is to silence this sect of Sabbath-keepers. We must excite popular indignation against them. We will enlist great men and worldly-wise men upon our side, and induce those in authority to carry out our purposes. Then the Sabbath which I have set up shall be enforced by laws the most severe and exacting. Those who disregard them shall be driven out from the cities and villages, and made to suffer hunger and privation." —*4SP, p. 338*

Satan Accuses the Brethren

Every manifestation of God's power for his people arouses the enmity of Satan. Every time God works in their behalf, Satan with his angels works with renewed vigor to compass their ruin. He is jealous of all who make Christ their strength. His object is to instigate evil, and when he has succeeded, throw all the blame upon the tempted ones. He points to their filthy garments, their defective characters. He presents their weakness and folly, their sins of ingratitude, their unlikeness to Christ, which have dishonored their Redeemer.

All this he urges as an argument proving his right to work his will in their destruction. He endeavors to affright their souls with the thought that their case is hopeless, that the stain of their defilement can never be washed away. He hopes so to destroy their faith that they will yield fully to his temptations, and turn from their allegiance to God. —*COL, p. 168*

Israel Blamed Moses for Disasters

There is nothing which will please the people better than to be praised and flattered when they are in wrong and darkness, and deserve reproof. Korah gained the attention of the people, and next their sympathies, by representing Moses as an overbearing leader. He said that Moses was too harsh, too exacting, and dictatorial, and that he reproved the people as though they were sinners, when they were a holy people, and the Lord was among them.

Korah rehearsed the incidents in their experience in their travels through the wilderness, where they had been brought into strait places, and where many of them had died because of murmuring and disobedience, and with their perverted senses they thought they saw very clearly that all their trouble might have been saved if Moses had pursued a different course. He was too unyielding, too exacting, and they decided that all their disasters in the wilderness were chargeable to Moses. Korah, the leading spirit, professed great wisdom in discerning the true reason for their trials and affliction.

— *ST, Sept. 9, 1880*

Sabbathkeepers are Condemned

God never forces the will or the conscience; but Satan's constant resort—to gain control of those whom he cannot otherwise seduce—is compulsion by cruelty. Through fear or force he endeavors to rule the conscience and to secure homage to himself. To accomplish this, he works through both religious and secular authorities, moving them to the enforcement of human laws in defiance of the law of God. Those who honor the Bible Sabbath will be denounced as enemies of law and order, as breaking down the moral restraints of society, causing anarchy and corruption, and calling down the judgments of God upon the earth.

Their conscientious scruples will be pronounced obstinacy, stubbornness, and contempt of authority. They will be accused of disaffection toward the government. Ministers who deny the obligation of the divine law will present from the pulpit the duty of yielding obedience to the civil authorities as ordained of God. In legislative halls and courts of justice, commandment keepers will be misrepresented and condemned. A false coloring will be given to their words; the worst construction will be put upon their motives.

— *GC, pp. 591, 592*

World Leaders are Furious

Errors are presented to the world by the various churches, and thus the Scriptures are fulfilled that say, "For all nations have drunk of the wine of the wrath of her fornication." It is a wrath which is created by false doctrines, and when kings and presidents drink this wine of the wrath of her fornication, they are stirred with anger against those who will not come into harmony with the false and Satanic heresies which exalt the false Sabbath, and lead men to trample underfoot God's memorial. — *RH, Sept. 12, 1893*

Spirits Accuse the Remnant

The miracle-working power manifested through spiritualism will exert its influence against those who choose to obey God rather than men. Communications from the spirits will declare that God has sent them to convince the rejecters of Sunday of their error, affirming that the laws of the land should be obeyed as the law of God. They will lament the great wickedness in the world and second the testimony of religious teachers that the degraded state of morals is caused by the desecration of Sunday. Great will be the indignation excited against all who refuse to accept their testimony.

Satan's policy in this final conflict with God's people is the same that he employed in the opening of the great controversy in heaven. He professed to be seeking to promote the stability of the divine government, while secretly bending every effort to secure its overthrow. And the very work which he was thus endeavoring to accomplish he charged upon the loyal angels. The same policy of deception has marked the history of the Roman Church. It has professed to act as the vicegerent of heaven, while seeking to exalt itself above God and to change his law.

Under the rule of Rome, those who suffered death for their fidelity to the gospel were denounced as evildoers; they were declared to be in league with Satan; and every possible means was employed to cover them with reproach, to cause them to appear in the eyes of the people and even to themselves as the vilest of criminals. So it will be now. While Satan seeks to destroy those who honor God's law, he will cause them to be accused as lawbreakers, as men who are dishonoring God and bringing judgments upon the world.

— *GC, pp. 590, 591*

People are Excited by False Charges

While appearing to the children of men as a great physician who can heal all their maladies, he (Satan) will bring disease and disaster, until populous cities are reduced to ruin and desolation...

And then the great deceiver will persuade men that those who serve God are causing these evils. The class that have provoked the displeasure of heaven will charge all their troubles upon those whose obedience to God's commandments is a perpetual reproof to transgressors. It will be declared that men are offending God by the violation of the Sunday sabbath; that this sin has brought calamities which will not cease until Sunday observance shall be strictly enforced; and that those who present the claims of the fourth commandment, thus destroying reverence for Sunday, are troublers of the people, preventing their restoration to divine favor and temporal prosperity.

Thus the accusation urged of old against the servant of God will be repeated and upon grounds equally well established: "And it came to pass, when Ahab saw Elijah, that Ahab said unto him, 'Art thou he that troubleth Israel?' And he answered, 'I have not troubled Israel; but thou, and thy father's house, in that ye have forsaken the commandments of the Lord, and thou hast followed Baalim.'" As the wrath of the people shall be excited by false charges, they will pursue a course toward God's ambassadors very similar to that which apostate Israel pursued toward Elijah. — GC, p. 590

Discussion Questions

1. Can you think of any recent calamities that people claimed were judgments from God?

2. Who is responsible for creating natural disasters?

3. Why will the seven last plagues enrage the wicked against the righteous?

4. What will it be like when the Remnant are universally hated?

5. How could Satan's agents be instrumental in convincing world leaders that God's people are responsible for worldwide desolation?

The Greater

Time of Trouble

— 15 —

The Tribulation Begins

"For in the time of trouble He shall hide me in his pavilion; in the secret place of his tabernacle He shall hide me; He shall set me high upon a rock." — Psalm 27:5

Ezek. 34:25	Isa. 26:20, 21	Jer. 31:15-17	Daniel 12:1	Matt. 24:15-22
Prov. 30:24-28	Isa. 33:15, 16	Ezek. 7:16	Nahum 1:7	Luke 17:30-36

A) Many are Laid to Rest

Children are Taken Away

Ere long we are to be brought into strait and trying places, and the many children brought into the world will in mercy be taken away before the time of trouble comes. Then why entail so much responsibility upon the wife? Souls that are perishing in their sins must be labored for, yet this work we have scarcely touched with the tips of our fingers. — *Ms 152, 1899*

Pray for God's Will to be Done

The Lord "doth not afflict willingly nor grieve the children of men." "Like as a father pitieth his children, so the Lord pitieth them that fear Him; for He knoweth our frame: He remembereth that we are dust." He knows our heart, for He reads every secret of the soul. He knows whether or not those for whom petitions are offered would be able to endure the trial and test that would come upon them if they lived. He knows the end from the beginning.

Many will be laid away to sleep in Jesus before the fiery ordeal of the time of trouble shall come upon our world. This is another reason why we should say after our earnest petition: "Nevertheless not my will, but thine, O Lord, be done." Such a petition will never be registered in heaven as a faithless prayer. — *GCDB, Feb. 26, 1897*

Kids are Swept Away

It is really not wise to have children now. Time is short, the perils of the last days are upon us, and the little children will be largely swept off before this.

—Lt 48, 1876

Most Children are Spared

Did you consider that it is far better to be childless in these days of wickedness and peril than to have children to suffer with the parents? I have been shown that most of the rising generation will be swept off by death prior to the time of trouble. Some will live, but most children of believing and unbelieving parents will be spared the day of trial for God's people. *—Lt 51a, 1878*

The Saving Faith of Parents

I know that some questioned whether the little children of even believing parents would be saved, because they have had no test of character and all must be tested and their character determined by trial. The question is asked, "How can little children have this test and trial?" I answer that the faith of the believing parents covers the children, as when God sent his judgments upon the first-born of the Egyptians... Christ blessed the children brought to Him by the faithful mothers. He will do this now, if mothers will do their duty to their children and teach their children and educate them in obedience and submission. Then they will bear the test and will be obedient to the will of God, for parents stand in the place of God to their children. *—Ms 26, 1885*

We will See Our Children Again

Remember the prophecy, "Thus saith the Lord; A voice was heard in Ramah, lamentation, and bitter weeping; Rachel weeping for her children refused to be comforted. ... Thus saith the Lord, Refrain thy voice from weeping and thine eyes from tears: for thy work shall be rewarded, saith the Lord; and they shall come again from the land of the enemy. And there is hope in thine end, saith the Lord, that thy children shall come again to thine own border." Jeremiah 31:15-17.

This promise is yours. You may be comforted and trust in the Lord. The Lord has often instructed me that many little ones are to be laid away before the time of trouble. We shall see our children again. We shall meet them and know them in the heavenly courts. Put your trust in the Lord, and be not afraid. *—Lt 196, 1899*

218

B) Great Trouble Commences

New Scenes of Commotion

Let not an impure thought lodge in your mind one moment. Troublous times are before us. You may yet be tested—your faith tried. Commotions in the nation will bring such scenes in the world as we have heretofore been strangers to. —*Lt 7, 1868*

Awful Affliction and Distress

The people of God will then be plunged into those scenes of affliction and distress which prophets have described as the time of Jacob's trouble. The cries of the faithful, persecuted ones ascend to heaven. And as the blood of Abel cried from the ground, there are voices also crying to God from martyrs' graves, from the sepulchers of the sea, from mountain caverns, from convent vaults: "How long, O Lord, holy and true, dost thou not judge and avenge our blood on them that dwell on the earth?" —*5T, p. 451*

The Greatest Time of Trouble

We thank God that in your poverty you can call God your Father. Poverty is coming upon this world, and there will be a time of trouble such as never was since there was a nation. There will be wars and rumors of wars, and the faces of men will gather paleness. You may have to suffer distress, you may go hungry sometimes, but God will not forsake you in your suffering. He will test your faith. We are not to live to please ourselves. We are here to manifest Christ to the world, to represent Him and his power to mankind. —*Ms 37, 1894*

A Vision of Jacob's Time of Trouble

About four months since, I had a vision of events, all in the future. And I saw the time of trouble, such as never was—Jesus told me it was the time of Jacob's trouble, and that we should be delivered out of it by the voice of God. Just before we entered it, we all received the seal of the living God.

Then I saw the four Angels cease to hold the four winds. And I saw famine, pestilence and sword, nation rose against nation, and the whole world was in confusion. Then we cried to God for deliverance day and night till we began to hear the bells on Jesus' garment. —*DS, Mar. 14, 1846*

Satan's Wrath Reaches Its Peak

The apostle John in vision heard a loud voice in heaven exclaiming: "Woe to the inhabiters of the earth and of the sea! For the devil is come down unto you, having great wrath, because he knoweth that he hath but a short time." Revelation 12:12. Fearful are the scenes which call forth this exclamation from the heavenly voice. The wrath of Satan increases as his time grows short, and his work of deceit and destruction will reach its culmination in the time of trouble. — *GC, p. 623*

Every Case Has Been Decided

The day of God's vengeance is just before us. "And at that time shall Michael stand up, the great prince that standeth for the children of thy people; and there shall be a time of trouble, such as never was since there was a nation, even to that same time; and at that time thy people shall be delivered, every one that shall be found written in the book." Daniel 12:1.

When the time of trouble comes, every case will have been decided. No longer will probation linger; no longer will there be mercy for the impenitent. Our own course of action is determining whether we shall be destroyed with the workers of iniquity, or delivered with the people of God. The Lord is willing to help us. While his face "is against them that do evil," his eyes "are over the righteous, and his ears are open unto their prayer." — *SW, Mar. 24, 1908*

Earth Plunges into the Final Trouble

Jesus ceases his intercession in the sanctuary above... When He leaves the sanctuary, darkness covers the inhabitants of the earth. In that fearful time the righteous must live in the sight of a holy God without an intercessor. The restraint which has been upon the wicked is removed, and Satan has entire control of the finally impenitent. God's long-suffering has ended. The world has rejected his mercy, despised his love, and trampled upon his law.

The wicked have passed the boundary of their probation; the Spirit of God, persistently resisted, has been at last withdrawn. Unsheltered by divine grace, they have no protection from the wicked one. Satan will then plunge the inhabitants of the earth into one great, final trouble. As the angels of God cease to hold in check the fierce winds of human passion, all the elements of strife will be let loose. The whole world will be involved in ruin more terrible than that which came upon Jerusalem of old. — *GC, p. 614*

C) Flee to the Mountains

Forced into the Mountains
The time will come when Christ said that if you are on your housetop, don't you go to gathering up the things that are there; don't you go down below to gather things. Why? Because they are driven right into the mountains. You do not know what is coming before us. — *Ms 189, 1907*

God Helps His People Hide
The last great crisis is at hand. The time is near when God will say, "Come, my people, enter thou into thy chambers and shut thy doors; hide thyself as it were for a little moment, until the indignation be overpast. For, behold, the Lord cometh out of his place to punish the inhabitants of the earth for their iniquity; the earth also shall disclose her blood, and shall no more cover her slain." Isaiah 26:20, 21. — *Ms 61, 1900*

The Remnant Flee in Groups
As the decree issued by the various rulers of Christendom against commandment keepers shall withdraw the protection of government and abandon them to those who desire their destruction, the people of God will flee from the cities and villages and associate together in companies, dwelling in the most desolate and solitary places. Many will find refuge in the strongholds of the mountains. Like the Christians of the Piedmont valleys, they will make the high places of the earth their sanctuaries and will thank God for "the munitions of rocks." Isaiah 33:16. — *GC, p. 626*

Angels Guide Christians to Safety
I did not sleep much the night after the Sabbath; for during the night a very impressive scene passed before me. There seemed to be great confusion and the conflict of armies. A messenger from the Lord stood before me, and said, "Call your household. I will lead you; follow me." He led me down a dark passage, through a forest, then through the clefts of mountains, and said, "Here you are safe." There were others who had been led to this retreat. The heavenly messenger said, "The time of trouble has come as a thief in the night, as the Lord warned you it would come." I awoke at twelve o'clock, with such an impression on my mind as I shall never forget. — *Ms 178, 1905*

221

Mountain Clouds Provide Refuge

The scenery seems to resemble Colorado scenery... These white clouds are advancing, rolling first down the mountain sides and then rising higher and spreading over the snow-capped mountains. They appear like mountains of snow in the noon-day sun... Was it not such a cloud as this that was sometimes the refuge of God's people, that they might escape in its friendly shelter from the sight of their persecutors? —*Ms 29, 1885*

The Wicked Pursue the Remnant

I saw the saints leaving the cities and villages, and associating together in companies, and living in the most solitary places. Angels provided them food and water, while the wicked were suffering from hunger and thirst... As the saints left the cities and villages, they were pursued by the wicked, who sought to slay them. But the swords that were raised to kill God's people broke and fell as powerless as a straw. Angels of God shielded the saints. —*EW, p. 282*

Waldenses Fled to the Mountains

Behind the lofty bulwarks of the mountains,—in all ages the refuge of the persecuted and oppressed,—the Waldenses found a hiding-place. Here the lamp of truth was kept burning during the long night that descended upon Christendom. Here for a thousand years they maintained their ancient faith.

God had provided for his people a sanctuary of awful grandeur, befitting the mighty truths committed to their trust. To those faithful exiles the mountains were an emblem of the immutable righteousness of Jehovah. They pointed their children to the heights towering above them in unchanging majesty, and spoke to them of Him with whom there is no variableness nor shadow of turning, whose word is as enduring as the everlasting hills.

God had set fast the mountains, and girded them with strength; no arm but that of infinite power could move them out of their place. In like manner had he established his law, the foundation of his government in heaven and upon earth. The arm of man might reach his fellow-men and destroy their lives; but that arm could as readily uproot the mountains from their foundations, and hurl them into the sea, as it could change one precept of the law of Jehovah, or blot out one of his promises to those who do his will. In their fidelity to his law, God's servants should be as firm as the unchanging hills. —*4SP, pp. 70, 71*

Flee before Infuriated Mobs

Houses and lands will be of no use to the saints in the time of trouble, for they will then have to flee before infuriated mobs, and at that time their possessions cannot be disposed of to advance the cause of present truth.

—EW, p. 56

Rocky Hideouts are a Refuge

The mountain heights and rocky fastnesses have ever been the friendly refuge of God's people when oppressed and hunted by their enemies. For hundreds of years the Waldenses worshiped God amid the mountain solitudes, and there defied the armies of kings and emperors. On their rocky heights, in sight of their enemies, they sang the praise of Him who made the hills; and no opposing power could silence their hymns of lofty cheer:

> *For the strength of the hills we bless thee,*
> *Our God, our fathers' God!*
> *Thou hast made thy children mighty*
> *By the touch of the mountain sod.*
>
> *Thou hast fixed our ark of refuge*
> *Where the spoiler's foot ne'er trod;*
> *For the strength of the hills we bless thee,*
> *Our God, our fathers' God!* — ST, Feb. 2, 1882

Discussion Questions

1. What action does Jesus take that triggers a great time of trouble?

2. The young and the elderly will be laid to rest before the tribulation begins. What Bible verses give assurance that we will see them again?

3. What signs might indicate that it is time to flee to the mountains?

4. Should we leave for wilderness areas by ourselves or in small groups?

5. What can we learn from the Waldenses? During the time of trouble, which encouraging hymns would you like to sing from the mountaintops?

— 16 —

The Death Decree

"For if we live, we live to the Lord, and if we die, we die to the Lord. So then, whether we live or whether we die, we are the Lord's." — Romans 14:8

Daniel 3:14-29	Matt. 10:34	Luke 21:17-19	2 Cor. 4:11	2 Tim. 2:11, 12
Malachi 3:17	Luke 12:4, 5	Rom. 8:35-39	Phil. 1:21	Rev. 12:11; 13:15

A Law Threatening Death

The end of all things is at hand. The time of trouble is about to come upon the people of God. Then it is that the decree will go forth forbidding those who keep the Sabbath of the Lord to buy or sell, and threatening them with punishment, and even death, if they do not observe the first day of the week as the sabbath. — *RH, Nov. 19, 1908*

World Leaders Pass a Decree

I saw the leading men of the earth consulting together, and Satan and his angels busy around them. I saw a writing, copies of which were scattered in different parts of the land, giving orders that unless the saints should yield their peculiar faith, give up the Sabbath, and observe the first day of the week, the people were at liberty after a certain time to put them to death. — *EW, p. 282*

A Law to Disregard the Sabbath

I saw that God would in a wonderful manner preserve his people through the time of trouble. As Jesus poured out his soul in agony in the garden, they will earnestly cry and agonize with Him day and night for deliverance. The decree will go forth that they must disregard the Sabbath of the fourth commandment, and honor the first day, or lose their lives; but they will not yield, and trample under their feet the Sabbath of the Lord, and honor an institution of the Papacy. — *RH, May 27, 1862*

An Attempt at Annihilation

Satan will have full control of those who have rejected mercy. They will endeavor to destroy God's people; but as Noah was shut into the ark, so the righteous will be shielded by divine power. —*PP, p. 98*

Men Risk Freedom and Life

The time will come when men will not only forbid Sunday work, but they will try to force men to labor on the Sabbath, and to subscribe to Sunday observance or forfeit their freedom and their lives. But the time for this has not yet come. —*RH, Apr. 6, 1911*

The Plagues Enrage the Wicked

Plagues enraged the wicked against the righteous; they thought that we had brought the judgments of God upon them, and that if they could rid the earth of us, the plagues would then be stayed. A decree went forth to slay the saints, which caused them to cry day and night for deliverance. This was the time of Jacob's trouble. —*EW, p. 36*

Demons Threaten the Remnant

Satan and his evil angels exultingly told the angels who ministered to these suffering saints that they were all to be killed, so that there would not be left a true Christian upon the earth. I saw that the church of God was then pure. There was no danger of men with corrupt hearts coming into it; for the true Christian, who dared to declare his faith, was in danger of the rack, the stake, and every torture which Satan and his evil angels could invent or inspire in the mind of man. —*EW, p. 221*

One Night to Kill God's People

As the time appointed in the decree against God's people comes, the inhabitants of the earth unite to destroy the disturbers of their peace. In one night they determine to strike the decisive blow that shall forever silence the voice of the reprover. The waiting ones, in their solitary retreats, are still pleading for divine protection. In every quarter, companies of armed men, urged on by hosts of evil angels, are preparing for the work of death. With shouts of triumph, with jeers and imprecations, they are about to rush upon their prey. —*4SP, p. 452*

The Worst Crimes Occur in Darkness

"Then led they Jesus from Caiaphas unto the hall of judgment, and it was early." The night was the most appropriate hour for their works of darkness. In these religious zealots we have a sample of what humanity will do when they have the Word that lighted every man that cometh into the world, and work directly contrary to it, irrespective of the consequence, the future retribution upon their neighbors or themselves. "We have a law," they say, "and by that law, he ought to die." — *Ms 104, 1897*

Satan Works to Inspire the Wicked

Christ has said, "If they have persecuted Me, they will also persecute you." There is no greater evidence that Satan is working than that those who profess to be sanctified to God's service persecute their fellow beings because they do not believe the same doctrine that they themselves believe. These will rush with fury against God's people, stating as true that which they know to be untrue. Thus they show that they are inspired by him who is an accuser of the brethren, and a murderer of the saints of God. — *RH, Dec. 28, 1897*

Satan Wants to Blot Out Adventists

Satanic agencies have been moved from beneath, and they have inspired men to unite in a confederacy of evil, that they may perplex, harass, and cause the people of God great distress. The whole world is to be stirred with enmity against Seventh-day Adventists, because they will not yield homage to the papacy, by honoring Sunday, the institution of this anti-Christian power. It is the purpose of Satan to cause them to be blotted from the earth, in order that his supremacy of the world may not be disputed. — *RH, Aug. 22, 1893*

An Evil Plan to Kill Sabbathkeepers

Says the great deceiver: ... "We led the Romish Church to inflict imprisonment, torture, and death upon those who refused to yield to her decrees, and now that we are bringing the Protestant churches and the world into harmony with this right arm of our strength, we will finally have a law to exterminate all who will not submit to our authority. When death shall be made the penalty of violating our Sabbath, then many who are now ranked with commandment-keepers will come over to our side." — *4SP, pp. 337, 338*

226

Protestants Betray Adventists

I saw that the nominal churches and nominal Adventists, like Judas, would betray us to the Catholics, to obtain their influence to come against the saints. The saints will be an obscure people, but little known to the Catholics, but the church and nominal Adventists will know of our faith and customs, and will betray the saints and report them to the Catholics, as those who disregard the institution of the pope, that is they keep the Sabbath and disregard Sunday.

Then the Catholics bid the Protestants to go forward and issue a decree that all who will not observe the first day of the week instead of the seventh shall be slain, and the Catholics, whose numbers are large, will stand by the Protestants. The Catholics will give their power to the image of the beast and then Protestants will work as their mother worked before them to destroy the saints. But before their decrees bring forth or bear fruit, the saints will be delivered by the voice of God. —*Ms 15, 1850*

Satan Incites Men to Kill the Godly

"There shall be a time of trouble, such as never was since there was a nation even to that same time: and at that time thy people shall be delivered, every one that shall be found written in the book." Daniel 12:1. By this we see the importance of having our names written in the book of life. All whose names are registered there will be delivered from Satan's power, and Christ will command that their filthy garments be removed, and that they be clothed with his righteousness.

"And they shall be mine, saith the Lord of hosts, in that day when I make up my jewels; and I will spare them, as a man spareth his own son that serveth him." Malachi 3:17.

In the time of trouble, Satan stirs up the wicked, and they encircle the people of God to destroy them. But he does not know that "pardon" has been written opposite their names in the books of heaven. He does not know that the command has been given, "Take away the filthy garments" from them, clothe them with "change of raiment," and set "a fair miter" upon their heads. If we could only see the many dangers from which we are daily preserved by the holy angels, instead of complaining of our trials and misfortunes, we would talk continually of the mercies of God. —*RH, Nov. 19, 1908*

A War against the Remnant

The civil power is called to the aid of the Church in persecuting those who keep holy the seventh day. The Church and the world are united in trampling upon God's commandments, and those who obey these commandments they threaten with death. John declares, "The dragon was wroth with the woman, and went to make war with the remnant of her seed, which keep the commandments of God, and have the testimony of Jesus Christ." The decree goes forth that no man shall be allowed to buy or sell save he that has the mark or the number of the beast. — *RH, July 16, 1901*

Ahasuerus Passed a Similar Law

The world will lend to the church power to crush out the right of the people to worship God according to his Word. The decree which is to go forth against the people of God in the near future is in some respects similar to that issued by Ahasuerus against the Jews in the time of Esther. The Persian edict sprang from the malice of Haman against Mordecai. Not that Mordecai had done Haman harm, but he had refused to flatter his vanity by showing him the reverence which is due only to God.

The king's decision against the Jews was secured under false pretenses. Satan instigated this scheme in order to rid the earth of those who preserved a knowledge of the true God. But his plots were defeated by a counter-power that reigns among the children of men. Angels who excel in strength were commissioned to protect the people of God, and the plots of their adversaries returned upon their own heads.

History repeats itself. The same masterful mind that plotted against the faithful in ages past is now at work to gain control of the Protestant churches, that through them he may condemn and put to death all who will not worship the idol sabbath. We have not to battle with man, as it may appear. We wrestle not against flesh and blood, but against principalities, against powers, against the rulers of the darkness of this world, against spiritual wickedness in high places. But if the people of God will put their trust in Him, and by faith rely upon his power, the devices of Satan will be defeated in our time as signally as in the days of Mordecai. The decree is to go forth that all who will not receive the mark of the beast shall neither buy nor sell, and, finally, that they shall be put to death. — *ST, Nov. 8, 1899*

Jesus was Sentenced to Death

It is God's purpose that man shall stand before him upright and noble; and God will not be defeated by Satan. He sent his Son to this world to bear the death penalty of man's transgression, and to show man how to live a sinless life. There is no other way in which man can be saved. "Without me," Christ says, "ye can do nothing." Through him, and him alone, can the natural heart be changed, the affections transformed, the affections set flowing heavenward. Christ alone can give life to the soul dead in trespasses and sins.

— YI, Apr. 16, 1903

Be Faithful like the Three Hebrews

The three Hebrews declared to the whole nation of Babylon their faith in Him whom they worshiped. They relied on God. In the hour of their trial they remembered the promise, "When thou passest through the waters, I will be with thee; and through the rivers, they shall not overflow thee: when thou walkest through the fire, thou shalt not be burned; neither shall the flame kindle upon thee." Isaiah 43:2.

And in a marvelous manner their faith in the living Word had been honored in the sight of all. The tidings of their wonderful deliverance were carried to many countries by the representatives of the different nations that had been invited by Nebuchadnezzar to the dedication. Through the faithfulness of his children, God was glorified in all the earth.

Important are the lessons to be learned from the experience of the Hebrew youth on the plain of Dura. In this our day, many of God's servants, though innocent of wrongdoing, will be given over to suffer humiliation and abuse at the hands of those who, inspired by Satan, are filled with envy and religious bigotry. Especially will the wrath of man be aroused against those who hallow the Sabbath of the fourth commandment; and at last a universal decree will denounce these as deserving of death.

The season of distress before God's people will call for a faith that will not falter. His children must make it manifest that He is the only object of their worship, and that no consideration, not even that of life itself, can induce them to make the least concession to false worship. To the loyal heart the commands of sinful, finite men will sink into insignificance beside the word of the eternal God. Truth will be obeyed though the result be imprisonment or exile or death. *—PK, p. 512*

Global Eradication is Planned

When the protection of human laws shall be withdrawn from those who honor the law of God, there will be, in different lands, a simultaneous movement for their destruction. As the time appointed in the decree draws near, the people will conspire to root out the hated sect. It will be determined to strike in one night a decisive blow, which shall utterly silence the voice of dissent and reproof. — *GC, p. 635*

Rulers Say It is Better for a Few to Die

The forms of religion will be continued by a people from whom the Spirit of God has been finally withdrawn; and the satanic zeal with which the prince of evil will inspire them for the accomplishment of his malignant designs, will bear the semblance of zeal for God.

As the Sabbath has become the special point of controversy throughout Christendom, and religious and secular authorities have combined to enforce the observance of the Sunday, the persistent refusal of a small minority to yield to the popular demand will make them objects of universal execration.

It will be urged that the few who stand in opposition to an institution of the church and a law of the state ought not to be tolerated; that it is better for them to suffer than for whole nations to be thrown into confusion and lawlessness. The same argument many centuries ago was brought against Christ by the "rulers of the people." "It is expedient for us," said the wily Caiaphas, "that one man should die for the people, and that the whole nation perish not." John 11:50. This argument will appear conclusive; and a decree will finally be issued against those who hallow the Sabbath of the fourth commandment, denouncing them as deserving of the severest punishment and giving the people liberty, after a certain time, to put them to death.

Romanism in the Old World and apostate Protestantism in the New will pursue a similar course toward those who honor all the divine precepts. The people of God will then be plunged into those scenes of affliction and distress described by the prophet as the time of Jacob's trouble. "Thus saith the Lord: We have heard a voice of trembling, of fear, and not of peace... All faces are turned into paleness. Alas! For that day is great, so that none is like it: it is even the time of Jacob's trouble; but he shall be saved out of it." Jeremiah 30:5-7. — *GC, pp. 615, 616*

A Grim Proclamation is Made

An idol sabbath has been set up as the golden image was set up in the plains of Dura. And as Nebuchadnezzar, the king of Babylon, issued a decree that all who would not bow down and worship this image should be killed, so a proclamation will be made that all who will not reverence the Sunday institution will be punished with imprisonment and death. Thus the Sabbath of the Lord is trampled underfoot. But the Lord has declared, "Woe unto them that decree unrighteous decrees, and write grievousness which they have prescribed." Isaiah 10:1. — *Ms 7a, 1896*

A Law by the Highest Earthly Authority

"And at that time shall Michael stand up, the great Prince which standeth for the children of thy people: and there shall be a time of trouble, such as never was since there was a nation even to that same time: and at that time thy people shall be delivered, every one that shall be found written in the book."

When this time of trouble comes, every case is decided; there is no longer probation, no longer mercy for the impenitent. The seal of the living God is upon his people. This small remnant, unable to defend themselves in the deadly conflict with the powers of earth that are marshaled by the dragon host, make God their defense. The decree has been passed by the highest earthly authority that they shall worship the beast and receive his mark under pain of persecution and death. — *5T, p. 212*

Discussion Questions

1. When exactly do you think a universal death decree will be passed?

2. Why does Satan desire to destroy all of the Remnant?

3. What are some of the death decrees that were passed in Bible times?

4. Why might world rulers say it is better for a small group to suffer than the whole world to perish?

5. How can we spiritually get ready to someday face a death sentence?

— 17 —

Without a Mediator

"Alas! For that day is great, so that none is like it: it is even the time of Jacob's trouble, but he shall be saved out of it." — Jeremiah 30:7

| Gen. 32:24-28 | Jer. 30:5-7 | Micah 4:9, 10 | Mark 10:39 | 1 Cor. 10:13 |
| Isaiah 26:16-19 | Ezek. 14:20 | Zech. 3:1-5 | Luke 6:22, 23 | Rev. 2:10 |

Darkness before Deliverance

The darkest hour of the church's struggle with the powers of evil is that which immediately precedes the day of her final deliverance. But none who trust in God need fear; for "when the blast of the terrible ones is as a storm against the wall," God will be to his church "a refuge from the storm." Isaiah 25:4. In that day only the righteous are promised deliverance. — *PK, p. 725*

Sealed Christians Suffer Trials

The same angel who visited Sodom is sounding the note of warning, "Escape for thy life." The bottles of God's wrath cannot be poured out to destroy the wicked and their works until all the people of God have been judged, and the cases of the living as well as the dead are decided.

And even after the saints are sealed with the seal of the living God, his elect will have trials individually. Personal afflictions will come; but the furnace is closely watched by an eye that will not suffer the gold to be consumed. The indelible mark of God is upon them. God can plead that his own name is written there. The Lord has shut them in. Their destination is inscribed—"God, New Jerusalem." They are God's property, his possession.

Will this seal be put upon the impure in mind, the fornicator, the adulterer, the man who covets his neighbor's wife?... Holiness must be inwrought in our character. — *TM, p. 446*

"Why Hast Thou Forsaken Me?"

I saw that all minds were intensely looking and stretching their thoughts on the impending crisis before them. The sins of Israel must go to judgment beforehand. Every sin must be confessed at the sanctuary, then the work will move. It must be done now. The remnant in the time of trouble will cry, "My God! My God! Why hast thou forsaken me?" —*Ms 1, 1852*

Every Soul to Stand Alone

The "time of trouble, such as never was," is soon to open upon us; and we shall need an experience which we do not now possess and which many are too indolent to obtain. It is often the case that trouble is greater in anticipation than in reality; but this is not true of the crisis before us. The most vivid presentation cannot reach the magnitude of the ordeal. In that time of trial, every soul must stand for himself before God. "Though Noah, Daniel, and Job" were in the land, "as I live, saith the Lord God, they shall deliver neither son nor daughter; they shall but deliver their own souls by their righteousness." Ezekiel 14:20. Now, while our great High Priest is making the atonement for us, we should seek to become perfect in Christ. —*GC, p. 622*

The Oppressor Triumphs for a Time

With pity and compassion, with tender yearning, the Lord is looking upon his tempted and tried people. For a time the oppressors will permitted to triumph over those who know God's holy commandments. All are given the same opportunity that was granted to the first great rebel to demonstrate the spirit that moves them to action. It is God's purpose that everyone shall be tested and proved to see whether he will be loyal or disloyal to the laws which govern the kingdom of heaven.

To the last, God permits Satan to reveal his character as a liar, an accuser, and a murderer. Thus the final triumph of his people is made more marked, more glorious, more full and complete. The words of the prophet will then be fulfilled, "The day of vengeance is in my heart, and the year of my redeemed is come." Isaiah 63:4. The song of God's people will be, "The Lord reigneth; let the people tremble: He sitteth between the cherubims, let the earth be moved. The Lord is great in Zion; He is high above his people." Psalm 99:1, 2. —*Lt 5, 1883*

The Suffering will be Mental

I saw that a time of trouble was before us, when stern necessity will compel the people of God to live on bread and water; but I saw that God did not require his people to live so now... But in the time of trouble none will labor with their hands. Their sufferings will be mental, and God will provide food for them. —*Ms 2, 1858*

Satan Appears to be Triumphant

It will appear as though Satan is triumphant, and that truth is overborne with falsehood and error; because the people over whom God has spread his shield, and the country which has been an asylum to the conscience-oppressed lovers of God and the defenders of his truth, are placed in desperate jeopardy through its oppressive legislation. —*RH, Dec. 11, 1888*

Characters Must be Spotless

Says the prophet: "Who may abide the day of his coming? and who shall stand when He appeareth? for He is like a refiner's fire, and like fullers' soap: and He shall sit as a refiner and purifier of silver: and He shall purify the sons of Levi, and purge them as gold and silver, that they may offer unto the Lord an offering in righteousness." Malachi 3:2, 3.

Those who are living upon the earth when the intercession of Christ shall cease in the sanctuary above are to stand in the sight of a holy God without a mediator. Their robes must be spotless, their characters must be purified from sin by the blood of sprinkling. Through the grace of God and their own diligent effort they must be conquerors in the battle with evil. While the investigative judgment is going forward in heaven, while the sins of penitent believers are being removed from the sanctuary, there is to be a special work of purification, of putting away of sin, among God's people upon earth. This work is more clearly presented in the messages of Revelation 14.

When this work shall have been accomplished, the followers of Christ will be ready for his appearing. "Then shall the offering of Judah and Jerusalem be pleasant unto the Lord, as in the days of old, and as in former years." Malachi 3:4. Then the church which our Lord at his coming is to receive to Himself will be a "glorious church, not having spot, or wrinkle, or any such thing." Ephesians 5:27. —*GC, p. 425*

The Godly Cry for Deliverance

When Christ shall cease his work as mediator in man's behalf, then this time of trouble will begin. Then the case of every soul will have been decided, and there will be no atoning blood to cleanse from sin. When Jesus leaves his position as man's intercessor before God, the solemn announcement is made, "He that is unjust, let him be unjust still: and he which is filthy, let him be filthy still: and he that is righteous, let him be righteous still: and he that is holy, let him be holy still." Revelation 22:11.

Then the restraining Spirit of God is withdrawn from the earth. As Jacob was threatened with death by his angry brother, so the people of God will be in peril from the wicked who are seeking to destroy them. And as the patriarch wrestled all night for deliverance from the hand of Esau, so the righteous will cry to God day and night for deliverance from the enemies that surround them. — *PP, p. 201*

The Remnant Must be Baptized

Said the angel, "Look ye!" My attention was turned to the wicked, or unbelievers. They were all astir. The zeal and power with the people of God had aroused and enraged them. Confusion, confusion, was on every side. I saw measures taken against the company who had the light and power of God. Darkness thickened around them; yet they stood firm, approved of God, and trusting in Him.

I saw them perplexed; next I heard them crying unto God earnestly. Day and night their cry ceased not: "Thy will, O God, be done! If it can glorify thy name, make a way of escape for thy people! Deliver us from the heathen around about us! They have appointed us unto death; but thine arm can bring salvation."

These are all the words which I can bring to mind. All seemed to have a deep sense of their unworthiness and manifested entire submission to the will of God; yet, like Jacob, everyone, without an exception, was earnestly pleading and wrestling for deliverance.

Soon after they had commenced their earnest cry, the angels, in sympathy, desired to go to their deliverance. But a tall, commanding angel suffered them not. He said, "The will of God is not yet fulfilled. They must drink of the cup. They must be baptized with the baptism." — *EW, p. 272*

Everyone is Individually Tested

We must seek to separate sin from us, relying upon the merits of the blood of Christ; and then in the day of affliction, when the enemy presses us, we shall walk among the angels. They will be like a wall of fire about us; and we shall one day walk with them in the city of God. In the day of fierce trial Jesus will say, "Come, my people, enter thou into thy chambers, and shut thy doors about thee: hide thyself as it were for a little moment, until the indignation be overpast."

What are the chambers in which they are to hide? They are the protection of Christ and holy angels. The people of God are not at this time all in one place. They are in different companies, and in all parts of the earth; and they will be tried singly, not in groups. Everyone must stand the test for himself.

—RH, Nov. 19, 1908

Christ's Followers Feel Soul Anguish

The earnest prayers of this faithful few will not be in vain. When the Lord comes forth as an avenger, He will also come as a protector of all those who have preserved the faith in its purity and kept themselves unspotted from the world. It is at this time that God has promised to avenge his own elect which cry day and night unto Him, though He bear long with them...

In the time when his wrath shall go forth in judgments, these humble, devoted followers of Christ will be distinguished from the rest of the world by their soul anguish, which is expressed in lamentation and weeping, reproofs and warnings. While others try to throw a cloak over the existing evil, and excuse the great wickedness everywhere prevalent, those who have a zeal for God's honor and a love for souls will not hold their peace to obtain favor of any. Their righteous souls are vexed day by day with the unholy works and conversation of the unrighteous.

They are powerless to stop the rushing torrent of iniquity, and hence they are filled with grief and alarm. They mourn before God to see religion despised in the very homes of those who have had great light. They lament and afflict their souls because pride, avarice, selfishness, and deception of almost every kind are in the church. The Spirit of God, which prompts to reproof, is trampled underfoot, while the servants of Satan triumph. God is dishonored, the truth made of none effect. *—5T, p. 210*

Separated and Scattered

The time is coming when we shall be separated and scattered, and each one of us will have to stand without the privilege of communion with those of like precious faith; and how can you stand unless God is by your side, and you know that He is leading and guiding you? Whenever we come to investigate Bible truth, the Master of assemblies is with us. The Lord does not leave the ship one moment to be steered by ignorant pilots. We may receive our orders from the Captain of our salvation. — *RH, Mar. 25, 1890*

The Wicked Mock the Remnant

Friday night several heard my voice exclaiming, "Look, look!" Whether I was dreaming or in vision, I cannot tell. I slept alone. The time of trouble was upon us. I saw our people in great distress, weeping and praying, pleading the sure promises of God, while the wicked were all around us, mocking us and threatening to destroy us. They ridiculed our feebleness, they mocked at the smallness of our numbers, and taunted us with words calculated to cut deep. They charged us with taking an independent position from all the rest of the world. They had cut off our resources so that we could not buy or sell, and they referred to our abject poverty and stricken condition.

They could not see how we could live without the world. We were dependent on the world, and we must concede to the customs, practices, and laws of the world, or go out of it. If we were the only people in the world whom the Lord favored, the appearances were awfully against us. They declared that they had the truth, that miracles were among them; that angels from heaven talked with them and walked with them, that great power and signs and wonders were performed among them, and that this was the temporal millennium they had been expecting so long.

The whole world was converted and in harmony with the Sunday law, and this little feeble people stood out in defiance of the laws of the land and the law of God, and claimed to be the only ones right on the earth.

They declared, "The angels from heaven have spoken to us," Referring to those whom Satan personated that had died and they claimed had gone to heaven. "You will bear the testimony of the heavenly messengers." They sneered, they mocked, they derided and abused the sorrowing ones. There was much more but I have not time to write it. — *Lt 6, 1884*

Those with the Seal are Tested

Those who bear the seal of the living God will be tested; for we read: "The dragon was wroth with the woman, and went to make war with the remnant of her seed, which keep the commandments of God, and have the testimony of Jesus Christ." —*Lt 47, 1902*

Christians are Cruelly Imprisoned

Many of all nations and of all classes, high and low, rich and poor, black and white, will be cast into the most unjust and cruel bondage. The beloved of God pass weary days, bound in chains, shut in by prison bars, sentenced to be slain, some apparently left to die of starvation in dark and loathsome dungeons. No human ear is open to hear their moans; no human hand is ready to lend them help.

Will the Lord forget his people in this trying hour? Did He forget faithful Noah when judgments were visited upon the antediluvian world? Did He forget Lot when the fire came down from heaven to consume the cities of the plain? Did He forget Joseph surrounded by idolaters in Egypt? Did He forget Elijah when the oath of Jezebel threatened him with the fate of the prophets of Baal? Did He forget Jeremiah in the dark and dismal pit of his prison house? Did He forget the three worthies in the fiery furnace? Or Daniel in the den of lions?

"Zion said, the Lord hath forsaken me, and my Lord hath forgotten me. Can a woman forget her sucking child, that she should not have compassion on the son of her womb? Yea, they may forget, yet will I not forget thee. Behold, I have graven thee upon the palms of my hands." Isaiah 49:14-16. The Lord of hosts has said: "He that toucheth you toucheth the apple of his eye." Zechariah 2:8.

Though enemies may thrust them into prison, yet dungeon walls cannot cut off the communication between their souls and Christ. One who sees their every weakness, who is acquainted with every trial, is above all earthly powers; and angels will come to them in lonely cells, bringing light and peace from heaven. The prison will be as a palace; for the rich in faith dwell there, and the gloomy walls will be lighted up with heavenly light as when Paul and Silas prayed and sang praises at midnight in the Philippian dungeon.

— *GC, pp. 626, 627*

God's Servants are Greatly Tested

In times of proving and trial, in the day of trouble such as never was, it will be revealed who have built their characters from material that will stand the test. God's true workmen will be forced to speak the truth and unmask hypocrisy and deception in defending every portion of the Word of God. Accusation upon accusation from men of high position will come against those who would be true to God, and they will be compelled to stand in defense of the truth.

But the servants of the Lord will be men of opportunity, of energy and tact, and will be ready to promote the interests of truth under every circumstance. They will not be selfish, self-important, self-sufficient persons; they will be men who have the mind of Christ. They will be kind, affectionate, loving, prompt, tender, yet resolute. They will be God-fearing men, and in the face of opposition they will move forward, firm and steadfast, to defend Bible truth. Such men will press the triumphs of the cross of Christ to the very end of the conflict. They will boldly, and yet in the Spirit of Christ, confront the agents of Satan who will seek to suppress religious liberty, and they will not give place to them for an hour.

There will be those, who, after a feeble resistance, will yield one point of truth after another. The reason they will do this is that they have never valued truth as they should...

But those who stand firm to the truth will answer those who demand their surrender to the traditions of men and their compliance with the custom of the majority, that they owe allegiance to a higher authority than that of the State. They will declare that they cannot set aside the Sabbath of the great Creator for a man-made institution. They will declare that as partakers of the divine nature, they are placed in a position where the ordinances of men, when conflicting with the commands of God, are of no force nor value.

Those who are empowered with authority will say to them as they said to Paul, "Thou art beside thyself;" and when persuasion and entreaty are in vain, heavier pressure will be brought to bear, and the steadfastness of Christ's followers will be tested to the uttermost. Every conceivable device that men and demons can invent will be brought to bear against them to overcome them; but those who have learned how to cling to God will not abate one jot or tittle of truth. —*RH, Oct. 23, 1894*

God is the Source of Strength

When the Lord sees his disciples deficient in spiritual power, day by day losing ground, day by day wandering farther and farther from the Source of strength, He sends them affliction and adversity. Disappointed hopes cause them to stop and think, and there come to them repentance, and a desire to draw near to God. And as they return to Him, He draws near to them, saying, "Let him take hold of my strength, that he may make peace with Me, and he shall make peace with Me." He receives the repentant sinner with loving assurances of pardon. There is no power in repentance to change the life.

But when the helpless soul casts itself on Christ, there comes transformation of character. The Saviour declares, "A new heart also will I give you, and a new spirit will I put within you." God often brings men to a crisis to show them their weakness, and to point them to the Source of strength. If they will pray, and watch unto prayer, fighting bravely, their weak points will become their strong points. Jacob's experience contains many valuable lessons for us.

All night Jacob wrestled with the angel. Finally the strong wrestler was weakened by a touch on his thigh. He was now disabled, and suffering the keenest pain, but he would not lose his hold. All penitent and broken, he clung to the angel; "he wept, and made supplication," pleading for a blessing. He must have the assurance that his sin was pardoned. His determination grew stronger, his faith more earnest and persevering, until the very last.

The angel tried to release himself; he urged, "Let me go; for the day breaketh," but Jacob answered, "I will not let thee go, except thou bless me." Had this been a boastful, presumptuous confidence, Jacob would have been instantly destroyed; but his was the assurance of one who confesses his own unworthiness, yet trusts to the faithfulness of a covenant-keeping God.

Jacob "had power over the angel, and prevailed." Through humiliation, repentance, and self-surrender, this sinful, erring mortal prevailed with the Majesty of heaven. He had fastened his trembling grasp on the promises of God, and the heart of infinite Love could not turn away the sinner's plea.

As an evidence that Jacob had been forgiven, his name was changed from one that was a reminder of his sin to one that commemorated his victory. "Thy name," said the angel, "shall be no more Jacob, but Israel; for as a prince hast thou power with God, and with men, and hast prevailed." —*Ms 2, 1903*

The Wicked Pursue the Remnant

I saw a writing, and copies of it scattered in different parts of the land, giving orders, that unless the saints should yield their peculiar faith, give up the Sabbath, and observe the first day, they were at liberty, after such a time, to put them to death.

But in this time the saints were calm and composed, trusting in God, and leaning upon his promise, that a way of escape would be made for them. In some places, before the time for the writing to be executed, the wicked rushed upon the saints to slay them; but angels in the form of men of war fought for them. Satan wished to have the privilege of destroying the saints of the Most High; but Jesus bade his angels watch over them, for God would be honored by making a covenant with those who had kept his law in the sight of the heathen round about them; and Jesus would be honored by translating the faithful, waiting ones, who had so long expected him, without their seeing death.

Soon I saw the saints suffering great mental anguish. They seemed to be surrounded with the wicked inhabitants of earth. Every appearance was against them. Some began to fear that God had left them at last to perish by the hand of the wicked. But if their eyes could have been opened, they would have seen themselves surrounded by angels of God. Next came the multitude of the angry wicked, and next a mass of evil angels, hurrying on the wicked to slay the saints.

But as they would attempt to approach them, they would first have to pass this company of mighty, holy angels, which was impossible. The angels of God were causing them to recede, and also causing the evil angels who were pressing around them, to fall back. It was an hour of terrible, fearful agony to the saints. They cried day and night unto God for deliverance. To outward appearance, there was no possibility of their escape.

The wicked had already commenced their triumphing, and were crying out, "Why doesn't your God deliver you out of our hands? Why don't you go up, and save your lives?" The saints heeded them not. They were wrestling with God like Jacob. The angels longed to deliver them; but they must wait a little longer, and drink of the cup, and be baptized with the baptism. The angels, faithful to their trust, kept their watch. The time had about come when God was to manifest his mighty power, and gloriously deliver them.

God would not suffer his name to be reproached among the heathen. For his name's glory he would deliver every one of those who had patiently waited for him, and whose names were written in the book.

I was pointed back to faithful Noah. The rain descended, the floods came, Noah, and his family had entered the ark, and God shut them in. Noah had faithfully warned the inhabitants of the old world, while they had mocked and derided him. And as the waters descended upon the earth, and as one after another were being drowned, they beheld that ark that they had made so much sport of, riding safely upon the waters, preserving the faithful Noah and his family.

So I saw that the people of God, who had warned the world of his coming wrath, would be delivered. They had faithfully warned the inhabitants of the earth, and God would not suffer the wicked to destroy those who were expecting translation, and who would not bow to the decree of the beast, or receive his mark. I saw that if the wicked were permitted to slay the saints, Satan and all his evil host, and all who hate God, would be gratified.

And oh, what a time of triumph it would be for his Satanic majesty, to have power, in the last closing struggle, over those who had so long waited to behold Him whom they loved. Those who have mocked at the idea of the saints going up, will witness the care of God for his people, and their glorious deliverance. — *1SG, pp. 201-203*

The Vision of Joshua and the Angel

Zechariah's vision of Joshua and the Angel applies with peculiar force to the experience of God's people in the closing up of the great day of atonement. The remnant church will be brought into great trial and distress.

Those who keep the commandments of God and the faith of Jesus will feel the ire of the dragon and his hosts. Satan numbers the world as his subjects, he has gained control of the apostate churches; but here is a little company that are resisting his supremacy. If he could blot them from the earth, his triumph would be complete. As he influenced the heathen nations to destroy Israel, so in the near future he will stir up the wicked powers of earth to destroy the people of God.

All will be required to render obedience to human edicts in violation of the divine law. Those who will be true to God and to duty will be menaced, denounced, and proscribed. They will "be betrayed both by parents, and brethren, and kinsfolks, and friends." Their only hope is in the mercy of God; their only defense will be prayer.

As Joshua was pleading before the Angel, so the remnant church, with brokenness of heart and earnest faith, will plead for pardon and deliverance through Jesus their Advocate. They are fully conscious of the sinfulness of their lives, they see their weakness and unworthiness, and as they look upon themselves they are ready to despair. The tempter stands by to accuse them, as he stood by to resist Joshua. He points to their filthy garments, their defective characters. He presents their weakness and folly, their sins of ingratitude, their unlikeness to Christ, which has dishonored their Redeemer.

He endeavors to affright the soul with the thought that their case is hopeless, that the stain of their defilement will never be washed away. He hopes to so destroy their faith that they will yield to his temptations, turn from their allegiance to God, and receive the mark of the beast.

Satan urges before God his accusations against them, declaring that they have by their sins forfeited the divine protection, and claiming the right to destroy them as transgressors. He pronounces them just as deserving as himself of exclusion from the favor of God. "Are these," he says, "the people who are to take my place in heaven and the place of the angels who united with me? While they profess to obey the law of God, have they kept its precepts? Have they not been lovers of self more than of God? Have they not placed their own interests above his service? Have they not loved the things of the world? Look at the sins which have marked their lives. Behold their selfishness, their malice, their hatred toward one another."

The people of God have been in many respects very faulty. Satan has an accurate knowledge of the sins which he has tempted them to commit, and he presents these in the most exaggerated light, declaring: "Will God banish me and my angels from his presence, and yet reward those who have been guilty of the same sins? Thou canst not do this, O Lord, in justice. Thy throne will not stand in righteousness and judgment. Justice demands that sentence be pronounced against them."

But while the followers of Christ have sinned, they have not given themselves to the control of evil. They have put away their sins, and have

243

sought the Lord in humility and contrition, and the divine Advocate pleads in their behalf. He who has been most abused by their ingratitude, who knows their sin, and also their repentance, declares: "The Lord rebuke thee, O Satan. I gave my life for these souls. They are graven upon the palms of my hands."

The assaults of Satan are strong, his delusions are terrible; but the Lord's eye is upon his people. Their affliction is great, the flames of the furnace seem about to consume them; but Jesus will bring them forth as gold tried in the fire. Their earthliness must be removed that the image of Christ may be perfectly reflected; unbelief must be overcome; faith, hope, and patience are to be developed.

The people of God are sighing and crying for the abominations done in the land. With tears they warn the wicked of their danger in trampling upon the divine law, and with unutterable sorrow they humble themselves before the Lord on account of their own transgressions. The wicked mock their sorrow, ridicule their solemn appeals, and sneer at what they term their weakness.

But the anguish and humiliation of God's people is unmistakable evidence that they are regaining the strength and nobility of character lost in consequence of sin. It is because they are drawing nearer to Christ, and their eyes are fixed upon his perfect purity, that they so clearly discern the exceeding sinfulness of sin. Their contrition and self-abasement are infinitely more acceptable in the sight of God than is the self-sufficient, haughty spirit of those who see no cause to lament, who scorn the humility of Christ, and who claim perfection while transgressing God's holy law. Meekness and lowliness of heart are the conditions for strength and victory.

The crown of glory awaits those who bow at the foot of the cross. Blessed are these mourners, for they shall be comforted. The faithful, praying ones are, as it were, shut in with God. They themselves know not how securely they are shielded. Urged on by Satan, the rulers of this world are seeking to destroy them; but could their eyes be opened, as were the eyes of Elisha's servant at Dothan, they would see the angels of God encamped about them, by their brightness and glory holding in check the hosts of darkness.

—5T, pp. 472-475

The Time of Jacob's Trouble

Jacob and Esau represent two classes. Jacob, the righteous; and Esau, the wicked. Jacob's night of wrestling and anguish represents the time of trouble through which the people of God must pass just prior to the Second Coming of Christ. Jeremiah refers to this time: "Wherefore do I see every man with his hands on his loins, as a woman in travail, and all faces are turned into paleness? Alas! for that day is great so that none is like it: it is even the time of Jacob's trouble; but he shall be saved out of it."

Daniel, in prophetic vision looking down to this point, says: "And at that time shall Michael stand up, the great prince which standeth for the children of thy people; and there shall be a time of trouble such as never was since there was a nation even to that same time; and at that time thy people shall be delivered, every one that shall be found written in the book." ...

In his distress, Jacob laid hold of the angel, and held him and wrestled with him all night. So also will the righteous, in the time of their trouble wrestle with God in prayer. Jacob prayed all night for deliverance from the hand of Esau. The righteous in their mental anguish will cry to God day and night for deliverance from the hands of the wicked who surround them. Jacob confessed his unworthiness: "I am not worthy of the least of all the mercies and of all the truth which thou hast showed unto thy servant." The righteous will have a deep sense of their shortcomings, and with many tears will acknowledge their utter unworthiness, and, like Jacob, will plead the promises of God through Christ, made to just such dependent, helpless, repenting sinners.

Jacob took firm hold of the angel and would not let him go. As he made supplication with tears, the angel reminded him of his past wrongs, and endeavored to escape from him, to test and prove him. So will the righteous in the day of their anguish, be tested, proved, and tried, to manifest their strength of faith, their perseverance, and unshaken confidence in the power of God to deliver them.

Jacob would not be turned away. He knew that God was merciful, and he appealed to his mercy. He pointed back to his past sorrow for, and repentance of, his wrongs, and urged his petition for deliverance from the hand of Esau. Thus his importuning continued all night. As he reviewed his past wrongs, he was driven almost to despair. But he knew that he must have help from

God or perish. He held the angel fast, and urged his petition with agonizing, earnest cries, until he prevailed. Thus will it be with the righteous. As they review the events of their past lives, their hopes will almost sink. But as they realize that it is a case of life or death, they will earnestly cry unto God, and appeal to Him in regard to their past sorrow for, and humble repentance of, their many sins, and then will refer to his promise: "Let him take hold of my strength, that he may make peace with Me, and he shall make peace with Me."

Thus will their earnest petitions be offered to God day and night. God would not have heard the prayer of Jacob, and mercifully saved his life, if he had not previously repented of his wrongs in obtaining the blessing by fraud. Every effort was put forward by Satan and his host to discourage Jacob and break his hold upon God by forcing upon him a sense of the sin of his falsehood and deception. But Jacob was not left alone; the Captain of the Lord's host, attended by an army of angels, was close beside the depressed, fear-stricken man, that he might not perish.

The righteous, like Jacob, will manifest unyielding faith and earnest determination, which will take no denial. They will feel their unworthiness, but will have no concealed wrongs to reveal. If they had sins, unconfessed and unrepented of, to appear then before them, while tortured with fear and anguish, they would be overwhelmed. Despair would cut off their earnest faith, and they could not have confidence to plead with God thus earnestly for deliverance, their precious moments would be spent in confessing hidden sins, and bewailing their hopeless condition.

In these days of peril those who have been unfaithful in their duties in life, and whose mistakes and sins of neglect are registered against them in the book in heaven, unrepented of and unforgiven, will be overcome by Satan. Every one is to be tested and severely tried. Satan will exert all his energies, and call to his aid his evil host, who will exercise all their experience, artifice, and cunning, to deceive souls and wrest them from the hands of Jesus Christ. He makes them believe they may be unfaithful in the minor duties of life, and God will not see, God will not notice; but that Being who numbers the hairs of our head, and marks the fall of the little sparrow, notices every deviation from truth, every departure from honor and integrity in both secular and religious things. These errors and sins corrupt the man, and disqualify him for the society of heavenly angels. By his defiled character he has placed himself under the flag of Satan. The archdeceiver has power over this class.

The more exalted their profession, the more honorable the position they have held, the more grievous their course in the sight of God, the more sure the triumph of Satan. These will have no shelter in the time of Jacob's trouble. Their sins will then appear of such magnitude that they will have no confidence to pray, no heart to wrestle as did Jacob. On the other hand, those who have been of like passion, erring and sinful in their lives, but who have repented of their sins, and in genuine sorrow confessed them, will have pardon written against their names in the heavenly records. They will be hid in the day of the Lord's anger. Satan will attack this class, but like Jacob they have taken hold of the strength of God, and true to his character He is at peace with them, and sends angels to comfort and bless and sustain them in their time of peril. The time of Jacob's trouble will test every one, and distinguish the genuine Christian from the one who is so only in name.

Those professed believers who come up to the time of trouble unprepared, will, in their despair, confess their sins before the world in words of burning anguish, while the wicked exult over their distress. The case of all such is hopeless. When Christ stands up, and leaves the most holy place, the time of trouble commences, the case of every soul is decided, and there will be no atoning blood to cleanse from sin and pollution. As Jesus leaves the most holy, He speaks in tones of decision and kingly authority: "He that is unjust, let him be unjust still; and he which is filthy, let him be filthy still; and he that is righteous, let him be righteous still; and he that is holy, let him be holy still. And, behold, I come quickly; and my reward is with Me, to give every man according as his work shall be." Rev. 22:11, 12.

Those who have delayed a preparation for the day of God, cannot obtain it in the time of trouble, or at any future period. The righteous will not cease their earnest, agonizing cries for deliverance. They cannot bring to mind any particular sins; but in their whole life they can see little good. Their sins have gone beforehand to judgment, and pardon has been written. Their sins have been borne away into the land of forgetfulness, and they can not bring them to remembrance. Certain destruction threatens them, and, like Jacob, they will not suffer their faith to grow weak because their prayers are not immediately answered. Though suffering the pangs of hunger, they will not cease their intercessions. They lay hold of the strength of God, as Jacob laid hold of the angel; and the language of their soul is, "I will not let thee go except thou bless me."

That season of distress and anguish will require an effort of earnestness and determined faith that can endure delay and hunger, and will not fail under weakness, though severely tried. The period of probation is the time granted to all to prepare for the day of God. If any neglect the preparation, and heed not the faithful warnings given, they will be without excuse. Jacob's course in wrestling with the angel, should be an example for Christians. Jacob prevailed because he was persevering and determined. All who desire the blessing of God, as did Jacob, and who will lay hold of the promises as he did, and be as earnest and persevering as he was, will succeed as he succeeded.

The reason there is so little exercise of true faith, and so little of the weight of truth resting upon many professed believers, is they are indolent in spiritual things. They are unwilling to make exertions, to deny self, to agonize before God, to pray long and earnestly for the blessing, and therefore they do not obtain it. That faith which will live through the time of trouble must be developed now. Those who do not make strong efforts now to exercise persevering faith, will be unable to stand in the day of trouble.

At the transfiguration, Jesus was glorified by his Father. From his lips came these words: "Now is the Son of man glorified, and God is glorified in Him." Before his betrayal and crucifixion He was strengthened for his last dreadful sufferings. As the members of Christ's body approach the period of their final conflict they will grow up into Him, and will possess symmetrical characters. As the message of the third angel swells to a loud cry, great power and glory will attend the closing work. It is the latter rain, which revives and strengthens the people of God to pass through the time of Jacob's trouble referred to by the prophets. The glory of that light which attends the third angel will be reflected upon them. God will preserve his people through that time of peril.

By self-surrender and confiding faith Jacob gained what he had failed to gain by conflict in his own strength. God would here fully make known to his servant that it was divine power and grace alone that could give him the life and peace he so much craved. This lesson is for all time. Those who live in the last days must pass through an experience similar to that of Jacob. Foes will be all around them, ready to condemn and destroy. Alarm and despair will seize them, for it appears to them as to Jacob in his distress, that God Himself has become an avenging enemy.

It is the design of God to arouse the dormant energies of his people to look out of and away from self to One who can bring help and salvation, that the promises given for just such a time may be seen in their preciousness, and relied upon with unwavering trust. Here faith is proved.

Deep anguish of soul will be felt by the people of God, yet their sufferings cannot be compared with the agony endured by our adorable Redeemer in the garden of Gethsemane. He was bearing the weight of our sins; we endure anguish on our own account. Wrestling with God—how few know what it is! To wrestle with God is to have the soul drawn out with intensity of desire until every power is on the stretch, while waves of despair that no language can express sweep over the soul; and yet the suppliant will not yield, but clings with deathlike tenacity to the promise.

Jacob specified no particular thing for the Lord to bestow upon him; he sought only a blessing; he knew that the Lord would give him a blessing appropriate to meet the necessities of the case at that time. God blessed him then and there; and on the field of conflict he was made a prince among men. Thus will it be with the agonized ones who prevail with God in the time of Jacob's trouble. — *ST, Nov. 27, 1879*

Discussion Questions

1. Even though Jesus has left the sanctuary, will divine forces still protect God's people during the great tribulation?

2. Can godly Christians help their friends to survive the time of trouble?

3. Why does Satan accuse the Remnant before God?

4. What can we learn from Jacob's experience of wrestling the angel?

5. Why will the worst suffering at the end of time be mental instead of physical? How can we begin to prepare for this harrowing experience?

— 18 —

Aided by Angels

"The angel of the Lord encampeth round about them that fear Him, and delivereth them."

— Psalm 34:7

1 Samuel 2:9	Ps. 37:39, 40	Ps. 121:5-7	Isa. 49:14-16	Zech. 12:8
Ps. 23:1-6	Ps. 50:14, 15	Isa. 25:1-9	Nahum 1:7	Luke 18:7, 8
Ps. 37:18, 19	Ps. 91:3-11	Isa. 40:31; 43:2	Zech. 2:8	Rev. 3:9, 10

The Lord will Intervene

When the defiance of God's law is almost universal, when his people are oppressed and afflicted by their fellow men, the Lord will interpose.

— COL, p. 178

Angels Support the Godly

What should we do in the hour that tries the soul without a Saviour? Ministering angels are around about them, giving them to drink of the water of life to refresh their souls in the closing scenes of life. *— Lt 78, 1890*

The Righteous are Preserved

In the time of trouble just before the coming of Christ, the righteous will be preserved through the ministration of heavenly angels; but there will be no security for the transgressor of God's law. Angels cannot then protect those who are disregarding one of the divine precepts. *— PP, p. 256*

Angels Wait for a Call to Help

The dangers coming upon us are continually increasing. It is high time that we put on the whole armor of God and worked to keep Satan from gaining any further advantage. Angels of God, that excel in strength, are waiting for us to call them to our aid, that our faith may not be eclipsed by the fierceness of the conflict. *— Lt 263, 1904*

God Covers His People
I saw a covering that God was drawing over his people to protect them in the time of trouble, and every soul that was decided on the truth was to be covered with this covering of Almighty God. Satan knew this and was also at work in mighty power. —*Ms 1, 1849*

Strengthening Power from God
The time of trouble is just before us; and then stern necessity will require the people of God to deny self, and to eat merely enough to sustain life; but God will prepare us for that time. In that fearful hour our necessity will be God's opportunity to impart his strengthening power, and to sustain his people.
—*1T, p. 206*

Strong Angels Guard the Remnant
Fearful tests and trials await the people of God. The spirit of war is stirring the nations from one end of the earth to the other. But in the midst of the time of trouble that is coming—a time of trouble such as has not been since there was a nation—God's chosen people will stand unmoved. Satan and his host cannot destroy them, for angels that excel in strength will protect them.
—*9T, p. 17*

The Lord will be a Protector
When declension and danger threaten the church, there will be more praying, more fasting, by the faithful few, and the Lord will answer the prayers offered to Him in sincerity, and at the same time He will come forth as an avenger because of the guiltiness of the evil-workers. He will be a protector; for He will "avenge his own elect, which cry day and night unto Him, though He bear long with them." —*RH, Dec. 11, 1888*

Angels Protect Humble Christians
Today, while earth's history is closing, the Lord requires of his children a vigilance that knows no relaxation. But though the conflict is a ceaseless one, none are left to struggle alone. Angels help and protect those who walk humbly before God. Never will our Lord betray one who trusts in Him. As his children draw near to Him for protection from evil, in pity and love He lifts up for them a standard against the enemy. "Touch them not," He says; "for they are mine. I have graven them upon the palms of my hands."
—*PK, p. 570*

Bread and Water is Guaranteed

That God who cared for Elijah in the time of famine, will not pass by one of his self-sacrificing children. He who has numbered the hairs of their head will care for them, and in days of famine they will be satisfied. While the wicked are perishing from hunger and thirst, their bread and water will be sure. Those who cling to their earthly treasure, and will not make a right disposition of that which is lent them of God, will lose the heavenly treasure, eternal life. — *RH, Sept. 16, 1884*

Ravens Help Feed the Remnant

The Lord has shown me repeatedly that it is contrary to the Bible to make any provision for our temporal wants in the time of trouble... Then will be the time for us to trust wholly in God, and He will sustain us. I saw that our bread and water will be sure at that time, and that we shall not lack or suffer hunger; for God is able to spread a table for us in the wilderness. If necessary He would send ravens to feed us, as He did to feed Elijah, or rain manna from heaven, as He did for the Israelites. — *EW, p. 56*

God Can Make a Refuge Anywhere

When we see what God can and will do for us, when we know that his church is the supreme object of his regard in this world, why are we not more willing to believe his Word? The powers of darkness will assail us, but we have a God who is above all. He can take care of his people. He can make a refuge for his people wherever they are. What He wants us to do is to stand where He can reveal his glory through us, that it may be known that there is a God in Israel, and that in behalf of his people He will manifest his power. — *Ms 10, 1903*

Be Inspired by the 144,000

Satan is marshaling his forces for the last great struggle, "to make war with the remnant of her seed, which keep the commandments of God, and have the testimony of Jesus Christ." If we would be true to God, we cannot escape the conflict. But we are not left in doubt as to the issue. Beyond the smoke and heat of the battle, we behold "them that had gotten the victory" standing on Mount Zion with the Lamb. And still there come to us down through the ages, those words of our Saviour, "In the world ye shall have tribulation; but be of good cheer, I have overcome the world." — *RH, July 18, 1882*

Christ will Not Forget His People

Christ reveals to his people the fearful conflict which they must meet before his Second Coming. Before the scenes of their bitter struggle are opened to them, they are reminded that their brethren also have drunk of the cup and been baptized with the baptism. He who sustained these early witnesses to the truth will not forsake his people in the final conflict. — *PP, pp. 166, 167*

God's Pledge of Security

In the time of trial just before us, God's pledge of security will be placed upon those that have kept the word of his patience. If you have complied with the conditions of God's Word, Christ will be to you a refuge from the storm. He will say to his faithful ones, "Come, my people, enter thou into thy chambers, and shut thy doors about thee; hide thyself as it were for a little moment, until the indignation be overpast." — *RH, Jan. 11, 1887*

God Avenges His Elect

The days will come when the righteous will be stirred to zeal for God because of the abounding iniquity. None but divine power can stay the arrogance of Satan united with evil men; but in the hour of the church's greatest danger most fervent prayer will be offered in her behalf by the faithful remnant, and God will hear and answer at the very time when the guilt of the transgressor has reached its height. He will "avenge his own elect, which cry day and night unto Him, though He bear long with them." They will be jealous for the honor of God. They will be zealous in prayer, and their faith will grow strong.
— *5T, p. 524*

Angels Eagerly Wait to Protect

Angels of God are waiting the mandate from the divine Advocate which shall place man above the wrath of Satan. The Lord of heaven and of earth sorrows and rejoices over his repenting, believing children. Their steadfast adherence to principle was attended by loss, sacrifice, and peril. Their adherence to the commandments of God provoked calumny and the hatred of the disloyal and apostate churches. Whatsoever is not sustained by the Bible standard must not be entertained. Those who are the agents of Satan are vindictive, cruel, and like their master. Those who make the Bible their standard must expect abuse, outrage. In the cause of truth there can be no compromise. — *Ms 16, 1884*

Christ Tasted Death for Us

All humanity must be tested and tried. All of us must drink the cup and be baptized with affliction. But Christ has tasted death for every man in its bitterest form. He knows how to pity, how to sympathize. Only rest in his arms; He loves you, and He has redeemed you with his everlasting love. Be thou faithful unto death, and thou shalt receive a crown of life. —*Lt 312, 1906*

A Light Shines on the Godly

Efforts will be put forth by evil angels, united with evil men to harass, persecute, and destroy, but the Lord God of Israel will not forsake those who trust in Him. Amid the strengthening of infidelity and apostasy, amid pretended illumination, which is the blindest presumption and delusion, there will be a light shining upon God's people from the sanctuary above. The truth of God will triumph. —*Lt 30a, 1892*

God will Arise in His Power

God's people are not to fear. Satan cannot go beyond his limit. The Lord will be the defense of his people. He regards the injury done to his servants for the truth's sake as done to Himself. When the last decision has been made, when all have taken sides, either for Christ and the commandments or for the great apostate, God will arise in his power, and the mouths of those who have blasphemed against Him will be forever stopped. Every opposing power will receive its punishment. —*Lt 28, 1900*

God Works Where Tyranny is Greatest

The commandment-keeping people of God ere long will be placed in a most trying position; but all those who have walked in the light, and have diffused the light, will realize that God interposes in their behalf. When everything looks most forbidding, then the Lord will reveal his power to his faithful ones. When the nation for which God has worked in such a marvelous manner, and over which He has spread the shield of Omnipotence, abandons Protestant principles, and through its legislature gives countenance and support to Romanism in limiting religious liberty, then God will work in his own power for his people that are true. The tyranny of Rome will be exercised, but Christ is our refuge. —*Lt 61, 1895*

Christ will Reveal Himself

The appearance of Christ to John should be to all, believers and unbelievers, an evidence that we have a risen Christ. It should give living power to the church. At times dark clouds surround God's people. It seems as if oppression and persecution would extinguish them. But at such times the most instructive lessons are given. Christ often enters prisons, and reveals Himself to his chosen ones. He is in the fire with them at the stake. As in the darkest night the stars shine the brightest, so the most brilliant beams of God's glory are revealed in the deepest gloom. The darker the sky, the more clear and impressive are the beams of the Sun of Righteousness, the risen Saviour.

— *YI, Apr. 5, 1900*

The Chosen Ones Stand Unmoved

As in the days of Shadrach, Meshach, and Abednego, so in the closing period of earth's history the Lord will work mightily in behalf of those who stand steadfastly for the right. He who walked with the Hebrew worthies in the fiery furnace will be with his followers wherever they are. His abiding presence will comfort and sustain. In the midst of the time of trouble—trouble such as has not been since there was a nation—his chosen ones will stand unmoved. Satan with all the hosts of evil cannot destroy the weakest of God's saints. Angels that excel in strength will protect them, and in their behalf Jehovah will reveal Himself as a "God of gods," able to save to the uttermost those who have put their trust in Him. — *PK, p. 513*

Angels Shield the Righteous

The people of God will not be free from suffering; but while persecuted and distressed, while they endure privation and suffer for want of food they will not be left to perish. That God who cared for Elijah will not pass by one of his self-sacrificing children. He who numbers the hairs of their head will care for them, and in time of famine they shall be satisfied.

While the wicked are dying from hunger and pestilence, angels will shield the righteous and supply their wants. To him that "walketh righteously" is the promise: "Bread shall be given him; his waters shall be sure." "When the poor and needy seek water, and there is none, and their tongue faileth for thirst, I the Lord will hear them, I the God of Israel will not forsake them." Isaiah 33:15, 16; 41:17. — *GC, p. 629*

Satan Cannot Touch the Righteous

In all ages Satan has persecuted the people of God. He has tortured them and put them to death, but in dying they became conquerors. They revealed in their steadfast faith a mightier One than Satan. Satan could torture and kill the body, but he could not touch the life that was hid with Christ in God. He could incarcerate in prison walls, but he could not bind the spirit. They could look beyond the gloom to the glory, saying, "I reckon that the sufferings of this present time are not worthy to be compared with the glory which shall be revealed in us." "Our light affliction, which is but for a moment, worketh for us a far more exceeding and eternal weight of glory." *—MB, p. 30*

God Vindicates and Hides the Remnant

When all arguments fail, the slanderers frequently open their galling fire upon the besieged servants of God; but their lying tongues eventually bring curses upon themselves. God will finally vindicate the right, honor the guiltless, and hide them in the secret of his pavilion from the strife of tongues.

God's servants have always suffered reproach; but the great work moves on, amid persecution, imprisonments, stripes, and death. The character of the persecution changes with the times, but the principle—the spirit that underlies it—is the same that stoned and beat and slew the chosen of the Lord centuries ago. There was never one who walked a man among men more cruelly slandered than the Son of God. *—2SP, p. 212*

God is Our Tower of Defense

Satan claims the world, but there is a little company who withstand his devices, and contend earnestly for the faith once delivered to the saints. Satan sets himself to destroy this commandment-keeping company. But God is their tower of defense. He will raise up for them a standard against the enemy. He will be to them "as an hiding place from the wind," and "as the shadow of a great rock in a weary land."

He will say to them, "Come, my people, enter thou into thy chambers, and shut thy doors about thee: hide thyself as it were for a little moment, until the indignation be overpast. For, behold, the Lord cometh out of his place to punish the inhabitants of the earth for their iniquity: the earth also shall disclose her blood, and shall no more cover her slain." *—RH, Sept. 17, 1901*

Mighty Angels Halt the Wicked

The heavenly sentinels, faithful to their trust, continue their watch. Though a general decree has fixed the time when commandment keepers may be put to death, their enemies will in some cases anticipate the decree, and before the time specified, will endeavor to take their lives. But none can pass the mighty guardians stationed about every faithful soul. Some are assailed in their flight from the cities and villages; but the swords raised against them break and fall powerless as a straw. Others are defended by angels in the form of men of war. —*PK, p. 512*

God Avenges His People

Those who keep God's memorial Sabbath are hated, and every charge which can be invented to make them trouble, is carried into effect. But this is the last great effort which satanic agencies, united with deceived and corrupted churches, will make. When all human calculation seems powerless and the case is desperate, God will interfere, and will be distinctly recognized. He will no longer be robbed of the honor due to his name through the perversity of men who seek glory for themselves. He will work when every human power is of no avail. When the height of guiltiness is reached, when the laws of men are made supreme and the law of God made void, God avenges the people who have vindicated his law. —*Ms 71, 1896*

Angels Walk with the Remnant

God adapts his grace to the peculiarities of each one's necessities. "My grace is sufficient for you." As your burden grows heavier, look up and by faith cling more firmly to the hand of Jesus, your mighty helper. As difficulties thicken about his people amid the perils of the last days, He sends his angels to walk all the way by our side, drawing us closer and still closer to the bleeding side of Jesus. And as the greater trials come, lesser trials are forgotten; the heart feels the need of more firm trust and become calm. You must remain pure and true and firm, remembering your character is being imprinted upon books of heaven—just as the features are imprinted upon the polished plate of the artist. There is no circumstance or place or difficulty or hardship where we cannot live beautiful lives of Christian fidelity and approved conduct.

—*Lt 29, 1884*

Christ Endured Worse Temptations

No one will be called to pass through temptations so severe as were those our Saviour endured. Because of this, our great High Priest knows how to succor those who are tempted. He knows how to sympathize with us when in our great need we call for help. There are severe trials before every one of us, yet we need not fail. In the hour of temptation, Christ will not leave his children, but will send his angels to minister unto us. He will answer our prayers for deliverance. — *RH, July 9, 1908*

Prayers Go as Arrows to God's Throne

The Captain of our salvation strengthens his followers, not with scientific falsehoods, but with genuine faith in the Word of a personal God. This Word is repeated over and over and over again with deeper affirmative power. Satan brings all his powers to the assault in close conflict, and the endurance of the follower of Christ is taxed to the utmost. At times it seems that he must yield.

But a word of prayer to the Lord Jesus goes like an arrow to the throne of God, and angels of God are sent to the field of battle. The tide is turned. The wondrous light that shines in the face of Jesus Christ has stopped the mouth of the caviling opponents. Under the power of the spell that is upon them, their lips are closed, and the oppressed are delivered. The believing, harassed souls are borne up as on eagles' wings, and the victory is gained. — *Ms 53, 1905*

God's Angels Comfort His People

Jacob's history is also an assurance that God will not cast off those who have been deceived and tempted and betrayed into sin, but who have returned unto Him with true repentance. While Satan seeks to destroy this class, God will send his angels to comfort and protect them in the time of peril. The assaults of Satan are fierce and determined, his delusions are terrible; but the Lord's eye is upon his people, and his ear listens to their cries. Their affliction is great, the flames of the furnace seem about to consume them; but the Refiner will bring them forth as gold tried in the fire.

God's love for his children during the period of their severest trial is as strong and tender as in the days of their sunniest prosperity; but it is needful for them to be placed in the furnace of fire; their earthliness must be consumed, that the image of Christ may be perfectly reflected. — *GC, p. 621*

Angels Form a Wall of Fire

You need not be worried. You need not be thinking that there is a special time coming when you are to be crucified; the time to be crucified is just now. Every day, every hour, self is to die; self is to be crucified; and then, when the time comes that the test shall come to God's people in earnest, the everlasting arms are around you. The angels of God make a wall of fire around about and deliver you. —*Ms 35, 1891*

Our Extremity is God's Opportunity

God has thrust his people into the gap, to make up the hedge, to raise up the foundation of many generations. The heavenly intelligences, angels that excel in strength, are waiting, obedient to his command, to unite with human agencies; and the Lord will interpose when matters have come to such a pass that none but a divine power can counteract the satanic agencies at work. When his people shall be in the greatest danger, seemingly unable to stand against the power of Satan, God will work in their behalf. Man's extremity is God's opportunity. —*Ms 48, 1891*

Power from God is Necessary

Oh, how I wish the church to arise and shine because the glory of the Lord has risen upon her. What can we not do in God if every human agency is doing its very utmost. "Without Me ye can do nothing." John 15:5.

We would lose faith and courage in the conflict if we were not sustained by the power of God. Every form of evil is to spring into intense activity. Evil angels unite their powers with evil men and, as they have been in constant conflict and attained an experience in the best modes of deception and battle, and have been strengthening for centuries, they will not yield the last great final contest without a desperate struggle.

All the world will be on one side or the other of the question. The battle of Armageddon will be fought. And that day must find none of us sleeping. Wide awake we must be, as wise virgins having oil in our vessels with our lamps. What is this? Grace, grace! The power of the Holy Ghost must be upon us and the Captain of the Lord's host will stand at the head of the angels of heaven to direct the battle. Solemn events before us are yet to transpire.

—*Lt 112, 1890*

The Deliverance is More Prominent

From time to time the Lord has made known his manner of working. He is mindful of what is passing upon the earth; and when a crisis has come, He has revealed Himself, and has interposed to hinder the working of Satan's plans. He has often permitted matters with nations, with families, and with individuals, to come to a crisis, that his interference might become marked.

Then He has let the fact be known that there was a God in Israel who would sustain and vindicate his people. When the defiance of the law of Jehovah shall be almost universal, when his people shall be pressed in affliction by their fellow men, God will interpose.

The fervent prayers of his people will be answered; for He loves to have his people seek Him with all their heart, and depend upon Him as their deliverer. He will be sought unto to do these things for his people, and He will arise as the protector and avenger of his people. The promise is, "Shall not God avenge his own elect, which cry day and night unto Him?" ... I tell you that He will avenge them speedily. — *RH, June 15, 1897*

The Faith of the Godly will Not Fail

Jacob would not be turned away. He had learned that God is merciful, and he cast himself upon his mercy. He pointed back to his repentance for his sin, and pleaded for deliverance. As he reviewed his life, he was driven almost to despair; but he held fast the Angel, and with earnest, agonizing cries urged his petition until he prevailed.

Such will be the experience of God's people in their final struggle with the powers of evil. God will test their faith, their perseverance, their confidence in his power to deliver them. Satan will endeavor to terrify them with the thought that their cases are hopeless; that their sins have been too great to receive pardon. They will have a deep sense of their shortcomings, and as they review their lives their hopes will sink.

But remembering the greatness of God's mercy, and their own sincere repentance, they will plead his promises made through Christ to helpless, repenting sinners. Their faith will not fail because their prayers are not immediately answered. They will lay hold of the strength of God, as Jacob laid hold of the Angel, and the language of their souls will be, "I will not let thee go, except thou bless me." — *PP, pp. 201, 202*

The Children of God are Fed

When we learn the power of his word, we shall not follow the suggestions of Satan in order to obtain food or to save our lives. Our only questions will be, "What is God's command? And what his promise?" Knowing these, we shall obey the one, and trust the other. In the last great conflict of the controversy with Satan those who are loyal to God will see every earthly support cut off.

Because they refuse to break his law in obedience to earthly powers, they will be forbidden to buy or sell. It will finally be decreed that they shall be put to death. See Revelation 13:11-17. But to the obedient is given the promise, "He shall dwell on high: his place of defense shall be the munitions of rocks: bread shall be given him; his waters shall be sure." Isaiah 33:16. By this promise the children of God will live. When the earth shall be wasted with famine, they shall be fed. "They shall not be ashamed in the evil time: and in the days of famine they shall be satisfied." Psalm 37:19. —*DA, pp. 121, 122*

God will Turn the Captivity

With his eye upon the church, the Lord has again and again allowed matters to come to a crisis, that in their extremity his people should look alone for his help. Their prayers, their faith, together with their steadfast purpose to be true, have called for the interference of God, and then He has fulfilled his promise, "Then shalt thou call, and the Lord shall answer; thou shalt cry, and He shall say, Here I am." His mighty arm has been stretched out for the deliverance of his people.

God reserves his gracious interposition in their behalf till the time of their extremity; thus He makes their deliverance more marked, and their victories more glorious. When all human wisdom fails, the Lord's interference will be more clearly recognized, and He will receive the glory that is his due. Even the enemies of our faith, persecutors, will perceive that God is working for his people in turning their captivity.

What is needed in this, our time of danger, is fervent prayer, mingled with earnest faith, a reliance upon God when Satan casts his shadow over God's people. Let every one bear in mind that God delights to listen to the supplications of his people; for the prevailing iniquity calls for more earnest prayer, and God has promised that He will avenge his own elect, who cry day and night unto Him, though He bear long with them. —*Ms 48, 1891*

261

Jesus will Deliver His People

To human sight it will appear that the people of God must soon seal their testimony with their blood as did the martyrs before them. They themselves begin to fear that the Lord has left them to fall by the hand of their enemies. It is a time of fearful agony. Day and night they cry unto God for deliverance. The wicked exult, and the jeering cry is heard: "Where now is your faith? Why does not God deliver you out of our hands if you are indeed his people?"

But the waiting ones remember Jesus dying upon Calvary's cross and the chief priests and rulers shouting in mockery: "He saved others; Himself He cannot save. If He be the King of Israel, let Him now come down from the cross, and we will believe Him." Matthew 27:42. Like Jacob, all are wrestling with God. Their countenances express their internal struggle. Paleness sits upon every face. Yet they cease not their earnest intercession.

Could men see with heavenly vision, they would behold companies of angels that excel in strength stationed about those who have kept the word of Christ's patience. With sympathizing tenderness, angels have witnessed their distress and have heard their prayers. They are waiting the word of their Commander to snatch them from their peril. But they must wait yet a little longer. The people of God must drink of the cup and be baptized with the baptism. The very delay, so painful to them, is the best answer to their petitions. As they endeavor to wait trustingly for the Lord to work they are led to exercise faith, hope, and patience, which have been too little exercised during their religious experience.

Yet for the elect's sake the time of trouble will be shortened. "Shall not God avenge his own elect, which cry day and night unto Him? ... I tell you that He will avenge them speedily." Luke 18:7, 8...

With earnest longing, God's people await the tokens of their coming King. As the watchmen are accosted, "What of the night?" the answer is given unfalteringly, "The morning cometh, and also the night." Isaiah 21:11, 12. Light is gleaming upon the clouds above the mountaintops. Soon there will be a revealing of his glory. The Sun of Righteousness is about to shine forth. The morning and the night are both at hand—the opening of endless day to the righteous, the settling down of eternal night to the wicked.

As the wrestling ones urge their petitions before God, the veil separating them from the unseen seems almost withdrawn. The heavens glow with the dawning of eternal day, and like the melody of angel songs the words fall upon the ear: "Stand fast to your allegiance. Help is coming." Christ, the almighty Victor, holds out to his weary soldiers a crown of immortal glory; and his voice comes from the gates ajar: "Lo, I am with you. Be not afraid. I am acquainted with all your sorrows; I have borne your griefs. You are not warring against untried enemies. I have fought the battle in your behalf, and in my name you are more than conquerors."

The precious Saviour will send help just when we need it. The way to heaven is consecrated by his footprints. Every thorn that wounds our feet has wounded his. Every cross that we are called to bear He has borne before us. The Lord permits conflicts, to prepare the soul for peace. The time of trouble is a fearful ordeal for God's people; but it is the time for every true believer to look up, and by faith he may see the bow of promise encircling him. Isaiah 51:11-16, 21-23 quoted.

The eye of God, looking down the ages, was fixed upon the crisis which his people are to meet, when earthly powers shall be arrayed against them. Like the captive exile, they will be in fear of death by starvation or by violence. But the Holy One who divided the Red Sea before Israel, will manifest his mighty power and turn their captivity. "They shall be mine, saith the Lord of hosts, in that day when I make up my jewels; and I will spare them, as a man spareth his own son that serveth him." Malachi 3:17.

If the blood of Christ's faithful witnesses were shed at this time, it would not, like the blood of the martyrs, be as seed sown to yield a harvest for God. Their fidelity would not be a testimony to convince others of the truth; for the obdurate heart has beaten back the waves of mercy until they return no more. If the righteous were now left to fall a prey to their enemies, it would be a triumph for the prince of darkness.

Says the psalmist: "In the time of trouble He shall hide me in his pavilion: in the secret of his tabernacle shall He hide me." Psalm 27:5. Christ has spoken: "Come, my people, enter thou into thy chambers, and shut thy doors about thee: hide thyself as it were for a little moment, until the indignation be overpast. For, behold, the Lord cometh out of his place to punish the inhabitants of the earth for their iniquity." Isaiah 26:20, 21. Glorious will be the deliverance of those who have patiently waited for his coming and whose names are written in the book of life. — *GC, pp. 630-634*

We will Receive Christ's Strength

As Satan tempted Christ, so he will tempt Christ's followers. The Son of man was betrayed into the hands of sinners. Many, for Christ's sake, will undergo a similar experience. Priests and rulers will instigate men to testify falsely against them. Christ has told us of the persecution that will come upon those that love and fear God through men who are working in co-partnership with Satan. Under the teaching of the Holy Spirit, God's people will learn more of the terrible character of sin as they feel the cruelty of those who are controlled by it. But all the cruelty manifested toward them is charged against the doers as done to Christ, who has redeemed human souls with his own blood, and has called them by his name.

The strength given to Christ in the hour of bodily suffering and mental anguish in the Garden of Gethsemane, has been and will be given to those who suffer for his dear name's sake. The same grace given to Jesus, the same comfort, the more than mortal steadfastness, will be given to every believing child of God, who is brought into perplexity and suffering, and threatened with imprisonment and death, by Satan's agents. Never has a soul that trusts in Christ been left to perish. The rack, the stake, the many inventions of cruelty, may kill the body, but they cannot touch the life that is hid with Christ in God. — *ST, June 3, 1897*

Discussion Questions

1. What global events could signal that God is about to deliver his people?

2. Why will it appear that Satan is triumphant?

3. What are some of the ways that angels will support and protect the righteous during the final hours of earth's history?

4. Can Satan harm Christians who have taken refuge with Christ?

5. Why will strength and grace from Jesus be necessary to stand through the tribulation?

The Second Coming

— 19 —

The Messiah Returns

"But who may abide the day of his coming? And who shall stand when He appeareth? For He is like a refiner's fire, and like fullers' soap." — Malachi 3:2

1 Kings 18:44	Isa. 13:4-13	Isa. 40:4, 5	Ezek. 43:2	Matt. 24:27-31	Rev. 11:13-19
Ps. 18:1-19	Isa. 24:18-20	Jer. 4:27-29	Joel 2:1-11	Mark 13:24-27	Rev. 14:14-20
Ps. 50:1-6	Isa. 30:30	Dan. 7:13, 14	Joel 3:15, 16	Heb. 9:28	Rev. 16:17-21
Isa. 2:10-21	Isa. 34:4	Ez. 38:18-20	Nahum 1:2-7	2 Pet. 3:10-12	Rev. 19:11-16

A) Signs in the Heavens

The Earth is Filled with Glory

The gospel of Christ is the law exemplified in character. The deceptions practiced against it, every device for vindicating falsehood, every error forged by satanic agencies, will eventually be eternally broken, and the triumph of truth will be like the appearing of the sun at noonday. The Sun of Righteousness shall shine forth with healing in his wings, and the whole earth shall be filled with his glory. —*Ms 32, 1896*

The Voice of God Thunders

The voice of God is heard from heaven, declaring the day and hour of Jesus' coming, and delivering the everlasting covenant to his people. Like peals of loudest thunder his words roll through the earth. The Israel of God stand listening, with their eyes fixed upward. Their countenances are lighted up with his glory, and shine as did the face of Moses when he came down from Sinai. The wicked cannot look upon them. And when the blessing is pronounced on those who have honored God by keeping his Sabbath holy, there is a mighty shout of victory. —*GC, p. 640*

The Great Apostasy is Ended

The great apostasy is working to a point, and will develop into darkness deep as midnight, impenetrable as sackcloth of hair... The apostasy will exist in this night of spiritual darkness. It will be destroyed by the brightness and exceeding glory of Christ's coming. Oh, what a day of gladness for the righteous that will be! What a breaking up of the spell of fanaticism and delusive sentiments when Christ shall shine forth before his ancients gloriously! Then the system of satanic delusion, which souls have preferred to the truth that involves a cross, will be broken up. —*Lt 31, 1897*

Glorious Mountains of Clouds

The scenery seems to resemble Colorado scenery.... We see banks of cloud—white as the whitest snow—looming up in the mountain clefts and increasing in dimensions. It is a beautiful sight. It looks like the billows of the sea, but perfectly white. These white clouds are advancing, rolling first down the mountain sides and then rising higher and spreading over the snow-capped mountains. They appear like mountains of snow in the noon-day sun. It was a picture of loveliness upon which I delighted to gaze. Some took the shape of thrones. I thought of Christ's coming in the clouds of heaven with power and great glory. I can never give in language a description of this sublime scene. —*Ms 29, 1885*

The Greatest Wonders are Seen

"Bow thy heavens, O Lord, and come down: touch the mountains, and they shall smoke. Cast forth lightning, and scatter them: shoot out thine arrows, and destroy them." Psalm 144:5, 6. Greater wonders than have yet been seen will be witnessed by these upon the earth a short time previous to the coming of Christ. "And I will show wonders in heaven above, and signs in the earth beneath; blood, and fire, and vapor of smoke."

"And there were voices, and thunders, and lightnings; and there was a great earthquake, such as was not since men were upon the earth, so mighty an earthquake, and so great." "And every island fled away, and the mountains were not found. And there fell upon men a great hail out of heaven, every stone about the weight of a talent; and men blasphemed God because of the plague of the hail; for the plague thereof was exceeding great." —*ST, Mar. 13, 1879*

Mountains Burn like a Furnace

In the day of the Lord, just before the coming of Christ, God will send lightnings from heaven in his wrath, which will unite with fire in the earth. The mountains will burn like a furnace, and will pour forth terrible streams of lava, destroying gardens and fields, villages and cities; and as they pour their melted ore, rocks and heated mud into the rivers, will cause them to boil like a pot, and send forth massive rocks and scatter their broken fragments upon the land with indescribable violence. Whole rivers will be dried up.

The earth will be convulsed, and there will be dreadful eruptions and earthquakes everywhere. God will plague the wicked inhabitants of the earth until they are destroyed from off it. The saints are preserved in the earth in the midst of these dreadful commotions, as Noah was preserved in the ark at the time of the flood. Christ appears in his glory, and calls forth the righteous dead. The living saints are changed, and, with the resurrected dead, are borne away from the earth by angels to meet their Lord in the air. The earth is left like a desolate wilderness. —*3SG, pp. 82, 83*

God's Temple in Heaven Opens

Writing of the last days, John says: "The nations were angry, and thy wrath is come, and the time of the dead, that they should be judged, and that thou shouldest give reward unto thy servants the prophets, and to the saints, and them that fear thy name, small and great: and shouldest destroy them which destroy the earth. And the temple of God was opened in heaven, and there was seen in his temple the ark of his testament: and there were lightnings, and voices, and thunderings, and an earthquake, and great hail." Revelation 11:18, 19.

When God's temple in heaven is opened, what a triumphant time that will be for all who have been faithful and true! In the temple will be seen the ark of the testament in which were placed the two tables of stone, on which are written God's law. These tables of stone will be brought forth from their hiding place, and on them will be seen the ten commandments engraved by the finger of God. These tables of stone now lying in the ark of the testament will be a convincing testimony to the truth and binding claims of God's law.

—*Lt 47, 1902*

A Brilliant Star Beams Hope

Through a rift in the clouds there beams a star whose brilliancy is increased fourfold in contrast with the darkness. It speaks hope and joy to the faithful, but severity and wrath to the transgressors of God's law. Those who have sacrificed all for Christ are now secure, hidden as in the secret of the Lord's pavilion. They have been tested, and before the world and the despisers of truth they have evinced their fidelity to Him who died for them.

A marvelous change has come over those who have held fast their integrity in the very face of death. They have been suddenly delivered from the dark and terrible tyranny of men transformed to demons. Their faces, so lately pale, anxious, and haggard, are now aglow with wonder, faith, and love. Their voices rise in triumphant song: "God is our refuge and strength, a very present help in trouble. Therefore will not we fear, though the earth be removed, and though the mountains be carried into the midst of the sea; though the waters thereof roar and be troubled, though the mountains shake with the swelling thereof." Psalm 46:1-3. — *GC, p. 638*

The Seventh Plague Jolts the Earth

Now in regard to the coming of the Son of Man. This will not take place until after the mighty earthquake shakes the earth. After the people have heard the voice of God they are in despair and trouble such as never was since there was a nation, and in this the people of God will suffer affliction. The clouds of heaven will clash, and there will be darkness.

Then that voice comes from heaven and the clouds begin to roll back like a scroll, and there is the bright, clear sign of the Son of Man. The children of God know what that cloud means. The sound of music is heard; and as it nears, the graves are opened and the dead are raised and there are thousands of thousands and ten thousand times ten thousand of angels that compose that glory and encircle the Son of Man...

Now there are many signs that will take place before the coming of the Son of Man, but when the white cloud is seen, this will be the sign of the coming of the Son of Man. There will be signs in the sun, moon, and stars, and the nations in perplexity. These all testify that Christ is coming, and He is revealed in the clouds with power and great glory. — *Ms 81, 1886*

The Remnant Hear God Speak

Jacob specified no particular thing for the Lord to bestow upon him; he sought only a blessing; he knew that the Lord would give him a blessing appropriate to meet the necessities of the case at that time. God blessed him then and there; and on the field of conflict he was made a prince among men.

Thus will it be with the agonized ones who prevail with God in the time of Jacob's trouble. Dangers thicken on every side, and it is difficult to fix the eye of faith upon the promises amidst the certain evidences of immediate destruction. But in the midst of revelry and violence, there falls upon the ear peal upon peal of the loudest thunder.

The heavens have gathered blackness and are only illuminated with the blazing light and terrible glory from heaven. God utters his voice from his holy habitation. The captivity of his people is turned. With sweet and subdued voices they say to one another, "God is our friend. We shall be safe from the power of wicked men." In solemn awe they listen to the words proceeding from the throne of God. — *ST, Nov. 27, 1879*

Everything in Nature Convulses

Before the Son of man appears in the clouds of heaven, everything in nature will be convulsed. Lightning from heaven, uniting with the fire in the earth, will cause the mountains to burn like a furnace and pour out their floods of lava over villages and cities. Molten masses of rock, thrown into the water by the upheaval of things hidden in the earth, will cause the water to boil, and they will send forth rocks and earth. There will be mighty earthquakes and great destruction of human life.

But as in the days of the great deluge Noah was preserved in the ark that God had prepared for him, so in these days of destruction and calamity God will be the refuge of his believing ones. Through the psalmist, He declares: "Because thou hast made the Lord, which is my refuge, even the Most High, thy habitation; there shall no evil befall thee, neither shall any plague come nigh thy dwelling." "For in the time of trouble He shall hide me in his pavilion: in the secret of his tabernacle shall He hide me; He shall set me up upon a rock." Then shall we not make the Lord our surety and our defense?

—*Lt 258, 1907*

The Heavens are Shaken

The Lord gave me a view of the shaking of the powers of the heavens. I saw that when the Lord said "heaven," in giving the signs recorded by Matthew, Mark, and Luke, He meant heaven, and when He said "earth" He meant earth. The powers of heaven are the sun, moon, and stars. They rule in the heavens. The powers of earth are those that rule on the earth.

The powers of heaven will be shaken at the voice of God. Then the sun, moon, and stars will be moved out of their places. They will not pass away, but be shaken by the voice of God...

I saw that the powers of earth are now being shaken and that events come in order. War, and rumors of war, sword, famine, and pestilence are first to shake the powers of earth, then the voice of God will shake the sun, moon, and stars, and this earth also. — *EW, p. 41*

The Faces of the Righteous Light Up

Satan's host, and wicked men, will surround them, and exult over them, because there will seem to be no way of escape for them. But in the midst of their revelry and triumph, there is peal upon peal of the loudest thunder.

The heavens have gathered blackness, and are only illuminated by the blazing light and terrible glory from heaven, as God utters his voice from his holy habitation. The foundations of the earth shake, buildings totter and fall with a terrible crash. The sea boils like a pot, and the whole earth is in terrible commotion. The captivity of the righteous is turned, and with sweet and solemn whisperings they say to each other, "We are delivered. It is the voice of God." With solemn awe they listen to the words of the voice. The wicked hear, but understand not the words of the voice of God. They fear and tremble, while the saints rejoice.

Satan and his angels, and wicked men, who had been exulting that the people of God were in their power, that they might destroy them from off the earth, witness the glory conferred upon those who have honored the holy law of God. They behold the faces of the righteous lighted up, and reflecting the image of Jesus. Those who were so eager to destroy the saints could not endure the glory resting upon the delivered ones, and they fell like dead men to the earth. Satan and evil angels fled from the presence of the saints glorified. Their power to annoy them was gone forever. — *RH, May 27, 1862*

The Majesty of God's Law

The Son of man will come in the clouds of heaven in his own glory, and the glory of his Father, and of all the holy angels. There will be no lack of honor and glory. In that day the law of God is to be revealed in its majesty, and man who has broken that law, and stood in defiant rebellion against its holy precepts, will understand that that law which they have despised, discarded, and trampled underfoot is God's standard of character. Every commandment-keeping soul, every transgressor will have placed before him the scene when the Sabbath was first given to man in Eden... and all the sons of God shouted for joy... This scene will be vividly brought before every mind. — *Ms 39, 1898*

Light Shines Out of the Darkness

The coming of the bridegroom was at midnight—the darkest hour. So the coming of Christ will take place in the darkest period of this earth's history. The days of Noah and Lot pictured the condition of the world just before the coming of the Son of man. The Scriptures pointing forward to this time declare that Satan will work with all power and "with all deceivableness of unrighteousness." 2 Thessalonians 2:9, 10.

His working is plainly revealed by the rapidly increasing darkness, the multitudinous errors, heresies, and delusions of these last days. Not only is Satan leading the world captive, but his deceptions are leavening the professed churches of our Lord Jesus Christ. The great apostasy will develop into darkness deep as midnight, impenetrable as sackcloth of hair. To God's people it will be a night of trial, a night of weeping, a night of persecution for the truth's sake. But out of that night of darkness God's light will shine.

He causes "the light to shine out of darkness." 2 Corinthians 4:6. When "the earth was without form, and void, and darkness was upon the face of the deep," "the Spirit of God moved upon the face of the waters. And God said, Let there be light; and there was light." Genesis 1:2, 3. So in the night of spiritual darkness, God's Word goes forth, "Let there be light." To his people He says, "Arise, shine; for thy light is come, and the glory of the Lord is risen upon thee." Isaiah 60:1. "Behold," says the Scripture, "the darkness shall cover the earth, and gross darkness the people; but the Lord shall arise upon thee, and his glory shall be seen upon thee." Isaiah 60:2. — *COL, pp. 414, 415*

God Speaks from Orion

Dark heavy clouds came up, and clashed against each other. The atmosphere parted and rolled back; then we could look up through the open space in Orion, whence came the voice of God. The Holy City will come down through that open space. — *EW, p. 41*

Deliverance Comes at Midnight

It was at midnight that God chose to deliver his people. As the wicked were mocking around them, suddenly the sun appeared, shining in his strength, and the moon stood still. The wicked looked upon the scene with amazement, while the saints beheld with solemn joy the tokens of their deliverance. Signs and wonders followed in quick succession. Everything seemed turned out of its natural course. The streams ceased to flow. Dark, heavy clouds came up and clashed against each other. But there was one clear place of settled glory, whence came the voice of God like many waters, shaking the heavens and the earth.

There was a mighty earthquake. The graves were opened, and those who had died in faith under the third angel's message, keeping the Sabbath, came forth from their dusty beds, glorified, to hear the covenant of peace that God was to make with those who had kept his law. The sky opened and shut and was in commotion. The mountains shook like a reed in the wind and cast out ragged rocks all around. The sea boiled like a pot and cast out stones upon the land. And as God spoke the day and the hour of Jesus' coming and delivered the everlasting covenant to his people, He spoke one sentence, and then paused, while the words were rolling through the earth. The Israel of God stood with their eyes fixed upward, listening to the words as they came from the mouth of Jehovah and rolled through the earth like peals of loudest thunder. It was awfully solemn.

At the end of every sentence the saints shouted, "Glory! Hallelujah!" Their countenances were lighted up with the glory of God, and they shone with glory as did the face of Moses when he came down from Sinai. The wicked could not look upon them for the glory. And when the never-ending blessing was pronounced on those who had honored God in keeping his Sabbath holy, there was a mighty shout of victory over the beast and over his image. Then commenced the jubilee, when the land should rest. — *EW, pp. 285, 286*

The Mystery of Iniquity Ends

The mystery of iniquity, which had already begun to work in Paul's day, will continue its work until it be taken out of the way at our Lord's Second Coming. — *ST, June 12, 1893*

Mountains Tremble and Bow

The lovely home God had given to man was turned to a broken, uneven surface, and the earth was a frightful solitude. Here before me was the evidences of the destruction of the old world by a flood because the law of God was not observed. Then I looked forward in prospect to the day of the Lord's coming, cruel both with wrath and fierce anger, to lay the land desolate and destroy the sinners thereof out of it. The mountains shake and tremble before the tread of the Lord's hosts. The Lion of the tribe of Judah, the Conqueror, comes to be glorified in his saints—those who love his appearing.

Before the glory of Him who is to reign, the mountains will tremble and bow, the rocks will be moved out of their place; for once more will the Lord shake not alone the earth, but the heavens also. The scattered ones who have fled for their lives to the rocks, the dens, the caverns of the earth, because of the fury of the oppressor, will be made glad at the voice of God. — *Ms 56, 1886*

A Glorious Rainbow Appears

With shouts of triumph, jeering, and imprecation, throngs of evil men are about to rush upon their prey, when, lo, a dense blackness, deeper than the darkness of the night, falls upon the earth. Then a rainbow, shining with the glory from the throne of God, spans the heavens and seems to encircle each praying company. The angry multitudes are suddenly arrested. Their mocking cries die away. The objects of their murderous rage are forgotten. With fearful forebodings they gaze upon the symbol of God's covenant and long to be shielded from its overpowering brightness.

By the people of God a voice, clear and melodious, is heard, saying, "Look up," and lifting their eyes to the heavens, they behold the bow of promise. The black, angry clouds that covered the firmament are parted, and like Stephen they look up steadfastly into heaven and see the glory of God and the Son of man seated upon his throne. In his divine form they discern the marks of his humiliation; and from his lips they hear the request presented before his Father and the holy angels: "I will that they also, whom Thou hast given Me, be with Me where I am." John 17:24. Again a voice, musical and triumphant, is heard, saying: "They come! They come! Holy, harmless, and undefiled. They have kept the word of my patience; they shall walk among the angels;" and the pale, quivering lips of those who have held fast their faith utter a shout of victory.

It is at midnight that God manifests his power for the deliverance of his people. The sun appears, shining in its strength. Signs and wonders follow in quick succession. The wicked look with terror and amazement upon the scene, while the righteous behold with solemn joy the tokens of their deliverance. Everything in nature seems turned out of its course. The streams cease to flow. Dark, heavy clouds come up and clash against each other. In the midst of the angry heavens is one clear space of indescribable glory, whence comes the voice of God like the sound of many waters, saying: "It is done." Revelation 16:17.

That voice shakes the heavens and the earth. There is a mighty earthquake, "such as was not since men were upon the earth, so mighty an earthquake, and so great." The firmament appears to open and shut. The glory from the throne of God seems flashing through. The mountains shake like a reed in the wind, and ragged rocks are scattered on every side. There is a roar as of a coming tempest. The sea is lashed into fury.

There is heard the shriek of a hurricane like the voice of demons upon a mission of destruction. The whole earth heaves and swells like the waves of the sea. Its surface is breaking up. Its very foundations seem to be giving way. Mountain chains are sinking. Inhabited islands disappear. The seaports that have become like Sodom for wickedness are swallowed up by the angry waters. Babylon the great has come in remembrance before God, "to give unto her the cup of the wine of the fierceness of his wrath." Great hailstones, every one "about the weight of a talent," are doing their work of destruction.

The proudest cities of the earth are laid low. The lordly palaces, upon which the world's great men have lavished their wealth in order to glorify themselves, are crumbling to ruin before their eyes. Prison walls are rent asunder, and God's people, who have been held in bondage for their faith, are set free. — *GC, pp. 635, 636*

B) The Saviour Appears

A Great White Cloud

I have not the slightest knowledge as to the time spoken by the voice of God. I heard the hour proclaimed, but had no remembrance of that hour after I came out of vision. Scenes of such thrilling, solemn interest passed before me as no language is adequate to describe. It was all a living reality to me, for close upon this scene appeared the great white cloud upon which was seated the Son of man. —*Lt 38, 1888*

Jesus Comes as a Divine Conqueror

Now this Saviour is our intercessor, making an atonement for us before the Father. "If we sin we have an advocate with the Father, even Jesus Christ the righteous." 1 John 2:1. And that precious Saviour is coming again. Many spiritualize this Second Coming all away. But the very same Jesus that ascended up into heaven, the angels said He would come in like manner. Those eyes will behold Him in his beauty as He comes to this earth, and those who have waited for Him and loved Him He will crown with glory, honor, immortality, eternal life.

When He cometh the second time, it is not to wear the crown of thorns, it is not to have that old purple robe placed upon his divine form; the voices will not be raised, "Crucify, Him, crucify Him," but there is a shout from the angelic host and from those who are waiting to receive Him, "Worthy, worthy is the Lamb that was slain." A divine conqueror. In the place of the crown of thorns, He will wear the crown of glory; in the place of that old kingly robe, that they put in mockery upon Him, He will wear a robe whiter than the whitest white.

And these hands that were bruised with the cruel nails will shine like gold. His eyes are like a flame of fire to search creation through. And the righteous dead come forth from their graves, and they that are alive and remain are caught up together with them to meet the Lord in the air: and so shall they ever be with the Lord. And they will listen to the voice of Jesus, sweeter than any music that ever fell on mortal ear, "Your warfare is accomplished, come ye blessed of my Father, enter into the kingdom prepared for you from the foundation of the earth." —*Ms 11, 1886*

Christ's Followers Rejoice

"Arise, shine; for thy light is come, and the glory of the Lord is risen upon thee." Isaiah 60:1. Christ is coming with power and great glory. He is coming with his own glory and with the glory of the Father. And the holy angels will attend Him on his way. While all the world is plunged in darkness, there will be light in every dwelling of the saints. They will catch the first light of his second appearing. The unsullied light will shine from his splendor, and Christ the Redeemer will be admired by all who have served Him. While the wicked flee, Christ's followers will rejoice in his presence. Then it is that the redeemed from among men will receive their promised inheritance.

Thus God's purpose for Israel will meet with literal fulfillment. That which God purposes, man is powerless to disannul. Even amid the working of evil, God's purposes have been moving steadily forward to their accomplishment. It was thus with the house of Israel throughout the history of the divided monarchy; it is thus with spiritual Israel today. — *PK, p. 720*

A Small Black Cloud Appears

Soon there appears in the east a small black cloud, about half the size of a man's hand. It is the cloud which surrounds the Saviour and which seems in the distance to be shrouded in darkness. The people of God know this to be the sign of the Son of man. In solemn silence they gaze upon it as it draws nearer the earth, becoming lighter and more glorious, until it is a great white cloud, its base a glory like consuming fire, and above it the rainbow of the covenant.

Jesus rides forth as a mighty conqueror. Not now a "Man of Sorrows," to drink the bitter cup of shame and woe, He comes, victor in heaven and earth, to judge the living and the dead. "Faithful and True," "in righteousness He doth judge and make war." And "the armies which were in heaven" (Revelation 19:11, 14) follow Him. With anthems of celestial melody the holy angels, a vast, unnumbered throng, attend Him on his way.

The firmament seems filled with radiant forms—"ten thousand times ten thousand, and thousands of thousands." No human pen can portray the scene; no mortal mind is adequate to conceive its splendor. "His glory covered the heavens, and the earth was full of his praise. And his brightness was as the light." Habakkuk 3:3, 4. — *GC, p. 640*

Every Eye Sees the Prince of Life

As the living cloud comes still nearer, every eye beholds the Prince of life. No crown of thorns now mars that sacred head; but a diadem of glory rests on his holy brow. His countenance outshines the dazzling brightness of the noonday sun. "And He hath on his vesture and on his thigh a name written, King of kings, and Lord of lords." Revelation 19:16.

Before his presence "all faces are turned into paleness;" upon the rejecters of God's mercy falls the terror of eternal despair. "The heart melteth, and the knees smite together, ... and the faces of them all gather blackness." Jeremiah 30:6; Nahum 2:10. The righteous cry with trembling: "Who shall be able to stand?" The angels' song is hushed, and there is a period of awful silence. Then the voice of Jesus is heard, saying: "My grace is sufficient for you." The faces of the righteous are lighted up, and joy fills every heart. And the angels strike a note higher and sing again as they draw still nearer to the earth.

The King of kings descends upon the cloud, wrapped in flaming fire. The heavens are rolled together as a scroll, the earth trembles before Him, and every mountain and island is moved out of its place. "Our God shall come, and shall not keep silence: a fire shall devour before Him, and it shall be very tempestuous round about Him. He shall call to the heavens from above, and to the earth, that He may judge his people." Psalm 50:3, 4. — *GC, pp. 640, 641*

Christ Returns as King of Heaven

When Christ came to this earth the first time, He came in lowliness and obscurity, and his life here was one of suffering and poverty... At his Second Coming all will be changed. Not as a prisoner surrounded by a rabble will men see Him, but as heaven's King. Christ will come in his own glory, in the glory of his Father, and in the glory of the holy angels. Ten thousand times ten thousand and thousands of thousands of angels, the beautiful, triumphant sons of God, possessing surpassing loveliness and glory, will escort Him on his way.

In the place of a crown of thorns, He will wear a crown of glory—a crown within a crown. In the place of that old purple robe, He will be clothed in a garment of whitest white, "so as no fuller on earth can white" it. And on his vesture and on his thigh a name will be written, "King of kings, and Lord of lords." — *RH, Nov. 13, 1913*

Everyone Recognizes Jesus

In that day of final punishment and reward, both saints and sinners will recognize in Him who was crucified the Judge of all living. — *RH, Nov. 22, 1898*

The Contrast between the Two Advents

Obedience or disobedience to the authority of the Lord is to decide the case of every soul. Christ is coming in the clouds of heaven with power and great glory. Who of you in this congregation will meet Him in peace? Who will be among that number to whom the words apply, "He shall come to be glorified in his saints, and to be admired of all them that believe." It is called the glorious appearing of the great God and our Saviour Jesus Christ. His coming surpasses in glory all that the eye has ever seen. Far exceeding anything the imagination has conceited will be his personal revelation in the clouds of heaven.

Then there will be a perfect contrast to the humility which attended his first advent. Then He came as the Son of the Infinite God, but his glory was concealed by the garb of humanity. Then He came without any worldly distinction of royalty, without any visible manifestation of glory; but at his second appearing He comes with his own glory and the glory of the Father and attended by the angelic host of heaven. In the place of that crown of thorns which marred his brow, He wears a crown within a crown. No longer is He clad with the garments of humility, with the old kingly robe placed upon Him by his mockers. No; He comes clad in a robe whiter than the whitest white. Upon his vesture and thigh a name is inscribed, "King of kings, and Lord of lords." Revelation 19:6.

As the representative of God, Christ appeared in human flesh. Though in the form of a man, He was the Son of God, and the world was given an opportunity to see how it would treat God. Christ declared, "He that hath seen Me hath seen the Father." John 14:9. But when He comes the second time, divinity is no longer concealed. He comes as one equal with God, as his own beloved Son, Prince of heaven and earth. He is also the Redeemer of his people, the Lifegiver. The glory of the Father and the Son are seen to be one. His claim to being one with the Father is now substantiated. His glory is the glory of the Son, and the glory of God. Then shall He shine forth before his ancients gloriously. — *Lt 90, 1898*

A Vision of the Second Coming

Soon we heard the voice of God like many waters, which gave us the day and hour of Jesus' coming. The living saints, 144,000 in number, knew and understood the voice, while the wicked thought it was thunder and an earthquake. When God spoke the time, He poured upon us the Holy Ghost, and our faces began to light up and shine with the glory of God, as Moses' did when he came down from Mount Sinai.

The 144,000 were all sealed and perfectly united. On their foreheads was written, God, New Jerusalem, and a glorious star containing Jesus' new name. At our happy, holy state the wicked were enraged, and would rush violently up to lay hands on us to thrust us into prison, when we would stretch forth the hand in the name of the Lord, and they would fall helpless to the ground. Then it was that the synagogue of Satan knew that God had loved us who could wash one another's feet and salute the brethren with a holy kiss, and they worshipped at our feet.

Soon our eyes were drawn to the east, for a small black cloud had appeared, about half as large as a man's hand, which we all knew was the sign of the Son of man. We all in solemn silence gazed on the cloud as it drew nearer and became lighter, glorious, and still more glorious, till it was a great white cloud. The bottom appeared like fire; a rainbow was over the cloud, while around it were ten thousand angels, singing a most lovely song; and upon it sat the Son of man. His hair was white and curly and lay on his shoulders; and upon his head were many crowns. His feet had the appearance of fire; in his right hand was a sharp sickle; in his left, a silver trumpet. His eyes were as a flame of fire, which searched his children through and through. Then all faces gathered paleness, and those that God had rejected gathered blackness. Then we all cried out, "Who shall be able to stand? Is my robe spotless?"

Then the angels ceased to sing, and there was some time of awful silence, when Jesus spoke: "Those who have clean hands and pure hearts shall be able to stand; my grace is sufficient for you." At this our faces lighted up, and joy filled every heart. And the angels struck a note higher and sang again, while the cloud drew still nearer the earth. Then Jesus' silver trumpet sounded, as He descended on the cloud, wrapped in flames of fire. He gazed on the graves of the sleeping saints, then raised his eyes and hands to heaven, and cried, "Awake! Awake! Awake! Ye that sleep in the dust, and arise." — *EW, pp. 14-16*

The Armies of Heaven

The battle of Armageddon is soon to be fought. He on whose vesture is written the name, "King of Kings and Lord of Lords," leads forth the armies of heaven on white horses, clothed in fine linen, clean and white. *— Ms 172, 1899*

A Living Cloud of Majesty

Soon appeared the great white cloud, upon which sat the Son of man. When it first appeared in the distance, this cloud looked very small. The angel said that it was the sign of the Son of man. As it drew nearer the earth, we could behold the excellent glory and majesty of Jesus as He rode forth to conquer. A retinue of holy angels, with bright, glittering crowns upon their heads, escorted Him on his way.

No language can describe the glory of the scene. The living cloud of majesty and unsurpassed glory came still nearer, and we could clearly behold the lovely person of Jesus. He did not wear a crown of thorns, but a crown of glory rested upon his holy brow. Upon his vesture and thigh was a name written, KING OF KINGS, and LORD OF LORDS. His countenance was as bright as the noonday sun, his eyes were as a flame of fire, and his feet had the appearance of fine brass. His voice sounded like many musical instruments. The earth trembled before Him, the heavens departed as a scroll when it is rolled together, and every mountain and island were moved out of their places. *— EW, p. 286*

Discussion Questions

1. Why will the great apostasy be destroyed when Christ returns?

2. How will the remnant respond to the glory of the Second Coming?

3. What will it be like to see and hear Jesus when he comes? Can you imagine a voice that sounds like many musical instruments?

4. Why does Jesus tell the Remnant that his grace is sufficient for them?

5. How will the wicked react when they see celestial glory for the first time?

The Joy of the Righteous

"And He shall send his angels with a great sound of a trumpet, and they shall gather together his elect from the four winds, from one end of heaven to the other." — Matthew 24:31

Job 19:25-27	Isa. 24:13-15	Dan. 12:2, 3	Mal. 3:17, 18	Rom. 8:30	1 Thes. 4:13-18
Psalm 17:15	Isa. 25:5-9	Hosea 13:14	John 5:28, 29	1 Cor. 15:51-55	2 Thes. 1:10
Isa. 13:12	Isa. 26:19	Zech. 9:16	John 10:10	Phil. 3:21	1 John 3:2, 3

A) The Dead are Raised

Abel is Resurrected

A few graves were opened at the resurrection of Christ; but at his Second Coming all the precious dead, from righteous Abel to the last saint that dies, shall awake to glorious, immortal life. —*3SP, p. 193*

The Righteous Dead Awaken

There is a pledge from Him who is the resurrection and the life that those who sleep in Jesus will Christ bring with Him from the grave. The trump will sound, the dead will awaken to life, to die no more. The eternal morning has come to them for there will be no night in the city of God. —*Lt 78, 1890*

The Trumpet of God is Heard

When Christ the great Lifegiver shall come in the clouds of heaven, to raise the dead, there will be a terrible earthquake. The trump of God will be heard resounding through earth's remotest bounds, and the voice of Jesus will call forth the dead from their graves to immortal life. You have not seen Christ coming with power and great glory which shall illuminate the earth from east to west, from north to south, like the lightning's flash. —*Lt 2, 1874*

Jesus Delivers Patient Souls

I saw that while Jesus was in the most holy place He would be married to the New Jerusalem; and after his work should be accomplished in the holiest, He would descend to the earth in kingly power and take to Himself the precious ones who had patiently waited his return. — *EW, p. 251*

Converts of Enoch Come Up

Enoch was the light to the world in his day, and how far that light extended! The light that Enoch reflected from God was broad and deep, and there were those who walked in this light, were blessed in this light, and died in this light, and will come up in the first resurrection. — *Ms 83, 1886*

Sleeping Saints are Glorified

The day of exile is nearly ended. The time is at hand when all who are sleeping in their graves will hear his voice and come forth, some to everlasting life, and some to final destruction. Christ will raise all his saints, glorify them with an immortal body, and open to them the gates of the city of God. — *Ms 69, 1912*

A Bright Reward for Martyrs

We may look back through centuries, and see the living stones gleaming like jets of light through the rubbish of moral darkness, errors, and superstition. These precious jewels shine with continually increasing luster, not alone for time, but for eternity. Although dead, the words and deeds of the righteous of all ages testify to the truth of God. The names of the martyrs for Christ's sake are immortalized among the angels in heaven; and a bright reward awaits them when the Life-giver shall call them from their graves. — *Rd, p. 80*

The Waldenses Come to Life

Here the Catholics came from Turin to persecute the Waldenses in these valleys and mountains. Our informer told us that thousands upon thousands of Protestants have been thrown from the precipice I have mentioned. What a scene will these mountains and hills in Switzerland present when Christ, the Lifegiver, shall call forth the dead! They will come from caverns, from dungeons, from deep wells, where their bodies have been buried. They will come forth with the sound of the trumpet and the voice of God at that last great and terrible day of the Lord. — *Lt 97, 1886*

A Vision of the Resurrection

Jesus' silver trumpet sounded, as He descended on the cloud, wrapped in flames of fire. He gazed on the graves of the sleeping saints, then raised his eyes and hands to heaven, and cried, "Awake! Awake! Awake! Ye that sleep in the dust, and arise."

Then there was a mighty earthquake. The graves opened, and the dead came up clothed with immortality. The 144,000 shouted, "Alleluia!" as they recognized their friends who had been torn from them by death, and in the same moment we were changed and caught up together with them to meet the Lord in the air. *— EW, p. 16*

Humans Receive Holy Flesh

When human beings receive holy flesh, they will not remain on the earth, but will be taken to heaven. While sin is forgiven in this life, its results are not wholly removed. It is at his coming that Christ is to "change our vile body, that it may be fashioned like unto his glorious body." Philippians 3:21.

When Christ shall come with a great sound of a trumpet, and shall call the dead from their prison house, then the saints will receive holy flesh. Then this mortal shall put on immortality, and this corruptible shall put on incorruption. Then Christ will be admired in all them that believe. He will see of the travail of his soul, and will be satisfied. Then will break forth from immortal beings the song of triumph, "Worthy, worthy is the Lamb."

— Ms 39, 1907

"O Grave, Where is Thy Victory?"

The earth mightily shook as the voice of the Son of God called forth the sleeping saints. They responded to the call and came forth clothed with glorious immortality, crying, "Victory, victory, over death and the grave! O death, where is thy sting? O grave, where is thy victory?" Then the living saints and the risen ones raised their voices in a long, transporting shout of victory. Those bodies that had gone down into the grave bearing the marks of disease and death came up in immortal health and vigor. The living saints are changed in a moment, in the twinkling of an eye, and caught up with the risen ones, and together they meet their Lord in the air. Oh, what a glorious meeting! Friends whom death had separated were united, nevermore to part.

— EW, p. 287

God's People are the Majority

In comparison with the millions of the world, God's people will be, as they have ever been, a little flock; but if they stand for the truth as revealed in his word, God will be their refuge. They stand under the broad shield of Omnipotence. God is always a majority. When the sound of the last trump shall penetrate the prison house of the dead, and the righteous shall come forth with triumph, exclaiming, "O death, where is thy sting? O grave, where is thy victory?" (1 Corinthians 15:55)—standing then with God, with Christ, with the angels, and with the loyal and true of all ages, the children of God will be far in the majority. —*AA, p. 590*

Two Classes Meet Christ

When Christ comes in the clouds of heaven only two classes, the obedient and the disobedient, will meet Him. And only those who, having had the light upon God's requirements, have been obedient to Him, can meet Him with joy. Those who have persisted in a course of disobedience, will flee in terror, hiding in the dens of the mountains, and saying to the rocks and the mountains, "Fall on us, and hide us from the face of Him that sitteth on the throne, and from the wrath of the Lamb." But those who have honored God by their obedience, will look up, and say, "Lo, this is our God; we have waited for Him, and He will save us; this is the Lord, we have waited for Him; we will be glad and rejoice in his salvation." —*ST, Feb. 11, 1897*

The Lifegiver Calls the Dead

Our Saviour promised that He would come again. Those heavenly gates are again to be lifted up, and Christ as conqueror, with a thousand times ten thousand and thousands of thousands, will march out of those gates in triumph, to honor those who have loved Him and kept his commandments, and to take them to Himself. And He says that He has not forgotten them nor his promise. The Lifegiver will call the dead from their prison-house, and as they come up from the grave, they will receive the finishing touch of immortality. They will rise from their dusty beds and exclaim, "O Death, where is thy sting? O Grave, where is thy victory!" And they will be caught up with those who are translated to heaven without seeing death, to meet their Lord in the air. —*RH, July 29, 1890*

God Rewards Martyrs

If it is his will that we lose our lives in his service, we will find eternal life in his everlasting kingdom. At the call of the archangel we shall come forth in the first resurrection to claim our right of entrance to the city of God and to eat of the tree of life which is in the midst of the Paradise of God. Let us thank God for the abundant provision that has been made for our race.

— *Ms 95, 1909*

Thoughts Begin as They Ended

Blessed rest for the weary righteous! Time, be it long or short, is but a moment to them. They sleep; they are awakened by the trump of God to a glorious immortality. "For the trumpet shall sound, and the dead shall be raised incorruptible... So when this corruptible shall have put on incorruption, and this mortal shall have put on immortality, then shall be brought to pass the saying that is written, Death is swallowed up in victory." 1 Corinthians 15:52-54.

As they are called forth from their deep slumber they begin to think just where they ceased. The last sensation was the pang of death; the last thought, that they were falling beneath the power of the grave. When they arise from the tomb, their first glad thought will be echoed in the triumphal shout: "O death, where is thy sting? O grave, where is thy victory?" — *GC, p. 549*

Imagine the Resurrection

I look forward in imagination to the time when the trump of God shall sound and all that are in their graves shall hear his voice and come forth, those that have done good to the resurrection of life, and they that have done evil to the resurrection of damnation. Oh, what a scene will we then see—some coming forth to life eternal at the first resurrection. Upon them the second death shall have no power. And then at the end of a thousand years the wicked dead come forth. I cannot endure to think of this.

I dwell with pleasure upon the resurrection of the just, who shall come forth from all parts of the earth, from rocky caverns, from dungeons, from caves of the earth, from the waters of the deep—not one is overlooked. Everyone shall hear his voice. They will come forth with triumph and victory. Then there is to be no more death, no more sin, no more sorrow. — *Lt 113, 1886*

The Prison House is Emptied

"Marvel not at this: for the hour is coming, in which all that are in the graves shall hear his voice, and shall come forth" John 5:28, 29. This voice is soon to resound through all the nations of the dead, and every saint who sleeps in Jesus shall awake and leave his prison house. —*Ms 137, 1897*

Balaam Saw the Glorious Reward

Not only was Balaam shown the history of the Hebrew people as a nation, but he beheld the increase and prosperity of the true Israel of God to the close of time. He saw the special favor of the Most High attending those who love and fear Him. He saw them supported by his arm as they enter the dark valley of the shadow of death. And he beheld them coming forth from their graves, crowned with glory, honor, and immortality. He saw the redeemed rejoicing in the unfading glories of the earth made new.

Gazing upon the scene, he exclaimed, "Who can count the dust of Jacob, and the number of the fourth part of Israel?" And as he saw the crown of glory on every brow, the joy beaming from every countenance, and looked forward to that endless life of unalloyed happiness, he uttered the solemn prayer, "Let me die the death of the righteous, and let my last end be like his!" —*PP, p. 447*

The Resurrection Justifies the Bible

Christ declared to his hearers that if there were no resurrection of the dead, the Scriptures which they professed to believe would be of no avail. He said, "But as touching the resurrection of the dead, have ye not read that which was spoken unto you by God, saying, I am the God of Abraham, and the God of Isaac, and the God of Jacob? God is not the God of the dead, but of the living." God counts the things that are not as though they were. He sees the end from the beginning, and beholds the result of his work as though it were now accomplished.

The precious dead, from Adam down to the last saint who dies, will hear the voice of the Son of God, and will come forth from the grave to immortal life. God will be their God, and they shall be his people. There will be a close and tender relationship between God and the risen saints. This condition, which is anticipated in his purpose, He beholds as if it were already existing. The dead live unto Him. —*DA, p. 606*

Martyrs Freed from Catacombs

Beneath the hills outside the city of Rome, long galleries had been tunneled through earth and rock; the dark and intricate network of passages extended for miles beyond the city walls. In these underground retreats the followers of Christ buried their dead; and here also, when suspected and proscribed, they found a home. When the Life-giver shall awaken those who have fought the good fight, many a martyr for Christ's sake will come forth from those gloomy caverns. — *GC, p. 40*

A Loud Trumpet Calls the Dead

Between the first and the Second Advent of Christ a wonderful contrast will be seen. No human language can portray the scenes of the Second Coming of the Son of man in the clouds of heaven. He is to come with his own glory, and with the glory of the Father and of the holy angels. He will come clad in the robe of light, which He has worn from the days of eternity. Angels will accompany Him. Ten thousand times ten thousand will escort Him on his way. The sound of the trumpet will be heard, calling the sleeping dead from the grave. The voice of Christ will penetrate the tomb, and pierce the ears of the dead, "and all that are in the graves... shall come forth." — *RH, Sept. 5, 1899*

Death is but a Small Matter

"Whoso eateth my flesh, and drinketh my blood, hath eternal life; and I will raise him up at the last day." John 10:10; 4:14; 6:54. To the believer, death is but a small matter. Christ speaks of it as if it were of little moment. "If a man keep my saying, he shall never see death," "he shall never taste of death." To the Christian, death is but a sleep, a moment of silence and darkness. The life is hid with Christ in God, and "when Christ, who is our life, shall appear, then shall ye also appear with Him in glory." John 8:51, 52; Colossians 3:4.

The voice that cried from the cross, "It is finished," was heard among the dead. It pierced the walls of sepulchers, and summoned the sleepers to arise. Thus will it be when the voice of Christ shall be heard from heaven. That voice will penetrate the graves and unbar the tombs, and the dead in Christ shall arise. At the Saviour's resurrection a few graves were opened, but at his Second Coming all the precious dead shall hear his voice, and shall come forth to glorious, immortal life. — *DA, pp. 786, 787*

Kind Characters are Immortalized

God's messengers are to hold aloft the standard of truth until the hand is palsied in death. When they sleep in death, the places that once knew them know them no more. The churches in which they preached, the places they visited to hold forth the word of life, still remain. The mountains, the hills, the things seen by mortal vision, are still there. All these things must at last pass away. The time is coming when the earth shall reel to and fro, and shall be removed like a cottage. But the thoughts, the purposes, the acts of God's workers, although now unseen, will appear at the great day of final retribution and reward. Things now forgotten will then appear as witnesses, either to approve or to condemn.

Love, courtesy, self-sacrifice—these are never lost. When God's chosen ones are changed from mortality to immortality, their words and deeds of goodness will be made manifest, and will be preserved through the eternal ages. No act of unselfish service, however small or simple, is ever lost. Through the merits of Christ's imputed righteousness, the fragrance of such words and deeds is forever preserved. — *RH, Mar. 10, 1904*

A Vision of the Second Coming

Soon I heard the voice of God, which shook the heavens and the earth. There was a mighty earthquake. Buildings were shaken down, and fell on every side. I then heard a triumphant shout of victory, loud, musical and clear. I looked upon this company who, a short time before were in such distress and bondage. Their captivity was turned. A glorious light shone upon them. How beautiful they then looked. All weariness and marks of care were gone. Health and beauty were seen in every countenance.

Their enemies, the heathen around them, fell like dead men. They could not endure the light that shone upon the delivered, holy ones. This light and glory remained upon them, until Jesus was seen in the clouds of heaven, and the faithful, tried company was changed in a moment, in the twinkling of an eye, from glory to glory. And the graves were opened and the saints came forth, clothed with immortality, crying victory over death and the grave, and together with the living saints, were caught up to meet their Lord in the air; while the rich, musical shouts of glory and victory were upon every immortal tongue, and proceeding from every sanctified, holy lip. — *1SG, p. 187*

Similar to the First Resurrection

The captives brought up from the graves at the time of the resurrection of Jesus were his trophies as a conquering Prince. Thus He attested his victory over death and the grave; thus He gave a pledge and an earnest of the resurrection of all the righteous dead. Those who were called from their graves went into the city, and appeared unto many in their resurrected forms, and testified that Jesus had indeed risen from the dead, and that they had risen with Him. The voice that cried, "It is finished," was heard among the dead. It pierced the walls of sepulchers, and summoned the sleepers to arise.

Thus shall it be when God's voice shall be heard shaking the heavens and earth. That voice will penetrate the graves and unbar the tombs. A mighty earthquake will then cause the world to reel to and fro like a drunkard. Then Christ, the King of Glory, shall appear, attended by all the heavenly angels. The trumpet shall sound, and the Life-giver shall call forth the righteous dead to immortal life. — *3SP, p. 223*

Jesus is Coming to Raise the Righteous

Jesus is coming! But not to listen to the woes of mankind, and to hear the guilty sinner confess his sins, and to speak pardon to him; for everyone's case will then be decided for life or death. Those who have lived in sin will remain sinners forever. Those who have confessed their sins to Jesus in the Sanctuary, have made Him their friend and have loved his appearing, will have pardon written for all their sins, and they, having purified their souls "in obeying the truth," will remain pure and holy forever. Jesus is coming as He ascended into heaven, only with additional splendor. He is coming with the glory of his Father, and all the holy angels with Him, to escort Him on his way.

Instead of the cruel crown of thorns to pierce his holy temples, a crown of dazzling glory will deck his sacred brow. He will not then appear, the man of sorrows and acquainted with grief; but his countenance will shine brighter than the noon-day sun. He will not wear a plain seamless coat, but a garment whiter than snow—of dazzling brightness. Jesus is coming! But not to reign as a temporal prince. He will raise the righteous dead, change the living saints to a glorious immortality, and, with the saints, take the kingdom under the whole heaven. This kingdom will never end. Then those who have patiently waited for Jesus, will be made like Him. — *YI, Apr. 1, 1854*

The Victory of the Saints

So those who had been raised were to be presented to the universe as a pledge of the resurrection of all who believe in Christ as their personal Saviour. The same power that raised Christ from the dead will raise his church, and glorify it with Christ, as his bride, above all principalities, above all powers, above every name that is named, not only in this world, but also in the heavenly courts, the world above.

The victory of the sleeping saints will be glorious on the morning of the resurrection. Satan's triumph will end, while Christ will triumph in glory and honor. The Life-giver will crown with immortality all who come forth from the grave. — *YI, Aug. 11, 1898*

A Long, Glad Shout of Victory

Amid the reeling of the earth, the flash of lightning, and the roar of thunder, the voice of the Son of God calls forth the sleeping saints. He looks upon the graves of the righteous, then, raising his hands to heaven, He cries: "Awake, awake, awake, ye that sleep in the dust, and arise!" Throughout the length and breadth of the earth the dead shall hear that voice, and they that hear shall live. And the whole earth shall ring with the tread of the exceeding great army of every nation, kindred, tongue, and people. From the prison house of death they come, clothed with immortal glory, crying: "O death, where is thy sting? O grave, where is thy victory?" 1 Corinthians 15:55. And the living righteous and the risen saints unite their voices in a long, glad shout of victory.

All come forth from their graves the same in stature as when they entered the tomb. Adam, who stands among the risen throng, is of lofty height and majestic form, in stature but little below the Son of God. He presents a marked contrast to the people of later generations; in this one respect is shown the great degeneracy of the race. But all arise with the freshness and vigor of eternal youth. In the beginning, man was created in the likeness of God, not only in character, but in form and feature. Sin defaced and almost obliterated the divine image; but Christ came to restore that which had been lost. He will change our vile bodies and fashion them like unto his glorious body. The mortal, corruptible form, devoid of comeliness, once polluted with sin, becomes perfect, beautiful, and immortal. All blemishes and deformities are left in the grave. — *GC, p. 644*

Jesus Comes for His Purchased Possessions

Those who believe in Jesus are sacred to his heart; for their life is hid with Christ in God. The command will come from the Life-giver, "Awake and sing, ye that dwell in dust: for thy dew is as the dew of herbs and the earth shall cast out her dead." Isaiah 26:19.

The Life-giver will call up his purchased possession in the first resurrection, and until that triumphant hour, when the last trump shall sound and the vast army shall come forth to eternal victory, every sleeping saint will be kept in safety and will be guarded as a precious jewel, who is known to God by name. By the power of the Saviour that dwelt in them while living, and because they were partakers of the divine nature, they are brought forth from the dead.

Christ claimed to be the only begotten of the Father, but men encased in unbelief, barricaded with prejudice, denied the holy and the just One. He was charged with blasphemy, and was condemned to a cruel death, but He burst the fetters of the tomb, and rose from the dead triumphant, and over the rent sepulchre of Joseph He declared, "I am the resurrection and the Life." John 11:25. All power in heaven and in earth was vested in Him, and the righteous will also come forth from the tomb free in Jesus. They shall be accounted worthy to obtain that world and the resurrection from the dead. "Then shall the righteous shine forth as the sun in the kingdom of their Father." Matthew 13:43.

What a glorious morning will the resurrection morning be! What a wonderful scene will open when Christ shall come to be admired of them that believe! All who were partakers with Christ in his humiliation and sufferings will be partakers with Him in his glory. By the resurrection of Christ from the dead every believing saint who falls asleep in Jesus will come forth from his prison house in triumph. The resurrected saint will proclaim, "O death where is thy sting! O grave where is thy victory!" 1 Corinthians 15:55. "If we believe that Jesus died and rose again, even so also those which sleep in Jesus will God bring with Him." 1 Thessalonians 4:14.

Jesus Christ has triumphed over death and rent the fetters of the tomb, and all who sleep in the tomb will share in the victory; they will come forth from their graves as did the conqueror. — *Lt 65a, 1894*

The Dead are Immortalized First

Paul showed that those living when Christ should come would not go to meet their Lord in advance of those who had fallen asleep in Jesus. The voice of the Archangel and the trump of God would reach the sleeping ones, and the dead in Christ should rise first, before the touch of immortality should be given to the living. "Then we which are alive and remain shall be caught up together with them in the clouds, to meet the Lord in the air: and so shall we ever be with the Lord. Wherefore comfort one another with these words." 1 Thes. 4:17, 18…

"Even so them also which sleep in Jesus will God bring with Him," Paul wrote. Many interpret this passage to mean that the sleeping ones will be brought with Christ from heaven; but Paul meant that as Christ was raised from the dead, so God will call the sleeping saints from their graves and take them with Him to heaven. Precious consolation! Glorious hope! —*AA, p. 258*

B) Reunited with Family and Friends

All Wrinkles Disappear

When our friends go into the grave they are beautiful to us. It may be our father or mother that we lay away; when they come forth those wrinkles are all gone, but the figure is there, and we know them and they know Christ. We want to be prepared to meet these dear friends as they come forth in the resurrection morning. Can any of us bear the thought that we should refuse the mercy of Him who has paid such an infinite price for us? —*Ms 80, 1886*

Separated Friends are United

The living righteous are changed "in a moment, in the twinkling of an eye." At the voice of God they were glorified; now they are made immortal and with the risen saints are caught up to meet their Lord in the air. Angels "gather together his elect from the four winds, from one end of heaven to the other." Little children are borne by holy angels to their mothers' arms. Friends long separated by death are united, nevermore to part, and with songs of gladness ascend together to the City of God. —*GC, p. 645*

Raised Friends are Recognized

The resurrection of Jesus was a type of the final resurrection of all who sleep in Him. The countenance of the risen Saviour, his manner, his speech, were all familiar to his disciples. As Jesus arose from the dead, so those who sleep in Him are to rise again. We shall know our friends, even as the disciples knew Jesus. They may have been deformed, diseased, or disfigured, in this mortal life, and they rise in perfect health and symmetry; yet in the glorified body their identity will be perfectly preserved. Then shall we know even as also we are known. 1 Corinthians 13:12. In the face radiant with the light shining from the face of Jesus, we shall recognize the lineaments of those we love. —*DA, p. 804*

Loved Ones Rise with Immortality

We should have hearts overflowing with sympathy for souls for whom Christ died. We should seek to educate our children in the fear of God, teaching them that Christ died for them, and that they may have salvation without money and without price. It will only be a little while before Jesus will come to save his children and to give them the finishing touch of immortality. "This corruptible shall put on incorruption, and this mortal shall put on immortality." The graves will be opened, and the dead will come forth victorious, crying, "O death, where is thy sting? O grave, where is thy victory?" Our loved ones who sleep in Jesus will come forth clothed with immortality. —*ST, Apr. 15, 1889*

Every Saint Knows Family Members

God's greatest gift is Christ, whose life is ours, given for us. He died for us, and was raised for us, that we might come forth from the tomb to a glorious companionship with heavenly angels, to meet our loved ones and to recognize their faces, for the Christlikeness does not destroy their image, but transforms it into his glorious image.

Every saint connected in family relationship here will know each other there. When we are redeemed, the Bible will be understood in a higher, broader, and clearer sense than it now is. The veil that has hung between mortality and immortality will be rent away. We shall see his face. The Bible tells us that we gain immortality through Jesus Christ. Our life must be hid with Christ in God. —*Lt 79, 1898*

Every Deformity is Removed

In the great day of God, all who are faithful and true will receive the healing touch of the divine Restorer. The Lifegiver will remove every deformity, and will give them eternal life. — *Lt 207, 1899*

Parents Receive Their Children

Calling Gehazi, Elisha bade him send the mother to him. "And when she was come in unto him, he said, Take up thy son. Then she went in, and fell at his feet, and bowed herself to the ground, and took up her son, and went out."

So was the faith of this woman rewarded. Christ, the great Life-giver, restored her son to her. In like manner will his faithful ones be rewarded, when, at his coming, death loses its sting and the grave is robbed of the victory it has claimed. Then will He restore to his servants the children that have been taken from them by death. — *PP, p. 239*

Personal Identity is Preserved

Our personal identity is preserved in the resurrection, though not the same particles of matter or material substance as went into the grave. The wondrous works of God are a mystery to man. The spirit, the character of man is returned to God there to be preserved. In the resurrection every man will have his own character.

God in his own time will call forth the dead, giving again the breath of life, and bidding the dry bones live. The same form will come forth, but it will be free from disease and every defect. It lives again bearing the same individuality of features, so that friend will recognize friend. There is no law of God in nature which shows that God gives back the same identical particles of matter which composed the body before death. God shall give the righteous dead a body that will please Him.

Paul illustrates this subject by a kernel of grain sown in the field. The planted kernel decays, but there comes forth a new kernel. The natural substance in the grain that decays is never raised as before, but God giveth it a body as it hath pleased Him. A much finer material will compose the human body, for it is a new creation, a new birth. It is sown a natural body, it is raised a spiritual body. — *Ms 76, 1900*

Infants Fly to Their Mothers

Our loved ones are torn from us by death. We close their eyes and habit them for the tomb, and lay them away from our sight. But hope bears our spirits up. We are not parted forever, but shall meet the loved ones who sleep in Jesus. They shall come again from the land of the enemy. The Life-giver is coming. Myriads of holy angels escort Him on his way. He bursts the bands of death, breaks the fetters of the tomb, the precious captives come forth in health and immortal beauty.

As the little infants come forth immortal from their dusty beds, they immediately wing their way to their mother's arms. They meet again never more to part. But many of the little ones have no mother there. We listen in vain for the rapturous song of triumph from the mother. The angels receive the motherless infants and conduct them to the tree of life. Jesus places the golden ring of light, the crown upon their little heads. God grant that the dear mother of "Eva" may be there, that her little wings may be folded upon the glad bosom of her mother. — *YI, Apr. 1, 1858*

The Resurrection Unites Families

"Then shall the King say unto them on his right hand, Come, ye blessed of my Father, inherit the kingdom prepared for you from the foundation of the world." Thus He welcomes them, to live hereafter in eternal communion with Himself. And every voice in the heavenly mansions echoes and echoes the welcome, "Come, ye blessed of my Father, inherit the kingdom prepared for you from the foundation of the world."

Jesus is coming, coming with clouds and great glory. A multitude of shining angels will attend Him. He will come to honor those who have loved Him and kept his commandments, and to take them to Himself. He has not forgotten them or his promise.

There will be a re-linking of the family chain. When we look upon our dead, we may think of the morning when the trump of God shall sound, when "the dead shall be raised incorruptible, and we shall be changed." That time is near. A little while, and we shall see the King in his beauty. A little while, and He will present his faithful ones "faultless before the presence of his glory with exceeding joy." — *RH, Nov. 22, 1906*

C) The Remnant are Immortalized

Elijah was a Type of Saint

Elijah was a type of the saints who will be living on the earth at the time of the Second Advent of Christ and who will be "changed, in a moment, in the twinkling of an eye, at the last trump," without tasting of death. — *PP, p. 227*

Slaves Shake Off Their Chains

I saw the pious slave rise in victory and triumph, and shake off the chains that bound him, while his wicked master was in confusion and knew not what to do; for the wicked could not understand the words of the voice of God.

— EW, p. 286

Enoch Represents the Righteous

Enoch's translation to heaven just before the destruction of the world by a flood, represents the translation of all the living righteous from the earth previous to its destruction by fire. The saints will be glorified in the presence of those who have hated them for their loyal obedience to God's righteous commandments. — *ST, Feb. 20, 1879*

Lowly Ones Become Truly Lofty

What a day that will be when the unsullied light will shine from his splendor, and Christ the Redeemer will be admired by all who have received Him. All who have served Him will catch the undimmed rays of the glory and brightness of the King in his majesty. In that day those who have been counted as the lowly ones will be the truly lofty. — *Ms 91, 1898*

The Lion of Judah Gathers His People

The Lion of Judah, whose wrath will be so terrible to the rejecters of his grace, will be the Lamb of God to the obedient and faithful. The pillar of cloud will speak terror and wrath to the transgressor of God's law, but light and mercy and deliverance to those who have kept his commandments. The Arm strong to smite the rebellious, will be strong to deliver the loyal. Every faithful one will surely be gathered. "He shall send his angels with a great sound of a trumpet, and they shall gather together his elect from the four winds, from one end of heaven to the other." — *RH, Jan. 11, 1887*

The 144,000 are Translated

The hundred and forty-four thousand... having been translated from the earth, from among the living, are counted as "the first fruits unto God and to the Lamb." Revelation 14:4. —*GC, p. 648*

Christ Comes for His Faithful Ones

Christ has declared that He will come the second time to gather his faithful ones to Himself: "Then shall all the tribes of the earth mourn, and they shall see the Son of man coming in the clouds of heaven with power and great glory. And He shall send his angels with a great sound of a trumpet, and they shall gather together his elect from the four winds, from one end of heaven to the other." Matthew 24:30, 31. —*GC, p. 37*

Do Not Worry about the Transition

Elder B. asked me... if I would not rather die easy on a bed, than to pass through the pain of being changed from mortal to immortality. I answered that I wished Jesus to come and save his children; and that I was willing to live or die; that I could endure all the pain that could be borne in a moment in the twinkling of an eye; and that I desired the wheels of time to roll swiftly round, and bring the welcome day, when these vile bodies should be changed, and fashioned like unto Christ's glorious body. —*2SG, p. 22*

Jesus Calls the Remnant from Caves

"Kings shall see and arise, princes also shall worship, because of the Lord that is faithful, and the Holy One of Israel, for He shall choose thee." Isaiah 49:7. The hidden ones have been scattered because of man's enmity against the law of Jehovah. They have been oppressed by all the powers of the earth. They have been scattered in the dens and caves of the earth through the violence of their adversaries, because they are true and obedient to the laws of Jehovah.

But deliverance comes to the people of God. To their enemies God will show Himself as a God of just retribution... From the dens and the caves of the earth, that have been the secret hiding places of God's people, they are called forth as his witnesses, true and faithful. The people who have braved out their rebellion will fill the description given in Revelation 6:15-17. In these very caves and dens they find the very statement of truth in the letters and in the publications as witness against them. —*Lt 86, 1900*

298

Godly Youth Greet Jesus

Youth who strive against sin, who believe and wait and watch for Christ's appearing, who submit to parental authority, and who love the Lord Jesus will be among those who love his appearing and who meet Him in peace.

These will stand without spot or wrinkle before the throne of God and enjoy his favor forever. They have formed lovely characters; they have guarded their speech; they have not spoken falsely; they have guarded their actions, that they should not do any evil thing, and they are crowned with everlasting life. —*Ms 67, 1909*

Christlike Men will See Jesus

I see wonderful glory in the prospect before us, when Christ shall come in all his glory, to be admired in all them that believe. I want to be among the number who welcome the Redeemer with joy, among the number who will see his face. Moses asked to see God's face, but the Lord told him that he could not see his face and live. He told him that He would hide him in the cleft of the rock, and cover him with his hand, and would then pass by before him and proclaim his name. And He passed by and proclaimed, "The Lord, the Lord God, merciful and gracious, longsuffering, and abundant in goodness and truth." This is God's character. And those who see his face must be like Him in character. —*Ms 28, 1901*

Moses Saw the Joy of the Saints

Moses looked and saw the covenant of peace made with God's commandment-keeping people when He spoke from his holy habitation, shaking the heavens and the earth by his voice. Moses saw that God is the hope of his people, while the despisers of the law, those who had crucified Jesus Christ afresh, bowed and groveled at the feet of the saints in fear of God's voice. He saw the countenances of the saints lighted up with glory, and beaming upon those around them as the faces of Himself and those who were with him shone when the law was given on Mount Sinai.

The commandment-keepers, those who had honored the law, were glorified. At the appearing of Christ in splendor and glory, they were translated to heaven without seeing death, rising with songs of triumph to enter through the gates into the city, into the land of Eden. —*Ms 69, 1912*

The Saved are Pure like Christ

"Behold what manner of love the Father hath bestowed upon us, that we should be called the sons of God. Therefore the world knoweth us not, because it knew Him not. Beloved, now are we the sons of God, and it doth not yet appear what we shall be: but we know that, when He shall appear, we shall be like Him, for we shall see Him as He is. And every man that hath this hope in Him, purifieth himself, even as He is pure." 1 John 3:1-3. The Father's wisdom and glory shines forth in his (Christ's) majesty. He is exalted and precious to all who believe. —*Lt 90, 1898*

The Saints Receive a Higher Nature

When Christ comes, He takes those who have purified their souls by obeying the truth. Some will go into the grave who are now in active life, and some will be alive and be changed when Christ shall come. This mortal shall put on immortality, and these corruptible bodies, subject to disease, will be changed from mortal to immortal. We shall then be gifted with a higher nature. The bodies of all who purify their souls by obeying the truth shall be glorified. They will have fully received and believed in Jesus Christ. To all who follow his example in his life in this world, He has given power to become the sons of God. —*Ms 36, 1906*

The Righteous Hear God's Voice

Then the last trump will sound, the voice of God will speak, and the whole earth, from the summits of the loftiest mountains to the lowest recesses of the deepest mines, will hear that voice. It will be heard in the dungeons of men, in the caverns of the deep, in the rocks and caves of the earth, and it will be obeyed. It is the same voice that said, "Come unto Me, all ye that labor and are heavy-laden, and I will give you rest,"—the same voice that said, "Thy sins be forgiven thee."

And those who obeyed that voice when it said, "If any man will come after Me, let him deny himself, and take up his cross, and follow Me," will now hear the words, "Well done, thou good and faithful servant, enter thou into the joy of thy Lord." To them that voice will mean rest, peace, and everlasting life. They will recognize it as the voice of the One who has been touched with the feeling of their infirmities. —*RH, Nov. 13, 1913*

The Saints Cry "Lo, This is our God"

Jesus is coming, but not as at his first advent, a babe in Bethlehem; not as He rode into Jerusalem, when the disciples praised God with a loud voice and cried, "Hosanna"; but in the glory of the Father and with all the retinue of holy angels to escort Him on his way to earth. All heaven will be emptied of the angels, while the waiting saints will be looking for Him and gazing into heaven, as were the men of Galilee when He ascended from the Mount of Olivet.

Then only those who are holy, those who have followed fully the meek Pattern, will with rapturous joy exclaim as they behold Him, "Lo, this is our God; we have waited for Him, and He will save us." And they will be changed "in a moment, in the twinkling of an eye, at the last trump"—that trump which wakes the sleeping saints, and calls them forth from their dusty beds, clothed with glorious immortality, and shouting, "Victory! Victory over death and the grave!" The changed saints are then caught up together with the angels to meet the Lord in the air, never more to be separated from the object of their love. —EW, p. 110

Christ Creates Glorious New Bodies

The stones were not prepared for their respective places just as they were about to be laid in the wall of the temple; all the fitting and planning was done previous to their being brought to the place of building. So it is that all the hewing, fitting and polishing of character must be done during man's probation. When Christ shall come again to earth it will not be to purify and refine the characters of men, and to fit them for heaven. His work then will only be to change their corruptible bodies and fashion them like unto Christ's most glorious body. Only a symmetrical and perfect character will in that day entitle men to the finishing touch of immortality.

Earth is the quarry and the work-shop where men are to be fitted and refined for the courts of heaven. As the stones composing Solomon's temple came together in the wall a perfect fit, without the touch of ax or hammer or any other instrument, so will the resurrected saints, and those who are alive at the time of his coming be caught up together to meet the Lord in the air, each one fitted for the great change and taking his proper place in the temple of God's love. —3SP, pp. 40, 41

Eternal Life is Cheap Enough

I was shown the saints' reward, the immortal inheritance. Then I was shown how much God's people had endured for the truth's sake, and that they would count heaven cheap enough. They reckoned that the sufferings of this present time were not worthy to be compared with the glory which should be revealed in them. The people of God in these last days will be tried. But soon their last trial will come, and then they will receive the gift of eternal life. — *1T, p. 432*

The Righteous are as the Three Hebrews

At this time, when wickedness is at its height, ministers of the gospel are crying, "Peace and safety." Upon the minds of those who are thus set at rest, "sudden destruction cometh." Unprepared, they shall not escape. Christ will not come with a still, small voice when He comes to bring hope and peace and joy to those who have proved faithful. In the day of his coming, the last great trumpet is heard, and there is a terrible shaking of earth and heaven. The whole earth, from the loftiest mountains to the deepest mines, will hear.

Everything will be penetrated by fire. The tainted atmosphere will be cleansed by fire. The fire having fulfilled its mission, the dead that have been laid away in the grave will come forth—some to the resurrection of life, to be caught up to meet their Lord in the air; and some to behold the coming of Him whom they have despised, and whom they now recognize as the judge of all the earth.

All the righteous are untouched by the flames. They can walk through the fire, as Shadrach, Meshach, and Abednego walked in the midst of the furnace heated seven times hotter than it was wont to be heated. The Hebrew worthies could not be consumed because the form of the fourth, the Son of God, was with them.

So in the day of the coming of the Lord, smoke and flame will be powerless to harm the righteous. Those who are united with the Lord will escape unscathed. Earthquakes, hurricanes, flame, and flood cannot injure those who are prepared to meet their Saviour in peace. But those who rejected our Saviour, and scourged and crucified Him, will be among those who will be raised from the dead to behold his coming in the clouds of heaven, attended by the heavenly host—ten thousand times ten thousand, and thousands of thousands. — *Ms 159, 1903*

The Revelation of Christ's Glory

The revelation of his own glory in the form of humanity will bring heaven so near to men that the beauty adorning the inner temple will be seen in every soul in whom the Saviour dwells. Men will be captivated by the glory of an abiding Christ. And in currents of praise and thanksgiving from the many souls thus won to God, glory will flow back to the great Giver.

"Arise, shine; for thy light is come, and the glory of the Lord is risen upon thee." Isaiah 60:1. To those who go out to meet the Bridegroom is this message given. Christ is coming with power and great glory. He is coming with his own glory and with the glory of the Father. He is coming with all the holy angels with Him. While all the world is plunged in darkness, there will be light in every dwelling of the saints. They will catch the first light of his second appearing. The unsullied light will shine from his splendor, and Christ the Redeemer will be admired by all who have served Him. While the wicked flee from his presence, Christ's followers will rejoice.

The patriarch Job, looking down to the time of Christ's Second Advent, said, "Whom I shall see for myself, and mine eyes shall behold, and not a stranger." Job 19:27.

To his faithful followers Christ has been a daily companion and familiar friend. They have lived in close contact, in constant communion with God. Upon them the glory of the Lord has risen. In them the light of the knowledge of the glory of God in the face of Jesus Christ has been reflected. Now they rejoice in the undimmed rays of the brightness and glory of the King in his majesty. They are prepared for the communion of heaven; for they have heaven in their hearts.

With uplifted heads, with the bright beams of the Sun of Righteousness shining upon them, with rejoicing that their redemption draweth nigh, they go forth to meet the Bridegroom, saying, "Lo, this is our God; we have waited for Him, and He will save us." Isaiah 25:9.

"And I heard as it were the voice of a great multitude, and as the voice of many waters, and as the voice of mighty thunderings, saying, Alleluia; for the Lord God omnipotent reigneth. Let us be glad and rejoice, and give honor to Him; for the marriage of the Lamb is come, and his wife hath made herself ready..." Revelation 19:6-9. — *COL, pp. 420, 421*

The Remnant are Pardoned and Honored

As the people of God afflict their souls before Him, pleading for purity of heart, the command is given, "Take away the filthy garments" from them, and the encouraging words are spoken, "Behold, I have caused thine iniquity to pass from thee, and I will clothe thee with change of raiment." The spotless robe of Christ's righteousness is placed upon the tried, tempted, yet faithful children of God. The despised remnant are clothed in glorious apparel, nevermore to be defiled by the corruptions of the world. Their names are retained in the Lamb's book of life, enrolled among the faithful of all ages. They have resisted the wiles of the deceiver; they have not been turned from their loyalty by the dragon's roar. Now they are eternally secure from the tempter's devices. Their sins are transferred to the originator of sin.

And the remnant are not only pardoned and accepted, but honored. "A fair miter" is set upon their heads. They are to be as kings and priests unto God. While Satan was urging his accusations and seeking to destroy this company, holy angels, unseen, were passing to and fro, placing upon them the seal of the living God. These are they that stand upon Mount Zion with the Lamb, having the Father's name written in their foreheads. They sing the new song before the throne, that song which no man can learn save the hundred and forty and four thousand, which were redeemed from the earth.

"These are they which follow the Lamb whithersoever He goeth. These were redeemed from among men, being the first fruits unto God and to the Lamb. And in their mouth was found no guile: for they are without fault before the throne of God." Revelation 14:4. Now is reached the complete fulfillment of those words of the Angel: "Hear now, O Joshua the high priest, thou, and thy fellows that sit before thee: for they are men wondered at: for, behold, I will bring forth my servant the Branch."

Christ is revealed as the Redeemer and Deliverer of his people. Now indeed are the remnant "men wondered at," as the tears and humiliation of their pilgrimage give place to joy and honor in the presence of God and the Lamb. "In that day shall the branch of the Lord be beautiful and glorious, and the fruit of the earth shall be excellent and comely for them that are escaped of Israel. And it shall come to pass, that he that is left in Zion, and he that remaineth in Jerusalem, shall be called holy, even every one that is written among the living in Jerusalem." —*5T, pp. 475, 476*

304

Moses and Elijah Typify the Saints

Moses passed under the dominion of death, but he was not to remain in the tomb. Christ Himself called him forth to life. Satan the tempter had claimed the body of Moses because of his sin; but Christ the Saviour brought him forth from the grave.

Moses upon the mount of transfiguration was a witness to Christ's victory over sin and death. He represented those who shall come forth from the grave at the resurrection of the just. Elijah, who had been translated to heaven without seeing death, represented those who will be living upon the earth at Christ's Second Coming, and who will be "changed, in a moment, in the twinkling of an eye, at the last trump;" when "this mortal must put on immortality," and "this corruptible must put on incorruption."

Jesus was clothed with the light of heaven, as He will appear when He shall come "the second time without sin unto salvation." For He will come "in the glory of his Father with the holy angels." Hebrews 9:28; Mark 8:38. The Saviour's promise to the disciples was now fulfilled. Upon the mount the future kingdom of glory was represented in miniature—Christ the King, Moses a representative of the risen saints, and Elijah of the translated ones.

—DA, pp. 421, 422

Men are Strengthened to Meet Jesus

As John, exiled upon the Isle of Patmos, was startled from his contemplation of the works of God in nature and as on bended knees he was praying to Him, he hears a voice, saying, "I am Alpha and Omega, the first and the last." At the sound of the voice, John falls down in astonishment as if dead. He is unable to bear the sight of the divine glory. But a Hand raises John up, and the voice he remembers as the voice of his Master. He is strengthened and can endure to talk with the Lord Jesus.

So will it be with the remnant people of God who are scattered—some in the mountain fastness, some exiled, some pursued, some persecuted. When the voice of God is heard, and the brightness of the glory is revealed, and the trial is over, the dross removed, they know they are in the presence of One who has redeemed them by his own blood. Just what Christ was to John in his exile, He will be to his people who are made to feel the hand of oppression for the faith and testimony of Jesus Christ.

305

These very martyrs will one day be resplendent with the glory of God because He has faithful ones who have been loyal where the world, the churches, have made void his holy law. These were driven by the storm and tempest of persecution to the crevices of the rocks, but were hiding in the Rock of Ages; and in the fastness of the mountains, in the caves and dens of the earth, the Saviour reveals his presence and his glory.

Yet a little while, and He that is to come will come and will not tarry. His eyes as a flame of fire penetrate into the fast-closed dungeons and hunt out the hidden ones, for their names are written in the Lamb's book of life. These eyes of the Saviour are above us, around us, noting every difficulty, discerning every danger; and there is no place where his eyes cannot penetrate, no sorrows and sufferings of his people where the sympathy of Christ does not reach. They reach the persecuted ones everywhere. "Inasmuch as ye have done this to one of the least of my brethren, ye have done it unto Me." Every deed of darkness that Satan united with wicked men may do, Christ's eyes like a flame of fire detect, and it is noted and registered by the great Heartsearcher.

The child of God will be terror-stricken at the first sight of the majesty of Jesus Christ. He feels that he cannot live in his holy presence. But the word comes to him as to John, "Fear not." Jesus laid his right hand upon John; He raised him up from his prostrate position. So will He do unto his loyal, trusting ones, for there are greater revelations of the glory of God to be given them. — *Ms 56, 1886*

Discussion Questions

1. What events will announce the resurrection?

2. How do Moses and Elijah typify the living and dead saints?

3. What will joyful Christians say as they spring forth from the graves?

4. Which family members and friends are you looking forward to seeing at the resurrection?

5. Why will the children of God someday be the majority?

— 21 —

The Terror of the Wicked

"Behold, He cometh with clouds; and every eye shall see Him, and they also which pierced Him: and all kindreds of the earth shall wail because of Him. Even so, Amen."

— Revelation 1:7

Job 11:20	Isaiah 33:14	Jer. 23:1, 2	Ezekiel 34:10	2 Thes. 1:7-9
Proverbs 1:27	Isaiah 63:5, 6	Jer. 47:2, 3	Nahum 2:10	Rev. 6:14-17
Isaiah 28:17, 18	Jer. 8:19, 20	Daniel 12:2	Zech. 12:10	Rev. 18:15-17

A) Consciences are Awakened

The Sinfulness of Sin
What is sin? The Lord defines it as "the transgression of the law"—the law of Him who holds the life of every human being in his hands and by whom everyone will be judged according to his works. Hereafter, when the Lord shall come in the clouds of heaven with power and great glory, every man will know who God is. Those who have trampled upon his law will then realize the sinfulness of sin. —*Lt 38, 1906*

False Shepherds are Powerless
Regarding the rapidly approaching advent of our Lord, the prophet Malachi raises the question, "Who may abide the day of his coming? And who shall stand when He appeareth?" Surely the arrows of God's wrath will pierce where the arrows of conviction could not. Where will the sinner flee when God pronounces judgment against him? Where will be the men in whom he trusted? Where are the false shepherds that led him astray? They can pay no ransom for his soul; for they themselves will be pressed under a still heavier load of guilt. The dens and caves of the earth afford no shelter for either deceiver or deceived. —*SW, June 23, 1908*

Surprised in Unfaithfulness

Those not found waiting and watching are finally surprised in their unfaithfulness. The Master comes, and instead of their being ready to open unto Him immediately, they are locked in worldly slumber, and are lost at last. —*2T, p. 191*

Foolish Virgins are Lost

The class represented by the foolish virgins have been content with a superficial work... When startled from their lethargy, they discern their destitution, and entreat others to supply their lack; but in spiritual things no man can make up another's deficiency. —*COL, p. 411*

A Dream of an Unprepared Group

I had a dream once in which I saw a large company gathered together, and suddenly the heavens gathered blackness, the thunder rolled, the lightning flashed, and a voice louder than the heaviest peals of thunder, sounded through the heavens and the earth, saying, "It is done." Part of the company, with pallid faces, sprang forward with a wail of agony, crying out, "Oh, I am not ready." The question was asked, "Why are you not ready? Why have you not improved the opportunities I graciously gave you?" I awoke with the cry ringing in my ears, "I am not ready; I am unsaved—lost! Lost! Eternally lost!"

—YI, July 21, 1892

Transgressors Cannot Look at Jesus

Those who trample upon God's authority, and show open contempt to the law given in such grandeur at Sinai, virtually despise the Lawgiver, the great Jehovah. The children of Israel who transgressed the first and second commandments, were charged not to be seen anywhere near the mount, where God was to descend in glory to write the law a second time upon tables of stone, lest they should be consumed with the burning glory of his presence.

And if they could not even look upon the face of Moses for the glory of his countenance, because he had been communing with God, how much less can the transgressors of God's law look upon the Son of God when He shall appear in the clouds of heaven in the glory of his Father, surrounded by all the angelic host, to execute judgment upon all who have disregarded the commandments of God, and have trodden underfoot his blood! —*1SP, p. 260*

All Wish for Christ's Favor

Christ is soon coming in glory, and when his majesty is revealed, the world will wish that they had his favor. At that time we shall all desire a place in the mansions of heaven; but those who do not confess Christ now in word, in life, in character, can not expect that He will confess them then before his Father and the holy angels. By those who have denied Him, the cry will be raised, even to the mountains, "Fall on us, and hide us from the face of Him that sitteth on the throne, and from the wrath of the Lamb: for the great day of his wrath is come; and who shall be able to stand?" — *RH, Jan. 2, 1913*

Sinners Hide from God's Face

The earth trembled before Him… "The kings of the earth, and the great men, and the rich men, and the chief captains, and the mighty men, and every bondman, and every freeman, hid themselves in the dens and in the rocks of the mountains; and said to the mountains and rocks, Fall on us, and hide us from the face of Him that sitteth on the throne, and from the wrath of the Lamb: for the great day of his wrath is come; and who shall be able to stand?"

Those who a short time before would have destroyed God's faithful children from the earth, now witnessed the glory of God which rested upon them. And amid all their terror they heard the voices of the saints in joyful strains, saying, "Lo, this is our God; we have waited for Him, and He will save us." — *EW, p. 286*

Evil Men Remain Impure

Do you think when the Lord shall come in the clouds of heaven, in the glory of his Father, with the holy retinue of angels, that He will give to you probation, that you may have another opportunity to form your characters for heaven? Is it to give you time to obtain moral fitness to enter the kingdom of glory? No opportunity is granted you then. It is then too late. No atoning blood then pleads in your behalf to wash away the stain of sin.

Just as you then are, you will remain. Just as you fall, so you must come up in the resurrection. And if you are living when the Son of Man is revealed, just as you are then found when He shall appear, if unready, so you must remain. The impure cannot then obtain perfection of Christian character. No work of purification can then be performed. — *RH, April 12, 1870*

Valuables are Thrown Away

In that day when every work shall be brought into judgment, when the Lord Jesus, with the marks of the crucifixion on his body, shall come in the clouds of heaven with power and great glory, those who, while holding positions of trust, have caused God's people to suffer, will cast their idols of silver and gold to the moles and to the bats; "to go into the clefts of the rocks, and into the tops of the ragged rocks, for fear of the Lord, and for the glory of his majesty, when He ariseth to shake terribly the earth." —*ST, May 13, 1897*

Former Sabbathkeepers Wail

I was shown a company who were howling in agony. On their garments was written in large characters, "Thou art weighed in the balance, and found wanting." I asked who this company were. The angel said, "These are they who have once kept the Sabbath and have given it up." I heard them cry with a loud voice, "We have believed in thy coming, and taught it with energy."

And while they were speaking, their eyes would fall upon their garments and see the writing, and then they would wail aloud. I saw that they had drunk of the deep waters, and fouled the residue with their feet—trodden the Sabbath underfoot—and that was why they were weighed in the balance and found wanting. —*EW, p. 36*

Skeptics are Surprised to See Jesus

Skepticism and that which is called science have undermined the faith to a large degree of the Christian world in their Bibles. Error and fables are gladly accepted, that they may pursue the path of self-indulgence and be not alarmed, for they are striving not to retain God in their knowledge. They say tomorrow will be as this day and much more abundant. But in the midst of their unbelief and godless pleasure, the shout of the archangel and the trump of God are heard. The fatal deception is broken at last, and they find themselves weighed in the balance and found wanting.

"Behold I come as a thief." Just when the world has been rocked to sleep by the peace and safety cry of the professed watchman, just when the scoffer is uttering his bold challenge, "Where is the promise of his coming;" when everything in our world is busy activity immersed in selfish ambition for gain, Jesus comes as a thief in the night. —*Ms 15b, 1886*

310

Remorse and Despair

When Christ suffered for the human race, He felt neither remorse, despair, or hatred. Far different will be the feelings of the sinner who has not availed himself of Christ's atoning sacrifice. Too late, he will realize what he has lost by refusing to accept the salvation of God. His heart will then be filled with an agony of remorse and despair, even though still fired by satanic hatred against God. — *Ms 87, 1903*

Jesus Appears in Flaming Fire

Many think lightly of Christ now. They despise and reject Him and say, "Where is the promise of his coming? For since the fathers fell asleep all things continue as they were from the beginning." But we read, "He shall come to judgment," and "every eye shall see Him." Mal 3:5; Rev. 1:7.

The same Jesus whose atonement has been rejected, whose followers have been despised and reviled, will be revealed from heaven "in flaming fire taking vengeance upon them that know not God and that obey not the gospel of our Lord Jesus Christ, who shall be punished with everlasting destruction from the presence of the Lord, and from the glory of his power." 2 Thessalonians 1:7-9. "Then shall all the kindreds of the earth wail because of Him." Revelation 1:7. — *Ms 39, 1898*

The Indescribable Terror of Sinners

It was a great cross for me to relate to the erring what had been shown me concerning them. It caused me great distress to see others troubled or grieved. And when obliged to declare the messages, I would often soften them down, and make them appear as favorable for the individual as I could, and then would go by myself and weep in agony of spirit...

I did not realize the danger and sin of such a course, until in vision I was taken into the presence of Jesus. He looked upon me with a frown, and turned his face from me. It is not possible to describe the terror and agony I then felt. I fell upon my face before Him, but had no power to utter a word. Oh, how I longed to be covered and hid from that dreadful frown! Then could I realize, in some degree, what the feelings of the lost will be when they cry: "Mountains and rocks, fall on us, and hide us from the face of Him that sitteth on the throne, and from the wrath of the Lamb." — *1T, pp. 73, 74*

Many are Terror-Stricken

There is also to be a revelation to the transgressors of the law of Jehovah—them that made void the law of God, that have taken their stand on the side of him who thought to change times and laws. From the terror-stricken myriads comes the cry, "The great day of his wrath is come; and who shall be able to stand?" Revelation 6:17. —*Ms 56, 1886*

A Cry of Agony and Despair Echoes

Too well do the unprepared inhabitants of earth know what to expect. Satan cannot pay a ransom for their souls, and poor deluded, professed Christians, who have been content to let the ministers do their searching of the Scriptures, see that they will receive as their works have been. Those, too, who have wrested the Scriptures and taught for doctrine the commandments of men, see that they must answer for the souls of those whom they have led into error and apostasy. A wail of despair and agony reaches heavenward, but it is echoed back to earth. Louder, far louder than any human cry, is the last trumpet's sound, and far above all is heard the voice of Omnipotence: "Depart from Me, ye that work iniquity." —*Ms 39, 1898*

Sinners Recall Statements against Jesus

Riches, power, genius, eloquence, pride, perverted reason, and passion, are enlisted as Satan's agents in doing his work in making the broad road attractive, strewing it with tempting flowers. But every word they have spoken against the world's Redeemer will be reflected back upon them, and will one day burn into their guilty souls like molten lead. They will be overwhelmed with terror and shame as they behold the exalted one coming in the clouds of heaven with power and great glory. Then shall the bold defier, who lifted himself up against the Son of God, see himself in the true blackness of his character.

The sight of the inexpressible glory of the Son of God will be intensely painful to those whose characters are stained with sin. The pure light and glory emanating from Christ will awaken remorse, shame, and terror. They will send forth wails of anguish to the rocks and mountains, "Fall on us, and hide us from the face of Him who sitteth on the throne, and from the wrath of the Lamb; for the great day of his wrath is come, and who shall be able to stand?" —*RH, Apr. 1, 1875*

The Wicked Face Millions of Angels

If the soldiers at the sepulcher were so filled with terror at the appearance of one angel clothed with heavenly light and strength, that they fell as dead men to the ground, how will his enemies stand before the Son of God, when He comes in power and great glory, accompanied by ten thousand times ten thousand, and thousands of thousands of angels from the courts of heaven? Then the earth shall reel to and fro like a drunkard, and be removed as a cottage. The elements shall be in flames, and the heavens shall be rolled together as a scroll. —*3SP, p. 193*

Mysterious Voices Declare Awful Doom

Thick clouds still cover the sky; yet the sun now and then breaks through, appearing like the avenging eye of Jehovah. Fierce lightnings leap from the heavens, enveloping the earth in a sheet of flame. Above the terrific roar of thunder, voices, mysterious and awful, declare the doom of the wicked.

The words spoken are not comprehended by all; but they are distinctly understood by the false teachers. Those who a little before were so reckless, so boastful and defiant, so exultant in their cruelty to God's commandment-keeping people, are now overwhelmed with consternation and shuddering in fear. Their wails are heard above the sound of the elements. Demons acknowledge the deity of Christ and tremble before his power, while men are supplicating for mercy and groveling in abject terror.

Said the prophets of old, as they beheld in holy vision the day of God: "Howl ye; for the day of the Lord is at hand; it shall come as a destruction from the Almighty." Isaiah 13:6. "Enter into the rock, and hide thee in the dust, for fear of the Lord, and for the glory of his majesty. The lofty looks of man shall be humbled, and the haughtiness of men shall be bowed down, and the Lord alone shall be exalted in that day. For the day of the Lord of hosts shall be upon every one that is proud and lofty, and upon every one that is lifted up; and he shall be brought low."

"In that day a man shall cast the idols of his silver, and the idols of his gold, which they made each one for himself to worship, to the moles and to the bats; to go into the clefts of the rocks, and into the tops of the ragged rocks, for fear of the Lord, and for the glory of his majesty, when He ariseth to shake terribly the earth." Isaiah 2:10-12, 20, 21. — *GC, pp. 637, 638*

False Teachers are Surprised

The advent of Christ will surprise the false teachers. They are saying, "Peace and safety." Like the priests and teachers before the fall of Jerusalem, they look for the church to enjoy earthly prosperity and glory. The signs of the times they interpret as foreshadowing this. But what saith the word of Inspiration? "Sudden destruction cometh upon them." 1 Thessalonians 5:3. Upon all who dwell on the face of the whole earth, upon all who make this world their home, the day of God will come as a snare. It comes to them as a prowling thief. —*DA, p. 635*

The Wrath of the Lamb is Understood

When Christ shall come in his own glory, and the glory of the Father, escorted by the armies of heaven, a crown within a crown upon his sacred head, his searching eye as a flame of fire burns into the very souls of those who are his enemies. He is clothed in a garment of the whitest white, such as no fuller on earth can white it, and girded about the breasts with a golden girdle, then the men who have acted out all this farce and debasing mockery will see Him as He is. They will understand what is comprehended in the wrath of the Lamb. This very scene they have enacted will stand out in all its degrading particulars in living, speaking symbols. Then they will have a knowledge of the value of the human soul, and the virtue of character, the Christlikeness they might have obtained and did not.

The tree of knowledge of evil, withheld from them for their good, they have greedily plucked of, and eaten, and continued to eat until unlawful deeds poisoned their thoughts and degraded their aspirations for healthful piety and eternal good. They have separated from God and united with their disobedience, boldness and cunning and cruelty. They see it all, their entrusted capabilities tainted, corrupted, degraded. They sense then what they have done. They see then that the power of their entrusted capacities they might have employed for good, and not for evil. The whole work of their lives fills them with abhorrence of themselves.

And as they view the hopelessness of their case, they cry out in awful agony and horror, "Rocks and mountains, fall on us, and hide us from the face of Him that sitteth upon the throne, and from the wrath of the Lamb, for the great day of his wrath is come, and who shall be able to stand?" —*Ms 112, 1897*

The Sad Fate of Apostates

You think, that those who worship before the saint's feet, Revelation 3:9, will at last be saved. Here I must differ with you; for God showed me that this class were professed Adventists, who had fallen away, and "crucified to themselves the Son of God afresh, and put Him to an open shame." And in the "hour of temptation," which is yet to come, to show out everyone's true character, they will know that they are forever lost; and overwhelmed with anguish of spirit, they will bow at the saint's feet. — *WLF, p. 12*

Wicked Consciences Awaken

When the voice of God turns the captivity of his people, there is a terrible awakening of those who have lost all in the great conflict of life. While probation continued they were blinded by Satan's deceptions, and they justified their course of sin. The rich prided themselves upon their superiority to those who were less favored; but they had obtained their riches by violation of the law of God. They had neglected to feed the hungry, to clothe the naked, to deal justly, and to love mercy. They had sought to exalt themselves and to obtain the homage of their fellow creatures.

Now they are stripped of all that made them great and are left destitute and defenseless. They look with terror upon the destruction of the idols which they preferred before their Maker. They have sold their souls for earthly riches and enjoyments, and have not sought to become rich toward God.

The result is, their lives are a failure; their pleasures are now turned to gall, their treasures to corruption. The gain of a lifetime is swept away in a moment. The rich bemoan the destruction of their grand houses, the scattering of their gold and silver. But their lamentations are silenced by the fear that they themselves are to perish with their idols.

The wicked are filled with regret, not because of their sinful neglect of God and their fellow men, but because God has conquered. They lament that the result is what it is; but they do not repent of their wickedness. They would leave no means untried to conquer if they could. The world see the very class whom they have mocked and derided, and desired to exterminate, pass unharmed through pestilence, tempest, and earthquake. He who is to the transgressors of his law a devouring fire, is to his people a safe pavilion.

— GC, p. 654

315

Sinners Realize What They Lost

The scene upon which the impenitent look makes them realize what they might have been had they received Christ and improved the opportunities granted them. —*Lt 131, 1900*

Unfaithful Ministers Fall and Confess

The minister who has sacrificed truth to gain the favor of men now discerns the character and influence of his teachings. It is apparent that the omniscient eye was following him as he stood in the desk, as he walked the streets, as he mingled with men in the various scenes of life. Every emotion of the soul, every line written, every word uttered, every act that led men to rest in a refuge of falsehood, has been scattering seed; and now, in the wretched, lost souls around him, he beholds the harvest.

Saith the Lord: "They have healed the hurt of the daughter of my people slightly, saying, Peace, peace; when there is no peace." "With lies ye have made the heart of the righteous sad, whom I have not made sad; and strengthened the hands of the wicked, that he should not return from his wicked way, by promising him life." Jeremiah 8:11; Ezekiel 13:22.

"Woe be unto the pastors that destroy and scatter the sheep of my pasture! ... Behold, I will visit upon you the evil of your doings." "Howl, ye shepherds, and cry; and wallow yourselves in the ashes, ye principal of the flock: for your days for slaughter and of your dispersions are accomplished; ... and the shepherds shall have no way to flee, nor the principal of the flock to escape." Jeremiah 23:1, 2; 25:34, 35. Ministers and people see that they have not sustained the right relation to God. They see that they have rebelled against the Author of all just and righteous law. The setting aside of the divine precepts gave rise to thousands of springs of evil, discord, hatred, iniquity, until the earth became one vast field of strife, one sink of corruption.

This is the view that now appears to those who rejected truth and chose to cherish error. No language can express the longing which the disobedient and disloyal feel for that which they have lost forever—eternal life. Men whom the world has worshipped for their talents and eloquence now see these things in their true light. They realize what they have forfeited by transgression, and they fall at the feet of those whose fidelity they have despised and derided, and confess that God has loved them. —*GC, pp. 654, 655*

Copenhagen is Surprised like Sodom

While in Copenhagen we… one day ascended the "round tower," a very large and high tower connected with an old church… nine stories high… A few stairs take us to the roof, which commands an extensive view of the city and the surrounding towns and islands…

As I looked down upon the great city, I could but think of the scenes that will be witnessed here when Christ shall come. This city is given up to pleasure and worldliness. Beer-drinking and card-playing, dancing and reveling, absorb the attention of the people. The multitudes will mock at the message of warning.

Like the dwellers in Sodom, they will be awakened only when it is too late. As the sun arose for the last time upon the cities of the plain, the people thought to commence another day of godless riot. All were eagerly planning their business or their pleasure, and the messenger of God was derided for his fears and his warnings. Suddenly as the thunder peal from an unclouded sky, fell balls of fire on the doomed capital.

"So shall also the coming of the Son of man be." The people will be eating and drinking, planting and building, marrying and giving in marriage, until the wrath of God shall be poured out without mixture of mercy. The world will be rocked to sleep in the cradle of carnal security. They have been taught by their ministers to believe that the second advent of Christ is to be spiritual or to take place in the distant future, and the warning of his soon coming is denounced as fanaticism or heresy. Skepticism and "science falsely so-called" have undermined faith in the Bible. The multitudes are striving to forget God, and they eagerly accept fables, that they may pursue the path of self-indulgence undisturbed. The people are hurrying to and fro, the lovers of pleasure intent upon amusement, the money-makers seeking wealth, and all are saying, "Where is the promise of his coming?"

Then it is that the voice of the archangel and the trump of God are heard. Oh, what terror will then overwhelm the wicked! What cries of anguish will be heard from those who have derided the overtures of mercy from God's messengers! The bolts and bars by which they sought to guard their treasures are rent asunder by the mighty earthquake. The grand and magnificent buildings are shaken down, and the guilty triflers are buried in the ruins.

—RH, Oct. 26, 1886

A Hand Appears Holding the Decalogue

While these words of holy trust ascend to God, the clouds sweep back, and the starry heavens are seen, unspeakably glorious in contrast with the black and angry firmament on either side. The glory of the celestial city streams from the gates ajar. Then there appears against the sky a hand holding two tables of stone folded together. Says the prophet: "The heavens shall declare his righteousness: for God is judge Himself." Psalm 50:6.

That holy law, God's righteousness, that amid thunder and flame was proclaimed from Sinai as the guide of life, is now revealed to men as the rule of judgment. The hand opens the tables, and there are seen the precepts of the Decalogue, traced as with a pen of fire. The words are so plain that all can read them. Memory is aroused, the darkness of superstition and heresy is swept from every mind, and God's ten words, brief, comprehensive, and authoritative, are presented to the view of all the inhabitants of the earth.

It is impossible to describe the horror and despair of those who have trampled upon God's holy requirements. The Lord gave them his law; they might have compared their characters with it and learned their defects while there was yet opportunity for repentance and reform; but in order to secure the favor of the world, they set aside its precepts and taught others to transgress. They have endeavored to compel God's people to profane his Sabbath. Now they are condemned by that law which they have despised. With awful distinctness they see that they are without excuse. They chose whom they would serve and worship. "Then shall ye return, and discern between the righteous and the wicked, between him that serveth God and him that serveth Him not." Malachi 3:18.

The enemies of God's law, from the ministers down to the least among them, have a new conception of truth and duty. Too late they see that the Sabbath of the fourth commandment is the seal of the living God. Too late they see the true nature of their spurious sabbath and the sandy foundation upon which they have been building. They find that they have been fighting against God. Religious teachers have led souls to perdition while professing to guide them to the gates of Paradise. Not until the day of final accounts will it be known how great is the responsibility of men in holy office and how terrible are the results of their unfaithfulness. Only in eternity can we rightly estimate the loss of a single soul. *— GC, pp. 639, 640*

The King of Glory is Acknowledged

The Father's wisdom and glory shines forth in his (Christ's) majesty. He is exalted and precious to all who believe. But his own personal glory, who can describe it? He comes with his divine nature plainly revealed—He who was denied and rejected by man, who stood at the bar of Pilate as a criminal. Where is that priest who rent his robe in hypocritical horror as he charged Him with blasphemy? Look at Him as He comes forth from the dead. What think ye of Jesus now? Will men now withhold from Him recognition and honor? Will those who were actors at the bar of Pilate refuse Him worship now? ...

Christ is now acknowledged as the King of Glory. "Blessed is He that cometh in the name of the Lord." Matthew 23:39. The question of his divinity is forever settled. Where are those who held the Saviour bound at Pilate's bar, who smote Him in the face, who scourged Him, who drove the nails through his hands and feet; those who mocked Him, saying, "He saved others; himself He cannot save. If he be the King of Israel, let Him now come down from the cross, and we will believe Him. He trusted in God; let Him deliver Him now, if He will have Him; for He said, I am the Son of God"? Matthew 27:42, 43.

Where is the puny arm that will be lifted against Him now? The scene is changed. "At the name of Jesus every knee shall bow, and every tongue shall confess that Jesus is Christ, Lord of heaven and earth, to the glory of God the Father." Philippians 2:10, 11. The angels of heaven bow in adoration before him. His enemies discern the mistake they have made, and every tongue confesses his divinity.

The glory of Christ's humanity did not appear when He was upon the earth. He was regarded as a man of sorrows, and acquainted with grief. We hid as it were our faces from Him. But He was pursuing the path the plan of God had devised. That same humanity now appears as He descends from heaven, robed in glory, triumphant, exalted. His priestly character appears. He has taken the blood of his own atonement into the holiest of all, sprinkled it there upon the mercy seat, and upon his own garments, and blessed the people. He has come and offered Himself a sacrifice, and appears the second time to declare that there is to be no more sacrifice for sin. —*Lt 90, 1898*

319

The Wicked Recognize Christ's Voice

The derisive jests have ceased. Lying lips are hushed into silence. The clash of arms, the tumult of battle, "with confused noise, and garments rolled in blood" (Isaiah 9:5), is stilled. Naught now is heard but the voice of prayer and the sound of weeping and lamentation. The cry bursts forth from lips so lately scoffing: "The great day of his wrath is come; and who shall be able to stand?" The wicked pray to be buried beneath the rocks of the mountains rather than meet the face of Him whom they have despised and rejected.

That voice which penetrates the ear of the dead, they know. How often have its plaintive, tender tones called them to repentance. How often has it been heard in the touching entreaties of a friend, a brother, a Redeemer. To the rejecters of his grace no other could be so full of condemnation, so burdened with denunciation, as that voice which has so long pleaded: "Turn ye, turn ye from your evil ways; for why will ye die?" Ezekiel 33:11.

Oh, that it were to them the voice of a stranger! Says Jesus: "I have called, and ye refused; I have stretched out my hand, and no man regarded; but ye have set at naught all my counsel, and would none of my reproof." Proverbs 1:24, 25. That voice awakens memories which they would fain blot out—warnings despised, invitations refused, privileges slighted. — *GC, p. 642*

Men Beg for Jesus to Save Them

Those who choose to make excuses and continue in sin and conformity to the world will be left to their idols. There will be a day when they will not beg to be excused, when not one will wish to be excused. When Christ shall come in his glory and the glory of his Father, with all the heavenly angels surrounding Him, escorting Him on his way with voices of triumph, while strains of the most enchanting music fall upon the ear, all will then be interested; there will not be one indifferent spectator.

Speculations will not then engross the soul. The miser's piles of gold, which have feasted his eyes, are no more attractive. The palaces which the proud men of earth have erected, and which have been their idols, are turned from with loathing and disgust. No one pleads his lands, his oxen, his wife that he has just married, as a reason why he should be excused from sharing the glory that bursts upon his astonished vision.

All want a share, but know that it is not for them. In earnest, agonizing prayer they call for God to pass them not by. The kings, the mighty men, the lofty, the proud, the mean man, alike bow together under a pressure of woe, desolation, misery inexpressible; heart-anguished prayers are wrung from their lips. "Mercy! Mercy! Save us from the wrath of an offended God!" A voice answers them with terrible distinctness, sternness, and majesty: "Because I have called, and ye refused; I have stretched out my hand, and no man regarded; but ye have set at nought all my counsel, and would none of my reproof: I also will laugh at your calamity; I will mock when your fear cometh."

Then kings and nobles, the mighty man, and the poor man, and the mean man, alike, cry there most bitterly. They who in the days of their prosperity despised Christ and the humble ones who followed in his footsteps, men who would not humble their dignity to bow to Christ, who hated his despised cross, are now prostrate in the mire of the earth. Their greatness has all at once left them, and they do not hesitate to bow to the earth at the feet of the saints. They then realize with terrible bitterness that they are eating the fruit of their own way, and are filled with their own devices.

In their supposed wisdom they turned away from the high, eternal reward, rejected the heavenly inducement, for earthly gain. The glitter and tinsel of earth fascinated them, and in their supposed wisdom they became fools. They exulted in their worldly prosperity as though their worldly advantages were so great that they could through them be recommended to God, and thus secure heaven.

Money was power among the foolish of earth, and money was their god; but their very prosperity has destroyed them. They became fools in the eyes of God and his heavenly angels, while men of worldly ambition thought them wise. Now their supposed wisdom is all foolishness, and their prosperity their destruction. Again ring forth shrieks of fearful, heart-rending anguish: "Rocks and mountains, fall on us, and hide us from the face of Him that sitteth on the throne, and from the wrath of the Lamb; for the great day of his wrath is come, and who shall be able to stand?" To the caves of the earth they flee as a covert, but these fail to be such then. —2T, pp. 41, 42

321

B) The Crucifiers are Raised

Violent Persecutors are Raised

Graves are opened, and "many of them that sleep in the dust of the earth...
awake, some to everlasting life, and some to shame and everlasting
contempt." Daniel 12:2. All who have died in the faith of the third angel's
message come forth from the tomb glorified, to hear God's covenant of peace
with those who have kept his law. "They also which pierced Him" (Revelation
1:7), those that mocked and derided Christ's dying agonies, and the most
violent opposers of his truth and his people, are raised to behold Him in his
glory and to see the honor placed upon the loyal and obedient. — *GC, p. 637*

Christ's Crucifiers Come Up

When Christ comes to gather to Himself those who have been faithful, the
last trump will sound, and the whole earth from the summits of the loftiest
mountains to the lowest recesses of the deepest mines will hear. The righteous
dead will hear the sound of the trump and will come forth from their graves,
to be clothed with immortality and to meet their Lord. And those who
pierced the Saviour, those who scourged and crucified Him will also be raised,
to behold Him whom they mocked and despised coming in the clouds of
heaven, attended by the heavenly host, ten thousand times ten thousand and
thousands of thousands. — *Ms 184, 1905*

Roman Soldiers Wail in Terror

The sound of music is heard; and as it nears, the graves are opened and the
dead are raised and there are thousands of thousands and ten thousand times
ten thousand of angels that compose that glory and encircle the Son of man.
Those who have acted the most prominent part in the rejection and
crucifixion of Christ come forth to see Him as He is, and those who have
rejected Christ come up and see the saints glorified, and it is at that time that
the saints are changed in a moment, in the twinkling of an eye, and are caught
up to meet their Lord in the air. The very ones who placed upon Him the
purple robe, and put the crown of thorns upon his brow, and those who put
the nails through his hands and feet, look upon Him and bewail. — *Ms 81, 1886*

Awful Sins Pierced Jesus

What a day that will be, when those who rejected Christ will look upon Him whom their sins have pierced. They will then know that He proffered them all heaven if they would but stand by his side as obedient children; that He paid an infinite price for their redemption; but that they would not accept freedom from the galling slavery of sin. They chose to stand under the black banner of rebellion to the close of mercy's hour. — *RH, Sept. 5, 1899*

John Saw a Dreadful Scene

To John were opened the great events of the future, that were to shake the thrones of kings and cause all earthly powers to tremble. He beheld the close of all earthly scenes, the ushering in of his reign, who is to be King of kings, and whose kingdom shall endure forever. "Behold," he said, "He cometh with clouds; and every eye shall see Him, and they also which pierced Him: and all kindreds of the earth shall wail because of Him." — *Ms 100, 1893*

A Perpetual Curse on the Jews

Looking upon the smitten Lamb of God, the Jews had cried, "His blood be on us, and on our children." That awful cry ascended to the throne of God. That sentence, pronounced upon themselves, was written in heaven. That prayer was heard. The blood of the Son of God was upon their children and their children's children, a perpetual curse. Terribly was it realized in the destruction of Jerusalem. Terribly has it been manifested in the condition of the Jewish nation for eighteen hundred years—a branch severed from the vine, a dead, fruitless branch, to be gathered up and burned. From land to land throughout the world, from century to century, dead, dead in trespasses and sins!

Terribly will that prayer be fulfilled in the great judgment day. When Christ shall come to the earth again, not as a prisoner surrounded by a rabble will men see Him. They will see Him then as heaven's King. Christ will come in his own glory, in the glory of his Father, and the glory of the holy angels. Ten thousand times ten thousand, and thousands of thousands of angels, the beautiful and triumphant sons of God, possessing surpassing loveliness and glory, will escort Him on his way. — *DA, p. 739*

Jesus Returns as the King of Glory

Jesus' life was without worldly grandeur, or extravagant show. His humble, self-denying life was a great contrast to the lives of the priests and elders, who loved ease and worldly honor, and the strict and holy life of Jesus was a continual reproof to them, on account of their sins. They despised Him for his humbleness, holiness and purity.

But those who despised Him here, will one day see Him in the grandeur of heaven, and the unsurpassed glory of his Father. He was surrounded with enemies in the judgment hall, who were thirsting for his blood; but those hardened ones who cried out, "His blood be on us and on our children," will behold Him an honored King. All the heavenly host will escort Him on his way with songs of victory, majesty and might, to Him that was slain, yet lives again a mighty conqueror.

Poor, weak, miserable man spit in the face of the King of glory, while a shout of brutal triumph arose from the mob at the degrading insult. They marred that face with blows and cruelty which filled all heaven with admiration. They will behold that face again, bright as the noon-day sun, and will seek to flee from before it. Instead of that shout of brutal triumph, in terror they will wail because of Him.

Jesus will present his hands with the marks of his crucifixion. The marks of this cruelty He will ever bear. Every print of the nails will tell the story of man's wonderful redemption, and the dear price that purchased it. The very men who thrust the spear into the side of the Lord of life, will behold the print of the spear, and will lament with deep anguish the part they acted in marring his body. His murderers were greatly annoyed by the superscription, "The King of the Jews," placed upon the cross above his head.

But then they will be obliged to see Him in all his glory and kingly power. They will behold on his vesture and on his thigh, written in living characters, King of kings, and Lord of lords. They cried to Him mockingly, as He hung upon the cross, "Let Christ the King of Israel descend from the cross, that we may see and believe." They will behold Him then with kingly power and authority. They will demand no evidence then of his being the King of Israel; but overwhelmed with a sense of his majesty and exceeding glory, they will be compelled to acknowledge, "Blessed is He that cometh in the name of the Lord." — *1SG, p. 61*

324

Priests and Rulers Remember Calvary

There are those who mocked Christ in his humiliation. With thrilling power come to their minds the Sufferer's words, when, adjured by the high priest, He solemnly declared: "Hereafter shall ye see the Son of man sitting on the right hand of power, and coming in the clouds of heaven." Matthew 26:64. Now they behold Him in his glory, and they are yet to see Him sitting on the right hand of power.

Those who derided his claim to be the Son of God are speechless now. There is the haughty Herod who jeered at his royal title and bade the mocking soldiers crown Him king. There are the very men who with impious hands placed upon his form the purple robe, upon his sacred brow the thorny crown, and in his unresisting hand the mimic scepter, and bowed before Him in blasphemous mockery. The men who smote and spit upon the Prince of life now turn from his piercing gaze and seek to flee from the overpowering glory of his presence. Those who drove the nails through his hands and feet, the soldier who pierced his side, behold these marks with terror and remorse.

With awful distinctness do priests and rulers recall the events of Calvary. With shuddering horror they remember how, wagging their heads in satanic exultation, they exclaimed: "He saved others; Himself He cannot save. If He be the King of Israel, let Him now come down from the cross, and we will believe Him. He trusted in God; let Him deliver Him now, if He will have Him." Matthew 27:42, 43.

Vividly they recall the Saviour's parable of the husbandmen who refused to render to their lord the fruit of the vineyard, who abused his servants and slew his son. They remember, too, the sentence which they themselves pronounced: The lord of the vineyard "will miserably destroy those wicked men." In the sin and punishment of those unfaithful men the priests and elders see their own course and their own just doom.

And now there rises a cry of mortal agony. Louder than the shout, "Crucify Him, crucify Him," which rang through the streets of Jerusalem, swells the awful, despairing wail, "He is the Son of God! He is the true Messiah!" They seek to flee from the presence of the King of kings. In the deep caverns of the earth, rent asunder by the warring of the elements, they vainly attempt to hide. In the lives of all who reject truth there are moments when conscience awakens, when memory presents the torturing recollection

325

of a life of hypocrisy and the soul is harassed with vain regrets. But what are these compared with the remorse of that day when "fear cometh as desolation," when "destruction cometh as a whirlwind!" Proverbs 1:27.

Those who would have destroyed Christ and his faithful people now witness the glory which rests upon them. In the midst of their terror they hear the voices of the saints in joyful strains exclaiming: "Lo, this is our God; we have waited for Him, and He will save us." Isaiah 25:9. *— GC, pp. 643, 644*

Sinners Chose Barabbas over Jesus

When sinners are compelled to look upon Him who clothed his divinity with humanity, and who still wears this garb, their confusion is indescribable. The scales fall from their eyes, and they see that which before they would not see. They realize what they might have been had they received Christ, and improved the opportunities granted them. They see the law which they have spurned, exalted even as God's throne is exalted. They see God Himself giving reverence to his law.

What a scene that will be! No pen can describe it! The accumulated guilt of the world will be laid bare, and the voice of the Judge will be heard saying to the wicked, "Depart from Me, ye that work iniquity." Then those who pierced Christ will remember how they slighted his love and abused his compassion; how they chose in his stead Barabbas, a robber and murderer; how they crowned the Saviour with thorns, and caused Him to be scourged and crucified; how, in the agony of his death on the cross, they taunted Him, saying, "Let Him now come down from the cross, and we will believe Him."

"He saved others; Himself He cannot save." They will seem to hear again his voice of entreaty. Every tone of solicitude will vibrate as distinctly in their ears as when the Saviour spoke to them. Every act of insult and mockery done to Christ will be as fresh in their memory as when the satanic deeds were done. They will call on the rocks and mountains to fall on them and hide them from the face of Him that sitteth on the throne and from the wrath of the Lamb. "The wrath of the Lamb,"—One who ever showed Himself full of tenderness, patience, and long-suffering, who, having given Himself up as the sacrificial offering, was led as a lamb to the slaughter, to save sinners from the doom now falling upon them because they would not allow Him to take away their guilt. *— RH, June 18, 1901*

Evil Men Look upon Christ

The angels of God faithfully recorded every insulting look, word, and act directed against their beloved Commander; and the base men who scorned and spat upon the calm, pale face of Christ, were one day to look upon it in its glory, shining brighter than the sun. In that awful time they would pray to the rocks and the mountains: "Hide us from the face of Him who sitteth upon the throne, and from the wrath of the Lamb." —*3SP, p. 122*

Zechariah's Vision is Fulfilled

The triumphal ride of Christ into Jerusalem was the dim foreshadowing of his coming in the clouds of heaven with power and glory, amid the triumph of angels and the rejoicing of the saints. Then will be fulfilled the words of Christ to the priests and Pharisees: "Ye shall not see Me henceforth, till ye shall say, Blessed is He that cometh in the name of the Lord." Matthew 23:39.

In prophetic vision Zechariah was shown that day of final triumph; and he beheld also the doom of those who at the first advent had rejected Christ: "They shall look upon Me whom they have pierced, and they shall mourn for Him, as one mourneth for his only son, and shall be in bitterness for Him, as one that is in bitterness for his first-born." Zechariah 12:10. This scene Christ foresaw when He beheld the city and wept over it. In the temporal ruin of Jerusalem He saw the final destruction of that people who were guilty of the blood of the Son of God. —*DA, p. 580*

Discussion Questions

1. Will the wicked be surprised to see Christ coming in clouds of glory?

2. What causes evildoers to be unable to look upon the face of Jesus?

3. Why will unfaithful Adventists howl in agony when Christ returns?

4. How will sinners respond to the Messiah's grand entrance?

5. Why does Jesus resurrect the men who persecuted Him?

— 22 —

Sinners are Destroyed

"For the time is come that judgment must begin at the house of God: and if it first begin at us, what shall the end be of them that obey not the gospel of God?" — 1 Peter 4:17

Job 19:29	Isaiah 34:1-8	Jer. 51:47-58	Ezek. 38:21-23	Matt. 13:37-43
Psalm 37:20-22	Isaiah 66:15-18	Ezek. 9:1-6	Zeph. 1:1-18	Luke 17:29, 30
Isaiah 13:11-16	Jer. 25:30-38	Ezek. 33:11	Zech. 14:12, 13	1 Thes. 5:1-3

A) The Doom of False Ministers

False Shepherds are Punished

God's Word is made of none effect by false shepherds... Their work will soon react upon themselves. Then will be witnessed the scenes described in Revelation 18 when the judgments of God shall fall upon mystical Babylon.

— Ms 60, 1900

Wrath Falls on Evil Watchmen

The day of woe, of wasting, and destruction is upon all who do unrighteousness. Especially will the Lord's hand fall upon the watchmen who have failed to place before the people in clear lines their obligation to God, who by creation and by redemption is their Owner. *— Lt 74, 1900*

Men Turn on Their Ministers

Those surrounding the righteous are then in their time of distress and inexpressible fear. The horror of despair seizes them, and these poor infatuated ones seem now to understand themselves. Those who have been deceived by the fables preached to them by their ministers now charge upon them the loss of their souls: "You have preached to us falsehoods. We have believed a lie, and are lost, forever lost." *— ST, Nov. 27, 1879*

False Prophets are Destroyed

The end of all things is at hand. The coming of the Lord in the clouds of heaven, with power and great glory, is very near. At this time, when wickedness is at its height, ministers of the gospel are crying, "Peace and safety." Upon those whose minds are thus set at rest, sudden destruction cometh. Unprepared, they shall not escape. —*Ms 184, 1905*

Deceitful Pastors are Condemned

The people turned upon their ministers with bitter hate and reproached them, saying, "You have not warned us. You told us that all the world was to be converted, and cried, 'Peace, peace,' to quiet every fear that was aroused. You have not told us of this hour; and those who warned us of it you declared to be fanatics and evil men, who would ruin us." —*EW, p. 282*

Ministers are Blamed for Loss of Souls

The shepherds who lead the sheep in false paths will hear the charge made against them, "It was you who made light of truth. It was you who told us that God's law was abrogated, that it was a yoke of bondage. It was you who voiced the false doctrines when I was convicted that these Seventh-day Adventists had the truth. The blood of our souls is upon your priestly garments. The persecution brought upon those who kept God's commandments did not destroy them or their influence."

"I could not read my Bible with its condemnatory words, and I laid it aside. Now will you pay the ransom for my soul? You said you would stand between my soul and God, but you are now full of anguish yourself. What shall we do who listened to your garbling of the Scriptures and your turning into a lie the truth that if obeyed would have saved us?"

When Christ comes to take vengeance on those who have educated and trained the people to trample on God's Sabbath, to tear down his memorial, and tread down with their feet the feed of his pastures, lamentations will be in vain. Those who trusted in the false shepherds had the Word of God to search for themselves, and they find that God will judge every man who has had the truth and turned from the light because it involved self-denial and the cross. Rocks and mountains cannot screen them from the indignation of Him that sitteth on the throne and from the wrath of the Lamb. —*Lt 86, 1900*

Strife and Bloodshed Everywhere

The people see that they have been deluded. They accuse one another of having led them to destruction; but all unite in heaping their bitterest condemnation upon the ministers. Unfaithful pastors have prophesied smooth things; they have led their hearers to make void the law of God and to persecute those who would keep it holy. Now, in their despair, these teachers confess before the world their work of deception. The multitudes are filled with fury. "We are lost!" they cry, "and you are the cause of our ruin;" and they turn upon the false shepherds.

The very ones that once admired them most will pronounce the most dreadful curses upon them. The very hands that once crowned them with laurels will be raised for their destruction. The swords which were to slay God's people are now employed to destroy their enemies. Everywhere there is strife and bloodshed. — *GC, pp. 654, 655*

Some Wish to Tear Ministers Apart

With his own finger God wrote his commandments on two tables of stone. These tables were not left in the keeping of men, but were placed in the ark; and in the great day when every case is decided, these tables, inscribed with the commandments, will be placed so that all the world will see and understand. The witness against them will be unanswerable. And upon those, who have taken upon them the work of shepherds of the flock, will be visited the heaviest judgments, because they have presented to the people fables instead of truth. Children will rise up and curse their parents.

Church members, who have seen the light and been convicted, but who have trusted the salvation of their souls to the minister, will learn in the day of God that no other soul can pay the ransom for their transgression.

A terrible cry will be raised, "I am lost, eternally lost." Men will feel as though they could rend in pieces the ministers who have preached falsehoods and condemned the truth. The pure truth for this time requires a reformation in the life, but they separate themselves from the love of the truth, and of them it can be said, "O Israel, thou hast destroyed thyself." The Lord sends a message to the people: "Set a trumpet to thy mouth. He shall come as an eagle against the house of the Lord, because they have transgressed my covenant and trespassed against my law." Hosea 8:1. — *Lt 30, 1900*

B) The Destroying Angel

The Wicked are Gathered

In the harvest of the world there will be no likeness between good and evil. The wicked will be gathered from the righteous, to trouble them no more forever. —*2SP, p. 249*

Two Angels Fly Forth

The angel with the writer's inkhorn is to place a mark upon the foreheads of all who are separated from sin and sinners, and the destroying angel follows this angel. —*Lt 12, 1886*

One Angel Looks for the Seal

What is the seal of the living God, which is placed in the foreheads of his people? It is a mark which angels, but not human eyes, can read; for the destroying angel must see this mark of redemption. —*Lt 126, 1898*

Vengeance is Executed

Vengeance will be executed against those who sit in the gate, deciding what the people should have and what they should not have. These take away the key of knowledge. They refuse to enter in themselves, and those that would enter they hinder. These bear not the seal of the living God. All who now occupy responsible positions should be solemnly and terribly afraid lest in this time they shall be found as unfaithful stewards. —*Ms 15, 1886*

A Moving Sword of Flame

Today I received a letter from Elder Daniells regarding the destruction of the Review office by fire. I feel very sad as I consider the great loss to the cause. I know that this must be a very trying time for the brethren in charge of the work... But I was not surprised by the sad news, for in the visions of the night I have seen an angel standing with a sword as of fire stretched over Battle Creek. Once, in the daytime, while my pen was in my hand, I lost consciousness, and it seemed as if this sword of flame were turning first in one direction and then in another. Disaster seemed to follow disaster because God was dishonored by the devising of men to exalt and glorify themselves.

—8T, p. 97

Ezekiel Describes a Slaughter

Read the ninth chapter of Ezekiel... The general slaughter of all those who do not thus see the wide contrast between sin and righteousness, and do not feel as those do who stand in the counsel of God and receive the mark, is described in the order to the five men with slaughter weapons: "Go ye after him through the city, and smite: let not your eye spare, neither have ye pity: slay utterly old and young, both maids, and little children, and women: but come not near any man upon whom is the mark; and begin at my sanctuary."

—3T, p. 267

The Angel of Death Goes Forth

The mark of deliverance has been set upon those "that sigh and that cry for all the abominations that be done." Now the angel of death goes forth, represented in Ezekiel's vision by the men with the slaughtering weapons, to whom the command is given: "Slay utterly old and young, both maids, and little children, and women: but come not near any man upon whom is the mark; and begin at my sanctuary." Says the prophet: "They began at the ancient men which were before the house." Ezekiel 9:1-6.

The work of destruction begins among those who have professed to be the spiritual guardians of the people. The false watchmen are the first to fall. There are none to pity or to spare. Men, women, maidens, and little children perish together. *— GC, p. 656*

The Wicked Die by the Sword

"A noise shall come even to the ends of the earth; for the Lord hath a controversy with the nations, He will plead with all flesh; He will give them that are wicked to the sword." Jeremiah 25:31. For six thousand years the great controversy has been in progress; the Son of God and his heavenly messengers have been in conflict with the power of the evil one, to warn, enlighten, and save the children of men.

Now all have made their decisions; the wicked have fully united with Satan in his warfare against God. The time has come for God to vindicate the authority of his downtrodden law. Now the controversy is not alone with Satan, but with men. "The Lord hath a controversy with the nations;" "He will give them that are wicked to the sword." *— GC, p. 656*

Ezekiel 9 is Literally Fulfilled

Study the ninth chapter of Ezekiel. These words will be literally fulfilled; yet the time is passing, and the people are asleep. They refuse to humble their souls and to be converted. Not a great while longer will the Lord bear with the people who have such great and important truths revealed to them, but who refuse to bring these truths into their individual experience. —*Lt 106, 1909*

Vengeance against Evil Pastors

The church—the Lord's sanctuary—was the first to feel the stroke of the wrath of God. The ancient men, those to whom God had given great light and who had stood as guardians of the spiritual interests of the people, had betrayed their trust. They had taken the position that we need not look for miracles and the marked manifestation of God's power as in former days.

Times have changed. These words strengthen their unbelief, and they say: "The Lord will not do good, neither will He do evil. He is too merciful to visit his people in judgment." Thus "Peace and safety" is the cry from men who will never again lift up their voice like a trumpet to show God's people their transgressions and the house of Jacob their sins. These dumb dogs that would not bark are the ones who feel the just vengeance of an offended God. Men, maidens, and little children all perish together. —*5T, p. 211*

Spoiled Children are Cut Down

I saw that the destroying angel was to slay utterly old and young, men and women, and little children. I then saw that if the Advent parents would have their children saved in the time of trouble from the destroying sword they must take care of them now. They must subdue their passions and correct their wrongs faithfully and with vigilance, and suffer not a wrong in them for a moment.

I saw that the parents, many of them who believe the present truth, will see their children cut down before their eyes because they have been so tender of their children. They have not used the rod as they should, and their evil propensities have been indulged, and God cannot save them because He cannot cover iniquity. I saw that the parents stood in the place of God to their children. God had entrusted them to the parents' care and they would have to render an account if they had been unfaithful of their trust. —*Ms 7, 1854*

Angels Engage in Warfare

When Satan's sophistries are heeded, when men and women reject light and evidence, gradually they become converted to the theories that Satan offers. Too late, too late they will see that angels of God are in the warfare against all who have departed from the faith. — *RH, Sept. 30, 1909*

Unrepentant Christians are Killed

The class who do not feel grieved over their own spiritual declension, nor mourn over the sins of others, will be left without the seal of God. The Lord commissions his messengers, the men with slaughtering weapons in their hands: "Go ye after him through the city, and smite: let not your eye spare, neither have ye pity: slay utterly old and young, both maids, and little children, and women: but come not near any man upon whom is the mark; and begin at my sanctuary. Then they began at the ancient men which were before the house." — *5T, p. 211*

Those Ashamed of Christ are Slain

Those who have left all to follow Christ in this world, denied themselves and endured reproach for his sake, choosing Christ before the world and every earthly friend, and esteem the cross of Christ greater riches than any worldly treasure, will save their lives. Their names are read by the recording angel and Jesus repeats their names with his own dear voice. He acknowledges them as his jewels before his Father and the heavenly host. They are counted worthy of everlasting life. Their every error and past sin is blotted out. Every transgression is covered, and He bids the angel with the writer's inkhorn to place a mark or sign upon their foreheads that the destroying angel may pass them over and not hurt them.

Then He gives another angel, clad in warlike garments, directions to go forth and follow the angel with the writer's inkhorn and slay utterly old and young, both men, women, and little children. Those who were ashamed of Christ are appointed among the number to be cut down by the destroying angel. That name they cherished too highly to be given to Christ, that they wished to preserve to be honored by the world, they lose. It finds no place in the book of life. It lives not among the holy angels. It finds its place in the book of death to be lost among those appointed unto death. — *Ms 7, 1875*

C) The Wicked are Blotted Out

Sinners are Unprepared to See Jesus

If one angel from heaven caused the Roman guard to fall as dead men, how can those who are unprepared, unholy, bear the sight and live, of seeing Jesus in the glory of his Father and ten thousand angels accompanying Him. Oh how can sinners bear this sight! They will cry for rocks and mountains to fall on them, and hide them from the face of Him that sitteth on the throne, and from the wrath of the Lamb. — *YI, Apr. 1, 1854*

Evil Leaders Reap Eternal Loss

Rulers and teachers who have caused souls to stumble over their perverted teachings, statesmen, senators, governors, all people who might have understood the prophecies, but who did not read and search to see if they were applicable for this time and concerned their individual selves, will be taken in the snare. They will reap eternal loss. They will suddenly be destroyed, and that without remedy. — *Ms 104, 1897*

Sudden Destruction Comes upon Men

When the reasoning of philosophy has banished the fear of God's judgments; when religious teachers are pointing forward to long ages of peace and prosperity, and the world are absorbed in their rounds of business and pleasure, planting and building, feasting and merrymaking, rejecting God's warnings and mocking his messengers—then it is that sudden destruction cometh upon them, and they shall not escape. — *PP, p. 104*

Wicked Lawmakers are Destroyed

As the advisers of Nebuchadnezzar hit upon the scheme of ensnaring the Hebrew captives, and causing them to bow to the idol by leading the king to proclaim that every knee should bow to the image, so men will strive today to turn God's people from their allegiance. But the men who sought to destroy Shadrach, Meshach, and Abednego, were themselves destroyed. Those who make cruel enactments, seeking to destroy, are destroyed by the recoil of their actions. — *Lt 90, 1897*

God's Glory is a Consuming Fire

"Then shall they that obey not the gospel be consumed with the spirit of his mouth and be destroyed with the brightness of his coming." 2 Thessalonians 2:8. Like Israel of old the wicked destroy themselves; they fall by their iniquity. By a life of sin, they have placed themselves so out of harmony with God, their natures have become so debased with evil, that the manifestation of his glory is to them a consuming fire. — *GC, p. 37*

Boastful Tongues are Consumed

The law of God is the golden link to unite finite man to the infinite God. It links earth to heaven, and man to God. The transgressor is about to meet the great Law-giver over his broken law. The wrath of God has long slumbered, but soon, with terrible justice and crushing weight will his wrath fall upon the transgressor. And that arm that has been stretched forth in rebellion against God's law, and would sever the golden link binding earth to heaven and man to God, will wither while the transgressor shall stand upon his feet.

That tongue that has boastingly and proudly spoken against God's law, and has made the fourth commandment of none effect, will consume in his mouth while he stands upon his feet. Terrible will be the fate of those who transgress God's law, and lead others in the same heaven-daring path of rebellion. — *2SG, p. 274*

The Bodies are Fed to the Birds

With what pride Satan looks upon the world whom we number as his subjects. With the union of church and state, he is ruler as far as it is possible for him to being the world. The great rebel who originated rebellion in heaven, is worshipped and the church rules the state, and a corrupt harmony exists... But his rebellion has an end; for the wicked are consumed by the brightness of his coming whose right it is to rule.

"And I saw an angel standing in the sun; and he cried with a loud voice, saying to all the fowls that fly in the midst of heaven, Come and gather yourselves together unto the supper of the great God; That ye may eat the flesh of kings, and the flesh of captains, and the flesh of mighty men, and the flesh of horses, and of them that sit on them, and the flesh of all men, both free and bond, both small and great." Rev. 19:17, 18. — *Ms 104, 1893*

Evil Shepherds Face Divine Wrath

The message God gives through his servants will be scorned and derided by the unfaithful shepherds, who tread down with their feet the feed of the pastures, giving the flock as food that which they have defiled. "Woe to the pastors that destroy and scatter the sheep of my pastures," saith the Lord. No outward nearness to God, no acceptance of sacred work, will screen from the divine wrath those who trample under feet the law of Jehovah. — *Ms 35, 1900*

Impenitent Jews are Demolished

When God called for fruit in its season, the Jewish people were surprised that He expected anything of the kind. They professed to be the most pious people on the earth. They had been employed as guardians and almoners of truth, and they should have used the Lord's goods to bless and benefit the world.

But they abused the messengers sent to them; and when God sent his Son, the heir to the inheritance, they lifted Him upon the cross of Calvary. One day they will see the result of their impenitence. No longer will be heard the pleadings of infinite love; but the wrath of the Lamb, the power they defied, will fall upon them as a rock, grinding them to powder. — *RH, July 17, 1900*

Christ is an Avenging Mountain

On "whomsoever it shall fall, it will grind him to powder." The people who rejected Christ were soon to see their city and their nation destroyed. Their glory would be broken, and scattered as the dust before the wind. And what was it that destroyed the Jews? It was the rock which, had they built upon it, would have been their security. It was the goodness of God despised, the righteousness spurned, the mercy slighted. Men set themselves in opposition to God, and all that would have been their salvation was turned to their destruction. All that God ordained unto life they found to be unto death.

In the Jews' crucifixion of Christ was involved the destruction of Jerusalem. The blood shed upon Calvary was the weight that sank them to ruin for this world and for the world to come. So it will be in the great final day, when judgment shall fall upon the rejecters of God's grace. Christ, their rock of offense, will then appear to them as an avenging mountain. The glory of his countenance, which to the righteous is life, will be to the wicked a consuming fire. Because of love rejected, grace despised, the sinner will be destroyed. — *DA, p. 600*

God's Wrath Falls on All Sinners

"The Lord cometh out of his place to punish the inhabitants of the earth for their iniquity: the earth also shall disclose her blood, and shall no more cover her slain." Isaiah 26:21.

"And this shall be the plague wherewith the Lord will smite all the people that have fought against Jerusalem; their flesh shall consume away while they stand upon their feet, and their eyes shall consume away in their holes, and their tongue shall consume away in their mouth. And it shall come to pass in that day, that a great tumult from the Lord shall be among them; and they shall lay hold everyone on the hand of his neighbor, and his hand shall rise up against the hand of his neighbor." Zechariah 14:12, 13.

In the mad strife of their own fierce passions, and by the awful outpouring of God's unmingled wrath, fall the wicked inhabitants of the earth—priests, rulers, and people, rich and poor, high and low. "And the slain of the Lord shall be at that day from one end of the earth even unto the other end of the earth: they shall not be lamented, neither gathered, nor buried." Jeremiah 25:33. —*GC, p. 656*

Evil Men Look for a Hiding Place

When the earth is reeling to and fro like a drunkard, when the heavens are shaking, and the great day of the Lord has come, who shall be able to stand? One object they behold in trembling agony from which they will try in vain to escape. "Behold, He cometh with clouds, and every eye shall see Him." The unsaved utter wild imprecations to dumb nature—their god: Mountains and rocks, "Fall on us, and hide us from the face of Him that sitteth on the throne, and from the wrath of the Lamb."

Creation is loyal to her God, and deaf to the frenzied call. That unrequited love is now turned to wrath. Sinners who would not let Jesus take away their sins are rushing from place to place in search of a hiding place, crying, "The harvest is past, the summer is ended, and our souls are not saved!"

Oh that they had seen the Rock of shelter and perfect safety—the Cleft of the Rock—where they might flee until the indignation be overpast! "A man shall be as a hiding place from the wind, and a covert from the tempest." That Lamb whose wrath will be so terrible to the scorners of his grace, will be grace and righteousness and love and blessing to all who have received Him.

—*Lt 137, 1896*

The Earth is Emptied

At the coming of Christ the wicked are blotted from the face of the whole earth—consumed with the spirit of his mouth and destroyed by the brightness of his glory. Christ takes his people to the City of God, and the earth is emptied of its inhabitants.

"Behold, the Lord maketh the earth empty, and maketh it waste, and turneth it upside down, and scattereth abroad the inhabitants thereof." "The land shall be utterly emptied, and utterly spoiled: for the Lord hath spoken this word." "Because they have transgressed the laws, changed the ordinance, broken the everlasting covenant. Therefore hath the curse devoured the earth, and they that dwell therein are desolate: therefore the inhabitants of the earth are burned." Isaiah 24:1, 3, 5, 6. — GC, p. 657

The Ground Holds God's Weapons

The depths of the earth are the Lord's arsenal, whence were drawn weapons to be employed in the destruction of the old world. Waters gushing from the earth united with the waters from heaven to accomplish the work of desolation. Since the Flood, fire as well as water has been God's agent to destroy very wicked cities. These judgments are sent that those who lightly regard God's law and trample upon his authority may be led to tremble before his power and to confess his just sovereignty.

As men have beheld burning mountains pouring forth fire and flames and torrents of melted ore, drying up rivers, overwhelming populous cities, and everywhere spreading ruin and desolation, the stoutest heart has been filled with terror and infidels and blasphemers have been constrained to acknowledge the infinite power of God...

Thus God will destroy the wicked from off the earth. But the righteous will be preserved in the midst of these commotions, as Noah was preserved in the ark. God will be their refuge, and under his wings shall they trust.

Says the psalmist: "Because thou hast made the Lord, which is my refuge, even the Most High, thy habitation; there shall no evil befall thee." Psalm 91:9, 10. "In the time of trouble He shall hide me in his pavilion: in the secret of his tabernacle shall He hide me." Psalm 27:5. God's promise is, "Because he hath set his love upon Me, therefore will I deliver him: I will set him on high, because he hath known my name." Psalm 91:14. — PP, p. 110

Worthless Men Burn Up

Those who do not hold the beginning of their confidence steadfast unto the end will find in the last great day that they have brought to the foundation worthless material represented by wood, hay, and stubble, which must be consumed by fire. — *Ms 90, 1903*

A Sudden Shower of Fire

After John's description in Revelation 16 of that miracle-working power which was to gather the world to the last great conflict, the symbols are dropped and the trumpet voice once more gives a certain sound: "Behold, I come as a thief. Blessed is he that watcheth, and keepeth his garments, lest he walk naked, and they see his shame." Revelation 16:15. After the transgression of Adam and Eve they were naked, for the garment of light and security had departed from them.

The world will have forgotten the admonition and warnings of God as did the inhabitants of the Noatic world, as did also the dwellers in Sodom. They awoke with all their plans and inventions of iniquity, but suddenly the shower of fire came from heaven and consumed the godless inhabitants. "Thus shall it be in the day when the Son of man is revealed." Luke 17:30. The world full of rioting, full of godless pleasure, is asleep, asleep in carnal security, putting afar off the coming of the Lord, laughing at warnings, calling those who try to arouse their attention, almost fanatics, enthusiasts, not levelheaded. The lovers of pleasure more than lovers of God are taken unawares. — *Ms 7a, 1896*

Discussion Questions

1. Why will Christians who have been deceived turn on their ministers?

2. Is Ezekiel 9 literal or symbolic? What does it mean for Adventists?

3. Why does the brightness of Christ's presence destroy the wicked?

4. What are the depths of the Lord's arsenal?

5. Why are sinners responsible for destroying themselves?

— 23 —

Satan is Chained

"I have cut off the nations: their towers are desolate; I made their streets waste, that none passeth by: their cities are destroyed, so that there is no man, that there is none inhabitant."

— Zeph. 3:6

Genesis 1:2	Isaiah 24:1-12	Isaiah 66:24	Jer. 16:4	Rev. 12:10
Lev. 16:21, 22	Isaiah 24:21-23	Jer. 4:23-26	Ezekiel 29:5	Rev. 19:17, 18
Isaiah 14:9-23	Isaiah 34:8-12	Jer. 7:32-34	Luke 17:36, 37	Rev. 20:1-3

Satan is Bound by His Chain

The heavenly universe had witnessed the weapons that were chosen by the Prince of Life—the words of Scripture, "It is written," and the weapons used by the prince of the world—falsehood and deception. They had seen the Prince of Life deal in straightforward lines of truth, honesty, and integrity...

When God expressed his abhorrence of Satan, and his indignation against him, the whole universe responded. They had been convinced. The last vestige of affection for the fallen angels had been uprooted; the last tie had been severed. The Lord had demonstrated his wisdom and justice in banishing Satan from heaven.

By his own course of action Satan has forged a chain by which he will be bound. The inhabitants of the heavenly universe will bear witness to God's justice in his destruction. Heaven itself has seen what heaven would be, if he were allowed to remain in it. All the unfallen beings are now united in regarding God's law as changeless. They support the government of Him, who, to redeem the transgressor, spared not his own Son. His law has been proved faultless. His government is forever secure. The Father, the Son, and Lucifer have been revealed in their true relation to one another. God has given unmistakable evidence of his justice and his love. — *ST, Aug. 27, 1902*

Revelation Depicts Satan's Fate

In the nineteenth chapter, the time is pictured when the beast and the false prophet are taken and cast into a lake of fire. The dragon, who was the instigator of the great rebellion against heaven, is bound and cast into the bottomless pit for a thousand years. —*Ms 75, 1906*

The Desolated Earth is Lucifer's Home

The wicked had been destroyed, and their dead bodies were lying upon its surface. The wrath of God in the seven last plagues had been visited upon the inhabitants of the earth, causing them to gnaw their tongues from pain and to curse God. The false shepherds had been the signal objects of Jehovah's wrath. Their eyes had consumed away in their holes, and their tongues in their mouths, while they stood upon their feet. After the saints had been delivered by the voice of God, the wicked multitude turned their rage upon one another. The earth seemed to be deluged with blood, and dead bodies were from one end of it to the other. The earth looked like a desolate wilderness. Cities and villages, shaken down by the earthquake, lay in heaps.

Mountains had been moved out of their places, leaving large caverns. Ragged rocks, thrown out by the sea, or torn out of the earth itself, were scattered all over its surface. Large trees had been uprooted and were strewn over the land. Here is to be the home of Satan with his evil angels for a thousand years. Here he will be confined, to wander up and down over the broken surface of the earth and see the effects of his rebellion against God's law. For a thousand years he can enjoy the fruit of the curse which he has caused. Limited alone to the earth, he will not have the privilege of ranging to other planets, to tempt and annoy those who have not fallen.

During this time, Satan suffers extremely. Since his fall his evil traits have been in constant exercise. But he is then to be deprived of his power, and left to reflect upon the part which he has acted since his fall, and to look forward with trembling and terror to the dreadful future, when he must suffer for all the evil that he has done and be punished for all the sins that he has caused to be committed. I heard shouts of triumph from the angels and from the redeemed saints, which sounded like ten thousand musical instruments, because they were to be no more annoyed and tempted by Satan and because the inhabitants of other worlds were delivered from his presence and his temptations. —*EW, p. 290*

Satan is Banished for a Millennium

The revelator foretells the banishment of Satan and the condition of chaos and desolation to which the earth is to be reduced, and he declares that this condition will exist for a thousand years.

After presenting the scenes of the Lord's Second Coming and the destruction of the wicked, the prophecy continues: "I saw an angel come down from heaven, having the key of the bottomless pit and a great chain in his hand. And he laid hold on the dragon, that old serpent, which is the devil, and Satan, and bound him a thousand years, and cast him into the bottomless pit, and shut him up, and set a seal upon him, that he should deceive the nations no more, till the thousand years should be fulfilled: and after that he must be loosed a little season." Revelation 20:1-3.

That the expression "bottomless pit" represents the earth in a state of confusion and darkness is evident from other Scriptures. Concerning the condition of the earth "in the beginning," the Bible record says that it "was without form, and void; and darkness was upon the face of the deep." Genesis 1:2. The Hebrew word here translated "deep" is rendered in the Septuagint (Greek) translation of the Hebrew Old Testament by the same word rendered "bottomless pit" in Revelation 20:1-3. Prophecy teaches that it will be brought back, partially at least, to this condition.

Looking forward to the great day of God, the prophet Jeremiah declares: "I beheld the earth, and, lo, it was without form, and void; and the heavens, and they had no light. I beheld the mountains, and, lo, they trembled, and all the hills moved lightly. I beheld, and, lo, there was no man, and all the birds of the heavens were fled. I beheld, and, lo, the fruitful place was a wilderness, and all the cities thereof were broken down." Jeremiah 4:23-26.

Here is to be the home of Satan with his evil angels for a thousand years. Limited to the earth, he will not have access to other worlds to tempt and annoy those who have never fallen. It is in this sense that he is bound: there are none remaining, upon whom he can exercise his power. He is wholly cut off from the work of deception and ruin which for so many centuries has been his sole delight.

The prophet Isaiah, looking forward to the time of Satan's overthrow, exclaims: "How art thou fallen from heaven, O Lucifer, son of the morning! How art thou cut down to the ground, which didst weaken the nations! ...

343

Thou hast said in thine heart, I will ascend into heaven, I will exalt my throne above the stars of God: ... I will be like the Most High. Yet thou shalt be brought down to hell, to the sides of the pit. They that see thee shall narrowly look upon thee, and consider thee, saying, is this the man that made the earth to tremble, that did shake kingdoms; that made the world as a wilderness, and destroyed the cities thereof; that opened not the house of his prisoners?" Isaiah 14:12-17.

For six thousand years, Satan's work of rebellion has "made the earth to tremble." He had "made the world as a wilderness, and destroyed the cities thereof." And he "opened not the house of his prisoners." For six thousand years his prison house has received God's people, and he would have held them captive forever; but Christ had broken his bonds and set the prisoners free.

Even the wicked are now placed beyond the power of Satan, and alone with his evil angels he remains to realize the effect of the curse which sin has brought. "The kings of the nations, even all of them, lie in glory, everyone in his own house (the grave). But thou art cast out of thy grave like an abominable branch... Thou shalt not be joined with them in burial, because thou hast destroyed thy land, and slain thy people." Isaiah 14:18-20.

For a thousand years, Satan will wander to and fro in the desolate earth to behold the results of his rebellion against the law of God. During this time his sufferings are intense. Since his fall his life of unceasing activity has banished reflection; but he is now deprived of his power and left to contemplate the part which he has acted since first he rebelled against the government of heaven, and to look forward with trembling and terror to the dreadful future when he must suffer for all the evil that he has done and be punished for the sins that he has caused to be committed.

To God's people the captivity of Satan will bring gladness and rejoicing. Says the prophet: "It shall come to pass in the day that Jehovah shall give thee rest from thy sorrow, and from thy trouble, and from the hard service wherein thou wast made to serve, that thou shalt take up this parable against the king of Babylon (representing Satan), and say, How hath the oppressor ceased! ... Jehovah hath broken the staff of the wicked, the scepter of the rulers; that smote the peoples in wrath with a continual stroke, that ruled the nations in anger, with a persecution that none restrained." Isaiah 14:3-6. — *GC, pp. 658-660*

The Scapegoat Represents Satan

As the priest, in removing the sins from the sanctuary, confessed them upon the head of the scapegoat, so Christ will place all these sins upon Satan, the originator and instigator of sin. The scapegoat, bearing the sins of Israel, was sent away "unto a land not inhabited" (Leviticus 16:22); so Satan, bearing the guilt of all the sins which he has caused God's people to commit, will be for a thousand years confined to the earth, which will then be desolate, without inhabitant, and he will at last suffer the full penalty of sin in the fires that shall destroy all the wicked. Thus the great plan of redemption will reach its accomplishment in the final eradication of sin and the deliverance of all who have been willing to renounce evil. — *GC, p. 485*

Satan is Led Away during the Plagues

Then I saw that Jesus' work in the sanctuary was almost finished, almost finished, and after his work there is finished He will come to the door of the tabernacle, or door of the first apartment, and confess the sins of Israel upon the head of the scapegoat. Then He will put on the garments of vengeance.

Then the plagues come upon the wicked, and they do not come until Jesus puts on the garments of vengeance and takes his seat upon the great white cloud. Then while the plagues are falling the scapegoat is being led away. He makes a mighty struggle to escape, but he is held fast by the hand that bears him away. If he should effect his escape Israel would be destroyed (or slain). I saw that it would take time to bear him away into the land of forgetfulness after the sins were put upon his head. — *Ms 15, 1850*

Discussion Questions

1. What happens to Satan during the Seven Last Plagues?

2. Why is Satan bound by his chain?

3. How is the earth's form similar during its creation and its ending?

4. Why is a thousand years of captivity an awful punishment for the devil?

5. How is Lucifer represented by the scapegoat of Leviticus?

The Millennium
in Heaven

— 24 —

The Award of Crowns

"Blessed is the man that endureth temptation: for when he is tried, he shall receive the crown of life, which the Lord hath promised to them that love Him." — James 1:12

Psalm 21:2-4	Isaiah 62:2-4	2 Tim. 2:5	1 Peter 5:4	Rev. 3:11, 12
Isaiah 28:5, 6	Matthew 25:34	2 Tim. 4:6-8	Rev. 2:10	Rev. 15:2-4

Soul Winners Shine Forever

Look at the sun and the stars marshaled in the heavens and known by their names. The Lord says, "They that turn many to righteousness shall shine as the stars forever and ever." —*Ms 83, 1886*

The Scarred Hands of Christ

Every crown that is given to the saints of the Most High will be bestowed by the hands of Christ—those hands that cruel priests and rulers condemned to be nailed to the cross. He alone can give to men the consolation of eternal life. —*RH, Nov. 22, 1898*

Converted by the Sabbath Truth

We cannot afford to miss one opportunity of working for the salvation of souls, one opportunity of explaining the truths of the Word to others. Those who do their duty in this matter will reap a rich reward in the kingdom of God.

In heaven souls whom you have tried to instruct and help, and to whom you have given the light of the Sabbath truth, will fall upon your neck and say, "It was your presentation of the truth that cleared from my mind the mists and fog." They will join you in the song of thanksgiving, that they are saved in the kingdom of God, that they have a right to enter through the gates of the city and have right to the tree of life. —*Ms 31, 1909*

The Infinite Blessing of Souls

The converted soul lives in Christ. His darkness passes away, and a new and heavenly light shines into his soul. "He that winneth souls is wise."... What is done through the co-operation of men with God is a work that shall never perish, but endure through the eternal ages. — *RH, Dec. 15, 1891*

Angels Build Crowns

When the Lord makes up his jewels, the true, the frank, the honest, will be looked upon with pleasure. Angels are employed in making crowns for such ones, and upon these star-gemmed crowns will be reflected, with splendor, the light which radiates from the throne of God. — *5T, p. 96*

The Shortness of Probation

When we shall stand with the redeemed upon the sea of glass, with harps of God and crowns of glory, and before us the unmeasured eternity, we shall then see how short was the waiting period of probation. "Blessed are those servants who when the Lord cometh shall be found watching." — *Lt 21, 1886*

Samuel Praises His Mother

Hannah... did not labor to place the hand of her son in that of the world, that he might follow its customs and practices; but she sought to place his hand in the hand of the Lord, thus connecting him with the Source of all wisdom, goodness, and power. When Samuel shall receive the crown of glory, he will wave it in honor before the throne, and gladly acknowledge that the faithful lessons of his mother, through the merits of Christ, have crowned him with immortal glory. — *GdH, Mar. 1, 1880*

Some Crowns are Star Heavy

We all entered the cloud together, and were seven days ascending to the sea of glass, when Jesus brought the crowns, and with his own right hand placed them on our heads. He gave us harps of gold and palms of victory. Here on the sea of glass the 144,000 stood in a perfect square. Some of them had very bright crowns, others not so bright. Some crowns appeared heavy with stars, while others had but few. All were perfectly satisfied with their crowns. And they were all clothed with a glorious white mantle from their shoulders to their feet. — *EW, p. 16*

The Saints Thank Jesus

When in the city of God the crowns are brought and placed upon the heads of the overcomers, they remember what words this one spoke to them, and that one spoke to them in their faithfulness, and they cast their crowns at the feet of Jesus, and clasp their arms around his neck and say, "Your words saved me. I should have lost all this if you had not helped me." —*Ms 140, 1909*

Jesus is Our Personal Saviour

"And there shall be no more curse; but the throne of God and of the Lamb shall be in it; and his servants shall serve Him; and they shall see his face; and his name shall be in their foreheads." Revelation 22:3, 4.

Who are these?—God's denominated people; those who on this earth have witnessed to their loyalty. Who are they?—those who have kept the commandments of God and the testimony of Jesus Christ; those who have owned the crucified One as their Saviour. —*Ms 132, 1903*

Overcomers were Never Famous

The crown of immortal glory will be placed upon each brow. What a wonderful sight are these exalted ones! The world knew them not, but they are the overcomers! Palm branches of victory will be placed in their hands, and again the gates will be opened, and they will enter into the city with Jesus, and all the angels of God will strike their harps, and the heavenly arches will ring with the victory achieved through their God. They will stand before the throne of God, clothed with the white linen which is the righteousness of Christ. —*RH, July 29, 1890*

A Rich Crown of Glory Awaits

I see a crown of glory that is laid up for us who wait, and love, and long for, the appearing of the Saviour. It is the waiting ones who are to be crowned with glory, honor, and immortality. You need not talk to me of the honors of the world, or the praise of its great ones. They are all vanity. Let but the finger of God touch them, and they would soon go back to dust again. I want honor that is lasting, honor that is immortal, honor that will never perish; a crown that is richer than any crown that ever decked the brow of a monarch. Oh! To have the approbation of high heaven! This is what we want.

—RH, Aug. 17, 1869

God's People are Rewarded

Whatever crosses they have been called to bear, whatever losses they have sustained, whatever persecution they have suffered, even to the loss of their temporal life, the children of God are amply recompensed. "They shall see his face; and his name shall be in their foreheads." Revelation 22:4. — *COL, p. 180*

Richer than Any Earthly Crown

Jesus, the Majesty of heaven, proposes to elevate to companionship with Himself those who come to Him with their burdens, their weaknesses, and their cares. He will count them as his children, and finally give them an inheritance of more value than the empires of kings, a crown of glory richer than has ever decked the brow of the most exalted earthly monarch.

— *ST, Mar. 17, 1887*

A Welcome of Heavenly Music

What a song that will be when the ransomed of the Lord meet at the gate of the Holy City, which is thrown back on its glittering hinges and the nations that have kept his word—his commandments—enter into the city, the crown of the overcomer is placed upon their heads, and the golden harps are placed in their hands! All heaven is filled with rich music, and with songs of praise to the Lamb. Saved, everlastingly saved, in the kingdom of glory! To have a life that measures with the life of God—that is the reward. — *Ms 92, 1908*

Many are Grateful to Soul Winners

When you enter within the gates into the city, and the crown of life is placed upon your brow, and on the brows of the very ones you have worked to save, they will cast themselves upon your neck, and say, "It was you that saved my soul; I should have perished if you had not saved me from myself. You had to take a good while; but you were patient with me and won me to a knowledge of the truth."

And then, as they lay their crowns at the feet of Jesus, and touch the golden harps that have been placed in their hands, and unite in praising and glorifying their Redeemer; and they realize that theirs is the great blessing of life, everlasting life, there will be rejoicing indeed. And oh, the thought that we may be instrumental, under God, in helping to show men and women the way of salvation, while living on this earth! — *Ms 15, 1909*

No More Temptation and Sin

Oh what a scene of rejoicing it will be when the Lamb of God shall place upon the heads of the redeemed the victor's crown! Never, nevermore will you be led into temptation and sin. You will see the King in his beauty. And those whom you have helped heavenward will meet you there. They will throw their arms about you and acknowledge what you have done for them. "You watched over me," they will say; "you prayed for me; you helped me to gain heaven." God grant that all who are here may hear the Saviour's words of welcome, and hear the grateful thanks of souls whom they have labored for in this life. —*Ms 49, 1909*

Parents Rejoice to See Children

There stand the host of the redeemed, the palm branch of victory in their hand, the crown upon their head. These are the ones who by faithful, earnest labor have obtained a fitness for heaven. The life-work performed on earth is acknowledged in the heavenly courts as a work well done.

With joy unutterable parents see the crown, the robe, the harp, given to their children. The days of hope and fear are ended. The seed sown in tears and prayers may have seemed to be sown in vain, but their harvest is reaped with joy at last. Their children have been redeemed. Fathers, mothers, shall the voices of your children swell the song of gladness in that day?

—RH, Sept. 15, 1904

Souls Won are an Eternal Reward

The messengers should watch for souls as they that must give account. Theirs must be a life of toil and anguish of spirit, while the weight of the precious but often-wounded cause of Christ rests upon them. They will have to lay aside worldly interests and comforts and make it their first object to do all in their power to advance the cause of present truth and save perishing souls.

They will also have a rich reward. In their crowns of rejoicing those who are rescued by them and finally saved will shine as stars forever and ever. And to all eternity they will enjoy the satisfaction of having done what they could in presenting the truth in its purity and beauty, so that souls fell in love with it, were sanctified through it, and availed themselves of the inestimable privilege of being made rich, and being washed in the blood of the Lamb and redeemed unto God. — *EW, p. 61*

The Joy of Jesus Christ

Let us, everyone, learn of Jesus. Take his yoke. Love Him because He first loved you, and we shall have a most precious victory by and by. He will open the gates of the City of God and bid us come in. He will welcome us and give us a heavenly benediction. To all who have tested their obedience that they will obey the law of God, He says, "Well done thou good and faithful servant, enter thou into the joy of thy Lord." What is that joy? The joy of seeing sinners converted. They will be brought to Jesus Christ, and this is his joy.

—Ms 12, 1894

Martyrs Shout in Triumph

What an example have the martyrs for Jesus left us... As these shall enter the portals of glory they will shout in triumph: "We overcame by the blood of the Lamb, and by the word of our testimony. We were faithful unto death, and now receive a crown of life." Shouts of triumph will come from lips that never triumphed before. Those who were too timid to praise God vocally were not too timid to die for their Lord. They struggled and fought the good fight of faith. They were steadfast to the end. They will unite their glad voices in the universal songs of triumph and victory, praising God that they were accounted worthy to receive the heavenly benediction "well done" from the Master they loved, and for whom they suffered. His own right hand will place upon their brows crowns of immortal glory that fade not away. *—RH, Dec. 2, 1875*

No Starless Crowns in Heaven

There will be no one saved in heaven with a starless crown. If you enter, there will be some soul in the courts of glory that has found an entrance there through your instrumentality. Then why not entreat the Lord to put upon you his Spirit, that you may be able to awaken an interest in the truth in the minds of those around you? Think of your neighbors and friends and relatives who are out of Christ. Think of those you have left in various foreign lands; how much do you care for their souls?

You should be so filled with love for the lost that you cannot forbear working for the salvation of souls. What you need is Jesus. He says, "Whosoever drinketh of the water that I shall give him shall never thirst; but the water that I shall give him shall be in him a well of water springing up into everlasting life." *— ST, June 6, 1892*

A Single Gem Shines Forever

Souls are perishing all around us, and what are you doing, my young friends, to win souls to Christ? Oh that you would use you powers of mind in seeking to approach sinners, so that you might win even one soul to the path of righteousness! What a thought! One soul to praise God through eternity! One soul to enjoy happiness and eternal life! One gem in your crown, to shine forever and ever! But you may be able, by the grace of Christ, to win more than one from sin to holiness, and your reward will be great in the kingdom of heaven. — *YI, Jan. 1, 1907*

The Happiness of Heaven

When Christ shall appear, then we all want to stand with the redeemed. The gates of the city will swing back on their glittering hinges, and the nations that have kept the truth will enter in. A crown will be placed on every head. The words will be spoken, "Come, ye blessed of my Father, inherit the kingdom prepared for you from the foundation of the world."

Whom is it prepared for?—For the obedient, those who keep his commandments and do his will... God wants to put the harp in your hand and the crown of gold on your head. As holy angels touch their harps, He wants you to follow, singing the song of triumph in the city of God. There you will see souls saved through your influence. That will be happiness.

—Ms 113, 1908

Bring Your Family to Paradise

God help us to elevate the standard in our homes, lest the standard of Satan be established there. You want a family for God, a household for God. You want to take them with you to the gates of the city, and say, "Here am I, Lord, and the children which thou hast given me." They may be grown to manhood and womanhood, but they are your children still. Your training, your patience, your prayers, your watchfulness, has been blessed of God till they stand with you as overcomers.

And this does not include those only who are your children by birth. Every soul that has been brought to a knowledge of the truth by you, and has been born again, stand before the Lord, as your children. "They that be wise, shall shine as the brightness of the firmament, and they that turn many to righteousness as the stars forever and ever." *—EA, p. 212*

Youth We Befriended are There

The brows of those who do this work will wear the crown of sacrifice. But they will receive their reward. In heaven we shall see the youth whom we helped, those whom we invited to our homes, whom we led from temptation. We shall see their faces reflecting the radiance of the glory of God. They shall see his face; and his name shall be in their foreheads. Revelation 22:4.

—6T, p. 348

A Reward of Infinite Gratitude

When the gates of that beautiful city on high are swung back on their glittering hinges, and the nations that have kept the truth shall enter in, crowns of glory will be placed on their heads, and they will ascribe honor and glory and majesty to God. And at that time some will come to you, and will say, "If it had not been for the words you spoke to me in kindness, if it had not been for your tears and supplications and earnest efforts, I should never have seen the King in his beauty." What a reward is this! How insignificant is the praise of human beings, in this earthly, transient life, in comparison with the infinite rewards that await the faithful in the future, immortal life!

—Ms 15, 1909

Thankfulness for God's Workers

Who will be among the happy throng that will sing praise around the throne of God? Who will serve God, whatever may be the consequences? I see in Jesus matchless charms. Let us lift up the Man of Calvary. If those who are burdened with sin will come and give their hearts to Jesus, and then go forth to gather sheaves for Him, what joy will be theirs by and by.

Although glory will be given to Jesus for full redemption, there will be those in heaven who will say to the co-workers with God, "I never would have had the light if you had not opened the Word of God to me. I never would have accepted the truth if you had not manifested Christ in your life."

God would have us co-laborers with Himself, that, when the pearly gates of the city of God shall be swung back upon their glittering hinges, He may say to us, "Come, ye blessed of my Father, inherit the kingdom prepared for you from the foundation of the world." "Thou hast been faithful over a few things, I will make thee ruler over many things; enter thou into the joy of thy Lord." *— ST, Aug. 4, 1890*

Sabbathkeepers are Crowned

Keep his commandments holy. Do not speak your own words on the holy Sabbath, but talk of heavenly things. Talk of Jesus, his loveliness and glory, and of his undying love for you, and let your heart flow out in love and gratitude to Him, who died to save you. Oh, get ready to meet your Lord in peace. Those who are ready will soon receive an unfading crown of life, and will dwell forever in the kingdom of God, with Christ, with angels, and with those who have been redeemed by the precious blood of Christ. — *YI, Dec. 1, 1852*

The Saints Feel Undeserving

Supreme love of God will sanctify the affections, and the fruit of love to God will be love to mankind. Those who have been tested and proved on this matter of loving others as themselves, will be pronounced meet for an inheritance with the saints in light. They will not become exalted, as did Lucifer in the courts of light. They will not create rebellion in heaven, because another has a brighter crown than they have. Heaven will be the home of the pure and undefiled, and those who reach that home of joy will feel rich, receiving a reward that they do not in the least feel that they deserve.

— ST, July 2, 1894

The Poor Widow is Rewarded

Every impulse of the Holy Spirit leading men to goodness and to God is noted in the books of heaven, and in the day of God everyone who has given himself as an instrument for the Holy Spirit's working will be permitted to behold what his life has wrought.

The poor widow who cast her two mites into the Lord's treasury little knew what she was doing. Her example of self-sacrifice has acted and reacted upon thousands of hearts in every land and in every age. It has brought to the treasury of God gifts from the high and the low, the rich and the poor. It has helped to sustain missions, to establish hospitals, to feed the hungry, clothe the naked, heal the sick, and preach the gospel to the poor. Multitudes have been blessed through her unselfish deed.

And the outworking of all these lines of influence she, in the day of God, will be permitted to see. So with Mary's precious gift to the Saviour. How many have been inspired to loving service by the memory of that broken alabaster box! And how she will rejoice as she beholds all this! — *6T, p. 310*

Anthems of Praise Reverberate

There is a day just about to burst upon us when God's mysteries will be seen, and all his ways vindicated; when justice, mercy, and love will be the attributes of his throne. When the earthly warfare is accomplished, and the saints are all gathered home, our first theme will be the song of Moses, the servant of God. The second theme will be the song of the Lamb, the song of grace and redemption. This song will be louder, loftier, and in sublimer strains, echoing and re-echoing through the heavenly courts. Thus the song of God's providence is sung, connecting the varying dispensations; for all is now seen without a veil between the legal, the prophetical, and the gospel.

The church history upon the earth and the church redeemed in heaven all center around the cross of Calvary. This is the theme, this is the song—Christ all and in all—in anthems of praise resounding through heaven from thousands and ten thousand times ten thousand and an innumerable company of the redeemed host. All unite in this song of Moses and of the Lamb. It is a new song, for it was never before sung in heaven. —*TM, p. 433*

John Heard the Song of the Lamb

The Spirit of God rested upon Moses, and he led the people in a triumphant anthem of thanksgiving, the earliest and one of the most sublime that are known to man... It was taken up by the women of Israel, Miriam, the sister of Moses, leading the way, as they went forth with timbrel and dance. Far over desert and sea rang the joyous refrain, and the mountains re-echoed the words of their praise—"Sing ye to Jehovah, for He hath triumphed gloriously."

This song and the great deliverance which it commemorates, made an impression never to be effaced from the memory of the Hebrew people. From age to age it was echoed by the prophets and singers of Israel, testifying that Jehovah is the strength and deliverance of those who trust in Him. That song does not belong to the Jewish people alone. It points forward to the destruction of all the foes of righteousness and the final victory of the Israel of God. The prophet of Patmos beholds the white-robed multitude that have "gotten the victory," standing on the "sea of glass mingled with fire," having "the harps of God. And they sing the song of Moses the servant of God, and the song of the Lamb." Revelation 15:2, 3. —*PP, pp. 287-289*

The Joy of Meeting Jesus

Christ accepted humanity, and lived on this earth a pure, sanctified life. For this reason He has received the appointment of judge. He who occupies the position of judge is God manifest in the flesh. What a joy it will be to recognize in Him our Teacher and Redeemer, bearing still the marks of the crucifixion, from which shine beams of glory, giving additional value to the crowns which the redeemed receive from his hands, the very hands outstretched in blessing over his disciples as He ascended. The very voice which said, "Lo, I am with you alway, even unto the end of the world," bids his ransomed ones welcome to his presence.

The very One who gave his precious life for them, who by his grace moved their hearts to repentance, who awakened them to their need of repentance, receives them now into his joy. Oh, how they love Him! The realization of their hope is infinitely greater than their expectation. Their joy is complete, and they take their glittering crowns and cast them at their Redeemer's feet.

— RH, June 18, 1901

Christlike Characters are Rewarded

The Lord has bidden us to draw nigh to Him and He will draw nigh to us; and drawing nigh to Him, we receive the grace by which to do those works which will be rewarded at his hands. The reward, the glories of heaven, bestowed upon the overcomers, will be proportionate to the degree in which they have represented the character of Christ to the world. "He which soweth sparingly shall reap also sparingly."

Thank God that it is our privilege to sow on earth the seed that will be harvested in eternity. The crown of life will be bright or dim, will glitter with many stars, or be lighted by few gems, in accordance with our own course of action. Day by day we may be laying up a good foundation against the time to come. By self-denial, by the exercise of the missionary spirit, by crowding all the good works possible into our life, by seeking so to represent Christ in character that we shall win many souls to the truth, we shall have respect unto the recompense of reward.

It rests with us to walk in the light, to make the most of every opportunity and privilege, to grow in grace and in the knowledge of our Lord Jesus Christ, and so we shall work the works of Christ, and ensure for ourselves treasure in the heavens. *— RH, Jan. 29, 1895*

The Happiness of Our Lord

As their reward, the faithful undershepherds will hear from the Chief Shepherd: "Well done, good and faithful servant." He will then place the crown of glory upon their heads and bid them enter into the joy of their Lord.

What is that joy? It is beholding with Christ the redeemed saints, reviewing with Him their travail for souls, their self-denial and self-sacrifice, their giving up of ease, of worldly gain, and every earthly inducement, and choosing the reproach, the suffering, the self-abasement, the wearing labor, and the anguish of spirit as men would oppose the counsel of God against their own souls; it is calling to remembrance the chastening of their souls before God, their weeping between the porch and the altar, and their becoming a spectacle unto the world, to angels, and to men.

All this is then ended, and the fruits of their labors are seen; souls are saved through their efforts in Christ. The ministers who have been co-workers with Christ enter into the joy of their Lord and are satisfied. —*2T, p. 709*

Jesus Bestows Emblems of Victory

Before entering the City of God, the Saviour bestows upon his followers the emblems of victory and invests them with the insignia of their royal state. The glittering ranks are drawn up in the form of a hollow square about their King, whose form rises in majesty high above saint and angel, whose countenance beams upon them full of benignant love. Throughout the unnumbered host of the redeemed every glance is fixed upon Him, every eye beholds his glory whose "visage was so marred more than any man, and his form more than the sons of men."

Upon the heads of the overcomers, Jesus with his own right hand places the crown of glory. For each there is a crown, bearing his own "new name" (Revelation 2:17), and the inscription, "Holiness to the Lord." In every hand are placed the victor's palm and the shining harp. Then, as the commanding angels strike the note, every hand sweeps the harp strings with skillful touch, awaking sweet music in rich, melodious strains. Rapture unutterable thrills every heart, and each voice is raised in grateful praise: "Unto Him that loved us, and washed us from our sins in his own blood, and hath made us kings and priests unto God and his Father; to Him be glory and dominion for ever and ever." Revelation 1:5, 6. —*GC, p. 645*

The Joy of Seeing Our Children

I will try to overcome my own neglect, my own sins, my own errors, that when I shall enter the gates of the city of God, I shall say, "Here am I and the children which thou hast given me."

And what do we see then? Oh, we see a retinue of angels on either side of the gate, and as we pass in, Jesus speaks, "Come ye blessed of my Father, inherit the kingdom that is prepared for you from the foundation of the world." Here He tells you to be a partaker of his joy, and what is that? It is the joy of seeing of the travail of your soul, fathers. It is the joy of seeing that your efforts, mothers, are rewarded. Here are your children; the crown of life is upon their heads, and the angels of God immortalize the name of the mothers whose efforts have won their children to Jesus Christ. —*Ms 12, 1895*

Practice to Sing in the Heavenly Choir

We can be filled with all the fullness of God. Our lives may measure with the life of God. Then can we press back the powers of darkness. Glory to God in the highest! I love Him because He first loved me. I will magnify his name. I rejoice in his love, and when we shall enter in through the gates into the city, it will be the highest privilege to cast my crown at his feet. Why? Because He gave me the victory, because He wrought out the plan of salvation.

And when I look at the glory, and at the saints redeemed, just like a flash will I cast my crown at the feet of my Redeemer. It is his; it was He who purchased my redemption. Glory to God in the highest! Let us praise Him and talk of his mightiness and of what He will do for us. Let us keep his law, and then He can trust us, for He has a law and He will reward obedience to that law; He will give us a crown of glory.

Now, brethren, we are almost home; we shall soon hear the voice of the Saviour, richer than any music, saying, "Your warfare is accomplished. Enter into the joy of thy Lord." Blessed, blessed benediction; I want to hear it from his immortal lips. I want to praise Him; I want to honor Him that sitteth on the throne. I want my voice to echo and re-echo through the courts of heaven. Will you be there? Then you must educate your voice to praise Him on earth, and then you can join the heavenly choir and sing the song of Moses and the Lamb. God help us and fill us with all fullness and power, and then we can taste of the joys of the world to come. —*Ms 8, 1888*

White Robes and a Crown

Women can do good work in the missionary field... The souls saved through their efforts will be more precious to them than costly and fashionable dress. The white robes and jeweled crown given them by Christ as the reward for their unselfish efforts in the salvation of souls, will be more valuable than needless adornments. The stars in their crowns will shine forever and ever, and will a thousand times repay them for the self-denial and self-sacrifice they have exercised in the cause of God. — *ST, Sept. 16, 1886*

The Joy of Faithful Laborers

There is reward for the wholehearted, unselfish workers who enter this (Southern) field, and also for those who contribute willingly for their support... Every wise steward of the means entrusted to him, will enter into the joy of his Lord. What is this joy?—"Likewise, I say unto you, there is joy in the presence of the angels of God over one sinner that repenteth." There will be a blessed commendation, a holy benediction, on the faithful winners of souls. They will join the rejoicing ones in heaven, who shout the harvest home.

How great will be the joy when the redeemed of the Lord shall all meet— gathered into the mansions prepared for them! Oh, what rejoicing for all who have been impartial, unselfish laborers together with God in carrying forward his work in the earth! What satisfaction will every reaper have, when the clear, musical voice of Jesus shall be heard, saying, "Come, ye blessed of my Father, inherit the kingdom prepared for you from the foundation of the world." "Enter thou into the joy of thy Lord."

The Redeemer is glorified because He has not died in vain. With glad, rejoicing hearts, those who have been co-laborers with God see of the travail of their soul for perishing, dying sinners, and are satisfied. The anxious hours they have spent, the perplexing circumstances they have had to meet, the sorrow of heart because some refused to see and receive the things which make for their peace, are forgotten. The self-denial they have practiced in order to support the work, is remembered no more. As they look upon the souls they sought to win to Jesus, and see them saved, eternally saved— monuments of God's mercy and of a Redeemer's love—there ring through the arches of heaven shouts of praise and thanksgiving. — *RH, Oct. 10, 1907*

The 144,000 Rejoice on the Sea of Glass

Upon the crystal sea before the throne, that sea of glass as it were mingled with fire—so resplendent is it with the glory of God—are gathered the company that have "gotten the victory over the beast, and over his image, and over his mark, and over the number of his name."

With the Lamb upon Mount Zion, "having the harps of God," they stand, the hundred and forty and four thousand that were redeemed from among men; and there is heard, as the sound of many waters, and as the sound of a great thunder, "the voice of harpers harping with their harps." And they sing "a new song" before the throne, a song which no man can learn save the hundred and forty and four thousand. It is the song of Moses and the Lamb—a song of deliverance.

None but the hundred and forty-four thousand can learn that song; for it is the song of their experience—an experience such as no other company have ever had. "These are they which follow the Lamb whithersoever He goeth." These, having been translated from the earth, from among the living, are counted as "the first fruits unto God and to the Lamb." Revelation 15:2, 3; 14:1-5.

"These are they which came out of great tribulation;" they have passed through the time of trouble such as never was since there was a nation; they have endured the anguish of the time of Jacob's trouble; they have stood without an intercessor through the final outpouring of God's judgments.

But they have been delivered, for they have "washed their robes, and made them white in the blood of the Lamb." "In their mouth was found no guile: for they are without fault" before God. "Therefore are they before the throne of God, and serve Him day and night in his temple: and He that sitteth on the throne shall dwell among them." They have seen the earth wasted with famine and pestilence, the sun having power to scorch men with great heat, and they themselves have endured suffering, hunger, and thirst.

But "they shall hunger no more, neither thirst anymore; neither shall the sun light on them, nor any heat. For the Lamb which is in the midst of the throne shall feed them, and shall lead them unto living fountains of waters: and God shall wipe away all tears from their eyes." Revelation 7:14-17.

— GC, p. 648

Worthy is the Lamb that was Slain

We have a living, risen Saviour. He burst the fetters of the tomb after He had lain there three days, and in triumph He proclaimed over the rent sepulcher of Joseph, "I am the resurrection and the life." John 11:25…

The Lifegiver is soon to come. The Lifegiver is coming to break the fetters of the tomb. He is to bring forth the captives and proclaim, "I am the resurrection, and the Life." There stands the risen host. The last thought was of death and its pangs. The last thoughts they had were of the grave and the tomb, but now they proclaim, "O death, where is thy sting? O grave, where is thy victory?" The pangs of death was the last thing they felt. "O death, where is thy sting?" The last thing they acknowledged were the pangs of death. When they awake the pain is all gone. "O grave, where is thy victory?"

Here they stand, and the finishing touch of immortality is put upon them, and they go up to meet their Lord in the air. The gates of the City of God swing back upon their hinges, and the nations that have kept the truth enter in. There are the columns of angels on either side, and the ransomed of God walk in through the cherubims and seraphims. Christ bids them welcome and puts upon them his benediction. "Well done, good and faithful servants, enter thou into the joy of thy Lord." What is that joy? He sees the travail of his soul and is satisfied. That is what we labor for.

Here is one, who in the night season we pleaded with God on his behalf. There is one that we talked with on his dying bed, and he hung his helpless soul upon Jesus. Here is one who was a poor drunkard. We tried to get his eyes fixed upon Him who is mighty to save and we told him that Christ could give him the victory.

There are the crowns of immortal glory upon their heads, and then the redeemed cast their glittering crowns at the feet of Jesus. Then the angelic choir strikes the note of victory and the angels in the two columns take up the song and the redeemed host join as though they had been singing the song on the earth, and they had been. Oh, what music! There is not an inharmonious note. Every voice proclaims, "Worthy is the Lamb that was slain and lives again." "He sees of the travail of his soul, and is satisfied." Do you think anyone there will take time to tell of his trials and terrible difficulties? "The former shall not be remembered, nor come into mind." "God shall wipe away all tears from their eyes." —*Ms 18, 1894*

362

The Redeemed Recognize Converts

Wonderful will be the revealing as the lines of holy influence, with their precious results, are brought to view. What will be the gratitude of souls that will meet us in the heavenly courts as they understand the sympathetic, loving interest which has been taken in their salvation! All praise, honor, and glory will be given to God and to the Lamb for our redemption; but it will not detract from the glory of God to express gratitude to the instrumentality He has employed in the salvation of souls ready to perish.

The redeemed will meet and recognize those whose attention they have directed to the uplifted Saviour. What blessed converse they have with these souls! "I was a sinner," it will be said, "without God and without hope in the world, and you came to me, and drew my attention to the precious Saviour as my only hope. And I believed in Him. I repented of my sins, and was made to sit together with his saints in heavenly places in Christ Jesus."

Others will say: "I was a heathen in heathen lands. You left your friends and comfortable home, and came to teach me how to find Jesus and believe in Him as the only true God. I demolished my idols and worshipped God, and now I see Him face to face. I am saved, eternally saved, ever to behold Him whom I love. I then saw Him only with the eye of faith, but now I see Him as He is. I can now express my gratitude for his redeeming mercy to Him who loved me and washed me from my sins in his own blood."

Others will express their gratitude to those who fed the hungry and clothed the naked. "When despair bound my soul in unbelief, the Lord sent you to me," they say, "to speak words of hope and comfort. You brought me food for my physical necessities, and you opened to me the Word of God, awakening me to my spiritual needs. You treated me as a brother. You sympathized with me in my sorrows and restored my bruised and wounded soul so that I could grasp the hand of Christ that was reached out to save me."

"In my ignorance you taught me patiently that I had a Father in heaven who cared for me. You read to me the precious promises of God's Word. You inspired in me faith that He would save me. My heart was softened, subdued, broken, as I contemplated the sacrifice which Christ had made for me. I became hungry for the bread of life, and the truth was precious to my soul. I am here, saved, eternally saved, ever to live in his presence, and to praise Him who gave his life for me."

What rejoicing there will be as these redeemed ones meet and greet those who have had a burden in their behalf! And those who have lived, not to please themselves, but to be a blessing to the unfortunate who have so few blessings—how their hearts will thrill with satisfaction! They will realize the promise: "Thou shalt be blessed; for they cannot recompense thee: for thou shalt be recompensed at the resurrection of the just."

"Thou shalt delight thyself in the Lord; and I will cause thee to ride upon the high places of the earth, and feed thee with the heritage of Jacob thy father: for the mouth of the Lord hath spoken it." Isaiah 58:14.

"Fear not: ... I am thy shield, and thy exceeding great reward." Genesis 15:1. "I am thy part and thine inheritance." Numbers 18:20. "Where I am, there shall also my servant be." John 12:26. —*6T, pp. 310-312*

A Vision of Jesus Awarding Crowns

On each side of the cloudy chariot were wings, and beneath it were living wheels; and as the chariot rolled upward, the wheels cried, "Holy," and the wings, as they moved, cried, "Holy," and the retinue of holy angels around the cloud cried, "Holy, holy, holy, Lord God Almighty!" And the saints in the cloud cried, "Glory! Alleluia!" And the chariot rolled upward to the Holy City. Before entering the city, the saints were arranged in a perfect square, with Jesus in the midst. He stood head and shoulders above the saints and above the angels. His majestic form and lovely countenance could be seen by all in the square.

Then I saw a very great number of angels bring from the city glorious crowns—a crown for every saint, with his name written thereon. As Jesus called for the crowns, angels presented them to Him, and with his own right hand, the lovely Jesus placed the crowns on the heads of the saints. In the same manner the angels brought the harps, and Jesus presented them also to the saints. The commanding angels first struck the note, and then every voice was raised in grateful, happy praise, and every hand skillfully swept over the strings of the harp, sending forth melodious music in rich and perfect strains.

Then I saw Jesus lead the redeemed company to the gate of the city. He laid hold of the gate and swung it back on its glittering hinges and bade the nations that had kept the truth enter in. Within the city there was everything to feast the eye. Rich glory they beheld everywhere. Then Jesus looked upon his redeemed saints; their countenances were radiant with glory; and as He fixed his loving eyes upon them, He said, with his rich, musical voice, "I behold the travail of my soul, and am satisfied. This rich glory is yours to enjoy eternally. Your sorrows are ended. There shall be no more death, neither sorrow nor crying, neither shall there be any more pain."

— EW, pp. 287, 288

The Saints Take the Kingdom

There was a great excitement in London last week. The Queen was coming. All wanted to see their sovereign. But there is One greater than the Queen coming. "The glorious appearing of the great God and our Saviour Jesus Christ." Titus 2:13.

Can we not get up an excitement on this subject? Jesus will bring the dead from their graves, and they shall be caught up to meet the Lord in the air. They shall enter into the city of God. There they shall see the gates open wide to receive them, and shall eat of the tree of life. There are angels there, who never fell. The saints of all ages are to be there, and take the kingdom, and it shall be theirs. Why cannot we make some excitement on this subject?

"In my Father's house are many mansions: if it were not so, I would have told you. I go to prepare a place for you. And if I go and prepare a place for you, I will come again, and receive you unto myself; that where I am, there ye may be also." John 14:2, 3. Now there is a great reward to be given to the saints. It is eternal life. Is it not enough to cause gladness in our hearts?

— Ms 25, 1887

Discussion Questions

1. What does each star in a crown represent?

2. What will it be like to stand on the sea of glass and talk to the people who helped lead you to Christ?

3. Why is it significant that Christ's scarred hands will give us our crowns?

4. What is the meaning behind the white robe that the saints will wear?

5. Why will there be no starless crowns in heaven?

The Splendor of Paradise

"But as it is written, 'Eye hath not seen, nor ear heard, neither have entered into the heart of man, the things which God hath prepared for them that love Him.'" — 1 Corinthians 2:9

Psalm 24:7-10	Isaiah 65:25	Joel 3:16-18	John 14:1-3	Rev. 7:13-17	Rev. 21:3, 4
Isaiah 11:6-10	Jer. 23:3, 4	Matthew 8:11	Jude 1:24	Rev. 14:1-5	Rev. 22:3-5

The Singing is Glorious

We shall have our insurance policy for the inheritance—the inheritance in the kingdom of glory, the city of God, that we shall have our portion there; and we shall be welcomed by Jesus Christ; and we shall receive a crown of life that never will be taken away from us. We will have the most glorious singing, we will have harps of gold. Oh what a happy time! — *Ms 142, 1906*

Worship at the Feet of Jesus

I want to see Jesus. I want you to see Him. I want to see the One who endured temptation in my behalf, and who wore the crown of thorns for sinners. Then He will be crowned with glory, and we shall see Him as He is. We shall fall at his feet in worship. He will place the harp in our hands, our voices will be raised in such music as we have never heard on earth. — *RH, Jan. 21, 1909*

The Heroes of Faith are Exalted

Heroes of faith have the promise of an inheritance of greater value than any earthly riches—an inheritance that will satisfy the longings of the soul. They may be unknown and unacknowledged of the world, but they are enrolled as citizens in the record books of heaven. An exalted greatness, an enduring, eternal weight of glory, will be the final reward of those whom God has made heirs of all things. — *4T, p. 526*

True Wealth in Heaven

Wealth we shall have when we are welcomed to the heavenly courts, to tread the streets of gold in the city of God. We shall not exalt earthly gain, human genius, when we see light in God's light. —*Lt 55, 1902*

Heaven is Cheap Enough

Our work here is soon to close, and every man will receive his reward according to his own labor. I was shown the saints' reward, the immortal inheritance, and saw that those who had endured the most for the truth's sake will not think they have had a hard time, but will count heaven cheap enough.

—*1T, p. 381*

Bring Children to the City of God

What we want, if possible, is to get into this city... What are the greatest riches any of us can have? Can you tell? The greatest riches that any one of us can have is to have the benefits of a life which measures with the life of God. And if you can get this blessing to your children, if you can get it to your families, then they can be with you when you come up to the gate of the city of God—"Here am I and the children that thou hast given me."

—*Ms 124, 1909*

God's Name is on Their Foreheads

All who enter will have on the robe of Christ's righteousness and the name of God will be seen in their foreheads. This name is the symbol which the apostle saw in vision, and signifies the yielding of the mind to intelligent and loyal obedience to all of God's commandments. There will be no covering up of sins and faults to hide the deformity of character; no robes will be half washed; but all will be pure and spotless. —*YI, Aug. 18, 1886*

The Saints Behold Christ's Glory

Christ has carried his humanity into eternity. He stands before God as the representative of our race. When we are clothed with the wedding garment of his righteousness, we become one with Him, and He says of us, "They shall walk with Me in white: for they are worthy." His saints will behold Him in his glory, with no dimming veil between. Since such is the privilege of those who are clothed in the righteousness of Christ, shall we not each seriously consider the question, "Have I on the wedding garment?"

—*YI, Oct. 28, 1897*

Jesus Shines Brighter than Sun

The love of God was shed abroad in my heart, my whole being was ravished with the glory of God and I was taken off in vision. I saw the exceeding loveliness and glory of Jesus. His countenance was brighter than the sun at noonday. His robe was whiter than the whitest white. How can I... describe to you the glories of heaven, and the lovely angels singing and playing upon their harps of ten strings? —*Lt 3, 1851*

A Grand Meeting Takes Place

Let us remember that there is a grand meeting to take place ere long. Everlasting life is before us, and the city of God. Angels of God will be there, and Christ will be there. They will bid us welcome to the joys of heaven because we have kept the commandments of God. Then there will be no more death, no sorrow, no sin. Let us do all we can to help one another to gain the eternal joys that are awaiting the redeemed. —*Ms 101, 1908*

The Shock of Seeing Who is There

Often we regard as hopeless subjects the very ones whom Christ is drawing to Himself. Were we to deal with these souls according to our imperfect judgment, it would perhaps extinguish their last hope. Many who think themselves Christians will at last be found wanting. Many will be in heaven who their neighbors supposed would never enter there. Man judges from appearance, but God judges the heart. The tares and the wheat are to grow together until the harvest; and the harvest is the end of probationary time.

—*COL, p. 71*

Heaven Means a Lot to Soul Winners

Now these white-robed ones are gathered into the fold of the Great Shepherd. The faithful worker and the soul saved through his labor are greeted by the Lamb in the midst of the throne, and are led to the tree of life and to the fountain of living waters. With what joy does the servant of Christ behold these redeemed ones, who are made to share the glory of the Redeemer! How much more precious is heaven to those who have been faithful in the work of saving souls! "And they that be wise shall shine as the brightness of the firmament; and they that turn many to righteousness, as the stars for ever and ever." —*5T, p. 621*

Everyone is Completely Unselfish

Everything in heaven is noble and elevated. All are seeking the interest and happiness of others. No mind is devoted to looking out and caring for self. It is the chief joy of all holy beings to witness the joy and happiness of those around them. — *PH, p. 34*

The Incalculable Value of Paradise

Language fails to express the value of the immortal inheritance. The glory, riches, and honor offered by the Son of God are of such infinite value that it is beyond the power of men or even angels to give any just idea of their worth, their excellence, their magnificence. — *2T, p. 40*

No Longer Branded as Criminals

May God help us in the great work of overcoming. He has crowns for those that overcome. He has white robes for the righteous. He has an eternal world of glory for those who seek for glory, honor, and immortality. Everyone who enters the city of God will enter it as a conqueror. He will not enter it as a condemned criminal, but as a son of God. And the welcome given to everyone who enters there will be, "Come, ye blessed of my Father, inherit the kingdom prepared for you from the foundation of the world." Matthew 25:34. — *CTBH, p. 149*

Worship around the Throne of God

In this morning's meeting, as we were listening to the testimonies borne here, and as the last hymn was sung—"When shall we meet again, meet ne'er to sever?"—I almost forgot myself. My mind reached over to the other shore, to the time when there will be a grand meeting in the city of God around the great white throne, and the redeemed will be singing there of triumph and of victory and of praise to God and to the Lamb.

Well now, it brought such a solemn, sweet feeling upon me; it softened my heart, and I could not prevent the tears from flowing. Oh, what happiness we shall enjoy, gathered round about the throne, clothed in the white robes of the righteousness of Christ! No more sorrow, no more separation, but to dwell in peace, to dwell in happiness, to dwell in glory throughout the ceaseless ages of eternity. What a happy, happy company we may be!

— *Ms 5, 1883*

Only Conquerors Enter Heaven

All who ever enter heaven's gates will enter as conquerors. When the redeemed throng surround the throne of God, with palm branches in their hands and crowns on their heads, it will be known what victories have been won. It will be seen how Satan's power has been exercised over minds, how he has linked with himself souls who flattered themselves that they were doing God's will. It will then be seen that his power and subtlety could not have been successfully resisted had not divine power been combined with human effort. — *5T, p. 384*

Inexpressible Glory on Every Side

I saw the beauty, the glory and majesty of Jesus. The sun could not shine in his presence any more than a star at noonday when the sun shone in its splendor. Oh how rich the inheritance of the saints looked to me. How glorious! Tongue cannot describe it. On every side and all around was glory, glory, glory, that cannot be expressed.

My soul was enchanted with the sight. I longed to see more and more. It seemed that I could plunge in the glory, that I could swim in it. Praise the name of the Lord. Oh shall we not go on with perseverance? Shall we sink down now? No, no, we shall soon see Jesus and reign with Him in glory. Hold fast, hold fast, hold fast. — *Lt 8, 1849*

The Pure in Heart are God's Jewels

Not only the wise, the great, the beneficent, will gain a passport into the heavenly courts,—not only the busy worker, full of zeal and restless activity. No; the pure in heart, in whose lips there is found no guile; the poor in spirit, who are actuated by the Spirit of an abiding Christ; the peacemaker, whose highest ambition is to do God's will,—these will gain an abundant entrance. They are God's jewels, and will be among that number of whom John writes:

"I heard as it were the voice of a great multitude, and as the voice of many waters, and as the voice of mighty thunderings, saying, Alleluia: for the Lord God omnipotent reigneth." They have washed their robes, and made them white in the blood of the Lamb. "Therefore are they before the throne of God, and serve Him day and night in his temple: and He that sitteth on the throne shall dwell among them." — *RH, May 11, 1897*

The Heavenly Theme Song

Oh how sweet it will be to meet all the blood-washed throng in the city of our God. Tis then we'll sing the song of Moses and the Lamb as we march through the gates into the city, bearing the palms of victory and wearing the crowns of glory. — *Lt 3, 1847*

The Glory is Indescribable

I am striving for heaven, and I mean by God's grace to obtain it. I want to be among the redeemed in the kingdom of glory and to see the King in his beauty. Oh what a joy it will be to look into the faces of those who have turned aside from the allurements of wealth and pleasure and have pressed their way through difficulties and trial to the kingdom of heaven. Their great desire in this life has been to use their possessions for the glory of God, and now God has crowned them with eternal glory.

The glories of heaven—who can describe them! Sometimes I have thought to speak more fully than I have done of that which has been revealed; but when I attempt it, I am unable to find words to tell what I would say. The prospect before us is a glorious one; and we are now being tried and tested, that it may be determined whether we are prepared for that which God is preparing for his faithful ones. — *Ms 51, 1912*

Behold the King in His Beauty

I love Him, because He first loved me. I love Him, because He has given his life for me. Nothing can separate me from his love. I am willing to be a partaker with Christ of his sufferings, but heaven I must have. I want to see the King in his beauty. I want the crown of life. I want to go home with the redeemed, as we are brought from the grave, and the living are changed from mortality to immortality and caught up to meet our Lord in the air.

As the gates of the city of God are thrown back upon their glittering hinges, I want the welcome as we enter in. I want to see Jesus in his glory and majesty. He says, "You shall sit upon my throne." Just think of it—as I sit upon my Father's throne, and as we enter in through the gates into the city of God, every crown is taken from our heads, after we have received them, and cast at the feet of Jesus, and there praise and glory comes forth from the lips of the saved to honor and to glorify the Redeemer. — *Ms 188, 1903*

The Badge of Admission

It is right to love beauty and to desire it; but God desires us to love and seek first the highest beauty, that which is imperishable. No outward adorning can compare in value or loveliness with that "meek and quiet spirit," the "fine linen, white and clean" (Revelation 19:14), which all the holy ones of earth will wear. This apparel will make them beautiful and beloved here, and will hereafter be their badge of admission to the palace of the King. His promise is, "They shall walk with Me in white: for they are worthy." Revelation 3:4.

—AA, p. 523

A Welcome for the Faithful

Those who are faithful during the closing work of the message will be given an abundant entrance through the pearly gates into the city of God; and there everyone will be greeted with the words, "Well done, good and faithful servant; enter thou into the joy of thy Lord." A glittering crown will be placed upon every brow, a golden harp in every hand. With strains of sweetest music the redeemed will unite in ascribing praise and thanksgiving to Christ. The language of every heart will be, "Worthy, worthy, worthy is the Lamb, who gave his life for me." Brethren and sisters, are we prepared to stand the test that will soon be brought to bear upon us? *—Ms 110, 1904*

Pastoral Rest for the Remnant

Oh, the home of the blest, I cannot afford to lose it! I shall, if saved in the kingdom of God, be constantly discerning new depths in the plan of salvation. All the redeemed saints will see and appreciate, as never before, the love of the Father and the Son, and songs of praise will burst forth from immortal tongues. He loved us, He gave his life for us.

With glorified bodies, with enlarged capacities, with hearts made pure, with lips undefiled, we shall sing the riches of redeeming love. There will be no suffering ones in heaven, no skeptics whom we must labor to convince of the reality of eternal things, no prejudices to uproot; but all will be susceptible of that love which passeth knowledge. Rest, thank God, there is a rest for the people of God where Jesus will lead the redeemed into green pastures, by the streams of living waters which make glad the city of our God. Then the prayer of Jesus to his Father will be answered, "I will that those also whom thou hast given Me, be with Me where I am." *—Lt 27, 1890*

All of Heaven Adores Jesus

To John were opened the great events of the future... He saw Christ receiving the adoration of all the hosts of heaven and heard the promise that whatever tribulation might come upon God's people, if they would but patiently endure, they should be more than conquerors through Him that loved them. And Jesus said of the overcomer, "I will not blot out his name out of the book of life, but I will confess his name before my Father and before his angels." Revelation 3:5. —Ms 100, 1893

The Lost Angels are Replaced

"As every man hath received the gift, even so minister the same one to another, as good stewards of the manifold grace of God." 1 Peter 4:10.

Thus it is that God desires to fulfill for us his purpose of grace. By the power of his love, through obedience, fallen men, a worm of the dust, is to be transformed, fitted to be a member of the heavenly family, a companion through eternal ages of God and Christ and the holy angels. Heaven will triumph, for the vacancies made by the fall of Satan and his host will be filled by the redeemed of the Lord. —Ms 21, 1900

Jesus Leads the Saints to the Tree of Life

I saw the redeemed host bow and cast their glittering crowns at the feet of Jesus, and then, as his lovely hand raised them up, they touched their golden harps and filled all heaven with their rich music and songs to the Lamb. I then saw Jesus leading his people to the tree of life, and again we heard his lovely voice, richer than any music that ever fell on mortal ear, saying, "The leaves of this tree are for the healing of the nations. Eat ye all of it."

Upon the tree of life was most beautiful fruit, of which the saints could partake freely. In the city was a most glorious throne, from which proceeded a pure river of water of life, clear as crystal. On each side of this river was the tree of life, and on the banks of the river were other beautiful trees bearing fruit which was good for food. Language is altogether too feeble to attempt a description of heaven. As the scene rises before me, I am lost in amazement. Carried away with the surpassing splendor and excellent glory, I lay down the pen, and exclaim, "Oh, what love! What wondrous love!" The most exalted language fails to describe the glory of heaven or the matchless depths of a Saviour's love. —EW, pp. 288, 289

Christians Wear God's Name

We want the light of the glory of God to shine upon us. Paul says, "For this cause I bow my knees unto the Father of our Lord Jesus Christ." It is the Father who "so loved the world that He gave his only begotten Son, that whosoever believeth in Him should not perish, but have everlasting life." "Of whom the whole family in heaven and earth is named."

The family is named after the Father. Those who enter the heavenly mansions will have the name of the Father and the name of the city of God written in their foreheads. They will bear the divine superscription, and be partakers of the divine nature, having escaped the corruptions that are in the world through lust. — *RH, July 19, 1892*

Christ's Character Shines Through

By and by the gates of heaven will be thrown open to admit God's children, and from the lips of the King of glory the benediction will fall on their ears like richest music, "Come, ye blessed of my Father, inherit the kingdom prepared for you from the foundation of the world." Matthew 25:34.

Then the redeemed will be welcomed to the home that Jesus is preparing for them. There their companions will not be the vile of earth, liars, idolaters, the impure, and unbelieving; but they will associate with those who have overcome Satan and through divine grace have formed perfect characters.

Every sinful tendency, every imperfection, that afflicts them here has been removed by the blood of Christ, and the excellence and brightness of his glory, far exceeding the brightness of the sun, is imparted to them. And the moral beauty, the perfection of his character, shines through them, in worth far exceeding this outward splendor. They are without fault before the great white throne, sharing the dignity and the privileges of the angels.

In view of the glorious inheritance that may be his, "what shall a man give in exchange for his soul?" Matthew 16:26. He may be poor, yet he possesses in himself a wealth and dignity that the world could never bestow. The soul redeemed and cleansed from sin, with all its noble powers dedicated to the service of God, is of surpassing worth; and there is joy in heaven in the presence of God and the holy angels over one soul redeemed, a joy that is expressed in songs of holy triumph. — *SC, pp. 125, 126*

Jesus Alone Makes Heaven Happy

The pure and heavenly mansions which Christ has gone to prepare for his children are such as the redeemed alone can value by being made meet for them by the inward work of grace in their hearts. I might picture to you the blessedness of heaven, the crowns laid up for the conquerors, the white linen which is the righteousness of Christ, the palm branches of victory, and the harps of gold. But all these alone will not make heaven a place of bliss for any one of us. Without any of these, if we had pure and holy characters, we would be happy, for we would have Jesus and his love. Purity and innocence and conformity to Christ's character will make heaven enjoyable. All the faculties will be strengthened, all in harmony. —*Lt 4, 1885*

Many Kind Heathen are in Paradise

All who have been born into the heavenly family are in a special sense the brethren of our Lord. The love of Christ binds together the members of his family, and wherever that love is made manifest there the divine relationship is revealed. "Everyone that loveth is born of God, and knoweth God." 1 John 4:7.

Those whom Christ commends in the judgment may have known little of theology, but they have cherished his principles. Through the influence of the divine Spirit they have been a blessing to those about them. Even among the heathen are those who have cherished the spirit of kindness; before the words of life had fallen upon their ears, they have befriended the missionaries, even ministering to them at the peril of their own lives.

Among the heathen are those who worship God ignorantly, those to whom the light is never brought by human instrumentality, yet they will not perish. Though ignorant of the written law of God, they have heard his voice speaking to them in nature, and have done the things that the law required. Their works are evidence that the Holy Spirit has touched their hearts, and they are recognized as the children of God.

How surprised and gladdened will be the lowly among the nations, and among the heathen, to hear from the lips of the Saviour, "Inasmuch as ye have done it unto one of the least of these my brethren, ye have done it unto me!" How glad will be the heart of Infinite Love as his followers look up with surprise and joy at his words of approval! —*DA, pp. 638, 639*

Commandment Keepers Rejoice

Think ye that the commandment-keepers will be sorry, and mourn when the pearly gates of the Golden City of God are swung back upon their glittering hinges, and they are welcomed in? No, never. They will then rejoice, that they are not under the bondage of the law, but that they have kept God's law, and therefore are free from it. They will have right to the tree of life, a right to its healing leaves. They will hear the lovely voice of Jesus, richer than any music that ever fell on mortal ear, saying, "There will be no more sorrow, pain or death; sighing and crying have fled away." — *RH, June 10, 1852*

The End of Pain and Weeping

The heirs of God have come from garrets, from hovels, from dungeons, from scaffolds, from mountains, from deserts, from the caves of the earth, from the caverns of the sea. On earth they were "destitute, afflicted, tormented." Millions went down to the grave loaded with infamy because they steadfastly refused to yield to the deceptive claims of Satan. By human tribunals they were adjudged the vilest of criminals.

But now "God is judge Himself." Psalm 50:6. Now the decisions of earth are reversed. "The rebuke of his people shall He take away." Isaiah 25:8. "They shall call them, The holy people, The redeemed of the Lord." He hath appointed "to give unto them beauty for ashes, the oil of joy for mourning, the garment of praise for the spirit of heaviness." Isaiah 62:12; 61:3.

They are no longer feeble, afflicted, scattered, and oppressed. Henceforth they are to be ever with the Lord. They stand before the throne clad in richer robes than the most honored of the earth have ever worn. They are crowned with diadems more glorious than were ever placed upon the brow of earthly monarchs. The days of pain and weeping are forever ended.

The King of glory has wiped the tears from all faces; every cause of grief has been removed. Amid the waving of palm branches they pour forth a song of praise, clear, sweet, and harmonious; every voice takes up the strain, until the anthem swells through the vaults of heaven: "Salvation to our God which sitteth upon the throne, and unto the Lamb." And all the inhabitants of heaven respond in the ascription: "Amen: Blessing, and glory, and wisdom, and thanksgiving, and honor, and power, and might, be unto our God for ever and ever." Revelation 7:10, 12. — *GC, p. 650*

No Chilling Winds in Heaven

The future life is to be secured. The promises are rich and full and glorious. These must be appropriated to yourself. Jesus the dear Saviour loves you. He has white robes and crowns of everlasting life for you. The dear Saviour will lead you by the fountains of living waters. There will be no chilling winds, no wintry colds, but an eternal summer. There is light for the intellect; love that is abiding, sincere. There will be health and immortality; vigor for every faculty. There will be shut out forever every sorrow and every grief. — *Lt 4, 1885*

The Redeemed Enter the Holy City

Before the ransomed throng is the Holy City. Jesus opens wide the pearly gates, and the nations that have kept the truth enter in. There they behold the Paradise of God, the home of Adam in his innocency. Then that voice, richer than any music that ever fell on mortal ear, is heard, saying: "Your conflict is ended." "Come, ye blessed of my Father, inherit the kingdom prepared for you from the foundation of the world."

Now is fulfilled the Saviour's prayer for his disciples: "I will that they also, whom thou hast given Me, be with Me where I am." "Faultless before the presence of his glory with exceeding joy." Jude 1:24. Christ presents to the Father the purchase of his blood, declaring: "Here am I, and the children whom thou hast given me." "Those that thou gavest me I have kept." Oh, the wonders of redeeming love! The rapture of that hour when the infinite Father, looking upon the ransomed, shall behold his image, sin's discord banished, its blight removed, and the human once more in harmony with the divine!

With unutterable love, Jesus welcomes his faithful ones to the joy of their Lord. The Saviour's joy is in seeing, in the kingdom of glory, the souls that have been saved by his agony and humiliation. And the redeemed will be sharers in his joy, as they behold, among the blessed, those who have been won to Christ through their prayers, their labors, and their loving sacrifice. As they gather about the great white throne, gladness unspeakable will fill their hearts, when they behold those whom they have won for Christ, and see that one has gained others, and these still others, all brought into the haven of rest, there to lay their crowns at Jesus' feet and praise Him through the endless cycles of eternity. — *GC, pp. 646, 647*

The Wonderful Reward of the Righteous

Glorious will be the reward bestowed when the faithful workers gather about the throne of God and of the Lamb. When John in his mortal state beheld the glory of God, he fell as one dead; he was not able to endure the sight. But when the children of God shall have put on immortality, they will "see Him as He is." 1 John 3:2. They will stand before the throne, accepted in the Beloved. All their sins have been blotted out, all their transgressions borne away. Now they can look upon the undimmed glory of the throne of God. They have been partakers with Christ in his sufferings, they have been workers together with Him in the plan of redemption, and they are partakers with Him in the joy of seeing souls saved in the kingdom of God, there to praise God through all eternity...

In that day the redeemed will shine forth in the glory of the Father and the Son. The angels, touching their golden harps, will welcome the King and his trophies of victory—those who have been washed and made white in the blood of the Lamb. A song of triumph will peal forth, filling all heaven. Christ has conquered. He enters the heavenly courts, accompanied by his redeemed ones, the witnesses that his mission of suffering and sacrifice has not been in vain. The resurrection and ascension of our Lord is a sure evidence of the triumph of the saints of God over death and the grave, and a pledge that heaven is open to those who wash their robes of character and make them white in the blood of the Lamb. Jesus ascended to the Father as a representative of the human race, and God will bring those who reflect his image to behold and share with Him his glory.

There are homes for the pilgrims of earth. There are robes for the righteous, with crowns of glory and palms of victory. All that has perplexed us in the providences of God will in the world to come be made plain. The things hard to be understood will then find explanation. The mysteries of grace will unfold before us. Where our finite minds discovered only confusion and broken promises, we shall see the most perfect and beautiful harmony. We shall know that infinite love ordered the experiences that seemed most trying. As we realize the tender care of Him who makes all things work together for our good, we shall rejoice with joy unspeakable and full of glory.

Pain cannot exist in the atmosphere of heaven. In the home of the redeemed there will be no tears, no funeral trains, no badges of mourning.

"The inhabitant shall not say, I am sick: the people that dwell therein shall be forgiven their iniquity." Isaiah 33:24. One rich tide of happiness will flow and deepen as eternity rolls on. We are still amidst the shadows and turmoil of earthly activities. Let us consider most earnestly the blessed hereafter.

Let our faith pierce through every cloud of darkness and behold Him who died for the sins of the world. He has opened the gates of paradise to all who receive and believe on Him. To them He gives power to become the sons and daughters of God. Let the afflictions which pain us so grievously become instructive lessons, teaching us to press forward toward the mark of the prize of our high calling in Christ. Let us be encouraged by the thought that the Lord is soon to come. Let this hope gladden our hearts. "Yet a little while, and He that shall come will come, and will not tarry." Hebrews 10:37. Blessed are those servants who, when their Lord comes, shall be found watching.

— 9T, pp. 285, 286

Jesus Bestows the Greatest Honor

It will be greater, far greater honor than the world can bestow upon you, for Jesus, when He rides forth a mighty Conqueror, attended with a retinue of holy angels, to acknowledge you as his, and in the presence of his angels, to acknowledge you an heir of God and joint heir with Jesus Christ. Oh, what honor is like this? To be owned and honored of Him who takes the kingdom under the whole heaven to possess it for ever and ever, and his kingdom to know no end! He reigns in majesty and splendor, and yet elevates those He has redeemed to be equal heirs with Him to his Father's estates.

Yes, He will receive you, if faithful, Lucia, to his heavenly mansion He has prepared for you, which is beautiful and adorned as no earthly mansion. And your companions will be the heavenly angels, and the redeemed host who have come up through great tribulation and washed their robes and made them white in the blood of the Lamb.

Close by the side of that dear mother who bore you, you can range the earth made new, and with her cry, "Worthy, worthy is the Lamb that was slain, and lives again." Together can you bow in adoration at the feet of that dear Saviour, and cast your glittering crowns at his feet, because He won them for you by his own blood. Which will you choose, heaven with the self-denial and the cross, or earthly pleasures, banishment from the presence of the Lord, and death? Choose ye this day whom ye will serve. *— Lt 23, 1862*

The Sunshine of God

I want not only to be pardoned for the transgression of God's holy law, but I want to be lifted into the sunshine of God's countenance. Not simply to be admitted to heaven, but to have an abundant entrance. —*Lt 55, 1886*

The Joy of Seeing God's Face

Our knowledge of God is partial and imperfect. When the conflict is ended and the Man Christ Jesus acknowledges before the Father his faithful workers, who, in a world of sin, have borne true witness for Him, they will understand clearly what now are mysteries to them.

Christ took with Him to the heavenly courts his glorified humanity. To those who receive Him, He gives power to become the sons of God, that at last God may receive them as his, to dwell with Him throughout eternity. If, during this life, they are loyal to God, they will at last "see his face; and his name shall be in their foreheads." Revelation 22:4. And what is the happiness of heaven but to see God? What greater joy could come to the sinner saved by the grace of Christ than to look upon the face of God and know Him as Father? —*8T, p. 267*

The Saints and Angels Praise Christ

There are revealed in these last days visions of future glory, scenes pictured by the hand of God, and these should be dear to his church. What sustained the Son of God in his betrayal and trial? He saw of the travail of his soul and was satisfied. He caught a view of the expanse of eternity and saw the happiness of those who through his humiliation should receive pardon and everlasting life. He was wounded for their transgressions, bruised for their iniquities. The chastisement of their peace was upon Him, and with his stripes they were healed. His ear caught the shout of the redeemed. He heard the ransomed ones singing the song of Moses and the Lamb.

We must have a vision of the future and of the blessedness of heaven. Stand on the threshold of eternity, and hear the gracious welcome given to those who in this life have cooperated with Christ, regarding it as a privilege and an honor to suffer for his sake. As they unite with the angels, they cast their crowns at the feet of the Redeemer, exclaiming: "Worthy is the Lamb that was slain to receive power, and riches, and wisdom, and strength, and honor, and glory, and blessing... Honor, and glory, and power, be unto Him that sitteth upon the throne, and unto the Lamb for ever and ever." Revelation 5:12, 13.

There the redeemed ones greet those who directed them to the uplifted Saviour. They unite in praising Him who died that human beings might have the life that measures with the life of God. The conflict is over. All tribulation and strife are at an end. Songs of victory fill all heaven as the redeemed stand around the throne of God. All take up the joyful strain: "Worthy, worthy is the Lamb that was slain, and lives again, a triumphant conqueror."

"I beheld, and, lo, a great multitude, which no man could number, of all nations, and kindreds, and people, and tongues, stood before the throne, and before the Lamb, clothed with white robes, and palms in their hands; and cried with a loud voice, saying, Salvation to our God which sitteth upon the throne, and unto the Lamb." Revelation 7:9, 10.

"These are they which came out of great tribulation, and have washed their robes, and made them white in the blood of the Lamb. Therefore are they before the throne of God, and serve Him day and night in his temple: and He that sitteth on the throne shall dwell among them. They shall hunger no more, neither thirst any more; neither shall the sun light on them, nor any heat. For the Lamb which is in the midst of the throne shall feed them, and shall lead them unto living fountains of waters: and God shall wipe away all tears from their eyes."

"And there shall be no more death, neither sorrow, nor crying, neither shall there be any more pain: for the former things are passed away." Will you catch the inspiration of the vision? Will you let your mind dwell upon the picture? Will you not be truly converted? —*8T, pp. 43-45*

A Vision of Heaven

Angels were all about us as we marched over the sea of glass to the gate of the City. Jesus raised his mighty glorious arm, laid hold of the gate and swung it back on its golden hinges, and said to us, "You have washed your robes in my blood, stood stiffly for my truth, enter in." We all marched in and felt we had a perfect right in the City.

Here we saw the tree of life, and the throne of God. Out of the throne came a pure river of water, and on either side of the river was the tree of life.

On one side of the river was a trunk of a tree and a trunk on the other side of the river, both of pure transparent gold. At first I thought I saw two trees. I looked again and saw they were united at the top in one tree. So it was the tree of life, on either side of the river of life; its branches bowed to the place where we stood; and the fruit was glorious, which looked like gold mixed with silver.

We all went under the tree, and sat down to look at the glory of the place, when brothers Fitch and Stockman, who had preached the gospel of the kingdom, and whom God had laid in the grave to save them, came up to us and asked us what we had passed through while they were sleeping. We tried to call up our greatest trials, but they looked so small compared with the far more exceeding and eternal weight of glory that surrounded us, that we could not speak them out, and we all cried out "Hallelujah, heaven is cheap enough," and we touched our glorious harps and made heaven's arches ring. And as we were gazing at the glories of the place our eyes were attracted upwards to something that had the appearance of silver. I asked Jesus to let me see what was within there.

In a moment we were winging our way upward, and entering in; here we saw good old father Abraham, Isaac, Jacob, Noah, Daniel, and many like them. And I saw a veil with a heavy fringe of silver and gold, as a border on the bottom; it was very beautiful. I asked Jesus what was within the veil. He raised it with his own right arm, and bade me take heed. I saw there a glorious ark, overlaid with pure gold, and it had a glorious border, resembling Jesus' crowns; and on it were two bright angels—their wings were spread over the ark as they sat on each end, with their faces turned towards each other and looking downward.

In the ark, beneath where the angels' wings were spread, was a golden pot of Manna, of a yellowish cast; and I saw a rod, which Jesus said was Aaron's; I saw it bud, blossom and bear fruit. And I saw two long golden rods, on which hung silver wires, and on the wires most glorious grapes; one cluster was more than a man here could carry. And I saw Jesus step up and take of the manna, almonds, grapes and pomegranates, and bear them down to the city, and place them on the supper table. I stepped up to see how much was taken away, and there was just as much left; and we shouted Hallelujah—Amen. — *WLF, pp. 14-16*

A Life Parallel to God's Life

Oh, how happy will be all those who have made themselves ready for the marriage supper of the Lamb, who are robed in the righteousness of Christ, and reflect his lovely image! They will have on the pure white linen which is the righteousness of the saints, and Christ will lead them by the side of living waters; God will wipe away all tears from their eyes, and they will have the life that runs parallel with the life of God. — *RH, Jan. 2, 1913*

Imagine the Glory of Heaven

I met a company of fifty assembled in a little park belted with trees and surrounded with rugged mountains... While seated in this beautiful, retired park, free from all confusion and bustle, a sweet peace came over my spirits. I seemed to be taken away from myself, and the bright home of the saints was presented vividly before me.

In imagination I gathered with the saints around the wide-spreading tree of life. Friends and dear relatives who had been separated from us by death were gathered there. The redeemed, white-robed multitude, who had washed their robes and made them white in the blood of the Lamb, were there. No flashing guard stood around the tree of life, barring our approach. With happy, joyous songs of praise, the voices were blended in perfect harmony as we plucked of the fruit from the tree of life.

For a time I lost all thought of time, of place, or occasion—of everything earthly. Heaven was the subject of my contemplation—heaven, the much longed-for heaven. I seemed to be there, where all was peace, where no stormy conflicts of earth could ever come. Heaven, a kingdom of righteousness where all the holy and pure and blest are congregated—ten thousand times ten thousand and thousands of thousands—living and walking in happy, pure intimacy, praising God and the Lamb who sitteth on the throne! Their voices were in perfect harmony. They never do each other wrong. Princes of heaven, the potentates of this mighty realm, are rivals only in good, seeking the happiness and joy of each other.

The greatest there is least in self-esteem, and the least is greatest in his gratitude and wealth of love. There are no dark errors to cloud the intellect. Truth and knowledge, clear, strong, and perfect, have chased every doubt away, and no gloom of doubt casts its baleful shadow upon its happy inhabitants. No voices of contention mar the sweet and perfect peace of heaven. Its inhabitants know no sorrow, no grief, no tears. All is in perfect harmony, in perfect order and perfect bliss. Our company was thirsty for water which could only be obtained from the river.

My imagination saw the "pure river of water of life, clear as crystal, proceeding out of the throne of God and of the Lamb." On either side of this river was the tree of life "which bare twelve manner of fruits, and yielded her fruit every month: and the leaves of the tree were for the healing of the nations." The Great Shepherd was leading his flock to living fountains of water and to green pastures, new and delightful scenery opening continually before his people.

Heaven, sweet heaven, the saints' eternal home, the abode for the toilers, where the weary who have borne the heavy burdens through life find rest, peace, and joy! They sowed in tears, they reap with joy and triumph. Heaven is a home where sympathy is alive in every heart, expressed in every look.

Love reigns there. There are no jarring elements, no discord or contentions or war of words. With our deepest study and our broadest experience we shall never be able to describe heaven or our senses to comprehend it. All that is pure, all that is excellent and lovely are there. The possession of heaven is endless bliss, infinite glory, riches, and knowledge. The character of heaven is perfect love, holiness, peace. —*Lt 30, 1882*

Discussion Questions

1. What will it be like to finally meet Jesus and embrace Him?

2. All of our earthly treasures are destroyed at the Second Coming. What will our true wealth in heaven be?

3. What is the significance of the saints having God's name written in their foreheads?

4. What would life be like if our greatest goal was to make others happy?

5. Why will the saints say that heaven is cheap enough?

— 26 —

Eden is Restored

"And the Lord God took the man, and put him into the Garden of Eden to dress it and to keep it." — Genesis 2:15

Gen. 2:9; 3:22	Prov. 11:30	Prov. 15:4	Eph. 1:13, 14	Rev. 22:1, 2
Psalm 46:4	Prov. 13:12	Isa. 33:20-24	Rev. 2:7	Rev. 22:14

Eden is Even More Glorious

After their sin Adam and Eve were no longer to dwell in Eden... They were told that their nature had become depraved by sin...

The Garden of Eden remained upon the earth long after man had become an outcast from its pleasant paths. The fallen race were long permitted to gaze upon the home of innocence, their entrance barred only by the watching angels. At the cherubim-guarded gate of Paradise the divine glory was revealed. Hither came Adam and his sons to worship God. Here they renewed their vows of obedience to that law the transgression of which had banished them from Eden.

When the tide of iniquity overspread the world, and the wickedness of men determined their destruction by a flood of waters, the hand that had planted Eden withdrew it from the earth. But in the final restitution, when there shall be "a new heaven and a new earth" (Revelation 21:1), it is to be restored more gloriously adorned than at the beginning.

Then they that have kept God's commandments shall breathe in immortal vigor beneath the tree of life; and through unending ages the inhabitants of sinless worlds shall behold, in that garden of delight, a sample of the perfect work of God's creation, untouched by the curse of sin—a sample of what the whole earth would have become, had man but fulfilled the Creator's glorious plan. — *PP, p. 62*

Eden Blooms Once Again

The principles of righteousness embodied in the Decalogue are as immutable as the eternal throne. Not one command has been annulled, not a jot or tittle has been changed. Those principles that were made known to man in Paradise as the great law of life will exist unchanged in Paradise restored. When Eden shall bloom on earth again, God's law of love will be obeyed by all beneath the sun. —*MB, p. 50*

Leaves to Heal the Nations

I have a faith that looks over into the future, and sees the tree of life. Upon it grow precious fruits, and the leaves of the tree are for the healing of the nations. No more broken hearts, no more sadness, no more sins, no more sorrow, no more suffering, in that kingdom of glory. If I am faithful, I expect to meet the loved ones there. Oh! I have everything to be thankful for. I expect to see Jesus, in whom our hopes of eternal life shall have glad fulfillment. —*RH, Dec. 23, 1884*

The Redeemed Grow Taller

Restored to the tree of life in the long-lost Eden, the redeemed will "grow up" (Malachi 4:2) to the full stature of the race in its primeval glory. The last lingering traces of the curse of sin will be removed, and Christ's faithful ones will appear in "the beauty of the Lord our God," in mind and soul and body reflecting the perfect image of their Lord. Oh, wonderful redemption! long talked of, long hoped for, contemplated with eager anticipation, but never fully understood. —*GC, p. 644*

The Tree of Life is like Christ

The fruit of the tree of life in the Garden of Eden possessed supernatural virtue. To eat of it was to live forever. Its fruit was the antidote of death. It leaves were for the sustaining of life and immortality... The tree of life was a type of the one great source of immortality. Of Christ it is written, "In Him was life, and the life was the light of men." He is the fountain of life. Obedience to Him is the life-giving, vivifying power that gladdens the soul. Through sin man shut himself off from access to the tree of life. Now, life and immortality are brought to light through Jesus Christ. —*Ms 41, 1902*

A Sign of God's Handiwork

Eden had been caught up from the earth; for God would not suffer it to feel the marks of the curse. He preserved it as a specimen of his handiwork at the beginning. —*Ms 69, 1912*

Eden was Temporarily Taken Away

The pure and lovely garden of Eden, from which our first parents were driven, remained until God purposed to destroy the earth by a flood. God had planted that garden, and especially blessed it, and in his wonderful providence withdrew it from the earth, and will return it to the earth again, more gloriously adorned than before it was removed from the earth. God purposed to preserve a specimen of his perfect work of creation free from the curse wherewith He had cursed the earth. —*3SG, p. 55*

The Indescribable Joy of Adam

When the faithful dead shall be resurrected, and the king of glory shall open before them the gates of the city of God, and the nations who have kept the truth enter in, what beauty and glory will meet the astonished sight of those who have seen no greater beauties in the earth than that which they beheld in decaying nature after the threefold curse was upon the earth.

It is impossible to describe Adam's transports of joy as he again beholds Paradise, the Garden of Eden, his once happy home, from which, because of his transgression, he had been so long separated. He beholds the lovely flowers and trees, of every description for fruit and beauty, every one of which to designate them he had named while in his innocence. He sees the luxuriant vines, which had once been his delight to train upon bowers and trees.

But when he again beholds the widespread tree of life with its extended branches and glowing fruit, and to him again is granted access to its fruit and leaves, his gratitude is boundless. He first in adoration bows at the feet of the King of glory, and then with the redeemed host swells the song, "Worthy, worthy is the Lamb that was slain." Adam had lost Eden by disobeying the commandments of God. He has now regained that lovely garden by repentance and faithful obedience. The curse rested upon him for disobedience, the blessing now for his obedience. —*3SG, pp. 88, 89*

A Tree that Perpetuates Life

The tree of life possessed the power to perpetuate life, and as long as they ate of it, they could not die. The lives of the antediluvians were protracted because of the life-giving power of this tree, which was transmitted to them from Adam and Eve. Christ is the source of our life, the source of our immortality. He is the tree of life, and to all who come to Him He gives spiritual life. — *RH, Jan. 26, 1897*

The Destiny of the Earth

The Garden of Eden was a representation of what God desired the whole earth to become, and it was his purpose that, as the human family increased in numbers, they should establish other homes and schools like the one He had given. Thus in course of time the whole earth might be occupied with homes and schools where the words and the works of God should be studied, and where the students should thus be fitted more and more fully to reflect, throughout endless ages, the light of the knowledge of his glory. — *Ed, p. 22*

The Two Adams Meet

As the ransomed ones are welcomed to the City of God, there rings out upon the air an exultant cry of adoration. The two Adams are about to meet. The Son of God is standing with outstretched arms to receive the father of our race—the being whom He created, who sinned against his Maker, and for whose sin the marks of the crucifixion are borne upon the Saviour's form.

As Adam discerns the prints of the cruel nails, he does not fall upon the bosom of his Lord, but in humiliation casts himself at his feet, crying: "Worthy, worthy is the Lamb that was slain!" Tenderly the Saviour lifts him up and bids him look once more upon the Eden home from which he has so long been exiled.

After his expulsion from Eden, Adam's life on earth was filled with sorrow. Every dying leaf, every victim of sacrifice, every blight upon the fair face of nature, every stain upon man's purity, was a fresh reminder of his sin. Terrible was the agony of remorse as he beheld iniquity abounding, and, in answer to his warnings, met the reproaches cast upon himself as the cause of sin. With patient humility he bore, for nearly a thousand years, the penalty of transgression. Faithfully did he repent of his sin and trust in the merits of the promised Saviour, and he died in the hope of a resurrection. The Son of God redeemed man's failure and fall; and now, through the work of the atonement, Adam is reinstated in his first dominion.

Transported with joy, he beholds the trees that were once his delight—the very trees whose fruit he himself had gathered in the days of his innocence and joy. He sees the vines that his own hands have trained, the very flowers that he once loved to care for. His mind grasps the reality of the scene; he comprehends that this is indeed Eden restored, lovelier now than when he was banished from it. The Saviour leads him to the tree of life and plucks the glorious fruit and bids him eat. He looks about him and beholds a multitude of his family redeemed, standing in the Paradise of God.

Then he casts his glittering crown at the feet of Jesus and, falling upon his breast, embraces the Redeemer. He touches the golden harp, and the vaults of heaven echo the triumphant song: "Worthy, worthy, worthy is the Lamb that was slain, and lives again!"

The family of Adam take up the strain and cast their crowns at the Saviour's feet as they bow before Him in adoration. This reunion is witnessed by the angels who wept at the fall of Adam and rejoiced when Jesus, after his resurrection, ascended to heaven, having opened the grave for all who should believe on his name. Now they behold the work of redemption accomplished, and they unite their voices in the song of praise. — *GC, pp. 647, 648*

Discussion Questions

1. Why did Adam and his sons worship God at the guarded gate of Eden?

2. How tall do you think the redeemed saints will be when they are done growing?

3. Why did God remove Eden from the Earth?

4. What will the leaves of the Tree of Life be used for?

5. How will Adam feel when he sees the deep scars in Christ's hands?

— 27 —

The Saints Judge Angels

"Do ye not know that the saints shall judge the world? And if the world shall be judged by you, are ye unworthy to judge the smallest matters? Do you not know that we shall judge angels? How much more, things that pertain to this life?" — 1 Corinthians 6:2, 3

Psalm 49:14	Psalm 149:5-9	Matthew 7:2	1 Cor. 4:5	Jude 1:6
Psalm 122:4, 5	Zech. 3:7	Luke 22:28-30	2 Peter 2:4	Rev. 20:4-6

Men Who Discern Good from Evil

Men who know God, and trust in Him, who are working for his name's glory, are to have keen discernment to discover any influence which would demerit the work and hinder the advancement of God's institution. Those who will be faithful guardians of the sacred work of God, who will keep all their powers in vital connection with Him, will discern between good and evil, and to those who have proved faithful and true and steadfast, connection with the King of righteousness will be their reward. They will be as gods, knowing good and evil. "Know ye not," says the apostle, "that the saints shall judge the world?"

—Lt 39, 1898

Overcomers are Ranked in Heaven

By patience, kindness, forbearance, we are to show that we are not of the world, that day by day we are learning the lessons that will fit us to enter the higher school. When God's redeemed ones are called to heaven, they will not leave behind the advancement they have made in this life by beholding Christ. They will go on, learning more and still more of God. They will carry their spiritual attainments into the courts above, leaving nothing of heavenly origin in this world. As the books of heaven are opened, each overcomer is assigned his lot and place in heaven, in accordance with the advancement he has made in this life. *—Ms 31, 1903*

Servants are Priests and Kings

God has promised that his faithful, obedient servants shall be exalted to be priests and kings. "Do ye not know that the saints shall judge the world?"

—ST, Nov. 16, 1888

The Weakest are the Greatest

The humblest and poorest of the true disciples of Christ, who are rich in good works, are more blessed and more precious in the sight of God than the men who boast of their great riches. They are more honorable in the courts of heaven than the most exalted kings and nobles who are not rich toward God.

—2T, p. 682

Evil Characters Cannot Judge

Angels of God are now testing and proving character. Angels are weighing moral worth. Know ye not that the saints, in unison with Christ, are to judge the world? But judgment will never be committed to those whose character is revealed in a tirade against their brethren. These men simply do not know themselves. They are bringing from the treasure of the heart evil things, and unless they are thoroughly converted, so that they possess the meekness of a little child, will never enter the kingdom of heaven. They may possess some good qualifications as businessmen, but when some things do not meet their ideas, they manifest the same accusing spirit that Judas displayed in his complaint against the woman who poured the ointment on the head and feet of Christ. *—Ms 35, 1893*

Satan is Judged by the Saints

Then I saw thrones, and Jesus and the redeemed saints sat upon them; and the saints reigned as kings and priests unto God. Christ, in union with his people, judged the wicked dead, comparing their acts with the statute book, the Word of God, and deciding every case according to the deeds done in the body. Then they meted out to the wicked the portion which they must suffer, according to their works; and it was written against their names in the book of death. Satan also and his angels were judged by Jesus and the saints.

Satan's punishment was to be far greater than that of those whom he had deceived. His suffering would so far exceed theirs as to bear no comparison with it. After all those whom he had deceived had perished, Satan was still to live and suffer on much longer. *—EW, p. 290*

The Power and Purity of Angels

Those who will be saved in the kingdom of God will be those who have washed their robes and made them white in the blood of the Lamb. The image of Christ will be perfected in every soul who accepts the gift of his grace, and those who are perfected through his grace, will stand before God equal in elevation, in power and purity, to the angels, and will be honored with them before the eternal throne. The angels of heaven will love those whom Christ has loved, and has bought with his own precious blood.

— ST, Dec. 30, 1889

A Few are in Christ's Inner Circle

All heaven rejoices over the weak, faulty human soul that gives itself to Jesus and lives a life of purity. Those who overcome much, love Jesus the most, and are put next to Christ, next to the great white throne, within the inner circle; yes, greatly honored. "Thou hast a few names even in Sardis which have not defiled their garments; and they shall walk with Me in white: for they are worthy. He that overcometh, the same shall be clothed in white raiment; and I will not blot out his name out of the book of life, but I will confess his name before my Father, and before his angels." Revelation 3:4, 5. Every moment is exceedingly precious. *— Lt 37, 1896*

Men are Placed above the Angels

Christ calls upon those who stand under his banner to engage in the conflict with Him as faithful soldiers, that they may inherit the crown of life. They have been adopted as sons and daughters of God. Christ has left them his assured promise that great will be the reward in the kingdom of heaven of those who partake of his humiliation and suffering for the truth's sake.

The cross of Calvary challenges, and will finally vanquish, every earthly and hellish power. In the cross all influence centers, and from it all influence goes forth. It is the great center of attraction, for on it Christ gave up his life for the human race. This sacrifice was offered for the purpose of restoring man to his original perfection. Yea, more, it was offered to give him an entire transformation of character, making him more than a conqueror. Those who in the strength of Christ overcome the great enemy of God and man, will occupy a position in the heavenly courts above angels who have never fallen.

— Ms 56, 1899

Christ's Attributes Allow Men to Judge

We are not inclined to associate kingly glory and judicial authority with the self-denial, patience, love, and forgiveness shown in the life of Christ; yet these attributes qualified the Saviour for his exalted position. The qualities of character which He developed on earth constitute his exaltation in glory. His triumphs were gained by love, not by force. In coming to Christ the sinner consents to be elevated to the noblest ideal of man.

"Do ye not know that the saints shall judge the world?" The attributes which exalted Christ, if obtained by his followers, will place the scepter in their hands, and they shall be kings and priests with God. Christ pledged Himself to keep the law which Adam transgressed, and to magnify that law and make it honorable by demonstrating that it was not arbitrary, and could be kept inviolate by man. Christ showed by his life that the law of God is faultless, and that man, by disobeying it, brings upon himself the evils which its restrictions seek to avert from him. —*3SP, pp. 256, 257*

Men are Distinguished by Their Piety

The qualities which shine with greatest luster in the kingdoms of the world, have no place in Christ's spiritual kingdom. That which is highly exalted among men, and brings exaltation to its possessor, such as caste, rank, position, or wealth, is not esteemed in the spiritual kingdom. The Lord says, "Them that honor Me, I will honor."

In Christ's kingdom men are distinguished according to their piety. Jesus said: "Whosoever therefore shall break one of these least commandments, and shall teach men so, he shall be called the least in the kingdom of heaven; but whosoever shall do and teach them, the same shall be called great in the kingdom of heaven. For I say unto you, That except your righteousness shall exceed the righteousness of the scribes and Pharisees, ye shall in no case enter into the kingdom of heaven."

The kingdom of heaven is of a higher order than any earthly kingdom. Whether we shall have a higher position or a lower position, will not be determined by our rank, wealth, or education, but by the character of the obedience rendered to the Word of God. Those who have been actuated by selfishness and human ambition, who have been striving to be greatest... will have no place in the kingdom of God. —*RH, Mar. 26, 1895*

393

Disobedient Souls will Never Judge

Those who are reckless in regard to obeying the law of God in this world, can never be entrusted with the judgment of the world hereafter. Those who have not special respect and reverence for a "Thus saith the Lord" in this world, will not have a place among the saints who are to judge the world.

Transgressors of the law of God would not feel at home in society that is pure and holy, for they would not cheerfully submit to the law of Jehovah which is to govern all the universe. How then could they judge the unlawful? Not being in harmony with the law of God in this life, they would be unfitted to have a place among those who hearken unto his commandments and cheerfully obey his statutes. — *ST, Jan. 17, 1895*

The Righteous Sit on Thrones to Judge

During the thousand years between the first and the second resurrection the judgment of the wicked takes place. The apostle Paul points to this judgment as an event that follows the Second Advent. "Judge nothing before the time, until the Lord come, who both will bring to light the hidden things of darkness, and will make manifest the counsels of the hearts." 1 Corinthians 4:5. Daniel declares that when the Ancient of Days came, "judgment was given to the saints of the Most High." Daniel 7:22. At this time the righteous reign as kings and priests unto God.

John in the Revelation says: "I saw thrones, and they sat upon them, and judgment was given unto them." "They shall be priests of God and of Christ, and shall reign with Him a thousand years." Revelation 20:4, 6. It is at this time that, as foretold by Paul, "the saints shall judge the world." 1 Corinthians 6:2. In union with Christ they judge the wicked, comparing their acts with the statute book, the Bible, and deciding every case according to the deeds done in the body. Then the portion which the wicked must suffer is meted out, according to their works; and it is recorded against their names in the book of death.

Satan also and evil angels are judged by Christ and his people. Says Paul: "Know ye not that we shall judge angels?" And Jude declares that "the angels which kept not their first estate, but left their own habitation, He hath reserved in everlasting chains under darkness unto the judgment of the great day." Jude 1:6. — *GC, pp. 660, 661*

The Sentence Equals the Crimes

I was shown that the seven last plagues will be poured out after Jesus leaves the sanctuary. Said the angel, "It is the wrath of God and the Lamb that causes the destruction or death of the wicked. At the voice of God the saints will be mighty and terrible as an army with banners, but they will not then execute the judgment written. The execution of the judgment will be at the close of the one thousand years."

After the saints are changed to immortality and caught up together with Jesus, after they receive their harps, their robes, and their crowns, and enter the city, Jesus and the saints sit in judgment. The books are opened—the book of life and the book of death. The book of life contains the good deeds of the saints; and the book of death contains the evil deeds of the wicked.

These books are compared with the statute book, the Bible, and according to that men are judged. The saints, in unison with Jesus, pass their judgment upon the wicked dead. "Behold ye," said the angel, "the saints, in unison with Jesus, sit in judgment, and mete out to the wicked according to the deeds done in the body, and that which they must receive at the execution of the judgment is set off against their names." This, I saw, was the work of the saints with Jesus through the one thousand years in the Holy City before it descends to the earth. —*EW, p. 52*

Discussion Questions

1. Why will the saints be like gods when they judge the world?

2. How will the redeemed be ranked in heaven? Who will be in Christ's inner circle?

3. In which ways are the saints equal to angels? What experiences might enable the redeemed to occupy a place above the angels?

4. Why are disobedient characters not worthy to judge?

5. Who will work together to determine the just penalty of the wicked? Do you think the punishment will be mental or physical?

The Final

Judgment

— 28 —

The Third Coming

"Before the Lord: for He cometh, for He cometh to judge the earth: He shall judge the world with righteousness, and the people with his truth." — Psalm 96:13

Joel 3:9-16	Micah 7:8, 9	John 5:28-30	Jude 1:14, 15	Rev. 17:14	Rev. 20:7, 8
Obad. 1:21	Zech. 14:3, 4	John 12:31	Rev. 16:16	Rev. 19:19, 20	Rev. 22:12

A) The Holy City Descends

The Mount of Olives Divides

Christ descends upon the Mount of Olives, whence, after his resurrection, He ascended, and where angels repeated the promise of his return. Says the prophet: … "His feet shall stand in that day upon the Mount of Olives, which is before Jerusalem on the east, and the Mount of Olives shall cleave in the midst thereof..." As the New Jerusalem, in its dazzling splendor, comes down out of heaven, it rests upon the place purified and made ready to receive it, and Christ, with his people and the angels, enters the Holy City. — *GC, p. 662*

Jesus and the Saints Return Home

After the judgment of the wicked dead had been finished, at the end of the one thousand years, Jesus left the city, and the saints and a train of the angelic host followed Him. Jesus descended upon a great mountain, which as soon as his feet touched it, parted asunder and became a mighty plain. Then we looked up and saw the great and beautiful city, with twelve foundations, and twelve gates, three on each side, and an angel at each gate. We cried out, "The city! The great city! It is coming down from God out of heaven!" And it came down in all its splendor and dazzling glory and settled in the mighty plain which Jesus had prepared for it. — *EW, p. 291*

Jerusalem and Eden Descend

At the end of one thousand years, Jesus, the king of glory, descends from the holy city, clothed with brightness like the lightning, upon the Mount of Olives—the same mount from whence He ascended after his resurrection. As his feet touch the mountain, it parts asunder, and becomes a very great plain, and is prepared for the reception of the holy city in which is the paradise of God, the Garden of Eden, which was taken up after man's transgression.

—3SG, p. 83

B) The Wicked are Resurrected

The Second Resurrection Occurs

At the close of the thousand years the second resurrection will take place. Then the wicked will be raised from the dead and appear before God for the execution of "the judgment written." Thus the revelator, after describing the resurrection of the righteous, says: "The rest of the dead lived not again until the thousand years were finished." Revelation 20:5. And Isaiah declares, concerning the wicked: "They shall be gathered together, as prisoners are gathered in the pit, and shall be shut up in the prison, and after many days shall they be visited." Isaiah 24:22. *— GC, p. 661*

Balaam is outside the Holy City

Before returning to his people, Balaam uttered a most beautiful and sublime prophecy of the world's Redeemer, and the final destruction of the enemies of God: "I shall see Him, but not now. I shall behold Him, but not nigh. There shall come a Star out of Jacob, and a Scepter shall rise out of Israel, and shall smite the corners of Moab, and shall destroy the children of Sheth."

He was permitted to look down through the ages to the first advent of Christ, and then forward to his second appearing, in power and glory. He would see the King above all kings, but not at present. He would behold his majesty and glory, but at a great distance. He would be among the number of the wicked dead, who should come forth in the second resurrection, to hear the awful doom, "Depart from Me, ye cursed." He would behold the redeemed ones in the city of God, while he himself would be shut out with the wicked. *— ST, Dec. 16, 1880*

Thomas Paine Awakens

Thomas Paine, whose body has moldered to dust... is to be called forth at the end of the 1000 years, at the second resurrection, to receive his reward, and suffer the second death. — *1SG, p. 175*

Evil Propensities are Resurrected

The very bodies that are sown in corruption will be raised in incorruption. That which is sown in dishonor will be raised in glory; sown in weakness it will be raised in power; sown a natural body it will be raised a spiritual body.

— *Lt 65a, 1894*

Deceitful Men are Kept Out

Only those who have brought into their lives the strictest integrity can enter through the gates into the holy city of God. Those who at the day of judgment are found to be standing under the rebuke of God, for unfair dealing, for covetous practices, for their multitude of deceptions and lies, will never pass the portals of the holy city. — *Ms 116, 1905*

The Wicked Still Hate Christ

At the close of the thousand years, Christ again returns to the earth. He is accompanied by the host of the redeemed and attended by a retinue of angels. As He descends in terrific majesty He bids the wicked dead arise to receive their doom. They come forth, a mighty host, numberless as the sands of the sea. What a contrast to those who were raised at the first resurrection! The righteous were clothed with immortal youth and beauty. The wicked bear the traces of disease and death.

Every eye in that vast multitude is turned to behold the glory of the Son of God. With one voice the wicked hosts exclaim: "Blessed is He that cometh in the name of the Lord!" It is not love to Jesus that inspires this utterance. The force of truth urges the words from unwilling lips. As the wicked went into their graves, so they come forth with the same enmity to Christ and the same spirit of rebellion. They are to have no new probation in which to remedy the defects of their past lives. Nothing would be gained by this. A lifetime of transgression has not softened their hearts. A second probation, were it given them, would be occupied as was the first in evading the requirements of God and exciting rebellion against Him. — *GC, p. 662*

Many Famous Men are Present

Each actor recalls the part which he performed. Herod, who slew the innocent children of Bethlehem that he might destroy the King of Israel; the base Herodias, upon whose guilty soul rests the blood of John the Baptist; the weak, timeserving Pilate; the mocking soldiers; the priests and rulers and the maddened throng who cried, "His blood be on us, and on our children!"—all behold the enormity of their guilt... There is Nero, that monster of cruelty and vice, beholding the joy and exaltation of those whom he once tortured, and in whose extremest anguish he found satanic delight... There are papist priests and prelates, who claimed to be Christ's ambassadors, yet employed the rack, the dungeon, and the stake to control the consciences of his people.

— GC, pp. 667, 668

The Wicked are Cursed by Sin

Then Jesus leaves the city surrounded by the redeemed host, and is escorted on his way by the angelic throng. In fearful majesty He calls forth the wicked dead. They are wakened from their long sleep. What a dreadful waking! They behold the Son of God in his stern majesty and resplendent glory.

All, as soon as they behold Him, know that He is the crucified one who died to save them, whom they had despised and rejected. They are in number like the sand upon the seashore. At the first resurrection all come forth in immortal bloom, but at the second, the marks of the curse are visible upon all. All come up as they went down into their graves. Those who lived before the flood, come forth with their giant-like stature, more than twice as tall as men now living upon the earth, and well proportioned. The generations after the flood were less in stature. There was a continual decrease through successive generations, down to the last that lived upon the earth.

The contrast between the first wicked men who lived upon the earth, and those of the last generation, was very great. The first were of lofty height and well proportioned—the last came up as they went down, a dwarfed, feeble, deformed race. A mighty host of kings, warriors, statesmen and nobles, down to the most degraded, came up together upon the desolate earth. When they behold Jesus in his glory they are affrighted, and seek to hide from his terrible presence. They are overwhelmed with his exceeding glory, and with one accord are compelled to exclaim in anguish, "Blessed is He who cometh in the name of the Lord." *—3SG, p. 83*

Lawbreakers are outside the Wall

The soul that has had light in regard to the Lord's Sabbath, his memorial of creation, and to save himself from inconvenience and reproach has chosen to remain disloyal, has sold his Lord. He has dishonored the name of Christ. He has taken his stand with the armies of Antichrist. With them at the last great day he will be found outside the city of God, not with the loyal, the true and righteous, in the heavenly kingdom. —*Ms 9, 1900*

Those Who Crucified Christ Arise

Then Jesus and all the retinue of holy angels, and all the redeemed saints, left the city. The angels surrounded their Commander and escorted Him on his way, and the train of redeemed saints followed. Then, in terrible, fearful majesty, Jesus called forth the wicked dead; and they came up with the same feeble, sickly bodies that went into the grave. What a spectacle! What a scene! At the first resurrection all came forth in immortal bloom; but at the second the marks of the curse are visible on all. The kings and noblemen of the earth, the mean and low, the learned and unlearned, come forth together.

All behold the Son of man; and those very men who despised and mocked Him, who put the crown of thorns upon his sacred brow, and smote Him with the reed, behold Him in all his kingly majesty. Those who spit upon Him in the hour of his trial now turn from his piercing gaze and from the glory of his countenance. Those who drove the nails through his hands and feet now look upon the marks of his crucifixion. Those who thrust the spear into his side behold the marks of their cruelty on his body. And they know that He is the very one whom they crucified and derided in his expiring agony. And then there arises one long protracted wail of agony, as they flee to hide from the presence of the King of kings and Lord of lords.

All are seeking to hide in the rocks, to shield themselves from the terrible glory of Him whom they once despised. And, overwhelmed and pained with his majesty and exceeding glory, they with one accord raise their voices, and with terrible distinctness exclaim, "Blessed is He that cometh in the name of the Lord!" Then Jesus and the holy angels, accompanied by all the saints, again go to the city, and the bitter lamentations and wailings of the doomed wicked fill the air. —*EW, p. 292*

C) Satan Prepare His Army

Satan Energizes the Wicked

Then at the close of the one thousand years, Jesus, with the angels and all the saints, leaves the Holy City, and while He is descending to the earth with them, the wicked dead are raised, and then the very men that "pierced Him," being raised, will see Him afar off in all his glory, the angels and saints with Him, and will wail because of Him. They will see the prints of the nails in his hands and in his feet, and where they thrust the spear into his side. The prints of the nails and the spear will then be his glory.

It is at the close of the one thousand years that Jesus stands upon the Mount of Olives, and the mount parts asunder and becomes a mighty plain. Those who flee at that time are the wicked, who have just been raised. Then the Holy City comes down and settles on the plain. Satan then imbues the wicked with his spirit. He flatters them that the army in the city is small, and that his army is large, and that they can overcome the saints and take the city.

— EW, p. 52

Satanic Forces Plan an Attack

Jesus and the saints return to the city. Satan goes forth among the vast multitude of resurrected wicked, and makes the feeble strong. He then points them to the countless millions who have been raised, and makes them believe that he, by his power, had brought them up from their graves. He points to the powerful race who lived before the flood, and to kings and warriors who were well skilled in battle, and flatters his subjects that their numbers are much greater than those in the city, that they can make war with them, and dethrone God and his Son Jesus Christ, and take the throne and occupy the city, and enjoy its richness and glory.

As the wicked come forth from their graves, they resume the current of their thoughts where it ceased in death. The antediluvian race perished blaspheming God. Many perished in battle; they fell while thirsting to conquer; they rise with the same spirit of war that they possessed when they fell. They accept Satan as their general, and his angels as their officers. Satan and his angels were once inhabitants of the city; and they profess to understand just how to attack the city and take possession of it. *— 3SG, p. 85*

Satan Believes in His Armies

Satan has not yet given up the idea that the world's armies will be so large that they will be able to overcome the heavenly host. —*Lt 90, 1906*

The Wicked Surround the City

Then I saw that Satan again commenced his work. He passed around among his subjects, and made the weak and feeble strong, and told them that he and his angels were powerful. He pointed to the countless millions who had been raised. There were mighty warriors and kings who were well skilled in battle and who had conquered kingdoms. And there were mighty giants and valiant men who had never lost a battle. There was the proud, ambitious Napoleon, whose approach had caused kingdoms to tremble. There stood men of lofty stature and dignified bearing, who had fallen in battle while thirsting to conquer.

As they come forth from their graves, they resume the current of their thoughts where it ceased in death. They possess the same desire to conquer which ruled when they fell. Satan consults with his angels, and then with those kings and conquerors and mighty men. Then he looks over the vast army, and tells them that the company in the city is small and feeble, and that they can go up and take it, and cast out its inhabitants, and possess its riches and glory themselves.

Satan succeeds in deceiving them, and all immediately begin to prepare themselves for battle. There are many skillful men in that vast army, and they construct all kinds of implements of war. Then with Satan at their head, the multitude move on. Kings and warriors follow close after Satan, and the multitude follow after in companies. Each company has its leader, and order is observed as they march over the broken surface of the earth to the Holy City. Jesus closes the gates of the city, and this vast army surround it, and place themselves in battle array, expecting a fierce conflict. —*EW, p. 293*

The Greatest Army is Formed

Now Satan prepares for a last mighty struggle for the supremacy. While deprived of his power and cut off from his work of deception, the prince of evil was miserable and dejected; but as the wicked dead are raised and he sees the vast multitudes upon his side, his hopes revive, and he determines not to yield the great controversy. He will marshal all the armies of the lost under his banner and through them endeavor to execute his plans. The wicked are Satan's captives.

In rejecting Christ they have accepted the rule of the rebel leader. They are ready to receive his suggestions and to do his bidding. Yet, true to his early cunning, he does not acknowledge himself to be Satan. He claims to be the prince who is the rightful owner of the world and whose inheritance has been unlawfully wrested from him. He represents himself to his deluded subjects as a redeemer, assuring them that his power has brought them forth from their graves and that he is about to rescue them from the most cruel tyranny.

The presence of Christ having been removed, Satan works wonders to support his claims. He makes the weak strong and inspires all with his own spirit and energy. He proposes to lead them against the camp of the saints and to take possession of the City of God. With fiendish exultation he points to the unnumbered millions who have been raised from the dead and declares that as their leader he is well able to overthrow the city and regain his throne and his kingdom.

In that vast throng are multitudes of the long-lived race that existed before the Flood; men of lofty stature and giant intellect, who, yielding to the control of fallen angels, devoted all their skill and knowledge to the exaltation of themselves; men whose wonderful works of art led the world to idolize their genius, but whose cruelty and evil inventions, defiling the earth and defacing the image of God, caused Him to blot them from the face of his creation. There are kings and generals who conquered nations, valiant men who never lost a battle, proud, ambitious warriors whose approach made kingdoms tremble. In death these experienced no change. As they come up from the grave, they resume the current of their thoughts just where it ceased. They are actuated by the same desire to conquer that ruled them when they fell.

Satan consults with his angels, and then with these kings and conquerors and mighty men. They look upon the strength and numbers on their side, and declare that the army within the city is small in comparison with theirs, and that it can be overcome. They lay their plans to take possession of the riches and glory of the New Jerusalem. All immediately begin to prepare for battle. Skillful artisans construct implements of war. Military leaders, famed for their success, marshal the throngs of warlike men into companies and divisions.

At last the order to advance is given, and the countless host moves on— an army such as was never summoned by earthly conquerors, such as the combined forces of all ages since war began on earth could never equal. Satan, the mightiest of warriors, leads the van, and his angels unite their forces for this final struggle. Kings and warriors are in his train, and the multitudes follow in vast companies, each under its appointed leader. With military precision the serried ranks advance over the earth's broken and uneven surface to the City of God. By command of Jesus, the gates of the New Jerusalem are closed, and the armies of Satan surround the city and make ready for the onset. — *GC, pp. 663, 664*

D) Jesus Appears Again

Christ Appears on a Throne

Now Christ again appears to the view of his enemies. Far above the city, upon a foundation of burnished gold, is a throne, high and lifted up. Upon this throne sits the Son of God, and around Him are the subjects of his kingdom. The power and majesty of Christ no language can describe, no pen portray. The glory of the Eternal Father is enshrouding his Son. The brightness of his presence fills the City of God, and flows out beyond the gates, flooding the whole earth with its radiance. — *GC, p. 665*

The Wicked are Captivated

As if entranced, the wicked have looked upon the coronation of the Son of God. They see in his hands the tables of the divine law, the statutes which they have despised and transgressed. They witness the outburst of wonder, rapture, and adoration from the saved; and as the wave of melody sweeps over the multitudes without the city, all with one voice exclaim, "Great and marvelous are thy works, Lord God Almighty; just and true are thy ways, thou King of saints" (Revelation 15:3); and, falling prostrate, they worship the Prince of life. — *GC, p. 668*

Sinners Try to Hide

Jesus stood meek and humble before the infuriated multitude, while they offered Him the vilest abuse. They spit in his face—that face from which they will one day desire to hide, which will give light to the city of God and shine brighter than the sun. —*EW, p. 170*

The Wicked See the Happy Saints

Jesus and all the angelic host and all the saints, with the glittering crowns upon their heads, ascend to the top of the wall of the city. Jesus speaks with majesty, saying, "Behold, ye sinners, the reward of the just! And behold, my redeemed, the reward of the wicked!" The vast multitude behold the glorious company on the walls of the city.

And as they witness the splendor of their glittering crowns and see their faces radiant with glory, reflecting the image of Jesus, and then behold the unsurpassed glory and majesty of the King of kings and Lord of lords, their courage fails. A sense of the treasure and glory which they have lost rushes upon them, and they realize that the wages of sin is death. They see the holy, happy company whom they have despised, clothed with glory, honor, immortality, and eternal life, while they are outside the city with every mean and abominable thing. —*EW, p. 293*

The Gates of the City are Shut

While Satan was rallying his army, the saints were in the city, beholding the beauty and glory of the Paradise of God. Jesus was at their head, leading them. All at once the lovely Saviour was gone from our company; but soon we heard his lovely voice, saying, "Come, ye blessed of my Father, inherit the kingdom prepared for you from the foundation of the world." We gathered about Jesus, and just as He closed the gates of the city, the curse was pronounced upon the wicked. The gates were shut.

Then the saints used their wings and mounted to the top of the wall of the city. Jesus was also with them; his crown looked brilliant and glorious. It was a crown within a crown, seven in number. The crowns of the saints were of the most pure gold, decked with stars. Their faces shone with glory, for they were in the express image of Jesus; and as they arose and moved all together to the top of the city, I was enraptured with the sight. —*EW, p. 53*

E) Christ Acknowledges the Saints

The Saints Rejoice over Children

The day of God will reveal how much the world owes to the holy influences of the home for men who have been unflinching advocates of truth and reform. When the Judgment shall sit, and the books shall be opened, when the "Well done" of the great Judge is pronounced, what joy unspeakable will fill our hearts, if, as we gather around the great white throne, we shall see our children, saved through our instrumentality, with the crown of immortal glory upon their brows.

How shall we feel as we look upon that company and see that those whom we have won for Christ have saved others, and these still others—a large assembly all brought into the haven of rest as the result of our labors, there to lay their crowns at Jesus's feet, and to praise Him through the endless cycles of eternity? — *ST, May 4, 1888*

Christ is Satisfied with His Purchase

Before the universe has been clearly presented the great sacrifice made by the Father and the Son in man's behalf. The hour has come when Christ occupies his rightful position and is glorified above principalities and powers and every name that is named. It was for the joy that was set before Him—that He might bring many sons unto glory—that He endured the cross and despised the shame. And inconceivably great as was the sorrow and the shame, yet greater is the joy and the glory. He looks upon the redeemed, renewed in his own image, every heart bearing the perfect impress of the divine, every face reflecting the likeness of their King. He beholds in them the result of the travail of his soul, and He is satisfied.

Then, in a voice that reaches the assembled multitudes of the righteous and the wicked, He declares: "Behold the purchase of my blood! For these I suffered, for these I died, that they might dwell in my presence throughout eternal ages." And the song of praise ascends from the white-robed ones about the throne: "Worthy is the Lamb that was slain to receive power, and riches, and wisdom, and strength, and honor, and glory, and blessing."

— *GC, p. 671*

The Reward of Soul Winners

When the redeemed stand before God, precious souls will respond to their names who are there because of the faithful, patient efforts put forth in their behalf, the entreaties and earnest persuasions to flee to the Stronghold. Thus those who in this world have been laborers together with God will receive their reward. —*8T, p. 196*

The Saints Stand Honored

Christ would have all understand that the end of all things is at hand, that the solemn scenes of the final judgment are soon to take place. In that great day, those whose characters the Judge of all the earth can vindicate will stand before the world glorified and honored. On this earth they manifested forth the light and glory of God, and He now rewards them according to their works. —*Lt 363, 1904*

Christ Acknowledges the Faithful

On Christ's coronation day, He will not acknowledge as his any who bear spot or wrinkle or any such thing. But to his faithful ones He will give crowns of immortal glory. Those who will not that He should reign over them will see Him surrounded by the army of the redeemed, each of whom bears the sign, "The Lord Our Righteousness." They will see the head once crowned with thorns crowned with a diadem of glory. —*Ms 168, 1902*

The Righteous Sing Triumphantly

In the day of final awards, when the righteous Judge of all the earth shall "sift the nations," and those that have kept the truth shall be permitted to enter the City of God, heaven's arches will ring with the triumphant songs of the redeemed.

"Ye shall have a song," the prophet declares, "as in the night when a holy solemnity is kept; and gladness of heart, as when one goeth with a pipe to come into the mountain of the Lord, to the Mighty One of Israel. And the Lord shall cause his glorious voice to be heard... Through the voice of the Lord shall the Assyrian be beaten down, which smote with a rod. And in every place where the grounded staff shall pass, which the Lord shall lay upon him, it shall be with tabrets and harps." Isaiah 30:29-32. —*PK, p. 366*

Jesus Welcomes Sabbathkeepers

John saw the holy city, the New Jerusalem, with its twelve gates of pearl and twelve foundations of precious stones, coming down from God out of heaven. The streets are of transparent gold, clear as crystal. Everyone who shall enter those gates and walk those streets will here have been changed and purified by the power of the truth; and the crown of immortal glory will adorn the brow of the overcomer. The nations that have kept the truth shall enter in, and the voice of the Son of God will pronounce the glad welcome, "Blessed are they that do his commandments, that they may have right to the tree of life, and may enter in through the gates into the city." — *ST, Dec. 22, 1887*

The Redeemed Sing Songs of Praise

The redeemed raise a song of praise that echoes and re-echoes through the vaults of heaven: "Salvation to our God which sitteth upon the throne, and unto the Lamb." And angel and seraph unite their voices in adoration. As the redeemed have beheld the power and malignity of Satan, they have seen, as never before, that no power but that of Christ could have made them conquerors. In all that shining throng there are none to ascribe salvation to themselves, as if they had prevailed by their own power and goodness. Nothing is said of what they have done or suffered; but the burden of every song, the keynote of every anthem, is: "Salvation to our God and unto the Lamb." — *GC, p. 665*

Many Owe Salvation to Their Mother

The day of God will reveal how much the world owes to godly mothers for men who have been unflinching advocates of truth and reform—men who have been bold to do and dare, who have stood unshaken amid trials and temptations; men who chose the high and holy interests of truth and the glory of God, before worldly honor or life itself.

When the judgment shall sit, and the books shall be opened; when the "well done" of the great Judge is pronounced, and the crown of immortal glory is placed upon the brow of the victor, many will raise their crowns in sight of the assembled universe, and pointing to their mother say, "She made me all I am through the grace of God. Her instruction, her prayers, have been blessed to my eternal salvation." — *ST, Nov. 3, 1881*

The True Worth of the Character

The life and its work stand daguerreotyped in heaven, and the close of the day is the proof of the picture. When the day of life is over, we can see and estimate human character at its true worth. We hope to meet this sister when the people of God shall be gathered around the great white throne, with many souls saved through her instrumentality to shine as stars in her crown of glory. "And they that be wise shall shine as the brightness of the firmament; and they that turn many to righteousness as the stars for ever and ever."

— RH, Oct. 14, 1884

Overcomers Stand around the Throne

Those who overcome in the name of Jesus will stand about the great white throne, with crowns of immortal glory, waving the palm branches of victory. They will be sons of God, children of the heavenly King, their lives running parallel with the life of God. The joy of the Lord will be their joy, and no shadow will ever darken their heavenly home.

Said Christ, "Blessed are they that do his commandments, that they may have right to the tree of life, and may enter in through the gates into the city." While mercy lingers, I beseech you to make the most of the probationary time left you, in preparing for eternity, that life may not be an utter failure, and that in the time of solemn scrutiny you may be found with those who are accepted of God, and are called the sons of God. *— ST, Aug. 1, 1878*

The Faithful are Truly Beautiful

Beauty of spirit, soul, heart, and life will never perish. These may not be appreciated here by a fashionable class, but will be appreciated of high heaven. There is a beauty which perishes not, such as angels wear. It forms the white robes of that company who stand before the throne of God, having come up through great tribulation. They washed their robes of character in the blood of the Lamb.

This beauty sets with a divine grace upon the countenance of every well-doer. It adorns the face of everyone whose life is virtuous and honest and true. This beauty molds the hands of charity and sweetens the voice of sympathy. If the features and form are not beautiful, the spirit may be beautiful by borrowing heaven's light and grace... Wisdom and virtue are jewels which will not dim with age or lose their luster in sickness and affliction. *— Lt 65, 1874*

A Great Multitude Surrounds the Throne

Nearest the throne are those who were once zealous in the cause of Satan, but who, plucked as brands from the burning, have followed their Saviour with deep, intense devotion. Next are those who perfected Christian characters in the midst of falsehood and infidelity, those who honored the law of God when the Christian world declared it void, and the millions, of all ages, who were martyred for their faith.

And beyond is the "great multitude, which no man could number, of all nations, and kindreds, and people, and tongues, ... before the throne, and before the Lamb, clothed with white robes, and palms in their hands." Revelation 7:9. Their warfare is ended, their victory won. They have run the race and reached the prize. The palm branch in their hands is a symbol of their triumph, the white robe an emblem of the spotless righteousness of Christ which now is theirs. — *GC, p. 665*

Many See the Foolishness of Their Plans

When we stand in the presence of God, we shall see how shortsighted we have been in our conclusions in regard to what heaven records as success. We shall see that the honor given to man is due to God alone, that the things for which in this world a man is exalted and glorified are of God, and that to Him belongs all the glory. From the lips of the inhabitants of the universe will peal forth the chorus, "Bring forth the royal diadem, and crown Him Lord of all."

And the redeemed host will join in the chorus, and will declare, "Great and marvelous are thy works, Lord God Almighty; just and true are thy ways, thou King of saints. Who shall not fear thee, O Lord, and glorify thy name; for thou only art holy; for all nations shall come and worship before thee; for thy judgments are made manifest."

As the redeemed review their efforts to achieve success, they will see how foolish were their plans, how petty their supposed trials, how unreasonable their doubts, and how unnecessary their conflicts. They will see that if they had only taken God at his Word, they should have seen all things clearly. And one thing will stand out in clear lines: that position does not make a man a fit candidate for entrance into the heavenly courts. — *Lt 31, 1902*

Father God is Glorified

After the redeemed are taken to heaven, God the Father will be glorified in crowning the Lord Jesus, who gave his life a ransom for the world.

—RH, Oct. 13, 1904

The Triumphant Throng Praises God

All classes, all nations and kindreds and people and tongues will stand before the throne of God and the Lamb, with their spotless robes and jeweled crowns. Said the angel, "These are they that have come up through great tribulation, and have washed their robes and made them white, while the lovers of pleasure more than lovers of God, the self-indulgent and disobedient, have lost both worlds. They neither have the things of this life nor the immortal life."

That triumphant throng, with songs of victory and with crowns and harps, have trodden in the fiery furnace of earthly affliction when it was heated and intensely hot. From destitution, from hunger and torture they come, from deep self-denial and bitter disappointments. Look upon them now as conquerors, no longer poor, no longer in sorrow, in affliction and hatred of all men for Christ's sake. Behold their heavenly garments, white and shining, richer than any kingly robe. Look by faith upon their jeweled crowns; never did such a diadem deck the brow of any earthly monarch.

Listen to their voices as they sing loud hosannas and as they wave the palm branches of victory. Rich music fills heaven as their voices sing forth these words, "Worthy, worthy is the Lamb that was slain and rose again forevermore. Salvation unto our God which sitteth upon the throne, and unto the Lamb." And the angelic host, angels and archangels, covering cherub and glorious seraph, echo back the refrain of that joyous, triumphant song, saying, "Amen: Blessing, and glory, and wisdom, and thanksgiving, and honor, and power, and might, be unto our God for ever and ever."

Oh in that day it will be discovered that the righteous were the wise ones, while the sinful and disobedient were fools in their pride and vanity, in neglecting the things of eternal interest. Shame and everlasting contempt is their portion. Those who have been co-laborers for Christ will then be near the throne of God, girt with purity and the garments of eternal righteousness.

—Lt 71, 1878

Christ Acknowledges the Heathen

"The hour is coming," Christ said, "in the which all that are in the graves shall hear his voice, and shall come forth." That voice is to resound through all the habitations of the dead; and every saint who sleeps in Jesus will awake and leave his prison-house. Then the virtue of character we have received from Christ's righteousness will ally us to true greatness of the highest order.

Every action of ours in befriending God's people will be rewarded as done unto Himself. In the day of final reckoning, Christ does not present before men the great work He has done for them in giving his life for their redemption. He presents before them the faithful work they have done for Him. What surpassing love is this! He even mentions the work of the heathen, who have no intelligent knowledge of the law of the Lord, but who have done the very things the law required, because they have heeded the voice speaking to them in the things of nature.

When the Holy Spirit implants Christ's Spirit in the heart of the savage, and he befriends God's servants, the quickening of the heart's sympathy is contrary to his nature, contrary to his education. The grace of God, working upon the darkened mind, has softened the savage nature untaught by the wisdom of men. And these uneducated heathen, in all their cruelty, are regarded in a more favorable light than are those who have had great light and evidence, but who have rejected the mercy and reproof of God.

— RH, Sept. 20, 1898

Discussion Questions

1. What is significant about Jesus descending onto the Mount of Olives?

2. Which famous people will be found outside of the New Jerusalem?

3. How is Satan able to deceive the wicked once again, convincing them to attack the Holy City?

4. Why is Jesus satisfied with the purchase of his blood?

5. What did the heathen do to earn a special acknowledgment from Christ?

The Books are Opened

"But I say to you that for every idle word men may speak, they will give account of it in the day of judgment." — Matt. 12:36

Isaiah 11:1-5	Isaiah 45:23-25	Matt. 25:31-46	Acts 17:30, 31	Rev. 3:5; 11:18
Isaiah 5:14-16	Dan. 7:9, 10	John 5:22-27	Rom. 14:11, 12	Rev. 20:11-13

A) Jesus is the Judge

God Gives Jesus Authority

"The Father judgeth no man, but hath committed all judgment unto the Son." "He hath given Him authority to execute judgment also, because He is the Son of man." In his super-added humanity consists the reason of Christ's appointment. God has committed all judgment unto the Son, for without controversy He is God manifest in the flesh. —*RH, Nov. 22, 1898*

Jesus Christ is a Worthy Judge

To prepare Himself to be the Judge of all the world, Christ endured the hardships and trials of mankind, suffering in all points like as we suffer, thus familiarizing Himself with the power of Satan's temptations. The enemy beset Him on every point, but He was victorious over the powers of darkness. If He had failed in a single instance, there would be no salvation for us.

But He has fought the battle for us, overcoming in our behalf. He rebuked those possessed of devils, and the evil spirits acknowledged his name, asking Him if He had come to torment them before the time. What a wonderful salvation has been worked out for us! To every sinner with whom we come in contact, we are to tell the infinite pains heaven has taken to bring us into right relation to God —*Ms 105, 1901*

The Triumph of the Law

The last day will be the triumph of law. Then the scales will fall from all eyes. That which seemed of little importance in spiritual and eternal things is in the mind of Omnipotence of vast consequence, and that which now seems to claim the mind, heart and affections, viewed by finite beings as of unmeasurable consequence, is estimated of God as an atom. The controlling power of appearances and professions will be seen as it is. The law of God is spoken of, argued, controverted, but sad to say, is not obeyed. There is profession and semblance of right but the law is disregarded, disobeyed with a carelessness that is painful. God calls for works, for character. —*Lt 52, 1891*

The Prince of Sufferers is Judge

God designed that the Prince of sufferers in humanity should be judge of the whole world. He who submitted to be arraigned before an earthly tribunal, He who came from the heavenly courts to save man from eternal death, He whom men despised, rejected, and upon whom they heaped all the contempt of which human beings inspired by Satan are capable, He who suffered the ignominious death of the cross—He alone was to pronounce the sentence of reward or of punishment. When every man shall be judged as his works have been, then the words spoken by Him in the judgment hall, "Hereafter shall the Son of man sit on the right hand of the power of God," will appear before them as if written in letters of fire. —*Ms 39, 1898*

Jesus Judged the Temple of Jerusalem

Jesus ascended the steps of the temple... the confusion was hushed. The sound of traffic and bargaining ceased. The silence became painful. A sense of awe overpowered the entire assembly. It was as if they were arraigned before the tribunal of God to answer for their deeds.

The Majesty of heaven stood as the Judge will stand at the last day, and every one of that vast crowd for the time acknowledged Him their Master. His eye swept over the multitude, taking in every individual. His form seemed to tower above them in commanding dignity, and a divine light illuminated his countenance. He spoke, and his clear, ringing voice, echoing through the arches of the temple, was like the voice that shook Mount Sinai, of old: "My house shall be called the house of prayer; but ye have made it a den of thieves."

—*2SP, p. 117*

Two Classes are Recognized

There are only two classes in the world today, and only two classes will be recognized in the judgment—those who violate God's law, and those who keep his law. Two great opposing powers are revealed in the last great battle. On one side stands the Creator of heaven and earth. All on his side bear his signet. They are obedient to his commands. On the other side stands the Prince of darkness, with those who have chosen apostasy and rebellion.

—RH, May 7, 1901

Justice Replaces Grace and Mercy

Christ is coming in power and great glory, and the dead are to be "judged out of those things which are written in the books, according to their works." The One who has stood as our intercessor; who hears all penitential prayers and confessions; who is represented with a rainbow, the symbol of grace and love, encircling his head, is soon to cease his work in the heavenly sanctuary. Grace and mercy will then descend from the throne, and justice will take their place. He for whom his people have looked will assume his right—the office of Supreme Judge. "The Father ... hath committed all judgment unto the Son... And He hath given Him authority to execute judgment also, because He is the Son of man." *—RH, Jan. 1, 1889*

Jehovah's Searching Eye Sees All

"Did not I deliver you from the Egyptians, and from the Amorites, from the children of Ammon, and from the Philistines? Yet ye have forsaken Me, and served other gods; wherefore I will deliver you no more." ...

As we ponder the solemn words of warning addressed to Israel, we are in imagination brought before the great white throne, wherein the presence of the assembled universe, every man will be judged according to the deeds done in the body. Then will be seen the true value of a Christian life and character. There must they render an account who have devoted their God-given talents of time, of means, or of intellect, to serving the gods of this world.

The searching eye of Jehovah will rest upon all; and that voice which amid the thunders of Sinai spake to man, "Thou shalt have no other gods before Me"—that voice will answer the sinner's imploring cry for pardon, "Go and cry unto the gods which ye have chosen. Let them deliver you in the time of your tribulation." *— ST, Aug. 18, 1881*

The Time of the Judgment

The general judgment shall take place at the end of the one thousand years. Whoever then has disowned Christ, betrayed Him in the person of his saints, will see the result of their work. Then the virtue of character we have received from Christ's righteousness will ally us to true greatness of the highest order.

—Ms 137, 1897

Judged by the Tables of Stone

What is the test of true religion? Knowing and doing the will of God, in accordance with every word that proceedeth out of the mouth of God. There is a sanctuary, and in that sanctuary is the ark: and in the ark are the tables of stone, on which are written the law spoken from Sinai amidst scenes of awful grandeur.

These tables of stone are in the heavens, and they will be brought forth in that day when the judgment shall sit, and the books shall be opened, and men shall be judged according to the things written in the books. They will be judged by the law written by the finger of God and given to Moses to be deposited in the ark. A record is kept of the deeds of all men, and according to his works will every man receive sentence, whether they be good or whether they be evil. *—Ms 20, 1906*

The Majesty of God's Law is Revealed

In his teachings, Christ sought to impress men with the certainty of the coming judgment, and with its publicity. This is not the judgment of a few individuals, or even of a nation, but of a whole world of human intelligences, of accountable beings. It is to be held in the presence of other worlds, that the love, the integrity, the service, of man for God, may be honored to the highest degree. There will be no lack of glory and honor. The Son of man will come in the clouds of heaven with his own glory, with the glory of his Father, and the glory of the holy angels.

The law of God will be revealed in its majesty; and those who have stood in defiant rebellion against its holy precepts will understand that the law that they have discarded, and despised, and trampled underfoot is God's standard of character. Vividly before the mind of every commandment-keeper, and before every transgressor, will be brought the scene when the Sabbath was first given to man in Eden. *—RH, Nov. 22, 1898*

God's Government is Vindicated

The final judgment is a most solemn, awful event. This must take place before the universe. To the Lord Jesus the Father has committed all judgment. He will declare the reward of loyalty to all who obey the law of Jehovah. God will be honored and his government vindicated and glorified, and that in the presence of the inhabitants of the unfallen worlds. On the largest possible scale will the government of God be vindicated and exalted. It is not the judgment of one individual or of one nation, but of the whole world.

Oh, what a change will then be made in the understanding of all created beings. Then all will see the value of eternal life. When God honors his commandment-keeping people, He would not have one of the enemies of truth and righteousness absent. And when the transgressors of his law receive their condemnation, He would have all the righteous behold the result of sin.

— Lt 131, 1900

Comparable to the Terrors of Sinai

The time is not far distant when God will arise to vindicate his insulted authority. "The Lord cometh out of his place to punish the inhabitants of the earth for their iniquity." Isaiah 26:21. "But who may abide the day of his coming? And who shall stand when He appeareth?" Malachi 3:2. The people of Israel, because of their sinfulness, were forbidden to approach the mount when God was about to descend upon it to proclaim his law, lest they should be consumed by the burning glory of his presence.

If such manifestations of his power marked the place chosen for the proclamation of God's law, how terrible must be his tribunal when He comes for the execution of these sacred statutes. How will those who have trampled upon his authority endure his glory in the great day of final retribution?

The terrors of Sinai were to represent to the people the scenes of the judgment. The sound of a trumpet summoned Israel to meet with God. The voice of the Archangel and the trump of God shall summon, from the whole earth, both the living and the dead to the presence of their Judge. The Father and the Son, attended by a multitude of angels, were present upon the mount. At the great judgment day Christ will come "in the glory of his Father with his angels." Matthew 16:27. He shall then sit upon the throne of his glory, and before Him shall be gathered all nations. *— PP, p. 339*

God's Law is Seen as Holy

When the judgment shall sit, and everyone shall be judged by the things written in the books, the authority of God's law will be looked upon in a light altogether different from that in which it is now regarded by the Christian world. Satan has blinded their eyes and confused their understanding, as he blinded and confused Adam and Eve, and led them into transgression. The law of Jehovah is great, even as its Author is great. In the judgment it will be recognized as holy, just, and good in all its requirements. Those who transgress this law will find that they have a serious account to settle with God; for his claims are decisive. — *RH, May 7, 1901*

Caiaphas Saw the Final Judgment

"Nevertheless I say unto you, Hereafter shall ye see the Son of man sitting on the right hand of power, and coming in the clouds of heaven."

For a moment the divinity of Christ flashed through his guise of humanity. The high priest quailed before the penetrating eyes of the Saviour. That look seemed to read his hidden thoughts, and burn into his heart. Never in afterlife did he forget that searching glance of the persecuted Son of God.

"Hereafter," said Jesus, "shall ye see the Son of man sitting on the right hand of power, and coming in the clouds of heaven." In these words Christ presented the reverse of the scene then taking place. He, the Lord of life and glory, would be seated at God's right hand. He would be the judge of all the earth, and from his decision there could be no appeal. Then every secret thing would be set in the light of God's countenance, and judgment be passed upon every man according to his deeds.

The words of Christ startled the high priest. The thought that there was to be a resurrection of the dead, when all would stand at the bar of God, to be rewarded according to their works, was a thought of terror to Caiaphas. He did not wish to believe that in future he would receive sentence according to his works. There rushed before his mind as a panorama the scenes of the final judgment. For a moment he saw the fearful spectacle of the graves giving up their dead, with the secrets he had hoped were forever hidden. For a moment he felt as if standing before the eternal Judge, whose eye, which sees all things, was reading his soul, bringing to light mysteries supposed to be hidden with the dead. — *DA, pp. 707, 708*

The Law Demands Purity

The law of God existed before man was created. It was adapted to the condition of holy beings; even angels were governed by it. After the fall, the principles of righteousness were unchanged. Nothing was taken from the law; not one of its holy precepts could be improved. And as it has existed from the beginning, so will it continue to exist throughout the ceaseless ages of eternity. "Concerning thy testimonies," says the psalmist, "I have known of old that thou hast founded them forever." By this law, which governs angels, which demands purity in the most secret thoughts, desires, and dispositions, and which "shall stand fast forever," all the world is to be judged in the rapidly approaching day of God. — *ST, Apr. 15, 1886*

A Vision of the Great Judgment Day

On the morning of October 23, 1879, about two o'clock, the Spirit of the Lord rested upon me, and I beheld scenes in the coming judgment. Language fails me in which to give an adequate description of the things which passed before me and of the effect they had upon my mind.

The great day of the execution of God's judgment seemed to have come. Ten thousand times ten thousand were assembled before a large throne, upon which was seated a person of majestic appearance. Several books were before Him, and upon the covers of each was written in letters of gold, which seemed like a burning flame of fire: "Ledger of Heaven."

One of these books, containing the names of those who claim to believe the truth, was then opened. Immediately I lost sight of the countless millions about the throne, and only those who were professedly children of the light and of the truth engaged my attention. As these persons were named, one by one, and their good deeds mentioned, their countenances would light up with a holy joy that was reflected in every direction. But this did not seem to rest upon my mind with the greatest force.

Another book was opened, wherein were recorded the sins of those who profess the truth. Under the general heading of selfishness came every other sin. There were also headings over every column, and underneath these, opposite each name, were recorded, in their respective columns, the lesser sins. Under covetousness came falsehood, theft, robbery, fraud, and avarice; under ambition came pride and extravagance; jealousy stood at the head of malice, envy, and hatred; and intemperance headed a long list of fearful crimes, such as lasciviousness, adultery, indulgence of animal passions, etc.

As I beheld I was filled with inexpressible anguish and exclaimed: "Who can be saved? Who will stand justified before God? Whose robes are spotless? Who are faultless in the sight of a pure and holy God?"

As the Holy One upon the throne slowly turned the leaves of the ledger, and his eyes rested for a moment upon individuals, his glance seemed to burn into their very souls, and at the same moment every word and action of their lives passed before their minds as clearly as though traced before their vision in letters of fire. Trembling seized them, and their faces turned pale. Their first appearance when around the throne was that of careless indifference.

But how changed their appearance now! The feeling of security is gone, and in its place is a nameless terror. A dread is upon every soul, lest he shall be found among those who are wanting. Every eye is riveted upon the face of the One upon the throne; and as his solemn, searching eye sweeps over that company, there is a quaking of heart; for they are self-condemned without one word being uttered. In anguish of soul each declares his own guilt and with terrible vividness sees that by sinning he has thrown away the precious boon of eternal life.

One class were registered as cumberers of the ground. As the piercing eye of the Judge rested upon these, their sins of neglect were distinctly revealed. With pale, quivering lips they acknowledged that they had been traitors to their holy trust. They had had warnings and privileges, but they had not heeded nor improved them. They could now see that they had presumed too much upon the mercy of God. True, they had not such confessions to make as had the vile and basely corrupt; but, like the fig tree, they were cursed because they bore no fruit, because they had not put to use the talents entrusted to them.

This class had made self supreme, laboring only for selfish interests. They were not rich toward God, not having responded to his claims upon them. Although professing to be servants of Christ, they brought no souls to Him. Had the cause of God been dependent on their efforts, it would have languished; for they not only withheld the means lent them of God, but they withheld themselves...

421

Like Meroz, the curse of God rested upon them for what they had not done. They had loved that work which would bring the greatest profit in this life; and opposite their names in the ledger devoted to good works there was a mournful blank. The words spoken to these were most solemn:

"You are weighed in the balances, and found wanting. You have neglected spiritual responsibilities because of busy activity in temporal matters, while your very position of trust made it necessary that you should have more than human wisdom and greater than finite judgment. This you needed in order to perform even the mechanical part of your labor; and when you disconnected God and his glory from your business, you turned from his blessing." The question was then asked: "Why have you not washed your robes of character and made them white in the blood of the Lamb?"

"God sent his Son into the world, not to condemn the world, but that through Him it might be saved. My love for you has been more self-denying than a mother's love. It was that I might blot out your dark record of iniquity, and put the cup of salvation to your lips, that I suffered the death of the cross, bearing the weight and curse of your guilt."

"The pangs of death, and the horrors of the darkness of the tomb, I endured, that I might conquer him who had the power of death, unbar the prison house, and open for you the gates of life. I submitted to shame and agony because I loved you with an infinite love, and would bring back my wayward, wandering sheep to the paradise of God, to the tree of life. That life of bliss which I purchased for you at such a cost, you have disregarded."

Shame, reproach, and ignominy, such as your Master bore for you, you have shunned. The privileges He died to bring within your reach have not been appreciated. You would not be partaker of his sufferings, and you cannot now be partaker with Him of his glory." Then were uttered these solemn words: "He that is unjust, let him be unjust still: and he which is filthy, let him be filthy still: and he that is righteous, let him be righteous still: and he that is holy, let him be holy still." The book then closed, and the mantle fell from the Person on the throne, revealing the terrible glory of the Son of God.

The scene then passed away, and I found myself still upon the earth, inexpressibly grateful that the day of God had not yet come, and that precious probationary time is still granted us in which to prepare for eternity.

—*4T, pp. 384-387*

B) The Wicked Realize Their Guilt

The Lost Blame Others

In the judgment the lost may point to you and say, "If it had not been for his influence, I would not have stumbled and made a mock of religion. He had light, he knew the way to heaven. I was ignorant, and went blindfolded on my way to destruction." — *YI, Feb. 2, 1893*

Men See the Souls They Lost

Those who are working on the side of Satan do not know what a fearful loss they are incurring. At the last great day, those who have given themselves to anarchy, and war, and strife will see how many souls have been lost as a result of their failure to take their stand under the rule of Christ. — *Ms 131, 1903*

Many Misrepresented Christ

A Christian is one who is Christlike. When the judgment sits, and all are judged according to the deeds done in the body, they will learn that they have misrepresented Christ in practical life and have not made themselves a savor of life unto life, but a savor of death unto death. In fellowship with them will be a numerous company who have conformed to lustful practices, but numbers will neither excuse their iniquity nor lessen their condemnation for destroying the brain nerve power and the physical health. All will be judged personally. They will stand before God to hear their sentence. — *Ms 123, 1901*

Scales Fall from All Eyes

In the last great day, Jehovah's law will triumph. Then shall the scales fall from all eyes. What now is regarded by the transgressors of the law of God as of no special consequence, or of but little importance in the standard of morality and holiness, will appear as it is, holy, just, and good. It will be seen as taking immeasurable compass. The law of the Lord is perfect, converting the soul. Then character and law alone will seem to be as large as eternity. The reign of appearance and deception will cease. Semblance and pretence will drop their mask. People will see themselves just as they are, obedient or disobedient, loyal or disloyal to the law of Jehovah. Then the division of the whole family will be made. — *Lt 29, 1897*

Children Condemn Parents

The curse of God will surely rest upon unfaithful parents. Not only are they planting thorns which will wound them here, but they must meet their own unfaithfulness when the judgment shall sit. Many children will rise up in judgment and condemn their parents for not restraining them, and charge upon them their destruction. — *1T, p. 219*

The Results of Unwise Love

Parents who have neglected their God-given responsibilities must meet that neglect in the judgment. The Lord will then inquire: "Where are the children that I gave you to train for me? Why are they not at my right hand?" Many parents will then see that unwise love blinded their eyes to their children's faults and left those children to develop deformed characters, unfit for heaven. Others will see that they did not give their children time and attention, love and tenderness; their own neglect of duty made the children what they are.

— *4T, p. 424*

God Ways are Vindicated

God carries with Him the sympathy and approval of the whole universe as step by step his great plan advances to its complete fulfillment. He will carry it with Him in the final eradication of rebellion. It will be seen that all who have forsaken the divine precepts have placed themselves on the side of Satan, in warfare against Christ. When the prince of this world shall be judged, and all who have united with him shall share his fate, the whole universe as witnesses to the sentence will declare, "Just and true are thy ways, thou King of saints." Revelation 15:3. — *PP, p. 79*

Everyone Gives an Account to God

When the books are opened, the character will be revealed, and every mouth will be stopped. You will be convicted of guilt before the revelation of your own life. Everyone unsaved will see where he departed from right, and will realize the influence his life of disobedience exerted to turn others from the way of truth. "Every one of us shall give account of himself to God," and the quick and the dead shall stand before the judgment seat of Christ. The secret things will be made known. There was an eye that saw and a hand that registered the hidden deeds. — *ST, Dec. 29, 1887*

Infidelity is Exposed

The day of final settlements is just before us. In that solemn and awful hour the unfaithfulness of the husband will be opened to the wife, and the unfaithfulness of the wife, to the husband. — *RH, Mar. 27, 1888*

Evil Men See Who They Tortured

Christ had such an experience in his humanity that He would be close beside everyone who passes through suffering for the truth's sake—those who are tortured, imprisoned in dungeons, and bound in chains. Christ ministered unto these. It was Christ in the person of his saints who suffered. And all who cause his people to suffer, will experience this suffering in their own bodies, be they pope, legate, priests, or people. They will understand in that day that they were dealing with Christ in the person of his saints. Then they will understand the wrath of the Lamb. — *Ms 137, 1897*

The Unjust Actions of Lawmakers

At the present time there are those placed as jurors, senators, lawyers, and judges, who forget that God is a party to all their transactions, and that He will call them to give account of all their injustice toward their fellow men, in causing the innocent to suffer and the guilty to escape. Men have so long done this that they have forgotten God. "Because sentence against an evil work is not executed speedily, therefore the hearts of the sons of men are fully set in them to do evil." But the God of truth is a witness to every false oath, and the Holy One that inhabiteth eternity will not serve with their sins.

— *Lt 89, 1898*

Secret Confessions Astonish the World

The time is at hand when every secret thing shall be brought into judgment, and then there will be many confessions made that will astonish the world. The secrets of all hearts will be revealed. The confession of sin will be most public. The sad part of it is that confession then made will be too late to benefit the wrong-doer or to save others from deception. It only testifies that his condemnation is just. He gained nothing by his pride and self-sufficiency and stubbornness, for his own life was embittered, he ruined his own character so that he was not a fit subject of heaven, and by his influence he led others to ruin. — *RH, Dec. 16, 1890*

The Obedient and the Disobedient

The difference between those who have sincerely worshiped God and those who have opposed Him will be seen by men and angels. The obedient and the disobedient will stand out plainly and distinctly, each wearing the badge of the one they serve. The disobedient are written as commandment-breakers, the obedient as commandment-keepers, who wear the God-given seal. Those who have worshiped God only in name will be seen just as they are, and they will be treated in accordance with their works. Those who have served God in wholehearted obedience will receive the gift of eternal life. Obedience unto obedience is as far-reaching as eternity. —*Lt 20, 1900*

Satan Has a New Appreciation for God

Satan, the first apostate, looked upon the fruit of his apostasy in the vast army under his banner, and his mind was made to comprehend the meaning of warfare against God and his Son. He saw how many he had by his subtlety led away from God, from happiness and holiness. The truth of his position and his efforts to overthrow God and assume his place, when he took with him vast numbers of angels who might have been a happy family in heaven, flashed over him. Never had the arch-deceiver such an appreciation of God and his throne, his holiness, his justice, his goodness, his amazing love, as when Christ hung on the cross. Mercy and truth had met together, righteousness and peace had embraced each other. —*Ms 94, 1899*

The Mixed Web of Human Influence

In the judgment when every case is decided, there will be revealed in its fullness the responsibility of every man. You will realize the influence you might have had over other souls had you stood under the bloodstained banner of Jesus Christ. How interwoven is the web of human influence! The course of action followed by every man has a direct bearing upon the life of others.

I have had presented to me the solemn scenes of the judgment, and I now ask you to stop and consider, "How is it with my soul?" Shall not the prayer go forth from your lips, "Wash me thoroughly from my sin, and cleanse me from mine iniquity?" Psalm 51:2. The Lord will hear the prayer that is offered to Him in sincerity. Believe in Christ as your personal Saviour. Grasp the promises before it is everlastingly too late. —*Lt 52, 1899*

Selfish Ministers are Lost

There are those in the ministry who have had light and a knowledge of the truth who will not be overcomers. They will not restrict their appetite and passions, or deny themselves for Christ's sake, and many of the poor outcasts, even publicans and sinners, will grasp the hope set before them in the gospel, and will go into the kingdom of heaven before the ones who have had great opportunities and great light, but who have walked in darkness. In the last great day, many will say, "Lord, Lord, open unto us." But the door will be shut, and their knock will be in vain. —*Lt 51b, 1898*

Many are Guilty of Secret Sins

Many of those who profess to believe the Bible, and even to expound its sacred truths, are yet living in the indulgence of some cherished sin—living as though there were no God whose eye could search the inmost recesses of the soul. They are blessed with heaven's bounties, and yet they express no more gratitude to the Giver than do the beasts of the field. They may now have no sense of their own sinfulness; but when summoned before the great white throne, they will in speechless terror stand condemned. The excuses now so flippantly urged to shield themselves from the divine requirements, they dare not mention with the eye of the Judge looking upon them. They knew their Master's will, but did it not, and they will be beaten with many stripes. —*ST, Mar. 9, 1882*

God Photographed Each Character

God's law reaches the feelings and motives, as well as the outward acts. It reveals the secrets of the heart, flashing light upon things before buried in darkness. God knows every thought, every purpose, every plan, every motive. The books of heaven record the sins that would have been committed had there been opportunity. God will bring every work into judgment, with every secret thing. By his law He measures the character of every man.

As the artist transfers to the canvas the features of the face, so the features of each individual character are transferred to the books of heaven. God has a perfect photograph of every man's character, and this photograph He compares with his law. He reveals to man the defects that mar his life, and calls upon him to repent and turn from sin. —*ST, July 31, 1901*

False Pastors Remember Sinai

Those who have ministered in word and doctrine; who by smooth words and fair speeches have taught that the law of God is no longer binding, that the Sabbath of the fourth commandment was given for the Jews only; who have educated their hearers to show contempt for the warnings sent by the Lord's prophets and apostles and delegated servants, will have brought to their minds the scenes of Sinai in all their grandeur—God the Father, and the holy angels, the blackness and darkness, the lightning's blazing flash, the thunder, the tempest, the earthquake, the sound of the trumpet waxing louder and louder, and the voice of God proclaiming his holy law. —*RH, Nov. 22, 1898*

The World Has Rejected Jesus

God has a controversy with the world. When the judgment shall sit, and the books shall be opened, he has an awful account to settle, which would now make the world fear and tremble, were men not blinded and bewitched by satanic delusions and deceptions. God will call the world to account for the death of his only begotten Son, whom to all intents and purposes the world has crucified afresh, and put to open shame in the persecution of his people.

The world has rejected Christ in the person of his saints, has refused his messages in the refusal of the messages of prophets, apostles, and messengers. They have rejected those who have been co-laborers with Christ, and for this they will have to render an account. —*RH, Aug. 29, 1893*

The Cross Makes Everyone Speechless

The whole world stands condemned before the great moral standard of righteousness. In the great day of judgment every soul that has lived on the earth will receive sentence in accordance as to whether his deeds have been good or evil in the light of the law of God. Every mouth will be stopped as the cross with its dying Victim shall be presented, and its real bearing shall be seen by every mind that has been sin blinded and corrupted.

Sinners will stand condemned before the cross, with its mysterious Victim bowing beneath the infinite burden of human transgression. How quickly will be swept away every subterfuge, every lying excuse! Human apostasy will appear in its heinous character. Men will see what their choice has been. They will then understand that they have chosen Barabbas instead of Christ, the Prince of Peace. —*ST, Mar. 7, 1895*

Only One Question is Asked

The only question asked in the judgment will be, "Are they obedient to my commandments?" The petty strife and contention over questions of no importance is an education which our people do not need. Let them seek instead to answer the prayer of Christ, "That they all may be one, as thou, Father, art in Me, and I in thee, that they also may be one in us; that the world may believe that thou hast sent Me." —*Ms 11, 1901*

Every Man Stands Revealed

The time will come when all must stand before angels and before men revealed in their true light. As the artist reproduces upon the polished plate the features of the human countenance, so their characters are being transferred to the books of heaven. The great Master-artist faithfully delineates every phase of the character. Every manifestation of selfishness or greed is noted by Him. In the judgment every man will stand revealed just as he is, either fashioned after the divine similitude, or disfigured by the idolatrous sins of selfishness and covetousness. —*Ms 53, 1903*

Parents and Children Meet Again

Those who indulge the appetite of their children, and do not control their passions, will see the terrible mistake they have made... When parents and children meet at the final reckoning, what a scene will be presented! Thousands of children who have been slaves to appetite and debasing vice, whose lives are moral wrecks, will stand face to face with the parents who made them what they are. Who but the parents must bear this fearful responsibility? Did the Lord make these youth corrupt? Oh, no! He made them in his image, a little lower than the angels.

Who, then, has done the fearful work of forming the life character? Who changed their characters so that they do not bear the impress of God, and must be forever separated from his presence as too impure to have any place with the pure angels in a holy heaven? Were the sins of the parents transmitted to the children in perverted appetites and passions? And was the work completed by the pleasure-loving mother in neglecting to properly train them according to the pattern given her? All these mothers will pass in review before God just as surely as they exist. —*3T, p. 568*

Satan Has No Excuse

In the final execution of the judgment it will be seen that no cause for sin exists. When the Judge of all the earth shall demand of Satan, "Why hast thou rebelled against Me, and robbed Me of the subjects of my kingdom?" the originator of evil can render no excuse. Every mouth will be stopped, and all the hosts of rebellion will be speechless. — *GC, p. 503*

Rich Men are Greatly Pitied

A worldly rich man will be, in the day of judgment, the poorest and most to be pitied of any man before the judgment throne. They sold themselves for paltry gain and their reward will be as their works have been. These rich men, poor as far as the knowledge of God is concerned, placed themselves higher than men who had moral worth, because the world regarded it in this light— not because the Saviour regarded it thus. They would not be practical Christians themselves, and those who would, they hindered. — *Lt 1, 1882*

Families Learn Hidden Secrets

In view of the solemn responsibilities that rest upon us, let us contemplate the future, that we may understand what we must do in order to meet it. In that day shall we be confronted with neglect and contempt of God and his mercy, with rejection of his truth and love? In the solemn assembly of the last day, in the hearing of the universe, will be read the reason of the condemnation of the sinner.

For the first time parents will learn what has been the secret life of their children. Children will see how many wrongs they have committed against their parents. There will be a general revealing of the secrets and motives of the heart; for that which is hid will be made manifest. Those who have made sport of solemn things connected with the judgment, will be sobered as they face its terrible reality.

Those who have despised the Word of God, will then face the Author of the inspired oracles. We cannot afford to live with no reference to the day of judgment; for though long delayed, it is now near, even at the door, and hasteth greatly. The trumpet of the archangel will soon startle the living, and wake the dead. At that day the wicked will be separated from the just, as the shepherd divides the goats from the sheep. — *YI, July 21, 1892*

The Unseen Witnesses

The thoughts, the purposes, the acts of God's workers, although now unseen, will appear at the great day of final retribution and reward. Things now forgotten will then appear as witnesses, either to approve or to condemn.

—Ms 161, 1897

Men Remember Their Sins

Each one in the day of investigative Judgment will stand in character as he really is; he will render an individual account to God. Every word uttered, every departure from integrity, every action that sullies the soul, will be weighed in the balances of the sanctuary. Memory will be true and vivid in condemnation of the guilty one, who in that day is found wanting. The mind will recall all the thoughts and acts of the past; the whole life will come in review like the scenes in a panorama. Thus everyone will be condemned or acquitted out of his own mouth, and the righteousness of God will be vindicated. *— RH, Nov. 4, 1884*

Men are Judged by Their Character

God will not treat men according to the position they occupy, according to their color, or their poverty, but according to the character they have formed. Thus will be decided the destiny of every one. Those who have had opportunity to know the truth, who have had great light, but who in blindness of mind contend against God's messengers, contend against God and his truth. They do what they know to be contrary to the truth. Their punishment will be proportionate to the light they have received.

God greatly favored them, giving them peculiar advantages and gifts, that they might let their light shine forth to others. But in their perversity they lead others astray. God will judge them for all the good they might have done and did not do. He will call them to account for their misused opportunities.

They turned from God's way to their own way, and God will judge them according to their work. They became fools in the sight of God by turning the truth of God into a lie. By walking contrary to the principles of the truth they greatly dishonored God. As God has distinguished them above all other nations of the earth by his wonderful mercy and grace, so He will make their punishment conspicuous. This He will do that all may see that He is a God of justice, and that his ways are equal. *— Ms 35, 1900*

There is No Excuse for Sin

Sin is a mysterious, unexplainable thing. There was no reason for its existence; to seek to explain it is to seek to give a reason for it, and that would be to justify it. Sin appeared in a perfect universe, a thing that was shown to be inexcusable and exceeding sinful. The reason of its inception or development was never explained and never can be, even at the last great day when the judgment shall sit and the books be opened, when every man shall be judged according to the deeds done in the body, when the sins of God's repentant, sanctified people shall be heaped upon the scapegoat, the originator of sin.

At that day it will be evident to all that there is not, and never was, any cause for sin. At the final condemnation of Satan and his angels and of all men who have finally identified themselves with him as transgressors of God's law, every mouth will be stopped. When the hosts of rebellion, from the first great rebel to the last transgressor, are asked why they have broken the law of God, they will be speechless. — *ST, Apr. 28, 1890*

Confession Comes Sooner or Later

Confession must come sooner or later—if not voluntarily now, then finally before the universe of heaven and the multitude that shall compose Satan's vast army encircling the city of God in the vain supposition that numbers will prevail. Those who persist in refusing to confess now will then be forced to confess their errors, their unfaithful, underhand dealing, and all their transgression of the law of God.

Oh, how much better to confess errors now, than to leave them until the opening of the records in the books of heaven, when every act shall be revealed, and even the motives that led to action! God reads the secrets of every heart. And the day draws near when all who have united in calling the actions of the unrighteous man just and righteous will see that they have acted a part in deceiving the man and that they have been partakers of his unrighteous deeds. They will then understand that because they have strengthened his evil propensities by passing them by without reproof, they are united with him in the sin; and as surely as the Lord has spoken, they will share the punishment when it will be administered in the presence of an assembled universe. — *Lt 136, 1906*

The Sins of Men are Revealed

When the judgment shall sit, and the books shall be opened, there will be many astonishing disclosures. Men will not then appear as they appear to the human eyes and finite judgments. Secret sins will then be laid open to the view of all. Motives and intentions which have been hidden in the dark chambers of the heart will be revealed. Designing ambitions, selfish purposes, will be seen where the outward appearance told only of a desire to honor God and to do good to men.

What revelations will then be made. Men of pure motives and true and noble purpose may now be slighted, neglected, slandered, and despised; but they will then appear as they are, and will be honored with the commendation of God. Hypocritical, ambitious teachers may now be admired and exalted by men; but God, who knows the secrets of the heart will strip off the deceptive covering, and reveal them as they are. Every hypocrite will be unmasked, every slandered believer will be justified, and every faithful steward of God will be approved and rewarded. — *RH, Jan. 1, 1884*

A Terrible Day for Sunday Worshipers

What a terrible day that will be for those who have refused God's sign, who have exalted a spurious rest day, and have claimed authority over the consciences of their fellow men! They have disregarded the law of Jehovah, and Satan has deceived them, to their ruin. They have received the falsehoods framed by him to make of none effect God's commands. As they stand before the bar of God, they will see the great sacrifice the Father made in giving his only begotten Son to the world, that men and women might hear the message of salvation, and live.

Christ was the light of the world, but when He came to his own, they received Him not. Inspired with the spirit of Satan, the Jewish leaders killed the Saviour because He condemned their practices. In the day of judgment, those who have refused the light and have led others to honor the false Sabbath will see the course Satan has pursued in causing men to transgress the law of God. They will see and fully comprehend the virtue of God's sign. They will understand that they might have been saved had they accepted God's message of mercy to a fallen world. But they turned from the truth and rejected the sign of God. — *Ms 27, 1900*

The Sin of Wasting God's Money

I wish I could impress on every mind the grievous sinfulness of wasting the Lord's money on fancied wants. The expenditure of sums that look small, may start a train of circumstances that will reach into eternity. When the Judgment shall sit, and the books are opened, the losing side will be presented to your view—the good that you might have done with the accumulated mites and the larger sums that were used for wholly selfish purposes.

And what will it reveal?—Just that deficiency in the bank of heaven,—robbery toward God, some destitute bodies not clothed, some poor souls praying for light and knowledge robbed of the bread of life. Your money went to gratify perverted appetite, or to indulge vanity. Oh, what shame and grief will come to your souls as you see how much you have lost! Look about you, and see if there is not a work which the Lord has given you. The Isaiah 58:1 presents before you a work that has been neglected. *—RH, Aug. 11, 1891*

Men are Conscious of Every Sin

In the presence of the assembled inhabitants of earth and heaven the final coronation of the Son of God takes place. And now, invested with supreme majesty and power, the King of kings pronounces sentence upon the rebels against his government and executes justice upon those who have transgressed his law and oppressed his people.

Says the prophet of God: "I saw a great white throne, and Him that sat on it, from whose face the earth and the heaven fled away; and there was found no place for them. And I saw the dead, small and great, stand before God; and the books were opened: and another book was opened, which is the book of life: and the dead were judged out of those things which were written in the books, according to their works." Revelation 20:11, 12.

As soon as the books of record are opened, and the eye of Jesus looks upon the wicked, they are conscious of every sin which they have ever committed. They see just where their feet diverged from the path of purity and holiness, just how far pride and rebellion have carried them in the violation of the law of God. The seductive temptations which they encouraged by indulgence in sin, the blessings perverted, the messengers of God despised, the warnings rejected, the waves of mercy beaten back by the stubborn, unrepentant heart—all appear as if written in letters of fire. *— GC, p. 666*

Pleasures and Riches Lose Importance

Sad will be the retrospect in that day when men stand face to face with eternity. The whole life will present itself just as it has been. The world's pleasures, riches, and honors will not then seem so important. Men will then see that the righteousness they despised is alone of value. They will see that they have fashioned their characters under the deceptive allurements of Satan. The garments they have chosen are the badge of their allegiance to the first great apostate. Then they will see the results of their choice. They will have a knowledge of what it means to transgress the commandments of God.

There will be no future probation in which to prepare for eternity. It is in this life that we are to put on the robe of Christ's righteousness. This is our only opportunity to form characters for the home which Christ has made ready for those who obey his commandments. — *COL, pp. 318, 319*

Destinies were Determined by Actions

In that great day all will see that their course of action decided their destiny. They will be rewarded or punished according as they have obeyed or violated the law of God. In that great day the character of each individual will be plainly and distinctly revealed. God will look into all the feelings and motives. No one can then occupy middle ground. Men and women are either saints or sinners, either entitled to a glorious life of eternity, or doomed to eternal death.

What a scene that will be! No pen can describe it! The aggravated guilt of the world will be laid bare, and the voice of the eternal Judge will be heard saying, "Depart from me; I never knew you." The judgment will be conducted in accordance with the rules given in order that man might have eternal life. The law of God, which men are now called upon to obey and to make their rule of life, but which many refused to accept, is the law by which they will be judged. We are judged by our works. Obedience or disobedience means everything to us.

The last great day will witness the triumph of the law of Jehovah. As the impenitent look upon the cross of Calvary, the scales fall from their eyes, and they see that which before they would not see. The law, God's standard of righteousness, is exalted even as his throne is exalted. God Himself gives reverence to his law. — *Lt 131, 1900*

435

Many Hide Their Sins like Achan

Achan acknowledged his guilt, but when it was too late for the confession to benefit himself. He had seen the armies of Israel return from Ai defeated and disheartened; yet he did not come forward and confess his sin. He had seen Joshua and the elders of Israel bowed to the earth in grief too great for words. Had he then made confession, he would have given some proof of true penitence; but he still kept silence. He had listened to the proclamation that a great crime had been committed, and had even heard its character definitely stated. But his lips were sealed. Then came the solemn investigation.

How his soul thrilled with terror as he saw his tribe pointed out, then his family and his household! But still he uttered no confession, until the finger of God was placed upon him. Then, when his sin could no longer be concealed, he admitted the truth. How often are similar confessions made.

There is a vast difference between admitting facts after they have been proved and confessing sins known only to ourselves and to God. Achan would not have confessed had he not hoped by so doing to avert the consequences of his crime. But his confession only served to show that his punishment was just. There was no genuine repentance for sin, no contrition, no change of purpose, no abhorrence of evil.

Confessions will be made by the guilty when they stand before the bar of God, after every case has been decided for life or death. The consequences to result to himself will draw from each an acknowledgment of his sin. It will be forced from the soul by an awful sense of condemnation and a fearful looking for of judgment. But such confessions cannot save the sinner.

So long as they can conceal their transgressions from their fellow men, many, like Achan, feel secure, and flatter themselves that God will not be strict to mark iniquity. All too late their sins will find them out in that day when they shall not be purged with sacrifice or offering forever. When the records of heaven shall be opened, the Judge will not in words declare to man his guilt, but will cast one penetrating, convicting glance, and every deed, every transaction of life, will be vividly impressed upon the memory of the wrongdoer. The person will not, as in Joshua's day, need to be hunted out from tribe to family, but his own lips will confess his shame. The sins hidden from the knowledge of men will then be proclaimed to the whole world.

— PP, pp. 497, 498

God Executes the Judgment

Enoch, the seventh from Adam, prophesied of that day, saying, "Behold, the Lord cometh with ten thousand of his saints, to execute judgment upon all." And Solomon, when in the capacity of a preacher he tried to present the strongest motive to holy obedience—the motive that was above all estimate in view of the judgment to come—said, "Let us hear the conclusion of the whole matter: Fear God, and keep his commandments; for this is the whole duty of man. For God shall bring every work into judgment, with every secret thing, whether it be good, or whether it be evil."

God places every action in the scale. What a scene it will be! What impressions will be made regarding the holy character of God and the terrible enormity of sin, when the judgment, based on the law, is carried forward in the presence of all the worlds. Then before the mind of the unrepentant sinner there will be opened all the sins that he has committed, and he will see and understand the aggregate of sin and his own guilt.

When the loyal overcomers are crowned, God would have present all who have transgressed his law and broken their covenant with Him. And not one of the righteous will be absent. They see, in the Judge, Christ Jesus, the One whom every sinner has crucified. The Son of man shall come in his glory, and before Him shall be gathered all nations. The Father judgeth no man, but hath committed all judgment to the Son. But the trumpet is waxing louder and louder, and the wicked dead come forth to confront Christ.

When the multitude of the lost, those whom God has favored with great light, shall look upon the goodness, mercy, and love of Jesus; when those who might have been saved if they had accepted the light and the blessings of God's Word, but who refused to obey his law, see the great sacrifice made in their behalf, they understand the unmeasured love of the Redeemer; they understand his incarnation, the sweat drops of blood, the marks of the nails in his hands and feet, the pierced side; and they ask to be hidden from the face of Him that sitteth on the throne and from the wrath of the Lamb.

They see as in reality the condemnation of Christ, they hear the loud cry, "Release unto us Barabbas." They hear the question, "What shall be done with Jesus?" and the answer, "Crucify Him, crucify Him." The reign of appearance and pretense is over. The voice of the righteous Judge speaks with awful emphasis, as He utters the sentence, "Depart from Me; I never knew you." —*Ms 77, 1906*

A Vivid Memory of Forgotten Deeds

What disclosure will the judgment reveal when the books are opened and every man is judged according to the deed done in the body! What an awakening will then come! How vividly will come back the memory of deeds that have now been forgotten! What intense, searching inspection will be made of all the life's actions. Hidden things will all be revealed. The sinful secrets of life and heart which have not been confessed and washed away in the blood of the Lamb will be made manifest.

The unfaithfulness of those who have taken upon them sacred responsibilities and have failed to fulfill them will stand revealed. Those whose consciences have become seared until sin was not sin to them, through whose influence others will be led to lightly regard sin will see things in their true light. Their great ambition to be first, to be highly honored of men, will stand forth in all its unhallowed aspects. —*Ms 25, 1892*

A Panoramic View of Redemption

Above the throne is revealed the cross; and like a panoramic view appear the scenes of Adam's temptation and fall, and the successive steps in the great plan of redemption. The Saviour's lowly birth; his early life of simplicity and obedience; his baptism in Jordan; the fast and temptation in the wilderness; his public ministry, unfolding to men heaven's most precious blessings; the days crowded with deeds of love and mercy, the nights of prayer and watching in the solitude of the mountains; the plottings of envy, hate, and malice which repaid his benefits; the awful, mysterious agony in Gethsemane beneath the crushing weight of the sins of the whole world.

His betrayal into the hands of the murderous mob; the fearful events of that night of horror—the unresisting prisoner, forsaken by his best-loved disciples, rudely hurried through the streets of Jerusalem; the Son of God exultingly displayed before Annas, arraigned in the high priest's palace, in the judgment hall of Pilate, before the cowardly and cruel Herod, mocked, insulted, tortured, and condemned to die—all are vividly portrayed.

And now before the swaying multitude are revealed the final scenes—the patient Sufferer treading the path to Calvary; the Prince of heaven hanging upon the cross; the haughty priests and the jeering rabble deriding his expiring agony; the supernatural darkness; the heaving earth, the rent rocks, the open graves, marking the moment when the world's Redeemer yielded up his life.

The awful spectacle appears just as it was. Satan, his angels, and his subjects have no power to turn from the picture of their own work. Each actor recalls the part which he performed. Herod, who slew the innocent children of Bethlehem that he might destroy the King of Israel; the base Herodias, upon whose guilty soul rests the blood of John the Baptist; the weak, timeserving Pilate; the mocking soldiers; the priests and rulers and the maddened throng who cried, "His blood be on us, and on our children!"—all behold the enormity of their guilt. They vainly seek to hide from the divine majesty of his countenance, outshining the glory of the sun, while the redeemed cast their crowns at the Saviour's feet, exclaiming: "He died for me!"

Amid the ransomed throng are the apostles of Christ, the heroic Paul, the ardent Peter, the loved and loving John, and their truehearted brethren, and with them the vast host of martyrs; while outside the walls, with every vile and abominable thing, are those by whom they were persecuted, imprisoned, and slain. There is Nero, that monster of cruelty and vice, beholding the joy and exaltation of those whom he once tortured, and in whose extremest anguish he found satanic delight. His mother is there to witness the result of her own work; to see how the evil stamp of character transmitted to her son, the passions encouraged and developed by her influence and example, have borne fruit in crimes that caused the world to shudder.

There are papist priests and prelates, who claimed to be Christ's ambassadors, yet employed the rack, the dungeon, and the stake to control the consciences of his people. There are the proud pontiffs who exalted themselves above God and presumed to change the law of the Most High.

Those pretended fathers of the church have an account to render to God from which they would fain be excused. Too late they are made to see that the Omniscient One is jealous of his law and that He will in no wise clear the guilty. They learn now that Christ identifies his interest with that of his suffering people; and they feel the force of his own words: "Inasmuch as ye have done it unto one of the least of these my brethren, ye have done it unto me." Matthew 25:40. — *GC, pp. 666-668*

Sinners See What They Lost

At the day of judgment there comes to the lost a full realization of the meaning of the sacrifice made on Calvary. They see what they have lost by refusing to be loyal. They think of the high, pure association it was their privilege to gain. But it is too late. The last call has been made. The wail is heard: "The harvest is past, the summer is ended, and we are not saved." Jeremiah 8:20. — *7T, p. 16*

Satan Recalls His Former Life

Satan seems paralyzed as he beholds the glory and majesty of Christ. He who was once a covering cherub remembers whence he has fallen. A shining seraph, "son of the morning;" how changed, how degraded! From the council where once he was honored, he is forever excluded. He sees another now standing near to the Father, veiling his glory. He has seen the crown placed upon the head of Christ by an angel of lofty stature and majestic presence, and he knows that the exalted position of this angel might have been his.

Memory recalls the home of his innocence and purity, the peace and content that were his until he indulged in murmuring against God, and envy of Christ. His accusations, his rebellion, his deceptions to gain the sympathy and support of the angels, his stubborn persistence in making no effort for self-recovery when God would have granted him forgiveness—all come vividly before him. He reviews his work among men and its results—the enmity of man toward his fellow man, the terrible destruction of life, the rise and fall of kingdoms, the overturning of thrones, the long succession of tumults, conflicts, and revolutions. He recalls his constant efforts to oppose the work of Christ and to sink man lower and lower. He sees that his hellish plots have been powerless to destroy those who have put their trust in Jesus.

As Satan looks upon his kingdom, the fruit of his toil, he sees only failure and ruin. He has led the multitudes to believe that the City of God would be an easy prey; but he knows that this is false. Again and again, in the progress of the great controversy, he has been defeated and compelled to yield. He knows too well the power and majesty of the Eternal.

The aim of the great rebel has ever been to justify himself and to prove the divine government responsible for the rebellion. To this end he has bent all the power of his giant intellect. He has worked deliberately and systematically, and with marvelous success, leading vast multitudes to accept his version of the great controversy which has been so long in progress. For thousands of years this chief of conspiracy has palmed off falsehood for truth.

But the time has now come when the rebellion is to be finally defeated and the history and character of Satan disclosed. In his last great effort to dethrone Christ, destroy his people, and take possession of the City of God, the archdeceiver has been fully unmasked. Those who have united with him see the total failure of his cause. Christ's followers and the loyal angels behold the full extent of his machinations against the government of God. He is the object of universal abhorrence.

Satan sees that his voluntary rebellion has unfitted him for heaven. He has trained his powers to war against God; the purity, peace, and harmony of heaven would be to him supreme torture. His accusations against the mercy and justice of God are now silenced. The reproach which he has endeavored to cast upon Jehovah rests wholly upon himself. And now Satan bows down and confesses the justice of his sentence.

"Who shall not fear thee, O Lord, and glorify thy name? For thou only art holy: for all nations shall come and worship before thee; for thy judgments are made manifest." Revelation 15:4. — *GC, pp. 669, 670*

Men and Evil Angels Realize Their Guilt

In the day when everyone shall be rewarded according to his work, how will transgressors appear in their own sight as for a few moments they are permitted to see the record of their life as they have chosen to make it, regardless of the law which through the eternal ages will govern the universe? They will then see what God desired them to do. They will realize that they should have used their blood-bought privileges in behalf of truth and righteousness. They will see that instead of placing their talents and influence on the side of rebellion, thus strengthening the forces of the enemy, they should have devoted their powers to being and doing good...

In the day of judgment men will see what they might have become through the power of Christ. They will see the robbery that they have practiced toward God. They will realize that they have apostatized from their Creator. They will see the good they might have done but did not do. They utterly refused to be made better. The efforts put forth in their behalf were in vain. They knew the claims of God, but they refused to comply with the conditions laid down in his Word. By their own choice they were united with demons. The power given them to use in God's service they used in the service of self. They made self their god, refusing to submit to any other control. They deceived themselves, and made themselves contemptible in the sight of God.

As they worked on the side of the power of darkness, they encouraged others to do the same. They arrayed themselves, soul, body, and spirit on the side of the enemy, laying as a willing offering on the altar of Satan that which they should have given to God. Although there was among themselves jealousy, envy, and discord, yet they were linked together as with iron bands in opposition to the laws which bring peace and harmony to the world. Fallen men and fallen angels are sure to join in desperate companionship. He who fell because of apostasy works constantly against goodness and obedience. He is leagued with those who refuse to keep God's law. In the day of judgment all this opens up before the impenitent.

Scene after scene passes before them. As plainly as in the light of the noon-day sun, they all see what they might have been had they cooperated with God instead of opposing Him. The picture cannot be changed. Their cases are forever decided. They must perish with the one whose ways and works they followed. A flash of light will come to all lost souls. They will see clearly the mystery of godliness, which during their lifetime they despised and hated.

And the fallen angels, endowed with higher intelligence than man, will realize what they have done in using their powers to lead human beings to choose deception and falsehood.

All who have united with the deceiver, all who have learned his ways and practiced his deceptions, must perish with him because they have the seeds of rebellion in them and have worked in their own way, carrying out their own devisings. Companies are formed in this world to strengthen Satan's methods to destroy the influence of God's appointed agencies. Where these should have been almost innumerable multitudes that expect to be saved, they have joined the rebel leader and would, if they only had a chance, carry on the work they began in this world to mold minds to their ideas. The Lord Jesus looks pityingly upon them and says, "Depart." At that time Zechariah, chapters 3 and 4, will be understood. — *Ms 37, 1900*

C) Unfruitful Christians

Fraudulent Christians

There are men, in the church and in the world, who have educated themselves to practice fraud, and for this they will be brought into judgment, for they have not only treated their soul, body, and spirit, as worthless, but have deprived God of his own blood-bought possession. "Ye are not your own," He says, "for ye are bought with a price." Consider the price paid for your salvation, that you might become members of the royal family, children of the heavenly king. —*Lt 89, 1898*

The Curse of Meroz

The judgment of the great day seems to pass before me. I see these souls as they will stand in the day when the judgment shall sit and the books be opened, and everyone is judged according to the deeds done in the body.

Before my mind's eye there seem to stand those who will share the curse of Meroz: "Curse ye Meroz; curse ye bitterly the inhabitants thereof; because they came not up to the help of the Lord, to the help of the Lord against the mighty." Judges 5:23. The pages of their history, as far as God and heaven are concerned, is one mournful blank. They are trees without fruit. They bring no sheaves to the Master. —*Ms 8, 1889*

Condemned by Neighbors

In the day of judgment, when everyone will be rewarded according to his works, many of the lost will charge their neighbors with neglect, saying, "You knew the truth regarding the requirements of the Bible, but you did not stop to think that close beside your own door there were souls who were in error, and who needed to be given instruction."

The judgment will reveal sins of omission as well as sins of commission. When Seventh-day Adventists know that the world is perishing in ignorance of Bible truth, why do they not go forth to hunt and fish for souls? If they do not do this, how will they be able to answer the question that in the great day of reckoning will be put to them by the lost, "Why did you not give to us the warning regarding God's requirements?" —*RH, Dec. 22, 1910*

Most Christians are Disappointed

The great mass of professing Christians will meet with bitter disappointment in the day of God. They have not upon their foreheads the seal of the living God. Lukewarm and half-hearted, they dishonor God far more than the avowed unbeliever. They grope in darkness, when they might be walking in the noonday light of the Word, under the guidance of One who never errs.

—Lt 121, 1903

Justified by Faith and by Works

The Lord is soon to come and take this matter in hand, and He will give to every man according as his works have been. What a scene that will be when the wrath of God shall come upon the guilty world! Then the words will stand before the eyes of men as if written in letters of fire: "Justified by faith, Justified by works." Their day of trust, with its burden of record is now ended in the day of reckoning. Every man has had the call, "Go, work today in my vineyard," and every man will receive according to the opportunities and privileges he has had. *—Ms 139, 1899*

Christians Plead to be Let into the City

As the wicked look upon the redeemed, and see their faces radiant with glory, and glittering crowns upon their heads, their courage fails, and they wail in anguish as they realize that they chose a life of rebellion against God, and Jesus Christ their Saviour, and for their disloyalty have lost eternal life, and an imperishable treasure.

Then many who had professed to be Christ's followers, but who had not honored God in their lives, enumerate their good deeds performed when they lived upon the earth, and entreat to be admitted into the city. They plead that their names were upon the church books, and they had prophesied in the name of Christ, and in his name cast out devils, and done many wonderful works.

Christ answers, "Your cases have been decided. Your names are not found enrolled in the book of life. You professed to believe in my name, but you trampled upon the law of God. I know you not, depart from Me ye workers of iniquity." Satan and his angels try to encourage the wicked multitude to action; but fire descends from heaven, and unites with the fire in the earth, and aids in the general conflagration. *—3SG, p. 86*

Many Robbed God of His Tithes

Those who follow their selfish, natural inclination, do not make their hearts an abiding place for Christ… The last great day will reveal to them and to the whole universe what good might have been done, had they not followed their selfish inclinations, and thus robbed God in tithes and offerings. They might have placed their treasure in the bank of heaven, and preserved it in bags that wax not old; but instead of doing this, they expended it upon themselves and their children, and seemed to feel afraid that the Lord would get any of their money or their influence, and thus they met with eternal loss. Let them contemplate the consequence of withholding from God. The slothful servant, who puts not out his Lord's money to usury, loses an eternal inheritance in the kingdom of glory. —*RH, Jan. 22, 1895*

Talents are Taken from the Unworthy

In the great judgment day those who have not worked for Christ, those who have drifted along, carrying no responsibility, thinking of themselves, pleasing themselves, will be placed by the Judge of all the earth with those who did evil. They receive the same condemnation.

Many who profess to be Christians neglect the claims of God, and yet they do not feel that in this there is any wrong. They know that the blasphemer, the murderer, the adulterer, deserves punishment; but as for them, they enjoy the services of religion. They love to hear the gospel preached, and therefore they think themselves Christians. Though they have spent their lives in caring for themselves, they will be as much surprised as was the unfaithful servant in the parable to hear the sentence, "Take the talent from him." Like the Jews, they mistake the enjoyment of their blessings for the use they should make of them.

Many who excuse themselves from Christian effort plead their inability for the work. But did God make them so incapable? No, never. This inability has been produced by their own inactivity and perpetuated by their deliberate choice. Already, in their own characters, they are realizing the result of the sentence, "Take the talent from him." The continual misuse of their talents will effectually quench for them the Holy Spirit, which is the only light. The sentence, "Cast ye the unprofitable servant into outer darkness," sets heaven's seal to the choice which they themselves have made for eternity. —*COL, p. 365*

The World Accuses Christians

The world has claims upon you. If you fail to shine as lights in the world, some will rise in the judgment, and charge upon you the blood of their souls. It will be seen that you were an agent in the hands of the enemy of God and man to mislead and deceive by your profession of Christianity. You did not lead souls to piety and devotion. You had a name to live, but were spiritually dead. You had not the vitalizing influence of the Spirit of God, which is abundantly provided for all who, in faith, make demands upon it. If man turns away, and does not act his part, he not only imperils his own soul, but deprives those who are in darkness of the light he could bring them. —*RH, Aug. 16, 1898*

Less Favored than Some Sinners

Sinners who have not had the light and privileges that Seventh-day Adventists have enjoyed will, in their ignorance, be in a more favorable position before God than those who have been unfaithful while in close connection with his work and professing to love and serve Him. The tears of Christ upon the mount came from an anguished, breaking heart because of his unrequited love and the ingratitude of his chosen people. He had labored untiringly to save them from the fate that they seemed determined to bring upon themselves, but they refused his mercy and knew not the time of their visitation. Their day of privilege was ending, yet they were so blinded by sin that they knew it not. —*4T, p. 191*

Discussion Questions

1. Why is Jesus specially qualified to oversee the final judgment?

2. What two classes are recognized in the judgment?

3. What are some of the secret sins that will finally be revealed?

4. During the final judgment, the wicked cast blame on each other. What does this say about their character?

5. Why will many Christians be guilty of committing the sin of Meroz?

— 30 —

Sinners are Sentenced

"For we must all appear before the judgment seat of Christ; that every one may receive the things done in his body, according to that he hath done, whether it be good or bad."

— 2 Cor. 5:10

1 Sam. 2:10	Isaiah 60:14	Jeremiah 8:1-3	Nahum 1:2	Phil. 2:8-11
Isaiah 2:4	Isaiah 65:6, 7	Ezekiel 18:23	Matt. 7:21-23	2 Peter 2:20-22

A) Heaven Would be Spoiled

Rebellion Would be Immortalized

Should God permit a transgressor of his law to enter into the portals of bliss, rebellion would be immortalized, and heaven would be no better than the earth. Jesus added to the statement as to how the transgressor would be regarded, and said, "For I say unto you, That except your righteousness shall exceed the righteousness of the scribes and Pharisees, ye shall in no case enter into the kingdom of heaven." —*RH, Aug. 6, 1895*

Selfish Men Would Snatch Crowns

If we are so selfish here that we have no interest for one another to make them obedient, and to bless them with the good things that He has provided for us in this life, how will we manifest anything like unselfishness in the kingdom of glory? How will we do it? We would be wanting to snatch the crown from another's head because it is more brilliant than ours. Another would become jealous, and we should have as bad a time as when Satan set up that work in heaven of rebellion against God... If we manifest the attributes of Satan, it is that character that can find no place in the heavenly courts above. —*Ms 43a, 1894*

447

Heaven Would be Spoiled

God will accept nothing less than unreserved surrender. Half-hearted, sinful, professing Christians would spoil heaven were they permitted to enter. They would stir up a second rebellion there. Those who know the truth, yet do not exalt the Author of truth, will never enter the city of God. Heaven would be purgatory to them, because they know nothing of the high, holy principles that govern the members of the royal family above. The directions that Christ has given are so distinct and so definite that no one need take a false step.

—Ms 61, 1903

There Would be Anarchy

When the judgment shall sit, and the books are opened, what excuse will they give for taking sides with the first great rebel, thus making the Word of God of none effect in their lives? God's wisdom and truthfulness are changeless, and in that great day when sentence is executed against the despisers of his law, the cross of Christ will show that He is a God of love in thus executing judgment. Those who refuse to obey his law during probationary time could not with safety be received into his kingdom; for they would labor as earnestly and zealously against the law of his government as did the first apostate. There would be a second rebellion in heaven. *— ST, April 7, 1898*

Sinners Would be Miserable

The mind controlled by Satan is weak in moral power. Can such a one without change be taken into a holy heaven?—Oh, no; it would be no mercy to the impenitent sinner to place him in the society of the angels.

When the wicked dead are raised from the grave, they come up with the tastes, habits, and characters that they formed in the time of probation. A sinner is not raised a saint, neither is a saint raised a sinner. The sinner could not be happy in the companionship of the saints in light, with Jesus, with the Lord of hosts; for on every side will be heard the song of praise and thanksgiving; and honor will be ascribed to the Father and the Son.

A song will be raised that the unsanctified, unholy ones have never learned, and it will be out of harmony with their depraved tastes and desires. It will be unbearable to them. The apostle John heard this song... It is impossible for the sinner to enjoy the bliss of heaven. *—RH, Feb. 17, 1891*

448

A Revolt in the Heavenly Courts

God, in his wisdom and mercy, tests men and women here, to see if they will obey his voice and respect his law, or rebel as Satan did. If they choose the side of Satan, putting his way above God's, it would not be safe to admit them into heaven; for they would cause another revolt against the government of God in the heavenly courts. He who fulfills the law in every respect, demonstrates that perfect obedience is possible. — *RH, July 21, 1891*

A Rebellion Ten Times Worse

Is God going to take man with all his disobedience and transgression into heaven as he is? There would be tenfold worse rebellion than there was when Satan was there. We cannot afford to go on in this, so delusive as it is. We want eternal life, and we want it in Christ's way. We want to keep the way of the Lord as Abram kept it, and taught his household and his children to keep the way of the Lord, to do judgment and justice, and then God can co-operate with man. You are partakers of the divine nature, and Christ puts his spirit upon every one that will earnestly co-operate with Him. — *Ms 49, 1894*

The Wicked Would Criticize Angels

Men who have a large opinion of themselves are frequently in error, but they will not confess this. Envy and jealousy are diseases which disorder all the faculties of the being... These persons generally are incurable, and as nothing that defileth can enter into heaven, they will not be there. They would criticize the angels. They would covet another's crown. They would not know what to do, or what subjects to converse upon, unless they could be finding some errors, some imperfections, in others.

Oh that such ones would become changed by following Christ! Oh that they would become meek and lowly of heart by learning in the school of Christ! Then they would go forth, not as missionaries for Satan, to cause disunion or alienation, but as missionaries for Christ, to be peacemakers, to work with Christ in restoring, not to bruise and wound and mangle character. Let the Holy Spirit of God come in and expel this unholy passion, which cannot in the slightest degree survive in heaven. Let it die. Let it be crucified. Open the heart to the attributes of Christ, who was pure, holy, undefiled, without guilt. — *Lt 97, 1896*

Sinful Men Can Never be Holy

Could that transported, unready one, mingle with the heavenly throng, participate in their songs, and receive the high purity, the exalted spiritual, transporting, glory that emanates from God and the Lamb? Oh, no! Their probation was lengthened for years that they might learn the language of heaven, that they might be "partakers of the divine nature, having escaped the corruption that is in the world through lust." 2 Peter 1:4.

But they have had a selfish business of their own to engage the powers of their mind and the energies of their being. They could not afford to serve God unreservedly and make this a business. Worldly enterprises must come first and take the best of their powers, and a transient thought is devoted to God. Are such to be transformed after the final decision: "He that is holy, let him be holy still," "he which is filthy, let him remain so forever?" Revelation 22:11. Such a time is coming. —*Lt 17, 1868*

Heaven Would Torture Sinners

In his sinless state, man held joyful communion with Him "in whom are hid all the treasures of wisdom and knowledge." Colossians 2:3. But after his sin, he could no longer find joy in holiness, and he sought to hide from the presence of God. Such is still the condition of the unrenewed heart. It is not in harmony with God, and finds no joy in communion with Him. The sinner could not be happy in God's presence; he would shrink from the companionship of holy beings.

Could he be permitted to enter heaven, it would have no joy for him. The spirit of unselfish love that reigns there—every heart responding to the heart of Infinite Love—would touch no answering chord in his soul. His thoughts, his interests, his motives, would be alien to those that actuate the sinless dwellers there. He would be a discordant note in the melody of heaven. Heaven would be to him a place of torture; he would long to be hidden from Him who is its light, and the center of its joy.

It is no arbitrary decree on the part of God that excludes the wicked from heaven; they are shut out by their own unfitness for its companionship. The glory of God would be to them a consuming fire. They would welcome destruction, that they might be hidden from the face of Him who died to redeem them. —*SC, pp. 17, 18*

Paradise Would be an Enigma

As in the natural, so in the spiritual world: every power unused will weaken and decay. Activity is the law of life; idleness is death. "The manifestation of the Spirit is given to every man to profit withal." 1 Corinthians 12:7. Employed to bless others, his gifts increase. Shut up to self-serving they diminish, and are finally withdrawn…

Let none suppose that they can live a life of selfishness, and then, having served their own interests, enter into the joy of their Lord. In the joy of unselfish love they could not participate. They would not be fitted for the heavenly courts. They could not appreciate the pure atmosphere of love that pervades heaven. The voices of the angels and the music of their harps would not satisfy them. To their minds the science of heaven would be as an enigma.

— COL, pp. 363, 364

Sinful Youth Cannot Grasp Calvary

How little do the young suffer, or deny self, for their religion! To sacrifice is scarcely thought of among them. They entirely fail of imitating the Pattern in this respect. I saw that the language of their lives is: "Self must be gratified, pride must be indulged." They forget the Man of Sorrows, who was acquainted with grief.

The sufferings of Jesus in Gethsemane, his sweating as it were great drops of blood in the garden, the platted crown of thorns that pierced his holy brow, do not move them. They have become benumbed. Their sensibilities are blunted, and they have lost all sense of the great sacrifice made for them. They can sit and listen to the story of the cross, hear how the cruel nails were driven through the hands and feet of the Son of God, and it does not stir the depths of the soul.

Said the angel: "If such should be ushered into the city of God, and told that all its rich beauty and glory was theirs to enjoy eternally, they would have no sense of how dearly that inheritance was purchased for them. They would never realize the matchless depths of a Saviour's love. They have not drunk of the cup, nor been baptized with the baptism. Heaven would be marred if such should dwell there. Those only who have partaken of the sufferings of the Son of God, and have come up through great tribulation, and have washed their robes and made them white in the blood of the Lamb, can enjoy the indescribable glory and unsurpassed beauty of heaven." *— 1T, p. 155*

Celestial Music Would Not Satisfy

If we do not receive the religion of Christ by feeding upon the Word of God, we shall not be entitled to an entrance into the city of God. Having lived on earthly food, having educated our tastes to love worldly things, we would not be fitted for the heavenly courts; we could not appreciate the pure, heavenly current that circulates in heaven. The voices of the angels and the music of their harps would not satisfy us. The science of heaven would be as an enigma to our minds. We need to hunger and thirst for the righteousness of Christ; we need to be molded and fashioned by the transforming influence of his grace, that we may be fitted for the society of heavenly angels. — *RH, May 4, 1897*

Men Awake Desiring Worldly Pleasures

When the voice of God awakes the dead, he will come from the grave with the same appetites and passions, the same likes and dislikes, that he cherished when living. God works no miracle to re-create a man who would not be re-created when he was granted every opportunity and provided with every facility. During his lifetime he took no delight in God, nor found pleasure in his service. His character is not in harmony with God, and he could not be happy in the heavenly family.

Today there is a class in our world who are self-righteous. They are not gluttons, they are not drunkards, they are not infidels; but they desire to live for themselves, not for God. He is not in their thoughts; therefore they are classed with unbelievers. Were it possible for them to enter the gates of the city of God, they could have no right to the tree of life, for when God's commandments were laid before them with all their binding claims they said, "No." They have not served God here; therefore they would not serve Him hereafter. They could not live in his presence, and they would feel that any place was preferable to heaven.

To learn of Christ means to receive his grace, which is his character. But those who do not appreciate and utilize the precious opportunities and sacred influences granted them on earth, are not fitted to take part in the pure devotion of heaven. Their characters are not molded according to the divine similitude. By their own neglect they have formed a chasm which nothing can bridge. Between them and the righteous there is a great gulf fixed.

— *COL, pp. 270, 271*

The End of Heaven's Harmony

Were justice extinct, and were it possible for divine mercy to open the gates to the whole race, irrespective of character, there would be a worse condition of disaffection and rebellion in heaven than before Satan was expelled. The peace, happiness, and harmony of heaven would be broken. The change from earth to heaven will not change men's character; the happiness of the redeemed in heaven results from the character formed in this life after the image of Christ. The saints in heaven will first have been saints on earth.

—RH, Dec. 13, 1892

Five Virgins were Unfit for Heaven

The ten virgins are watching in the evening of this earth's history. All claim to be Christians. All have a call, a name, a lamp, and all profess to be doing God's service. All apparently wait for Christ's appearing. But five are unready. Five will be found surprised, dismayed, outside the banquet hall. At the final day, many will claim admission to Christ's kingdom, saying, "We have eaten and drunk in thy presence, and thou hast taught in our streets." "Lord, Lord, have we not prophesied in thy name? and in thy name have cast out devils? And in thy name done many wonderful works?" But the answer is, "I tell you, I know you not whence ye are; depart from Me."

In this life they have not entered into fellowship with Christ; therefore they know not the language of heaven, they are strangers to its joy. "What man knoweth the things of a man, save the spirit of man which is in him? Even so the things of God knoweth no man, but the Spirit of God." 1 Corinthians 2:11.

Saddest of all words that ever fell on mortal ear are those words of doom, "I know you not." The fellowship of the Spirit, which you have slighted, could alone make you one with the joyous throng at the marriage feast. In that scene you cannot participate. Its light would fall on blinded eyes, its melody upon deaf ears. Its love and joy could awake no chord of gladness in the world-benumbed heart. You are shut out from heaven by your own unfitness for its companionship. We cannot be ready to meet the Lord by waking when the cry is heard, "Behold, the Bridegroom!" and then gathering up our empty lamps to have them replenished. We cannot keep Christ apart from our lives here, and yet be fitted for his companionship in heaven. *— COL, pp. 412, 413*

No Possible Cure for the Wicked

Those who have chosen Satan as their leader and have been controlled by his power are not prepared to enter the presence of God. Pride, deception, licentiousness, cruelty, have become fixed in their characters. Can they enter heaven to dwell forever with those whom they despised and hated on earth? Truth will never be agreeable to a liar; meekness will not satisfy self-esteem and pride; purity is not acceptable to the corrupt; disinterested love does not appear attractive to the selfish. What source of enjoyment could heaven offer to those who are wholly absorbed in earthly and selfish interests?

Could those whose lives have been spent in rebellion against God be suddenly transported to heaven and witness the high, the holy state of perfection that ever exists there—every soul filled with love, every countenance beaming with joy, enrapturing music in melodious strains rising in honor of God and the Lamb, and ceaseless streams of light flowing upon the redeemed from the face of Him who sitteth upon the throne—could those whose hearts are filled with hatred of God, of truth and holiness, mingle with the heavenly throng and join their songs of praise? Could they endure the glory of God and the Lamb?

No, no; years of probation were granted them, that they might form characters for heaven; but they have never trained the mind to love purity; they have never learned the language of heaven, and now it is too late.

A life of rebellion against God has unfitted them for heaven. Its purity, holiness, and peace would be torture to them; the glory of God would be a consuming fire. They would long to flee from that holy place. They would welcome destruction, that they might be hidden from the face of Him who died to redeem them. The destiny of the wicked is fixed by their own choice. Their exclusion from heaven is voluntary with themselves, and just and merciful on the part of God.

Like the waters of the Flood the fires of the great day declare God's verdict that the wicked are incurable. They have no disposition to submit to divine authority. Their will has been exercised in revolt; and when life is ended, it is too late to turn the current of their thoughts in the opposite direction, too late to turn from transgression to obedience, from hatred to love.

— GC, pp. 542, 543

Sinners Cannot Bear God's Glory

Should your probation close today and you be brought just as you are this moment to the gate of the city, and it should open before you, and the rays of light that emanate from the throne of God should beam forth upon you, could you endure it? Could you bear it, in your sins and in your iniquity and imperfection? Could you enjoy that sacred and divine light?

Not for a moment. You would drop as powerless as the Roman guard, who watched around the sepulcher of Jesus Christ, when the angels there descended to resurrect the Son of God. As that light fell upon the Roman guard, they became as dead men. They fell to the earth. They could not endure the light from heaven, which was reflected from one mighty angel. Neither can you unless you have a fitness for it here.

Could you be brought through the gates into the holy city, your probation closed and sins upon you, pride, folly, envy, evil surmisings, lustful passions, covetousness and these evil things, and gaze upon sinless angels, who never have fallen, never been in disobedience and transgression, and behold in every countenance the light of the glory of God as it shineth in the face of Jesus Christ, and see the redeemed saints that have washed their robes and made them white in the blood of the Lamb, how would you feel? You hear a voice inquire, "Who are these?" And the answer is given, "These are they which have come up through great tribulation, and have washed their robes and made them white in the blood of the Lamb."

You look around and see those that have made a covenant with God by sacrifice. You then behold yourself. Impurity is upon you. Your garments are defiled with pollution of the world. Sin has left its disgusting impress upon your countenance. You cannot endure the glory and light. And you would say, "Anywhere but here to be pained with this glory and beauty and loveliness." You could not endure it. You were not worthy. No, you were not ready for it, and you could not dwell there. You would rather be anywhere else. You would prefer that rocks and mountains should fall upon you and hide you from the unbearable glory that you behold everywhere...

These things will seem to many like idle tales, nevertheless they are true, and without preparation, without readiness, without moral fitness, you can have no place in the kingdom of glory. — *RH, Apr. 12, 1870*

B) Condemned by the Law

The Wicked Cannot be Reformed

In sparing the life of Cain the murderer, God gave the world an example of what would be the result of permitting the sinner to live to continue a course of unbridled iniquity. Through the influence of Cain's teaching and example, multitudes of his descendants were led into sin, until "the wickedness of man was great in the earth" and "every imagination of the thoughts of his heart was only evil continually." — *GC, p. 543*

Nominal Christians are Doomed

The Lord will not be trifled with. Those who neglect his mercies and blessings in this day of opportunities will bring impenetrable darkness upon themselves and will be candidates for the wrath of God. Sodom and Gomorrah were visited with the curse of the Almighty for their sins and iniquities. There are those in our day who have equally abused the mercies of God and slighted his warnings. It will be more tolerable for Sodom and Gomorrah in the day of judgment than for those who bear the name of Christ, yet dishonor Him by their unconsecrated lives. This class are laying up for themselves a fearful retribution when God in his wrath shall visit them with his judgments. — *4T, p. 191*

Cain's Life Shows Sin is Progressive

The dark history of Cain and his descendants was an illustration of what would have been the result of permitting the sinner to live on forever, to carry out his rebellion against God. The forbearance of God only rendered the wicked more bold and defiant in their iniquity. Fifteen centuries after the sentence pronounced upon Cain, the universe witnessed the fruition of his influence and example, in the crime and pollution that flooded the earth.

It was made manifest that the sentence of death pronounced upon the fallen race for the transgression of God's law was both just and merciful. The longer men lived in sin, the more abandoned they became. The divine sentence cutting short a career of unbridled iniquity, and freeing the world from the influence of those who had become hardened in rebellion, was a blessing rather than a curse. — *PP, p. 78*

Sodom Might Have Repented

Very few have an experimental knowledge of the sanctifying influence of the truths which they profess. Their obedience and devotion have not been in accordance with their light and privileges. They have no real sense of the obligation resting upon them to walk as children of the light, and not as children of darkness. If the light that has been given to these had been given Sodom and Gomorrah, they would have repented in sackcloth and ashes, and would have escaped the signal wrath of God. — *2T, p. 488*

No Excuse for Willful Blindness

None will be condemned for not heeding light and knowledge that they never had, and they could not obtain. But many refuse to obey the truth that is presented to them by Christ's ambassadors, because they wish to conform to the world's standard; and the truth that has reached their understanding, the light that has shone in the soul, will condemn them in the judgment.

In these last days we have the accumulated light that has been shining through all the ages, and we shall be held correspondingly responsible. The path of holiness is not on a level with the world; it is a way cast up. If we walk in this way, if we run in the way of the Lord's commandments, we shall find that the "path of the just is as the shining light, that shineth more and more unto the perfect day." Proverbs 4:18. — *RH, Nov. 25, 1884*

A Responsibility for Neglecting Truth

Many are going directly contrary to the light which God has given to his people, because they do not read the books which contain the light and knowledge in cautions, reproofs, and warnings. The cares of the world, the love of fashion, and the lack of religion have turned the attention from the light God has so graciously given, while books and periodicals containing error are traveling all over the country.

Skepticism and infidelity are increasing everywhere. Light so precious, coming from the throne of God, is hid under a bushel. God will make his people responsible for this neglect. An account must be rendered to Him for every ray of light He has let shine upon our pathway, whether it has been improved to our advancement in divine things or rejected because it was more agreeable to follow inclination. — *5T, p. 681*

No Hope for Many Great Men

The great military commander conquers nations and shakes the armies of half the world, but he dies of disappointment and in exile. The philosopher who ranges through the universe, everywhere tracing the manifestations of God's power and delighting in their harmony, often fails to behold in these marvelous wonders the Hand that formed them all. "Man that is in honor, and understandeth not, is like the beasts that perish." No hope of glorious immortality lights up the future of the enemies of God. —*4T, p. 526*

The Wicked Destroyed Themselves

In the day of judgment, everyone will receive sentence according to his deeds. Every mouth will be stopped, as the cross is presented, and its real bearing seen. Sinners will stand condemned. Every subterfuge, every excuse, will be swept away. Sin will appear in all its sinfulness. The mystery of the incarnation and the crucifixion of the Son of God will be plainly discerned, and every condemned soul will read clearly the result of a rejection of truth.

Those who have chosen to transgress will then understand that they have sinned, and come short. They will read the sentence, "Thou, O man, hast chosen to stand under the banner of the great apostate, and, in so doing, thou hast destroyed thyself." —*ST, Jan. 25, 1905*

The Cases of Sinners are Settled

Mighty, invisible powers are acting their part in the affairs of men in the last great conflict. The warfare will be so conducted that the power, which has exalted itself above God and has enlisted souls in rebellion against God, will work out fully the principles of disobedience. Every mouth shall confess the glory of God. It will be plainly seen that the principles of righteousness and obedience to God's law are above all powers, and that the retribution which falls upon transgressors is just.

The unfallen worlds and the heavenly universe will see the result of the apostasy of Satan and will acknowledge God as the living and only true God. The forces of rebellion will confess God's righteousness, but this acknowledgment will not give them another probation. Their cases are forever settled. After the second resurrection, Satan, the root, and his children the branches, will perish together. —*Lt 25, 1900*

Satan's Allies are Condemned

Those who do the work the enemy of all righteousness did in the heavenly court, and still does on this earth, will know very well what it means to answer for professedly being on the Lord's side when in reality they were on the side of the enemy, hindering others from receiving the Word of the Lord. The blood of the souls who have perished through their unfaithfulness will be found upon their heads. —*Ms 33, 1900*

No Miracle Can Save Evil Souls

God has appointed means, if we will use them diligently and prayerfully, that no vessel shall be shipwrecked, but outride the tempest and storm, and anchor in the haven of bliss at last. But if we despise and neglect these appointments and privileges, God will not work a miracle to save any of us, and we will be lost as were Judas and Satan.

Do not think that God will work a miracle to save those weak souls who cherish evil, who practice sin; or that some supernatural element will be brought into their lives, lifting them out of self into a higher sphere, where it will be comparatively easy work, without any special effort, any special fighting, without any crucifixion of self; because all who dally on Satan's ground for this to be done will perish with the evildoers. — *TM, p. 453*

Men See How They Rejected Truth

In the day of final judgment, every lost soul will understand the nature of his own rejection of truth. The cross will be presented, and its real bearing will be seen by every mind that has been blinded by transgression. Before the vision of Calvary with its mysterious Victim, sinners will stand condemned. Every lying excuse will be swept away. Human apostasy will appear in its heinous character. Men will see what their choice has been.

Every question of truth and error in the long-standing controversy will then have been made plain. In the judgment of the universe, God will stand clear of blame for the existence or continuance of evil. It will be demonstrated that the divine decrees are not accessory to sin. There was no defect in God's government, no cause for disaffection. When the thoughts of all hearts shall be revealed, both the loyal and the rebellious will unite in declaring, "Just and true are thy ways, thou King of saints." —*DA, p. 58*

The Law Condemns All Sinners

The ministers have taught the people that the law of God is not binding. But God certainly does not say so, and in the day of judgment that law, written with the finger of God on tables of stone, will condemn all impenitent transgressors. The Ten Commandments are an expression of the character of God. It is our duty to obey God's Word, to love to do his will. It was ordained by God that faithful ministers should be appointed to study the Scriptures and feed the flock, not with the words of men, but with the living Word of God — *Ms 33, 1900*

No Second Chance for Fallen Angels

It was Satan's design that the state of man should be the same with that of the fallen angels in rebellion against God, uncheered by a gleam of hope. He reasoned that if God pardoned sinful man whom he had created, he would also pardon and receive into favor him and his angels. But he was disappointed. The divine Son of God saw that no arm but his own could save fallen man. He determined to help man. He left the fallen angels to perish in their rebellion, but stretched forth his hand to rescue perishing man.

The angels who were rebellious were dealt with according to the light and experience they had abundantly enjoyed in heaven. Satan, the chief of the fallen angels, once had an exalted position in heaven. He was next in honor to Christ. The knowledge which he, as well as the angels who fell with him, had of the character of God, of his goodness, his mercy, wisdom, and excellent glory, made their guilt unpardonable.

There was no possible hope for those ever to be redeemed, who had witnessed and enjoyed the inexpressible glory of heaven and had seen the terrible majesty of God, and, in presence of all this glory, had rebelled against Him. There were no new and more wonderful exhibitions of God's exalted power that could ever impress them as deeply as those they had already experienced. If they could rebel in the very presence of the weight of glory inexpressible, they could not be placed in any more favorable condition to be proved. There was no reserve force of power, nor were there any greater heights and depths of infinite glory to overpower their jealous doubts and rebellious murmuring. Their guilt and their punishment must be in proportion to their exalted privileges in the heavenly courts. — *RH, Feb. 24, 1874*

C) The Wicked are Sentenced

Lawmakers are Sentenced

The Lord will judge according to their works those who are seeking to establish a law of the nations that will cause men to violate the law of God. In proportion to their guilt will be their punishment. —*Lt 90, 1908*

Satan Judges Himself

Satan will be judged by his own ideas of justice. It was his plea that every sin should meet its punishment. "If God remitted the punishment," he said, "He was not a God of truth or justice." Satan will meet the judgment which he said God should exercise. —*Ms 111, 1897*

God Asks the Wicked to Depart

There is a day appointed when men who have bowed to the mandates of Satan will find themselves the subjects of the wrath of God, when the Judge of all the earth shall pronounce the sentence against Satan and his adherents, "Depart from Me, ye cursed, into everlasting fire, prepared for the devil and his angels." —*Lt 244, 1907*

Doom for Unconverted Souls

Those who do not receive in faith God's plan for redeeming the race do despite to the Spirit of grace, and at the last great day their sentence will be, "Depart from Me." They have hated righteousness and fostered iniquity, and they must be banished forever from the presence of God, exiled from happiness to death—eternal death. —*Lt 232, 1903*

The Reward of Breaking the Law

If we serve sin, we shall meet the reward of the transgressor of the law of Jehovah before the judgment seat of Christ. The Lord Jesus is to judge the world. He can read the purpose of every life, see through every soul, discern the thoughts of every heart, estimate the feelings that prompt to every action. All the invitations of a gracious God-given, but slighted and refused and rejected—will be presented to every individual, and the sentence which will fix the destiny of the soul in eternal bliss or to be punished with the fiery element of the wrath of God will close the history of the wicked forever.

—*Ms 59, 1895*

The Penalty Equals the Hurt

The Ruler of the universe bears long with the perversity of men, but He keeps a record of their works, and in proportion as they have caused pain to others, they will themselves be punished. —*Ms 42, 1899*

A Fine for Dishonoring God

Those who have had great light and have disregarded it stand in a worse position than those who have not been given so many advantages. They exalt themselves but not the Lord. The punishment inflicted on human beings will in every case be proportionate to the dishonor they have brought on God.

—*Lt 159, 1901*

The Reward of Their Doings

Transgressors may flatter themselves that the Most High does not know, that the Almighty does not consider; He will not always bear with them. Soon they will receive the reward of their doings, the death that is the wages of sin; while the righteous nation, that have kept the law, will be ushered through the pearly gates of the celestial city, and will be crowned with immortal life and joy in the presence of God and the Lamb. —*ST, Apr. 15, 1886*

Traitors will be Punished

In the camp there have been many traitors in disguise, and Christ knows every one of them. God has been dishonored by disloyal subjects, who, were Christ on the earth today in human form, would cry, "Crucify Him, crucify Him." How will it be with the unrepentant sinner hereafter? The higher the position and the greater the light accorded to the man who has become disloyal, and has denied his Saviour, the greater will be his punishment. —*Ms 108, 1905*

The Penalty is Retributive

I am instructed to present these words before those who have had light and evidence, but who have walked directly contrary to the light. The Lord will make the punishment of those who will not receive his admonitions and warnings as broad as the wrong has been. The purposes of those who have tried to cover their wrong, while they have secretly worked against the purposes of God, will be fully revealed. Truth will be vindicated. God will make manifest that He is God. —*Ms 125, 1907*

Judged by the Light Received

We have been given great light in regard to God's law. This law is the standard of character. To it man is now required to conform, and by it he will be judged in the last great day. In that day men will be dealt with according to the light they have received. — *RH, Jan. 1, 1901*

Death is the Fine for Transgression

When every case is decided in the courts of heaven, this covenant will be brought forth, plainly written with the finger of God. The world will be arraigned before the bar of infinite Justice to receive sentence—a life measuring with the life of God for obedience, and death for transgression.

— RH, Apr. 7, 1900

A Sentence for Refusing Light

The judgment will present a scene the like of which the universe has never beheld. To what a pass will they come who have made light of the work of the Holy Spirit, and called its workings a delusion. The sentence of death will be passed upon all who, having light and evidence, like the Jews have refused to come to the Light, that their deeds should be reproved. — *Ms 186, 1897*

A Double Punishment for Sins

The time is near when He will say, ... "Behold, the Lord cometh out of his place to punish the inhabitants of the earth for their iniquity; the earth also shall disclose her blood, and shall no more cover her slain." Isaiah 26:21.

Men who claim to be Christians may now defraud and oppress the poor; they may rob the widow and fatherless; they may indulge their satanic hatred because they cannot control the consciences of God's people; but for all this God will bring them into judgment. They "shall have judgment without mercy" that have "showed no mercy." James 2:13.

Not long hence they will stand before the Judge of all the earth, to render an account for the pain they have caused to the bodies and souls of his heritage. They may now indulge in false accusations, they may deride those whom God has appointed to do his work, they may consign his believing ones to prison, to the chain gang, to banishment, to death; but for every pang of anguish, every tear shed, they must answer. God will reward them double for their sins. — *COL, p. 178*

Lawbreakers to Die the Second Death

The Sabbath was made for man, for the benefit of man, and to knowingly transgress the holy commandment forbidding labor upon the seventh day is a crime in the sight of heaven which was of such magnitude under the Mosaic law as to require the death of the offender. But this was not all. The offender that was not deemed worthy to live was to suffer, for God would not take a transgressor of his law to heaven. He must suffer the second death, which was full and final penalty of the transgressor. —*Ms 8, 1866*

The Whole Multitude is Divided

The division of the whole multitude will be made. "When the Son of man shall come in his glory, and all the holy angels with Him, then shall He sit upon the throne of his glory. And before Him shall be gathered all nations: and He shall separate them one from another, as a shepherd divideth his sheep from the goats: and He shall set the sheep on his right hand, but the goats on the left." Those who have done good and those who have done evil will receive a reward according to their works.

Then shall Jesus say to those on his right hand, "Come, ye blessed of my Father, inherit the kingdom prepared for you from the foundation of the world." —*Ms 77, 1906*

The Penalty for Strange Infatuations

The whole wicked world stand arraigned at the bar of God on the charge of high treason against the government of heaven. They have none to plead their cause; they are without excuse; and the sentence of eternal death is pronounced against them.

It is now evident to all that the wages of sin is not noble independence and eternal life, but slavery, ruin, and death. The wicked see what they have forfeited by their life of rebellion. The far more exceeding and eternal weight of glory was despised when offered them; but how desirable it now appears. "All this," cries the lost soul, "I might have had; but I chose to put these things far from me. Oh, strange infatuation! I have exchanged peace, happiness, and honor for wretchedness, infamy, and despair." All see that their exclusion from heaven is just. By their lives they have declared: "We will not have this Man (Jesus) to reign over us." —*GC, p. 668*

Only a Few are Saved

The Word of God plainly tells us that few will be saved, and that the greater number of those, even, who are called will prove themselves unworthy of everlasting life. They will have no part in heaven, but will have their portion with Satan, and experience the second death. —*2T, p. 293*

Not All Sins are Equal

God does not regard all sins as of equal magnitude; there are degrees of guilt in his estimation, as well as in that of man; but however trifling this or that wrong act may seem in the eyes of men, no sin is small in the sight of God. Man's judgment is partial, imperfect; but God estimates all things as they really are. The drunkard is despised and is told that his sin will exclude him from heaven; while pride, selfishness, and covetousness too often go unrebuked.

But these are sins that are especially offensive to God; for they are contrary to the benevolence of his character, to that unselfish love which is the very atmosphere of the unfallen universe. He who falls into some of the grosser sins may feel a sense of his shame and poverty and his need of the grace of Christ; but pride feels no need, and so it closes the heart against Christ and the infinite blessings He came to give. —*SC, p. 30*

The Wages of Sin is Eternal Death

In mercy to the world, God blotted out its wicked inhabitants in Noah's time. In mercy He destroyed the corrupt dwellers in Sodom. Through the deceptive power of Satan the workers of iniquity obtain sympathy and admiration, and are thus constantly leading others to rebellion. It was so in Cain's and in Noah's day, and in the time of Abraham and Lot; it is so in our time. It is in mercy to the universe that God will finally destroy the rejecters of his grace.

"The wages of sin is death; but the gift of God is eternal life through Jesus Christ our Lord." Romans 6:23. While life is the inheritance of the righteous, death is the portion of the wicked. Moses declared to Israel: "I have set before thee this day life and good, and death and evil." Deuteronomy 30:15. The death referred to in these Scriptures is not that pronounced upon Adam, for all mankind suffer the penalty of his transgression. It is "the second death" that is placed in contrast with everlasting life. —*GC, pp. 543, 544*

The Recompense of Deeds
God permits the wicked to prosper and to reveal their enmity against Him, that when they shall have filled up the measure of their iniquity all may see his justice and mercy in their utter destruction. The day of his vengeance hastens, when all who have transgressed his law and oppressed his people will meet the just recompense of their deeds; when every act of cruelty or injustice toward God's faithful ones will be punished as though done to Christ Himself. — *GC, p. 48*

A Sentence for Brutal Torturers
Christians are filled with hatred because they cannot force the consciences of God's people. Not long hence they will stand before the Judge of all the earth, to render an account for the pain they have caused to the bodies and souls of God's heritage… For every drop of blood drawn forth by torture, for all they have burned with fire, they will receive punishment. God will reward them double for their sins. They have drunk the blood of the saints, and have become intoxicated with exultation. God says to his ministers of judgment: "Reward her even as she rewarded you, and double unto her double according to her works: in the cup which she hath filled fill to her double."

— RH, Dec. 28, 1897

Discussion Questions

1. Why will sinful youth never fully be able to appreciate the sacrifice made on Calvary?

2. What does the life of the Cain teach us about probation?

3. Why will fallen angels never receive a second chance?

4. Because not all sins are equal, does this mean that murderers will be punished worse than other sinners?

5. Why is there a terrible penalty for rejecting light? Could this include truth that God reveals to us from the Spirit of Prophecy?

— 31 —

The Eternal Death

"Upon the wicked He will rain coals; fire and brimstone and a burning wind shall be the portion of their cup." — Psalm 11:6

Job 4:9	Psalm 37:38	Isa. 9:4, 5	Ezek. 28:6-19	Obadiah 1:16	Heb. 2:14
Job 18:17	Psalm 75:7, 8	Isa. 9:17-19	Daniel 2:44	Malachi 4:1-3	Heb. 12:29
Psalm 9:5, 6	Isa. 1:28; 5:24	Isa. 47:14	Amos 5:18	1 Cor. 15:24-26	2 Peter 3:7

Fire Comes from the Ground

The places of the earth will be in confusion, as from its bowels pour forth its burning contents, to destroy the inhabitants of the world, who in their wickedness resemble the inhabitants of the antediluvian world. — *Ms 72, 1902*

The Candle of Life is Put Out

The candle of those who harden their hearts in iniquity will be put out by the Lord. They have lived only for themselves, and death must come to them. When the limit of grace is reached, God will give his command for the destruction of the transgressor. He will arise in his Almighty character as a God above all gods, and those who have worked against Him, in league with the great rebel, will be treated in accordance with their works. — *Ms 50, 1893*

The Penalty is Measured Out

Then the wicked saw what they had lost; and fire was breathed from God upon them and consumed them. This was the execution of the judgment. The wicked then received according as the saints, in unison with Jesus, had meted out to them during the one thousand years. The same fire from God that consumed the wicked purified the whole earth. The broken, ragged mountains melted with fervent heat, the atmosphere also, and all the stubble was consumed. — *EW, p. 54*

God is a Sun and a Shield

While the earth was wrapped in the fire of destruction, the righteous abode safely in the Holy City. Upon those that had part in the first resurrection, the second death has no power. While God is to the wicked a consuming fire, He is to his people both a sun and a shield. Revelation 20:6; Psalm 84:11.

—GC, p. 673

The Wicked Cease to Exist

I saw, that as Christ is the vine, and his children the branches: so Satan is the "root", and his children are the "branches;" and at the final destruction of "Gog and Magog," the whole wicked host will be burnt up, "root and branch," and cease to exist... All that were raised at the second resurrection, were burnt up, and ceased to exist. *— WLF, p. 12*

God Destroys Sodomitish Impurity

Church members need to fast and pray, striving earnestly to overcome by the blood of the Lamb and the word of their testimony. Not one particle of Sodomitish impurity will escape the wrath of God at the execution of the judgment. Those who do not repent and forsake all uncleanness will fall with the wicked. Those who become members of the royal family and who form God's kingdom in the earth made new, will be saints, not sinners. *—Lt 159, 1901*

The New Jerusalem is a Type of Ark

When the flood of waters was at its height upon the earth, it had the appearance of a boundless lake of water. When God finally purifies the earth, it will appear like a boundless lake of fire. As God preserved the ark amid the commotions of the flood, because it contained eight righteous persons, He will preserve the New Jerusalem, containing the faithful of all ages, from righteous Abel down to the last saint which lived.

Although the whole earth, with the exception of that portion where the city rests, will be wrapped in a sea of liquid fire, yet the city is preserved as was the ark, by a miracle of Almighty power. It stands unharmed amid the devouring elements. "But the day of the Lord will come as a thief in the night; in which the heavens shall pass away with a great noise, and the elements shall melt with fervent heat, the earth also, and the works that are therein shall be burned up." *—3SG, p. 87*

The Wicked Feel Christ's Agony

After all has been done that God could do to save men, if they show by their lives that they slight Jesus' offered mercy, death will be their portion, and it will be dearly purchased. It will be a dreadful death; for they will have to feel the agony that Christ felt upon the cross to purchase for them the redemption which they have refused. And they will then realize what they have lost—eternal life and the immortal inheritance. The great sacrifice that has been made to save souls shows us their worth. When the precious soul is once lost, it is lost forever. —*1T, p. 124*

The Unrepentant Destroy Themselves

Just what took place in Pharaoh's heart will take place in every soul that neglects to cherish the light and walk promptly in its rays. God destroys no one. The sinner destroys himself by his own impenitence. When a person once neglects to heed the invitations, reproofs, and warnings of the Spirit of God, his conscience becomes seared, and the next time he is admonished, it will be more difficult to yield obedience than before. And thus with every repetition. Conscience is the voice of God, heard amid the conflict of human passions; when it is resisted, the Spirit of God is grieved. —*5T, p. 120*

Fire from God Devours False Religion

It makes every difference what material is used in the character building. The long-expected day of God will soon test every man's work. "The fire shall try every man's work of what sort it is." As fire reveals the difference between gold, silver, and precious stones, and wood, hay, and stubble, so the day of judgment will test characters, showing the difference between characters formed after Christ's likeness, and characters formed after the likeness of the selfish heart.

All selfishness, all false religion, will then appear as it is. The worthless material will be consumed; but the gold of true, simple, humble faith will never lose its value. It can never be consumed; for it is imperishable. One hour of transgression will be seen to be a great loss, while the fear of the Lord will be seen to be the beginning of wisdom. The pleasure of self-indulgence will perish as stubble, while the gold of steadfast principle, maintained at any cost, will endure forever. —*RH, Dec. 11, 1900*

Jerusalem is Made Sacred

The city of Jerusalem is no longer a sacred place. The curse of God is upon it because of the rejection and crucifixion of Christ. A dark blot of guilt rests upon it, and never again will it be a sacred place until it has been cleansed by the purifying fires of heaven. — *RH, July 30, 1901*

Fire from Heaven and Earth Unite

As the waters of the flood cleansed the earth in the days of Noah, so will the fire of God purify it in the last great day. Then the water from the heavens united with the water in the bowels of the earth; and in the destruction that is coming, fire from heaven will unite with the fire that is stored up in the earth. — *ST, Apr. 17, 1901*

Satan Tries to Rally His Troops

Notwithstanding that Satan has been constrained to acknowledge God's justice and to bow to the supremacy of Christ, his character remains unchanged. The spirit of rebellion, like a mighty torrent, again bursts forth. Filled with frenzy, he determines not to yield the great controversy. The time has come for a last desperate struggle against the King of heaven. He rushes into the midst of his subjects and endeavors to inspire them with his own fury and arouse them to instant battle.

But of all the countless millions whom he has allured into rebellion, there are none now to acknowledge his supremacy. His power is at an end. The wicked are filled with the same hatred of God that inspires Satan; but they see that their case is hopeless, that they cannot prevail against Jehovah. Their rage is kindled against Satan and those who have been his agents in deception, and with the fury of demons they turn upon them.

Saith the Lord: "Because thou hast set thine heart as the heart of God; behold, therefore I will bring strangers upon thee, the terrible of the nations: and they shall draw their swords against the beauty of thy wisdom, and they shall defile thy brightness. They shall bring thee down to the pit." "I will destroy thee, O covering cherub, from the midst of the stones of fire... I will cast thee to the ground, I will lay thee before kings, that they may behold thee... I will bring thee to ashes upon the earth in the sight of all them that behold thee... Thou shalt be a terror, and never shalt thou be any more." Ezekiel 28:6-8, 16-19. — *GC, p. 671*

The Heavenly Host Says "Amen"

I saw the mercy and compassion of God in giving his Son to die for guilty man. Those who will not choose to accept salvation which has been so dearly purchased for them, must be punished. Beings whom God created have chosen to rebel against his government; but I saw that God did not shut them up in hell to endure endless misery. He could not take them to heaven; for to bring them into the company of the pure and holy would make them perfectly miserable.

God will not take them to heaven, neither will he cause them to suffer eternally. He will destroy them utterly, and cause them to be as though they had not been, and then his justice will be satisfied. He formed man out of the dust of the earth, and the disobedient and unholy will be consumed by fire, and return to dust again. I saw that the benevolence and compassion of God in this, should lead all to admire his character, and to adore Him; and after the wicked shall be destroyed from off the earth, all the heavenly host will say, "Amen!" — *1SG, p. 118*

A Storm of God's Desolating Wrath

From the highest peaks men looked abroad upon a shoreless ocean. The solemn warnings of God's servant no longer seemed a subject for ridicule and scorning. How those doomed sinners longed for the opportunities which they had slighted! How they pleaded for one hour's probation, one more privilege of mercy, one call from the lips of Noah! But the sweet voice of mercy was no more to be heard by them. Love, no less than justice, demanded that God's judgments should put a check on sin. The avenging waters swept over the last retreat, and the despisers of God perished in the black depths.

"By the Word of God ... the world that then was, being overflowed with water, perished: but the heavens and the earth, which are now, by the same word are kept in store, reserved unto fire against the day of judgment and perdition of ungodly men." 2 Peter 3:5-7. Another storm is coming. The earth will again be swept by the desolating wrath of God, and sin and sinners will be destroyed. The sins that called for vengeance upon the antediluvian world exist today. The fear of God is banished from the hearts of men, and his law is treated with indifference and contempt. — *PP, pp. 100, 101*

God Utilizes Coal and Oil

Satan and his angels try to encourage the wicked multitude to action; but fire descends from heaven, and unites with the fire in the earth, and aids in the general conflagration.

Those majestic trees which God had caused to grow upon the earth, for the benefit of the inhabitants of the old world, and which they had used to form into idols, and to corrupt themselves with, God has reserved in the earth, in the shape of coal and oil to use as agencies in their final destruction.

As he called forth the waters in the earth at the time of the flood, as weapons from his arsenal to accomplish the destruction of the antediluvian race, so at the end of the one thousand years He will call forth the fires in the earth as his weapons which he has reserved for the final destruction, not only of successive generations since the flood, but the antediluvian race who perished by the flood. —*3SG, pp. 86, 87*

The Wicked Sink into Eternal Oblivion

"All that are in the graves shall hear his voice, and shall come forth; they that have done good, unto the resurrection of life; and they that have done evil, unto the resurrection of damnation." John 5:28, 29. They who have been "accounted worthy" of the resurrection of life are "blessed and holy."

"On such the second death hath no power." Revelation 20:6. But those who have not, through repentance and faith, secured pardon, must receive the penalty of transgression—"the wages of sin." They suffer punishment varying in duration and intensity, "according to their works," but finally ending in the second death. Since it is impossible for God, consistently with his justice and mercy, to save the sinner in his sins, He deprives him of the existence which his transgressions have forfeited and of which he has proved himself unworthy. Says an inspired writer: "Yet a little while, and the wicked shall not be: yea, thou shalt diligently consider his place, and it shall not be."

And another declares: "They shall be as though they had not been." Psalm 37:10; Obadiah 16. Covered with infamy, they sink into hopeless, eternal oblivion. Thus will be made an end of sin, with all the woe and ruin which have resulted from it. Says the psalmist: "Thou hast destroyed the wicked, Thou hast put out their name forever and ever. O thou enemy, destructions are come to a perpetual end." Psalm 9:5, 6. —*GC, pp. 544, 545*

God Ends Human Perversity

Consider the wondrous power of our God, and then call to mind his love for fallen man. He "so loved the world, that He gave his only begotten Son, that whosoever believeth in Him should not perish, but have everlasting life." How can man, for whom God has done so much, for whom Christ has given his life, continue in his perversity? Can we wonder that at the close of the thousand years, all who have refused to accept Him shall be destroyed with fire from heaven outside of the city of God?

God declares that this shall be so. He says, "Behold, the day of the Lord cometh, cruel both with wrath and fierce anger, to lay the land desolate: and He shall destroy the sinners thereof out of it... And I will punish the world for their evil, and the wicked for their iniquity; and I will cause the arrogancy of the proud to cease, and will lay low the haughtiness of the terrible."

— GCB, Apr. 1, 1897

The Punishment is Not Arbitrary

The end will come. God will vindicate his law and deliver his people. Satan and all who have joined him in rebellion will be cut off. Sin and sinners will perish, root and branch, (Malachi 4:1)—Satan the root, and his followers the branches. The word will be fulfilled to the prince of evil, "Because thou hast set thine heart as the heart of God; ... I will destroy thee, O covering cherub, from the midst of the stones of fire... Thou shalt be a terror, and never shalt thou be any more." Then "the wicked shall not be: yea, thou shalt diligently consider his place, and it shall not be;" "they shall be as though they had not been." Ezekiel 28:6-19; Psalm 37:10; Obadiah 1:16.

This is not an act of arbitrary power on the part of God. The rejecters of his mercy reap that which they have sown. God is the fountain of life; and when one chooses the service of sin, he separates from God, and thus cuts himself off from life. He is "alienated from the life of God." Christ says, "All they that hate Me love death." Ephesians 4:18; Proverbs 8:36.

God gives them existence for a time that they may develop their character and reveal their principles. This accomplished, they receive the results of their own choice. By a life of rebellion, Satan and all who unite with him place themselves so out of harmony with God that his very presence is to them a consuming fire. The glory of Him who is love will destroy them.

— DA, pp. 763, 764

The Pride of Assyria is Put Down

The pride of Assyria and its fall are to serve as an object lesson to the end of time. Of the nations of earth today who in arrogance and pride array themselves against Him, God inquires, "To whom art thou thus like in glory and in greatness among the trees of Eden? Yet shalt thou be brought down with the trees of Eden unto the nether parts of the earth."

"The Lord is good, a stronghold in the day of trouble; and He knoweth them that trust in Him. But with an overrunning flood He will make an utter end" of all who endeavor to exalt themselves above the Most High. Nahum 1:7, 8. "The pride of Assyria shall be brought down, and the scepter of Egypt shall depart away." Zechariah 10:11. This is true not only of the nations that arrayed themselves against God in ancient times, but also of nations today who fail of fulfilling the divine purpose. —*PK, p. 366*

Satan and His Followers Destroyed

Satan rushes into the midst of his followers and tries to stir up the multitude to action. But fire from God out of heaven is rained upon them, and the great men, and mighty men, the noble, the poor and miserable, are all consumed together. I saw that some were quickly destroyed, while others suffered longer. They were punished according to the deeds done in the body. Some were many days consuming, and just as long as there was a portion of them unconsumed, all the sense of suffering remained.

Said the angel, "The worm of life shall not die; their fire shall not be quenched as long as there is the least particle for it to prey upon."

Satan and his angels suffered long. Satan bore not only the weight and punishment of his own sins, but also of the sins of the redeemed host, which had been placed upon him; and he must also suffer for the ruin of souls which he had caused. Then I saw that Satan and all the wicked host were consumed, and the justice of God was satisfied; and all the angelic host, and all the redeemed saints, with a loud voice said, "Amen!"

Said the angel, "Satan is the root, his children are the branches. They are now consumed root and branch. They have died an everlasting death. They are never to have a resurrection, and God will have a clean universe." I then looked and saw the fire which had consumed the wicked, burning up the rubbish and purifying the earth. —*EW, p. 294*

Adulterers Die the Second Death

Have you become so hardened that you have no fear of God, of the judgment, of eternity, when your acts however secret are to pass in review before God? Do you realize that your evil doings are faithfully chronicled in heaven, written in the book, and that the Word of God, the statute book, is to judge you in that day? What did God command Moses to do with those who were guilty of adultery? They should be stoned to death.

Does the punishment end there? No, they are to die the second death. The stoning system has been done away, but the penalty for transgressing God's law is not done away. If the transgressor does not heartily repent, he will be punished with everlasting destruction from the presence of the Lord.

—Lt 12, 1864

The Wicked Feel Black Despair

Doubts assailed the dying Son of God. He could not see through the portals of the tomb. Bright hope did not present to Him his coming forth from the tomb a conqueror and his Father's acceptance of his sacrifice. The sin of the world, with all its terribleness, was felt to the utmost by the Son of God.

The displeasure of the Father for sin, and its penalty, which is death, were all that He could realize through this amazing darkness. He was tempted to fear that sin was so offensive in the sight of his Father that He could not be reconciled to his Son. The fierce temptation that his own Father had forever left Him caused that piercing cry from the cross: "My God, my God, why hast thou forsaken Me?"

Christ felt much as sinners will feel when the vials of God's wrath shall be poured out upon them. Black despair, like the pall of death, will gather about their guilty souls, and then they will realize to the fullest extent the sinfulness of sin. Salvation has been purchased for them by the suffering and death of the Son of God. It might be theirs, if they would accept of it willingly, gladly; but none are compelled to yield obedience to the law of God.

If they refuse the heavenly benefit and choose the pleasures and deceitfulness of sin, they have their choice, and at the end receive their wages, which is the wrath of God and eternal death. They will be forever separated from the presence of Jesus, whose sacrifice they had despised. They will have lost a life of happiness and sacrificed eternal glory for the pleasures of sin for a season. *—2T, pp. 209, 210*

The Earth is Purified

The feet of the wicked will never desecrate the earth made new. Fire will come down from God out of heaven and devour them—burn them up root and branch. Satan is the root, and his children are the branches. The same fire that will devour the wicked will purify the earth. — *EW, p. 51*

Sinners Receive Their Reward

"Every battle of the warrior is with confused noise, and garments rolled in blood; but this shall be with burning and fuel of fire." "The indignation of the Lord is upon all nations, and his fury upon all their armies: He hath utterly destroyed them, He hath delivered them to the slaughter." "Upon the wicked He shall rain quick burning coals, fire and brimstone and a horrible tempest: this shall be the portion of their cup." Isaiah 9:5; 34:2; Psalm 11:6. Fire comes down from God out of heaven.

The earth is broken up. The weapons concealed in its depths are drawn forth. Devouring flames burst from every yawning chasm. The very rocks are on fire. The day has come that shall burn as an oven. The elements melt with fervent heat, the earth also, and the works that are therein are burned up. Malachi 4:1; 2 Peter 3:10. The earth's surface seems one molten mass—a vast, seething lake of fire. It is the time of the judgment and perdition of ungodly men—"the day of the Lord's vengeance, and the year of recompenses for the controversy of Zion." Isaiah 34:8.

The wicked receive their recompense in the earth. Proverbs 11:31. They "shall be stubble: and the day that cometh shall burn them up, saith the Lord of hosts." Malachi 4:1. Some are destroyed as in a moment, while others suffer many days. All are punished "according to their deeds." The sins of the righteous having been transferred to Satan, he is made to suffer not only for his own rebellion, but for all the sins which he has caused God's people to commit. His punishment is to be far greater than that of those whom he has deceived.

After all have perished who fell by his deceptions, he is still to live and suffer on. In the cleansing flames the wicked are at last destroyed, root and branch—Satan the root, his followers the branches. The full penalty of the law has been visited; the demands of justice have been met; and heaven and earth, beholding, declare the righteousness of Jehovah. — *GC, pp. 672, 673*

All of the Wicked are Cut Off

It will be seen that Satan's rebellion against God has resulted in ruin to himself and to all that chose to become his subjects. He has represented that great good would result from transgression; but it will be seen that "the wages of sin is death."

"For, behold, the day cometh, that shall burn as an oven; and all the proud, yea, and all that do wickedly, shall be stubble: and the day that cometh shall burn them up, saith the Lord of hosts, that it shall leave them neither root nor branch." Malachi 4:1.

Satan, the root of every sin, and all evil workers, who are his branches, shall be utterly cut off. An end will be made of sin, with all the woe and ruin that have resulted from it. Says the psalmist, "Thou hast destroyed the wicked, thou hast put out their name forever and ever. O thou enemy, destructions are come to a perpetual end." Psalm 9:5, 6.

But amid the tempest of divine judgment the children of God will have no cause for fear. "The Lord will be the hope of his people, and the strength of the children of Israel." Joel 3:16. The day that brings terror and destruction to the transgressors of God's law will bring to the obedient "joy unspeakable and full of glory" "Gather my saints together unto Me," saith the Lord, "those that have made a covenant with Me by sacrifice. And the heavens shall declare his righteousness: for God is Judge Himself." — *PP, p. 341*

Discussion Questions

1. Who had the job of deciding how much the wicked will be punished?

2. How is the New Jerusalem comparable to Noah's Ark?

3. Why will some of the wicked remain alive for many days after the judgments from God fall?

4. Why is Satan called a branch and his followers are referred to as roots?

5. Should we be afraid of suffering the second death? Will God's children have anything to fear when fire and brimstone is raining from heaven?

— 32 —

Sin is Forever Ended

"What do ye imagine against the Lord? He will make an utter end: affliction shall not rise up the second time." — Nahum 1:9

Psalm 37:9-11	Psalm 111:7, 8	Psalm 145:10	Zeph. 3:9-20	Eph. 2:4-7
Psalm 46:10	Psalm 113:3	Daniel 7:18	Zech. 14:9	2 Pet. 3:12, 13
Psalm 104:35	Psalm 119:89	Habakkuk 3:4	1 Cor. 4:9	Rev. 5:13

All Traces of Sin are Gone

"I saw a new heaven and a new earth: for the first heaven and the first earth were passed away." Revelation 21:1. The fire that consumes the wicked purifies the earth. Every trace of the curse is swept away. No eternally burning hell will keep before the ransomed the fearful consequences of sin. — *GC, p. 674*

No Sounds of Blasphemy

John, in the Revelation, looking forward to the eternal state, hears a universal anthem of praise undisturbed by one note of discord. "Every creature in heaven and earth was heard ascribing glory to God." Revelation 5:13. There will then be no lost souls to blaspheme God as they writhe in never-ending torment; no wretched beings in hell will mingle their shrieks with the songs of the saved. — *GC, p. 545*

Wealth and Fame are Gone

The message of warning is to be given with a deep sense of individual responsibility. Wealth, fame, renown, selfish exaltation will be extinguished, to be forever in the dust. The life-giving power from Christ in the human agent will not die. Saints will appear just what grace has made them. They praise God who sitteth on the throne, and the Lamb. They live forever and forever through the ceaseless ages of eternity. — *Ms 59, 1895*

No Chance of Another Rebellion

The death of Christ upon the cross made sure the destruction of him who has the power of death, who was the originator of sin. When Satan is destroyed, there will be none to tempt to evil; the atonement will never need to be repeated; and there will be no danger of another rebellion in the universe of God. That which alone can effectually restrain from sin in this world of darkness, will prevent sin in heaven. The significance of the death of Christ will be seen by saints and angels. Fallen men could not have a home in the paradise of God without the Lamb slain from the foundation of the world. Shall we not then exalt the cross of Christ? — *ST, Dec. 30, 1889*

Evil will Never Happen Again

The whole universe will have become witnesses to the nature and results of sin. And its utter extermination, which in the beginning would have brought fear to angels and dishonor to God, will now vindicate his love and establish his honor before the universe of beings who delight to do his will, and in whose heart is his law. Never will evil again be manifest. Says the Word of God: "Affliction shall not rise up the second time." Nahum 1:9. The law of God, which Satan has reproached as the yoke of bondage, will be honored as the law of liberty. A tested and proved creation will never again be turned from allegiance to Him whose character has been fully manifested before them as fathomless love and infinite wisdom. — *GC, p. 504*

One Reminder of Sin Remains

One reminder alone remains: Our Redeemer will ever bear the marks of his crucifixion. Upon his wounded head, upon his side, his hands and feet, are the only traces of the cruel work that sin has wrought. Says the prophet, beholding Christ in his glory: "He had bright beams coming out of his side: and there was the hiding of his power." Habakkuk 3:4.

That pierced side whence flowed the crimson stream that reconciled man to God—there is the Saviour's glory, there "the hiding of his power." "Mighty to save," through the sacrifice of redemption, He was therefore strong to execute justice upon them that despised God's mercy. And the tokens of his humiliation are his highest honor; through the eternal ages the wounds of Calvary will show forth his praise and declare his power. — *GC, p. 674*

Songs of Praise Burst Forth

In dying, Christ proclaimed Satan's death sentence. This victory was heralded by all the heavenly host. All the angelic family, cherubs and seraphs, sang the praise of the wonderful work which united earth to heaven, and finite man to the infinite God. And when the conflict is forever ended, what songs of praise will burst forth from the redeemed host! That will indeed be music. Without a discordant note, the rich, full anthem will arise from immortal voices, "Worthy, worthy is the Lamb." — *ST, Feb. 14, 1900*

Christ Bears Human Traits Forever

Christ ascended to heaven, bearing a sanctified, holy humanity. He took this humanity with Him into the heavenly courts, and through the eternal ages He will bear it, as the One who has redeemed every human being in the city of God, the One who has pleaded before the Father, "I have graven them upon the palms of my hands." The palms of his hands bear the marks of the wounds that He received. If we are wounded and bruised, if we meet with difficulties that are hard to manage, let us remember how much Christ suffered for us. Let us sit together with our brethren in heavenly places in Christ. Let us bring heaven's blessing into our hearts. — *RH, Mar. 9, 1905*

Every Question is Made Plain

Every question of truth and error in the long-standing controversy has now been made plain. The results of rebellion, the fruits of setting aside the divine statutes, have been laid open to the view of all created intelligences. The working out of Satan's rule in contrast with the government of God has been presented to the whole universe. Satan's own works have condemned him. God's wisdom, his justice, and his goodness stand fully vindicated.

It is seen that all his dealings in the great controversy have been conducted with respect to the eternal good of his people and the good of all the worlds that He has created. "All thy works shall praise thee, O Lord; and thy saints shall bless thee." Psalm 145:10. The history of sin will stand to all eternity as a witness that with the existence of God's law is bound up the happiness of all the beings He has created. With all the facts of the great controversy in view, the whole universe, both loyal and rebellious, with one accord declare: "Just and true are thy ways, thou King of saints." — *GC, p. 670*

The Cross Protects the Angels

Through the eternal ages the offensive character of sin will be seen in what it cost the Father and the Son in the humiliation, suffering, and death of Christ. All the worlds will behold in Him a living testimony to the malignity of sin, for in his divine form He bears the marks of the curse. He is in the midst of the throne as the Lamb that had been slain.

Not only men but angels will ascribe honor and glory to the Redeemer, for even they are secure only through the sufferings of the Son of God. It is through the efficacy of the cross that the inhabitants of unfallen worlds have been guarded from apostasy. It is this that has effectually unveiled the deceptions of Satan and refuted his claims. Not only those that are washed by the blood of Christ, but also the holy angels, are drawn to Him by his crowning act of giving his life for the sins of the world. God's dealing with the rebellion of Satan is justified before the universe. The justice and mercy of God are fully vindicated, so that to all eternity, rebellion will never again arise. —*Ms 41, 1892*

All that was Lost by Sin is Restored

The great plan of redemption results in fully bringing back the world into God's favor. All that was lost by sin is restored. Not only man but the earth is redeemed, to be the eternal abode of the obedient. For six thousand years Satan has struggled to maintain possession of the earth. Now God's original purpose in its creation is accomplished.

"The saints of the Most High shall take the kingdom, and possess the kingdom forever, even forever and ever." Daniel 7:18. "From the rising of the sun unto the going down of the same the Lord's name is to be praised." Psalm 113:3. "In that day shall there be one Lord, and his name one." "And Jehovah shall be king over all the earth." Zechariah 14:9. Says the Scripture, "Forever, O Lord, thy word is settled in heaven." "All his commandments are sure. They stand fast forever and ever." Psalm 119:89; 111:7, 8.

The sacred statutes which Satan has hated and sought to destroy, will be honored throughout a sinless universe. And "as the earth bringeth forth her bud, and as the garden causeth the things that are sown in it to spring forth; so the Lord God will cause righteousness and praise to spring forth before all nations." Isaiah 61:11. —*PP, p. 342*

The Saved are an Eternal Testimony

The working out of the great plan of redemption, as manifest in the history of this world, is not only to men but to angels, a revelation of the Father. Here is seen the work of Satan in the degradation and ruin of the race by sin, and, on the other hand, the work of God in man's recovery and uplifting through the grace of Christ. Every soul that develops a righteous character and withstands the power of the wicked one is a testimony to the falsehood of Satan's charges against the divine government.

Through the eternal ages the exaltation of the redeemed will be a testimony to God's love and mercy. This is set forth in the touching and beautiful words of the apostle Paul. He says that "we are a spectacle unto the world, to angels, and to men." 1 Corinthians 4:9. "God, who is rich in mercy, for his great love wherewith He loved us, even when we were dead in sins, hath quickened us together with Christ, ... that in the ages to come He might show the exceeding riches of his grace, in his kindness toward us through Jesus Christ." Ephesians 2:4-7. —*Ms 41, 1892*

The Wounds in Christ's Side

The priests wished to make sure of the death of Jesus, and at their suggestion a soldier thrust a spear into the Saviour's side. From the wound thus made, there flowed two copious and distinct streams, one of blood, the other of water. This was noted by all the beholders, and John states the occurrence very definitely. He says, "One of the soldiers with a spear pierced his side, and forthwith came there out blood and water. And He that saw it bare record, and his record is true: and He knoweth that He saith true, that ye might believe. For these things were done, that the Scripture should be fulfilled, A bone of Him shall not be broken. And again another Scripture saith, They shall look on Him whom they pierced." John 19:34-37.

After the resurrection the priests and rulers circulated the report that Christ did not die upon the cross, that He merely fainted, and was afterward revived... But it was not the spear thrust, it was not the pain of the cross, that caused the death of Jesus. That cry, uttered "with a loud voice" (Matthew 27:50; Luke 23:46), at the moment of death, the stream of blood and water that flowed from his side, declared that He died of a broken heart. His heart was broken by mental anguish. He was slain by the sin of the world.

—*DA, pp. 771, 772*

Satan's Reign is Forever Ended

Satan's work of ruin is forever ended. For six thousand years he has wrought his will, filling the earth with woe and causing grief throughout the universe. The whole creation has groaned and travailed together in pain. Now God's creatures are forever delivered from his presence and temptations. "The whole earth is at rest, and is quiet: they (the righteous) break forth into singing." Isaiah 14:7. And a shout of praise and triumph ascends from the whole loyal universe. "The voice of a great multitude," "as the voice of many waters, and as the voice of mighty thunderings," is heard, saying: "Alleluia: for the Lord God omnipotent reigneth." Revelation 19:6. — GC, p. 673

All the Worlds Understand God's Justice

Through the plan of salvation, the precepts of the law were to be proved perfect and immutable, that at last one tide of glory and love might go up throughout the universe, ascribing glory and honor and praise to Him that sitteth upon the throne, and to the Lamb forever and ever.

The inhabitants of all worlds will be convinced of the justice of the law in the overthrow of rebellion and the eradication of sin. When man, beguiled by Satan's power, disobeyed the divine law, God could not, even to save the lost race, change that law. God is love, and to change the law would be to deny Himself, to overthrow those principles with which are bound up the good of the universe. The working out of the plan of salvation reveals not only to men, but to angels, the character of God, and through the ages of eternity the malignant character of sin will be understood by the cost to the Father and the Son of the redemption of a rebel race.

In Christ, the Lamb slain from the foundation of the world, all worlds will behold the marks of the curse, and angels as well as men will ascribe honor and glory to the Redeemer, through whom they are all made secure from apostasy. The efficiency of the cross guards the redeemed race from the danger of a second fall. The life and death of Christ effectually unveils the deceptions of Satan, and refutes his claims. The sacrifice of Christ for a fallen world draws not only men, but angels, unto Him in bonds of indissoluble union. Through the plan of salvation the justice and mercy of God are fully vindicated, and to all eternity rebellion will never again arise, affliction never again touch the universe of God. — BE, July 15, 1893

God's Love and Honor are Vindicated

By a life of rebellion, Satan and all who unite with him place themselves so out of harmony with God that his very presence is to them a consuming fire. The glory of Him who is love will destroy them. At the beginning of the great controversy, the angels did not understand this. Had Satan and his host then been left to reap the full result of their sin, they would have perished; but it would not have been apparent to heavenly beings that this was the inevitable result of sin. A doubt of God's goodness would have remained in their minds as evil seed, to produce its deadly fruit of sin and woe.

But not so when the great controversy shall be ended. Then, the plan of redemption having been completed, the character of God is revealed to all created intelligences. The precepts of his law are seen to be perfect and immutable. Then sin has made manifest its nature, Satan his character.

Then the extermination of sin will vindicate God's love and establish his honor before a universe of beings who delight to do his will, and in whose heart is his law. Well, then, might the angels rejoice as they looked upon the Saviour's cross; for though they did not then understand all, they knew that the destruction of sin and Satan was forever made certain, that the redemption of man was assured, and that the universe was made eternally secure. Christ Himself fully comprehended the results of the sacrifice made upon Calvary. To all these He looked forward when upon the cross He cried out, "It is finished." —*DA, p. 764*

Discussion Questions

1. Why will there never be a chance of a second rebellion?

2. What is the significance of the marks on Christ's body?

3. Why did Christ decide to trade some of his divinity for humanity?

4. How will the history of sin stand for all eternity as a witness?

5. Why will the character and honor of God be fully vindicated?

The Ages
of Eternity

— 33 —

The New Earth

"For as the new heavens and the new earth, which I will make, shall remain before Me, saith the Lord, so shall your seed and your name remain." — Isaiah 66:22

Deut. 30:3-5	Psalm 87:3	Isa. 30:26	Isa. 61:11	Haggai 2:9	Zech. 8:3
1 Samuel 2:8	Isa. 14:3-8	Isa. 45:18	Isa. 65:17	Zeph. 3:8-13	Rev. 21:1-5
Psalm 37:29	Isa. 29:18-24	Isa. 60:18-21	Daniel 2:44	Zech. 2:10-12	Rev. 21:10-27

No Sadness in the Holy City

We are homeward bound. He who loved us so much as to die for us has built us a city. The New Jerusalem is our place of rest. There will be no sadness in the city of God. No wail of sorrow, no dirge of crushed hopes and buried affections, will evermore be heard. Soon the garments of heaviness will be changed for the wedding garment. Soon we shall witness the coronation of our King. Those whose lives have been hidden with Christ, those who on this earth have fought the good fight of faith, will shine forth with the Redeemer's glory in the kingdom of God. — *9T, p. 287*

The Earth is Our Eternal Home

Christ, by his sacrifice paying the penalty of sin, would not only redeem man, but recover the dominion which man had forfeited. All that was lost by the first Adam will be restored by the second. The prophet says, "O Tower of the flock, the stronghold of the daughter of Zion, to thee shall it come, even the first dominion."

And Paul points forward to the "redemption of the purchased possession." God created the earth to be the abode of holy, happy beings. That purpose will be fulfilled when, renewed by the power of God, and freed from sin and sorrow, it shall become the eternal home of the redeemed. — *RH, Oct. 22, 1908*

Our Inheritance to be Revealed

Then the wicked saw what they had lost; and fire was breathed from God upon them and consumed them… The same fire from God that consumed the wicked purified the whole earth. The broken, ragged mountains melted with fervent heat, the atmosphere also, and all the stubble was consumed. Then our inheritance opened before us, glorious and beautiful, and we inherited the whole earth made new. We all shouted with a loud voice, "Glory; Alleluia!" — *EW, p. 54*

Earth is Purified from the Curse

I looked and saw the earth purified. There was not a single sign of the curse. The broken, uneven surface of the earth now looked like a level, extensive plain. God's entire universe was clean, and the great controversy was forever ended. Wherever we looked, everything upon which the eye rested was beautiful and holy. And all the redeemed host, old and young, great and small, cast their glittering crowns at the feet of their Redeemer, and prostrated themselves in adoration before Him, and worshipped Him that liveth forever and ever. The beautiful New Earth, with all its glory, was the eternal inheritance of the saints. The kingdom and dominion, and the greatness of the kingdom under the whole heaven, was then given to the saints of the Most High, who were to possess it forever, even forever and ever.

— EW, p. 295

Jesus Brightens the New Jerusalem

Jesus has gone to prepare mansions for those who are waiting and watching for his appearing. There they will meet the pure angels and the redeemed host, and will join their songs of praise and triumph. There the Saviour's love surrounds his people, and the city of God is irradiated with the light of his countenance—a city whose walls, great and high, are garnished with all manner of precious stones, whose gates are pearls, and whose streets are pure gold, as it were transparent glass.

"There shall in no wise enter into it anything that defileth, neither whatsoever worketh abomination, or maketh a lie; but they which are written in the Lamb's book of life." The shadows of night never fall on that city; it has no need of the sun, neither of the moon; its inhabitants rejoice in the undimmed glory of the Lamb of God. — *RH, June 3, 1880*

Heavenly Riches will Endure

A new heavens and a new earth are promised to all who are loyal and true to God's commandments. When all things earthly are dissolved, when the treasures of the wicked are lost to them forever, the righteous will take possession of the riches that endure—the heavenly treasures, incorruptible, undefiled, and that fadeth not away. —*Ms 81, 1900*

Abraham Saw the Earth Restored

The patriarch begged for some visible token as a confirmation of his faith and as an evidence to after-generations that God's gracious purposes toward them would be accomplished... The plan of redemption was here opened to him, in the death of Christ, the great sacrifice, and his coming in glory. Abraham saw also the earth restored to its Eden beauty, to be given him for an everlasting possession, as the final and complete fulfillment of the promise.

—*PP, p. 137*

Moses was Shown the New Earth

The servant of God was carried still farther. He saw the earth purified by fire, and cleansed from every vestige of sin, every mark of the curse, and renovated, and given to the saints to possess forever and ever. He saw the kingdoms of the earth given to the saints of the Most High. No impurity, nothing to mar their peace and happiness, was in the earth made new.

In the new earth the prophecies which the Jews applied to the first advent of Christ will be fulfilled. The saints will then be redeemed and made immortal. Upon their heads will be crowns of immortality, and joy and glory will be pictured on their countenances, which will reflect the image of their Redeemer. Moses saw the land of Canaan as it will appear when it becomes the home of the saints. John the Revelator was given a view of this same land, of which he writes: "I saw a new heaven and a new earth: for the first heaven and the first earth were passed away; and there was no more sea." ...

As Moses beheld this scene, joy and triumph were expressed in his countenance. He could understand the force of all the angels revealed to him. He took in the whole scene as it was presented before him. His mind was firm, his intellect clear. His strength was unabated, his eye was undimmed. Then he closed his eyes in death, and the angels of God buried him in the mount. —*Ms 69, 1912*

No Marriage in the New Earth

The Sadducees reasoned that if the body is to be composed of the same particles of matter in its immortal as in its mortal state, then when raised from the dead it must have flesh and blood, and must resume in the eternal world the life interrupted on earth. In that case they concluded that earthly relationships would be resumed, husband and wife would be reunited, marriages consummated, and all things go on the same as before death, the frailties and passions of this life being perpetuated in the life beyond.

In answer to their questions, Jesus lifted the veil from the future life. "In the resurrection," He said, "they neither marry, nor are given in marriage, but are as the angels of God in heaven." He showed that the Sadducees were wrong in their belief. Their premises were false. "Ye do err," He added, "not knowing the Scriptures, nor the power of God." He did not charge them, as He had charged the Pharisees, with hypocrisy, but with error of belief. The Sadducees had flattered themselves that they of all men adhered most strictly to the Scriptures. —DA, p. 605

The New Earth is a Country

In the Bible the inheritance of the saved is called "a country." Hebrews 11:14-16. There the heavenly Shepherd leads his flock to fountains of living waters. The tree of life yields its fruit every month, and the leaves of the tree are for the service of the nations. There are ever-flowing streams, clear as crystal, and beside them waving trees cast their shadows upon the paths prepared for the ransomed of the Lord. There the wide-spreading plains swell into hills of beauty, and the mountains of God rear their lofty summits.

On those peaceful plains, beside those living streams, God's people, so long pilgrims and wanderers, shall find a home. "My people shall dwell in a peaceable habitation, and in sure dwellings, and in quiet resting places." ...

There, "the wilderness and the solitary place shall be glad for them; and the desert shall rejoice, and blossom as the rose." "Instead of the thorn shall come up the fir tree, and instead of the brier shall come up the myrtle tree." "The wolf also shall dwell with the lamb, and the leopard shall lie down with the kid; ... and a little child shall lead them." "They shall not hurt nor destroy in all my holy mountain," saith the Lord. Isaiah 35:1; 55:13; Isaiah 11:6, 9.

—GC, p. 675

Jeremiah Saw the Covenant Renewed

Yet amid the general ruin into which the nation was rapidly passing, Jeremiah was often permitted to look beyond the distressing scenes of the present to the glorious prospects of the future, when God's people should be ransomed from the land of the enemy and planted again in Zion. He foresaw the time when the Lord would renew his covenant relationship with them. "Their soul shall be as a watered garden; and they shall not sorrow any more at all." Jeremiah 31:12.

Of his call to the prophetic mission, Jeremiah himself wrote: "The Lord put forth his hand, and touched my mouth. And the Lord said unto me, Behold, I have put my words in thy mouth. See, I have this day set thee over the nations and over the kingdoms, to root out, and to pull down, and to destroy, and to throw down, to build, and to plant." Jeremiah 1:9, 10. Thank God for the words, "to build, and to plant." By these words Jeremiah was assured of the Lord's purpose to restore and to heal. — *PK, pp. 408, 409*

Earth is Honored above All Other Worlds

Through Christ's redeeming work the government of God stands justified. The Omnipotent One is made known as the God of love. Satan's charges are refuted, and his character unveiled. Rebellion can never again arise. Sin can never again enter the universe. Through eternal ages all are secure from apostasy. By love's self-sacrifice, the inhabitants of earth and heaven are bound to their Creator in bonds of indissoluble union. The work of redemption will be complete.

In the place where sin abounded, God's grace much more abounds. The earth itself, the very field that Satan claims as his, is to be not only ransomed but exalted. Our little world, under the curse of sin the one dark blot in his glorious creation, will be honored above all other worlds in the universe of God. Here, where the Son of God tabernacled in humanity; where the King of glory lived and suffered and died—here, when He shall make all things new, the tabernacle of God shall be with men, "and He will dwell with them, and they shall be his people, and God Himself shall be with them, and be their God." And through endless ages as the redeemed walk in the light of the Lord, they will praise Him for his unspeakable Gift—Immanuel, "God with us." — *DA, p. 26*

Promises to Abraham are Fulfilled

The Bible plainly teaches that the promises made to Abraham are to be fulfilled through Christ. All that are Christ's are "Abraham's seed, and heirs according to the promise"—heirs to "an inheritance incorruptible, and undefiled, and that fadeth not away"—the earth freed from the curse of sin. Galatians 3:29; 1 Peter 1:4.

For "the kingdom and dominion, and the greatness of the kingdom under the whole heaven, shall be given to the people of the saints of the Most High;" and "the meek shall inherit the earth; and shall delight themselves in the abundance of peace." Daniel 7:27; Psalm 37:11. —*PP, p. 169*

The Incredible Glory of God's Paradise

"O Tower of the flock, the stronghold of the daughter of Zion, unto thee shall it come, even the first dominion." Micah 4:8. The time has come to which holy men have looked with longing since the flaming sword barred the first pair from Eden, the time for "the redemption of the purchased possession." Ephesians 1:14. The earth originally given to man as his kingdom, betrayed by him into the hands of Satan, and so long held by the mighty foe, has been brought back by the great plan of redemption. All that was lost by sin has been restored.

"Thus saith the Lord ... that formed the earth and made it; He hath established it, He created it not in vain, He formed it to be inhabited." Isaiah 45:18. God's original purpose in the creation of the earth is fulfilled as it is made the eternal abode of the redeemed. "The righteous shall inherit the land, and dwell therein forever." Psalm 37:29.

A fear of making the future inheritance seem too material has led many to spiritualize away the very truths which lead us to look upon it as our home. Christ assured his disciples that He went to prepare mansions for them in the Father's house. Those who accept the teachings of God's Word will not be wholly ignorant concerning the heavenly abode.

And yet, "eye hath not seen, nor ear heard, neither have entered into the heart of man, the things which God hath prepared for them that love Him." 1 Corinthians 2:9. Human language is inadequate to describe the reward of the righteous. It will be known only to those who behold it. No finite mind can comprehend the glory of the Paradise of God. — *GC, p. 674*

The New Jerusalem Shines with Glory

There is the New Jerusalem, the metropolis of the glorified New Earth, "a crown of glory in the hand of the Lord, and a royal diadem in the hand of thy God." "Her light was like unto a stone most precious, even like a jasper stone, clear as crystal." "The nations of them which are saved shall walk in the light of it: and the kings of the earth do bring their glory and honor into it." Saith the Lord: "I will rejoice in Jerusalem, and joy in my people." "The tabernacle of God is with men, and He will dwell with them, and they shall be his people, and God Himself shall be with them, and be their God." Isaiah 62:3; Revelation 21:11, 24; Isaiah 65:19; Revelation 21:3.

In the City of God "there shall be no night." None will need or desire repose. There will be no weariness in doing the will of God and offering praise to his name. We shall ever feel the freshness of the morning and shall ever be far from its close. "And they need no candle, neither light of the sun; for the Lord God giveth them light." Revelation 22:5. The light of the sun will be superseded by a radiance which is not painfully dazzling, yet which immeasurably surpasses the brightness of our noontide. The glory of God and the Lamb floods the Holy City with unfading light. The redeemed walk in the sunless glory of perpetual day.

"I saw no temple therein: for the Lord God Almighty and the Lamb are the temple of it." Revelation 21:22. The people of God are privileged to hold open communion with the Father and the Son. "Now we see through a glass, darkly." 1 Corinthians 13:12. We behold the image of God reflected, as in a mirror, in the works of nature and in his dealings with men; but then we shall see Him face to face, without a dimming veil between. We shall stand in his presence and behold the glory of his countenance.

There the redeemed shall know, even as also they are known. The loves and sympathies which God Himself has planted in the soul shall there find truest and sweetest exercise. The pure communion with holy beings, the harmonious social life with the blessed angels and with the faithful ones of all ages who have washed their robes and made them white in the blood of the Lamb, the sacred ties that bind together "the whole family in heaven and earth"—these help to constitute the happiness of the redeemed. Ephesians 3:15. — *GC, pp. 676, 677*

492

No Sea on the New Earth

The sea divides friends. It is a barrier between us and those whom we love. Our associations are broken up by the broad, fathomless ocean. In the New Earth there will be no more sea, and there shall pass there "no galley with oars." In the past many who have loved and served God have been bound by chains to their seats in galleys, compelled to serve the purpose of cruel, hardhearted men. The Lord has looked upon their suffering in sympathy and compassion. Thank God, in the earth made new there will be no fierce torrents, no engulfing ocean, no restless, murmuring waves. —*Ms 33, 1911*

A Vision of the New Earth

We began to look at the glorious things outside of the city. There I saw most glorious houses, that had the appearance of silver, supported by four pillars, set with pearls, most glorious to behold, which were to be inhabited by the saints; in them was a golden shelf; I saw many of the saints go into the houses, take off their glittering crowns and lay them on the shelf, then go out into the field by the houses to do something with the earth; not as we have to do with the earth here; no, no. A glorious light shone all about their heads, and they were continually shouting and offering praises to God.

And I saw another field full of all kinds of flowers, and as I plucked them, I cried out, "well they will never fade." Next I saw a field of tall grass, most glorious to behold; it was living green, and had a reflection of silver and gold, as it waved proudly to the glory of King Jesus. Then we entered a field full of all kinds of beasts—the lion, the lamb, the leopard and the wolf, altogether in perfect union; we passed through the midst of them, and they followed on peaceably after. Then we entered a wood, not like the dark woods we have here, no, no; but light, and all over glorious; the branches of the trees waved to and fro, and we all cried out, "we will dwell safely in the wilderness and sleep in this woods." We passed through the woods, for we were on our way to Mount Zion.

As we were traveling along, we met a company who were also gazing at the glories of the place. I noticed red as a border on their garments; their crowns were brilliant; their robes were pure white. As we greeted them, I asked Jesus who they were? He said they were martyrs that had been slain for Him. With them was an innumerable company of little ones; they had a hem of red on their garments also. Mount Zion was just before us, and on the Mount sat a glorious temple, and about it were seven other mountains, on which grew roses and lilies, and I saw the little ones climb, or if they chose, use their little wings and fly to the top of the mountains, and pluck the never fading flowers.

There were all kinds of trees around the temple to beautify the place; the box, the pine, the fir, the oil, the myrtle, the pomegranate, and the fig tree bowed down with the weight of its timely figs, that made the place look all over glorious. And as we were about to enter the holy temple, Jesus raised his lovely voice and said, "only the 144,000 enter this place," and we shouted Hallelujah. Well, bless the Lord, dear brethren and sisters, it is an extra meeting for those who have the seal of the living God.

This temple was supported by seven pillars, all of transparent gold, set with pearls most glorious. The glorious things I saw there, I cannot describe to you. Oh, that I could talk in the language of Canaan, then could I tell a little of the glory of the upper world; but, if faithful, you soon will know all about it. I saw there the tables of stone in which the names of the 144,000 were engraved in letters of gold; after we had beheld the glory of the temple, we went out.

Then Jesus left us, and went to the city; soon, we heard his lovely voice again, saying—"Come my people, you have come out of great tribulation, and done my will; suffered for me; come in to supper, for I will gird myself, and serve you." We shouted Hallelujah, glory, and entered into the city. And I saw a table of pure silver, it was many miles in length, yet our eyes could extend over it. And I saw the fruit of the tree of life, the manna, almonds, figs, pomegranates, grapes, and many other kinds of fruit.

We all reclined at the table. I asked Jesus to let me eat of the fruit. He said, "not now. Those who eat of the fruit of this land, go back to earth no more. But in a little while, if faithful, you shall both eat of the fruit of the tree of life, and drink of the water of the fountain;" and He said, "you must go back to the earth again, and relate to others, what I have revealed to you." Then an angel bore me gently down to this dark world. Sometimes I think I cannot stay here any longer, all things of earth look so dreary—I feel very lonely here, for I have seen a better land. Oh, that I had wings like a dove, then would I fly away, and be at rest. —*WLF, pp. 16-18*

No New Babies will be Born

There are men today who express their belief that there will be marriages and births in the new earth, but those who believe the Scriptures cannot accept such doctrines. The doctrine that children will be born in the new earth is not a part of the "sure word of prophecy." The words of Christ are too plain to be misunderstood. They should forever settle the question of marriages and births in the new earth. Neither those who shall be raised from the dead, nor those who shall be translated without seeing death, will marry or be given in marriage. They will be as the angels of God, members of the royal family.

—Ms 28, 1904

The Earth is Immeasurably Glorious

The glorious City of God has twelve gates, set with pearls most glorious. It also has twelve foundations of various colors. The streets of the City are of pure gold. In this city is the throne of God, and a pure, beautiful river proceeding out of it, as clear as crystal. Its sparkling purity and beauty makes glad the City of God. The saints will drink freely of the healing waters of the river of life.

On either side of this beautiful river is the tree of life. And the redeemed saints, who have loved God and kept his commandments here, will enter in through the gates of the City, and have right to the tree of life. They will eat freely of it, as our first parents did before their fall. The leaves of that immortal wide-spread tree will be for the healing of the nations. All their woes will then be gone. Sickness, sorrow and death they will never again feel, for the leaves of the tree of life have healed them.

Jesus will then see of the travail of his soul and be satisfied, when the redeemed, who have been subject to sorrow, toil and afflictions, who have groaned beneath the curse, are gathered up around that tree of life to eat of its immortal fruit, that our first parents forfeited all right to, by breaking God's commands. There will be no danger of their ever losing right to the tree of life again, for he that tempted our first parents to sin, will be destroyed by the second death.

All faces will reflect the image of their Redeemer. There will then be no anxious, troubled countenances, but all will be bright, and smiling in spotless purity. The angels will be there, also the resurrected saints with the martyrs, and the best of all, and what will cause us the most joy, our lovely Saviour who suffered and died that we might enjoy that happiness and freedom, will be there. His glorious face will shine brighter than the sun, and light up the beautiful City, and reflect glory all around.

Children will be there. They will never be engaged in strife or discord. Their love will be fervent and holy. They will also have a crown of gold upon their heads, and a harp in their hands. And their little countenances, that we here see so often troubled and perplexed, will beam with holy joy, expressive of their perfect freedom and happiness. They will express in child-like purity their wonder and delight, as they behold everything around them so new and lovely. They will look to the blessed Saviour who has given Himself for them, and, with admiration and love for Him who is smiling upon them, raise their voices and sing to his praise and glory, while they feel and realized the matchless depths of a Saviour's love.

This earth, dear children, is to be purified with fire; then it will be much more beautiful. The grass will be living green, and will never wither. There will be roses and lilies, and all kinds of flowers there. They will never blight or fade, or lose their beauty and fragrance. The lion, we should much dread and fear here, will then lie down with the lamb, and everything in the New Earth will be peace and harmony. The trees of the New Earth will be straight and lofty, without deformity.

The saints will have crowns of glory upon their heads, and harps of gold in their hands. They will play upon the golden harp, and sing redeeming love, and make melody unto God. Their former trials and suffering in this world will be forgotten and lost amid the glories of the New Earth. And they will ever have the approving smiles of Jesus upon them, and their happiness will be complete. There will be glory, glory all around. Dear children, the future abode of the saints will be all over glorious, and will you strive to be there?

Let your minds dwell upon the glories of heaven, for this you may do with safety, and this will bring substantial joys, and will make you heavenly minded. If you have trials here, and feel lonesome, look away from this dark world to the bright glories of heaven. Set your affections upon heavenly joys, and then you will not feel so deeply the trials and disappointments of this life, for you will feel that you have a home in glory, a crown, a harp, and a lovely Saviour there. Strive for that blest inheritance which God has promised to those that love Him, and keep his commandments. — *YI, Oct. 1, 1851*

All of Nature Constantly Praises God

At last the victory was gained. The army following the banner with the inscription, "The commandments of God, and the faith of Jesus," was gloriously triumphant. The soldiers of Christ were close beside the gates of the city, and with joy the city received her King. The kingdom of peace and joy and everlasting righteousness was established.

Now the church is militant. Now we are confronted with a world in midnight darkness, almost wholly given over to idolatry. But the day is coming in which the battle will have been fought, the victory won. The will of God is to be done on earth, as it is done in heaven. Then the nations will own no other law than the law of heaven. All will be a happy, united family, clothed with the garments of praise and thanksgiving—the robe of Christ's righteousness.

All nature, in its surpassing loveliness, will offer to God a constant tribute of praise and adoration. The world will be bathed in the light of heaven. The years will move on in gladness. The light of the moon will be as the light of the sun, and the light of the sun will be sevenfold greater than it is now. Over the scene the morning stars will sing together, and the sons of God will shout for joy, while God and Christ will unite in proclaiming: "There shall be no more sin, neither shall there be any more death." —*8T, pp. 41, 42*

Discussion Questions

1. The New Earth is called "a country." What will it be like to live in a world where there is no crime, car traffic, or shopping districts?

2. What are some of the promises to Abraham that will finally be fulfilled?

3. What will provide light for New Jerusalem and the New Earth?

4. Why do you think there will be no marriage or babies on the New Earth?

5. What are several ways that earth will be honored above all other planets?

— 34 —

The Tasks of Immortals

"Commit thy works unto the Lord, and thy thoughts shall be established." — Proverbs 16:3

| Isaiah 35:8-10 | Isaiah 55:12 | Isaiah 66:23 | Micah 4:6-8 | Col. 1:26, 27 |
| Isaiah 51:3 | Isaiah 65:18-23 | Amos 9:14, 15 | Matt. 5:18 | Rev. 22:3, 4 |

A) Workers for God

The Joy of Obeying God

The happiness and glory of the inhabitants of heaven is perfect because the will of God is their supreme delight. —*Lt 22, 1889*

Serving God will be Delightful

"Thy kingdom come. Thy will be done, as in heaven, so in earth." In heaven the will of God is perfectly carried out. Love to God makes service a joy.

—*ST, Mar. 29, 1905*

Build Houses and Plant Vineyards

The whole wicked host will be burnt up, "root and branch," and cease to exist. Then will appear the new heaven and the new earth. Then will the saints "build houses," and "plant vineyards." —*WLF, p. 12*

The Greatest Joys are in Service

In our life here, earthly, sin-restricted though it is, the greatest joy and the highest education are in service. And in the future state, untrammeled by the limitations of sinful humanity, it is in service that our greatest joy and our highest education will be found—witnessing, and ever as we witness learning anew "the riches of the glory of this mystery;" "which is Christ in you, the hope of glory." Colossians 1:27. —*Ed, p. 309*

The Homes are Permanent

"In my Father's house are many mansions." The word here translated mansion means permanent abodes, habitations that are not removed like tents, but which permanently endure for the family of the redeemed. The Father is there, to gather his children in his paternal arms, and bestow upon them his everlasting love. — *Lt 84, 1907*

Heavenly Employment is Restful

No man or woman who is converted to God can be anything but a worker. There certainly is and ever will be employment in heaven. The whole family of the redeemed will not live in a state of dreamy idleness. There remaineth therefore a rest to the people of God. In heaven activity will not be wearying and burdensome; it will be rest. The whole family of the redeemed will find their delight in serving Him whose they are by creation and by redemption.

— *Lt 11, 1899*

Activity is Essential for Happiness

Men would not have been happy in Paradise without employment. The curse does not consist in labor, but in the sin of disobedience which has made man a convicted rebel. Man is not made for contemplation only, or for idleness, but for action. Activity is essential for happiness and for health. Our faculties are precious, God-given talents to be exercised. Everything in relation to man in the human machinery means action. The wheels of nature and of providence are not made to roll backward or to stand motionless. — *Lt 241, 1899*

Adam and Eve Worked in Paradise

God made Adam and Eve in paradise, and surrounded them with everything that was useful and lovely. God planted for them a beautiful garden. No herb, nor flower, nor tree was wanting, which might be for use and ornament. The Creator of man knew that this workmanship of his hands could not be happy without employment. Paradise delighted their souls, but this was not enough; they must have labor to call into exercise the wonderful organs of the body.

The Lord had made the organs for use. If happiness consisted in doing nothing, man in his state of holy innocence would have been left unemployed. But He who formed man, knew what would be for his best happiness; and He no sooner made him, than He gave him his appointed work.

— *RH, July 27, 1886*

Heaven is a Place of Activity

Heaven is a place of interested activity; yet to the weary and heavy-laden, those who have fought the good fight of faith, it will be a glorious rest; for the youth and vigor of immortality will be theirs, and they will no longer have to contend against sin and Satan. To these energetic workers a state of eternal indolence would be irksome. It would be no heaven to them. *—Ms 58, 1890*

Houses are Built on the New Earth

We are heirs of God, and joint heirs with Christ to riches that are imperishable. Christ said to his followers, "I go to prepare a place for you. And if I go and prepare a place for you, I will come again, and receive you unto myself, that where I am there ye may be also." John 14:3.

We shall be with Christ until the city of God comes to earth, and we take possession of our future home. We shall build houses and inhabit them, we shall plant vineyards, and eat the fruit of them. Do you not want a place in the earth made new? I want to be there. I want to see the King in his beauty. I want to see the One who died a victim on Calvary for my sin. When He comes in power and great glory, the admired of all them that believe, I do not want to be found under the bondage of sin. *—EA, p. 151*

Both Angels and Saints Work with God

God designed that all should be workers. The toiling beast of burden answers the purpose of its creation better than does the indolent man, who does not develop his physical and mental powers, but neglects the tasks which God has set for him to do. In the cause of reform the indolence of the many necessitates the overwork of the few earnest and devoted laborers. Because these are allowed to do the work of others in addition to their own, they often fail beneath the burden. But though the path of the Christian reformer may be hard and narrow, it is honored by the footprints of the Redeemer, and he is safe who follows in that sacred way.

The angels are workers; they are ministers of God to the children of men. Those slothful spirits who look forward to a heaven of inaction will be disappointed; for the economy of the Creator prepares no place for the gratification of sinful indolence. But to the weary and heavy-laden, rest is promised. *—ST, Oct. 9, 1884*

The Reward of Helping Jesus

It is the faithfulness, the loyalty to God, the loving service, that wins the divine approval. Every impulse of the Holy Spirit leading men to goodness and to God, is noted in the books of heaven, and in the day of God the workers through whom He has wrought will be commended.

They will enter into the joy of the Lord as they see in his kingdom those who have been redeemed through their instrumentality. And they are privileged to participate in his work there, because they have gained a fitness for it by participation in his work here. What we shall be in heaven is the reflection of what we are now in character and holy service. Christ said of Himself, "The Son of man came not to be ministered unto, but to minister." Matthew 20:28. This, his work on earth, is his work in heaven. And our reward for working with Christ in this world is the greater power and wider privilege of working with Him in the world to come. — *COL, p. 361*

Isaiah Saw the Saints Working

As the prophet beholds the redeemed dwelling in the City of God, free from sin and from all marks of the curse, in rapture he exclaims, "Rejoice ye with Jerusalem, and be glad with her, all ye that love her: rejoice for joy with her."

The prophet caught the sound of music there, and song, such music and song as, save in the visions of God, no mortal ear has heard or mind conceived. "The ransomed of the Lord shall return, and come to Zion with songs and everlasting joy upon their heads: they shall obtain joy and gladness, and sorrow and sighing shall flee away." "Joy and gladness shall be found therein, thanksgiving, and the voice of melody." "As well the singers as the players on instruments shall be there." "They shall lift up their voice, they shall sing for the majesty of the Lord." Isaiah 35:10; 51:3; Psalm 87:7; Isaiah 24:14.

In the earth made new, the redeemed will engage in the occupations and pleasures that brought happiness to Adam and Eve in the beginning. The Eden life will be lived, the life in garden and field. "They shall build houses, and inhabit them; and they shall plant vineyards, and eat the fruit of them. They shall not build, and another inhabit; they shall not plant, and another eat: for as the days of a tree are the days of my people, and mine elect shall long enjoy the work of their hands." Isaiah 65:21, 22. — *PK, pp. 729, 730*

B) Worship on Sabbath

Harps of Ten Strings
How can I... describe to you the glories of heaven, and the lovely angels singing and playing upon their harps of ten strings? —*Lt 3, 1851*

The Key to Eternal Salvation
It means eternal salvation to keep the Sabbath holy unto the Lord. God says: "Them that honor Me I will honor." 1 Samuel 2:30. —*6T, p. 356*

The Air is Filled with Praise
The melody of praise is the atmosphere of heaven; and when heaven comes in touch with the earth, there is music and song—"thanksgiving, and the voice of melody." Isaiah 51:3. —*Ed, p. 161*

God's Law Endures Forever
Through the eternal ages God's law will endure. Its principles are unchangeable. From these principles there can be no sinless swerving. And naught but blessing follows those who reverentially obey. —*ST, Jan. 25, 1905*

The Song of Heaven is Eternal Joy
All who enter heaven will learn the song of heaven, and that song is praise, thankfulness, and joy... In heaven, there are no frowns, no whining, no complaining, but joy, joy, wholly, continually, through eternal ages. —*Lt 1, 1882*

God's Law Endures for All Eternity
If God's commandments are to be binding for a thousand generations, it will take them into the kingdom of God, into the presence of God and his holy angels. This is an argument that cannot be controverted. The commandments of God will endure through all time and eternity. —*Ms 8, 1896*

Sabbath Worship Continues Forever
The Sabbath, which God declares to be the sign of the loyalty of his people, is placed in the bosom of the Decalogue. Its sanctity reaches into eternity, for God declares that from one new moon to another, and from one Sabbath to another, his subjects shall come up to worship before Him in the earth made new. Isaiah 66:23. —*Ms 63, 1897*

Sabbath Worship in the Holy City

The Lord pronounced his blessing upon all who keep holy the Sabbath day. His commandments are given to a thousand generations, and when that period is ended the redeemed host shall be in the city of God and observe the Sabbath there, and especially come up to worship God from Sabbath to Sabbath and from one new moon to another. —Ms 173, 1897

The Highest Angel Leads the Singing

Only the pure and undefiled, only those who are without spot or wrinkle or any such thing will enter the city of God, when the gates are swung back and the nation that has kept the truth enters in. There the harp will be placed in the hand of the overcomer, and the song of redemption through Christ will be led by heaven's highest angel. You may have the privilege of joining that song and singing in triumph the glory of God. —Ms 95, 1909

John Heard the Music of the Saints

John was strengthened to live in the presence of his glorified Lord. Then before his wondering vision were opened the glories of heaven. He was permitted to see the throne of God and, looking beyond the conflicts of earth, to behold the white-robed throng of the redeemed. He heard the music of the heavenly angels and the triumphant songs of those who had overcome by the blood of the Lamb and the word of their testimony. —AA, p. 582

The Saints Sing with the Holy Angels

Then I was pointed to the glory of heaven, to the treasure laid up for the faithful. Everything was lovely and glorious. The angels would sing a lovely song, then they would cease singing and take their crowns from their heads and cast them glittering at the feet of the lovely Jesus, and with melodious voices cry, "Glory, Alleluia!"

I joined with them in their songs of praise and honor to the Lamb, and every time I opened my mouth to praise Him, I felt an unutterable sense of the glory that surrounded me. It was a far more, an exceeding and eternal weight of glory. Said the angel, "The little remnant who love God and keep his commandments and are faithful to the end will enjoy this glory and ever be in the presence of Jesus and sing with the holy angels." —EW, p. 66

The Sabbath is Fully Understood

I saw that we sensed and realized but little of the importance of the Sabbath... But we shall not see the Sabbath in all its glory and importance until the covenant of peace is made with us at the voice of God, and the pearly gates of the New Jerusalem are thrown open and swing back on their glittering hinges, and the glad and joyful voice of the lovely Jesus is heard, richer than any music that ever fell on mortal ear, bidding us to enter, that we had a perfect right in the city for we had kept the commandments of God, and heaven, sweet heaven is our home for we have kept the commandments of God. —*Lt 3, 1851*

The Sabbath is a Eternal Sign

The Sabbath was not for Israel merely, but for the world. It had been made known to man in Eden, and, like the other precepts of the Decalogue, it is of imperishable obligation. Of that law of which the fourth commandment forms a part, Christ declares, "Till heaven and earth pass, one jot or one tittle shall in nowise pass from the law." So long as the heavens and the earth endure, the Sabbath will continue as a sign of the Creator's power.

And when Eden shall bloom on earth again, God's holy rest day will be honored by all beneath the sun. "From one Sabbath to another" the inhabitants of the glorified New Earth shall go up "to worship before Me, saith the Lord." Matthew 5:18; Isaiah 66:23. —*DA, p. 283*

Heaven's Music is Rich and Melodious

I have been shown the order, the perfect order, of heaven, and have been enraptured as I listened to the perfect music there. After coming out of vision, the singing here has sounded very harsh and discordant. I have seen companies of angels, who stood in a hollow square, everyone having a harp of gold. At the end of the harp was an instrument to turn to set the harp or change the tunes. Their fingers did not sweep over the strings carelessly, but they touched different strings to produce different sounds.

There is one angel who always leads, who first touches the harp and strikes the note, then all join in the rich, perfect music of heaven. It cannot be described. It is melody, heavenly, divine, while from every countenance beams the image of Jesus, shining with glory unspeakable. —*1T, p. 146*

Angels Join the Singing

Angels have far more to do with the human family than many suppose. "Are they not all ministering spirits, sent forth to minister to those who shall be heirs of salvation?" Holy angels will join in the song of the redeemed. Though they cannot sing from experimental knowledge, "He hath washed us in his own blood, and redeemed us unto God," yet they understand the great peril from which the people of God have been saved. Were they not sent to lift up for them a standard against the enemy? They can fully sympathize with the glowing ecstasy of those who have overcome by the blood of the Lamb and the word of their testimony. —*Lt 79, 1900*

Immortal Tongues Praise God

Praise God here, and then you will be fitted to join the heavenly choir when you enter the city of God. Then you can cast your glittering crowns at the feet of Jesus, take your golden harps, and fill all heaven with melody. We shall praise Him with an immortal tongue. Do you not want to be there? We must get an education here that will enable us to live with God through the eternal ages. The education we begin here will be perfected in heaven. We will only just enter a higher grade. We sit in heavenly places with Christ Jesus, He reveals Himself to us, and we learn the mystery of the incarnation of Christ, and the great sacrifice which He made in our behalf. —*Ms 16, 1895*

Christ Established the Sabbath

The law of God is immutable in its character, for "it is easier for heaven and earth to pass, than for one tittle of the law to fail." The law of God is a revelation of the divine will, a transcript of the divine character, and must forever endure. Not one command has been annulled; not a jot or a tittle of the law has been changed. The Psalmist says, "Forever, O Lord, thy word is settled in heaven." "All his commandments are sure. They stand fast forever and ever." ...

The claim so often put forth that Christ changed the Sabbath is disproved by his own words. In the sermon on the mount He said: "Think not that I am come to destroy the law, or the prophets; I am not come to destroy, but to fulfill. For verily I say unto you, Till heaven and earth pass, one jot or one tittle shall in nowise pass from the law, till all be fulfilled..." —*ST, Nov. 12, 1894*

The Saints Meet Once a Week

God teaches that we should assemble in his house to cultivate the attributes of perfect love. This will fit the dwellers of earth for the mansions that Christ has gone to prepare for all who love Him. There they will assemble in the sanctuary from Sabbath to Sabbath, from one new moon to another, to unite in loftiest strains of song, in praise and thanksgiving to Him who sits upon the throne, and to the Lamb for ever and ever. —*6T, p. 368*

Sabbath is for Rest and Rejoicing

Glorious to the eyes of heavenly beings was the promise of the future. A restored creation, a redeemed race, that having conquered sin could never fall—this, the result to flow from Christ's completed work, God and angels saw. With this scene the day upon which Jesus rested is forever linked. For "His work is perfect;" and "whatsoever God doeth, it shall be forever."

When there shall be a "restitution of all things, which God hath spoken by the mouth of all his holy prophets since the world began" (Acts 3:21), the creation Sabbath, the day on which Jesus lay at rest in Joseph's tomb, will still be a day of rest and rejoicing. Heaven and earth will unite in praise, as "from one Sabbath to another" (Isaiah 66:23) the nations of the saved shall bow in joyful worship to God and the Lamb. —*DA, p. 769*

The Sabbath is Eternally Honored

I was shown that the law of God would stand fast forever, and exist in the New Earth to all eternity. At the creation, when the foundations of the earth were laid, the sons of God looked with admiration upon the work of the Creator, and all the heavenly host shouted for joy. It was then that the foundation of the Sabbath was laid. At the close of the six days of creation, God rested on the seventh day from all his work which He had made; and He blessed the seventh day and sanctified it, because that in it He had rested from all his work.

The Sabbath was instituted in Eden before the fall, and was observed by Adam and Eve, and all the heavenly host. God rested on the seventh day, and blessed and hallowed it. I saw that the Sabbath never will be done away; but that the redeemed saints, and all the angelic host, will observe it in honor of the great Creator to all eternity. —*EW, p. 217*

Glorify the Name of God

Shall we not arise to our high privilege? Shall we not labor as we have never before? Shall we not seek as did Jacob, for the blessing, saying, "I will not let thee go except thou bless me?" Oh, what a depth of love, what fullness and completeness there is in Christ Jesus. It is the purpose of God to exceed all our highest imaginations by glorifying his name, through the endless ages of eternity, in the redemption and glorification of the sons and daughters of God. — *Lt 42, 1898*

Members of the Heavenly Choir

Oh, let it be seen in the world that He has given you tongues and utterances, and you will praise Him with your hearts and souls and voices. You are then making melody to God in your hearts, and when the call comes, "Child, come up higher," when you enter the City of God through the gates that will sweep back on their glittering hinges, you will know just where to take up the immortal song. You will hear the music and know that the warfare is accomplished. And you will hear the voice of the Master, "Welcome thou into the joy of thy Lord. Thou hast been faithful over a few things; I will make you ruler over many things." You will know just where to begin that song. You learned it here.

You are not to groan and complain, but be learners in the school of Christ of his meekness and lowliness. We want to bear his yoke. He says that it is easy and that his burden is light. And if you have found it so, you know just how to catch the strains as the angel leads the heavenly choir. You will take the golden harp and fill all heaven with rich music to the Lamb. "Worthy, worthy is the Lamb that was slain for our transgression." You will cast your glittering crowns at his feet.

Then have faith and patience and hope and you will gain the richest experience. You will be a light to the world and they, seeing your good works, will glorify your Father which is in heaven. I want to meet you among the throng in the kingdom of glory. I want to see your faces all illuminated with the glory of God. I want them to shine with the image of Jesus reflected in you. All your sorrows will be ended and you will be free indeed. No more sorrow and sin, but it will be joy, eternal joy, through the eternal ages.

— *Ms 16, 1894*

C) Travel the Universe

A Vision of Two Other Worlds

The Lord has given me a view of other worlds. Wings were given me, and an angel attended me from the city to a place that was bright and glorious. The grass of the place was living green, and the birds there warbled a sweet song. The inhabitants of the place were of all sizes; they were noble, majestic, and lovely. They bore the express image of Jesus, and their countenances beamed with holy joy, expressive of the freedom and happiness of the place. I asked one of them why they were so much lovelier than those on the earth. The reply was, "We have lived in strict obedience to the commandments of God, and have not fallen by disobedience, like those on the earth."

Then I saw two trees, one looked much like the tree of life in the city. The fruit of both looked beautiful, but of one they could not eat. They had power to eat of both, but were forbidden to eat of one. Then my attending angel said to me, "None in this place have tasted of the forbidden tree; but if they should eat, they would fall."

Then I was taken to a world which had seven moons. There I saw good old Enoch, who had been translated. On his right arm he bore a glorious palm, and on each leaf was written "Victory." Around his head was a dazzling white wreath, and leaves on the wreath, and in the middle of each leaf was written "Purity," and around the wreath were stones of various colors, that shone brighter than the stars, and cast a reflection upon the letters and magnified them. On the back part of his head was a bow that confined the wreath, and upon the bow was written "Holiness."

Above the wreath was a lovely crown that shone brighter than the sun. I asked him if this was the place he was taken to from the earth. He said, "It is not; the city is my home, and I have come to visit this place." He moved about the place as if perfectly at home.

I begged of my attending angel to let me remain in that place. I could not bear the thought of coming back to this dark world again. Then the angel said, "You must go back, and if you are faithful, you, with the 144,000, shall have the privilege of visiting all the worlds and viewing the handiwork of God." —*EW, p. 39*

Travel from Planet to Planet

Oh that all might see the importance of carefully studying the Scriptures! Many seem to have the idea that this world and the heavenly mansions constitute the universe of God. Not so. The redeemed throng will range from world to world, and much of their time will be employed in searching out the mysteries of redemption. And throughout the whole stretch of eternity, this subject will be continually opening to their minds. The privileges of those who overcome by the blood of the Lamb and the word of their testimony are beyond comprehension. — *RH, Mar. 9, 1886*

The Redeemed Fly to Unfallen Worlds

All the treasures of the universe will be open to the study of God's redeemed. Unfettered by mortality, they wing their tireless flight to worlds afar—worlds that thrilled with sorrow at the spectacle of human woe and rang with songs of gladness at the tidings of a ransomed soul. With unutterable delight the children of earth enter into the joy and the wisdom of unfallen beings. They share the treasures of knowledge and understanding gained through ages upon ages in contemplation of God's handiwork. With undimmed vision they gaze upon the glory of creation—suns and stars and systems, all in their appointed order circling the throne of Deity. Upon all things, from the least to the greatest, the Creator's name is written, and in all are the riches of his power displayed. — *GC, p. 677*

Discussion Questions

1. Why will the happiness of the saints in heaven be perfect?

2. What will it be like to have a permanent home and never move again?

3. How will employment on the new earth differ from your current job?

4. Why will the Sabbath be fully understood when the saints worship together in the New Jerusalem?

5. What will be the purpose of flying across the universe?

— 35 —

The School of Christ

"For now we see through a glass, darkly; but then face to face: now I know in part; but then shall I know even as also I am known." — 1 Corinthians 13:12

| Deut. 29:29 | Prov. 1:5-7 | Prov. 9:9 | Matt. 4:4 | Rom. 16:25 | 1 Cor. 13:8-12 |
| Psalm 19:1, 2 | Prov. 4:1-2 | Isa. 2:2, 3 | John 3:16 | 1 Cor. 2:7, 8 | 1 John 3:1 |

A) Taught by Jesus

Never a Graduation

We talk of graduating from our colleges, but there is no graduation from the school of Christ. Throughout the ceaseless ages of eternity Christians will be learners in this school. —*Lt 6, 1885*

Study the Bible Forever

Time is too short for us to undertake to reveal all that might be opened to view. Eternity will be required for us to know all the length and breadth, the depth and height, of the Scriptures. —*6T, p. 58*

From Defeats to Blessings

In the future life the mysteries that here have annoyed and disappointed us will be made plain. We shall see that our seemingly unanswered prayers and disappointed hopes have been among our greatest blessings. —*MH, p. 474*

All Perplexities are Made Plain

All the perplexities of life's experience will then be made plain. Where to us have appeared only confusion and disappointment, broken purposes and thwarted plans, will be seen a grand, overruling, victorious purpose, a divine harmony. —*Ed, p. 305*

Dark Scriptures are Explained

All true knowledge obtained in this life will be retained by us in heaven. There our education is to be perfected. In the New Earth Christ will lead us by the side of the living waters and explain the dark passages of Scripture that we have never been able to understand. All his providences will then be made plain. — *Ms 102, 1904*

Continually Advance in Wisdom

In the school of Christ, students never graduate. Among the pupils are both the old and the young. Those who give heed to the instructions of the Divine Teacher, constantly advance in wisdom, refinement, and nobility of soul, and thus they are prepared to enter that higher school, where advancement will continue throughout eternity. — *RH, July 11, 1882*

The Eleventh Hour Convert

Some among the redeemed will have laid hold of Christ in the last hours of life, and in heaven instruction will be given to these, who, when they died, did not understand perfectly the plan of salvation. Christ will lead the redeemed one beside the river of life and will open to them that which while on this earth they could not understand. — *Lt 203, 1905*

The Burdens God Bore are Revealed

Our heavenly Father has the power of turning the flinty rock into life-giving and refreshing streams. We shall never know, until we are face to face with God, when we shall see as we are seen, and know as we are known, how many burdens He has borne for us, and how many burdens He would have been glad to bear if, with childlike faith, we had brought them to Him.

— *ST, Sept. 10, 1896*

Jesus Teaches the Heavenly School

Heaven is a school; its field of study, the universe; its teacher, the Infinite One. A branch of this school was established in Eden; and, the plan of redemption accomplished, education will again be taken up in the Eden school... Between the school established in Eden at the beginning and the school of the hereafter there lies the whole compass of this world's history— the history of human transgression and suffering, of divine sacrifice, and of victory over death and sin. — *Ed, pp. 301, 302*

Graduate to the Heavenly School

He who makes advancement in the school of Christ here below will at last pass through the pearly gates of the city of God, to enter the higher school, there to receive instruction from the divine Teacher. "Eye hath not seen, nor ear heard, neither have entered into the heart of man, the things which God hath prepared for them that love Him." — *ST, June 21, 1905*

Eternity will Reveal Biblical Wisdom

The Bible is the revelation of God to our world, telling us of the character we must have in order to reach the paradise of God. We are to esteem it as God's disclosure to us of eternal things, the things of most consequence for us to know. By the world it is thrown aside, as if the perusal of it were sufficient, but a thousand years of research would not exhaust the hidden treasure it contains. Eternity alone will disclose the wisdom of this book. The jewels buried in it are inexhaustible, for it is the wisdom of an infinite mind.

— *Ms 22, 1895*

Christ Unfolds the Mysteries of Nature

In the world to come, Christ will lead the redeemed beside the river of life, and will teach them wonderful lessons of truth. He will unfold to them the mysteries of nature. They will see that a Master-Hand holds the worlds in position. They will behold the skill displayed by the great Artist in coloring the flowers of the field, and will learn of the purposes of the merciful Father, who dispenses every ray of light, and with the holy angels the redeemed will acknowledge in songs of grateful praise God's supreme love to an unthankful world. — *RH, Jan. 3, 1907*

Mysterious Matters are Explained

We are not to let our imaginations work upon matters that God has not revealed to us. We are to plant our feet upon the Word of the living God, and when we reach the kingdom of heaven, we shall understand the mysteries of that country. Christ will lead us beside the river of life and open to our minds the truths of his Word. He will unfold to us mysteries that we cannot now grasp. In the school above we shall obtain the higher education. Till then we must be content to leave with God the mysteries that we cannot comprehend. — *Ms 17, 1903*

Explore Divine Mysteries

The more we know of his truth, the more we shall desire to know. There will be an eternity before us, in which to explore the mysteries of God. It will be the delight of our Lord to lead us in green pastures, beside flowing waters, and unfold to the redeemed the mysteries of redemption. — *ST, Apr. 8, 1889*

Attend Classes at the Tree of Life

Every family that finds entrance to the city of God will have been faithful workers in their earthly homes, fulfilling the responsibilities that Christ has laid upon them. There Christ the heavenly Teacher will lead his people to the tree of life that grows on either side of the river of life, and He will explain to them the truths they could not in this life understand. In that future life his people will gain the higher education in its completeness. — *Ms 31, 1909*

Learn How to Glorify God's Name

The truths contained in the Scriptures are grand, elevating, ennobling, and uplifting. If the lost image of God is restored during probationary time, these truths must be cherished. They are graced with such simplicity that they could not have originated in any human mind. A Sower from a higher world went forth to sow the seeds of truth. This higher education alone is able to prepare students for the highest life—the highest grade in the highest school, where, with Christ and God as teachers, we shall through the ceaseless ages of eternity learn how best to magnify and glorify God's name. — *EA, p. 262*

Christ Educates the Faithful

Take time to think of the pleasures that await those who are faithful. When this earthly pilgrimage is ended, you will have the Saviour's presence with you continually. He will lead you to behold the beautiful scenes of the earth made new. He will talk to you about the things most precious, and will teach you a fuller knowledge of his way. The education you gain in the things of God in this life will not end here. All that you gain you will take with you to the future life; and Christ, as your teacher, will continue the work of education through the eternal ages. And your love for Him will broaden and deepen as you realize more fully all that his sacrifice has purchased for you.

— YI, Apr. 28, 1908

The Saints Continually Improve

A character formed according to the divine likeness is the only treasure that we can take from this world to the next. Those who are under the instruction of Christ in this world will take every divine attainment with them to the heavenly mansions. And in heaven we are continually to improve.

How important, then, is the development of character in this life. The heavenly intelligences will work with the human agent who seeks with determined faith that perfection of character which will reach out to perfection in action. To everyone engaged in this work Christ says, "I am at your right hand to help you." — *COL, p. 332*

Jesus is Eager to Reveal Wonders

Jesus is waiting with longing desire to open before his people the glory that will attend his Second Advent, and to carry them forward to a contemplation of the landscapes of bliss. There are wonders to be revealed. A long lifetime of prayer and research will leave much unexplored and unexplained. But what we know not now will be revealed hereafter. The work of instruction begun here will be carried on to all eternity. The Lamb, as He leads the hosts of the redeemed to the Fountain of living waters, will impart rich stores of knowledge; He will unravel mysteries in the works and providence of God that have never before been understood. — *5T, p. 301*

Disobedience Shut the Door to Wisdom

In God's Word is found wisdom unquestionable, inexhaustible, wisdom that did not originate in finite minds, but in the Infinite mind. There is no time now to fill minds with false precepts and ideas of what is called higher education. There can be no higher education than that which comes from the Author of truth.

Disobedience has closed the door to a vast amount of knowledge that might have been gained from the Word of God. In eternity we shall learn that which, if we had received the enlightenment that it was possible for us to obtain here, would have opened our understanding. And understanding means obedience to all God's commandments. The plan of God's government would have been understood. The heavenly world would have opened its chambers of grace and glory for exploration. — *Ms 45, 1898*

Learn to Truly Know Jesus

I love Jesus now; and I want to know more and more of Him. I have only begun to know Him, but there is an eternity before us in which there will be revealings of his glory, and we shall become better and better acquainted with our divine Lord, and have a more comprehensive knowledge of Him.

— RH, Feb. 26, 1889

Find Out the Reason for Trials

Long have we waited for our Saviour's return. But nonetheless sure is the promise. Soon we shall be in our promised home. There Jesus will lead us beside the living stream flowing from the throne of God and will explain to us the dark providences through which on this earth He brought us in order to perfect our characters. There we shall behold with undimmed vision the beauties of Eden restored. Casting at the feet of the Redeemer the crowns that He has placed on our heads, and touching our golden harps, we shall fill all heaven with praise to Him that sitteth on the throne. *— 8T, p. 254*

An Eternity for Bible Truths to Unfold

God has worlds upon worlds that are obedient to his law. These worlds are conducted with reference to the glory of the Creator. As these inhabitants see the great price that has been paid to ransom man, they are filled with amazement. With intense interest they watch the controversy between Christ and Satan; and as this controversy progresses, and the glory of God shines brighter and brighter, they give praise to God.

And yet, because finite men can discern a little of God's marvelous power, they take the glory that belongs to the Creator. Oh, that the veil could be removed, and they could see beyond their wisdom! Every mouth would cease its boasting, and men would see the greatness of the plans of God.

God intends that to the earnest seeker the truths of his word shall be ever unfolding. The mysteries it contains are not such because God has sought to conceal truth; the inability to understand is not in his purpose, but in our inability to understand. But it is impossible for any human mind to exhaust even one truth or promise of the Bible. One catches the glory from one point of view, and another from another point; yet we can discern only gleamings. The full radiance is beyond our vision. It will take eternity to unfold it all.

— SW, Apr. 23, 1907

Mysteries Fade in Light from God

The education begun here will not be completed in this life; it will be going forward throughout eternity, ever progressing, never completed. Day by day the wonderful works of God, the evidences of his miraculous power in creating and sustaining the universe, will open before the mind in new beauty. In the light that shines from the throne, mysteries will disappear, and the soul will be filled with astonishment at the simplicity of the things that were never before comprehended. Now we see through a glass, darkly; but then face to face; now we know in part; but then shall we know even as also we are known.

—8T, p. 328

The Greatest Questions are Answered

How much that is acknowledged to be truth is mysterious and unexplainable to the human mind! How dark seem the dispensations of providence! What necessity there is for implicit faith and trust in God's moral government! We are ready to say with Paul, "How unsearchable are his judgments, and his ways past finding out!"

We are not now sufficiently advanced in spiritual attainments to comprehend the mysteries of God. But when we shall compose the family of heaven, these mysteries will be unfolded before us. Of the members of that family John writes: "They shall hunger no more, neither thirst any more; neither shall the sun light on them, nor any heat. For the Lamb which is in the midst of the throne shall feed them, and shall lead them unto living fountains of waters; and God shall wipe away all tears from their eyes." "And they shall see his face; and his name shall be in their foreheads."

Then much will be revealed in explanation of matters upon which God now keeps silence because we have not gathered up and appreciated that which has been made known of the eternal mysteries. The ways of providence will be made clear; the mysteries of grace through Christ will be unfolded. That which the mind cannot now grasp, which is hard to be understood, will be explained. We shall see order in that which has seemed unexplainable; wisdom in everything withheld; goodness and gracious mercy in everything imparted. Truth will be unfolded to the mind free from obscurity, in a single line, and its brightness will be endurable. The heart will be made to sing for joy. Controversies will be forever ended, and all difficulties will be solved.

—ST, Mar. 25, 1897

B) The Ministry of Angels

Angels Came to the Rescue

Shall we obtain strength from God, and win victory after victory, or shall we try in our own strength, and at last fall back defeated, worn out by vain effort? Victory is sure when self is surrendered to God. The Lord is not slack concerning his promise. He has given his angels charge over his children. Hereafter the witness will be heard, "My feet had well-nigh slipped, but the Lord upheld me." His way was best—to come in trial to the one He wished to help. — *ST, May 20, 1903*

The Angel Ministry is Explained

Not until the providences of God are seen in the light of eternity shall we understand what we owe to the care and interposition of his angels. Celestial beings have taken an active part in the affairs of men. They have appeared in garments that shone as the lightning; they have come as men, in the garb of wayfarers. They have accepted the hospitalities of human homes; they have acted as guides to benighted travelers. They have thwarted the spoiler's purpose and turned aside the stroke of the destroyer.

Though the rulers of this world know it not, yet often in their councils angels have been spokesmen. Human eyes have looked upon them. Human ears have listened to their appeals. In the council hall the court of justice, heavenly messengers have pleaded the cause of the persecuted and oppressed. They have defeated purposes and arrested evils that would have brought wrong and suffering to God's children. To the students in the heavenly school, all this will be unfolded.

Every redeemed one will understand the ministry of angels in his own life. The angel who was his guardian from his earliest moment; the angel who watched his steps, and covered his head in the day of peril; the angel who was with him in the valley of the shadow of death, who marked his resting place, who was the first to greet him in the resurrection morning—what will it be to hold converse with him, and to learn the history of divine interposition in the individual life, of heavenly co-operation in every work for humanity!

— Ed, pp. 304, 305

We Had Strong Helpers

In the future life we shall understand things that here greatly perplex us. We shall realize how strong a helper we had, and how angels of God were commissioned to guard us as we followed the counsel of the Word of God. To all who receive Him, Christ will give power to become the sons of God.

—RH, June 9, 1910

God's Providence is Revealed

In all ages, angels have been near to Christ's faithful followers. The vast confederacy of evil is arrayed against all who would overcome; but Christ would have us look to the things which are not seen, to the armies of heaven encamped about all who love God, to deliver them. From what dangers, seen and unseen, we have been preserved through the interposition of the angels, we shall never know, until in the light of eternity we see the providences of God. Then we shall know that the whole family of heaven was interested in the family here below, and that messengers from the throne of God attended our steps from day to day. *—DA, p. 240*

C) The Science of Redemption

Study Redemption for Eternity

When we are receiving a training, as did Moses in the school of Christ, what shall we learn?—to become puffed up?—to have an exalted opinion of ourselves?—No, indeed. The more we learn in this school, the more we shall advance in meekness and lowliness of mind. We are not to feel that we have learned everything worth knowing. We should put to the best use the talents God has given us, that when we are changed from mortality to immortality, we shall not leave behind that which we have attained, but may take it with us to the other side.

Throughout the ceaseless ages of eternity, Christ and his work of redemption will be the theme of our study. Let none of us think that we are ready to graduate. There are new lessons for us to learn every day. As did Moses, we may say, "Show us thy glory," and by living faith grasp the arm of power. *—Ms 36, 1885*

Jesus is Forever Bound to Men

By his life and his death, Christ has achieved even more than recovery from the ruin wrought through sin. It was Satan's purpose to bring about an eternal separation between God and man; but in Christ we become more closely united to God than if we had never fallen. In taking our nature, the Saviour has bound Himself to humanity by a tie that is never to be broken. Through the eternal ages He is linked with us... Christ is our brother. Heaven is enshrined in humanity, and humanity is enfolded in the bosom of Infinite love... By love's self-sacrifice, the inhabitants of earth and heaven are bound to their Creator in bonds of indissoluble union. —*RH, Feb. 25, 1915*

Imagine Christ's Amazing Love

I saw the beauty of heaven. I heard the angels sing their rapturous songs, ascribing praise, honor, and glory to Jesus. I could then realize something of the wondrous love of the Son of God. He left all the glory, all the honor which He had in heaven, and was so interested for our salvation that He patiently and meekly bore every indignity and slight which man could heap upon Him. He was wounded, smitten, and bruised; He was stretched on Calvary's cross and suffered the most agonizing death to save us from death, that we might be washed in his blood and be raised up to live with Him in the mansions He is preparing for us, to enjoy the light and glory of heaven, to hear the angels sing, and to sing with them. —*1T, p. 123*

Redemption is Love Inexpressible

He was eternally rich, yet for our sakes He became poor, that we through his poverty might be made rich. He was clothed with light and glory, and was surrounded with hosts of heavenly angels waiting to execute his commands. Yet He put on our nature and came to sojourn among sinful mortals. Here is love that no language can express. It passes knowledge.

Great is the mystery of godliness. Our souls should be enlivened, elevated, and enraptured with the theme of the love of the Father and the Son to man. The followers of Christ should here learn to reflect in some degree that mysterious love preparatory to joining all the redeemed in ascribing "blessing, and honor, and glory, and power, ... unto Him that sitteth upon the throne, and unto the Lamb for ever and ever." —*2T, p. 215*

God's Love for a Hateful World

The plan of salvation had been laid before the creation of the earth; for Christ is "the Lamb slain from the foundation of the world" (Revelation 13:8); yet it was a struggle, even with the King of the universe, to yield up his Son to die for the guilty race… Oh, the mystery of redemption! The love of God for a world that did not love Him! Who can know the depths of that love which "passeth knowledge?" Through endless ages immortal minds, seeking to comprehend the mystery of that incomprehensible love, will wonder and adore. — *PP, p. 63*

The Universe Focuses on the Cross

The attention of all the inhabitants of all worlds will be directed to the cross of Christ, around which will cluster the exceeding and eternal weight of glory. The imagination becomes exhausted in its stretch to comprehend the wonderful work of redemption. The plan of salvation is too high to be fully reached by human thought. It is too grand to be fully embraced by finite comprehension. The apostle says, "Eye hath not seen, nor ear heard, neither have entered into the heart of man, the things which God hath prepared for them that love Him." Can we wonder that heaven is amazed because men act as though the gift of God were valueless? What will be the eternal loss of those who reject so great a salvation, offered freely through the merits of God's only-begotten and well-beloved Son! — *ST, Dec. 30, 1889*

Forgiveness Leads to Great Gratitude

In all ages the Saviour's chosen have been educated and disciplined in the school of trial. They walked in narrow paths on earth; they were purified in the furnace of affliction. For Jesus' sake they endured opposition, hatred, calumny. They followed Him through conflicts sore; they endured self-denial and experienced bitter disappointments. By their own painful experience they learned the evil of sin, its power, its guilt, its woe; and they look upon it with abhorrence. A sense of the infinite sacrifice made for its cure humbles them in their own sight and fills their hearts with gratitude and praise which those who have never fallen cannot appreciate. They love much because they have been forgiven much. Having been partakers of Christ's sufferings, they are fitted to be partakers with Him of his glory. — *GC, p. 649*

The Incentives of Eternity

Let us contemplate the amazing sacrifice that has been made for us! Let us try to appreciate the labor and energy that heaven is expending to reclaim the lost, and bring them back to the Father's house. Motives stronger, and agencies more powerful, could never be brought into operation; the exceeding rewards for right-doing, the enjoyment of heaven, the society of the angels, the communion and love of God and his Son, the elevation and extension of all our powers throughout eternal ages—are these not mighty incentives and encouragements to urge us to give the heart's loving service to our Creator and Redeemer? — *SC, p. 21*

The Years Bring Richer Revelations

The years of eternity, as they roll, will bring richer and still more glorious revelations of God and of Christ. As knowledge is progressive, so will love, reverence, and happiness increase. The more men learn of God, the greater will be their admiration of his character. As Jesus opens before them the riches of redemption and the amazing achievements in the great controversy with Satan, the hearts of the ransomed thrill with more fervent devotion, and with more rapturous joy they sweep the harps of gold; and ten thousand times ten thousand and thousands of thousands of voices unite to swell the mighty chorus of praise. — *GC, p. 678*

There is Much More Knowledge Available

Human beings would have been altogether different from what they now are in form, in speech, in song, for by exploring the mines of truth, they would have been ennobled. The mystery of redemption, the knowledge of God, and of Jesus Christ in his mediatorial character, the incarnation of Christ our Redeemer, his atoning sacrifice, would not be, as they now are, vague in our mind. They would have been, not only better understood, but altogether more highly appreciated.

These themes will employ the hearts and minds and tongues of the redeemed through the everlasting ages, and new developments of them will be opened up, which Christ longed to open to his disciples, but which they did not have faith to seek and grasp. Forever and ever, new views of the perfection and glory of Christ will appear. — *Ms 45, 1898*

Contemplate Calvary Forever

The seed buried in the ground produces fruit, and in their turn the seeds of this fruit are planted. Thus the harvest is multiplied. So the death of Christ on the cross of Calvary will bear fruit unto eternal life. The contemplation of this sacrifice will be the glory of those who, as the fruit of it, will live through the eternal ages. — *ST, July 1, 1897*

Spend Eternity Studying Jesus

In the Scriptures we read of his incarnation, his teaching, his miracles, his death, and his resurrection. The effort to understand these wonderful subjects puts to the tax the highest powers of the mind, and then there is an infinity beyond which can not be exhausted. The oftener the mind is called to this study, the stronger and clearer it will become. In the daily life will be revealed the mysteries of godliness, which may be experienced, but can not be explained. Throughout the ceaseless ages of eternity the redeemed will study these subjects, ever gaining from them a deeper and clearer knowledge of God and of Christ. — *ST, Apr. 26, 1905*

The Science of Salvation is Christ's Focus

Christ intercedes in behalf of those who receive Him. To them He gives power by virtue of his own merits, to become members of the royal family—children of the heavenly King. And the Father demonstrates his infinite love for Christ, who paid our ransom by his blood, by receiving and welcoming Christ's friends as his friends. He is satisfied with the atonement made. He is glorified by the incarnation, the life, death, and meditation of his Son.

This is the science of salvation, the science of true godliness, the true science of all education which the students can take with them to the higher grade—the courts above. That which heaven deems important in all education is that kind of knowledge which has been revealed from eternity and which enters into the purposes of God, expressing his mind and revealing his glory. To obtain this education is the study of the angels of God and of all the heavenly intelligences. The themes which should absorb our attention in this life, and which will demand study throughout the eternal ages, are so momentous that they not only supersede the discoveries of man, but engross the undivided attention of the only begotten Son of God. — *EA, p. 260*

The Unsearchable Riches of Jesus

Great is the reward in heaven of those who are witnesses for Christ through persecution and reproach. While the people are looking for earthly good, Jesus points them to a heavenly reward. But He does not place it all in the future life; it begins here. The Lord appeared of old time to Abraham and said, "I am thy shield, and thy exceeding great reward." Genesis 15:1.

This is the reward of all who follow Christ. Jehovah Immanuel—He "in whom are hid all the treasures of wisdom and knowledge," in whom dwells "all the fullness of the Godhead bodily"—to be brought into sympathy with Him, to know Him, to possess Him, as the heart opens more and more to receive his attributes; to know his love and power, to possess the unsearchable riches of Christ, to comprehend more and more "what is the breadth, and length, and depth, and height; and to know the love of Christ, which passeth knowledge, that ye might be filled with all the fullness of God" (Ephesians 3:18, 19)—"this is the heritage of the servants of the Lord, and their righteousness is of Me, saith the Lord." Isaiah 54:17. —*MB, p. 34*

Christ Suffered Greatly for Our Sake

You never can begin to suffer nor to understand the depth and breadth of the humiliation that our Saviour went through. There is no one of us that can ever go through that. And then the priests and the rulers stood, while He was hanging in agony on the cross, saying "Oh, if you are the Son of man, come down, and we will believe on you." But no, no, He was to bear all this suffering in our behalf, that no one that lives on the face of the earth can say He never suffered as I suffered; He doesn't know how to suffer; He doesn't know how to pity us; for He never suffered as I suffered.

But He has gone through every phase of temptation, every phase of suffering, and I want you to have sympathy with my Lord. I want you to have that love for Him that you will try to imitate his life of character; because He wants you. He wants to put a crown of glory on your heads. He wants to throw back the gates of the city of God, that all the nations that have kept the truth may enter in. He pronounces his blessing upon them as they enter in, and they cast at his feet their glittering crowns that He has placed upon their heads, and they touch the golden harps, and fill all heaven with rich music and with songs to the Lamb. —*Ms 189, 1903*

The Lesson Book of the Universe

Our little world is the lesson book of the universe. God's wonderful purpose of grace, the mystery of redeeming love, is the theme into which "angels desire to look," and it will be their study throughout endless ages. Both the redeemed and the unfallen beings will find in the cross of Christ their science and their song. It will be seen that the glory shining in the face of Jesus is the glory of self-sacrificing love.

In the light from Calvary it will be seen that the law of self-renouncing love is the law of life for earth and heaven; that the love which "seeketh not her own" has its source in the heart of God; and that in the meek and lowly One is manifested the character of Him who dwelleth in the light which no man can approach unto. — *DA, p. 19*

The Greatest Subject to Contemplate

The plan of salvation, making manifest the justice and love of God, provides an eternal safeguard against defection in unfallen worlds, as well as among those who shall be redeemed by the blood of the Lamb. Our only hope is perfect trust in the blood of Him who can save to the uttermost all that come unto God by Him. The death of Christ on the cross of Calvary is our only hope in this world, and it will be our theme in the world to come. Oh, we do not comprehend the value of the atonement! If we did, we would talk more about it. The gift of God in his beloved Son was the expression of an incomprehensible love. It was the utmost that God could do to preserve the honor of his law, and still save the transgressor.

Why should man not study the theme of redemption? It is the greatest subject that can engage the human mind. If men would contemplate the love of Christ, displayed in the cross, their faith would be strengthened to appropriate the merits of his shed blood, and they would be cleansed and saved from sin. There are many who will be lost, because they depend on legal religion, or mere repentance for sin. But repentance for sin alone cannot work the salvation of any soul. Man cannot be saved by his own works. Without Christ it is impossible for him to render perfect obedience to the law of God; and heaven can never be gained by an imperfect obedience; for this would place all heaven in jeopardy, and make possible a second rebellion.

— *ST, Dec. 30, 1889*

Eternity Reveals Christ's Love

Christ loved the human race, and this love impelled Him to sacrifice his own happiness for the good of others. He took upon Himself human nature in order that He might unite divine power with human weakness. Although it cost Him a great sacrifice, He was willing to humble Himself, in order that He might elevate humanity and make all who believed in Him sharers of his own blessings, honor, and glory. Revelations of his love are among the great secrets which eternity will reveal. The highest glory of the love of God was manifested in the self-sacrifice of Christ, and the highest glory of the Christian is in imitating his Lord in self-denial and self-sacrifice. *— Lt 30, 1895*

The Science and Song of the Redeemed

In this life we can only begin to understand the wonderful theme of redemption. With our finite comprehension we may consider most earnestly the shame and the glory, the life and the death, the justice and the mercy, that meet in the cross; yet with the utmost stretch of our mental powers we fail to grasp its full significance. The length and the breadth, the depth and the height, of redeeming love are but dimly comprehended.

The plan of redemption will not be fully understood, even when the ransomed see as they are seen and know as they are known; but through the eternal ages new truth will continually unfold to the wondering and delighted mind. Though the griefs and pains and temptations of earth are ended and the cause removed, the people of God will ever have a distinct, intelligent knowledge of what their salvation has cost.

The cross of Christ will be the science and the song of the redeemed through all eternity. In Christ glorified they will behold Christ crucified. Never will it be forgotten that He whose power created and upheld the unnumbered worlds through the vast realms of space, the Beloved of God, the Majesty of heaven, He whom cherub and shining seraph delighted to adore—humbled Himself to uplift fallen man; that He bore the guilt and shame of sin, and the hiding of his Father's face, till the woes of a lost world broke his heart and crushed out his life on Calvary's cross. That the Maker of all worlds, the Arbiter of all destinies, should lay aside his glory and humiliate Himself from love to man will ever excite the wonder and adoration of the universe. *— GC, pp. 651, 652*

The Universe Marvels at Christ's Love

Christ has pledged Himself to be our substitute and surety, and He neglects no one... This is the mystery of godliness. That Christ should take human nature, and by a life of humiliation elevate men in the scale of moral worth with God; that He should carry his adopted nature to the throne of God and there present his children to the Father, to have conferred upon them an honor exceeding that conferred upon the angels, this is the marvel of the heavenly universe, the mystery into which angels desire to look. This is love that melts the sinner's heart. — *Ms 21, 1900*

Redemption is an Exhaustless Theme

The Lord Jesus, who is the image of the invisible God, gave his own life to save perishing man, and, oh, what light, what power, He brings with Him! In Him dwells all the fullness of the Godhead, bodily. What a mystery of mysteries! It is difficult for the reason to grasp the majesty of Christ, the mystery of redemption. The shameful cross has been upraised, the nails have been driven through his hands and feet, the cruel spear has pierced to his heart, and the redemption price has been paid for the human race. The spotless Lamb of God bore our sins in his own body upon the tree; He carried our sorrows.

Redemption is an inexhaustible theme, worthy of our closest contemplation. It passes the comprehension of the deepest thought, the stretch of the most vivid imagination. Who by searching can find out God? The treasures of wisdom and knowledge are opened to all men, and were thousands of the most gifted men to devote their whole time to setting forth Jesus always before us, studying how they might portray his matchless charms, they would never exhaust the subject.

Although great and talented authors have made known wonderful truths, and have presented increased light to the people, still in our day we shall find new ideas, and ample fields in which to work, for the theme of salvation is inexhaustible. The work has gone forward from century to century, setting forth the life and character of Christ, and the love of God as manifested in the atoning sacrifice. The theme of redemption will employ the minds of the redeemed through all eternity. There will be new and rich developments made manifest in the plan of salvation throughout eternal ages. — *RH, June 3, 1890*

The Cost is Not Yet Realized

Never can the cost of our redemption be realized until the redeemed shall stand with the Redeemer before the throne of God. Then as the glories of the eternal home burst upon our enraptured senses we shall remember that Jesus left all this for us, that He not only became an exile from the heavenly courts, but for us took the risk of failure and eternal loss. Then we shall cast our crowns at his feet, and raise the song, "Worthy is the Lamb that was slain to receive power, and riches, and wisdom, and strength, and honor, and glory, and blessing." Revelation 5:12. — *DA, p. 131*

Students Explore All of History

There will be open to the student, history of infinite scope and of wealth inexpressible. Here, from the vantage ground of God's Word, the student is afforded a view of the vast field of history and may gain some knowledge of the principles that govern the course of human events. But his vision is still clouded, and his knowledge incomplete. Not until he stands in the light of eternity will he see all things clearly.

Then will be opened before him the course of the great conflict that had its birth before time began, and that ends only when time shall cease. The history of the inception of sin; of fatal falsehood in its crooked working; of truth that, swerving not from its own straight lines, has met and conquered error—all will be made manifest. The veil that interposes between the visible and the invisible world will be drawn aside, and wonderful things will be revealed…

For what was the great controversy permitted to continue throughout the ages? Why was it that Satan's existence was not cut short at the outset of his rebellion? It was that the universe might be convinced of God's justice in his dealing with evil; that sin might receive eternal condemnation. In the plan of redemption there are heights and depths that eternity itself can never exhaust, marvels into which the angels desire to look. The redeemed only, of all created beings, have in their own experience known the actual conflict with sin; they have wrought with Christ, and, as even the angels could not do, have entered into the fellowship of his sufferings; will they have no testimony as to the science of redemption—nothing that will be of worth to unfallen beings? — *Ed, pp. 304, 308*

Love will Expand in Light

The richest gift, the most costly sacrifice, was selected by God to come to the world as his expression of the love of God to man. The gift of God to our world in sending Jesus is an exhibition of his grace which God Himself cannot surpass. There will be, while we live in this world, new developments of the extensive glory of the great love He had for the souls He has created even in this world. But that love will be extending and expanding before the saints in light, and in characters of new and increasing interest, seen and joyously realized throughout eternity. — *Lt 83, 1895*

The Mystery of Redemption

In giving us his word, God has put us in possession of every truth essential for our salvation. Thousands have drawn water from these wells of life, yet there is no diminishing of the supply. Thousands have set the Lord before them, and by beholding have been changed into the same image. Their spirit burns within them as they speak of his character, telling what Christ is to them, and what they are to Christ. But these searchers have not exhausted these grand and holy themes.

Thousands more may engage in the work of searching out the mysteries of salvation. As the life of Christ and the character of his mission are dwelt upon, rays of light will shine forth more distinctly at every attempt to discover truth. Each fresh search will reveal something more deeply interesting than has yet been unfolded. The subject is inexhaustible. The study of the incarnation of Christ, his atoning sacrifice and mediatorial work, will employ the mind of the diligent student as long as time shall last; and looking to heaven with its unnumbered years he will exclaim, "Great is the mystery of godliness."

In eternity we shall learn that which, had we received the enlightenment it was possible to obtain here, would have opened our understanding. The themes of redemption will employ the hearts and minds and tongues of the redeemed through the everlasting ages. They will understand the truths which Christ longed to open to his disciples, but which they did not have faith to grasp. Forever and forever new views of the perfection and glory of Christ will appear. Through endless ages will the faithful Householder bring forth from his treasure things new and old. — *COL, pp. 133, 134*

Love Inexpressible

The Majesty of heaven... has promised, "To him that overcometh will I grant to sit with Me in my throne, even as I also overcame, and am set down with my Father in his throne." Wonder of wonders! Man, a creature of the earth; dust, elevated to the throne of the King of the universe! Marvelous love! Inexpressible, incomprehensible love! — *RH, July 9, 1895*

Joy and Understanding of God Grows

There are mysteries in the plan of redemption—the humiliation of the Son of God, that He might be found in fashion as a man, the wonderful love and condescension of the Father in yielding up his Son—that are to the heavenly angels subjects of continual amazement. The apostle Peter, speaking of the revelations given to the prophets of "the sufferings of Christ, and the glory that should follow," says that these are things which "the angels desire to look into." And these will be the study of the redeemed through eternal ages.

As they contemplate the work of God in creation and redemption, new truth will continually unfold to the wondering and delighted mind. As they learn more and more of the wisdom, the love, and the power of God, their minds will be constantly expanding, and their joy will continually increase.

If it were possible for created beings to attain to a full understanding of God and his works, then, having reached this point, there would be for them no further discovery of truth, no growth in knowledge, no further development of mind or heart. God would no longer be supreme; and men, having reached the limit of knowledge and attainment, would cease to advance.

Let us thank God that it is not so. God is infinite; in Him are "all the treasures of wisdom and knowledge." And to all eternity men may be ever searching, ever learning, and yet they can never exhaust the treasures of his wisdom, his goodness, and his power.

God intends that, even in this life, truth shall be ever unfolding to his people. There is only one way in which this knowledge can be obtained. We can attain to an understanding of God's Word only through the illumination of that Spirit by which the word was given. "The things of God knoweth no man, but the Spirit of God;" "for the Spirit searcheth all things, yea, the deep things of God." — *5T, pp. 702, 703*

Angels Study Redemption

The theme of redemption is one that the angels desire to look into; it will be the science and the song of the ransomed throughout the ceaseless ages of eternity. Is it not worthy of careful thought and study now? Should we not praise God with heart and soul and voice "for his wonderful works to the children of men?" *—5T, p. 317*

The Central Theme of the Bible

The central theme of the Bible, the theme about which every other in the whole book clusters, is the redemption plan, the restoration in the human soul of the image of God. From the first intimation of hope in the sentence pronounced in Eden to that last glorious promise of the Revelation, "They shall see his face; and his name shall be in their foreheads" (Revelation 22:4), the burden of every book and every passage of the Bible is the unfolding of this wondrous theme—man's uplifting—the power of God, "which giveth us the victory through our Lord Jesus Christ." 1 Corinthians 15:57.

He who grasps this thought has before him an infinite field for study. He has the key that will unlock to him the whole treasure house of God's Word. The science of redemption is the science of all sciences; the science that is the study of the angels and of all the intelligences of the unfallen worlds; the science that engages the attention of our Lord and Saviour; the science that enters into the purpose brooded in the mind of the Infinite—"kept in silence through times eternal" (Romans 16:25); the science that will be the study of God's redeemed throughout endless ages. This is the highest study in which it is possible for man to engage. As no other study can, it will quicken the mind and uplift the soul.

"The excellency of knowledge is, that wisdom giveth life to them that have it." "The words that I speak unto you," said Jesus, "they are spirit, and they are life." "This is life eternal, that they should know thee the only true God, and Him whom thou didst send." Ecclesiastes 7:12; John 6:63; 17:3. The creative energy that called the worlds into existence is in the Word of God. This word imparts power; it begets life. Every command is a promise; accepted by the will, received into the soul, it brings with it the life of the Infinite One. It transforms the nature and re-creates the soul in the image of God. The life thus imparted is in like manner sustained. *—Ed, pp. 125, 126*

530

Eternal Redemption

It is impossible for finite minds to comprehend the work of redemption. Its mystery exceeds human knowledge; yet he who passes from death to life realizes that it is a divine reality. The beginning of redemption we may know here through a personal experience. Its results reach through the eternal ages.

—DA, p. 173

Christ's Character is Infinitely Perfect

During the night season I have listened to words that are of the deepest importance to me. Who by searching can find out God to perfection? The gospels set forth the character of Christ as infinitely perfect. I wish I could speak of this so that the whole world could hear the object of Christ's mission and work; but Infinity alone can do this work. Read and search the Scriptures, in which Christ is set forth as the divine object of our faith.

When finite man, under the influence of satanic agencies, comes to question the words of the One who is called, "Wonderful, Counsellor, The mighty God, The everlasting Father, The Prince of Peace" (Isaiah 9:6), his conceptions of himself increase and his conceptions of Christ and God decrease. "Search the Scriptures; for in them ye think ye have eternal life, and they are they which testify of Me." John 5:39. The sufferings of the Redeemer, the humility of his human-divine character, are not understood, and therefore his virtues are not practiced. The treasures of knowledge to be obtained from God are inexhaustible.

The most gifted men on the earth could all find abundant employment, from now until the judgment, for all their God-given powers in exalting the character of Christ. But they would fail decidedly to present Him as He is.

The mysteries of redemption, embracing Christ's divine-human character, his incarnation, his atonement for sin could employ the pens and the highest mental powers of the wisest men from now until Christ shall be revealed in the clouds of heaven in power and great glory. But though these men should seek with all their power to give a representation of Christ and his work, the representation would fall far short of the reality. The mysteries of redemption are not presented to the students in our schools as they should be. The themes of redemption will employ the minds and tongues of the redeemed through everlasting ages. The reflection of the glory of God will shine forth forever and ever from the Saviour's face. *—Lt 280a, 1904*

The Endless Love of God

"Behold, what manner of love the Father hath bestowed upon us, that we should be called the sons of God." What love, what matchless love, that, sinners and aliens as we are, we may be brought back to God, and adopted into his family! We may address Him by the endearing name, "Our Father," which is a sign of our affection for Him, and a pledge of his tender regard and relationship to us. And the Son of God, beholding the heirs of grace, "is not ashamed to call them brethren." They have even a more sacred relationship to God than have the angels who have never fallen.

All the paternal love which has come down from generation to generation through the channel of human hearts, all the springs of tenderness which have opened in the souls of men, are but as a tiny rill to the boundless ocean, when compared with the infinite, exhaustless love of God. Tongue cannot utter it; pen cannot portray it. You may meditate upon it every day of your life; you may search the Scriptures diligently in order to understand it; you may summon every power and capability that God has given you, in the endeavor to comprehend the love and compassion of the heavenly Father; and yet there is an infinity beyond.

You may study that love for ages; yet you can never fully comprehend the length and the breadth, the depth and the height, of the love of God in giving his Son to die for the world. Eternity itself can never fully reveal it. Yet as we study the Bible, and meditate upon the life of Christ and the plan of redemption, these great themes will open to our understanding more and more.

And it will be ours to realize the blessing which Paul desired for the Ephesian church, when he prayed "that the God of our Lord Jesus Christ, the Father of glory, may give unto you the Spirit of wisdom and revelation in the knowledge of Him: the eyes of your understanding being enlightened; that ye may know what is the hope of his calling, and what the riches of the glory of his inheritance in the saints, and what is the exceeding greatness of his power to usward who believe." Christ's redeemed ones are his jewels, his precious and peculiar treasure... Christ looks upon his people in their purity and perfection as the reward of all his sufferings, his humiliation, and his love, and the supplement of his glory—Christ the great center, from whom radiates all glory. — *RH, Oct. 22, 1908*

Calvary Explains All Mysteries

As the nations of the saved look upon their Redeemer and behold the eternal glory of the Father shining in his countenance; as they behold his throne, which is from everlasting to everlasting, and know that his kingdom is to have no end, they break forth in rapturous song: "Worthy, worthy is the Lamb that was slain, and hath redeemed us to God by his own most precious blood!" The mystery of the cross explains all other mysteries.

In the light that streams from Calvary the attributes of God which had filled us with fear and awe appear beautiful and attractive. Mercy, tenderness, and parental love are seen to blend with holiness, justice, and power. While we behold the majesty of his throne, high and lifted up, we see his character in its gracious manifestations, and comprehend, as never before, the significance of that endearing title, "Our Father."

It will be seen that He who is infinite in wisdom could devise no plan for our salvation except the sacrifice of his Son. The compensation for this sacrifice is the joy of peopling the earth with ransomed beings, holy, happy, and immortal. The result of the Saviour's conflict with the powers of darkness is joy to the redeemed, redounding to the glory of God throughout eternity. And such is the value of the soul that the Father is satisfied with the price paid; and Christ Himself, beholding the fruits of his great sacrifice, is satisfied. — *GC, p. 652*

Discussion Questions

1. Scholars who study in Christ's school will advance forever. What will it be like to have Jesus as our teacher?

2. Why will eleventh hour converts need to take special classes in Christ's school?

3. What are some of the mysteries that you would like Jesus to explain?

4. Why is Jesus eternally bound to men?

5. Is it possible to fully comprehend the amazing love of God?

— 36 —

The Glories of God

"For as the heavens are higher than the earth, so are my ways higher than your ways, and my thoughts than your thoughts." — Isaiah 55:8, 9

Num. 18:20	Psalm 93:1, 2	Prov. 3:19, 20	Isaiah 45:3	Eph. 3:14-21
1 Chron. 29:11	Psalm 99:1-5	Eccl. 7:12	Isaiah 66:1	Col. 2:1-3
Job 11:7-9	Psalm 104:1-7	Isaiah 33:5, 6	Jer. 9:24	Heb. 1:1-4
Psalm 19:1-6	Psalm 104:31-34	Isaiah 40:10-23	Hab. 3:3-6	1 John 3:2

God's Ways are Concealed

The Lord conceals Himself from us in the cloudy pillar, as from ancient Israel. His ways are past finding out. Yet all that He makes known of Himself, all that He can reveal to the most elevated mind, only convinces us of an infinity beyond, of wisdom, purity, and love. — *ST, Oct. 21, 1880*

An Infinity of Eternal Glory

The pure in heart shall see God. His presence can be revealed; comprehended it cannot be. This knowledge is too wonderful for us. There are feelings that cannot be communicated. Some things one cannot say. Words are tame, and our thoughts come far short of taking all in, for there is an infinity beyond our thoughts. — *Lt 55, 1897*

A Glorious Future Ahead of Us

Whatever clouds overcast the sky, whatever storms surge around the soul, this anchor holds firm, and we may be sure of the victory. With the eye of faith you may see the land that is afar off. Many have longed to penetrate into the glories of the future world, and to have the secrets of eternal mysteries disclosed to them, but they knock in vain. That which is revealed, is for us and for our children. — *Lt 30, 1893*

The Purpose of the Planets

The creation of the worlds, the mystery of the gospel, are for one purpose, to make manifest to all created intelligences, through nature and through Christ, the glories of the divine character. — *ST, Apr. 25, 1892*

Divinity Peopled the Worlds

Children may be made acquainted with God in his created works by having their minds directed to the glories of the heavens in the light of the setting sun. His hand has strewed the skies with everlasting gems of light. Worlds are peopled by his power, and yet the humblest creatures of the earth are the objects of his love and care. — *ST, Dec. 12, 1878*

The Word of Christ's Power

The Creator has given abundant evidence that his power is unlimited, that He can establish kingdoms, and overturn kingdoms. He upholds the world by the word of his power. He made the night, marshaling the shining stars in the firmament. He calls them all by name. The heavens declare the glory of God, and the firmament showeth his handiwork, showing man that this little world is but a jot in God's creation. — *YI, April 4, 1905*

Everything We Have is from God

All that man has—life, the means of existence, happiness, and other blessings unnumbered that come to him day by day—is from the Father above. Man is a debtor for all he proudly claims as his own. God gives his precious gifts, that they may be used in his service. Every particle of the glory of man's success belongs to God. It is his manifold wisdom that is displayed in the works of men, and to Him belongs the praise. — *YI, April 4, 1905*

Life is a Standing Memorial of God

What is life? A standing memorial of the only true God. The work of creation can never be explained by science. What intellect is there that can explain the science of life? Can we wonder that the materialist has no place for the existence of God? The fourth commandment declares to the whole universe, to the worlds unfallen and to the fallen world, that God created the world in six days and rested on the seventh. The evidence there given does not leave standing room for skepticism. — *Lt 7, 1900*

Love and Knowledge Grows Forever

In the City of God... immortal minds will contemplate with never-failing delight the wonders of creative power, the mysteries of redeeming love. There will be no cruel, deceiving foe to tempt to forgetfulness of God. Every faculty will be developed, every capacity increased. The acquirement of knowledge will not weary the mind or exhaust the energies. There the grandest enterprises may be carried forward, the loftiest aspirations reached, the highest ambitions realized; and still there will arise new heights to surmount, new wonders to admire, new truths to comprehend, fresh objects to call forth the powers of mind and soul and body. — *GC, p. 677*

Nobody Can Fully Comprehend God

Let none think that there is no more knowledge for them to gain. The depth of human intellect may be measured; the works of human authors may be mastered; but the highest, deepest, broadest flight of the imagination cannot find out God. There is infinity beyond all that we can comprehend. We have seen only the glimmering of divine glory and of the infinitude of knowledge and wisdom; we have, as it were, been working on the surface of the mine, when rich golden ore is beneath the surface, to reward the one who will dig for it. The shaft must be sunk deeper and yet deeper in the mine, and the result will be glorious treasure. Through a correct faith, divine knowledge will become human knowledge. — *COL, p. 113*

Ceaseless Sources of Glory and Bliss

Let men and women who are satisfied with their dwarfed, crippled position in divine things be suddenly transported to heaven and for an instant experience the high, holy state of perfection which ever abides there: The souls filled with love, joy beaming upon every countenance, the high and melodious strains of enchanting music in honor of God and the Lamb; the ceaseless streams of light which flow from the face of Him who sitteth upon the throne, and from the Lamb, upon the faces of his saints; and yet higher and greater joy to experience. The more they receive and exercise the enjoyment of God, the capacity is increased to bear more, to rise higher in eternal, immortal enjoyment, and thus continue to receive new and greater supplies from the ceaseless sources of glory and bliss inexpressible. — *Lt 17, 1868*

God's Hand Guides the Planets

The same creative energy that brought the world into existence is still exerted in upholding the universe and continuing the operations of nature. The hand of God guides the planets in their orderly march through the heavens. It is not because of inherent power that year by year the earth continues her motion round the sun and produces her bounties. The Word of God controls the elements. He covers the heavens with clouds and prepares rain for the earth. He makes the valleys fruitful and "grass to grow upon the mountains." Psalm 147:8. It is through his power that vegetation flourishes, that the leaves appear and the flowers bloom. — *Ms 74, 1896*

A Personal Connection with Jesus

The privileges granted to the children of God are without limit—to be connected with Jesus Christ, who, throughout the universe of heaven and worlds that have not fallen, is adored by every heart, and his praises sung by every tongue; to be children of God, to bear his name, to become a member of the royal family; to be ranged under the banner of Prince Immanuel, the King of kings and Lord of lords. His word is obeyed by the highest intelligences; his word marshals the hosts of heaven whose servants are mighty angels, excelling in strength. "They do his commandments, hearkening unto the voice of his word." The lowliest service done for Jesus is the greatest honor mortals can enjoy. — *YI, Oct. 20, 1886*

God Doesn't Need Man for Honor

Should all the inhabitants of this little world refuse obedience to God, He would not be left without glory. He could sweep every mortal from the face of the earth in a moment, and create a new race to people it and glorify his name. God is not dependent on man for honor. He could marshal the starry hosts of heaven, the millions of worlds above, to raise a song of honor and praise and glory to his name.

"And the heavens shall praise thy wonders, O Lord; thy faithfulness also in the congregation of the saints. For who in the heaven can be compared unto the Lord? Who among the sons of the mighty can be likened unto the Lord? God is greatly to be feared in the assembly of the saints, and to be had in reverence of all them that are about Him." Psalm 89:5-7. — *RH, Mar. 1, 1881*

The God of Nature is Infinite

Nature is a power, but the God of nature is unlimited in power. His works interpret his character. Those who judge Him from his handiworks, and not from the suppositions of great men, will see his presence in everything. They behold his smile in the glad sunshine, and his love and care for man in the rich fields of autumn. Even the adornments of the earth, as seen in the grass of living green, the lovely flowers of every hue, and the lofty and varied trees of the forest, testify to the tender, fatherly care of our God, and to his desire to make his children happy. — *ST, Mar. 13, 1884*

Eternity will Reveal Our Destiny

The education begun in this life will be continued in the life to come. Day by day the wonderful works of God, the evidences of his wisdom and power in creating and sustaining the universe, the infinite mystery of love and wisdom in the plan of redemption, will open to the mind in new beauty. "Eye hath not seen, nor ear heard, neither have entered into the heart of man, the things which God hath prepared for them that love Him." 1 Corinthians 2:9.

Even in this life we may catch glimpses of his presence and may taste the joy of communion with heaven, but the fullness of its joy and blessing will be reached in the hereafter. Eternity alone can reveal the glorious destiny to which man, restored to God's image, may attain. — *PP, p. 602*

The Holiness of God's Glory

Men exalt themselves among men, and speak of what they know of higher education. If they only knew more, they would wish to sink out of sight. They may think and reason to the utmost of their ability; but were the veil lifted, they would see infinity beyond. They know hardly anything of the mysteries of God, who holds supervision over the universe. It will take all eternity to unfold his plans.

Let those who think themselves competent to weigh and measure the counsels of divine wisdom be assured that they know not even the A B C of what is comprehended in higher education. When they gain even a glimpse of the true and living God, they will show a becoming humility. The sight will suggest the command, "Loose thy shoe from off thy foot; for the place whereon thou standest is holy." — *RH, Sept. 25, 1900*

New Light will Astonish Us

Every effort should be made in the education of youth to impress their minds with the loveliness and power of the truth as it is in Jesus. When the vail shall be removed which separates time from eternity, then will come to many minds the clear perception of the policy of human wisdom in comparison with the sure word of prophecy. All true science leads to harmony with, and obedience to God. When that which has seemed incomprehensible is seen in the light shining from the throne of God, it will fill the soul with the greatest astonishment that it was never seen and comprehended before.

—GCDB, Feb. 18, 1897

Lift Up Your Eyes on High

God calls men to look upon the heavens. See Him in the wonders of the starry heavens. "Lift up your eyes on high," He says, "and behold who hath created these things, that bringeth out their host by number: He called them all by name by the greatness of his might." Isaiah 40:26. We are not merely to gaze upon the heavens; we are to consider the works of God. He would have us study the works of infinity, and—then what?—from this study learn to love and reverence and obey Him. The heavens and the earth with their treasures are to teach the lessons of God's love, care, and power. As you look at the wonderful things God's hand has made, let your proud, foolish heart feel its dependence and inferiority. *—Ms 96, 1899*

Only Christ Has Inherent Eternal Life

"In Him was life; and the life was the light of men." It is not physical life that is here specified, but eternal life, the life which is exclusively the property of God. The Word, who was with God, and who was God, had this life.

Physical life is something which each individual received. It is not eternal or immortal; for God, the Life-giver, takes it again. Man has no control over his life. But the life of Christ was unborrowed. No one can take this life from Him. "I lay it down of myself," He said. In Him was life, original, unborrowed, underived.

This life is not inherent in man. He can possess it only through Christ. He can not earn it; it is given him as a free gift if he will believe in Christ as his personal Saviour. "This is life eternal, that they might know thee the only true God, and Jesus Christ, whom thou hast sent." John 17:3. *—ST, Feb. 13, 1912*

Eternity is Purity, Holiness, and Peace

Through Christ alone can you make sure of heaven, where all is purity, holiness, peace, and blessedness, where there are glories that mortal lips cannot describe. The nearest we can come to a description of the reward that awaits the overcomer is to say that it is a far more exceeding and eternal weight of glory. It will be an eternity of bliss, a blessed eternity, unfolding new glories throughout the ceaseless ages. You must be there. Whatever you lose here, be determined to make sure of eternal life. Never become discouraged. —*8T, p. 131*

Paul Could Not Fathom Eternal Glory

Paul had a view of heaven, and in discoursing on the glories there, the very best thing he could do was to not try to describe them. He tells us that "eye had not seen nor ear heard, neither hath it entered into the heart of man the things which God hath prepared for those that love Him." 1 Corinthians 2:9.

So you may put your imagination to the stretch, you may try to the very best of your abilities to take in and consider the eternal weight of glory, and yet your finite senses, faint and weary with the effort, cannot grasp it, for there is an infinity beyond. It takes all of eternity to unfold the glories and bring out the precious treasures of the Word of God. —*Ms 13, 1888*

God's Handiwork Reveals His Glory

The glory of God is displayed in his handiwork. Here are mysteries that the mind will become strong in searching out. Minds that have been amused and abused by reading fiction may in nature have an open book, and read truth in the works of God around them.

All may find themes for study in the simple leaf of the forest tree, the spires of grass covering the earth with their green velvet carpet, the plants and flowers, the stately trees of the forest, the lofty mountains, the granite rocks, the restless ocean, the precious gems of light studding the heavens to make the night beautiful, the exhaustless riches of the sunlight, the solemn glories of the moon, the winter's cold, the summer's heat, the changing, recurring seasons, in perfect order and harmony, controlled by infinite power; here are subjects which call for deep thought, for the stretch of the imagination.

—4T, p. 581

God the Father Looks like Jesus

I saw a throne, and on it sat the Father and the Son. I gazed on Jesus' countenance and admired his lovely person. The Father's person I could not behold, for a cloud of glorious light covered Him. I asked Jesus if his Father had a form like Himself. He said He had, but I could not behold it, for said He, "If you should once behold the glory of his person, you would cease to exist." —*EW, p. 54*

Created Things Declare God's Glory

All created things declare the glory of his excellence. There is nothing, save the selfish heart of man, that lives unto itself. No bird that cleaves the air, no animal that moves upon the ground, but ministers to some other life. There is no leaf of the forest, or lowly blade of grass, but has its ministry. Every tree and shrub and leaf pours forth that element of life without which neither man nor animal could live; and man and animal, in turn, minister to the life of tree and shrub and leaf. The flowers breathe fragrance and unfold their beauty in blessing to the world. The sun sheds its light to gladden a thousand worlds. The ocean, itself the source of all our springs and fountains, receives the streams from every land, but takes to give. The mists ascending from its bosom fall in showers to water the earth, that it may bring forth and bud.

—DA, p. 20

Finite Man Cannot Fathom Divinity

It is the duty and privilege of all to use reason as far as man's finite faculties can go; but there is a boundary where man's resources must cease. There are many things that can never be reasoned out by the strongest intellect, or discerned by the most penetrating mind. Philosophy cannot determine the ways and works of God; the human mind cannot measure infinity. Jehovah is the fountain of all wisdom, of all truth, of all knowledge.

There are high attainments that man can reach in this life through the wisdom that God imparts; but there is an infinity beyond that will be the study and the joy of the saints throughout eternal ages. Man can now only linger upon the borders of that vast expanse, and let imagination take its flight. Finite man cannot fathom the deep things of God; for spiritual things are spiritually discerned. The human mind cannot comprehend the wisdom and power of God. —*RH, Dec. 29, 1896*

Eternity Unfolds the Love of God

The mind of God to save the world was the mind of Christ. His own love was one with that of the Father, and that love constrained Him. Herein is the love of God manifested, inexpressible, immeasurable, and passing knowledge. The human mind cannot grasp it in its fullness; but we should put forth the most earnest efforts of which we are capable, that we may communicate redeeming love to others. Eternity, all eternity, will unfold that love, and then we shall know what here we cannot comprehend. — *BE, Nov. 25, 1895*

Study God's Character Forever

The contemplation and study of God's character as revealed in his created works will open a field of thought that will draw the mind away from low, debasing, enervating amusements. The knowledge of God's works and ways we can only begin to obtain in this world; the study will be continued throughout eternity. God has provided for man subjects of thought which will bring into activity every faculty of the mind. We may read the character of the Creator in the heavens above and the earth beneath, filling the heart with gratitude and thanksgiving. Every nerve and sense will respond to the expressions of God's love in his marvelous works. — *4T, p. 581*

God is the Source of All Wisdom

God is the source of all wisdom. He is infinitely wise, and just, and good. The wisest men that ever lived cannot comprehend Him. They may profess to be wise; they may glory in their great attainments; but mere intellectual knowledge, aside from the great truths that center in Christ, is as nothingness. "Let not the wise man glory in his wisdom; ... but let him that glorieth glory in this, that he understandeth and knoweth Me, that I am the Lord which exercise loving-kindness, judgment, and righteousness, in the earth."

If men could see for a moment beyond the finite vision, if they could catch a glimpse of the Eternal, every mouth would be stopped in its boasting. Men, living in this little atom of a world, are finite; God has unnumbered worlds that are obedient to his laws, and are conducted with reference to his glory. When men have gone as far in scientific research as their limited powers will permit, there is still an infinity beyond what they can apprehend. — *SpTEd, p. 49*

We Cannot Fully Understand God

The mightiest human being, whatever may be his claim, is not infinite. He cannot understand infinity. Christ plainly stated, "No man knoweth the Son but the Father." Matthew 11:27. A teacher was once endeavoring to present the exaltation of God, when a voice was heard, saying, "We cannot as yet understand who He is." The teacher nobly replied, "Were I able fully to set forth God, I should either be a god myself, or God Himself would cease to be God." — *Ms 128, 1897*

Eternal Life is an Infinite Gift

"By grace are ye saved through faith; and that not of yourselves; it is the gift of God." Ephesians 2:8. Here is truth that will unfold the subject to your mind if you do not close it to the rays of light. Eternal life is an infinite gift. This places it outside the possibility of our earning it, because it is infinite. It must necessarily be a gift. As a gift it must be received by faith, and gratitude and praise be offered to God... Do the work of Christ, and you will honor God and come off more than conquerors through Him that has loved us and given his life for us, that we should have life and salvation in Jesus Christ.

— Ms 36, 1890

An Infinity beyond All Knowledge

Men of the greatest intellect cannot understand the mysteries of Jehovah as revealed in nature. Divine inspiration asks many questions which the most profound scholar cannot answer. These questions were not asked that we might answer them, but to call our attention to the deep mysteries of God and to teach us that our wisdom is limited; that in the surroundings of our daily life there are many things beyond the comprehension of finite minds; that the judgment and purposes of God are past finding out. His wisdom is unsearchable.

Skeptics refuse to believe in God because with their finite minds they cannot comprehend the infinite power by which He reveals Himself to men. But God is to be acknowledged more from what He does not reveal of Himself than from that which is open to our limited comprehension. Both in divine revelation and in nature, God has given to men mysteries to command their faith. This must be so. We may be ever searching, ever inquiring, ever learning, and yet there is an infinity beyond. — *8T, p. 261*

Never Tire of Glorifying God

We are God's heritage. He has bought us with a price. He has given his own life for us, that we should have eternal life in the kingdom of God to glorify Him through the eternal ages. And I tell you it will be good business. You need not be afraid that you will get tired of glorifying God. There is everything in heaven that can be desired. There is everything that could make the soul happy and full of glory to God. I know what I am talking about.

—Ms 160, 1904

Learn More of God's Purposes

There is no mystery in the law of God. The feeblest intellect can grasp these rules to regulate the life and form the character after the divine Model. If the children of men would, to the best of their ability, obey this law, they would gain strength of intellect and power of discernment to comprehend still more of God's purposes and plans. And this advancement may not only be continued during the present life, but it may go forward during the eternal ages. However far we may advance in the knowledge of God's wisdom and his power, there is ever an infinity beyond. *—RH, Sept. 14, 1886*

The Glory Shared by Jesus and His Father

What will be the glory and the gain and the enjoyment of that eternal life that is to be given to those only for whom it has been prepared? The great joy of the overcomer will be that he is in the presence of Christ. "Where I am, there shall also my servant be," He declared.

And He prayed, "Father, I will that they also whom thou hast given Me be with Me where I am; that they may behold my glory." Christ is speaking of the glory of his Father's presence and his Father's house. The glory that is to be revealed to all who are saved is the glory which Christ had with his Father before the world was—the unapproachable splendor of their converse together.

The angels were not admitted to the interviews between the Father and the Son when the plan of salvation was laid. Those human beings who seek to intrude into the secrets of the Most High, who inhabiteth eternity, show their ignorance of spiritual and eternal things. Far better might they, while mercy's voice is still heard, humble themselves in the dust and plead with God to teach them his ways. *—Lt 232, 1903*

The Purpose of Adam's Creation

When Adam came from the Creator's hand, he bore, in his physical, mental, and spiritual nature, a likeness to his Maker. "God created man in his own image" (Genesis 1:27), and it was his purpose that the longer man lived the more fully he should reveal this image—the more fully reflect the glory of the Creator. All his faculties were capable of development; their capacity and vigor were continually to increase.

Vast was the scope offered for their exercise, glorious the field opened to their research. The mysteries of the visible universe—the "wondrous works of Him which is perfect in knowledge" (Job 37:16)—invited man's study. Face-to-face, heart-to-heart communion with his Maker was his high privilege. Had he remained loyal to God, all this would have been his forever.

Throughout eternal ages he would have continued to gain new treasures of knowledge, to discover fresh springs of happiness, and to obtain clearer and yet clearer conceptions of the wisdom, the power, and the love of God. More and more fully would he have fulfilled the object of his creation, more and more fully have reflected the Creator's glory. — *Ed, p. 15*

God is the Source of All Power

The high and lofty One who inhabiteth eternity claims and deserves our highest thoughts and holiest affections. God is the source of all power. From his infinite love flow blessings to every creature formed in his image. Our heavenly Father has hung out glories in the firmament of the heavens, that men may have an expression of his love in the revealing of his wondrous works. God would not have us indifferent to the symbols of the glories of his infinite power in the heavens. David delighted to dwell upon these glories. He composed psalms which the Hebrew singers chanted to the praise of God.

"The heavens declare the glory of God and the firmament showeth his handiwork. Day unto day uttereth speech, and night unto night showeth knowledge. There is no speech nor language, where their voice is not heard. Their line is gone out through all the earth, and their words to the end of the world. In them hath He set a tabernacle for the sun, which is as a bridegroom coming out of his chamber, and rejoiceth as a strong man to run a race. His going forth is from the end of the heaven, and his circuit unto the ends of it: and there is nothing hid from the heat thereof." Psalm 19:1-6. — *ST, Dec. 12, 1878*

God's Throne is from Everlasting

The Lord… says, "I am Alpha and Omega, the beginning and the ending, … which is, and which was, and which is to come, the Almighty." Revelation 1:8. What is the work of angels in comparison with his condescension? His throne is from everlasting. He has reared every arch and pillar in nature's great temple.

Behold Him, the beginning of the creation of God, who numbers the stars, who created the worlds—among which this earth is but a small speck, and would scarcely be missed from the many worlds more than a tiny leaf from the forest trees. The nations before Him are but "as a drop of a bucket," and "as the small dust of the balance." "He taketh up the isles as a very little thing." Isaiah 40:15.

Contemplate Him, the Lord, the all-glorious Redeemer, an inhabitant of the world He has created, and yet unacknowledged by the very ones He manifested so great interest to bless and save, that He might make them happy in this life and eternally happy in his kingdom. —*Ms 75, 1886*

Philosophers Cannot Understand God

The greatest philosopher may lift himself up in his pride, he may range through the harmonies and charms of the universe, tracing the wonderful manifestations of creative power and beholding the expressions of infinite wisdom in the formation of worlds, yet he has not wisdom to find God in his great and majestic works.

The mystery of God's hand discerned in his creative works he does not comprehend—wise in the world's knowledge, but a fool as far as the mystery of godliness is concerned. Yet just such human greatness attracts the world, and millions are ready to worship this world's gods which pass away to atoms of dust, to know nothing of the immortal life which runs parallel with the life of Jehovah. His glory has perished with his existence.

But that humble child of God has the promise of heirship to riches that will endure, glory that will never cease to brighten with the progress of the ages. The change wrought in his affections have brought him into harmony with the will of the Controller of the universe. His name angels have enrolled in the record book of heaven, and mansions are prepared for his reception.

—*Lt 36, 1877*

God Created Everything

God is the foundation of everything. All true science is in harmony with his works; all true education leads to obedience to his government. Science opens new wonders to our view; she soars high, and explores new depths; but she brings nothing from her research that conflicts with divine revelation. Ignorance may seek to support false views of God by appeals to science, but the book of nature and the written word shed light upon each other. We are thus led to adore the Creator and to have an intelligent trust in his word.

No finite mind can fully comprehend the existence, the power, the wisdom, or the works of the Infinite One. Says the sacred writer: "Canst thou by searching find out God? canst thou find out the Almighty unto perfection? It is as high as heaven; what canst thou do? deeper than hell; what canst thou know? The measure thereof is longer than the earth, and broader than the sea." Job 11:7-9. The mightiest intellects of earth cannot comprehend God. Men may be ever searching, ever learning, and still there is an infinity beyond.

—PP, pp. 115, 116

An Eternity of Perfect Happiness

Shall we, in the enjoyment of the gifts, forget the Giver? Let them rather lead us to contemplate his goodness and his love. Let all that is beautiful in our earthly home remind us of the crystal river and green fields, the waving trees and the living fountains, the shining city and the white-robed singers, of our heavenly home—that world of beauty which no artist can picture, no mortal tongue describe. "Eye hath not seen, nor ear heard, neither have entered into the heart of man, the things which God hath prepared for them that love Him."

To dwell forever in this home of the blest, to bear in soul, body, and spirit, not the dark traces of sin and the curse, but the perfect likeness of our Creator, and through ceaseless ages to advance in wisdom, in knowledge and holiness, ever exploring new fields of thought, ever finding new wonders and new glories, ever increasing in capacity to know and to enjoy and to love, and knowing that there is still beyond us joy and love and wisdom infinite—such is the object to which the Christian hope is pointing, for which Christian education is preparing. To secure this education, and to aid others to secure it, should be the object of the Christian's life. *—RH, July 11, 1882*

God Upholds All of Creation

The psalmist says: "The heavens declare the glory of God; and the firmament showeth his handiwork. Day unto day uttereth speech, and night unto night showeth knowledge. There is no speech nor language, where their voice is not heard." Some may suppose that these grand things in the natural world are God. They are not God. All these wonders in the heavens are only doing the work appointed them. They are the Lord's agencies. God is the superintendent, as well as the Creator, of all things. The divine Being is engaged in upholding the things that He has created. The same hand that holds the mountains and balances them in position, guides the worlds in their mysterious march around the sun. — *RH, Nov. 8, 1898*

The Treasures of the Universe

When the veil that darkens our vision shall be removed, and our eyes shall behold that world of beauty of which we now catch glimpses through the microscope; when we look on the glories of the heavens, now scanned afar through the telescope; when, the blight of sin removed, the whole earth shall appear in "the beauty of the Lord our God," what a field will be open to our study!

There the student of science may read the records of creation and discern no reminders of the law of evil. He may listen to the music of nature's voices and detect no note of wailing or undertone of sorrow. In all created things he may trace one handwriting—in the vast universe behold "God's name writ large," and not in earth or sea or sky one sign of ill remaining...

There shall be nothing to "hurt nor destroy in all my holy mountain, saith the Lord." Isaiah 65:25. There man will be restored to his lost kingship, and the lower order of beings will again recognize his sway; the fierce will become gentle, and the timid trustful...

All the treasures of the universe will be open to the study of God's children. With unutterable delight we shall enter into the joy and the wisdom of unfallen beings. We shall share the treasures gained through ages upon ages spent in contemplation of God's handiwork. And the years of eternity, as they roll, will continue to bring more glorious revelations. "Exceeding abundantly above all that we ask or think" will be, forever and forever, the impartation of the gifts of God. Ephesians 3:20. — *Ed, pp. 303-307*

The Glory will be Indescribable

The sanctification of the truth, confirming man's steadfastness in the faith, will constitute men laborers together with God. United with the Source of all power, persevering in duty, enlarging the apprehension of the love of God in Christ Jesus, they become one with Christ, until they are complete with Christ in God.

The glories that await the faithful overcomer are beyond any description. The Lord will greatly honor and exalt his faithful ones. They shall grow like the cedar, and their comprehension will be certainly increasing. And at every advanced stage of knowledge their anticipation will fall far beneath the reality.

"Eye hath not seen nor ear heard, neither hath entered into the heart of man the things which God hath prepared for them who love Him." Our work now is to prepare for those mansions that God is preparing for those who love Him and keep his commandments. — *Lt 71, 1900*

The Universe Declares God is Love

The great controversy is ended. Sin and sinners are no more. The entire universe is clean. One pulse of harmony and gladness beats through the vast creation. From Him who created all, flow life and light and gladness, throughout the realms of illimitable space. From the minutest atom to the greatest world, all things, animate and inanimate, in their unshadowed beauty and perfect joy, declare that God is love. — *GC, p. 678*

Discussion Questions

1. What treasures of the universe are you looking forward to seeing?

2. Have scientists had any success in determining how life originated?

3. Would God still be divine if scholars could fully comprehend Him?

4. Why did God create worlds and fill them with people?

5. What will it be like to live in a universe where all of creation, from the smallest atom to the most magnificent world, declares that God is love?

List of Acronyms

1SG	Spiritual Gifts, Vol. 1 (1858)
2SG	Spiritual Gifts, Vol. 2 (1860)
3SG	Spiritual Gifts, Vol. 3 (1864)
4aSG	Spiritual Gifts, Vol. 4a (1864)
4bSG	Spiritual Gifts, Vol. 4b (1864)
1SP	Spirit of Prophecy, Vol. 1 (1870)
2SP	Spirit of Prophecy, Vol. 2 (1877)
3SP	Spirit of Prophecy, Vol. 3 (1878)
4SP	Spirit of Prophecy, Vol. 4 (1884)
1T	Testimonies for the Church, Vol. 1 (1868)
2T	Testimonies for the Church, Vol. 2 (1871)
3T	Testimonies for the Church, Vol. 3 (1875)
4T	Testimonies for the Church, Vol. 4 (1881)
5T	Testimonies for the Church, Vol. 5 (1889)
6T	Testimonies for the Church, Vol. 6 (1901)
7T	Testimonies for the Church, Vol. 7 (1902)
8T	Testimonies for the Church, Vol. 8 (1904)
9T	Testimonies for the Church, Vol. 9 (1909)
AA	Acts of the Apostles (1911)
AUCR	Australasian Union Conference Record
BE	The Bible Echo
CM	Camp-meetings

COL	Christ's Object Lessons (1900)
CTBH	Christian Temperance and Bible Hygiene (1890)
DA	The Desire of Ages (1898)
EA	Experiences in Australia
Ed	Education (1903)
EW	Early Writings (1882)
GC	The Great Controversy (1911)
GCB	General Conference Bulletin
GCDB	General Conference Daily Bulletin
GdH	Good Health
GW	Gospel Workers (1915)
HS	Historical Sketches of the Foreign Adventist Missions
LP	Sketches from the Life of Paul (1883)
Lt	Letter
MB	Thoughts from the Mount of Blessing (1896)
MH	Ministry of Healing (1905)
Ms	Manuscript
PH	Counsels to Physicians and Medical Students (1885)
PK	Prophets and Kings (1917)
PP	Patriarchs and Prophets (1890)
PUR	Pacific Union Recorder
Rd	Redemption: or the Teachings of Paul (1878)
RH	Review and Herald
SC	Steps to Christ (1892)
SpTEd	Special Testimonies on Education (1897)
SSW	Sabbath-School Worker
ST	Signs of the Times
SW	The Southern Work (1901)
TM	Special Testimonies for Ministers and Workers
WLF	A Word to the "Little Flock" (1847)

www.ingramcontent.com/pod-product-compliance
Lightning Source LLC
Chambersburg PA
CBHW070643150426
42811CB00050B/517